Coconut Triple-Layer Cake (page 44)

Irish Bread Pudding with
Caramel-Whiskey Sauce (page 54)

Home-Style Meat Loaf (page 61)

Mashed Potatoes (page 61)

Polenta with Roasted Vegetables (page 66)

Linguine with White Clam Sauce (page 56)

Siam Stir-Fry Wrap (page 48)

German-Chocolate Cake (page 46)

$\mathscr{S}$ay Ahhhhhhhhhh...

Got the flu, a cold, or the winter blues? Try these soothing recipes that will help you feel in the pink again.

It's no longer considered just a wives' tale that a bowl of chicken soup has medicinal value, or that chocolate can lift your spirits. More and more scientific studies have shown just how healing and healthful everyday foods can be. The following recipes may not have you back in your aerobics class tomorrow or running a 10K this weekend, but they will give you nourishment and plenty of pleasure.

HOME-STYLE MEAT LOAF

(pictured on page 58)

An iron-rich food like meat loaf can help keep you warm on a cold winter night. When researchers at the U.S. Department of Agriculture deprived a group of women of iron, they became chilled more quickly when exposed to lower temperatures.

¾ cup ketchup, divided
½ cup quick-cooking oats
¼ cup minced fresh onion
2 tablespoons chopped fresh parsley
1 tablespoon brown sugar
¼ teaspoon salt
¼ teaspoon pepper
2 large egg whites, lightly beaten
1½ pounds ground round
Cooking spray

1. Preheat oven to 350°.
2. Combine ½ cup ketchup, oats, and next 6 ingredients in a large bowl. Add meat, and stir just until blended. Shape meat mixture into an 8 x 4-inch loaf on a broiler pan coated with cooking spray. Brush remaining ¼ cup ketchup over meat loaf. Bake at 350° for 1 hour and 10 minutes. Let stand 10 minutes before slicing. Yield: 6 servings (serving size: 1 slice).

CALORIES 242 (28% from fat); FAT 7.5g (sat 2.6g, mono 3.1g, poly 0.5g); PROTEIN 27.2g; CARB 15.5g; FIBER 1.4g; CHOL 70mg; IRON 3mg; SODIUM 527mg; CALC 21mg

MASHED POTATOES

(pictured on page 58)

Whatever your problem, mashed potatoes can help. Adding a little garlic doesn't hurt, either.

4 cups cubed peeled baking potato (about 1½ pounds)
1 garlic clove, sliced
¾ cup 1% low-fat milk
2 tablespoons grated Parmesan cheese
1 tablespoon stick margarine or butter
½ teaspoon salt
⅛ teaspoon pepper

1. Place potato and garlic in a medium saucepan; add water to cover. Bring to a boil; cover, reduce heat, and simmer 25 minutes or until tender. Drain. Return potato mixture to pan. Add milk and remaining ingredients; mash with a potato masher. Yield: 4 servings (serving size: 1 cup).

CALORIES 176 (21% from fat); FAT 4.2g (sat 1.4g, mono 1.6g, poly 1g); PROTEIN 5.7g; CARB 29.5g; FIBER 2.4g; CHOL 4mg; IRON 1.2mg; SODIUM 405mg; CALC 104mg

CHICKEN SOUP WITH ORZO

Researchers speculate that it's more than the hot, steamy nature of chicken soup that helps relieve congestion. Chances are there is an aromatic or flavoring compound in chicken soup that offers an extra measure of cold relief.

1 (3-pound) package chicken pieces
3 quarts water
1 medium onion, cut into 8 wedges
1 cup chopped carrot
1 cup chopped celery
1 tablespoon black peppercorns
1½ cups sliced carrot
1 cup diced celery
2 tablespoons chopped fresh or 2 teaspoons dried basil
1 teaspoon chopped fresh or ¼ teaspoon dried oregano
¾ teaspoon salt
1 bay leaf
½ cup uncooked orzo (rice-shaped pasta)

1. Remove and discard giblets and neck from chicken. Rinse chicken under cold water; pat dry. Trim excess fat. Combine chicken and 3 quarts water in a stockpot; bring to a boil. Add onion and next 3 ingredients; bring to a boil. Partially cover, reduce heat, and simmer 1 hour.
2. Remove chicken from broth, reserving broth; cool. Discard skin. Remove chicken from bones; cut meat into bite-size pieces. Strain chicken broth through a sieve over a bowl; discard solids. Add enough water to broth to measure 10 cups; pour broth mixture into stockpot. Add sliced carrot and next 5 ingredients; bring to a boil. Cover, reduce heat, and simmer 10 minutes. Add chicken and orzo; cook 8 minutes or until pasta is done. Yield: 8 servings (serving size: 1½ cups).

CALORIES 151 (24% from fat); FAT 4.1g (sat 1.1g, mono 1.4g, poly 1g); PROTEIN 16.9g; CARB 10.7g; FIBER 1.2g; CHOL 47mg; IRON 1.3mg; SODIUM 286mg; CALC 24mg

SPICY SAUSAGE CHILI

Have a stuffy nose? It's becoming more common for physicians to prescribe spicy foods as a remedy. Fiery foods can trigger a release of fluids that can help open nasal passages.

  2 **cups diced onion**
  ¾ **pound hot turkey Italian sausage, crumbled**
  2 **cups water**
  1½ **teaspoons dried oregano**
  1½ **teaspoons ground cumin**
  1½ **teaspoons chili powder**
  ½ **teaspoon salt**
  ¼ **teaspoon dried crushed red pepper**
  2 **(14.5-ounce) cans no-salt-added stewed tomatoes, undrained**
  1 **(15.5-ounce) can cannellini beans or other white beans, drained**
  1 **(4.5-ounce) can chopped green chiles, undrained**
  2 **large garlic cloves, minced**

1. Combine onion and sausage in a Dutch oven; cook over medium-high heat until sausage is browned, stirring constantly.
2. Stir in water and remaining ingredients; bring to a boil. Reduce heat, and simmer 30 minutes, stirring occasionally. Yield: 7 servings (serving size: 1 cup).

CALORIES 234 (31% from fat); FAT 8g (sat 2.4g, mono 2.9g, poly 2.5g); PROTEIN 16.7g; CARB 25.9g; FIBER 2.9g; CHOL 40mg; IRON 3.6mg; SODIUM 628mg; CALC 88mg

MILK-CHOCOLATE PUDDING

Many feel that chocolate is the ultimate "feel-good" food when you're down. Speculation is that it either contains mood-elevating substances or that it stimulates their production.

  ½ **cup sugar**
  2 **tablespoons cornstarch**
  2 **cups 1% low-fat milk**
  1½ **ounces semisweet chocolate, chopped**
  1 **large egg, lightly beaten**
  1 **teaspoon vanilla extract**

1. Combine sugar and cornstarch in a saucepan; gradually add milk, stirring with a whisk until well-blended. Stir in chocolate. Bring to a boil over medium heat; cook 7 minutes, stirring constantly. Gradually add hot milk mixture to egg, stirring constantly.
2. Return milk mixture to pan, and cook until thick and bubbly (about 30 seconds), stirring constantly. Remove from heat, and stir in vanilla. Spoon mixture into a bowl. Place plastic wrap over surface; cool to room temperature. Yield: 4 servings (serving size: ½ cup).

CALORIES 240 (24% from fat); FAT 6.4g (sat 3.3g, mono 2g, poly 0.3g); PROTEIN 6.1g; CARB 40.8g; FIBER 0.1g; CHOL 60mg; IRON 0.5mg; SODIUM 78mg; CALC 160mg

RASPBERRY-BUTTERMILK SHERBET

Remember when you had your tonsils out? The milk shakes were the best part. Here's a smooth, cool treat for the sorest of throats.

  1 **(14-ounce) bag frozen unsweetened raspberries, thawed**
  1 **cup sugar**
  1 **teaspoon vanilla extract**
  1 **cup 2% reduced-fat milk**
  1 **cup low-fat buttermilk**

1. Place frozen raspberries in a food processor, and process until smooth. Strain raspberries through a sieve into a bowl, reserving raspberry puree. Discard solids. Combine raspberry puree, sugar, and vanilla in a large bowl. Stir in milks.
2. Pour mixture into freezer can of an ice-cream freezer, and freeze according to manufacturer's instructions. Spoon sherbet into a freezer-safe container; cover and freeze 1 hour or until firm. Yield: 7 servings (serving size: ½ cup).

CALORIES 205 (6% from fat); FAT 1.3g (sat 0.8g, mono 0.4g, poly 0.1g); PROTEIN 2.8g; CARB 46.8g; FIBER 4g; CHOL 3mg; IRON 0.4mg; SODIUM 36mg; CALC 94mg

PASSION-CHERRY GELATIN

There's nothing scientific about gelatin's healing properties. It just feels good going down.

  1 **(6-ounce) package cherry-flavored gelatin**
  3 **cups boiling water, divided**
  1⅓ **cups cold water, divided**
  2 **cups ice cubes, divided**
  1 **(16½-ounce) can pitted dark sweet cherries, drained and halved**
  2 **(8-ounce) cans tropical fruit salad in light syrup and passionfruit juice (such as Dole), undrained**
  2 **(3-ounce) packages peach-passionfruit-flavored gelatin**

1. Combine cherry-flavored gelatin and 1½ cups boiling water in a bowl; stir until gelatin dissolves (about 3 minutes). Add 1 cup cold water and 1 cup ice cubes; stir until ice melts. Chill until consistency of unbeaten egg white (about 10 to 15 minutes). Fold in cherries; pour into a 13 x 9-inch baking dish. Cover and chill until set but not firm (about 30 minutes).
2. Drain fruit salad in a colander over a bowl, reserving ⅔ cup juice. Combine peach-passionfruit-flavored gelatin and 1½ cups boiling water in a bowl; stir until gelatin dissolves (about 3 minutes). Add reserved juice, ⅓ cup cold water, and 1 cup ice cubes; stir until ice melts. Chill until consistency of unbeaten egg white (about 10 to 15 minutes). Fold in fruit salad, and

spoon over cherry mixture. Chill until firm (about 8 hours). Yield: 9 servings. *Note:* You can substitute sugar-free gelatin for the regular variety. For a 6-ounce box of regular, substitute the 0.6-ounce box of sugar-free. For the 3-ounce box of regular, substitute the 0.3-ounce box of sugar-free.

CALORIES 205 (0% from fat); FAT 0g; PROTEIN 4.1g; CARB 49.7g; FIBER 0.5g; CHOL 0mg; IRON 0.3mg; SODIUM 165mg; CALC 3mg

LEMON-MERINGUE SURPRISE PIE

The "surprise" in this filling is tofu, one of the latest "superfoods." Researchers find that in Asian countries where women eat a lot of tofu and other foods made from soybeans, hot flashes are rare. Phytoestrogens (plant estrogens), hormonelike substances found in soy foods, may be responsible. New studies are underway to examine soy as a natural alternative to hormone replacement.

  1 cup firm tofu (about 7 ounces)
  1 teaspoon grated lemon rind
  ⅓ cup fresh lemon juice
 1½ cups water
  1 cup sugar
  ⅓ cup cornstarch
  2 large egg yolks, lightly beaten
  1 (9-inch) reduced-fat graham cracker crust (such as Keebler)
  3 large egg whites (at room temperature)
  ¼ teaspoon cream of tartar
  ⅛ teaspoon salt
  ⅓ cup sugar

1. Preheat oven to 325°.
2. Combine first 3 ingredients in a blender; process until smooth. Combine water, 1 cup sugar, and cornstarch in a medium saucepan. Bring to a boil; cook 1 minute or until thick, stirring constantly with a whisk. Gradually add sugar mixture to egg yolks, stirring constantly. Return yolk mixture to pan. Bring to a boil over medium heat; cook

1 minute, stirring constantly. Remove from heat, and stir in tofu mixture. Spread filling evenly in crust.
3. Beat egg whites, cream of tartar, and salt at high speed of a mixer until foamy. Gradually add ⅓ cup sugar, 1 tablespoon at a time, beating until stiff peaks form. Spread evenly over filling, sealing to edge of crust. Bake at 325° for 25 minutes; cool 1 hour on a wire rack. Cut with a sharp knife dipped in hot water. Yield: 8 servings (serving size: 1 wedge).

CALORIES 292 (17% from fat); FAT 5.5g (sat 1.6g, mono 1.7g, poly 1.3g); PROTEIN 5g; CARB 55.8g; FIBER 1.2g; CHOL 54mg; IRON 1.9mg; SODIUM 156mg; CALC 34mg

GINGERBREAD

Ginger ale has long been used as a remedy for an upset stomach. But a generous slice of gingerbread could be just as effective. Research shows that compounds in ginger can sometimes suppress an upset stomach and nausea.

  ⅓ cup granulated sugar
  ¼ cup stick margarine or butter, softened
  ⅓ cup molasses
  1 large egg
 1½ cups all-purpose flour
  1 teaspoon ground ginger
  ½ teaspoon baking soda
  ¼ teaspoon ground nutmeg
  ⅛ teaspoon salt
  ⅛ teaspoon ground cloves
  ⅔ cup 1% low-fat milk
Cooking spray
  2 teaspoons powdered sugar

1. Preheat oven to 350°.
2. Beat granulated sugar and margarine at medium speed of a mixer until well-blended (about 5 minutes). Add molasses and egg; beat well.
3. Lightly spoon flour into dry measuring cups, and level with a knife. Combine flour and next 5 ingredients. Add flour mixture to sugar mixture alternately with milk, beginning and ending with flour mixture.

4. Pour batter into an 8-inch square baking pan coated with cooking spray. Bake at 350° for 30 minutes or until a wooden pick inserted in center comes out clean. Cool in pan on a wire rack. Sift powdered sugar over cake, and serve warm. Yield: 9 servings.

CALORIES 201 (27% from fat); FAT 6.1g (sat 1.3g, mono 2.5g, poly 1.8g); PROTEIN 3.5g; CARB 33.2g; FIBER 0.6g; CHOL 25mg; IRON 1.7mg; SODIUM 183mg; CALC 55mg

It's in the Bag

With the "out to lunch" sign becoming a thing of the past, we've created jazzy new lunches that you can bring to work.

It's not every day that you can get out for lunch at some trendy bistro. Some days, you get stuck at your desk or on a plane. Well, know that you're not alone. Research shows that more Americans are either skipping lunch or brown-bagging it so that they can be more productive. On the days that you can't find the time for a two-hour expense-account lunch, don't fret. We've got the next best thing: recipes that will put new zip in your zip-top bag. These recipes are easy and can be made the night before. So when someone asks you where you're having lunch today, tell them you have reservations at the best place in town: Chez Desk.

COUSCOUS-AND-BLACK BEAN SALAD

  1 large orange
  ⅛ teaspoon salt
  ⅔ cup uncooked couscous
  1 cup canned black beans, rinsed and drained
  ½ cup chopped red bell pepper
  ¼ cup chopped green onions
  2 tablespoons chopped fresh parsley
  1 tablespoon seasoned rice vinegar
 1½ teaspoons vegetable oil
  ¼ teaspoon ground cumin

Continued

1. Grate ¼ teaspoon orange rind, and set aside. Squeeze juice from orange over a bowl; reserve ¼ cup juice, and set aside. Add water to remaining juice in bowl to equal 1 cup.

2. Bring water mixture and salt to a boil in a medium saucepan; gradually stir in couscous. Remove from heat; cover and let stand 5 minutes. Fluff with a fork. Cool slightly. Stir in orange rind, beans, and next 3 ingredients.

3. Combine reserved ¼ cup orange juice, vinegar, oil, and cumin. Add couscous mixture, and toss well. Store salad in an airtight container in refrigerator. Yield: 2 servings (serving size: 2 cups).

CALORIES 342 (13% from fat); FAT 4.8g (sat 0.8g, mono 1.1g, poly 2g); PROTEIN 14.7g; CARB 62.5g; FIBER 6.6g; CHOL 0mg; IRON 3.9mg; SODIUM 391mg; CALC 46mg

HAM-AND-RICE SALAD WITH SPINACH

1½ cups water
⅔ cup uncooked fast-cooking recipe long-grain and wild rice (such as Uncle Ben's)
¼ cup sweetened dried cranberries (such as Craisins)
4 cups chopped spinach leaves
1 cup diced cooked ham
¼ cup chopped red onion
2 teaspoons olive oil
1 (11-ounce) can mandarin oranges in light syrup, undrained

1. Bring water and rice to a boil in a saucepan. Cover, reduce heat, and simmer 22 minutes. Stir in cranberries; cover and cook 2 minutes. Remove from heat. Let stand, covered, 5 minutes or until liquid is absorbed. Cool. Combine rice mixture, spinach, and remaining ingredients in a large bowl; toss well. Store in an airtight container in refrigerator. Yield: 2 servings (serving size: 2 cups).

CALORIES 451 (28% from fat); FAT 14.2g (sat 3.6g, mono 7.5g, poly 1.6g); PROTEIN 20.7g; CARB 49.8g; FIBER 6.3g; CHOL 48mg; IRON 5.4mg; SODIUM 1,229mg; CALC 146mg

THAI SHRIMP-AND-PASTA SALAD

Store the shrimp-pasta mixture and vinaigrette separately in the refrigerator; toss just before serving. Fish sauce is a salty condiment that accounts for the high sodium content of this salad. It comes bottled and is sometimes labeled nam pla *in Asian markets or your supermarket's ethnic-food section.*

2 ounces uncooked linguine
½ cup shredded carrot
8 ounces medium shrimp, cooked and peeled
1 cup thinly sliced Boston lettuce leaves
¼ cup fresh cilantro leaves
2 tablespoons chopped unsalted, dry-roasted peanuts
¼ cup fresh lime juice
2 tablespoons fish sauce
2 tablespoons chopped fresh cilantro
1 tablespoon chopped green onions
2½ teaspoons sugar
2 teaspoons vegetable oil
1 teaspoon grated peeled fresh ginger
2 garlic cloves, minced

1. Cook pasta in boiling water 9½ minutes. Add carrot; cook an additional 30 seconds. Drain and cool. Combine pasta mixture, shrimp, and next 3 ingredients in a large bowl; toss well.

2. Combine lime juice and remaining 7 ingredients in a jar. Cover tightly, and shake vigorously. Pour over pasta mixture, tossing gently to coat. Yield: 2 servings (serving size: 2 cups).

CALORIES 367 (28% from fat); FAT 10.6g (sat 2g, mono 3.8g, poly 4.8g); PROTEIN 26.2g; CARB 37.4g; FIBER 3.2g; CHOL 166mg; IRON 4.9mg; SODIUM 1,512mg; CALC 80mg

CURRIED TOFU-EGG SALAD SANDWICHES

¾ cup finely chopped firm light tofu (about 5 ounces)
2 tablespoons chopped fresh cilantro
1 tablespoon chopped green onions
2 tablespoons light mayonnaise
2 tablespoons plain fat-free yogurt
1 teaspoon hot pepper sauce
½ teaspoon curry powder
¼ teaspoon salt
⅛ teaspoon pepper
2 hard-cooked large eggs, finely chopped
6 (1.2-ounce) slices whole-grain bread

1. Combine first 10 ingredients in a medium bowl, and stir until mixture is well-blended.

2. Spread ½ cup tofu mixture over each of 3 bread slices, and top with remaining bread slices. Store in small zip-top bags in refrigerator. Yield: 3 sandwiches.

CALORIES 272 (29% from fat); FAT 8.9g (sat 2.2g, mono 2g, poly 3g); PROTEIN 15g; CARB 35.3g; FIBER 3.3g; CHOL 147mg; IRON 2.6mg; SODIUM 729mg; CALC 127mg

CAESAR CHICKEN-SALAD SANDWICHES

2 (4-ounce) skinned, boned chicken breast halves
1 tablespoon fresh lemon juice, divided
2 teaspoons low-sodium soy sauce
Cooking spray
3 tablespoons light mayonnaise
2 tablespoons grated Parmesan cheese
1 teaspoon Dijon mustard
½ teaspoon anchovy paste
½ teaspoon bottled minced garlic
⅛ teaspoon pepper
4 (1.2-ounce) slices whole-grain bread
2 romaine lettuce leaves
4 (¼-inch-thick) slices tomato

1. Preheat broiler.

2. Combine chicken, 2 teaspoons lemon juice, and soy sauce in a large zip-top plastic bag; seal and marinate in refrigerator 10 minutes, turning bag once. Remove chicken from bag. Place chicken on rack of a broiler pan coated with cooking spray; broil 6 minutes on each side or until done. Cool; shred chicken with 2 forks.

3. Combine chicken, 1 teaspoon lemon juice, mayonnaise, and next 5 ingredients. Spread 1 cup chicken mixture over 2 bread slices. Top each with 1 lettuce leaf, 2 tomato slices, and 1 bread slice. Store sandwiches in small zip-top bags in refrigerator. Yield: 2 sandwiches.

CALORIES 366 (28% from fat); FAT 11.4g (sat 3.1g, mono 1.2g, poly 3.7g); PROTEIN 30g; CARB 37.3g; FIBER 3g; CHOL 63mg; IRON 2.4mg; SODIUM 1,054mg; CALC 155mg

SMOKED-SALMON SANDWICHES

- 2 ounces smoked salmon
- ⅓ cup tub-style light cream cheese
- 1 teaspoon lemon juice
- 2 teaspoons chopped fresh or ½ teaspoon dried dill
- 2 teaspoons minced red onion
- 4 (1-ounce) slices pumpernickel bread
- 4 (⅛-inch-thick) slices tomato
- 8 (⅛-inch-thick) slices cucumber

1. Combine first 3 ingredients in a food processor; process until smooth. Spoon into a bowl; stir in dill and onion.

2. Divide salmon mixture evenly between 2 bread slices; top each with 2 tomato slices, 4 cucumber slices, and 1 bread slice. Store in small zip-top bags in refrigerator. Yield: 2 sandwiches.

CALORIES 265 (28% from fat); FAT 8.3g (sat 4.1g, mono 0.7g, poly 0.8g); PROTEIN 14.7g; CARB 35g; FIBER 4g; CHOL 29mg; IRON 2mg; SODIUM 760mg; CALC 112mg

HUMMUS SPREAD

- ½ cup 1% low-fat cottage cheese
- ¼ cup fresh parsley leaves
- 2 tablespoons tahini (sesame-seed paste)
- ¼ teaspoon grated lemon rind
- 1 tablespoon fresh lemon juice
- ½ teaspoon ground coriander
- ⅛ teaspoon salt
- 1 garlic clove
- 1 (15-ounce) can chickpeas (garbanzo beans), rinsed and drained

1. Place all ingredients in a food processor; process until smooth, scraping sides of processor bowl once. Store in an airtight container in refrigerator. Serve with pita triangles or fresh vegetables. Yield: 4 servings (serving size: ½ cup).

CALORIES 184 (30% from fat); FAT 6.1g (sat 0.9g, mono 2g, poly 2.5g); PROTEIN 11.2g; CARB 22.7g; FIBER 3.4g; CHOL 1mg; IRON 3mg; SODIUM 342mg; CALC 92mg

FAST FOOD

Slice 'n Easy

Now that you can buy polenta in prepackaged rolls, try these entrées that showcase its versatility.

Once Americans caught on to polenta, it was inevitable that someone would make this rustic Italian favorite more convenient. Just as you can buy frozen pizzas, shrink-wrapped focaccia, and bottled marinara sauce, you can now buy slice-and-bake polenta. Good thing, too, because traditional polenta takes lots of time and effort. But with the packaged, premade rolls that resemble slice-and-bake cookie logs, there's no tedious preparation. And because polenta is basically cornmeal, it's receptive to all kinds of flavors.

So the next time *la famiglia* is hungry for Italian food, forget the boiling water. Just slice, and bake. After all, that's how it's done in America.

TRIPLE-MUSHROOM POLENTA

Preparation time: 15 minutes
Cooking time: 19 minutes

- 1 (3½-ounce) package fresh shiitake mushrooms
- 1 (3-ounce) package fresh chanterelle mushrooms
- 1 (3-ounce) package fresh oyster mushrooms
- 2 teaspoons olive oil
- ⅓ cup minced shallots
- 3 garlic cloves, minced
- 2 tablespoons all-purpose flour
- 1 (14¼-ounce) can no-salt-added beef broth
- 1½ tablespoons minced fresh or 1½ teaspoons dried thyme
- ½ teaspoon freshly ground pepper
- 1 (16-ounce) roll wild-mushroom polenta, cut crosswise into 12 slices

Cooking spray
- ½ cup (2 ounces) grated Asiago or Parmesan cheese

1. Preheat broiler.

2. Remove stems from mushrooms. Slice mushroom caps to equal 4 cups. Heat oil in a large nonstick skillet over medium heat. Add shallots; cook 3 minutes. Add mushrooms and garlic; cook 4 minutes, stirring occasionally. Sprinkle flour over mushroom mixture; cook 30 seconds, stirring constantly. Stir in broth, thyme, and pepper; cook 3 minutes or until sauce thickens, stirring frequently.

3. Place polenta on a baking sheet coated with cooking spray; broil 4 minutes on each side or until thoroughly heated. Top with mushroom mixture; sprinkle with cheese. Yield: 4 servings (serving size: ⅔ cup mushroom mixture, 3 polenta slices, and 2 tablespoons cheese).

CALORIES 212 (28% from fat); FAT 6.6g (sat 2.8g, mono 2.8g, poly 0.4g); PROTEIN 9.1g; CARB 26.9g; FIBER 3.3g; CHOL 15mg; IRON 2.2mg; SODIUM 376mg; CALC 169mg

POLENTA WITH ROASTED VEGETABLES

(pictured on page 59)

Preparation time: 20 minutes
Cooking time: 32 minutes

4 cups (1-inch) pieces zucchini
   (about 2 medium)
2½ cups (1-inch) pieces red bell
   pepper (about 2 peppers)
1 cup (1-inch) pieces red onion
1 tablespoon olive oil
Cooking spray
⅓ cup chopped fresh basil
1½ tablespoons balsamic vinegar
¼ teaspoon black pepper, divided
2 (16-ounce) rolls polenta, each
   cut crosswise into 12 slices
¼ teaspoon salt
½ cup (2 ounces) crumbled goat
   cheese or feta cheese
Basil sprigs (optional)

1. Preheat oven to 475°.
2. Combine first 4 ingredients in a large bowl; arrange in a single layer on a jelly-roll pan coated with cooking spray. Bake at 475° for 25 minutes or until tender, stirring after 15 minutes. Stir in chopped basil, vinegar, and ⅛ teaspoon black pepper.
3. Preheat broiler. Place polenta slices on a baking sheet coated with cooking spray; sprinkle with salt and ⅛ teaspoon black pepper. Broil 7 minutes on each side or until lightly browned. Spoon roasted vegetables over polenta; sprinkle with cheese. Garnish with basil sprigs, if desired. Yield: 4 servings (serving size: 1 cup vegetables, 6 polenta slices, and 2 tablespoons cheese).

CALORIES 288 (23% from fat); FAT 7.2g (sat 2.7g, mono 3.2g, poly 0.7g); PROTEIN 8.9g; CARB 45.3g; FIBER 7g; CHOL 13mg; IRON 3.4mg; SODIUM 713mg; CALC 109mg

---

MENU SUGGESTION

EASY POLENTA LASAGNA

Mesclun-and-beet salad with sweet-and-sour dressing*

*Combine 6 cups mesclun (gourmet salad greens), ½ cup sliced red onion, 2 tablespoons toasted slivered almonds, and 1 (15-ounce) can whole baby beets, drained. Toss with ¼ cup low-fat sweet-and-sour dressing. Serves 4.

EASY POLENTA LASAGNA

Preparation time: 10 minutes
Cooking time: 35 minutes

1 (16-ounce) roll polenta, cut
   crosswise into 12 slices
Cooking spray
1¼ cups part-skim ricotta cheese
½ teaspoon dried crushed red
   pepper
1 (10-ounce) package frozen
   chopped spinach, thawed,
   drained, and squeezed dry
1 large egg white
1 cup fat-free marinara sauce
½ cup (2 ounces) finely grated fresh
   Parmesan cheese
¼ cup thinly sliced fresh basil

1. Preheat oven to 400°.
2. Arrange polenta slices in an 11 x 7-inch baking dish coated with cooking spray. Combine ricotta cheese and next 3 ingredients in a medium bowl. Spread over polenta; spoon marinara sauce evenly over ricotta cheese mixture. Cover with foil; bake at 400° for 30 minutes. Uncover; sprinkle with Parmesan cheese. Bake an additional 5 minutes or until cheese melts. Sprinkle with basil. Yield: 4 servings.

CALORIES 291 (32% from fat); FAT 10.2g (sat 6.2g, mono 2.8g, poly 0.4g); PROTEIN 19.8g; CARB 28.6g; FIBER 5.3g; CHOL 33mg; IRON 3mg; SODIUM 740mg; CALC 511mg

---

SOUTHWESTERN BEAN STEW OVER POLENTA

Preparation time: 20 minutes
Cooking time: 22 minutes

2 teaspoons vegetable oil
1 cup chopped green bell pepper
1 cup chopped red bell pepper
½ cup chopped onion
3 garlic cloves, minced
½ cup bottled salsa
2 teaspoons ground cumin
1 (15-ounce) can black beans,
   rinsed and drained
1 (14.5-ounce) can no-salt-added
   diced tomatoes, undrained
1 (16-ounce) roll Mexican
   pepper polenta, cut crosswise
   into 12 slices
¼ cup fat-free sour cream
¼ cup chopped fresh cilantro
4 ounces ripe diced peeled
   avocado (about ½ small)

1. Heat oil in a medium saucepan over medium heat. Add bell peppers, onion, and garlic; sauté for 6 minutes. Stir in salsa and next 3 ingredients; bring to a boil. Cover, reduce heat, and simmer 10 minutes, stirring occasionally.
2. Quarter each polenta slice. Place in a shallow 2-quart microwave-safe baking dish. Microwave, uncovered, at HIGH for 2 minutes or until hot, tossing gently after 1 minute.
3. Divide polenta evenly among 4 bowls, and spoon ¾ cup of bean stew over each serving. Top each serving with 1 tablespoon sour cream, 1 tablespoon cilantro, and 2½ tablespoons avocado. Yield: 4 servings.

CALORIES 296 (23% from fat); FAT 7.7g (sat 1.3g, mono 3.6g, poly 2.1g); PROTEIN 11.4g; CARB 46.8g; FIBER 7.7g; CHOL 0mg; IRON 4.9mg; SODIUM 481mg; CALC 96mg

MOROCCAN CHICKEN WITH POLENTA

Preparation time: 15 minutes
Cooking time: 22 minutes

  2 tablespoons all-purpose flour
1½ teaspoons ground cumin
1½ teaspoons ground coriander
  ½ teaspoon ground red pepper
  ¼ teaspoon salt
  ¼ teaspoon ground cinnamon
  1 pound skinned, boned chicken
       breasts, cut into 1-inch pieces
  2 teaspoons olive oil
  ¾ cup low-salt chicken broth
  ⅓ cup raisins
  1 teaspoon ground turmeric
  1 (16-ounce) roll wild-mushroom
       polenta, cut crosswise into 12
       slices
     Cooking spray
  ¼ cup plain fat-free yogurt
  ¼ cup sliced almonds, toasted
  ¼ cup chopped fresh cilantro

1. Combine first 6 ingredients in a medium bowl; reserve 1 tablespoon flour mixture. Add chicken to flour mixture in bowl; toss gently to coat. Heat oil in a large nonstick skillet over medium-high heat. Add chicken; cook 5 minutes, stirring frequently. Stir in broth, raisins, and turmeric; bring to a boil. Reduce heat; simmer 8 minutes or until slightly thick.
2. Preheat broiler. Place polenta slices on a baking sheet coated with cooking spray, and sprinkle with reserved 1 tablespoon flour mixture. Broil 8 minutes or until thoroughly heated. Serve chicken mixture over polenta; top with yogurt, and sprinkle with almonds and cilantro. Yield: 4 servings (serving size: 1 cup chicken mixture, 3 polenta slices, 1 tablespoon yogurt, 1 tablespoon almonds, and 1 tablespoon cilantro).

CALORIES 333 (21% from fat); FAT 7.6g (sat 1.2g, mono 4.2g, poly 1.3g); PROTEIN 31.9g; CARB 32.4g; FIBER 3.8g; CHOL 67mg; IRON 3.4mg; SODIUM 457mg; CALC 84mg

SHRIMP AND FENNEL OVER POLENTA

To speed up prep time of this dish, buy peeled and deveined shrimp. Broil the polenta to warm the slices and give them a crispy crust.

Preparation time: 15 minutes
Cooking time: 19 minutes

  1 fennel bulb
  2 teaspoons olive oil
  3 garlic cloves, minced
  1 tablespoon all-purpose flour
  1 cup low-salt chicken broth
  ¼ cup dry vermouth or white wine
  2 tablespoons sun-dried tomato
       sprinkles
  ½ teaspoon hot sauce
  1 pound medium shrimp, peeled
       and deveined
  1 (16-ounce) roll polenta, cut
       crosswise into 12 slices
     Cooking spray
  ½ teaspoon pepper

1. Remove and discard stalks from fennel bulb. Cut fennel bulb in half lengthwise; discard core. Chop fennel bulb to measure 1½ cups.
2. Heat oil in a large nonstick skillet over medium-high heat. Add chopped fennel bulb and garlic; sauté 5 minutes or until tender. Add flour, and cook 1 minute, stirring constantly with a whisk. Stir in broth and next 3 ingredients; bring to a boil. Reduce heat, and simmer 5 minutes or until thick, stirring occasionally. Add shrimp, and cook 1 minute. Keep warm.
3. Preheat broiler. Place polenta on a baking sheet coated with cooking spray. Sprinkle polenta with pepper. Broil 6 minutes or until lightly browned. Serve shrimp mixture over polenta. Yield: 4 servings (serving size: ¾ cup shrimp mixture and 3 polenta slices).

CALORIES 229 (18% from fat); FAT 4.5g (sat 0.8g, mono 1.9g, poly 0.8g); PROTEIN 21.8g; CARB 23.1g; FIBER 2.4g; CHOL 130mg; IRON 4.1mg; SODIUM 397mg; CALC 96mg

COOKING CLASS

Tropical Trio

Spring is the time for pineapple, papaya, and mango. They're abundant and waiting to be picked.

To celebrate spring's bounty of exotic produce, we've created recipes that showcase three of its biggest stars—pineapple, papaya, and mango—both solo and in concert. These tropical beauties aren't just for desserts, either. They're perfect for light entrées, providing a sweet-tart contrast to chicken and seafood for some Floribbean flair.

MANGO-MUSTARD GLAZED CHICKEN

  1 cup chopped peeled mango
  1 cup pineapple juice
  ½ cup apricot or peach preserves
  ½ cup dry white wine
1½ tablespoons stone-ground
       mustard
  1 tablespoon cornstarch
  1 tablespoon water
  6 (4-ounce) skinned, boned
       chicken breast halves
  ¼ teaspoon salt
  ¼ teaspoon pepper
     Cooking spray

1. Combine first 7 ingredients in a bowl; stir well with a whisk.
2. Sprinkle chicken with salt and pepper. Heat a large nonstick skillet coated with cooking spray over medium-high heat until hot. Add chicken; cook 3 minutes on each side or until browned. Remove chicken. Add mango mixture, and bring to a boil. Return chicken to skillet; reduce heat, and simmer 15 minutes or until chicken is done and sauce thickens, stirring occasionally. Yield: 6 servings (serving size: 1 chicken breast half and 3 tablespoons sauce).

CALORIES 241 (7% from fat); FAT 1.9g (sat 0.4g, mono 0.4g, poly 0.4g); PROTEIN 26.9g; CARB 29.3g; FIBER 0.9g; CHOL 66mg; IRON 1.3mg; SODIUM 236mg; CALC 34mg

MANGO

The mango is originally from India but is now grown in temperate climates around the world, including California and Florida. Look for fruit with unblemished yellow skin, blushed with red. Very fragrant when ripe, mangoes are ready to eat when they become soft to the touch.

❶ *The mango can be tricky to cut because it has a rather large flat seed that grows inside the fruit. You must therefore cut around it on both sides. Hold the mango vertically on the cutting board.*

❷ *With a sharp knife, slice the fruit lengthwise on each side of the flat pit.*

❸ *Holding the mango half in the palm of your hand, score the pulp. Be sure that you slice to, but not through, the skin.*

❹ *Turn the mango inside out, and cut the chunks from the skin.*

MANGO TANGO CHICKEN SALAD

3¼ cups chopped ready-to-eat roasted skinned, boned chicken breast halves (such as Tyson) (about 4 breast halves)
½ cup diced peeled mango
½ cup diced fresh pineapple
½ cup drained, sliced water chestnuts
½ cup sliced celery
¼ cup sliced green onions
1 tablespoon mango chutney
1 tablespoon light mayonnaise
1 tablespoon low-fat sour cream
2 teaspoons lemon juice
½ teaspoon salt
1 teaspoon minced peeled fresh ginger
¼ teaspoon pepper
10 slices peeled papaya (about 1 large)

1. Combine first 6 ingredients in a large bowl. Combine chutney and next 6 ingredients in a small bowl; stir chutney mixture into chicken mixture. Arrange 2 papaya slices on each of 5 plates, and top with chicken salad. Yield: 5 servings (serving size: 1 cup salad and 2 papaya slices).

CALORIES 163 (15% from fat); FAT 2.8g (sat 1.1g, mono 0.8g, poly 0.8g); PROTEIN 8.7g; CARB 16.2g; FIBER 1.9g; CHOL 51mg; IRON 0.4mg; SODIUM 685mg; CALC 30mg

CARIBBEAN COBB SALAD

4 cups torn romaine lettuce
1 pound medium shrimp, cooked and peeled
1 cup cubed peeled papaya
1 cup cubed fresh pineapple
½ cup chopped peeled avocado
½ cup chopped red or green bell pepper
1 (15-ounce) can black beans, rinsed and drained
½ cup (2 ounces) shredded reduced-fat Monterey Jack cheese
½ cup Orange-Soy Vinaigrette
¼ cup chopped unsalted cashews, toasted

1. Arrange lettuce on a serving platter. Spoon shrimp down center of platter; arrange papaya and next 5 ingredients in rows on either side of shrimp. Drizzle 2 tablespoons Orange-Soy Vinaigrette over each salad; sprinkle each with 1 tablespoon cashews. Yield: 4 servings.

CALORIES 383 (35% from fat); FAT 14.7g (sat 3.7g, mono 6.3g, poly 2.7g); PROTEIN 30.6g; CARB 34.6g; FIBER 6.1g; CHOL 175mg; IRON 5.9mg; SODIUM 553mg; CALC 208mg

Orange-Soy Vinaigrette:

- ½ cup orange juice
- ½ cup pineapple juice
- 1 tablespoon minced fresh parsley
- 2 tablespoons fresh lime juice
- 2 tablespoons low-sodium soy sauce
- 1 tablespoon extra-virgin olive oil
- 1 tablespoon dark sesame oil
- 2 teaspoons sugar
- 1 teaspoon lemon pepper

1. Combine all ingredients in a jar; cover tightly, and shake vigorously. Yield: 1⅓ cups (serving size: 2 tablespoons).

CALORIES 43 (57% from fat); FAT 2.7g (sat 0.4g, mono 1.5g, poly 0.7g); PROTEIN 0.2g; CARB 4.3g; FIBER 0.1g; CHOL 0mg; IRON 0.1mg; SODIUM 79mg; CALC 5mg

SPICY TROPICAL GAZPACHO

This gazpacho, which combines Spanish and Caribbean flavors, has a slightly chunky texture.

- 1 cup tomato juice
- 1 cup pineapple juice
- ½ cup chopped peeled mango
- ½ cup chopped peeled papaya
- ½ cup chopped fresh pineapple
- ½ cup chopped seeded peeled cucumber
- ¼ cup chopped green bell pepper
- ¼ cup chopped red bell pepper
- 2 tablespoons minced fresh cilantro
- ¼ teaspoon salt
- ½ to 1 teaspoon hot sauce

1. Combine all ingredients in a food processor or blender; pulse 4 times or until combined. Cover and chill. Yield: 4 servings (serving size: 1 cup).

CALORIES 83 (4% from fat); FAT 0.4g (sat 0.1g, mono 0.1g, poly 0.1g); PROTEIN 1.3g; CARB 20.5g; FIBER 1.7g; CHOL 0mg; IRON 1mg; SODIUM 375mg; CALC 31mg

GOLD-COAST GROUPER WITH MOJO MARINARA

Mojo is a spicy, though not hot, sauce made with citrus and herbs. If grouper is not available, try any white, firm-fleshed fish.

- 2 teaspoons vegetable oil
- ½ cup chopped green onions
- ¼ cup chopped fresh pineapple
- ¼ cup chopped peeled mango
- ¼ cup chopped red bell pepper
- ¼ cup chopped green bell pepper
- 2 teaspoons minced seeded jalapeño pepper
- 2 teaspoons minced fresh thyme, divided
- ½ cup tomato puree
- 2 tablespoons fresh lime juice
- ½ teaspoon salt, divided
- ½ teaspoon black pepper
- 4 (6-ounce) grouper fillets
Cooking spray

1. Preheat oven to 400°.
2. Heat oil in a medium saucepan over medium heat until hot. Add green onions, pineapple, mango, bell peppers, jalapeño, and 1 teaspoon thyme; sauté 2 minutes. Add tomato puree, lime juice, ¼ teaspoon salt, and black pepper; bring to a boil. Cover, reduce heat, and simmer 5 minutes. Remove from heat; keep warm.
3. Rub fish with 1 teaspoon thyme and ¼ teaspoon salt. Place fish on rack of a broiler pan coated with cooking spray. Spoon mango mixture evenly over fish. Bake at 400° for 20 minutes or until fish flakes easily when tested with a fork. Yield: 4 servings (serving size: 5 ounces fish and ⅓ cup sauce).

CALORIES 214 (19% from fat); FAT 4.4g (sat 0.8g, mono 1.1g, poly 1.7g); PROTEIN 34.1g; CARB 9.1g; FIBER 1.8g; CHOL 63mg; IRON 2.4mg; SODIUM 511mg; CALC 66mg

PAPAYA

This fruit comes in many varieties, sizes, and colors. The most common is the Solo, grown in Hawaii and Florida. These can have a green or golden-colored skin and a sweet, perfumelike smell.

❶ *Cut about 1 inch from each end of the fruit.*

❷ *With a paring knife or vegetable peeler, remove the skin in ½-inch slices.*

❸ *Cut the papaya in half lengthwise, and remove the seeds with a spoon. The fruit can now be cut as needed for the recipe.*

A ripe pineapple should be deep golden-brown in color and have a slightly sweet smell; it should also be a bit soft to the touch. The leaves should pull out from the top without much effort. Avoid fruit that has dark, soft spots or a woody-looking or whitish appearance.

❶ *Cut about 1 inch from each end.*

❷ *Stand the pineapple vertically on the cutting board. Using a sharp knife, slice down about ½ inch into the skin. This should remove the eyes from the pineapple flesh.*

❸ *Keep turning the pineapple with one hand and slicing 1-inch-wide bands down in a straight line until the pineapple is peeled.*

❹ *Cut the fruit into quarters. While holding each pineapple quarter firmly, remove the core.*

❺ *Cut the pineapple wedges in half lengthwise; then cut as needed for the recipe.*

PINEAPPLE-COCONUT RICE

This lively side dish brightens up a simple fish or pork entrée.

- 2 teaspoons olive oil
- 1 cup diced onion
- 2 teaspoons minced fresh or ½ teaspoon dried thyme
- ¼ teaspoon pepper
- ¾ cup uncooked basmati or long-grain rice
- 1½ cups diced fresh pineapple
- 1 cup water
- ½ cup chopped green onions
- ½ cup pineapple juice
- 2 tablespoons flaked sweetened coconut
- ½ teaspoon salt

1. Heat olive oil in a large saucepan over medium heat. Add diced onion, thyme, and pepper; sauté 2 minutes. Add rice, and cook 1 minute. Stir in pineapple and remaining ingredients; bring to a boil. Cover, reduce heat, and simmer 20 minutes or until rice is done and liquid is absorbed. Yield: 4 servings (serving size: 1 cup).

CALORIES 228 (15% from fat); FAT 3.9g (sat 1.3g, mono 1.8g, poly 0.4g); PROTEIN 3.6g; CARB 45.4g; FIBER 2.6g; CHOL 0mg; IRON 2.2mg; SODIUM 306mg; CALC 39mg

PINEAPPLE-RUM BREAD PUDDING

- 1½ cups cubed fresh pineapple
- ¾ cup packed brown sugar
- ½ cup rum
- Cooking spray
- 8 cups (½-inch) cubed French bread (about 16 [1-ounce] slices)
- 3 cups 2% reduced-fat milk
- ½ cup packed brown sugar
- 1 tablespoon molasses
- 2 teaspoons minced peeled fresh ginger
- ¼ teaspoon ground cinnamon
- ¼ teaspoon ground allspice
- ¼ teaspoon ground nutmeg
- 5 large egg whites
- 2 large eggs

1. Preheat oven to 325°.
2. Combine first 3 ingredients in a bowl; toss gently to coat. Spoon into a 13 x 9-inch baking dish coated with cooking spray.
3. Place bread cubes in a single layer on a jelly-roll pan. Bake at 325° for 15 minutes or until toasted. Combine milk and remaining 8 ingredients in a large bowl. Add bread cubes, and toss gently. Let mixture stand 15 minutes. Spoon bread mixture over pineapple mixture. Bake at 325° for 35 minutes or until pudding is set. Serve warm or at room temperature. Yield: 12 servings.

CALORIES 241 (12% from fat); FAT 3.3g (sat 1.3g, mono 1.1g, poly 0.6g); PROTEIN 7.5g; CARB 46g; FIBER 1g; CHOL 43mg; IRON 1.6mg; SODIUM 242mg; CALC 128mg

ORANGE-SCENTED FLAN WITH ROASTED PINEAPPLE

Roasted pineapple can be served over low-fat ice cream or angel food cake.

    5   cups (½-inch-thick) chunks fresh pineapple
    1   tablespoon fresh lime juice
    1   tablespoon stick margarine or butter, melted
    1   teaspoon vanilla extract
    1   tablespoon minced fresh mint
    2   cups 2% reduced-fat milk
    2   teaspoons grated orange rind
    1   vanilla bean, split or ¾ teaspoon vanilla extract
 1½   cups sugar, divided
    ½   cup water
    3   large eggs
    2   large egg whites

1. Preheat oven to 450°.
2. Combine first 4 ingredients in a 3-quart casserole. Bake at 450° for 40 minutes, stirring once. Remove from oven. Stir in mint; set aside. Reduce oven temperature to 325°.
3. Combine milk, orange rind, and vanilla bean in a medium saucepan. Bring to a simmer over low heat; cook 10 minutes. Remove from heat; discard vanilla bean. (If using vanilla extract, remove mixture from heat; stir in extract.)

4. Combine ¾ cup sugar and water in a small heavy saucepan over medium heat; cook until golden (about 15 minutes). Immediately pour into a 9-inch round cake pan, tipping quickly until caramelized sugar coats bottom of pan.
5. Combine milk mixture, remaining ¾ cup sugar, eggs, and egg whites in a large bowl; stir well with a whisk. Pour mixture into prepared pan. Place cake pan in a large shallow pan; add hot water to shallow pan to a depth of 1 inch. Cover with foil; bake at 325° for 50 minutes or until a knife inserted in center comes out clean. Remove cake pan from water; cool completely on a wire rack. Cover and chill at least 3 hours.
6. Loosen edges of flan with a knife or rubber spatula. Place a plate, upside down, on top of pan; invert flan onto plate. Drizzle remaining caramelized syrup over flan. Cut flan into 8 wedges; top with pineapple mixture. Yield: 8 servings (serving size: 1 wedge flan and about ½ cup pineapple).

CALORIES 219 (17% from fat); FAT 4.2g (sat 1.9g, mono 1.3g, poly 0.4g); PROTEIN 4.4g; CARB 42.9g; FIBER 1.5g; CHOL 70mg; IRON 0.6mg; SODIUM 67mg; CALC 72mg

LAST HURRAH

Star Light

In honor of International Astrology Day, we've created a heavenly bean salad.

This month, your plate is in Pisces with a fork rising. That is to say, March 20 is International Astrology Day, which coincides with the vernal equinox. So here is our salute to celestial bodies everywhere: a Moon-Bean Salad made with blue cheese (which, after all, is what the moon is made of). One taste, and we predict that this recipe will never be in retrograde.

MOON-BEAN SALAD

    2   teaspoons olive oil, divided
    1   teaspoon dried oregano
    1   garlic clove, minced
    ¼   cup cider vinegar
    2   (16-ounce) cans cannellini beans or other white beans, rinsed and drained
 1½   cups diced plum tomato
    ½   cup chopped Vidalia or other sweet onion
    ½   cup (2 ounces) crumbled blue cheese
    ⅓   cup chopped fresh parsley
    ½   teaspoon salt
    ½   teaspoon pepper
Crostini

1. Heat 1 teaspoon oil in a nonstick skillet over medium-high heat. Add oregano and garlic; sauté 30 seconds. Add vinegar, and remove from heat. Combine vinegar mixture and beans in a large bowl. Cover and chill 30 minutes.
2. Add 1 teaspoon oil, tomato, and next 5 ingredients to bean mixture; toss well. Serve with Crostini. Yield: 8 servings (serving size: about ⅔ cup bean salad and 3 crostini).

CALORIES 289 (19% from fat); FAT 6g (sat 2g, mono 2.3g, poly 1.5g); PROTEIN 12.2g; CARB 46.8g; FIBER 4.3g; CHOL 7mg; IRON 3.5mg; SODIUM 640mg; CALC 103mg

Crostini:

   24   (½-inch-thick) slices diagonally-cut French bread baguette (about 12 ounces)
    1   garlic clove, halved
Olive oil-flavored cooking spray

1. Preheat oven to 400°.
2. Place bread slices in a single layer on a baking sheet. Bake at 400° for 5 minutes or until toasted. Rub cut sides of garlic over one side of each toasted bread slice. Coat with cooking spray. Bake at 400° 3 additional minutes. Yield: 8 servings (serving size: 3 crostini).

CALORIES 125 (6% from fat); FAT 0.9g (sat 0.3g, mono 0.4g, poly 0.4g); PROTEIN 3.9g; CARB 23.7g; FIBER 1g; CHOL 1mg; IRON 0.9mg; SODIUM 247mg; CALC 19mg

Reel Food

Because movies are on everybody's mind during Oscar month,
we decided to lighten up some tasty cinematic moments.

In honor of the Oscars, we decided to take a critical look at the movies and give recipes for dishes that have appeared in some of our favorite films. We've lightened them for today's audiences, and in some cases, we've reformatted and even colorized them.

"MYSTIC PIZZA" PIZZA

This pizza is our version of the ones served in the romantic comedy by the same name. In it, Leona, the owner of a local pizza parlor, closely guards her family's sauce recipe that's made with a secret blend of Portuguese spices.

1½ cups all-purpose flour, divided
1 teaspoon sugar
1 package quick-rise yeast
    (2½ teaspoons)
½ cup warm water (105° to 115°)
1 teaspoon olive oil
½ teaspoon salt, divided
Cooking spray
2 teaspoons cornmeal
3 garlic cloves, minced
1 tablespoon chopped fresh or
    1 teaspoon dried oregano
1 tablespoon minced fresh
    cilantro
¾ teaspoon fennel seeds
¼ teaspoon dried crushed red
    pepper
1 (8-ounce) can no-salt-added
    tomato sauce
1½ cups (6 ounces) shredded
    part-skim mozzarella cheese

1. Lightly spoon flour into dry measuring cups; level with a knife.
2. Dissolve sugar and yeast in warm water in a large bowl; let stand 5 minutes. Add 1¼ cups flour, 1 teaspoon oil, and ¼ teaspoon salt; stir to form a soft dough.
3. Turn dough out onto a lightly floured surface. Knead until smooth and elastic (about 10 minutes); add enough of remaining ¼ cup flour, 1 tablespoon at a time, to prevent dough from sticking to hands.
4. Place dough in a bowl coated with cooking spray; turn to coat top. Cover and let rise in a warm place (85°), free from drafts, 30 minutes or until doubled in bulk.
5. Preheat oven to 450°.
6. Punch dough down; roll dough into a 12-inch circle on a lightly floured surface. Place dough on a baking sheet or 12-inch pizza pan coated with cooking spray and sprinkled with cornmeal. Crimp edges of dough to form a rim. Let dough stand, covered, 10 minutes.
7. Place a small saucepan coated with cooking spray over medium heat until hot. Add garlic, and sauté 2 minutes. Add remaining ¼ teaspoon salt, oregano, and next 4 ingredients; reduce heat, and simmer, uncovered, 20 minutes or until mixture is thick, stirring occasionally. Spread sauce over pizza crust; sprinkle with cheese. Bake at 450° for 10 minutes or until cheese is melted and crust is golden. Remove pizza to a cutting board; cut into wedges. Yield: 6 servings.

CALORIES 221 (24% from fat); FAT 5.8g (sat 3g, mono 1.9g, poly 0.4g); PROTEIN 11.2g; CARB 30.4g; FIBER 1.4g; CHOL 16mg; IRON 2mg; SODIUM 338mg; CALC 199mg

"THE BIG EASY" CAJUN GUMBO

When The Big Easy *costars Dennis Quaid and Ellen Barkin dine out, Quaid's character banters with the chef about the amount of filé in his gumbo. Filé powder, which is made from dried sassafras leaves, is used to thicken and flavor gumbo.*

2 tablespoons all-purpose flour
1 tablespoon vegetable oil
1 cup chopped onion
1 cup chopped celery
1 cup chopped green bell pepper
4 garlic cloves, minced
¼ cup water
¾ teaspoon hot pepper sauce
1 (14.5-ounce) can no-salt-added
    stewed tomatoes, undrained
1 (10½-ounce) can low-salt chicken
    broth
2 bay leaves
½ pound turkey kielbasa, cut into
    ¼-inch-thick slices
½ pound medium shrimp, peeled
    and deveined
1 (10-ounce) package frozen cut
    okra, thawed
1 tablespoon filé powder
3 cups hot cooked rice

1. Place flour in a saucepan. Cook over medium-high heat 7 minutes or until very brown, stirring constantly with a whisk. (If flour browns too fast, remove from heat; stir constantly until it cools.) Place browned flour in a bowl.
2. Heat oil in pan over medium-high heat. Add onion and next 3 ingredients; sauté 8 minutes or until tender. Sprinkle with browned flour; cook 1 minute, stirring constantly. Stir in water and next 4 ingredients. Bring to a boil; reduce heat, and simmer, uncovered, 10 minutes. Add kielbasa; simmer, uncovered, 5 minutes. Add shrimp and okra; cover and simmer 5 minutes or until shrimp are done. Discard bay leaves. Stir in filé. Serve over rice. Yield: 6 servings (serving size: 1 cup gumbo and ½ cup rice).

CALORIES 301 (23% from fat); FAT 7.8g (sat 1.8g, mono 2.4g, poly 2.4g); PROTEIN 17.5g; CARB 40.9g; FIBER 2.2g; CHOL 70mg; IRON 3.3mg; SODIUM 445mg; CALC 111mg

"DESK SET" OVEN-FRIED CHICKEN BREASTS

In Desk Set, *Katharine Hepburn plays a corporate reference librarian and Spencer Tracy an efficiency expert. While falling in love, they discuss fried-chicken recipes. In one scene, Tracy even cooks the dish for Hepburn.*

¼ cup dry breadcrumbs
1 tablespoon grated Parmesan cheese
1 teaspoon paprika
1 teaspoon dried thyme
½ teaspoon garlic salt
¼ teaspoon ground red pepper
⅓ cup low-fat buttermilk
4 (6-ounce) skinned chicken breast halves
Cooking spray
1 tablespoon stick margarine or butter, melted

1. Preheat oven to 400°.
2. Combine first 6 ingredients in a shallow dish. Place buttermilk in a shallow dish. Dip chicken in buttermilk; dredge in breadcrumb mixture. Place chicken, bone sides down, in a jelly-roll pan coated with cooking spray. Drizzle margarine over chicken. Bake at 400° for 40 minutes or until done. Yield: 4 servings.

CALORIES 295 (27% from fat); FAT 9g (sat 2.3g, mono 3.2g, poly 2.1g); PROTEIN 44.1g; CARB 6.6g; FIBER 0.5g; CHOL 115mg; IRON 2.4mg; SODIUM 486mg; CALC 88mg

"LADY AND THE TRAMP" SPAGHETTI AND MEATBALLS

We've based this recipe on Disney's classic animated flick Lady and the Tramp, *which is about a romantic relationship between a lovable mongrel and a purebred cocker spaniel. In one scene, Tramp and Lady gaze adoringly at each other as they share a plate of spaghetti and meatballs.*

1 pound ground sirloin
¼ cup minced fresh onion
2 tablespoons dry breadcrumbs
¼ teaspoon garlic salt
¼ teaspoon pepper
1 large egg white, lightly beaten
1 (25.5-ounce) jar fat-free tomato-and-basil pasta sauce, divided
Cooking spray
5 cups hot cooked spaghetti (about 8 ounces uncooked pasta)
5 tablespoons grated Parmesan cheese
5 tablespoons chopped fresh basil

1. Combine first 6 ingredients and 2 tablespoons of pasta sauce in a medium bowl. Shape the meat mixture into 25 (1-inch) meatballs. Place a large non-stick skillet coated with cooking spray over medium heat until hot. Add meatballs, and cook 6 minutes, browning on all sides. Stir in remaining pasta sauce. Cover, reduce heat, and simmer 10 minutes or until the meatballs are done, stirring occasionally. Serve meatballs over spaghetti; sprinkle with Parmesan cheese and basil. Yield: 5 servings (serving size: 5 meatballs, ½ cup sauce, 1 cup pasta, 1 tablespoon cheese, and 1 tablespoon basil).

CALORIES 476 (19% from fat); FAT 10g (sat 3.8g, mono 3.7g, poly 0.8g); PROTEIN 38.2g; CARB 42.8g; FIBER 4.9g; CHOL 78mg; IRON 5.5mg; SODIUM 651mg; CALC 217mg

"TEQUILA SUNRISE" PASTA QUATTRO FORMAGGI

Two Hollywood hunks vie for the attentions of beautiful restaurant manager Michelle Pfeiffer in Tequila Sunrise. *But when Mel Gibson oohs and aahs over Pfeiffer's pasta with four cheeses, a food star is born.*

1 tablespoon stick margarine or butter
1 tablespoon all-purpose flour
½ teaspoon pepper
¼ teaspoon salt
1 (12-ounce) can evaporated skim milk
¼ cup (1 ounce) shredded fontina cheese
¼ cup (1 ounce) crumbled Gorgonzola or other blue cheese
¼ cup (1 ounce) diced Camembert cheese
6 cups hot cooked rigatoni (about 9 ounces uncooked pasta)
2 tablespoons chopped fresh basil
¼ cup (1 ounce) finely grated fresh Parmesan cheese

1. Melt margarine in a large saucepan over medium heat. Add flour; cook 30 seconds, stirring constantly with a whisk. Add pepper, salt, and milk; bring to a simmer, stirring frequently. Remove from heat; add fontina, Gorgonzola, and Camembert cheeses, stirring until cheeses melt. Stir in pasta and basil; spoon into 4 bowls. Sprinkle with Parmesan cheese. Yield: 4 servings (serving size: 1½ cups pasta and 1 tablespoon Parmesan).

CALORIES 485 (23% from fat); FAT 12.2g (sat 7g, mono 3.3g, poly 0.9g); PROTEIN 23.6g; CARB 68.9g; FIBER 3.3g; CHOL 35mg; IRON 3.3mg; SODIUM 548mg; CALC 453mg

"FRIED GREEN TOMATOES" BANANA CREAM PIE

In Fried Green Tomatoes, Mary-Louise Parker and Mary Stuart Masterson cook up a laundry list of freshly baked pies like this one.

1½ cups low-fat graham cracker crumbs (about 10 cracker sheets)
3 tablespoons reduced-calorie stick margarine, melted
2 tablespoons sugar
  Cooking spray
⅔ cup sugar
⅓ cup cornstarch
2½ cups 2% reduced-fat milk
2 large eggs, lightly beaten
1 large egg yolk, lightly beaten
2 teaspoons vanilla extract
2 drops yellow food coloring
2½ cups sliced ripe banana, divided
1 cup frozen reduced-calorie whipped topping, thawed

1. Preheat oven to 325°.
2. Combine first 3 ingredients in a medium bowl; toss with a fork until moist. Press into bottom and up sides of a 9-inch pie plate coated with cooking spray. Bake at 325° for 10 minutes; let cool.
3. Combine ⅔ cup sugar and cornstarch in a medium saucepan. Gradually add milk, stirring with a whisk. Bring to a boil over medium heat; cook 1 minute, stirring constantly. Gradually add hot milk mixture to eggs and egg yolk, stirring constantly with a whisk. Return milk mixture to pan; cook over medium heat until thick (about 4 minutes), stirring constantly. Remove from heat; stir in vanilla and food coloring.
4. Arrange 1¼ cups banana in prepared pie crust; pour half of custard over banana. Top with remaining banana and custard. Cover surface of custard with plastic wrap; chill 4 hours. Remove plastic wrap; spread whipped topping over pie. Yield: 8 servings.

CALORIES 256 (30% from fat); FAT 8.6g (sat 2.4g, mono 2.6g, poly 1.5g); PROTEIN 6.4g; CARB 55.5g; FIBER 2g; CHOL 89mg; IRON 1.1mg; SODIUM 220mg; CALC 111mg

"BREAKFAST AT TIFFANY'S" CINNAMON TWISTS

Here's our take on the pastry that Holly Golightly might have been munching on in the opening scene of Breakfast at Tiffany's.

1 package dry yeast (2½ teaspoons)
¼ cup warm water (105° to 115°)
3 cups all-purpose flour, divided
½ cup warm 2% reduced-fat milk (105° to 115°)
¼ cup granulated sugar
¼ cup stick margarine or butter, melted and divided
¼ teaspoon salt
1 large egg, lightly beaten
½ cup golden raisins
  Cooking spray
⅓ cup granulated sugar
2 teaspoons ground cinnamon
½ cup sifted powdered sugar
2½ teaspoons 2% reduced-fat milk
¼ teaspoon vanilla extract

1. Dissolve yeast in warm water in a large bowl; let stand 5 minutes. Lightly spoon flour into dry measuring cups; level with a knife. Add 2 cups flour, ½ cup warm milk, ¼ cup granulated sugar, 2 tablespoons margarine, salt, and egg to bowl; beat at medium speed of a mixer until mixture is smooth. Stir in ¾ cup flour and raisins to form a soft dough. Turn dough out onto a lightly floured surface. Knead until smooth and elastic (about 8 minutes); add enough of remaining flour, 1 tablespoon at a time, to prevent dough from sticking to hands.
2. Place dough in a large bowl coated with cooking spray, turning to coat top. Cover and let rise in a warm place (85°), free from drafts, 1 hour or until doubled in bulk. Punch dough down. Roll dough into a 12-inch square on a lightly floured surface. Brush with remaining 2 tablespoons margarine. Combine granulated sugar and cinnamon; sprinkle over dough. Cut dough in half crosswise. Cut each rectangle lengthwise into 12 strips. Place 2 strips together; twist. Pinch ends to seal. Place on a large baking sheet coated with cooking spray; gently press ends to baking sheet. Repeat procedure with remaining dough. Cover and let rise for 30 minutes or until doubled in bulk.
3. Preheat oven to 350°.
4. Bake at 350° for 15 minutes or until browned. Remove from baking sheet; cool on wire racks. Combine powdered sugar, 2½ teaspoons milk, and vanilla. Drizzle over twists. Yield: 1 dozen.

CALORIES 241 (18% from fat); FAT 4.9g (sat 1.1g, mono 2g, poly 1.4g); PROTEIN 4.6g; CARB 45.2g; FIBER 1.5g; CHOL 19mg; IRON 1.9mg; SODIUM 106mg; CALC 31mg

"GROUNDHOG DAY" BUTTERMILK PANCAKES

Bill Murray is a cynical weatherman who relives the same day over and over again in the comedy Groundhog Day. *After visiting the same restaurant for breakfast each day, he winds up ordering everything on the menu, from pancakes to angel food cake.*

1 cup all-purpose flour
1 teaspoon sugar
1 teaspoon baking powder
½ teaspoon baking soda
¼ teaspoon salt
1⅓ cups low-fat buttermilk
1 tablespoon stick margarine or butter, melted
1 large egg white
  Cooking spray
½ cup maple syrup

1. Lightly spoon flour into a dry measuring cup; level with a knife. Combine flour and next 4 ingredients. Combine buttermilk, margarine, and egg white. Add to flour mixture, stirring until smooth.
2. Spoon about ¼ cup pancake batter onto a hot nonstick griddle coated with cooking spray. Turn pancakes when tops are covered with bubbles and edges look cooked (about 2 minutes). Serve with syrup. Yield: 4 servings (serving size: 3 pancakes and 2 tablespoons syrup).

CALORIES 293 (15% from fat); FAT 4.8g (sat 2.7g, mono 1.2g, poly 0.3g); PROTEIN 7.1g; CARB 55.7g; FIBER 0.8g; CHOL 8mg; IRON 1.9mg; SODIUM 489mg; CALC 185mg

Taking the Heat

Roasting your meals at a high temperature reduces the cooking time and increases the flavor.

You open the oven door, careful to avoid the rush of hot air. The earthy aromas of meat or seafood and caramelized vegetables have your taste buds swooning. There it is: a complete dinner cooked in remarkable time, a rustic feast that can be served after work or for last-minute company. And there's only one pan to clean.

So what is this revolutionary cooking method that requires little preparation or attention? It's called roasting, a magical method that's been around for centuries. The oven dial is turned up to the max, a scorching 475° to 500°, and the natural flavors of foods are intensified. Thanks to caramelization, roasting concentrates flavors without added fat, giving foods a crispy exterior, tender interior, and rich, dark color.

Despite its simplicity, roasting can be as creative as any other kind of cooking. The seasonings can be varied to suit individual palates, and the combinations of meats and vegetables can be changed. Roasting is also the perfect antidote to those end-of-winter doldrums. Whose spirits wouldn't soar when presented with such a robust platter of soothing flavors?

WHEN TO DO WHAT

To speed up meal preparation even more, our recipes are designed so that meats and vegetables all cook in the same pan. The exceptions apply to chicken and Cornish game hens. They cook better on the broiler rack of a roasting pan; that way, the vegetables aren't sitting in fatty drippings.

Because vegetables and small or large pieces of meat require different amounts of roasting time, parts of the meal may go into the oven at different times. For example, in Filet Mignon with Roasted Potatoes and Asparagus, the potatoes go in first, and then the beef tenderloin is added 10 minutes later. Asparagus, which takes only 10 minutes to roast, comes last. Shrimp or lean cuts of meat such as pork tenderloin can roast together with vegetables in the bottom of the pan.

ROASTED CORNISH HENS AND JERUSALEM ARTICHOKES IN TOMATO-OLIVE SAUCE

Jerusalem artichokes are knobby, brown-skinned tubers with a crunchy texture and a slightly nutty flavor. If you prefer, potatoes can be substituted.

2 (1½-pound) Cornish hens
½ teaspoon salt, divided
¼ teaspoon pepper, divided
1 pound Jerusalem artichokes, peeled and cut into 1-inch pieces
10 large shallots, peeled and halved
1 teaspoon olive oil
4 medium tomatoes, cut into 1-inch pieces (about 1¾ pounds)
¼ cup sliced green olives, drained
1 tablespoon red wine vinegar

1. Preheat oven to 475°.
2. Remove and discard giblets and necks from hens. Rinse hens under cold water; pat dry. Split hens in half lengthwise. Sprinkle hen halves with ¼ teaspoon salt and ⅛ teaspoon pepper.
3. Combine artichokes and shallots in a large bowl. Toss with oil, ¼ teaspoon salt, and ⅛ teaspoon pepper. Place shallot mixture on the rack of a broiler pan. Bake at 475° for 10 minutes, stirring once. Arrange hen halves, skin sides up, over shallot mixture. Bake at 475° for 25 minutes or until hen juices run clear. Discard skin. Place hen halves on a serving platter; cover with foil, and keep warm. Add tomato and olives to shallot mixture. Bake at 475° for 10 minutes, stirring occasionally. Add tomato mixture to serving platter; drizzle with vinegar. Yield: 4 servings (serving size: 1 hen half and 1½ cups tomato-olive sauce).

CALORIES 317 (30% from fat); FAT 10.7g (sat 2.6g, mono 4.4g, poly 2.3g); PROTEIN 35.7g; CARB 19.8g; FIBER 3g; CHOL 101mg; IRON 4.2mg; SODIUM 484mg; CALC 47mg

---

TARRAGON-ROASTED CHICKEN WITH MUSHROOMS AND POTATOES

1 (3-pound) roasting chicken
Cooking spray
8 fresh tarragon sprigs
4 medium-size red potatoes, halved (about 1¼ pounds)
½ teaspoon salt, divided
½ teaspoon pepper, divided
6 cups quartered fresh mushrooms (about 1 pound)

1. Preheat oven to 500°.
2. Remove and discard giblets and neck from chicken. Rinse chicken under cold water, and pat dry. Trim excess fat from chicken. Place chicken, breast side up, on the rack of a broiler pan coated with cooking spray. Place tarragon sprigs in body cavity of chicken. Insert meat thermometer into meaty part of thigh, making sure not to touch bone. Arrange potato halves around chicken; sprinkle ¼ teaspoon salt and ¼ teaspoon pepper over potato.
3. Bake at 500° for 15 minutes; stir potato. Add mushrooms; sprinkle with ¼ teaspoon salt and ¼ teaspoon pepper. Bake at 500° for an additional 15 minutes. Stir mushrooms, and bake at 500° for 15 additional minutes or until thermometer registers 180° and chicken juices run clear. Discard skin. Yield: 4 servings (serving size: 3 ounces chicken, 2 potato halves, and ¾ cup mushrooms).

CALORIES 336 (23% from fat); FAT 8.6g (sat 2.3g, mono 2.8g, poly 2g); PROTEIN 36.1g; CARB 28.7g; FIBER 4g; CHOL 95mg; IRON 4.5mg; SODIUM 399mg; CALC 42mg

FILET MIGNON WITH ROASTED POTATOES AND ASPARAGUS

The asparagus is roasted after the beef and potatoes are pulled from the oven.

1½ pounds asparagus spears
¾ teaspoon salt, divided
3 baking potatoes, cut into 1-inch pieces (about 1½ pounds)
1 teaspoon olive oil
½ teaspoon pepper, divided
Cooking spray
1¼ pounds beef tenderloin
¼ cup water

1. Preheat oven to 500°.
2. Snap off tough ends of asparagus; sprinkle with ¼ teaspoon salt. Set aside.
3. Toss potato with oil, ¼ teaspoon salt, and ¼ teaspoon pepper. Arrange in a single layer in bottom of a broiler pan coated with cooking spray. Bake at 500° for 10 minutes.
4. Trim fat from tenderloin. Sprinkle tenderloin with ¼ teaspoon salt and ¼ teaspoon pepper. Insert meat thermometer into thickest portion of tenderloin. Add tenderloin to broiler pan, nestling it into potato mixture. Bake at 500° for 20 minutes or until thermometer registers 145° (medium-rare) to 160° (medium), stirring potato mixture once.
5. Place tenderloin and potato mixture on a serving platter; cover with foil. Let stand 10 minutes. Add asparagus and water to pan. Bake at 500° for 10 minutes or until asparagus is crisp-tender. Yield: 4 servings (serving size: 3 ounces tenderloin, 1 cup potatoes, and ¾ cup asparagus).

CALORIES 429 (23% from fat); FAT 10.9g (sat 3.9g, mono 4.4g, poly 0.7g); PROTEIN 35.3g; CARB 47.2g; FIBER 5.1g; CHOL 88mg; IRON 7.1mg; SODIUM 532mg; CALC 46mg

ROASTED PORK TENDERLOIN WITH APPLES AND SWEET POTATOES

1 teaspoon salt
½ teaspoon ground cinnamon
½ teaspoon ground cardamom
¼ teaspoon pepper
4½ cups (1-inch) cubed peeled sweet potato (about 1½ pounds)
4 teaspoons olive oil, divided
2 (¾-pound) pork tenderloins
Cooking spray
4 large Granny Smith apples, each peeled and cut into 6 wedges

1. Preheat oven to 500°.
2. Combine first 4 ingredients in a small bowl. Combine sweet potato, 1 teaspoon spice mixture, and 3 teaspoons oil; toss well. Trim fat from pork; rub remaining spice mixture over pork. Drizzle 1 teaspoon oil over pork.
3. Arrange sweet potato in a single layer in a 15 x 10-inch jelly-roll pan coated with cooking spray; bake at 500° for 10 minutes. Add apple and pork; bake 20 additional minutes or until a meat thermometer registers 160°, turning sweet potato, apple, and pork after 10 minutes. Yield: 6 servings (serving size: 3 ounces pork, ¾ cup sweet potato, and 4 apple wedges).

CALORIES 328 (18% from fat); FAT 6.6g (sat 1.5g, mono 3.5g, poly 0.8g); PROTEIN 25.6g; CARB 42.2g; FIBER 6.2g; CHOL 74mg; IRON 2.3mg; SODIUM 459mg; CALC 38mg

ROASTED LAMB WITH ACORN SQUASH AND BROCCOLI

Use the leftover lamb from this meal in a stir-fry, stew, or sandwich.

1 (4-pound) rolled boned leg of lamb
3 garlic cloves, halved
1 fresh rosemary sprig, broken into 6 pieces
1 teaspoon salt, divided
1 tablespoon coarsely ground pepper
2 teaspoons olive oil, divided
2 large acorn squash (about 1¼ pounds), cut into 1-inch wedges
12 (4-inch) broccoli spears
1 garlic clove, minced

1. Preheat oven to 500°.
2. Unroll leg of lamb; trim fat. Reroll lamb; secure at 1-inch intervals with heavy string. Make 6 (½-inch-deep) slits in lamb; place garlic halves and rosemary into each slit. Sprinkle lamb with ½ teaspoon salt and pepper. Place lamb on a broiler pan; insert meat thermometer into thickest portion of lamb. Bake at 500° for 10 minutes. Reduce oven temperature to 425° (do not remove lamb from oven).
3. Combine ¼ teaspoon salt, 1 teaspoon olive oil, and squash; arrange around roast. Bake at 425° for 22 minutes. Combine 1 teaspoon oil, ¼ teaspoon salt, broccoli, and minced garlic. Carefully turn roast, and arrange broccoli mixture around roast. Bake at 425° for an additional 25 minutes or until thermometer registers 145° (medium-rare). Let stand 5 minutes. Yield: 6 servings (serving size: 3 ounces lamb, ⅓ cup acorn squash, and 2 broccoli spears).

CALORIES 203 (26% from fat); FAT 5.8g (sat 1.7g, mono 2.7g, poly 0.7g); PROTEIN 20.7g; CARB 19.8g; FIBER 3.9g; CHOL 54mg; IRON 3.3mg; SODIUM 464mg; CALC 92mg

PRIL

Back to the Garden

A new trend in farming gives busy consumers a chance to feel connected to the land and have its bounty delivered from the garden right to their front doors.

For some, springtime arrives in a cardboard box. What makes the box special is that it signals the start of produce delivered directly from the farm to their doorstep every week through the end of the growing season in late autumn. It's one of the perks of being a member of a CSA farm.

CSA stands for "community-supported agriculture"—a new trend in farming aimed at creating sustainable farms and a deeper appreciation of the land and its bounty among consumers. CSA farmers grow fruits and vegetables for area consumers who have paid for weekly boxes of seasonal produce. The boxes are either picked up at the farm or at points where the produce is distributed to members.

Tom Brandtmeier owns a small, 4-acre farm, and he has only 18 members in his CSA. For $300, members get a box each week from late April through late November filled with seasonal produce. In springtime, the boxes are filled with spinach, chickweed, parsnips, herbs, lettuces, and, later on, radishes, peas, Swiss chard, kale, collards, cabbage, beets, and carrots. In summer, members can expect green beans, beets, zucchini, tomatoes, sweet corn, peppers, eggplant, cantaloupe, and watermelon. And in the fall, they get Brussels sprouts, pumpkins, rutabagas, garlic, turnips, squashes, and many other vegetables.

It can be difficult learning to cook with a box of assigned vegetables. Following are recipes that will help you make the most of this season's produce—whether you get it from a CSA or buy it at your local supermarket.

ONION PIZZA

2¼ cups bread flour
¾ teaspoon salt, divided
1 package quick-rise yeast
1 cup very warm water (120° to 130°)
2 tablespoons olive oil, divided
1 tablespoon cornmeal
½ cup (2 ounces) crumbled feta cheese
1 cup thinly sliced sweet onion
½ cup thinly sliced green onions
½ cup thinly sliced leek
1 tablespoon chopped fresh or 1 teaspoon dried oregano
2 tablespoons (½ ounce) grated fresh Parmesan cheese

1. Preheat oven to 425°.
2. Lightly spoon flour into dry measuring cups; level with a knife. Place flour, ½ teaspoon salt, and yeast in a food processor; pulse 2 times or until blended. With processor on, slowly add water and 1 tablespoon oil through food chute; process until dough forms a ball. Process an additional 45 seconds. Turn out onto a lightly floured surface; knead lightly 4 or 5 times. Cover and let rest 30 minutes.
3. Roll dough into a 14-inch circle on a lightly floured surface. Place dough on a baking sheet sprinkled with cornmeal. Crimp edges of dough with fingers to form a rim. Sprinkle feta cheese evenly over dough. Combine onions, leek, oregano, 1 tablespoon oil, and ¼ teaspoon salt; spread mixture evenly over crust. Sprinkle with cheese; bake at 425° for 25 minutes or until crust is lightly browned. Yield: 6 servings.

CALORIES 289 (26% from fat); FAT 8.2g (sat 2.6g, mono 4.1g, poly 0.9g); PROTEIN 9.6g; CARB 44.1g; FIBER 1.3g; CHOL 10mg; IRON 3.3mg; SODIUM 441mg; CALC 112mg

HOLLANDAISE-ASPARAGUS TART

1 cup all-purpose flour
2 tablespoons sugar
3 tablespoons vegetable shortening
3½ tablespoons ice water
Cooking spray
1 pound asparagus spears, trimmed
⅔ cup evaporated skim milk
½ teaspoon grated lemon rind
2 tablespoons fresh lemon juice
½ teaspoon dried tarragon
¼ teaspoon salt
1 large egg
1 large egg white, lightly beaten
½ cup (2 ounces) grated fresh Parmesan cheese

1. Preheat oven to 450°.
2. Lightly spoon flour into a dry measuring cup; level with a knife. Place flour and sugar in a food processor; pulse 3 times or until combined. Add shortening; pulse 6 times or until mixture resembles coarse meal. With processor on, add ice water through food chute, processing just until combined. Gently press mixture into a 6-inch circle on a lightly floured surface; roll dough into an 12-inch circle. Fit dough into a 9-inch pie plate coated with cooking spray; fold edges under, and flute. Pierce bottom and sides of dough with a fork; bake at 450° for 10 minutes or until lightly browned. Cool on a wire rack.
3. Reduce oven temperature to 375°.
4. Snap off tough ends of asparagus; remove scales with a knife or vegetable peeler, if desired. Steam asparagus, covered, 3 minutes or until crisp-tender. Rinse asparagus under cold water; drain well. Arrange asparagus spokelike in prepared crust with tips toward center. Combine milk and next 6 ingredients; stir well. Pour over asparagus; sprinkle with cheese. Bake at 375° for 30 minutes or until puffy and lightly browned. Serve warm. Yield: 6 servings.

CALORIES 212 (33% from fat); FAT 7.9g (sat 2.4g, mono 3g, poly 1.7g); PROTEIN 9.5g; CARB 26.2g; FIBER 1g; CHOL 41mg; IRON 1.6mg; SODIUM 240mg; CALC 158mg

PARSLEY, LEEK, AND GREEN ONION FRITTATA

½ cup chopped fresh flat-leaf parsley
½ cup part-skim ricotta cheese
2 tablespoons (½ ounce) grated fresh Parmesan cheese
2 tablespoons fat-free milk
¼ teaspoon salt
¼ teaspoon ground red pepper
4 large eggs
2 large egg whites
1 tablespoon olive oil
1 cup chopped leek
½ cup (1-inch) julienne-cut carrot
½ cup chopped green onions

1. Combine first 8 ingredients in a bowl; stir with a whisk until blended.
2. Heat olive oil in a large nonstick skillet over medium heat. Add leek, carrot, and green onions; sauté 5 minutes or until tender. Add egg mixture; cover and cook over low heat 8 minutes or until frittata is almost set. Yield: 6 servings.

CALORIES 203 (54% from fat); FAT 12.2g (sat 4.2g, mono 5.5g, poly 1.2g); PROTEIN 14.5g; CARB 9.4g; FIBER 1.4g; CHOL 233mg; IRON 2.2mg; SODIUM 354mg; CALC 200mg

COUSCOUS WITH SPRING VEGETABLES AND HARISSA SAUCE

(pictured on page 94)

Harissa is a fiery-hot sauce of Tunisian origin that can be bought at Middle Eastern markets. It's made from common ingredients and easy to prepare.

1 (5.8-ounce) package roasted-garlic-and-olive oil or plain couscous (such as Near East)
⅓ cup finely chopped plum tomato
⅛ teaspoon ground allspice
1 tablespoon olive oil
2 cups coarsely chopped leek
1 cup coarsely chopped yellow bell pepper
1 cup Sugar Snap peas, trimmed
½ cup peeled halved pearl onions
½ cup quartered radishes
6 baby carrots, cut in half lengthwise
3 garlic cloves, minced
2 cups torn spinach
½ cup chopped fresh parsley
½ teaspoon sugar
⅛ teaspoon salt
1 (15-ounce) can chickpeas (garbanzo beans), drained
Harissa Sauce

1. Prepare couscous according to package directions, omitting oil. Stir in tomato and allspice; keep warm.
2. Heat oil in a large nonstick skillet over medium-high heat. Add leek and next 6 ingredients; sauté 8 minutes. Add spinach and next 4 ingredients; sauté 2 minutes. Spoon vegetable mixture over couscous mixture, and serve with Harissa Sauce. Yield: 4 servings (serving size: 1 cup vegetable mixture, ½ cup couscous, and 1 tablespoon sauce).

CALORIES 423 (23% from fat); FAT 10.7g (sat 1.5g, mono 6g, poly 2.2g); PROTEIN 15.8g; CARB 70.8g; FIBER 9g; CHOL 0mg; IRON 6.8mg; SODIUM 626mg; CALC 151mg

Harissa Sauce:

2 teaspoons caraway seeds
½ teaspoon ground coriander
½ teaspoon ground cumin
½ teaspoon dried crushed red pepper
½ teaspoon black pepper
1 garlic clove, peeled
1 jalapeño pepper, seeded
2 tablespoons red wine vinegar
1 tablespoon olive oil

1. Place first 7 ingredients in a food processor; process until finely chopped. Add vinegar and oil; process until smooth. Cover and chill. Yield: ¼ cup (serving size: 1 tablespoon).
Note: Store sauce in an airtight container in refrigerator for up to 2 weeks.

CALORIES 39 (83% from fat); FAT 3.6g (sat 0.5g, mono 2.6g, poly 0.3g); PROTEIN 0.4g; CARB 1.8g; FIBER 0.4g; CHOL 0mg; IRON 0.5mg; SODIUM 2mg; CALC 14mg

SPINACH-AND-SUGAR SNAP RISOTTO

(pictured on page 96)

To trim Sugar Snap peas, pull the string at one end; it will come off the entire pod.

2 tablespoons olive oil, divided
1 cup finely chopped onion
¼ teaspoon sugar
3 cups chopped spinach
1¼ cups Sugar Snap peas, trimmed
2 tablespoons minced fresh or 2 teaspoons dried rubbed sage
¼ teaspoon salt
¼ teaspoon freshly ground pepper
1 garlic clove, minced
¾ cup water
1 (14½-ounce) can vegetable broth
1 cup uncooked Arborio or other short-grain rice
¼ cup dry white wine
½ cup (2 ounces) grated fresh Parmesan cheese

1. Heat 1 tablespoon oil in a large saucepan over medium-high heat. Add onion and sugar; sauté 30 seconds. Stir in spinach and next 5 ingredients; sauté 30 seconds or until spinach wilts. Remove spinach mixture from pan; set aside.
2. Bring water and broth to a simmer in a small saucepan (do not boil). Keep warm over low heat.
3. Heat 1 tablespoon oil in large saucepan; add rice. Cook 5 minutes, stirring constantly. Stir in wine; cook until wine is absorbed, stirring constantly. Stir in ½ cup broth mixture; cook 4 minutes or until liquid is nearly absorbed, stirring constantly. Add remaining broth mixture, ½ cup at a time, stirring constantly, until each portion of broth is absorbed before adding the next (about 22 minutes total). Stir in spinach mixture and cheese; cook 1 minute or until thoroughly heated. Yield: 6 servings (serving size: ¾ cup).

CALORIES 230 (30% from fat); FAT 7.6g (sat 2.3g, mono 4.1g, poly 0.6g); PROTEIN 7.5g; CARB 33g; FIBER 2.7g; CHOL 6mg; IRON 2.9mg; SODIUM 518mg; CALC 162mg

Orecchiette with Potatoes and Radishes

1 (8-ounce) bunch radishes with
    tops
8 ounces uncooked orecchiette
    ("little ears" pasta)
2 tablespoons olive oil
2 garlic cloves, minced
1 pound red potatoes, cut into
    1-inch cubes (about 3 cups)
¾ cup vegetable broth
2 cups (1-inch) diagonally sliced
    asparagus
½ teaspoon salt
2 tablespoons (½ ounce) grated
    fresh Parmesan cheese

1. Wash radishes and tops thoroughly. Cut radishes into thin slices to equal ½ cup; chop radish tops to equal ⅓ cup.
2. Cook pasta according to package directions, omitting salt and fat. Set aside, and keep warm.
3. Heat oil in a large nonstick skillet over medium-high heat. Add radishes, radish tops, and garlic; sauté 5 minutes, stirring frequently. Add potato and broth; bring to a boil. Cover, reduce heat, and simmer 7 minutes or until potato is tender. Add asparagus; cook 3 minutes. Add salt. Combine potato mixture and pasta; toss well. Sprinkle with cheese. Yield: 8 servings (serving size: 1 cup).

CALORIES 197 (21% from fat); FAT 4.6g (sat 0.9g, mono 2.7g, poly 0.5g); PROTEIN 6.4g; CARB 33g; FIBER 2.5g; CHOL 1mg; IRON 2.2mg; SODIUM 279mg; CALC 45mg

Spinach-Strawberry Salad with Goat-Cheese Bruschetta

(pictured on page 93)

¼ cup sugar
2 tablespoons sherry vinegar or
    white wine vinegar
1½ teaspoons sesame seeds, toasted
1½ teaspoons olive oil
1 teaspoon minced red onion
¾ teaspoon poppy seeds
¼ teaspoon Hungarian sweet paprika
⅛ teaspoon salt
6 cups torn spinach (about 1 pound)
2 cups halved strawberries
2 tablespoons slivered almonds,
    toasted
1 (3-ounce) log goat cheese, cut
    into 6 slices
6 (1-ounce) slices French bread,
    toasted

1. Combine first 8 ingredients in a jar; cover tightly, and shake vigorously.
2. Combine spinach and strawberries in a bowl; toss gently. Pour dressing over spinach mixture; toss gently. Spoon 1 cup salad onto each of 6 plates; sprinkle each serving with 1 teaspoon almonds. Spread cheese over toast; top each salad with 1 bruschetta. Yield: 6 servings.

CALORIES 213 (28% from fat); FAT 6.7g (sat 2.7g, mono 2.6g, poly 1.1g); PROTEIN 7.1g; CARB 31g; FIBER 4.5g; CHOL 13mg; IRON 2.7mg; SODIUM 446mg; CALC 163mg

Artichokes with Pesto-Cannellini Spread

3 medium artichokes
2 tablespoons lemon juice
1 (16-ounce) can cannellini or
    other white beans, drained
¼ cup chopped fresh parsley
2 tablespoons Italian-seasoned
    breadcrumbs
2 tablespoons (½ ounce) finely
    grated fresh Parmesan cheese
2 tablespoons water
1 tablespoon commercial pesto
    sauce
1 tablespoon balsamic vinegar

1. Cut off artichoke stems; remove bottom leaves. Trim about ½ inch from top of each artichoke. Place artichokes, stem ends down, in a large Dutch oven filled two-thirds with water. Add lemon juice to water; bring to a boil. Cover, reduce heat, and simmer 40 minutes or until a leaf near center of artichoke pulls out easily. Place artichokes, stem ends up, on a rack to drain.
2. Remove bottom leaves and tough outer leaves from artichokes; remove fuzzy thistles with a spoon.
3. Mash beans in a medium bowl; stir in parsley and remaining 5 ingredients. Spoon bean mixture into centers of artichokes. Yield: 3 servings (serving size: 1 artichoke and ⅓ cup spread).

CALORIES 286 (21% from fat); FAT 6.6g (sat 1.6g, mono 2.6g, poly 1.6g); PROTEIN 14.9g; CARB 46.8g; FIBER 10.3g; CHOL 4mg; IRON 5.9mg; SODIUM 558mg; CALC 214mg

INSPIRED VEGETARIAN

Spring Collection

Nutrition, value, and freshness are top picks in this season's fashion crop. And green is in.

Each spring the fashion world transforms itself with a burst of color and an array of new looks, and you can tell the world has spun another quarter turn. But in the produce markets there is a "spring collection" to rival any: bountiful baskets of asparagus, glistening shipments of artichokes, peppery watercress, ripe tomatoes, and crisp snap peas. It's a treat for the eye, nose, and palate—and also a boost for healthful cooking. During peak growing season, vegetables are especially rewarding, reaching the pinnacle of nutritional value and taste. And in the spring they're the most economical to prepare, often half the price you might pay for them out of season.

SPAGHETTI WITH SPRING PESTO

4   cups trimmed watercress (about 1 bunch)
1½ cups fresh parsley
1   cup basil leaves
½   cup pecan halves
½   cup frozen green peas, thawed
½   cup fat-free ricotta cheese
¼   cup (1 ounce) grated fresh Parmesan cheese
⅓   cup (1-inch) sliced green onions
½   teaspoon salt
¼   teaspoon pepper
3   garlic cloves
1½ tablespoons olive oil
6   cups hot cooked spaghetti (about 1 pound uncooked pasta)

1. Place first 11 ingredients in a food processor; process until smooth. With processor on, slowly pour oil through food chute; process until well-blended. Combine with pasta; toss gently to coat. Yield: 7 servings (serving size: 1 cup).

CALORIES 298 (31% from fat); FAT 10.3g (sat 1.7g, mono 5.9g, poly 1.9g); PROTEIN 12.2g; CARB 40.3g; FIBER 3.6g; CHOL 5mg; IRON 3mg; SODIUM 282mg; CALC 155mg

LINGUINE WITH GRILLED ASPARAGUS AND SHIITAKE MUSHROOM VINAIGRETTE

1½ tablespoons dark sesame oil
1   tablespoon minced peeled fresh ginger
¼   teaspoon dried crushed red pepper
3   garlic cloves, minced
1½ cups thinly sliced shiitake mushroom caps (about 1 [3½-ounce] package)
1   cup sliced button mushrooms (about 3 ounces)
¼   cup rice vinegar
¼   cup low-sodium soy sauce
¼   cup minced fresh parsley
¼   cup pineapple juice
2   tablespoons water
2   teaspoons sugar
1   pound asparagus spears
4   cups hot cooked linguine (about 8 ounces uncooked pasta)

1. Heat oil in a large nonstick skillet. Add ginger, pepper, and garlic; cook 1 minute. Add mushrooms; cook 2 minutes. Add vinegar and next 5 ingredients; remove from heat.
2. Snap off tough ends of asparagus; remove scales with a knife or vegetable peeler, if desired. Brush asparagus with mushroom vinaigrette; keep remaining vinaigrette warm.
3. Prepare grill or broiler. Grill or broil asparagus 3 minutes or until lightly browned. Place asparagus on pasta, and top with remaining mushroom vinaigrette. Yield: 4 servings (serving size: 1 cup pasta, 2 ounces asparagus, and ¼ cup vinaigrette).

CALORIES 300 (20% from fat); FAT 6.5g (sat 0.9g, mono 2.2g, poly 2.7g); PROTEIN 10.2g; CARB 50.9g; FIBER 3.7g; CHOL 0mg; IRON 3.6mg; SODIUM 498mg; CALC 38mg

STRUDEL VERDE

2   teaspoons olive oil
1   cup chopped onion
½   cup (½-inch) sliced asparagus
½   cup diced red bell pepper
½   cup sliced mushrooms
1   cup cooked long-grain brown rice
1   cup drained canned chickpeas (garbanzo beans), mashed
¼   cup frozen chopped spinach, thawed, drained, and squeezed dry
¼   cup frozen green peas, thawed
½   cup (2 ounces) crumbled feta cheese
¼   cup chopped fresh dill
½   teaspoon salt
¼   teaspoon black pepper
5   sheets frozen phyllo dough, thawed
Cooking spray
1   tablespoon sesame seeds

1. Preheat oven to 350°.
2. Heat oil in a large nonstick skillet over medium-high heat. Add onion and next 3 ingredients; sauté 2 minutes. Stir in rice and next 3 ingredients. Remove from heat; cool to room temperature. Stir in feta cheese and next 3 ingredients.

3. Place 1 phyllo sheet on work surface; lightly coat with cooking spray. Working with 1 phyllo sheet at a time, coat remaining 4 phyllo sheets with cooking spray, stacking each on top of the first. Place a sheet of plastic wrap over phyllo; press gently to seal sheets together. Discard plastic wrap.
4. Remove vegetable mixture from skillet with a slotted spoon. Spoon vegetable mixture along 1 long edge of phyllo, leaving a 3-inch border. Fold over short edges of phyllo to cover 2 inches of vegetable mixture on each end.
5. Starting at long edge with 2-inch border, roll up jelly-roll fashion. (Do not roll tightly, or strudel may split). Place, seam side down, on a jelly-roll pan coated with cooking spray. Lightly coat with cooking spray; sprinkle with sesame seeds. Bake at 350° for 40 minutes or until golden brown. Yield: 4 servings (serving size: 1 [3-inch] piece).

CALORIES 321 (27% from fat); FAT 9.6g (sat 3g, mono 3.4g, poly 2.3g); PROTEIN 12.8g; CARB 48.1g; FIBER 6.2g; CHOL 13mg; IRON 5.8mg; SODIUM 637mg; CALC 242mg

SPRING STUFFED ONIONS

6   large Vidalias or other sweet onions (about 1 pound each)
Cooking spray
½   teaspoon salt, divided
¼   teaspoon pepper, divided
1½ cups water
1   tablespoon extra-virgin olive oil
1   cup uncooked bulgur or cracked wheat
1   cup peeled, seeded, and cubed cucumber
1   cup finely chopped fresh parsley
½   cup minced red onion
½   cup diced seeded tomato
¼   cup chopped fresh mint
¼   cup fresh lemon juice
1   (16-ounce) can cannellini beans or other white beans, rinsed and drained

1. Preheat oven to 475°.
2. Peel onions; cut ½ inch off top and bottom of onions. Place onions in a
Continued

13 x 9-inch baking dish coated with cooking spray, and lightly coat onions with cooking spray. Sprinkle ¼ teaspoon salt and ⅛ teaspoon pepper over onions. Bake at 475° for 40 minutes or until golden. Cool to room temperature. Remove and discard cores from onions, leaving 1-inch-thick shells.

3. Combine water and oil in a saucepan; bring to boil. Pour over bulgur in a large bowl; cover and let stand 30 minutes. Stir in ¼ teaspoon salt, ⅛ teaspoon pepper, cucumber, and remaining ingredients. Spoon 1 cup bulgur mixture into each onion shell. Yield: 6 servings.

CALORIES 229 (17% from fat); FAT 4.2g (sat 0.6g, mono 2.1g, poly 1g); PROTEIN 9g; CARB 42.2g; FIBER 8.4g; CHOL 0mg; IRON 3mg; SODIUM 315mg; CALC 71mg

ARTICHOKES STUFFED WITH SMASHED POTATOES AND BROWNED GARLIC

4 large artichokes
1½ pounds baking potatoes, cut into ½-inch cubes
2 tablespoons olive oil
6 garlic cloves, minced
¼ cup dry sherry
¾ cup (3 ounces) shredded part-skim mozzarella cheese
½ cup chopped fresh basil
½ teaspoon salt
½ teaspoon pepper
1 tablespoon shredded fresh Parmesan cheese
Cooking spray
Fresh parsley sprigs (optional)

1. Cut off artichoke stems to the base. Remove bottom leaves and tough outer leaves, leaving tender heart and bottom; trim about 2 inches from top of artichokes. Steam artichokes, covered, 20 minutes; cool to room temperature. Gently spread leaves; remove fuzzy thistle from bottom with a spoon.
2. Preheat oven to 375°.
3. Place potato in a saucepan; cover with water. Bring to a boil. Reduce heat. Simmer 12 minutes or until

tender; drain. Beat at medium speed of a mixer or mash with a potato masher until coarsely mashed.
4. Heat oil in a nonstick skillet over medium-high heat. Add garlic; sauté 2 minutes or until golden. Remove from heat; add sherry, scraping skillet to loosen browned bits. Add sherry mixture, mozzarella, and next 3 ingredients to potatoes.
5. Stuff about 1 cup potato mixture into each artichoke. Sprinkle with Parmesan. Place stuffed artichokes in an 8-inch square baking dish coated with cooking spray. Bake at 375° for 20 minutes or until artichokes are tender. Garnish with parsley, if desired. Yield: 4 servings.

CALORIES 391 (26% from fat); FAT 11.3g (sat 3.5g, mono 6.1g, poly 0.9g); PROTEIN 13.8g; CARB 62.8g; FIBER 10.5g; CHOL 14mg; IRON 4.9mg; SODIUM 549mg; CALC 262mg

SWEET-PEA GUACAMOLE

1 cup fresh shelled green peas (about ¾ pound)
1 large ripe avocado, peeled and seeded
⅓ cup minced green onions
¼ cup bottled salsa
1½ tablespoons fresh lime juice
1 teaspoon hot sauce
½ teaspoon ground cumin
4 cilantro sprigs
2 garlic cloves
84 baked tortilla chips

1. Steam peas, covered, 4 minutes or until tender. Combine peas and next 8 ingredients in a food processor or blender; pulse just until combined. Serve guacamole with tortilla chips. Yield: 14 servings (serving size: 2 tablespoons guacamole and 6 chips).
Note: Frozen green peas may be substituted for fresh.

CALORIES 115 (30% from fat); FAT 3.8g (sat 0.6g, mono 2.2g, poly 0.7g); PROTEIN 3.0g; CARB 19.2g; FIBER 2.2g; CHOL 0mg; IRON 0.2mg; SODIUM 107mg; CALC 5mg

Raising the Anti

With research showing how important antioxidants are to your health, we cooked up some powerful recipes to boost your immune system.

Antioxidants can help keep the body's immune system in peak condition. Perhaps the most delicious news is that these nutrient soldiers (beta carotene, vitamin C, vitamin E, and the trace mineral selenium) are found in everyday foods. In light of such evidence, we came up with recipes that dish up a wealth of protection.

MEDITERRANEAN CHICKEN-AND-BROWN RICE SALAD

2 teaspoons olive oil
1 cup coarsely chopped onion
1 cup uncooked long-grain brown rice
1 cup water
1 (10½-ounce) can low-salt chicken broth
2 cups coarsely chopped plum tomato
1¾ cups cubed ready-to-eat roasted skinned, boned chicken breasts (about 2 breasts)
½ cup chopped fresh basil
¼ cup chopped fresh oregano
¼ cup coarsely chopped ripe olives
2 tablespoons white balsamic vinegar
¼ teaspoon salt
1 (19-ounce) can chickpeas (garbanzo beans), drained
2 garlic cloves, minced

1. Heat oil in a large saucepan over medium-high heat. Add onion; sauté 3 minutes. Add rice; sauté 1 minute. Stir in water and broth; bring to a boil. Cover, reduce heat to medium-low, and cook for 45 minutes or until liquid is absorbed. Spoon into a large bowl; fluff with a fork. Add tomato and remaining ingredients; toss well. Serve at room temperature or chilled. Yield 6 servings (serving size: 1½ cups).

CALORIES 304 (18% from fat); FAT 6g (sat 1.1g, mono 2.3g, poly 1.5g); PROTEIN 17g; CARB 47.5g; FIBER 5g; CHOL 21mg; IRON 3.9mg; SODIUM 460mg; CALC 112mg

---

MENU SUGGESTION

MOROCCAN ROASTED
SALMON WITH MANGO SALSA

Casablanca couscous *

*Combine 4 cups hot cooked couscous, 1 (15-ounce) can drained chickpeas, 2 tablespoons toasted pine nuts, 2 tablespoons minced fresh parsley, 2 tablespoons lemon juice, and 1 teaspoon minced garlic.
Serves 4.

MOROCCAN ROASTED SALMON WITH MANGO SALSA

Harissa is a hot sauce made with chile peppers, garlic, cumin, coriander, and caraway.

1½ cups chopped peeled mango (about 1 large)
2 tablespoons finely chopped red onion
2 tablespoons chopped fresh mint
2 tablespoons orange juice
1½ teaspoons commercial harissa
1 (1½-pound) salmon fillet, skinned and cut crosswise into 4 equal pieces
¼ teaspoon salt
Cooking spray

1. Preheat oven to 450°.
2. Combine first 4 ingredients in a bowl; cover and chill. Spread harissa over both sides of salmon; sprinkle with salt. Place salmon on a baking sheet coated with cooking spray. Bake at 450° for 20 minutes or until fish flakes easily when tested with a fork. Serve with mango salsa. Yield: 4 servings (serving size: 5 ounces fish and about ⅓ cup salsa).

CALORIES 334 (40% from fat); FAT 14.9g (sat 2.6g, mono 6.8g, poly 3.1g); PROTEIN 35.4g; CARB 13.3g; FIBER 1g; CHOL 112mg; IRON 0.8mg; SODIUM 310mg; CALC 17mg

---

SPINACH-AND-ROASTED RED-PEPPER PIZZA

1 (10-ounce) can refrigerated pizza crust dough
Cooking spray
1 tablespoon cornmeal
1 cup (4 ounces) shredded Asiago cheese, divided
¼ teaspoon ground nutmeg
⅛ teaspoon pepper
1 (10-ounce) package frozen chopped spinach, thawed, drained, and squeezed dry
1 (7-ounce) bottle roasted red bell peppers, drained and cut into 2-inch strips
½ teaspoon dried thyme

1. Preheat oven to 425°.
2. Pat dough into a 12-inch round pizza pan coated with cooking spray and sprinkled with cornmeal. Combine ½ cup cheese, nutmeg, pepper, and spinach in a bowl. Arrange mixture over dough. Top with bell pepper; sprinkle with thyme and remaining ½ cup cheese. Bake at 425° for 15 minutes or until crust is browned and cheese melts. Yield: 6 servings.

CALORIES 218 (28% from fat); FAT 6.8g (sat 3.5g, mono 1.9g, poly 0.7g); PROTEIN 8.9g; CARB 26.4g; FIBER 1.6g; CHOL 20mg; IRON 1.2mg; SODIUM 565mg; CALC 256mg

---

CURRIED SWEET POTATO BISQUE

2 teaspoons olive oil
1 cup chopped onion
2 teaspoons curry powder
¼ teaspoon ground allspice
1 cup water
3 (10½-ounce) cans low-salt chicken broth
5 cups cubed peeled sweet potato (about 3½ pounds)
½ teaspoon salt
1½ cups plain fat-free yogurt, divided

1. Heat olive oil in a Dutch oven over medium-high heat. Add onion; sauté 2 minutes. Stir in curry and allspice; cook 1 minute. Add water, broth, sweet potato, and salt. Cook 25 minutes or until potato is tender. Place half of mixture in a blender; process until smooth. Repeat procedure with remaining potato mixture. Return pureed mixture to pan. Bring to a boil; remove from heat. Stir in 1 cup yogurt until blended. Ladle bisque into bowls; top with yogurt. Yield: 7 servings (serving size: 1½ cups bisque and about 1 tablespoon yogurt).

CALORIES 258 (10% from fat); FAT 2.9g (sat 0.8g, mono 1.0g, poly 0.4g); PROTEIN 7.8g; CARB 51.3g; FIBER 6.1g; CHOL 3mg; IRON 1.3mg; SODIUM 289mg; CALC 152mg

---

A FOOD DEFENSE LINEUP

Here's a quick rundown of the antioxidants in foods that help keep your immune system healthy.

BETA CAROTENE is adept at destroying free radicals, substances that can weaken immune defenses and may leave the body open to a variety of chronic ills ranging from cataracts to heart disease. This antioxidant is a plant pigment that helps give sweet potatoes, pumpkins, and mangoes their orange color. Spinach is also rich in beta carotene, although its dark-green color masks the orange pigment.

VITAMIN E can help improve immune function in older adults when added to their diets, according to Boston researchers. Walnuts and wheat germ are particularly rich sources.

VITAMIN C is perhaps best known for its ability to help decrease the symptoms of the common cold, but it's also a powerful warrior against harmful free radicals. Aside from citrus fruits, other good sources of the vitamin include mangoes and tomatoes.

SELENIUM may play a role in warding off certain types of cancer, according to preliminary studies. It's also integral to helping heal wounds. Its best food sources are brown rice, seafood, poultry, and meat.

PUMPKIN-CRANBERRY CAKE

If you're using a glass baking dish, lower the oven temperature to 325°.

- ½ cup chopped walnuts
- 3 tablespoons brown sugar
- 1½ tablespoons toasted wheat germ
- ¼ teaspoon pumpkin-pie spice
- 1 cup all-purpose flour
- ½ cup whole-wheat flour
- ½ cup toasted wheat germ
- 2 teaspoons baking powder
- 1 teaspoon pumpkin-pie spice
- ¾ teaspoon salt
- ¼ teaspoon baking soda
- 1 cup plain fat-free yogurt
- ¾ cup canned pumpkin
- ½ cup packed brown sugar
- 2 tablespoons vegetable oil
- 1 large egg
- ½ cup sweetened dried cranberries (such as Craisins)
- 1 teaspoon grated orange rind
  Cooking spray

1. Preheat oven to 350°.
2. Combine first 4 ingredients in a small bowl; stir with fork. Set aside.
3. Lightly spoon flours into dry measuring cups; level with a knife. Combine flours and next 5 ingredients in a medium bowl; make a well in center of mixture. Combine yogurt and next 4 ingredients; stir well with a whisk. Add to flour mixture, stirring just until moist. Fold in cranberries and orange rind. Spoon batter into a 13 x 9-inch baking pan coated with cooking spray, spreading evenly. Sprinkle with walnut mixture. Bake at 350° for 25 minutes. Cool on a wire rack. Yield: 12 servings.

CALORIES 210 (28% from fat); FAT 6.6g (sat 0.9g, mono 1.6g, poly 3.6g); PROTEIN 6.2g; CARB 33.5g; FIBER 3g; CHOL 19mg; IRON 2mg; SODIUM 199mg; CALC 112mg

Planned to Perfection

Not by food alone can you pull off a great dinner party—the wise cook also uses sticky notes.

Do you find yourself with little time to devote to throwing a party?

Here's our system that really works. It's a list of guidelines for putting together a party menu that ensures you don't stay up all night cooking.

Have an adequate supply of sticky notes. Several nights ahead, pull out the serving utensils and platters for every dish on the menu and label them. Any food made in advance is stuck in the fridge with a label. This is particularly useful when you make parts of a dish, such as a spice rub or a dressing. For example, the hen marinade would carry the specific label "Marinade for Moroccan Cornish Hens, 4/10/98." It may sound silly, but if you have two similarly colored dressings, both in identical bowls, sticky notes could save you from culinary catastrophe.

Construct a predinner schedule that details everything you need to do while guests are in your home. Keep a list on your kitchen counter indicating what needs to be done and when to do it.

Select recipes that benefit by advance preparation, like marinated foods.

The food must look as delicious as it tastes, but not because of careful, artful arrangements. Good looks have to be inherent to the food, not a result of fussy, fancy finger work.

With our recipes and prep plan, beautiful, flavorful food is just what you'll get.

MENU

BEET-AND-BLUE CHEESE SPREAD

SPRINGTIME DIP

PITA CHIPS

GRAPEFRUIT-AND-FENNEL SALAD

MOROCCAN CORNISH HENS

MUSTARD-DRESSED ASPARAGUS

PARSNIP PUREE

CHOCOLATE-APRICOT STRUDEL

BEET-AND-BLUE CHEESE SPREAD

- 2 beets (about 1 pound)
- 2 Granny Smith apples, each peeled and cut into 8 wedges
- ¼ cup (1 ounce) crumbled blue cheese
- 1 tablespoon prepared horseradish

1. Preheat oven to 400°.
2. Leave root and 1-inch stem on beets; scrub with a brush. Wrap beets in foil; bake at 400° for 1 hour or until tender. Cool. Peel and trim off beet roots. Place beets, apple, cheese, and horseradish in a food processor; process until well-blended, scraping sides of processor bowl occasionally. Serve with Pita Chips. Yield: 3 cups (serving size: ¼ cup).

CALORIES 36 (20% from fat); FAT 0.8g (sat 0.5g, mono 0.2g, poly 0.1g); PROTEIN 1.1g; CARB 6.8g; FIBER 1g; CHOL 2mg; IRON 0.3mg; SODIUM 58mg; CALC 20mg

SPRINGTIME DIP

6 cups fresh parsley leaves
2 cups fresh mint leaves
6 canned anchovy fillets, drained
1 tablespoon sherry vinegar
¼ teaspoon salt
Dash of ground nutmeg
Dash of ground red pepper
Dash of black pepper
½ cup part-skim ricotta cheese
½ cup plain fat-free yogurt
¼ cup low-fat sour cream
1 tablespoon minced fresh
    onion
1 teaspoon unflavored gelatin
2 tablespoons water
Fresh parsley sprigs (optional)

1. Place parsley and mint leaves in a food processor; pulse 2 or 3 times or until combined. Add anchovy and next 5 ingredients; process until well-blended, scraping sides of bowl occasionally. Add ricotta; process until smooth. Spoon mixture into a bowl; stir in yogurt, sour cream, and onion.
2. Sprinkle gelatin over water in a saucepan; let stand 1 minute. Cook over low heat; stir until gelatin dissolves. Remove from heat; cool slightly. Stir into parsley mixture. Cover and chill. Garnish with parsley sprigs, if desired. Serve with Pita Chips. Yield: 2 cups (serving size: ¼ cup).

CALORIES 66 (38% from fat); FAT 2.8g (sat 1.4g, mono 0.8g, poly 0.2g); PROTEIN 5.4g; CARB 5.4g; FIBER 2g; CHOL 8mg; IRON 3.1mg; SODIUM 253mg; CALC 151mg

PITA CHIPS

3 (6-inch) pitas

1. Preheat oven to 350°.
2. Split pitas, and cut each into 8 wedges. Place wedges in a single layer on a baking sheet. Bake at 350° for 20 minutes or until crisp. Yield: 8 servings (serving size: 6 chips).

CALORIES 76 (11% from fat); FAT 0.9g (sat 0.3g, mono 0.4g, poly 0.3g); PROTEIN 2.4g; CARB 14.2g; FIBER 0.5g; CHOL 1mg; IRON 0.7mg; SODIUM 144mg; CALC 20mg

PARTY PLANNER

MONDAY Make Pita Chips; store in an airtight container.
Make strudel filling, and refrigerate.
Transfer phyllo dough from freezer to refrigerator.

TUESDAY Roast and peel beets, and chill.
Assemble strudel, and freeze.

WEDNESDAY Take the day off.

THURSDAY Make Parsnip Puree, and chill.
Prepare salad ingredients and dressing.

FRIDAY Make paste and marinade for Moroccan Cornish Hens, and chill.
Prepare Springtime Dip, and chill.
Prepare Beet-and-Blue Cheese Spread.
Clean and dry asparagus, and chill.

SATURDAY

Saturday morning
Marinate hens.
Cook asparagus.
Set table.
Prepare coffee or tea service.
Chill beverages.

2 hours before dinner
Preheat oven for hens and begin cooking.

1 hour before dinner
Prepare pitcher of water.
Measure out flavoring ingredients for asparagus.
Place large skillet on stove. Place asparagus in loosely covered bowl nearby.
Remove Parsnip Puree from refrigerator; stir. Allow to come to room temperature.

30 minutes before dinner
Remove strudel from freezer, and unwrap; place on a baking sheet.

15 minutes before dinner
Reheat Parsnip Puree in the microwave.
Check on hens.
Finish Mustard-Dressed Asparagus. Cover skillet loosely, and let sit until serving.
Assemble and dress salad; place on plates.

As guests are seated at the dinner table
Serve first-course salad when hens are ready. Remove hens from oven and cover loosely with foil. Start coffee.

To serve main course
Place oranges on plate; top with hens. Spoon sauce, olives, and dates on hens.
Place a mound of Parsnip Puree on each plate, and top with asparagus.
Just before sitting down to main course, place strudel in the oven. Set timer for strudel.

To serve dessert
Remove strudel from oven, then clear dinner dishes.
Cut warm strudel, transferring slices to chocolate-drizzled plates with a flat spatula. Let strudel servings cool slightly as you top with fruit garnish.
Serve strudels with coffee; sit back, relax, and enjoy.

GRAPEFRUIT-AND-FENNEL SALAD

4 pink grapefruit
12 cups gourmet salad greens
2 cups coarsely chopped fennel
   bulb (about 2 bulbs)
1 cup vertically sliced red onion
Sweet Pink Grapefruit Vinaigrette

1. Peel and section grapefruit over a bowl, and squeeze membranes to extract juice. Set 3 cups sections aside, and reserve ¼ cup juice for vinaigrette. Discard membranes.
2. Combine grapefruit sections, salad greens, fennel, and onion in a large bowl. Drizzle salad with vinaigrette, and toss gently to coat. Serve immediately. Yield: 8 servings (serving size: 1½ cups).

CALORIES 85 (22% from fat); FAT 2.1g (sat 0.3g, mono 1.3g, poly 0.3g); PROTEIN 2.7g; CARB 15.3g; FIBER 2.3g; CHOL 0mg; IRON 1.8mg; SODIUM 84mg; CALC 68mg

Sweet Pink Grapefruit Vinaigrette:

½ cup seasoned rice vinegar
¼ cup reserved grapefruit juice
2 tablespoons honey
1 tablespoon extra-virgin olive oil
1 teaspoon fennel seeds, crushed
¼ teaspoon salt

1. Combine all ingredients in a small bowl; stir well with a whisk. Yield: 1 cup (serving size: 2 tablespoons).

CALORIES 35 (44% from fat); FAT 1.7g (sat 0.2g, mono 1.3g, poly 0.2g); PROTEIN 0.1g; CARB 4.8g; FIBER 0g; CHOL 0mg; IRON 0.2mg; SODIUM 75mg; CALC 4mg

MOROCCAN CORNISH HENS

(pictured on page 96)

Paste:

2 cups cilantro sprigs
½ teaspoon ground cardamom
2 teaspoons ground cumin
¼ teaspoon ground coriander
12 garlic cloves

Marinade:

½ cup balsamic vinegar
½ cup dry Marsala wine
¼ cup honey

Remaining ingredients:

4 large oranges, sliced
2 cups whole pitted dates (about
   8 ounces)
4 (1½-pound) Cornish hens
½ cup pimento-stuffed olives

1. To prepare paste, place cilantro in a food processor; pulse 4 times or until coarsely chopped. Add cardamom and next 3 ingredients; process until finely chopped. Set aside.
2. To prepare marinade, combine vinegar, wine, and honey; stir well. Set aside or store in refrigerator for up to 2 days.
3. Arrange orange slices in 2 (13 x 9-inch) baking dishes; sprinkle with dates.
4. Remove and discard giblets and necks from hens. Rinse hens with cold water; pat dry. Remove skin, and trim excess fat. Split hens in half lengthwise. Place hen halves, meaty sides up, on top of dates. Pat cilantro mixture onto hens; arrange olives around hens.
5. Slowly pour marinade over hens. Cover; marinate in refrigerator 2 to 24 hours, basting once with marinade.
6. Preheat oven to 350°.
7. Uncover hens; bake at 350° for 1 hour and 25 minutes or until juices run clear, basting occasionally with marinade. Shield wings with foil, if needed. Yield: 8 servings.

CALORIES 412 (23% from fat); FAT 10.5g (sat 2.7g, mono 4.3g, poly 2.1g); PROTEIN 35.5g; CARB 46.9g; FIBER 8.3g; CHOL 101mg; IRON 3.5mg; SODIUM 1,198mg; CALC 111mg

MUSTARD-DRESSED ASPARAGUS

4 pounds asparagus
2 tablespoons Dijon mustard
2 tablespoons lemon juice
¼ teaspoon salt
1 tablespoon mustard seeds

1. Snap off tough ends of asparagus. Bring 4 quarts water to a boil in an 8-quart stockpot. Add half of asparagus; cook 3 minutes. Remove asparagus from stockpot. Rinse with cold water; drain and pat dry. Repeat procedure with remaining asparagus.
2. Combine mustard, lemon juice, and salt in a small bowl. Place a large non-stick skillet over medium heat until hot. Add mustard seeds; cook 1 minute, stirring constantly. Add asparagus and mustard mixture, and cook 2 minutes or until thoroughly heated. Yield: 8 servings.

CALORIES 51 (19% from fat); FAT 1.1g (sat 0.1g, mono 0.3g, poly 0.3g); PROTEIN 4.5g; CARB 8.3g; FIBER 4.4g; CHOL 0mg; IRON 1.3mg; SODIUM 222mg; CALC 74mg

PARSNIP PUREE

8 cups (1-inch-thick) sliced
   parsnip (about 4 pounds)
½ cup evaporated skim milk
½ teaspoon salt
¼ teaspoon pepper
1 (10½-ounce) can low-salt chicken
   broth

1. Cook parsnip in boiling water in a large saucepan 20 minutes or until tender; drain.
2. Combine milk and remaining 3 ingredients in a 2-cup glass measure. Place parsnip in a food processor; process until smooth, scraping sides of processor bowl occasionally. With processor on, slowly add milk mixture through food chute, processing until well-blended. Yield: 8 servings (serving size: ¾ cup).
Note: This dish can be made 3 days ahead and stored in the refrigerator. To reheat, place puree in the microwave

on MEDIUM for 5 minutes, stirring once halfway through.

CALORIES 143 (5% from fat); FAT 0.8g (sat 0.2g, mono 0.2g, poly 0.1g); PROTEIN 3.8g; CARB 32.4g; FIBER 4.2g; CHOL 1mg; IRON 1mg; SODIUM 198mg; CALC 107mg

CHOCOLATE-APRICOT STRUDEL

Filling:

⅓ cup amaretto (almond-flavored liqueur)
¼ cup sugar
2 tablespoons water
1 cup dried apricots, thinly sliced (about 6 ounces)
1 tablespoon chopped crystallized ginger
¼ cup semisweet chocolate chips

Remaining ingredients:

8 sheets frozen phyllo dough, thawed
Butter-flavored cooking spray
¼ cup semisweet chocolate chips
4 apricots, diced (optional)

1. To prepare filling, combine first 3 ingredients in a medium bowl. Microwave at HIGH 1½ minutes or until sugar dissolves, stirring after 45 seconds. Stir in dried apricots and ginger; cover. Microwave at HIGH 3 minutes; let stand 5 minutes. Place apricot mixture in a food processor or blender; process until coarsely chopped. Spoon apricot mixture into bowl; cover and cool completely. Stir in ¼ cup chips.
2. Preheat oven to 350°.
3. Place 1 phyllo sheet on work surface (cover remaining dough to keep from drying); lightly coat with cooking spray. Working with 1 phyllo sheet at a time, coat remaining 7 phyllo sheets with cooking spray, placing one on top of the other. Place a sheet of plastic wrap over phyllo, pressing gently to seal sheets; discard plastic wrap.
4. Spoon apricot filling along 1 long edge of phyllo, leaving a 2-inch border.

Fold short edges of phyllo to cover 2 inches of apricot mixture on each end.
5. Starting at long edge with 2-inch border, roll up jelly-roll fashion. Do not roll tightly, or strudel may split. (Strudel may be frozen for up to five days at this point.) Place strudel, seam side down, on a baking sheet coated with cooking spray. Score 7 diagonal slits into top using a sharp knife. Lightly coat with cooking spray. Bake at 350° for 30 minutes or until golden.
6. Place ¼ cup chips in a small heavy-duty, zip-top plastic bag, and seal. Submerge bag in very hot water until chips melt. Snip a tiny hole in 1 corner of bag; drizzle chocolate evenly over 8 dessert plates. Cut strudel diagonally into 16 slices using a serrated knife dipped in hot water; arrange 2 slices over chocolate drizzle on each plate. Garnish each serving with diced apricot, if desired. Yield: 8 servings.

CALORIES 217 (24% from fat); FAT 5.8g (sat 2.4g, mono 1.6g, poly 1.2g); PROTEIN 2.6g; CARB 38.8g; FIBER 1.8g; CHOL 0mg; IRON 2mg; SODIUM 95mg; CALC 17mg

Speed-Scratch Desserts

By using a few convenience products for these desserts, you can save time and have the taste of "from-scratch" baking.

When you serve a homemade dessert, people always sit up and take notice. "I made it from scratch" usually means that it has uncompromised taste and texture, which can involve a complicated and slow process. But the following dessert recipes have shortcuts that simplify and speed up their preparation, and they taste as if they were homemade all the way.

By using a cake or pudding mix, refrigerated cookie dough, or store-bought angel food cake, you save precious time. And with Caramel-Pineapple Upside-down Cake or a Mocha-Chocolate Trifle, you can put a spectacular dessert on the table without a hassle.

CARAMEL-PINEAPPLE UPSIDE-DOWN CAKE

This recipe makes two cakes, so plan on freezing one cake. It will keep for up to three weeks in the freezer.

1 (20-ounce) can pineapple tidbits in juice, undrained
Cooking spray
¼ cup fat-free milk
1 tablespoon stick margarine or butter
30 small soft caramel candies
1 cup canned mashed sweet potatoes or yams
¼ cup vegetable oil
1 teaspoon ground cinnamon
½ teaspoon ground nutmeg
3 large egg whites
1 large egg
1 (18.25-ounce) package light yellow cake mix

1. Preheat oven to 350°.
2. Drain pineapple in a colander over a bowl, reserving 1 cup juice. Arrange pineapple tidbits evenly in bottom of 2 (9-inch) round cake pans coated with cooking spray. Combine milk, margarine, and caramels in a small microwave-safe bowl; microwave at HIGH 2½ minutes or until caramels are melted, stirring every minute. Pour caramel mixture evenly over pineapple in pans.
3. Combine reserved pineapple juice, sweet potatoes, and remaining ingredients in a large bowl; beat at low speed of a mixer 30 seconds. Beat at medium speed 2 minutes or until well-blended. Pour batter evenly over caramel layers in pans; bake at 350° for 40 minutes or until a wooden pick inserted in center comes out clean. Cool in pans 5 minutes. Place a plate upside down on top of each pan, and invert cakes onto plates. Serve cakes warm. Yield: 16 servings (2 cakes, 8 servings per cake).

CALORIES 258 (25% from fat); FAT 7.3g (sat 2.6g, mono 1.5g, poly 1.9g); PROTEIN 3g; CARB 45.3g; FIBER 0.8g; CHOL 15mg; IRON 0.8mg; SODIUM 269mg; CALC 85mg

LEMON-BLUEBERRY POUND CAKE

Cooking spray
- 1 tablespoon all-purpose flour
- 1 (18.25-ounce) package light yellow cake mix
- 1 cup water
- ⅓ cup lemon juice
- 1 teaspoon vanilla extract
- 1 (8-ounce) block fat-free cream cheese, softened
- 3 large egg whites
- 1 large egg
- 1 cup fresh or frozen blueberries, thawed
- 1 cup sifted powdered sugar
- 4 teaspoons lemon juice

1. Preheat oven to 350°.
2. Coat a 12-cup Bundt pan with cooking spray; dust with flour. Combine cake mix and next 6 ingredients in a large bowl; beat at low speed of a mixer 30 seconds. Beat at medium speed 2 minutes; fold in blueberries. Pour batter into prepared pan. Bake at 350° for 50 minutes or until a wooden pick inserted in center comes out clean. Cool cake in pan 10 minutes; remove from pan. Cool completely on a wire rack.
3. Combine sugar and 4 teaspoons lemon juice in a small bowl; drizzle glaze over cake. Yield: 16 servings (serving size: 1 slice).

CALORIES 187 (9% from fat); FAT 1.9g (sat 0.9g, mono 0.1g, poly 0.1g); PROTEIN 3.9g; CARB 37.4g; FIBER 0.4g; CHOL 16mg; IRON 0.4mg; SODIUM 302mg; CALC 88mg

EASY COCONUT CAKE

Cooking spray
- 1 tablespoon all-purpose flour
- 1 (18.25-ounce) package light white cake mix
- 1 cup low-fat buttermilk
- ¼ cup vegetable oil
- 1 teaspoon coconut extract
- 2 large egg whites
- 1 large egg
- ¼ cup flaked sweetened coconut
- ¼ cup packed light brown sugar
- Coconut-Cream Cheese Frosting

1. Preheat oven to 350°.
2. Coat a 13 x 9-inch baking pan with cooking spray; dust with flour.
3. Combine cake mix and next 5 ingredients; beat at low speed of a mixer 30 seconds. Beat at medium speed 2 minutes. Pour half of batter into prepared pan. Sprinkle with flaked coconut and brown sugar; top with remaining batter. Bake at 350° for 30 minutes or until a wooden pick inserted in center comes out clean. Cool cake completely in pan. Spread Coconut-Cream Cheese Frosting over top of cake. Yield: 18 servings.

CALORIES 268 (28% from fat); FAT 8.4g (sat 3.7g, mono 2.1g, poly 1.6g); PROTEIN 3.6g; CARB 45g; FIBER 0.1g; CHOL 19mg; IRON 0.7mg; SODIUM 256mg; CALC 69mg

Coconut-Cream Cheese Frosting:

- 6 ounces ⅓-less-fat block-style cream cheese (Neufchâtel), softened
- 1 teaspoon vanilla extract
- 3 cups sifted powdered sugar
- ¼ cup flaked sweetened coconut

1. Beat cream cheese and vanilla at high speed of a mixer until creamy. Gradually add sugar, beating at low speed until well-blended. Stir in coconut. Yield: 1¾ cups.

STRAWBERRY ANGEL CAKE

- 4 cups sliced strawberries
- ¾ cup sugar, divided
- 2 tablespoons evaporated skim milk
- 1 (8-ounce) block ⅓-less-fat cream cheese (Neufchâtel), softened
- 1 (10-inch) round angel food cake
- 3 tablespoons triple sec (orange-flavored liqueur) or orange juice, divided
- 1 (8-ounce) carton frozen reduced-calorie whipped topping, thawed
- 2 tablespoons sliced almonds, toasted

1. Combine strawberries and ¼ cup sugar in a small bowl; cover and let stand 1 hour. Combine ½ cup sugar, milk, and cream cheese in a medium bowl; beat at medium speed of a mixer until smooth.
2. Cut cake horizontally into 3 layers, using a serrated knife; place bottom layer, cut side up, on a serving plate. Brush with 1 tablespoon liqueur, and spread half of cream cheese mixture over cake. Spoon one-third of strawberry mixture over cream cheese mixture using a slotted spoon. Repeat layers, ending with cake and liqueur. Spread whipped topping over top and sides of cake. Cover; chill 30 minutes. Arrange remaining strawberries on top of cake before serving; sprinkle with almonds. Yield: 16 servings.

CALORIES 203 (26% from fat); FAT 5.8g (sat 4g, mono 1.2g, poly 0.3g); PROTEIN 4.1g; CARB 33.5g; FIBER 1.1g; CHOL 11mg; IRON 0.3mg; SODIUM 214mg; CALC 58mg

TRIPLE-CHOCOLATE BUNDT CAKE

You can substitute one (1.4-ounce) package of sugar-free chocolate fudge instant pudding mix for the regular pudding mix.

- 1 (18.25-ounce) package light devil's food cake mix
- 1 cup fat-free sour cream
- ⅓ cup fat-free milk
- ¼ cup vegetable oil
- 1 teaspoon almond extract
- 3 large egg whites
- 1 large egg
- 1 (3.9-ounce) package chocolate pudding mix
- Cooking spray
- 1 cup sifted powdered sugar
- 4 teaspoons fat-free milk
- ⅓ cup semisweet chocolate chips

1. Preheat oven to 350°.
2. Combine first 8 ingredients in a large bowl; beat at low speed of a mixer 30 seconds. Beat at medium speed 2 minutes. Pour batter into a 12-cup Bundt pan coated with cooking spray.

Bake at 350° for 50 minutes or until a wooden pick inserted in center comes out clean. Cool in pan 10 minutes; remove from pan. Cool completely on a wire rack.

3. Combine sugar and 4 teaspoons milk in a small bowl; drizzle over cake. Let stand 10 minutes. Place chips in a small heavy-duty zip-top plastic bag; seal. Submerge bag in very hot water until chips melt or microwave at MEDIUM-HIGH (70% power) 1 minute. Snip a tiny hole in 1 corner of bag; drizzle chocolate over cake. Yield: 18 servings.

CALORIES 216 (22% from fat); FAT 5.2g (sat 1.5g, mono 1.2g, poly 1.5g); PROTEIN 2.8g; CARB 39.3g; FIBER 0.9g; CHOL 0mg; IRON 1mg; SODIUM 336mg; CALC 35mg

MOCHA-CHOCOLATE TRIFLE

This spectacular dessert serves a crowd and can be made ahead of time.

    1   (18.25-ounce) package light
          devil's food cake mix
 1⅓   cups water
    2   tablespoons vegetable oil
    2   large egg whites
    1   large egg
 Cooking spray
    3   cups cold fat-free milk
    1   (5.9-ounce) package chocolate
          instant pudding mix
  ½   cup Kahlúa (coffee-flavored
          liqueur) or ½ cup strong brewed
          coffee
    1   (8-ounce) carton frozen fat-free
          whipped topping, thawed
  ½   cup chopped reduced-fat
          chocolate toffee crisp bars
          (about 4 bars) (such as Hershey's
          Sweet Escapes)

1. Preheat oven to 350°.
2. Combine first 5 ingredients in a large bowl; beat at medium speed of a mixer until well-blended. Spoon batter into a 13 x 9-inch baking pan coated with cooking spray. Bake at 350° for 25 minutes or until a wooden pick inserted in center comes out clean. Cool in pan 10 minutes on a wire rack;

remove from pan. Cool completely on a wire rack.
3. Combine milk and pudding mix in a medium bowl; prepare according to package directions.
4. Tear cake into pieces; place half of pieces in a 3-quart bowl or trifle dish. Pour ¼ cup Kahlúa over cake; top with half of pudding, whipped topping, and chopped chocolate bars. Repeat procedure with remaining cake, Kahlúa, pudding, whipped topping, and chocolate bars. Cover; chill at least 4 hours. Yield: 16 servings (serving size: about 1 cup).

CALORIES 269 (14% from fat); FAT 4.2g (sat 1.3g, mono 0.7g, poly 0.9g); PROTEIN 4.1g; CARB 48.4g; FIBER 1.1g; CHOL 16mg; IRON 1mg; SODIUM 476mg; CALC 93mg

TROPICAL-FRUIT PIZZA

    1   (18-ounce) package refrigerated
          sugar cookie dough
 Cooking spray
  ⅓   cup sugar
 1½   teaspoons grated orange rind
    1   teaspoon coconut extract
    1   (8-ounce) block fat-free cream
          cheese, softened
    1   cup (1-inch) pieces peeled ripe
          mango
    1   cup sliced banana (about 1
          large)
    6   (½-inch) slices fresh pineapple,
          cut in half
    2   kiwifruit, each peeled and cut
          into 8 slices
  ¼   cup apricot preserves
    1   tablespoon triple sec (orange-
          flavored liqueur) or orange
          juice
    2   tablespoons flaked sweetened
          coconut, toasted

1. Preheat oven to 350°.
2. Cut cookie dough into 8 slices; firmly press slices into a 12-inch round pizza pan coated with cooking spray. Bake at 350° for 25 minutes or until lightly browned. Cool completely on a wire rack.
3. Combine sugar and next 3 ingredients in a bowl; beat at medium speed of a mixer until blended. Spread cream

cheese mixture over cookie crust, leaving a ½-inch margin around edges. Arrange mango, banana, pineapple, and kiwifruit on top of cream cheese mixture. Combine preserves and liqueur in a small microwave-safe bowl, and microwave at HIGH 30 seconds or until melted. Drizzle over fruit; sprinkle with toasted coconut. Chill 1 hour. Yield: 12 servings (serving size: 1 wedge).

CALORIES 283 (24% from fat); FAT 7.4g (sat 2.4g, mono 0.1g, poly 1g); PROTEIN 4.6g; CARB 48.2g; FIBER 1.7g; CHOL 10mg; IRON 1.3mg; SODIUM 203mg; CALC 63mg

CRUNCHY OAT-APRICOT BARS

Most any flavor of fruit preserves can be used in place of apricot.

 1¾   cups all-purpose flour
    2   cups regular oats
    1   cup packed brown sugar
  ⅔   cup reduced-calorie stick
          margarine
 1½   teaspoons vanilla extract
 Cooking spray
 1½   cups apricot preserves

1. Preheat oven to 350°.
2. Lightly spoon flour into dry measuring cups, and level with a knife. Place flour and next 4 ingredients in a food processor; pulse 4 or 5 times or until oat mixture resembles coarse meal. Press half of oat mixture into the bottom of a 13 x 9-inch baking pan coated with cooking spray. Spread apricot preserves over oat mixture. Sprinkle remaining oat mixture over preserves, and gently press. Bake at 350° for 35 minutes or until bubbly and golden brown. Cool completely in pan on a wire rack. Cut into bars. Yield: 3 dozen (serving size: 1 bar).

CALORIES 113 (20% from fat); FAT 2.5g (sat 0.5g, mono 1g, poly 0.8g); PROTEIN 1.4g; CARB 22.2g; FIBER 0.8g; CHOL 0mg; IRON 0.7mg; SODIUM 41mg; CALC 11mg

CHEWY CHOCOLATE COOKIES

1 (18.25-ounce) package light
    devil's food cake mix
2 tablespoons stick margarine or
    butter, softened
2 tablespoons water
2 large egg whites
1 large egg
¾ cup semisweet chocolate chips
Cooking spray

1. Preheat oven to 350°.
2. Combine first 5 ingredients in a
large bowl; beat at medium speed of a
mixer 2 minutes. Stir in chocolate
chips. Drop by rounded teaspoons 2
inches apart onto baking sheets coated
with cooking spray. Bake at 350° for
10 minutes. Remove from pans; cool
on wire racks. Store in an airtight container. Yield: 5 dozen (serving size: 1
cookie).

CALORIES 50 (27% from fat); FAT 1.5g (sat 0.6g, mono 0.4g,
poly 0.2g); PROTEIN 0.7g; CARB 8.4g; FIBER 0.2g;
CHOL 4mg; IRON 0.3mg; SODIUM 79mg; CALC 9mg

LIGHTEN UP

Ah, Sweet Mystery

*A New Hampshire couple asks for help in
solving a culinary mystery: how to
lighten their favorite scone recipe.*

New England readers Faith Wilson
and her husband, Jim, are scone
sleuths. When they taste a scone that's
really special, they set out to get the
recipe. Recently they sampled some
fruit-filled scones from a cozy café in a
New Hampshire bookstore. "They
were the best scones ever," Faith pro-
claims. But when the Wilsons got the
recipe, they were taken aback by the
high-fat ingredients.

So we put on our aprons and began
our lightening magic.

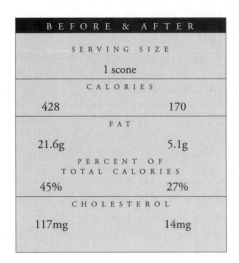

BEFORE & AFTER	
SERVING SIZE	
1 scone	
CALORIES	
428	170
FAT	
21.6g	5.1g
PERCENT OF TOTAL CALORIES	
45%	27%
CHOLESTEROL	
117mg	14mg

TRIPLE-FRUIT SCONES

*Dried cranberries and apricots, as well
as orange rind, give these scones a sweet,
tart flavor. But you can mix and match
any dried fruits to create your own
fruit scone.*

3 cups all-purpose flour
⅓ cup sugar
1 tablespoon baking powder
½ teaspoon baking soda
¼ teaspoon salt
6 tablespoons chilled stick
    margarine or butter
⅓ cup chopped dried apricots
⅓ cup sweetened dried cranberries
    (such as Craisins)
¾ cup low-fat buttermilk
2 teaspoons grated orange rind
1 large egg
1 large egg white
Cooking spray
1 tablespoon sugar

1. Preheat oven to 400°.
2. Lightly spoon flour into dry measuring cups; level with a knife. Combine flour, ⅓ cup sugar, and next 3
ingredients; cut in margarine with a
pastry blender or 2 knives until mixture resembles coarse meal. Stir in apricots and cranberries. Combine
buttermilk and next 3 ingredients; add
to flour mixture, stirring just until
moist.
3. Turn dough out onto a lightly floured
surface; knead lightly 4 times with
floured hands. Roll dough into a 12 x

6-inch rectangle. Cut dough into 8
(3-inch) squares using a dull knife or a
dough scraper. Cut each square into 2
triangles; place on a baking sheet coated
with cooking spray. Sprinkle with 1 tablespoon sugar; bake at 400° for 12
minutes or until golden. Serve warm.
Yield: 16 servings (serving size: 1 scone).

CALORIES 170 (27% from fat); FAT 5.1g (sat 1.1g, mono 2.1g,
poly 1.5g); PROTEIN 3.6g; CARB 27.6g; FIBER 0.8g;
CHOL 14mg; IRON 1.4mg; SODIUM 142mg; CALC 74mg

READER RECIPES

Sea of Love

*Our readers share their finest seafood
recipes with some new twists reeled in.*

For the last three years, Gary Fumicello has worked as a personal chef for
a Southern California client who likes
to eat and entertain with light, healthful foods. Fumicello enjoys creating
new recipes such as this salmon dish.
He says, "This job has made me see a
whole new side of cooking that I really
like. I'm close to the food I cook." Fumicello thinks he's found the California good life. He has.

CHILLED POACHED SALMON WITH PANZANELLA

*This is a twist on the Italian salad
called* panzanella *(pahn-zah-NEHL-
lah)—made with bread, onions, tomatoes, and a vinaigrette-style dressing.*
—*Gary Fumicello, Palm Dessert, California*

2 cups water
4 (6-ounce) salmon fillets (about
    1 inch thick)
2 cups diced tomato
1 cup finely chopped seeded
    peeled cucumber
½ cup finely chopped red onion
¼ cup coarsely chopped ripe olives
¼ cup balsamic vinegar
1 tablespoon chopped fresh or
    1 teaspoon dried basil

1 tablespoon capers
½ teaspoon pepper
¼ teaspoon salt
4 (1½-ounce) slices Italian bread, toasted
Basil sprigs (optional)

1. Bring water to a boil in a large skillet. Add salmon; reduce heat, and simmer 7 minutes or until fish flakes easily when tested with a fork. Remove from skillet; place in a shallow dish. Cover and chill.
2. Combine tomato and next 8 ingredients. Cover and chill 30 minutes.
3. Place 1 toast slice on each of 4 plates; top each with 1 cup tomato mixture and 1 fillet. Garnish with basil sprigs, if desired. Yield: 4 servings.

CALORIES 436 (32% from fat); FAT 15.6g (sat 2.7g, mono 7.5g, poly 3.4g); PROTEIN 40.2g; CARB 32.2g; FIBER 3.2g; CHOL 111mg; IRON 2.7mg; SODIUM 732mg; CALC 41mg

GROUPER WITH TOMATILLO-AND-GREEN CHILE CHUTNEY

This dish is based on a chile chutney recipe that I made at a cooking class in Santa Fe, New Mexico. It's a perfect complement to a mild fish like grouper, but it's also great with grilled steak or chicken.
—*Sally A. Travis, Bloomfield, New Mexico*

¾ pound tomatillos (about 5 large)
1 cup chopped onion
1 cup sugar
1 cup cider vinegar
½ cup chopped seeded jalapeño pepper
1 teaspoon ground red pepper
½ teaspoon salt
½ teaspoon ground cumin
½ teaspoon ground coriander
4 (6-ounce) grouper or other firm white fish fillets
Cooking spray
Lemon wedges (optional)

1. Discard husks and stems from tomatillos; chop. Place tomatillos, onion and next 7 ingredients in a saucepan, and bring to a boil. Reduce

heat, and simmer 1 hour or until mixture is thick, stirring occasionally. Spoon chutney into a bowl; cover and chill.
2. Prepare grill or broiler. Place grouper on a grill rack or broiler pan coated with cooking spray; cook 6 minutes on each side or until fish flakes easily when tested with a fork. Serve with chutney; garnish with lemon wedges, if desired. Yield: 4 servings (serving size: 5 ounces fish and about ⅓ cup chutney).

CALORIES 411 (7% from fat); FAT 3g (sat 0.5g, mono 0.5g, poly 1g); PROTEIN 34.7g; CARB 63.8g; FIBER 1.3g; CHOL 63mg; IRON 2.4mg; SODIUM 388mg; CALC 71mg

HALIBUT IN ZESTY TOMATO SAUCE

When I was a little girl my mother told me that fish was food for the brain, so fish is one of my favorite foods. If I did get smarter, why not attribute it to the fish?
—*Pearl E. Manne, Cranbury, New Jersey*

2½ quarts water
2 cups sliced onion
1 cup coarsely chopped celery
⅓ cup chopped carrot
1 tablespoon white vinegar
4 black peppercorns
2 bay leaves
6 (6-ounce) halibut fillets (about 1½ inches thick)
2 tablespoons vegetable oil
4½ cups sliced onion
1 cup chopped green bell pepper
2 tablespoons all-purpose flour
1 (14½-ounce) can plum tomatoes, undrained and chopped
1 teaspoon dried oregano
½ teaspoon salt
¼ teaspoon black pepper
3 cups hot cooked rice
6 lemon wedges

1. Combine first 7 ingredients in a Dutch oven; bring to a boil. Reduce heat; simmer 20 minutes. Add halibut; simmer 10 minutes. Remove from heat; let stand 20 minutes.
2. Heat oil in a large saucepan over medium heat. Add 4½ cups onion and

bell pepper, and sauté 5 minutes or until tender. Stir in flour. Add tomatoes and oregano; cover, reduce heat, and simmer 15 minutes.
3. Remove fish from cooking liquid with a slotted spoon; drain well. Discard cooking liquid and solids. Sprinkle fish with salt and black pepper. Arrange over rice. Top with tomato sauce. Serve with lemon wedges. Yield: 6 servings (serving size: 5 ounces fish, ½ cup rice, and ½ cup sauce).

CALORIES 402 (20% from fat); FAT 9g (sat 1.5g, mono 2.5g, poly 3.8g); PROTEIN 39.6g; CARB 38.8g; FIBER 3.1g; CHOL 80mg; IRON 3.5mg; SODIUM 402mg; CALC 135mg

SICHUAN SHRIMP

I love making this dish because it's so easy and quick, but at the same time, it's colorful and elegant.
—*Sheila Richardson, Los Banos, California*

2 teaspoons dark sesame oil, divided
4 cups small broccoli florets
2 pounds large shrimp, peeled and deveined
8 garlic cloves, minced
⅓ cup sugar
½ cup rice vinegar
¼ cup ketchup
2 tablespoons cornstarch
1 tablespoon red chili paste
1 (8-ounce) can sliced water chestnuts, drained
3 cups hot cooked rice
1½ tablespoons thinly sliced green onion tops

1. Heat 1 teaspoon sesame oil in a large nonstick skillet over medium-high heat. Add broccoli, and sauté 4 minutes. Add remaining 1 teaspoon sesame oil, shrimp, and garlic; sauté 4 minutes or until shrimp are done.
2. Combine sugar and next 4 ingredients. Add to skillet; cook 1 minute, stirring constantly. Stir in water chestnuts. Serve over rice, and sprinkle with green onions. Yield: 6 servings (serving size: 1 cup shrimp mixture and ½ cup rice).
Continued

Note: You can find red chili paste, which comes in a bottle, in the Asian section of your supermarket.

CALORIES 366 (10% from fat); FAT 4.1g (sat 0.7g, mono 0.9g, poly 1.5g); PROTEIN 27.7g; CARB 53.6g; FIBER 2.8g; CHOL 173mg; IRON 4.5mg; SODIUM 342mg; CALC 112mg

---

MENU SUGGESTION

SEAFOOD-STUFFED
POBLANOS WITH WARM
TOMATO SALSA

*Mexican corn-and-black
bean salad**

Saffron rice

*Combine 1 (15-ounce) can drained black
beans, 1 (11-ounce) can drained corn,
¼ cup chopped green onions,
2 tablespoons chopped cilantro, and
2 tablespoons low-fat Italian dressing.
Serves 4.

SEAFOOD-STUFFED POBLANOS WITH WARM TOMATO SALSA

I developed this recipe because my whole family loves seafood and chiles.
—Julie Seidel, Houston, Texas

 1 cup lump crabmeat, shell pieces removed
 ¼ cup (1 ounce) finely shredded reduced-fat sharp Cheddar cheese
 ¼ cup (1 ounce) finely shredded Monterey Jack cheese with jalapeño peppers
 ⅛ teaspoon salt
 ⅛ teaspoon pepper
 2 garlic cloves, minced
 2 large poblano chiles, halved and seeded
Cooking spray
 3 cups chopped peeled tomato (about 1¼ pounds)
 2 cups sliced onion
 ¼ cup water
 1 teaspoon white vinegar
 ¼ teaspoon salt
 1 jalapeño pepper, seeded and sliced

1. Preheat oven to 350°.
2. Combine first 6 ingredients in a bowl. Divide crab mixture evenly among chile halves.
3. Place stuffed chiles in an 11 x 7-inch baking dish coated with cooking spray.
4. Combine tomato and remaining ingredients in a saucepan; bring to a boil. Cover, reduce heat, and simmer 30 minutes or until onion is soft. Pour over chiles. Cover and bake at 350° for 45 minutes. Yield: 4 servings (serving size: 1 stuffed poblano half with sauce).

CALORIES 140 (31% from fat); FAT 4.8g (sat 2.3g, mono 1.2g, poly 0.6g); PROTEIN 12.7g; CARB 12.9g; FIBER 3g; CHOL 44mg; IRON 1.3mg; SODIUM 415mg; CALC 173mg

---

SHRIMP DIP

This is one of those tried-and-true family recipes that's become a favorite at parties over the years. A few years ago I lightened it, and no one has even noticed that it's low-fat. It's still a big hit.
—Kristy Rea, Naples, Florida

 ⅓ cup fat-free sour cream
 1 (8-ounce) block fat-free cream cheese, softened
 ½ cup chopped celery
 ½ cup diced onion
 2 tablespoons fresh lemon juice
 ¼ teaspoon salt
 ¼ teaspoon black pepper
 ⅛ teaspoon ground red pepper
 2 (7-ounce) cans tiny shrimp, drained

1. Combine sour cream and cream cheese in a medium bowl; beat at medium speed of a mixer until smooth. Stir in celery and remaining ingredients. Cover and chill. Yield: 2⅔ cups (serving size: 1 tablespoon).

CALORIES 16 (11% from fat); FAT 0.2g (sat 0g, mono 0g, poly 0.1g); PROTEIN 2.7g; CARB 0.7g; FIBER 0.1g; CHOL 15mg; IRON 0.2mg; SODIUM 61mg; CALC 21mg

---

LAST HURRAH

Pudding Panic in Perspective

If you're observing National Anxiety Month, we've created a praline pudding cake that's culinary therapy.

PRALINE PUDDING CAKE

(pictured on page 94)

 ¾ cup packed dark brown sugar
 1¼ cups plus 1 tablespoon all-purpose flour, divided
 ¾ cup granulated sugar
 ⅓ cup chopped pecans
 1 tablespoon baking powder
 ¼ teaspoon salt
 ½ cup 1% low-fat milk
 2 tablespoons stick margarine or butter, melted
 1½ teaspoons vanilla extract
 1¾ cups boiling water
 2 cups frozen fat-free whipped topping, thawed
Chopped pecans (optional)

1. Preheat oven to 350°.
2. Combine brown sugar and 1 tablespoon flour in a bowl. Lightly spoon 1¼ cups flour into dry measuring cups; level with a knife. Combine with granulated sugar and next 3 ingredients in a bowl; make a well in center. Combine milk, margarine, and vanilla; add to flour mixture. Stir just until moist.
3. Spread batter into an 8-inch square baking pan; sprinkle with brown sugar mixture. Pour boiling water over batter (do not stir). Bake at 350° for 35 minutes or until pudding is bubbly and cake springs back when touched lightly in center. Serve warm with whipped topping. Garnish with pecans, if desired. Yield: 8 servings (serving size: 1 square and ¼ cup whipped topping).

CALORIES 323 (18% from fat); FAT 6.6g (sat 1g, mono 3.4g, poly 1.8g); PROTEIN 3g; CARB 56.7g; FIBER 0.9g; CHOL 1mg; IRON 1.7mg; SODIUM 133mg; CALC 144mg

Broiled Shrimp with Spicy Chile Sauce Barra Vieja (page 10)

Spinach-Strawberry Salad with
Goat-Cheese Bruschetta (page 80)

Praline Pudding Cake (page 92)

Couscous with Spring Vegetables and Harissa Sauce (pages 79)

Confetti Quesadillas (page 97)

Spinach-and-Sugar Snap Risotto (page 79)

Moroccan Cornish Hens (page 86)

Nuevo Tex-Mex

The latest fusion of Texan and Mexican cooking brings a fresh, light, and modern spin to this old favorite.

Tex-Mex first blazed across American taste buds in the Wild West of the 1880s. But the term "Tex-Mex" as applied to food didn't come along until the 1970s, when Mexican cooking authorities convinced us that this sort of Texan-Mexican fusion cooking wasn't really Mexican food at all. The name was something of an insult to them, so they divided Mexican food into two categories: Things such as guacamole and tamales were authentic Mexican foods; the gloppy, cheese-covered platters and fast-food tacos were Tex-Mex. Suddenly, one of America's oldest and most popular regional cooking styles had been demoted to junk-food status.

The reality of Tex-Mex's newfound fame is only beginning to sink in at home. Over the course of this decade, the innovations of Southwestern cuisine have trickled down into the popular cooking style of the Southwest. Ingredients that used to seem exotic, like ancho chiles, black beans, and cilantro, are finding their way into more and more cupboards.

CONFETTI QUESADILLAS

(pictured on page 95)

1 tablespoon stick margarine or butter
1 cup chopped onion
1 cup fresh corn kernels (about 2 ears)
1 garlic clove, minced
⅔ cup chopped tomato
1½ teaspoons minced seeded jalapeño pepper
½ pound medium shrimp, peeled, deveined, and chopped
2 tablespoons fresh lemon juice
2 tablespoons minced fresh cilantro
¼ teaspoon salt
8 (8-inch) fat-free flour tortillas
1 cup (4 ounces) shredded part-skim mozzarella cheese, divided
1 cup Three-Pepper Salsa

1. Heat margarine in a medium non-stick skillet over medium heat. Add onion, corn, and garlic, and sauté 30 seconds. Add tomato and jalapeño; sauté 4 minutes. Stir in shrimp and next 3 ingredients; sauté 3 minutes. Remove corn mixture from skillet; keep warm.
2. Place 1 tortilla in a medium non-stick skillet over medium heat; top with ¼ cup cheese. Spoon ½ cup corn mixture over cheese; top with a tortilla. Cook 3 minutes, pressing down with a spatula until cheese melts. Turn carefully; cook until thoroughly heated (about 1 minute). Repeat procedure with remaining tortillas, cheese, and corn mixture. Cut each quesadilla into quarters; serve with Three-Pepper Salsa. Yield: 4 servings (serving size: 1 quesadilla and ¼ cup salsa).

CALORIES 430 (19% from fat); FAT 9.2g (sat 3.7g, mono 2.9g, poly 1.7g); PROTEIN 22.5g; CARB 66.9g; FIBER 6.1g; CHOL 81mg; IRON 2.1mg; SODIUM 1,125mg; CALC 231mg

THREE-PEPPER SALSA

This spicy salsa is for those who can take the heat.

1½ cups boiling water
3 dried ancho chiles or ½ teaspoon dried crushed red pepper
2 large poblano chiles
1 large yellow bell pepper
1 cup diced tomato
½ cup diced red onion
¼ cup chopped fresh cilantro
3 tablespoons orange juice
2 tablespoons lime juice
2 tablespoons minced seeded serrano chile
¼ teaspoon salt

1. Combine water and ancho chiles in a small bowl; cover, and let stand 30 minutes or until soft. Drain well; seed and chop.
2. Preheat broiler. Cut poblanos and bell pepper in half lengthwise; discard seeds and membranes. Place poblano and bell pepper halves, skin sides up, on a foil-lined baking sheet; flatten with hand. Broil 10 minutes or until blackened. Place in a zip-top plastic bag; seal. Let mixture stand 10 minutes. Peel and dice poblanos and bell pepper.
3. Combine anchos, poblanos, bell pepper, tomato, and remaining ingredients in a medium bowl; cover salsa, and chill. Yield: 2¼ cups (serving size: ¼ cup).

CALORIES 26 (14% from fat); FAT 0.4g (sat 0.1g, mono 0g, poly 0.2g); PROTEIN 1g; CARB 5.6g; FIBER 1.5g; CHOL 0mg; IRON 0.6mg; SODIUM 79mg; CALC 12mg

---

CHECKING ON CHILES

Chiles heat up even the mildest of recipes! The hottest ones are small and have pointed tips rather than blunt ones. (See serrano and jalapeño photos on page 98.)

Small chiles are hotter because, proportionately, they contain more seeds and veins than larger chiles. These seeds and membranes contain a potent compound that makes the chiles hot. If you want to reduce the amount of heat in a chile, remove its seeds and veins.

WILD-MUSHROOM NACHOS

Before making these simple nachos, you'll need to make the Refried White Beans and Roasted-Tomato Sauce.

> 4 (6-inch) flour tortillas, cut into quarters
> Cooking spray
> 2 small portobello mushrooms, sliced (about ½ pound)
> ¼ cup low-salt chicken broth
> 1 tablespoon fresh lemon juice
> 1 tablespoon low-sodium soy sauce
> 1 teaspoon olive oil
> 2 tablespoons chopped fresh or 2 teaspoons dried basil
> 1 tablespoon chopped fresh or 1 teaspoon dried thyme
> 1 cup Refried White Beans
> ⅓ cup Roasted-Tomato Sauce
> ⅓ cup (about 1½ ounces) crumbled feta cheese
> Lime rind (optional)

1. Preheat oven to 350°.
2. Place tortilla quarters on a baking sheet coated with cooking spray. Bake at 350° for 8 minutes or until crisp.
3. Place mushrooms in a shallow 2-quart baking dish. Combine broth and next 3 ingredients; drizzle over mushrooms. Sprinkle with basil and thyme; toss well. Cover and bake at 350° for 15 minutes or until tender. Drain mushrooms, discarding liquid.
4. Spread 1 tablespoon Refried White Beans over each tortilla quarter, and top evenly with mushrooms. Top each serving with 1 teaspoon Roasted-Tomato Sauce and 1 teaspoon feta cheese. Bake at 350° for 5 minutes or until tortillas are thoroughly heated. Garnish nachos with lime rind, if desired. Serve immediately. Yield: 4 servings (serving size: 4 nachos).

CALORIES 303 (25% from fat); FAT 8.5g (sat 2.5g, mono 2.8g, poly 2.1g); PROTEIN 11.2g; CARB 47g; FIBER 8.6g; CHOL 10mg; IRON 4mg; SODIUM 704mg; CALC 151mg

---

THE BIG CHILE It wouldn't be Tex-Mex if it didn't include lots of chile peppers. Be sure to handle chiles with care because they can irritate your skin. Here's a description of all the chiles found in these recipes.

ANCHO: The dried version of the poblano chile, the ancho is a deep reddish-brown and about 3 to 4 inches long. It is the sweetest of the dried chiles.

JALAPEÑO: This smooth, dark-green chile, which is bright red when ripe, can be very hot. It has a rounded tip and is about 2 inches long.

POBLANO: A dark-green chile used in classic chiles rellenos, the poblano is usually fairly mild. It is about 3 inches wide and 4 to 5 inches long, tapering from top to bottom in a triangular shape.

CHIPOTLE: This hot chile is really just a dried, smoked jalapeño. It has a wrinkled, dark skin and a smoky, sweet flavor. Chipotles (chih-POHT-lays) are often pickled and canned in adobo sauce.

SERRANO: A small, pointed chile (about 1½ inches long), the serrano is very hot. As it matures, it turns from bright green to scarlet red, then yellow.

REFRIED WHITE BEANS

Make ahead to use in Wild-Mushroom Nachos and Chicken-and-Rajas Enchiladas, or just for dipping. The beans can be stored in an airtight container in the refrigerator for up to two weeks.

> 2 teaspoons vegetable oil
> ½ cup finely chopped carrot
> 1 cup chopped green onions
> 3 large garlic cloves, minced
> 1½ teaspoons ground cumin
> 2 (15-ounce) cans cannellini beans or other white beans, undrained
> ¼ cup chopped fresh cilantro

1. Heat oil in a large nonstick skillet over medium-high heat. Add carrot; sauté 5 minutes. Add onions and garlic; sauté 2 minutes or until tender. Stir in cumin and beans; partially mash mixture with a potato masher. Cook 10 minutes or until thick, stirring frequently. Stir in cilantro. Yield: 2½ cups (serving size: ¼ cup).

CALORIES 118 (15% from fat); FAT 2g (sat 0.3g, mono 0.5g, poly 0.9g); PROTEIN 4.6g; CARB 21g; FIBER 6g; CHOL 0mg; IRON 1.6mg; SODIUM 259mg; CALC 42mg

ROASTED-TOMATO SAUCE

Roasting the tomatoes, pepper, and onion imparts a rich, caramelized flavor that stands up to the smoky taste of the chipotle.

2 pounds plum tomatoes, cut in half lengthwise
1 onion, cut into ½-inch-thick slices
1 jalapeño pepper, halved and seeded
Cooking spray
1 tablespoon fresh lime juice
¼ teaspoon salt
1 drained canned chipotle chile, seeded

1. Preheat oven to 500°.
2. Arrange first 3 ingredients on a jelly-roll pan coated with cooking spray, and bake at 500° for 30 minutes. Remove jalapeño pepper from pan. Bake tomato and onion slices an additional 15 minutes or until vegetables are soft. Combine tomato, onion, jalapeño pepper, lime juice, salt, and chipotle chile in a food processor; process until smooth. Yield: 2 cups (serving size: 1 tablespoon).

CALORIES 9 (10% from fat); FAT 0.1g; PROTEIN 0.3g; CARB 1.9g; FIBER 0.5g; CHOL 0mg; IRON 0.2mg; SODIUM 22mg; CALC 3mg

CHICKEN-AND-RAJAS ENCHILADAS

Rajas is Spanish for roasted-pepper strips. Red bell peppers can be substituted for the poblano chiles. Prepare Refried White Beans before starting this recipe.

2 large poblano chiles
Cooking spray
2 (4-ounce) skinned, boned chicken breasts, cut into ¼-inch strips
1 cup chopped tomato
¾ cup thinly sliced onion
¼ teaspoon freshly ground pepper
4 (10-inch) fat-free flour tortillas
1 cup Refried White Beans

1 cup (4 ounces) shredded fontina or Monterey Jack cheese
Fresh cilantro sprigs (optional)

1. Preheat broiler. Cut poblanos in half lengthwise, and discard seeds and membranes. Place poblano halves, skin sides up, on a foil-lined baking sheet; flatten with hand. Broil 10 minutes or until blackened. Place in a zip-top plastic bag, and seal. Let stand 10 minutes. Peel chiles and cut into ¼-inch strips.
2. Place a medium nonstick skillet coated with cooking spray over medium-high heat until hot. Add chicken, tomato, and onion; sauté 5 minutes or until chicken is done. Stir in ground pepper.
3. Warm tortillas according to package directions. Spread about ¼ cup Refried White Beans down center of each tortilla. Divide chicken mixture, chiles, and cheese evenly among tortillas, and roll up. Garnish with cilantro sprigs, if desired. Yield: 4 servings (serving size: 1 enchilada).

CALORIES 444 (24% from fat); FAT 11.9g (sat 6g, mono 3.2g, poly 1.6g); PROTEIN 28.3g; CARB 56.4g; FIBER 7.2g; CHOL 66mg; IRON 2.5mg; SODIUM 953mg; CALC 213mg

GREEN RICE

Texmati is a Texas-grown hybrid of long-grain and Indian basmati rices. In this recipe, the rice is cooked in a tomatillo mixture, making it exceptionally tangy. It makes an excellent accompaniment to the Chicken-and-Rajas Enchiladas.

6 large tomatillos (about ¾ pound)
2 tablespoons water
⅓ cup minced fresh cilantro
4 teaspoons minced seeded jalapeño pepper
½ teaspoon salt
1 garlic clove, minced
1¼ cups uncooked Texmati, basmati, or long-grain rice

1. Discard husks and stems from tomatillos. Cook tomatillos in boiling

water in a medium saucepan 4 minutes or until soft; drain. Combine tomatillos and 2 tablespoons water in a blender, and process until smooth. Pour tomatillo mixture into a 4-cup glass measure, and add enough water to measure 2½ cups.
2. Combine tomatillo mixture, cilantro, and next 3 ingredients in saucepan, and bring to a boil. Add rice; cover, reduce heat, and simmer 20 minutes or until liquid is absorbed. Let stand, covered, 5 minutes. Remove from heat, and fluff with a fork. Yield: 8 servings (serving size: ½ cup).

CALORIES 117 (3% from fat); FAT 0.4g (sat 0.1g, mono 0.1g, poly 0.1g); PROTEIN 2.7g; CARB 25.5g; FIBER 0.9g; CHOL 0mg; IRON 1.6mg; SODIUM 155mg; CALC 18mg

STRAWBERRY MARGARITAS

3½ cups strawberries
2½ cups crushed ice
½ cup tequila
½ cup fresh lime juice
¼ cup sugar
3 tablespoons Cointreau (orange-flavored liqueur)
Lime wedges (optional)

1. Combine first 6 ingredients in a blender, and process until mixture is smooth. Pour margaritas into 4 large glasses. Garnish with lime wedges, if desired. Serve immediately. Yield: 4 servings (serving size: 1 cup).

CALORIES 198 (2% from fat); FAT 0.5g (sat 0g, mono 0.1g, poly 0.3g); PROTEIN 0.9g; CARB 27.7g; FIBER 3.4g; CHOL 0mg; IRON 0.5mg; SODIUM 2mg; CALC 21mg

Sweet-Talking Onions

Boisterous when raw, onions turn mellow, rich, and ever so sweet when caramelized.

Onions are among the world's most pungent foods, capable of taking your breath (and your friends') away if eaten raw. But when cooked, onions begin to lose that sharp flavor. And when cooked to the point that their natural sugars caramelize, the transformation goes even further. The onions darken to a deep golden-brown color and take on an interesting sweetness. Caramelizing isn't difficult, but it does take a little time, a watchful eye, and a good attitude about stirring frequently. It's worth the effort, though, because this simple process can change an ordinary recipe into an extraordinary one.

Going for the Gold

1. *Slice onions in half vertically.* Place cut sides down on cutting board, and slice into thin slivers. (You can cut the onions any way you like, but they're prettiest vertically sliced.)
2. *10 minutes:* Cook over medium-high heat, stirring often. The onions begin to soften and release their liquid.
3. *15 minutes:* Keep stirring. The onions begin to turn golden, but they're not quite done yet.
4. *20 minutes:* The onions are a deep golden brown and done.

Caramelized Onions

To caramelize a larger quantity of onions (4 to 8 cups), use a large Dutch oven. You won't need additional oil.

1½ teaspoons olive oil
   Cooking spray
  3 **cups vertically sliced onion
      (sweet, yellow, white, or red
      onion), about 1 pound**

1. Heat oil in a 12-inch nonstick skillet coated with cooking spray over medium-high heat. Add sliced onion, and cook 5 minutes, stirring occasionally. Continue cooking 15 to 20 minutes or until deep golden brown, stirring frequently. Yield: 1 cup.

CALORIES 260 (28% from fat); FAT 8.2g (sat 1.1g, mono 5.1g, poly 0.9g); PROTEIN 5.9g; CARB 44g; FIBER 9.4g; CHOL 0mg; IRON 1.1mg; SODIUM 16mg; CALC 102mg

Risotto with Caramelized Onions

  4 **(10½-ounce) cans low-salt
      chicken broth**
  1 **tablespoon extra-virgin olive
      oil**
 ⅓ **cup finely chopped shallot**
1½ **cups uncooked Arborio rice or
      other short-grain rice**
  1 **cup Caramelized Onions (about
      3 cups uncooked)**
 ¼ **teaspoon salt**
 ¼ **teaspoon pepper**
 ½ **cup chopped flat-leaf parsley**
 ¼ **cup (1 ounce) grated fresh
      Parmesan cheese**

1. Bring broth to a simmer in a saucepan (do not boil). Keep warm over low heat.
2. Heat oil in a large saucepan over medium heat. Add shallot; sauté 1 minute. Add rice; cook 2 minutes, stirring constantly. Add ½ cup broth; cook until liquid is nearly absorbed, stirring constantly. Add remaining broth, ½ cup at a time, stirring constantly until each portion is absorbed. Stir in Caramelized Onions, salt, and pepper; cook 1 minute. Remove from heat; stir in parsley and cheese. Serve immediately. Yield: 5 servings (serving size: 1 cup).

CALORIES 355 (20% from fat); FAT 7.8g (sat 2.4g, mono 4.1g, poly 0.8g); PROTEIN 10.8g; CARB 60.3g; FIBER 3.1g; CHOL 8mg; IRON 3.3mg; SODIUM 328mg; CALC 118mg

CHICKEN AND RICE WITH CARAMELIZED ONIONS

1½ teaspoons olive oil
1 teaspoon grated lemon rind
1 teaspoon finely chopped fresh or ½ teaspoon dried rosemary
¼ teaspoon salt
⅛ teaspoon pepper
3 garlic cloves, crushed
4 (3-ounce) skinned, boned chicken thighs
Olive oil-flavored cooking spray
2 cups low-salt chicken broth
¼ cup dry white wine
3 cups Caramelized Onions (about 8 cups uncooked)
1 cup uncooked long-grain rice
1 tablespoon chopped fresh or 1 teaspoon dried thyme
½ teaspoon salt
1 large zucchini, quartered lengthwise and cut into 2-inch slices (about 8 ounces)
4 lemon wedges
Thyme sprigs (optional)

1. Combine first 6 ingredients in a small bowl; rub evenly over chicken. Cover and chill 1 hour.
2. Preheat oven to 350°.
3. Place a large nonstick skillet coated with cooking spray over medium-high heat until hot. Add chicken; cook 4 minutes on each side or until browned. Remove chicken from skillet. Add broth and wine to skillet, scraping skillet to loosen browned bits; add Caramelized Onions and next 3 ingredients. Add chicken and zucchini to skillet, nestling them into rice mixture. Bring mixture to a boil. Remove from heat; wrap handle of skillet with foil. Cover and bake at 350° for 20 minutes or until liquid is absorbed. Serve with lemon wedges; garnish with thyme sprigs, if desired. Yield: 4 servings (serving size: 1 chicken thigh and 1 cup rice mixture).

CALORIES 462 (17% from fat); FAT 8.8g (sat 1.9g, mono 3.7g, poly 1.4g); PROTEIN 26.4g; CARB 70.2g; FIBER 7.2g; CHOL 73mg; IRON 4.1mg; SODIUM 582mg; CALC 117mg

PIZZA WITH CARAMELIZED ONIONS, FETA, AND OLIVES

This pizza is a variation on a classic dish from the South of France called pissaladière. *Our version omits the original's anchovies.*

1 package dry yeast (about 2¼ teaspoons)
¼ teaspoon sugar
¼ cup warm water (105° to 115°)
⅓ cup cool water
1 tablespoon fat-free milk
1 teaspoon olive oil
2 cups all-purpose flour
½ teaspoon salt, divided
Cooking spray
1 tablespoon cornmeal
2½ cups Caramelized Onions (about 8 cups uncooked)
¼ teaspoon pepper
1 garlic clove, minced
1 cup (4 ounces) crumbled feta cheese
¼ cup coarsely chopped pitted kalamata olives

1. Dissolve yeast and sugar in warm water in a small bowl, and let stand 5 minutes. Stir in cool water, milk, and olive oil. Lightly spoon flour into dry measuring cups; level with a knife. Place flour and ¼ teaspoon salt in a food processor, and pulse 2 times or until blended. With processor on, slowly add yeast mixture through food chute, and process until dough forms a ball. Process dough an additional minute. Turn dough out onto a lightly floured surface, and knead lightly 4 or 5 times.
2. Place dough in a large bowl coated with cooking spray, turning to coat top. Cover, and let rise in a warm place (85°), free from drafts, 1 hour or until doubled in bulk.
3. Preheat oven to 450°.
4. Punch dough down; cover and let rest 15 minutes. Roll dough into a 14-inch circle on a lightly floured surface. Place dough on a 15-inch pizza pan or baking sheet sprinkled with cornmeal.
5. Combine Caramelized Onions, ¼ teaspoon salt, pepper, and garlic.

Spread onion mixture over dough. Top with feta and olives. Bake at 450° for 18 minutes or until crust is browned. Yield: 6 servings.

CALORIES 324 (21% from fat); FAT 7.6g (sat 3.3g, mono 2.8g, poly 0.7g); PROTEIN 10.4g; CARB 54.5g; FIBER 6g; CHOL 17mg; IRON 3.1mg; SODIUM 466mg; CALC 157mg

CARAMELIZATION BASICS

All onions become sweeter when caramelized. We used yellow onions to test these recipes, although white and red varieties work well, too.

• 1 pound of onions yields about 3 cups vertically sliced onion.

• 3 cups vertically sliced onion yield about 1 cup caramelized onions.

• 8 cups vertically sliced onion yield about 2½ to 3 cups caramelized onions.

• Stir occasionally during the first 5 minutes of caramelization, then more frequently during the last 15 to 20 minutes.

• The onions should be deep golden brown, but not burned, so watch them closely.

• Onions need lots of space to caramelize, so make sure your pan is large enough. Use a 12-inch skillet to caramelize 3 cups of onions; use a Dutch oven to caramelize 4 cups or more.

Caramelized-Onion, Spinach, and Bacon Quiche

1 (10-ounce) can refrigerated pizza crust dough
Cooking spray
1 (10-ounce) package frozen chopped spinach, thawed, drained, and squeezed dry
¼ cup low-fat sour cream
2 tablespoons minced shallot
1 cup evaporated skim milk
¼ teaspoon salt
⅛ teaspoon pepper
2 large egg whites
1 large egg
¾ cup Caramelized Onions (about 3 cups uncooked)
⅓ cup chopped Canadian bacon
¼ cup (1 ounce) shredded reduced-fat Monterey Jack cheese

1. Preheat oven to 350°.
2. Shape dough into a 4-inch circle; cover and let stand 5 minutes. Roll dough into an 11-inch circle on a lightly floured surface. Fit dough into a 9-inch pie plate coated with cooking spray, and flute.
3. Combine spinach, sour cream, and shallot in a small bowl. Combine evaporated milk and next 4 ingredients in a medium bowl, and stir well with a whisk. Stir ⅓ cup milk mixture into spinach mixture. Spoon spinach mixture into prepared crust. Add Caramelized Onions; top with bacon and cheese. Pour remaining milk mixture over cheese. Place pie plate on a baking sheet, and bake at 350° for 45 minutes or until set. Let quiche stand 10 minutes. Yield: 6 servings (serving size: 1 wedge).

CALORIES 261 (22% from fat); FAT 6.3g (sat 2.3g, mono 2.1g, poly 0.9g); PROTEIN 12.6g; CARB 35g; FIBER 2.7g; CHOL 50mg; IRON 1.5mg; SODIUM 607mg; CALC 244mg

Pasta with Caramelized Onions, Mushrooms, and Bell Pepper

1 tablespoon olive oil
Olive oil-flavored cooking spray
3 cups sliced fresh mushrooms (about 8 ounces)
2 cups (3 x ¼-inch) julienne-cut red bell pepper
2 garlic cloves, minced
2½ cups Caramelized Onions (about 8 cups uncooked)
1 cup low-salt chicken broth
½ teaspoon salt
¼ teaspoon black pepper
⅛ teaspoon dried crushed red pepper
¾ cup low-fat sour cream
1 tablespoon chopped fresh or 1 teaspoon dried oregano
8 cups hot cooked farfalle (about 1 pound uncooked bow tie pasta)
Oregano sprigs (optional)

1. Heat olive oil in a large nonstick skillet coated with cooking spray over medium-high heat. Add mushrooms and bell pepper; sauté 4 minutes. Add garlic, and sauté 30 seconds. Add Caramelized Onions and next 4 ingredients; bring to a simmer. Remove from heat; stir in sour cream and chopped oregano. Serve over pasta, and garnish with oregano sprigs, if desired. Yield: 6 servings (serving size: 1⅓ cups pasta and ⅔ cup onion mixture).

CALORIES 435 (19% from fat); FAT 9.3g (sat 3.1g, mono 3.7g, poly 1.2g); PROTEIN 13.7g; CARB 75.7g; FIBER 8.1g; CHOL 12mg; IRON 4mg; SODIUM 237mg; CALC 102mg

Menu Suggestion

*Raspberry-mint lamb chops**

Caramelized-Onion Custards

Steamed fresh asparagus

*Sprinkle 8 (4-ounce) lean lamb rib chops with ¼ teaspoon salt; grill 6 minutes on each side. Bring ⅓ cup raspberry jam and ¼ cup lemon juice to a boil; simmer 5 minutes. Stir in 1½ tablespoons minced fresh mint. Drizzle over chops. Serves 4.

Caramelized-Onion Custards

These savory custards are ideal accompaniments to beef, lamb, or game.

1 cup chopped Caramelized Onions, cooled (about 3 cups uncooked)
⅛ teaspoon salt
⅛ teaspoon pepper
⅛ teaspoon ground nutmeg
2 large eggs
2 large egg whites
1 (12-ounce) can evaporated skim milk
Cooking spray

1. Preheat oven to 325°.
2. Combine all ingredients except cooking spray in a large bowl. Spoon onion mixture into 6 (6-ounce) custard cups coated with cooking spray. Place custard cups in a 13 x 9-inch baking pan; add hot water to pan to a depth of 1 inch. Bake at 325° for 1 hour or until a knife inserted in center comes out clean. Yield: 6 servings.

CALORIES 120 (26% from fat); FAT 3.4g (sat 0.8g, mono 1.5g, poly 0.4g); PROTEIN 8.6g; CARB 14.2g; FIBER 1.6g; CHOL 76mg; IRON 0.6mg; SODIUM 156mg; CALC 191mg

The Gathering Place, Part I

From around the world come at-home menus that are meant to be shared with friends.

As you look on your calendar, why not search for a few evenings that could be set aside for dinner with friends? Share the work, and don't worry about the selection of china or the state of your housekeeping. Simply spend time in the kitchen with friends, and relax in the glow of the hospitality you have created.

We've provided the menus for you: a Mexican-style meal (below) and two island-style dinners in Part II (page 127).

(pictured on page 93)

MENU

BROILED SHRIMP WITH SPICY
CHILE SAUCE BARRA VIEJA

POSOLE

Green salad

Tortillas

PINEAPPLE NIEVE

BROILED SHRIMP WITH SPICY CHILE SAUCE BARRA VIEJA

(pictured on page 93)

- 6 dried New Mexico chiles
- 3 ancho chiles
- 1 cup boiling water
- ⅔ cup chopped onion
- 2 tablespoons molasses
- 1 tablespoon white vinegar
- ½ teaspoon ground cumin
- ½ teaspoon dried marjoram
- ½ teaspoon dried oregano
- ¼ teaspoon salt
- ⅛ teaspoon ground cloves
- 4 plum tomatoes, quartered (about 1 pound)
- 3 garlic cloves, minced
- 1 (8-ounce) carton plain fat-free yogurt
- 1 tablespoon fresh lime juice
- ¼ teaspoon salt
- Dash of saffron powder
- 24 large cherry tomatoes
- 18 jumbo shrimp (about 1 pound)
- Cooking spray
- 2 cups trimmed watercress (about 1 bunch)
- 1 tablespoon minced fresh cilantro
- 1 teaspoon chili powder

1. Cut a lengthwise slit in each chile; discard seeds and stems. Combine chiles and boiling water. Cover and let stand 10 minutes. Drain chiles through a fine sieve over a bowl, reserving ½ cup liquid. Place chiles, onion, and next 9 ingredients in a food processor; process until smooth. Combine chile mixture and reserved liquid in a small saucepan. Bring to a boil; reduce heat, and simmer 15 minutes.

2. Spoon yogurt onto several layers of heavy-duty paper towels; spread to ½-inch thickness. Cover with additional paper towels; let stand 5 minutes. Scrape into a bowl using a rubber spatula. Add juice, ¼ teaspoon salt, and saffron; stir well. Cover and refrigerate.

3. Place tomatoes in a nonstick skillet over medium-high heat. Sauté 10 minutes or until lightly browned, and cool. Cut a slit in each tomato; mash gently. Discard seeds.

4. Preheat broiler. Peel shrimp, leaving tails intact. Starting at tail end, butterfly each shrimp, cutting to, but not through, underside of shrimp. Brush shrimp with about ½ cup chile mixture; arrange shrimp on a broiler pan coated with cooking spray. Broil 6 minutes or until shrimp are done.

5. Place ½ cup yogurt mixture in a small heavy-duty, zip-top plastic bag, and seal. Snip a tiny hole in 1 corner of bag; drizzle yogurt mixture over 6 plates. Arrange ⅓ cup watercress evenly over yogurt. Top with 3 shrimp and 4 tomatoes. Sprinkle with fresh cilantro and chili powder. Yield: 6 servings.

Note: Store remaining chile mixture in an airtight container in the refrigerator. Serve with grilled chicken or enchiladas.

CALORIES 127 (13% from fat); FAT 1.9g (sat 0.4g, mono 0.2g, poly 0.5g); PROTEIN 15.4g; CARB 13.0g; FIBER 2.7g; CHOL 87mg; IRON 2.3mg; SODIUM 265mg; CALC 140mg

---

POSOLE

Mexican cooks spend two days preparing the hominy by pounding and soaking white-corn kernels. We opted for canned hominy in this earthy stew.

- 1 pound pork spareribs
- ¼ teaspoon black pepper
- 11 cups water, divided
- Cooking spray
- 1 (3½-pound) chicken
- 1 cup chopped onion
- ¼ teaspoon salt
- 3 bay leaves
- 2 garlic cloves, minced
- 8 cups torn kale (about 1 bunch)
- 2 (15.5-ounce) cans golden hominy or whole-kernel corn
- 6 tablespoons chopped fresh oregano
- 6 tablespoons chopped onion
- 1 lime, cut into 6 wedges
- 6 (6-inch) corn tortillas
- Dried crushed red pepper (optional)

1. Preheat oven to 350°.
2. Trim fat from pork; sprinkle pork with black pepper. Pour 1 cup water into a shallow roasting pan. Place pork on a rack coated with cooking spray; place rack in pan. Bake at 350° for 1 hour and 15 minutes or until tender. Remove pork from bones; reserve bones. Shred meat into bite-size pieces. Discard drippings.

Continued

3. Combine 10 cups water, chicken, and next 4 ingredients in a stockpot; bring to a boil. Reduce heat; simmer 1 hour. Remove from heat. Remove chicken from broth. Place chicken in a bowl; cool 15 minutes. Strain broth through a sieve into a bowl; discard solids. Remove chicken from bones; discard skin and reserve bones. Shred meat into bite-size pieces.

4. Return broth, pork bones, and chicken bones to pan. Bring to a boil; cook until stock is reduced to 6 cups (about 20 minutes). Strain stock through a sieve into a bowl; discard solids. Place a large zip-top plastic bag inside a 2-quart glass measure. Pour broth into bag; let stand 10 minutes (fat will rise to the top). Seal bag; snip off 1 bottom corner of bag. Drain broth into pan; stop before fat layer reaches opening. Discard fat. Add shredded pork, chicken, kale, and hominy; bring to a boil. Reduce heat; simmer 5 minutes.

5. Ladle posole into 6 bowls. Top each serving with 1 tablespoon oregano, 1 tablespoon onion, and 1 lime wedge. Serve with warm tortillas, and sprinkle with dried crushed red pepper, if desired. Yield: 6 servings (serving size: 1⅔ cups posole and 1 tortilla).

CALORIES 551 (37% from fat); FAT 22.6g (sat 7.8g, mono 9.4g, poly 4g); PROTEIN 46.4g; CARB 44.7g; FIBER 3.6g; CHOL 134mg; IRON 4.7mg; SODIUM 667mg; CALC 230mg

PINEAPPLE NIEVE

Nieve *is the Spanish word for 'snow.' One taste of this extraordinary ice, and you'll see why each bite tastes like freshly fallen snow drenched in lime and pineapple.*

    5 cups coarsely chopped pineapple
      (1 large pineapple)
    ¼ cup sugar
    ¼ cup fresh lime juice
    Cinnamon Chips

1. Place pineapple in a food processor, and process 2 minutes or until very smooth. Add sugar and lime juice;

pulse 2 times or until blended. Strain pineapple mixture through a sieve into a bowl. Discard solids.

2. Pour mixture into the freezer can of an ice-cream freezer; freeze according to manufacturer's instructions. Spoon into a freezer-safe container; cover and freeze 30 minutes or until firm. Serve with Cinnamon Chips. Yield: 6 servings (serving size: ¾ cup ice and 4 Cinnamon Chips).

Note: To prepare *nieve* without an ice-cream freezer, pour mixture into an 8-inch square baking dish; cover and freeze until firm, stirring occasionally.

CALORIES 157 (10% from fat); FAT 1.7g (sat 0.2g, mono 0.5g, poly 0.6g); PROTEIN 1.9g; CARB 36g; FIBER 2.5g; CHOL 0mg; IRON 1mg; SODIUM 76mg; CALC 31mg

Cinnamon Chips:

    1 tablespoon sugar
    ¼ teaspoon ground cinnamon
    2 (8-inch) flour tortillas
    1 tablespoon water

1. Preheat oven to 350°.

2. Combine sugar and cinnamon in a small bowl. Lightly brush both sides of tortillas with water, and sprinkle each side with cinnamon mixture. Cut each tortilla into 12 wedges. Arrange wedges in a single layer on a cookie sheet. Bake at 350° for 15 minutes or until crisp. Yield: 6 servings (serving size: 4 chips).

CALORIES 59 (17% from fat); FAT 1.1g (sat 0.2g, mono 0.5g, poly 0.4g); PROTEIN 1.4g; CARB 10.8g; FIBER 0.5g; CHOL 0mg; IRON 0.5mg; SODIUM 74mg; CALC 21mg

MAY

The Beauty of Age

*Green bell peppers turn to gold (and red and orange)
when left to vine-ripen. And May is prime time
for these sweeter, milder bells.*

For most of the year, red, yellow, and orange bell peppers are like precious gems: rare and costly. Then comes late spring, and suddenly grocery-store bins overflow with them for as little as two for a dollar. But why should you choose them over the usual green bell peppers?

First, there is the flavor difference. Green bell peppers, because they are picked before they're ripe, have a tangy, robust taste. But when left on the vine, their natural sugars develop as their hue changes. That makes red, yellow, and orange bells' flavor sweeter, milder, and more subtle. There's also a nutritional difference: As bells ripen, they become richer in vitamins A and C.

Bell peppers are more plentiful in May, which is their peak harvest season nationwide. Growers decide what color to harvest based on market price and demand. It's not unusual for immature green peppers and mature red, yellow, or orange peppers to be harvested from the same field.

What can you do with all the pepper bounty? We took the bell by the horns and created recipes that make the most of these colorful peppers.

CLASSIC SAUSAGE-AND-PEPPER GRILL

Cooking spray
1 pound red potatoes, quartered
5 garlic cloves
¼ teaspoon salt, divided
¼ teaspoon black pepper, divided
1 red onion, peeled and cut in half crosswise
4 red bell peppers, quartered
2 yellow bell peppers, quartered
5 (3-ounce) turkey Italian sausage links
2 tablespoons chopped fresh parsley
1 tablespoon minced fresh oregano

1. Coat grill rack with cooking spray.
2. Cut an 18 x 12-inch sheet of heavy-duty foil. Place potato and garlic in center of foil; sprinkle with ⅛ teaspoon salt and ⅛ teaspoon black pepper. Fold foil over vegetables, tightly sealing edges. Add foil pouch to grill rack. Grill 30 minutes, turning foil pouch occasionally.
3. Lightly coat onion and bell peppers with cooking spray; sprinkle with remaining ⅛ teaspoon salt and ⅛ teaspoon black pepper. Place onion on grill rack; grill 15 minutes. Turn onion; add bell peppers and sausage. Grill 15 additional minutes or until vegetables are tender and sausage is done; turn occasionally. Remove from grill.
4. Slice bell peppers into strips; coarsely chop onion. Combine bell pepper strips, chopped onion, and potato in a large bowl. Squeeze garlic cloves into a small bowl to extract garlic pulp; discard skins. Add parsley and oregano, tossing well. Add garlic mixture to potato mixture. Slice sausage into ½-inch-thick slices, and serve with bell pepper mixture. Yield: 5 servings (serving size: 2 ounces turkey sausage and 1 cup bell pepper mixture).

CALORIES 247 (32% from fat); FAT 8.7g (sat 2.5g, mono 3.5g, poly 2.4g); PROTEIN 18.6g; CARB 24.6g; FIBER 4.1g; CHOL 72mg; IRON 4mg; SODIUM 638mg; CALC 34mg

PIZZA WITH SWEET PEPPERS AND MOZZARELLA

You can use a premade pizza crust in place of the homemade crust, but it will raise the fat and sodium content of the recipe.

1 package dry yeast (about 2¼ teaspoons)
¾ cup warm water (105° to 115°)
1¾ cups all-purpose flour, divided
2 tablespoons cornmeal, divided
1 teaspoon olive oil
1 teaspoon salt
Cooking spray
1 cup (4 ounces) shredded part-skim mozzarella cheese, divided
½ cup (2 ounces) finely grated fresh Parmesan cheese, divided
2 red bell peppers, roasted, peeled, and cut into strips
2 orange bell peppers, roasted, peeled, and cut into strips
1 tablespoon minced fresh parsley
2 teaspoons minced fresh oregano
2 teaspoons olive oil
½ teaspoon dried crushed red pepper
4 garlic cloves, minced

1. Dissolve yeast in warm water in a large bowl; let stand 5 minutes. Lightly spoon flour into dry measuring cups; level with a knife. Add 1½ cups flour,

1 tablespoon cornmeal, oil, and salt to yeast mixture; stir until smooth (dough will be sticky). Turn dough out onto a lightly floured surface. Knead until smooth and elastic (about 10 minutes); add enough of remaining flour, 1 tablespoon at a time, to prevent dough from sticking to hands.

2. Place dough in a large bowl coated with cooking spray, turning to coat top. Cover and let rise in a warm place (85°), free from drafts, 1 hour or until doubled in bulk. Punch dough down; cover and let rest 5 minutes. Roll dough into a 10 x 8-inch rectangle on a lightly floured surface. Place dough on a baking sheet coated with cooking spray and sprinkled with remaining 1 tablespoon cornmeal. Cover and let rise 20 minutes or until puffy.

3. Preheat oven to 475°.

4. Sprinkle dough with ¾ cup mozzarella and ¼ cup Parmesan cheese, leaving a 1-inch margin. Combine bell peppers and remaining 5 ingredients; spoon evenly over cheese. Sprinkle remaining ¼ cup mozzarella and ¼ cup Parmesan cheese over bell pepper mixture. Bake at 475° for 18 minutes or until cheeses melt. Yield: 6 servings.

CALORIES 268 (30% from fat); FAT 9.0g (sat 4.1g, mono 3.4g, poly 0.7g); PROTEIN 13.4g; CARB 33.3g; FIBER 2.5g; CHOL 18mg; IRON 2.9mg; SODIUM 659mg; CALC 269mg

CHICKEN-AND-SWEET PEPPER FAJITAS

- 2 teaspoons vegetable oil, divided
- 2 cups vertically sliced onion
- 1 cup yellow bell pepper strips
- 1 cup red bell pepper strips
- 1 cup green bell pepper strips
- ¼ cup thinly sliced seeded jalapeño pepper (about 2 peppers)
- ⅓ cup chopped fresh cilantro
- ¼ teaspoon salt
- ⅛ teaspoon black pepper
- 12 ounces skinned, boned chicken breasts, cut into 2 x ¼-inch strips
- 4 (8-inch) flour tortillas
- 2 tablespoons light cream cheese with garlic and spices

1. Heat 1 teaspoon oil in a large non-stick skillet over medium-high heat. Add onion and next 4 ingredients; stir-fry 12 minutes or until crisp-tender. Remove mixture from skillet; stir in cilantro, salt, and black pepper.

2. Heat remaining 1 teaspoon oil in skillet over medium-high heat. Add chicken; sauté 3 minutes or until done. Return pepper mixture to skillet; cook 1 minute or until thoroughly heated.

3. Heat tortillas according to package directions. Spread 1½ teaspoons of cream cheese over each tortilla. Divide chicken mixture evenly among tortillas; roll up. Yield: 4 fajitas (serving size: 1 fajita).

CALORIES 334 (25% from fat); FAT 9.4g (sat 2.8g, mono 2.3g, poly 2.9g); PROTEIN 25.8g; CARB 36.6g; FIBER 4.1g; CHOL 57mg; IRON 3.7mg; SODIUM 480mg; CALC 98mg

BAKED GROUPER WITH TWO-PEPPER RELISH

- ⅓ cup chopped pitted kalamata olives
- 2 tablespoons minced fresh parsley
- 1 tablespoon extra-virgin olive oil
- 2 teaspoons red wine vinegar
- 1½ teaspoons minced fresh or ½ teaspoon dried thyme
- ¼ teaspoon salt
- 1 yellow bell pepper, roasted, peeled, and chopped
- 1 red bell pepper, roasted, peeled, and chopped
- 1 garlic clove, minced
- 6 (6-ounce) grouper fillets
- ¼ teaspoon salt
- ¼ teaspoon black pepper
- Cooking spray
- ⅓ cup dry white wine
- Thyme sprigs (optional)

1. Preheat oven to 375°.

2. Combine first 9 ingredients.

3. Sprinkle fish with ¼ teaspoon salt and black pepper. Place fish in a 13 x 9-inch baking dish coated with cooking spray. Add wine to baking dish. Bake at 375° for 24 minutes or until fish flakes easily when tested with a

fork. Serve with pepper relish. Garnish with thyme sprigs, if desired. Yield: 6 servings (serving size: 5 ounces fish and about ¼ cup relish).

CALORIES 225 (29% from fat); FAT 7.2g (sat 1g, mono 3.4g, poly 1.8g); PROTEIN 35.8g; CARB 2.4g; FIBER 0.7g; CHOL 80mg; IRON 2.2mg; SODIUM 355mg; CALC 96mg

---

MENU SUGGESTION

*Deviled beef tenderloin**

GOLDEN-PEPPER RISOTTO

Steamed fresh asparagus

*Combine 1 teaspoon hot sauce, 2 teaspoons mustard, and 2 teaspoons brown sugar; brush over 1 side of 4 (4-ounce) beef tenderloin steaks. Press ¾ teaspoon coarsely ground pepper into mustard mixture. Grill steaks, starting with pepper sides down, 6 minutes on each side or to desired doneness. Serves 4.

GOLDEN-PEPPER RISOTTO

- 4 small yellow bell peppers, roasted
- 2½ cups water
- 1 (10½-ounce) can low-salt chicken broth
- 2 teaspoons olive oil
- ½ cup minced onion
- 1½ cups uncooked Arborio rice or other short-grain rice
- ½ cup dry white wine
- ½ cup (2 ounces) finely grated fresh Parmesan cheese
- 2 tablespoons minced fresh parsley
- 2 teaspoons stick margarine or butter
- ½ teaspoon salt
- ¼ teaspoon black pepper

1. Place 2 roasted peppers in a food processor or blender, and process until smooth. Chop remaining peppers.

2. Bring water and broth to a simmer in a medium saucepan (do not boil). Keep warm over low heat.

3. Heat oil in a large saucepan over medium-high heat. Add onion; sauté 3 *Continued*

minutes or until tender. Add rice; cook 2 minutes, stirring constantly. Stir in wine; cook 2 minutes or until liquid is nearly absorbed, stirring constantly. Add simmering broth mixture, ½ cup at a time, stirring constantly until each portion of broth is absorbed before adding the next (about 20 minutes total). Stir in pureed and chopped peppers; cook 2 minutes, stirring constantly. Remove from heat; stir in cheese and remaining ingredients. Yield: 6 servings (serving size: 1 cup).

CALORIES 267 (21% from fat); FAT 6.1g (sat 2.3g, mono 2.5g, poly 0.8g); PROTEIN 8g; CARB 44.5g; FIBER 1.8g; CHOL 7mg; IRON 3mg; SODIUM 390mg; CALC 127mg

MEDITERRANEAN PEPPERS AND POTATOES

   2   teaspoons olive oil
   ½   cup chopped onion
   3   garlic cloves, minced
   1   cup minced seeded plum
         tomato
   1½ cups cubed peeled baking potato
   1   cup (1-inch) pieces red bell
         pepper
   1   cup (1-inch) pieces yellow bell
         pepper
   1   cup (1-inch) pieces orange bell
         pepper
   ¼   teaspoon salt
   ¼   teaspoon black pepper
   1   (10½-ounce) can low-salt chicken
         broth
   ⅓   cup coarsely chopped fresh basil
   ¼   cup sliced pimento-stuffed olives

1. Heat oil in a medium saucepan over medium-high heat. Add onion; sauté 10 minutes. Add garlic; sauté 1 minute. Add tomato; cook 5 minutes, stirring frequently. Add potato and next 6 ingredients; bring to a boil. Cover, reduce heat, and simmer 20 minutes or until potato is tender, stirring occasionally. Remove from heat; stir in basil and olives. Let stand, covered, 20 minutes. Yield: 5 servings (serving size: 1 cup).

CALORIES 105 (28% from fat); FAT 3.3g (sat 0.8g, mono 1.7g, poly 0.5g); PROTEIN 3.2g; CARB 17.5g; FIBER 3.2g; CHOL 1mg; IRON 2mg; SODIUM 215mg; CALC 32mg

ROASTED PEPPER-AND-CHICKPEA SALAD

   ½   cup vertically sliced red onion
   ⅓   cup minced fresh cilantro
   2   tablespoons fresh lemon juice
   1   tablespoon olive oil
   ½   teaspoon Hungarian sweet
         paprika
   ¼   teaspoon salt
   ¼   teaspoon black pepper
   3   red bell peppers, roasted, peeled,
         and cut into thin strips
   1   garlic clove, crushed
   1   (15½-ounce) can chickpeas
         (garbanzo beans), drained

1. Combine all ingredients in a medium bowl, and toss well. Yield: 4 servings (serving size: 1 cup).

CALORIES 178 (28% from fat); FAT 5.6g (sat 0.7g, mono 3g, poly 1.3g); PROTEIN 7.6g; CARB 26.6g; FIBER 4.1g; CHOL 0mg; IRON 3.3mg; SODIUM 302mg; CALC 56mg

YELLOW-AND-ORANGE PEPPER SOUP WITH RED-CHILE PUREE

This soup is equally good without the red-chile puree.

   1   tablespoon olive oil
   2   cups diced orange bell pepper
   2   cups diced yellow bell pepper
   ½   cup diced onion
   ½   cup diced carrot
   3   garlic cloves, minced
   3   cups diced peeled baking potato
         (about 1 pound)
   3   cups water, divided
   ½   teaspoon salt
   ¼   teaspoon black pepper
   1   (14½-ounce) can vegetable broth
   1   large ancho chile (about
         ¼ ounce)
   ⅛   teaspoon salt
         Chopped fresh cilantro (optional)

1. Heat oil in a Dutch oven over medium-high heat. Add bell peppers, onion, carrot, and garlic; sauté 10 minutes or until lightly browned. Add potato, 2 cups water, and next 3 ingredients; bring to a boil. Cover, reduce

heat, and simmer 30 minutes or until vegetables are tender.
2. Place half of bell pepper mixture in a blender; cover and process until smooth. Pour pureed bell pepper mixture into a large bowl. Repeat procedure with remaining mixture, and keep warm.
3. Remove stem and seeds from chile. Tear chile into large pieces; place in a small saucepan over medium heat. Cook 3 minutes or until thoroughly heated, turning pieces occasionally (be careful not to burn chile). Add remaining 1 cup water; bring to a simmer. Cover and simmer 5 minutes or until soft. Remove chile from pan with a slotted spoon, reserving 2 tablespoons cooking liquid. Discard remaining liquid.
4. Combine chile, 2 tablespoons cooking liquid, and ⅛ teaspoon salt in a blender; cover and process until smooth. Ladle soup into 7 bowls; top with chile puree, and garnish with cilantro, if desired. Yield: 7 servings (serving size: 1 cup soup and 1½ teaspoons puree).

CALORIES 114 (26% from fat); FAT 3.3g (sat 0.7g, mono 1.6g, poly 0.4g); PROTEIN 2.8g; CARB 19.9g; FIBER 3.3g; CHOL 2mg; IRON 1.8mg; SODIUM 483mg; CALC 23mg

High-Energy Eats

These recipes will keep you on an even keel throughout the day.

It's important to keep your body supplied with energy throughout the day. The following recipes do just that. Not only do they provide a balance of protein, fat, and carbohydrates, but they are also rich in nutrients, vitamins, minerals, and fiber. These recipes get you through the whole day: breakfast, lunch, dinner, and between-meal power snacks. In other words, if you want to keep your eyes open during that 4 p.m. meeting, we can help.

TEX-MEX CHICKEN SOUP WITH SPLIT PEAS

While the split peas rev up the carbohydrates in this chicken soup, the bell peppers pump up the vitamin C.

    2 teaspoons chili powder
    ½ teaspoon ground coriander
    ⅛ teaspoon salt
    ⅛ teaspoon garlic powder
    ⅛ teaspoon ground red pepper
    ⅛ teaspoon black pepper
    1 pound skinned, boned chicken
       breasts
    1 teaspoon vegetable oil
Cooking spray
 1½ cups vertically sliced onion
    ⅔ cup thinly sliced yellow bell
       pepper
    ⅔ cup thinly sliced green bell pepper
    ⅔ cup thinly sliced red bell pepper
    2 cups low-salt chicken broth
    2 cups water
    ½ cup green split peas
    ¼ teaspoon salt
    ½ cup bottled salsa
    1 tablespoon fresh lime juice
    3 (10-inch) flour tortillas, cut into
       ¼-inch-thick strips
    ¾ cup (3 ounces) shredded reduced-
       fat Monterey Jack cheese

1. Combine first 6 ingredients in a shallow dish. Dredge chicken in spice mixture. Heat oil in a large nonstick skillet coated with cooking spray over medium-high heat. Add chicken, and sauté 6 minutes on each side or until chicken is done. Remove chicken from pan, and cool. Cut chicken into ½-inch pieces.
2. Add onion and bell peppers to skillet; sauté 3 minutes. Add chicken, broth, and next 3 ingredients; bring to a boil. Partially cover, reduce heat, and simmer for 30 minutes or until peas are tender. Add salsa and lime juice; simmer 10 additional minutes.
3. Preheat broiler. Spread tortilla strips in a single layer on a baking sheet coated with cooking spray; lightly coat tortilla strips with cooking spray. Broil 4 minutes or until lightly browned, stirring once.
4. Ladle soup into 6 bowls; top with tortilla strips, and sprinkle with cheese. Yield: 6 servings (serving size: 1⅓ cups soup, about ¾ cup tortilla strips, and 2 tablespoons cheese).

CALORIES 322 (22% from fat); FAT 7.8g (sat 2.6g, mono 2.1g, poly 1.8g); PROTEIN 30.2g; CARB 33g; FIBER 3.6g; CHOL 55mg; IRON 3.1mg; SODIUM 526mg; CALC 193mg

ZESTY VEGETARIAN PITAS

Serve leftover chickpea spread with baked tortilla chips for a high-carbohydrate snack.

    ½ cup light mayonnaise
    ¼ cup chopped fresh basil
    2 tablespoons sun-dried tomato
       spread (such as California Sun
       Dry)
    1 teaspoon lemon juice
    ¼ teaspoon pepper
    1 (15-ounce) can chickpeas
       (garbanzo beans), drained
    2 cups chopped seeded tomato
    ½ cup peeled, seeded, and diced
       cucumber
    ¼ cup chopped red onion
    ¼ cup fat-free Italian dressing
    2 (6-inch) pitas, cut in half
    4 curly leaf lettuce leaves

1. Combine first 6 ingredients in a food processor; process until smooth. Cover and chill. Combine tomato and next 3 ingredients in a bowl; cover and marinate in refrigerator 1 hour. Drain vegetable mixture; discard marinade. Line each pita half with a lettuce leaf; spread each with 3 tablespoons chickpea mixture. Spoon about ⅔ cup marinated vegetables into each pita half. Yield: 4 servings (serving size: 1 filled pita half).

CALORIES 209 (27% from fat); FAT 6.2g (sat 0.8g, mono 1.8g, poly 2.9g); PROTEIN 6g; CARB 32.3g; FIBER 5.5g; CHOL 5mg; IRON 3.5mg; SODIUM 294mg; CALC 61mg

APRICOT STICKY MUFFINS

When your energy level is fading fast, these muffins are your ticket for a boost.

    1 cup apple juice
    ½ cup finely chopped dried apricots
 1¾ cups all-purpose flour
    ⅓ cup uncooked farina (such as
       Cream of Wheat)
    ⅓ cup sugar
    2 teaspoons baking powder
    ¼ teaspoon salt
    ⅛ teaspoon ground nutmeg
    ¼ cup stick margarine or butter,
       melted
    1 teaspoon vanilla extract
    3 large egg whites, lightly beaten
    1 (8-ounce) carton plain fat-free
       yogurt
Cooking spray
    2 tablespoons sugar

1. Preheat oven to 400°.
2. Combine apple juice and apricots in a microwave-safe bowl. Cover with heavy-duty plastic wrap, and vent. Microwave at HIGH 3 minutes or until mixture boils. Let stand, covered; cool completely. Drain apricots in a colander over a bowl, reserving apple juice.
3. Lightly spoon flour into dry measuring cups, and level with a knife. Combine flour and next 5 ingredients in a medium bowl; make a well in center of mixture. Combine 3 tablespoons reserved apple juice, margarine, and next 3 ingredients; stir well with a whisk. Add to flour mixture, stirring just until moist. Stir in apricots.
4. Spoon batter into 12 muffin cups coated with cooking spray. Bake at 400° for 20 minutes or until muffins spring back when touched lightly in center. Remove muffins from pans immediately; place on a wire rack. Dip muffin tops in remaining apple juice; sprinkle each with ½ teaspoon sugar. Yield: 1 dozen (serving size: 1 muffin).

CALORIES 189 (20% from fat); FAT 4.3g (sat 0.8g, mono 1.7g, poly 1.3g); PROTEIN 4.6g; CARB 33.1g; FIBER 0.9g; CHOL 0mg; IRON 2.9mg; SODIUM 142mg; CALC 116mg

Rice Pudding with Cider-Rhubarb Sauce

You could make this for dessert, then have it for breakfast the next day instead of hot cereal.

      2 cups cooked long-grain brown
         rice
   Butter-flavored cooking spray
   ¼ cup sugar
      2 ounces tub-style light cream
         cheese (about ½ cup)
   ¼ cup 2% reduced-fat milk
   ¼ cup evaporated skim milk
   ¼ teaspoon vanilla extract
   Dash of salt
      1 large egg
   Cider-Rhubarb Sauce

1. Preheat oven to 350°.
2. Spoon ½ cup rice into each of 4 (4-ounce) ramekins coated with cooking spray.
3. Combine sugar and cream cheese in a medium bowl; beat at medium speed of mixer until smooth. Add reduced-fat milk and next 4 ingredients; beat well. Divide mixture evenly among prepared ramekins. Place ramekins in a 13 x 9-inch baking dish; add hot water to dish to a depth of 1 inch. Bake at 350° for 40 minutes or until set. Remove ramekins from dish. Drizzle each with 1 tablespoon sauce. Yield: 4 servings.

CALORIES 251 (15% from fat); FAT 4.3g (sat 2g, mono 0.6g, poly 0.3g); PROTEIN 7g; CARB 45.7g; FIBER 0.6g; CHOL 65mg; IRON 1.2mg; SODIUM 124mg; CALC 115mg

Cider-Rhubarb Sauce:

   ½ cup thinly sliced fresh or frozen
         rhubarb, thawed
      2 tablespoons apple cider
      1 tablespoon sugar

1. Combine all ingredients in a small saucepan, and bring to a boil. Cover, reduce heat, and simmer 5 minutes, stirring occasionally. Yield: ¼ cup (serving size: 1 tablespoon).

Mocha Mudslide

Refuel with this creamy shake that's loaded with the potassium you need after a workout.

      1 cup fat-free milk
   ⅔ cup sliced ripe banana
      2 tablespoons sugar
      1 teaspoon instant coffee granules
   ¼ cup vanilla low-fat yogurt
   Banana slices (optional)

1. Place first 4 ingredients in a blender; cover and process until smooth. Place blender container in freezer; freeze 1 hour or until slightly frozen. Loosen frozen mixture from sides of blender container; add yogurt. Cover and process until smooth; garnish with sliced banana, if desired. Serve immediately. Yield: 2 servings (serving size: 1 cup).
Note: For a chocolate-flavored shake, use reduced-fat chocolate milk instead of plain fat-free milk, and reduce sugar to 1 tablespoon.

CALORIES 164 (4% from fat); FAT 0.8g (sat 0.5g, mono 0.2g, poly 0.1g); PROTEIN 6.2g; CARB 34.4g; FIBER 1.5g; CHOL 4mg; IRON 0.3mg; SODIUM 83mg; CALC 204mg

Peanut Butter-Granola Gorp

For a quick, on-the-go snack, store this crunchy trail mix in small, plastic zip-top bags.

   ¼ cup creamy peanut butter
   ¼ cup maple-flavored syrup
      1 cup low-fat granola with raisins
         (such as Kellogg's Low-fat
         Granola with Raisins)
   32 tiny fat-free pretzels, broken
         into small pieces
   Cooking spray
   ½ cup golden raisins
   ½ cup sweetened dried cranberries
         (such as Craisins)

1. Preheat oven to 300°.
2. Combine peanut butter and syrup in a small microwave-safe bowl.

Microwave at HIGH 30 seconds or until hot; stir well. Place granola and pretzels in a large bowl; pour peanut butter mixture over granola mixture, stirring to coat. Spread mixture in a single layer on a jelly-roll pan coated with cooking spray. Bake at 300° for 25 minutes, stirring twice. Stir in raisins and cranberries; return pan to oven. Turn oven off; cool mixture in closed oven 30 minutes. Remove from oven; cool completely. Yield: 3½ cups (serving size: ½ cup).

CALORIES 225 (23% from fat); FAT 5.7g (sat 0.8g, mono 2.7g, poly 1.9g); PROTEIN 5.1g; CARB 42g; FIBER 2.7g; CHOL 0mg; IRON 1.6mg; SODIUM 180mg; CALC 22mg

LAST HURRAH

Third Shift from the Sun

At last, a day where the 9-to-5 masses can pay tribute to those who work through the night.

Whether they're driving ambulances, patrolling the highways, delivering newspapers, or dispensing cups of joe in a diner, they're America's late-night heroes. For those who are at their jobs while the rest of us are asleep, May 13th, 1998 was set aside as National Third-Shift Worker's Day. What can you do to show your appreciation to these unsung heroes of the dark? Here's a suggestion: Why not make your favorite late-night employee something truly special? Try our Coffee Coffeecake. It may be just the invigorating treat they need when those 4 a.m. droopsies set in.

COFFEE COFFEECAKE

⅓ cup granulated sugar
4½ teaspoons instant espresso or
  3 tablespoons instant coffee
  granules
1½ teaspoons ground cinnamon
1½ cups all-purpose flour
½ cup granulated sugar
1 teaspoon baking powder
½ teaspoon baking soda
⅛ teaspoon salt
1 cup plain low-fat yogurt
2½ tablespoons stick margarine or
  butter, melted
1 teaspoon vanilla extract
1 large egg
Cooking spray
2 tablespoons finely chopped
  walnuts
2 teaspoons 1% low-fat
  milk
1 teaspoon instant espresso or
  2 teaspoons instant coffee
  granules
⅓ cup sifted powdered sugar

1. Preheat oven to 350°.
2. Combine first 3 ingredients, and set aside.
3. Lightly spoon flour into dry measuring cups, and level with a knife. Combine flour, granulated sugar, and next 3 ingredients in a large bowl. Combine yogurt and next 3 ingredients; add to flour mixture, stirring just until moist.
4. Spread half of batter into an 8-inch square cake pan coated with cooking spray, and sprinkle with half of espresso mixture. Top with remaining batter, spreading to cover; sprinkle with remaining espresso mixture. Swirl batters together using a knife, and sprinkle with walnuts. Bake at 350° for 35 minutes or until cake springs back when touched lightly in center. Cool on a wire rack.
5. Combine milk and 1 teaspoon espresso, stirring until coffee granules dissolve; stir in powdered sugar. Drizzle over cake. Yield: 9 servings.

CALORIES 234 (21% from fat); FAT 5.4g (sat 1.2g, mono 2g, poly 1.8g); PROTEIN 4.8g; CARB 41.8g; FIBER 0.8g; CHOL 26mg; IRON 1.4mg; SODIUM 131mg; CALC 77mg

INSPIRED VEGETARIAN

Great Pretenders

Readers challenged us to "de-meat" their favorite recipes. Come join us for dinner.

We hope "gardenizing" these recipes will open the path for many of you who are looking for a full-flavor experience without the meat.

We don't make that claim lightly. The taste of a juicy steak, medium burger, or slice of prime rib can't really be duplicated, and we shouldn't pretend otherwise. But what about bringing in other palate sensations to supplant the old cravings with something new and equally as mouth-watering? When prepared correctly, portobello mushrooms, pan-seared tofu, or a well-made vegetarian burger could make you forget all about that half-pounder at the drive-through window.

TEXAS BARBECUE WRAP

¼ cup barbecue sauce
1 teaspoon chili powder
½ teaspoon ground cumin
½ teaspoon dried oregano
1 (12.3-ounce) package light tofu,
  drained and sliced lengthwise
  into ¼-inch pieces
2 teaspoons olive oil
¼ cup chopped onion
1 teaspoon ground turmeric
2 garlic cloves, minced
1 jalapeño pepper, seeded and
  minced
1½ cups water
¾ cup uncooked basmati rice
4 curly leaf lettuce leaves
4 (10-inch) fat-free flour
  tortillas
1 cup (4 ounces) shredded
  reduced-fat Monterey Jack
  cheese
½ cup plain fat-free yogurt
8 (⅛-inch-thick) slices tomato, cut
  in half crosswise

1. Preheat broiler.
2. Combine first 4 ingredients in a small bowl. Brush barbecue sauce mixture over both sides of tofu. Broil tofu 4 minutes on each side or until bubbly.
3. Heat olive oil in a medium saucepan over medium-high heat. Add onion and next 3 ingredients; sauté 1 minute. Add water and rice; bring to a boil. Cover, reduce heat, and simmer 30 minutes or until rice is tender.
4. Place 1 lettuce leaf on each tortilla. Divide broiled tofu slices evenly among tortillas. Top each with ¾ cup rice mixture, ¼ cup shredded cheese, 2 tablespoons yogurt, and 2 tomato slices; roll up. Cut each tortilla diagonally in half. Yield: 4 servings (serving size: 2 halves).

CALORIES 439 (18% from fat); FAT 8.6g (sat 3.8g, mono 2.3g, poly 1.2g); PROTEIN 21g; CARB 67.7g; FIBER 1.6g; CHOL 19mg; IRON 2.6mg; SODIUM 823mg; CALC 315mg

GARDEN "SLOPPY JOES"

Tempeh is a chewy, rich-flavored soybean cake that can be found in health food stores. It's great marinated and grilled, or in stews and chilis.

2 teaspoons olive oil
1 cup chopped onion
1 cup chopped celery
½ cup diced carrot
1 (8-ounce) package tempeh,
  crumbled
2 cups canned crushed tomatoes
  in puree, undrained
¼ cup water
¼ cup bottled hot-and-spicy
  barbecue sauce
2 teaspoons chili powder
½ teaspoon dried oregano
½ teaspoon pepper
¼ teaspoon salt
8 (1½-ounce) whole-wheat
  hamburger buns

1. Heat oil in a nonstick skillet over medium heat. Add onion, celery, carrot, and tempeh; sauté 5 minutes. Stir in tomatoes and next 6 ingredients.
Continued

Bring to a boil; cover, reduce heat, and simmer 10 minutes, stirring occasionally. Uncover and cook an additional 3 minutes or until mixture is slightly thick. Serve on hamburger buns. Yield: 8 servings (serving size: 1 bun and ½ cup vegetable mixture).

CALORIES 208 (22% from fat); FAT 5g (sat 0.7g, mono 1.7g, poly 2g); PROTEIN 11.2g; CARB 33.1g; FIBER 2.9g; CHOL 1mg; IRON 2.6mg; SODIUM 496mg; CALC 102mg

COWBOY-STYLE "MEAT LOAF"

    2   teaspoons olive oil
    1   cup chopped onion
    ½   cup chopped celery
    ½   cup diced green bell pepper
    ½   cup diced red bell pepper
  1½   teaspoons ground cumin
    2   garlic cloves, minced
    1   jalapeño pepper, seeded and
          chopped
    ½   cup barbecue sauce, divided
    2   cups mashed cooked peeled
          baking potato (about 1 pound
          uncooked potatoes)
    1   cup regular oats, uncooked
    ¼   cup minced fresh cilantro
    ¼   cup ketchup
    1   tablespoon Dijon mustard
    ½   teaspoon salt
    ½   teaspoon pepper
    1   (16-ounce) can kidney beans,
          drained and mashed
        Cooking spray
    ¾   cup (3 ounces) shredded reduced-
          fat sharp Cheddar cheese

1. Preheat oven to 375°.
2. Heat oil in a large nonstick skillet over medium-high heat. Add onion and next 6 ingredients; sauté 3 minutes. Stir in ¼ cup barbecue sauce, potato, and next 7 ingredients. Spoon potato mixture into a 9 x 5-inch loaf pan coated with cooking spray. Bake at 375° for 30 minutes. Brush remaining ¼ cup barbecue sauce over loaf, and sprinkle with cheese. Bake an additional 10 minutes or until done. Yield: 6 servings.

CALORIES 266 (21% from fat); FAT 6.3g (sat 2.1g, mono 2.4g, poly 0.9g); PROTEIN 12.7g; CARB 41.2g; FIBER 5.4g; CHOL 9mg; IRON 3.3mg; SODIUM 765mg; CALC 178mg

ITALIAN VEGETABLE PIE

We used lasagna noodles instead of a deep-dish pie shell and tofu instead of ground beef.

    2   teaspoons olive oil
    1   cup chopped green bell pepper
    1   cup chopped onion
    1   cup chopped mushrooms
    1   (12.3-ounce) package firm tofu,
          drained and crumbled
    3   garlic cloves, minced
    3   tablespoons tomato paste
    1   teaspoon dried Italian seasoning
    1   teaspoon fennel seeds
    ¼   teaspoon dried crushed red
          pepper
    1   (25.5-ounce) jar fat-free
          marinara sauce
    6   cooked lasagna noodles, cut in
          half crosswise
        Cooking spray
  1½   cups (6 ounces) shredded part-
          skim mozzarella cheese
    ¼   cup grated Parmesan cheese

1. Preheat oven to 375°.
2. Heat oil in a large nonstick skillet over medium-high heat. Add bell pepper and next 4 ingredients; sauté 3 minutes or until vegetables are tender. Stir in tomato paste and next 4 ingredients; bring to a boil. Reduce heat; simmer 10 minutes.
3. Arrange noodles spokelike in the bottom of an 8-inch round baking dish coated with cooking spray. Spread 3 cups tomato mixture over noodles. Fold ends of noodles over tomato mixture, and top with remaining tomato mixture and cheeses. Bake at 375° for 20 minutes. Yield: 8 servings.

CALORIES 307 (30% from fat); FAT 10.4g (sat 4.4g, mono 3g, poly 2.1g); PROTEIN 19.7g; CARB 33.8g; FIBER 4.8g; CHOL 20mg; IRON 6.7mg; SODIUM 444g; CALC 340mg

BLACKENED PORTOBELLO-MUSHROOM SALAD

(pictured on page 116)

We've used portobellos in place of New York strip steak in this salad. To keep the protein up, we added white beans.

    ¼   cup red wine vinegar
    ¼   cup balsamic vinegar
    ¼   cup tomato juice
    1   tablespoon olive oil
    2   teaspoons Dijon mustard
    2   teaspoons stone-ground mustard
    ¼   teaspoon coarsely ground pepper
    4   (4-ounce) portobello mushroom
          caps (about 5 inches wide)
    1   tablespoon Cajun seasoning for
          steak (such as Chef Paul
          Prudhomme's Steak Magic)
    2   teaspoons olive oil
        Cooking spray
   16   cups gourmet salad greens
    1   large tomato, cut into 8 wedges
    ½   cup thinly sliced red onion,
          separated into rings
    1   (15-ounce) can cannellini or
          other white beans, rinsed and
          drained
    ¼   cup (1 ounce) crumbled blue
          cheese

1. Combine first 7 ingredients in a large zip-top plastic bag. Add mushrooms; seal bag. Marinate 10 minutes, turning occasionally. Remove mushrooms, reserving marinade.
2. Sprinkle mushrooms with Cajun seasoning. Heat oil in a large nonstick skillet coated with cooking spray over medium-high heat. Add mushrooms; cook 2 minutes on each side or until very brown. Cool; cut diagonally into thin slices.
3. Arrange 4 cups salad greens on 4 plates. Top with mushroom slices, 2 tomato wedges, and onion rings. Sprinkle each serving with ¼ cup beans and 1 tablespoon blue cheese. Drizzle reserved marinade evenly over salads. Yield: 4 servings.

CALORIES 260 (37% from fat); FAT 10.7g (sat 2.4g, mono 5.2g, poly 1.7g); PROTEIN 12.8g; CARB 31.4g; FIBER 7.7g; CHOL 5mg; IRON 5.4mg; SODIUM 669mg; CALC 165mg

Family Frittata (page 130)

Pan-Fried Garlic-Scallop Dumplings (page 117)

Soy-Sesame Dipping Sauce (page 118)

Barbecued Flank Steak with
Chutney-Bourbon Glaze (page 123)

Pasta with Arugula and Shaved Parmesan (page 124)

Spiced Spinach and Shrimp (page 128)

Raspberry-Almond Crumb Cake (page 121)

Lychee Sorbet with Fruit Salsa (page 128)

Blackened Portobello-Mushroom Salad (page 112)

A Culinary Revolution

A survivor of China's Cultural Revolution is working to redefine the way Americans see—and eat—Chinese food.

Since arriving in the United States 11 years ago, Ying Compestine—as she's now called—has fulfilled many hopes, for her father and herself. The latest is a cookbook, *Secrets of Fat-Free Chinese Cooking* (Avery, $14.95).

Although Ying is a sociologist by profession, she's now exploring the dynamics of food. "I can't believe what I had, and what I now have," she says. "Americans just don't know."

As grateful as she is for her success in America, Ying says she also regrets the years she could have spent with her parents in China.

"There were good things in the bad," she says, remembering. . . "I really miss the closeness that people in China have. If you don't want to make dinner, you go to somebody's house, and they feed you. You don't need a week's appointment to visit, like here. You just drop in."

"In China, it's very important for families to eat together," she says. "Even when my father [a surgeon] was in surgery, we'd wait hours for him to come home so we could eat. I insist that my family eats together every night. No TV. No music. Just us talking."

HOT-AND-SOUR SOUP

For a meatless version, use vegetable broth and add a little extra tofu to replace the pork.

10 dried shiitake mushrooms
   (about 1 ounce)
1½ cups boiling water
3 (10½-ounce) cans low-salt
   chicken broth
1 (4-ounce) boned center-cut loin
   pork chop, cut into thin strips
4 ounces firm tofu, cut into
   ½-inch cubes
2 tablespoons cornstarch
3 tablespoons white wine
   vinegar
3 tablespoons low-sodium soy
   sauce
2 teaspoons fish sauce
¼ teaspoon dried crushed red
   pepper
¼ teaspoon black pepper
¼ cup minced green onion tops
1 teaspoon dark sesame oil

1. Combine mushrooms and boiling water in a bowl; cover and let stand 15 minutes. Drain in a colander over a bowl, reserving 1 cup liquid. Discard mushroom stems; rinse and cut caps into thin strips.
2. Combine ½ cup reserved mushroom liquid and broth in a large saucepan; bring to a boil. Add mushrooms, pork, and tofu; reduce heat, and simmer 3 minutes. Combine remaining ½ cup reserved mushroom liquid, cornstarch, and next 5 ingredients in a small bowl. Add cornstarch mixture to saucepan; bring to a boil. Cook 1 minute, stirring constantly. Remove from heat; stir in onions and oil. Yield: 4 servings (serving size: 1¼ cups).

CALORIES 162 (34% from fat); FAT 6.1g (sat 1.8g, mono 1.7g, poly 1.5g); PROTEIN 12.9g; CARB 12.6g; FIBER 1.4g; CHOL 22mg; IRON 2.2mg; SODIUM 709mg; CALC 54mg

PAN-FRIED GARLIC-SCALLOP DUMPLINGS

(pictured on page 113)

Using less oil and water to pan-fry the dumplings makes them crisp on the bottom, tender on top, and just as delicious as traditional dumplings.

½ pound scallops, minced
¼ cup minced fresh onion
2 tablespoons low-sodium soy sauce
1 tablespoon minced peeled fresh
   ginger
½ teaspoon chili oil
4 garlic cloves, minced
36 round gyoza skins
2 teaspoons vegetable oil, divided
½ cup water, divided
¾ cup Soy-Sesame Dipping Sauce
   (page 118)
Sliced green onions (optional)
Edible flowers (optional)

1. Combine first 6 ingredients.
2. Spoon about 1½ teaspoons of scallop mixture into center of each gyoza skin, working with 1 skin at a time (cover remaining skins to keep them from drying). Moisten edges of skin with water. Fold in half, pinching edges together to seal. Place dumplings on a baking sheet; cover loosely with a towel to keep them from drying.
3. Heat 1 teaspoon oil in a large nonstick skillet over medium-high heat. Arrange half of dumplings in skillet; cover. Cook 5 minutes or until lightly browned. Add ¼ cup water; reduce heat to medium-low. Cover and simmer 5 minutes. Remove dumplings, and keep warm. Repeat procedure with remaining dumplings, 1 teaspoon oil, and ¼ cup water. Serve with Soy-Sesame Dipping Sauce. Garnish with green onions and edible flowers, if desired. Yield: 12 appetizer servings (serving size: 3 dumplings and about 1 tablespoon sauce).

CALORIES 111 (17% from fat); FAT 2.1g (sat 0.3g, mono 0.6g, poly 0.9g); PROTEIN 6.1g; CARB 16.5g; FIBER 0.1g; CHOL 8mg; IRON 1.2mg; SODIUM 492mg; CALC 22mg

SOY-SESAME DIPPING SAUCE

(pictured on page 113)

The longer this sauce stands, the more intense the flavor gets.

½ cup low-sodium soy sauce
¼ cup rice vinegar
2 tablespoons minced green onions
2 tablespoons fresh lemon juice
2 teaspoons dark sesame oil
4 large garlic cloves, minced

1. Combine all ingredients; stir well with a whisk. Cover; let stand at least 15 minutes before serving. Yield: 1 cup (serving size: 1 tablespoon).

CALORIES 12 (45% from fat); FAT 0.6g (sat 0g, mono 0.3g, poly 0.3g); PROTEIN 0.3g; CARB 1.2g; FIBER 0g; CHOL 0mg; IRON 0.3mg; SODIUM 243mg; CALC 3mg

SHREDDED CHICKEN IN HOT SAUCE

When the Chinese eat chicken, it is rarely served on its own. Most often, it is cooked with various vegetables.

2 tablespoons low-sodium soy sauce
1 tablespoon cornstarch
1 tablespoon rice vinegar
1 tablespoon minced peeled fresh ginger
¼ teaspoon dried crushed red pepper
1 pound skinned, boned chicken breasts, cut into ¼-inch-wide strips
2 tablespoons vegetable oil
1 cup coarsely chopped green onions
1 tablespoon minced peeled fresh ginger
3 garlic cloves, minced
¾ cup (1 x ¼-inch) julienne-cut red bell pepper
¾ cup (1 x ¼-inch) julienne-cut yellow bell pepper
2 tablespoons fresh lemon juice
½ to 1 teaspoon white pepper
¼ teaspoon salt
4 cups hot cooked rice

1. Combine first 5 ingredients in a medium bowl; add chicken. Cover and marinate in refrigerator 30 minutes.
2. Heat oil in a large nonstick skillet over medium-high heat. Add onions, ginger, and garlic; sauté 1 minute. Add chicken mixture, and sauté 2 minutes. Stir in bell peppers, lemon juice, white pepper, and salt; cook 1½ minutes or until chicken is done. Serve over rice. Yield: 4 servings (serving size: 1 cup chicken mixture and 1 cup rice).

CALORIES 445 (18% from fat); FAT 8.7g (sat 1.7g, mono 2.4g, poly 3.7g); PROTEIN 31.7g; CARB 58g; FIBER 2.3g; CHOL 66mg; IRON 3.7mg; SODIUM 469mg; CALC 61mg

CURRY BEEF

The Chinese always cook beef with aromatic vegetables and spices such as leeks, onions, and curry. This dish is very popular in southern China.

1 tablespoon curry powder
2 tablespoons low-sodium soy sauce
1 tablespoon rice vinegar
1 pound beef eye-of-round roast, cut into thin strips
1 leek
1 tablespoon vegetable oil
1 tablespoon minced peeled fresh ginger
4 garlic cloves, minced
1¼ cups vertically sliced onion
½ teaspoon white pepper
¼ teaspoon salt
4 cups hot cooked rice

1. Combine first 4 ingredients in a medium bowl; cover and marinate in refrigerator 30 minutes.
2. Remove roots, outer leaves, and top from leek, leaving 1½ to 2 inches of dark leaves. Rinse leek with cold water, and cut into 2-inch julienne strips to yield 1¼ cups.
3. Heat oil in a large nonstick skillet over medium-high heat. Add ginger and garlic; sauté 1½ minutes. Add beef mixture, and sauté 5 minutes. Add leek, onion, pepper, and salt; sauté 3 minutes. Serve over rice. Yield: 4 servings (serving size: 1 cup beef mixture and 1 cup rice).

CALORIES 471 (19% from fat); FAT 10g (sat 2.9g, mono 3.8g, poly 2g); PROTEIN 32.5g; CARB 60.1g; FIBER 2.6g; CHOL 64mg; IRON 5.1mg; SODIUM 455mg; CALC 67mg

LONGEVITY NOODLES

While Westerners celebrate their birthdays with cake, the Chinese celebrate with noodles to signify a wish for a long and happy life.

1 tablespoon dry white wine or water
1 tablespoon low-sodium soy sauce
1 teaspoon white pepper
1 teaspoon minced peeled fresh ginger
½ teaspoon cornstarch
20 medium shrimp, peeled and deveined (about ½ pound)
2 tablespoons vegetable oil
2 cups sliced fresh shiitake mushroom caps
1 cup diagonally sliced carrot
4 cups hot cooked whole-wheat spaghetti or spaghettini (about 8 ounces uncooked pasta)
1 tablespoon white wine vinegar
¼ teaspoon salt
2½ tablespoons minced green onions

1. Combine first 5 ingredients in a large zip-top plastic bag; add shrimp. Seal bag, and marinate shrimp in refrigerator 15 minutes.
2. Heat oil in a large nonstick skillet over medium-high heat. Add shrimp mixture, and sauté 3 minutes. Add mushrooms and carrot; stir-fry 2 minutes. Stir in pasta, vinegar, and salt; cook 2 minutes or until thoroughly heated. Sprinkle with minced onions. Yield: 4 servings (serving size: 1½ cups).

CALORIES 333 (28% from fat); FAT 10.5g (sat 1.8g, mono 3.4g, poly 4.3g); PROTEIN 17.3g; CARB 45.9g; FIBER 6.4g; CHOL 65mg; IRON 3.8mg; SODIUM 344mg; CALC 61mg

BROCCOLI WITH GARLIC

Broccoli doesn't need to cook very long—overcooking will destroy its beautiful green color and wonderful fresh taste.

      5 cups broccoli florets (about
            1 pound)
      1 teaspoon vegetable oil
      2 teaspoons minced seeded
            jalapeño pepper
    14 garlic cloves, minced (about
            3 tablespoons)
      1 tablespoon fresh lemon juice
      1 tablespoon rice vinegar

1. Steam broccoli, covered, 4 minutes. Heat oil in a nonstick skillet over medium-high heat. Add pepper and garlic; sauté 2 minutes. Remove from heat. Add broccoli, juice, and vinegar; toss well. Yield: 4 servings (serving size: 1 cup).

CALORIES 59 (24% from fat); FAT 1.6g (sat 0.3g, mono 0.4g, poly 0.8g); PROTEIN 4g; CARB 9.7g; FIBER 3.6g; CHOL 0mg; IRON 1.2mg; SODIUM 32mg; CALC 72mg

PINEAPPLE-AND-SCALLOP FRIED RICE

      1 tablespoon vegetable oil
      1 tablespoon minced peeled fresh
            ginger
      2 garlic cloves, minced
      4 ounces bay scallops
      3 cups cooked short-grain rice
      1 cup coarsely chopped pineapple
      1 tablespoon fresh lemon juice
    ¼ teaspoon salt
    ¼ to ½ teaspoon pepper
    ½ tablespoon minced fresh cilantro

1. Heat oil in a nonstick skillet over medium-high heat. Add ginger and garlic; stir-fry 2 minutes or until lightly browned. Add scallops; stir-fry 3 minutes or until done. Add rice and next 4 ingredients; stir-fry 2 minutes or until thoroughly heated. Sprinkle with cilantro. Yield: 4 servings (serving size: 1 cup).

CALORIES 228 (17% from fat); FAT 4.2g (sat 0.8g, mono 1.2g, poly 1.9g); PROTEIN 8.1g; CARB 39.1g; FIBER 1.3g; CHOL 9mg; IRON 1.8mg; SODIUM 197mg; CALC 39mg

Incredible Crumb Cakes

From one basic mixture spring eight easy crumb cakes.

Crumb cakes have a lowly moniker, but don't be misled. Unlike other cakes, they can be served for breakfast, brunch, lunch, at bridge parties, for an after-dinner dessert, or as a late-night snack. Their earthy, crumbly topping and homey taste and smell are irresistible. A crumb cake coming warm and sweet out of the oven—it doesn't get any better.

And it doesn't get any easier than using our recipes. That's because you only need to make one mixture of ingredients, which you then divide into two portions. While half the mixture becomes the basis for the crumb-cake batter, the other half is used as the topping. Then we let the crumbs fall where they might, adding enlivening ingredients ranging from apples and cinnamon to apricots and coffee.

GINGERBREAD CRUMB CAKE

    1¼ cups all-purpose flour
    ⅔ cup sugar
    ½ teaspoon ground cinnamon
    ½ teaspoon ground ginger
    ¼ teaspoon ground nutmeg
    ⅛ teaspoon salt
    ⅛ teaspoon ground cloves
    ¼ cup chilled stick margarine or
            butter, cut into small pieces
    ½ teaspoon baking powder
    ½ teaspoon baking soda
    ½ cup low-fat buttermilk
      2 tablespoons molasses
      1 large egg
    Cooking spray
    1½ teaspoons water

1. Preheat oven to 350°.
2. Lightly spoon flour into a dry measuring cups, and level with a knife.

Combine flour and next 6 ingredients; cut in margarine with a pastry blender or 2 knives until mixture resembles coarse meal. Reserve ½ cup flour mixture; set aside.
3. Combine remaining flour mixture, baking powder, and baking soda; add buttermilk, molasses, and egg. Beat at medium speed of a mixer until blended. Spoon into an 8-inch round cake pan coated with cooking spray. Combine reserved ½ cup flour mixture and 1½ teaspoons water; stir with a fork. Sprinkle over batter. Bake at 350° for 30 minutes or until cake springs back when touched lightly in center. Cool on a wire rack. Yield: 8 servings (serving size: 1 wedge).

CALORIES 219 (28% from fat); FAT 6.9g (sat 1.5g, mono 2.9g, poly 1.9g); PROTEIN 3.5g; CARB 36.2g; FIBER 0.6g; CHOL 28mg; IRON 1.4mg; SODIUM 200mg; CALC 57mg

BANANA-COCONUT CRUMB CAKE

    1¼ cups all-purpose flour
    ⅓ cup granulated sugar
    ⅓ cup packed dark brown sugar
    ¼ teaspoon ground allspice
    ⅛ teaspoon salt
    ¼ cup chilled stick margarine or
            butter, cut into small pieces
    ¾ teaspoon baking powder
    ½ teaspoon baking soda
    ½ cup mashed ripe banana
            (1 medium banana)
      3 tablespoons 1% low-fat milk
      1 large egg
    Cooking spray
    ¼ cup flaked sweetened coconut
      1 teaspoon water

1. Preheat oven to 350°.
2. Lightly spoon flour into dry measuring cups, and level with a knife. Combine flour and next 4 ingredients in a bowl; cut in margarine with a pastry blender or 2 knives until mixture resembles coarse meal. Reserve ½ cup flour mixture, and set aside.
3. Combine remaining flour mixture, baking powder, and baking soda; add

Continued

banana, milk, and egg. Beat at medium speed of a mixer until blended. Spoon batter into an 8-inch round cake pan coated with cooking spray. Combine reserved ½ cup flour mixture, coconut, and 1 teaspoon water; stir with a fork. Sprinkle crumb mixture over batter. Bake at 350° for 30 minutes or until cake springs back when touched lightly in center. Cool on a wire rack. Yield: 8 servings (serving size: 1 wedge).

CALORIES 229 (31% from fat); FAT 7.8g (sat 2.3g, mono 2.9g, poly 2g); PROTEIN 3.3g; CARB 37.3g; FIBER 1.1g; CHOL 28mg; IRON 1.3mg; SODIUM 205mg; CALC 50mg

---

┌─────────────────────────────────┐

MENU SUGGESTION

*Spring onion omelet**

CINNAMON CRUMB CAKE

*Sauté ¼ cup sliced green onions in an 8-inch skillet coated with cooking spray over medium heat. Add ¾ cup egg substitute; cook 3 minutes. Fold omelet in half; top with 2 tablespoons shredded reduced-fat sharp Cheddar cheese. Wrap handle of skillet with foil; place under broiler for 10 seconds. Garnish with red onion rings and a strawberry fan. Serves 1.

└─────────────────────────────────┘

CINNAMON CRUMB CAKE

1¼ cups all-purpose flour
⅔ cup packed brown sugar
¾ teaspoon ground cinnamon
⅛ teaspoon salt
¼ cup chilled stick margarine or butter, cut into small pieces
½ teaspoon baking powder
½ teaspoon baking soda
½ cup low-fat buttermilk
1 teaspoon vanilla extract
1 large egg
Cooking spray

1. Preheat oven to 350°.
2. Lightly spoon flour into dry measuring cups; level with a knife. Combine flour and next 3 ingredients; cut in margarine with a pastry blender or 2 knives until mixture resembles coarse meal. Reserve ½ cup flour mixture; set aside.

3. Combine remaining flour mixture, baking powder, and baking soda; add buttermilk, vanilla, and egg. Beat at medium speed of a mixer until blended. Spoon batter into an 8-inch round cake pan coated with cooking spray. Sprinkle reserved ½ cup flour mixture over batter. Bake at 350° for 30 minutes or until cake springs back when touched lightly in center. Cool on a wire rack. Yield: 8 servings (serving size: 1 wedge).

CALORIES 211 (29% from fat); FAT 6.9g (sat 1.5g, mono 2.9g, poly 2g); PROTEIN 3.5g; CARB 33.9g; FIBER 0.6g; CHOL 28mg; IRON 1.5mg; SODIUM 206mg; CALC 62mg

---

APPLE-OATMEAL CRUMB CAKE

Any firm cooking apple can be used in this recipe.

1 cup all-purpose flour
⅓ cup regular oats
⅓ cup granulated sugar
⅓ cup packed dark brown sugar
⅛ teaspoon salt
⅛ teaspoon ground nutmeg
¼ cup chilled stick margarine or butter, cut into small pieces
½ teaspoon baking powder
¼ teaspoon baking soda
⅓ cup apple juice
1 teaspoon vanilla extract
1 large egg
1½ cups coarsely chopped peeled McIntosh apple (about 2 apples)
Cooking spray

1. Preheat oven to 350°.
2. Lightly spoon flour into a dry measuring cup, and level with a knife. Combine flour and next 5 ingredients in a bowl; cut in margarine with a pastry blender or 2 knives until mixture resembles coarse meal. Reserve ½ cup flour mixture; set aside.
3. Combine remaining flour mixture, baking powder, and baking soda; add apple juice, vanilla extract, and egg. Beat at medium speed of a mixer until blended; fold in apple.
4. Spoon batter into an 8-inch round cake pan coated with cooking spray,

and sprinkle reserved ½ cup flour mixture over batter. Bake at 350° for 30 minutes or until cake springs back when touched lightly in center. Cool on a wire rack. Yield: 8 servings (serving size: 1 wedge).

CALORIES 204 (30% from fat); FAT 6.9g (sat 1.4g, mono 2.9g, poly 2g); PROTEIN 3.1g; CARB 33g; FIBER 1.3g; CHOL 28mg; IRON 1.2mg; SODIUM 154mg; CALC 33mg

---

MOCHA CRUMB CAKE

1¼ cups all-purpose flour
⅔ cup sugar
3 tablespoons unsweetened cocoa
1 tablespoon instant coffee granules
⅛ teaspoon salt
¼ cup chilled stick margarine or butter, cut into small pieces
½ teaspoon baking powder
¼ teaspoon baking soda
⅓ cup 1% low-fat milk
1 teaspoon vanilla extract
1 large egg
Cooking spray
1½ teaspoons water

1. Preheat oven to 350°.
2. Lightly spoon flour into dry measuring cups, and level with a knife. Combine flour and next 4 ingredients in a mixing bowl; cut in margarine with a pastry blender or 2 knives until mixture resembles coarse meal. Reserve ½ cup flour mixture, and set aside.
3. Combine remaining flour mixture, baking powder, and baking soda; add milk, vanilla, and egg. Beat at medium speed of a mixer until blended. Spoon batter into an 8-inch round cake pan coated with cooking spray. Combine reserved ½ cup flour mixture and 1½ teaspoons water; stir with a fork. Sprinkle crumb mixture over batter. Bake at 350° for 30 minutes or until cake springs back when touched lightly in center. Cool on a wire rack. Yield: 8 servings (serving size: 1 wedge).

CALORIES 213 (30% from fat); FAT 7g (sat 1.6g, mono 2.8g, poly 2g); PROTEIN 3.9g; CARB 33.6g; FIBER 0.5g; CHOL 28mg; IRON 1.4mg; SODIUM 156mg; CALC 42mg

RASPBERRY-ALMOND CRUMB CAKE

(pictured on page 115)

- 1 cup all-purpose flour
- ⅓ cup sugar
- ⅛ teaspoon salt
- ¼ cup chilled stick margarine or butter, cut into small pieces
- ½ teaspoon baking powder
- ¼ teaspoon baking soda
- ⅓ cup fat-free sour cream
- 2 tablespoons 1% low-fat milk
- 1 teaspoon vanilla extract
- ½ teaspoon almond extract
- 1 large egg
- Cooking spray
- 3 ounces block-style fat-free cream cheese, softened (about ⅔ cup)
- 2 tablespoons sugar
- 1 large egg white
- ¼ cup raspberry preserves
- ⅓ cup fresh raspberries
- 2 tablespoons sliced almonds

1. Preheat oven to 350°.
2. Lightly spoon flour into a dry measuring cup, and level with a knife. Combine flour, ⅓ cup sugar, and salt in a bowl; cut in margarine with a pastry blender or 2 knives until mixture resembles coarse meal. Reserve ½ cup flour mixture for topping; set aside.
3. Combine remaining flour mixture, baking powder, and baking soda; add sour cream and next 4 ingredients. Beat at medium speed of a mixer until mixture is blended. Spoon batter into an 8-inch round cake pan coated with cooking spray.
4. Combine cream cheese, 2 tablespoons sugar, and egg white; beat at medium speed until blended. Spread evenly over batter; dot with preserves. Top with raspberries. Combine reserved ½ cup flour mixture and almonds. Sprinkle crumb mixture over raspberries. Bake at 350° for 30 minutes or until cake springs back when touched lightly in center. Cool on a wire rack. Yield: 8 servings (serving size: 1 wedge).

CALORIES 217 (31% from fat); FAT 7.4g (sat 1.4g, mono 3.3g, poly 2.1g); PROTEIN 5.6g; CARB 31.7g; FIBER 0.7g; CHOL 30mg; IRON 1mg; SODIUM 234mg; CALC 66mg

❶ *Using a large spoon, stir flour gently before measuring, and spoon into a dry measuring cup.*

❷ *Level flour with a knife or small metal spatula. Don't shake the cup— it packs the flour.*

❸ *After combining flour, sugar, and salt, cut in chilled stick margarine or butter with a pastry blender or 2 knives until the mixture resembles coarse meal.*

❹ *Reserve ½ cup of crumb mixture, and set aside to use for topping. Combine remaining crumb mixture with other ingredients, and beat at medium speed of a mixer until blended.*

❺ *Spoon batter into an 8-inch round cake pan coated with cooking spray. Sprinkle with reserved ½ cup crumb mixture.*

APRICOT-ORANGE CRUMB CAKE

1¼ cups all-purpose flour
½ cup sugar
⅛ teaspoon salt
¼ cup chilled stick margarine or butter, cut into small pieces
3 tablespoons tub-style light cream cheese
½ teaspoon baking powder
¼ teaspoon baking soda
⅓ cup 1% low-fat milk
3 tablespoons part-skim ricotta cheese
1 teaspoon vanilla extract
1 teaspoon grated orange rind
1 large egg
¼ cup chopped dried apricots
Cooking spray
¼ cup apricot preserves

1. Preheat oven to 350°.
2. Lightly spoon flour into dry measuring cups, and level with a knife. Combine flour, sugar, and salt in a mixing bowl; cut in margarine and cream cheese with a pastry blender or 2 knives until mixture resembles coarse meal. Reserve ½ cup flour mixture for topping; set aside.
3. Combine remaining flour mixture, baking powder, and baking soda; add milk and next 4 ingredients. Beat at medium speed of a mixer until blended (batter will be lumpy); fold in chopped apricots. Spoon batter into an 8-inch round cake pan coated with cooking spray. Dot batter with apricot preserves, and swirl preserves into batter using a knife. Sprinkle reserved ½ cup flour mixture over batter. Bake at 350° for 30 minutes or until cake springs back when touched lightly in center. Cool on a wire rack. Yield: 8 servings (serving size: 1 wedge).

CALORIES 241 (30% from fat); FAT 8.1g (sat 2.2g, mono 3.2g, poly 2g); PROTEIN 4.7g; CARB 38.1g; FIBER 0.8g; CHOL 33mg; IRON 1.4mg; SODIUM 201mg; CALC 65mg

LEMON-ROSEMARY CRUMB CAKE

1¼ cups all-purpose flour
⅔ cup sugar
⅛ teaspoon salt
¼ cup chilled stick margarine or butter, cut into small pieces
¾ teaspoon minced fresh or ¼ teaspoon dried rosemary
½ teaspoon baking powder
¼ teaspoon baking soda
⅓ cup low-fat buttermilk
2 tablespoons fresh lemon juice
1 large egg
Cooking spray
2 teaspoons grated lemon rind
¾ teaspoon water
Rosemary sprigs (optional)
Lemon slices (optional)

1. Preheat oven to 350°.
2. Lightly spoon flour into dry measuring cups, and level with a knife. Combine flour, sugar, and salt in a bowl; cut in margarine with a pastry blender or 2 knives until mixture resembles coarse meal. Reserve ½ cup flour mixture, and set aside.
3. Combine remaining flour mixture, rosemary, baking powder, and baking soda; add buttermilk, lemon juice, and egg. Beat at medium speed of a mixer until blended. Spoon batter into an 8-inch round cake pan coated with cooking spray. Combine reserved ½ cup flour mixture, lemon rind, and ¾ teaspoon water; stir with a fork. Sprinkle crumb mixture over batter. Bake at 350° for 30 minutes. Cool on a wire rack. Garnish with rosemary sprigs and lemon slices, if desired. Yield: 8 servings (serving size: 1 wedge).

CALORIES 203 (30% from fat); FAT 6.8g (sat 1.4g, mono 2.8g, poly 2g); PROTEIN 3.3g; CARB 32.7g; FIBER 0.5g; CHOL 28mg; IRON 1.1mg; SODIUM 157mg; CALC 39mg

FAST FOOD

Chutney Change-Up

This fruit-based condiment has left its home in India to shake up conventional meals across America.

Fruits, vegetables, spices, and vinegars combine in chutneys to produce a range of flavors as varied and complex as the Indian subcontinent that inspired them. Today you can find these sweet, tangy condiments, in strengths from mild to hot, in almost any supermarket. Although once considered exotic, they've found a solid home in America as an alternative to tabletop traditions such as ketchup or mustard. Amenable to almost any food, chutneys can be used to glaze meat and poultry or to add zing to a salad dressing. And whether based on mangoes, bananas, raisins, or any other fruit, the bottled brands are usually low in fat, so you can easily adjust to taste. But remember, chutneys of any strength are piquant and flavorful, so a little goes a long way.

ASIAN PORK-AND-BROCCOLI STIR-FRY

Preparation time: 15 minutes
Cooking time: 12 minutes

⅓ cup mango chutney
2 tablespoons low-sodium soy sauce
1 tablespoon dry sherry
2 teaspoons dark sesame oil, divided
1 pound pork tenderloin, cut into 1-inch strips
4 cups broccoli florets
1 tablespoon water
2 cups fresh bean sprouts
2 garlic cloves, minced
1 (8-ounce) can sliced water chestnuts, drained

1. Combine first 3 ingredients.
2. Heat 1 teaspoon oil in a nonstick skillet over medium-high heat. Add pork; stir-fry 3 minutes. Remove pork from pan with a slotted spoon. Add remaining 1 teaspoon oil, broccoli, and water to skillet; stir-fry 5 minutes. Add chutney mixture, bean sprouts, garlic, and water chestnuts; stir-fry 2 minutes. Return pork to skillet; stir-fry 30 seconds. Yield: 4 servings (serving size: 1½ cups).

CALORIES 267 (19% from fat); FAT 5.5g (sat 1.4g, mono 2.2g, poly 1.4g); PROTEIN 29g; CARB 27.3g; FIBER 3.6g; CHOL 74mg; IRON 3.5mg; SODIUM 373mg; CALC 69mg

BARBECUED FLANK STEAK WITH CHUTNEY-BOURBON GLAZE

(pictured on page 114)

Preparation time: 15 minutes
Marinating time: 15 minutes
Cooking time: 17 minutes

1 (1-pound) flank steak
⅓ cup peach chutney
⅓ cup pineapple juice
3 tablespoons bourbon or apple juice
1½ tablespoons rice wine vinegar
1½ tablespoons hot pepper sauce
¼ teaspoon salt
2 garlic cloves, minced

1. Prepare grill or broiler.
2. Trim fat from steak. Combine steak and remaining ingredients in a large zip-top plastic bag. Seal and marinate in refrigerator 15 minutes. Remove steak from bag, reserving marinade.
3. Place steak on a grill rack or broiler pan. Cook 8 minutes on each side or until desired degree of doneness. Cut steak diagonally across grain into thin slices. Keep warm.
4. Bring reserved marinade to a boil in a small saucepan; cook 1 minute, stirring occasionally. Serve with steak. Yield: 4 servings (serving size: 3 ounces steak and 2 tablespoons glaze).

CALORIES 254 (39% from fat); FAT 11.1g (sat 4.6g, mono 4.3g, poly 0.4g); PROTEIN 22.8g; CARB 13.9g; FIBER 0.7g; CHOL 57mg; IRON 2.4mg; SODIUM 308mg; CALC 12mg

CURRIED LAMB-AND-SPINACH BURGERS

Preparation time: 25 minutes
Cooking time: 14 minutes

1 pound lean ground lamb
⅔ cup fresh breadcrumbs
⅓ cup savory chutney (such as Raffetto's Chut-Nut Colonial)
1 teaspoon curry powder
½ teaspoon salt
¼ teaspoon dried crushed red pepper
1 (10-ounce) package frozen chopped spinach, thawed, drained, and squeezed dry
2 garlic cloves, minced
4 (2-ounce) onion sandwich buns
¼ cup savory chutney

1. Combine first 8 ingredients in a medium bowl. Divide mixture into 4 equal portions; shape into ½-inch-thick patties. Prepare grill or broiler. Place patties on a grill rack or broiler pan; cook 7 minutes on each side or until done. Place patties on bottom halves of sandwich buns; spread each patty with 1 tablespoon chutney. Cover with bun tops. Yield: 4 servings.

CALORIES 420 (17% from fat); FAT 7.8g (sat 2.4g, mono 2.9g, poly 2.2g); PROTEIN 26.1g; CARB 61.9g; FIBER 2.6g; CHOL 56mg; IRON 4.9mg; SODIUM 701mg; CALC 131mg

MENU SUGGESTION

*West Indies Cornish hens**

CARIBBEAN SWEET POTATO-AND-BLACK BEAN SALAD

*Combine 1 teaspoon garlic powder, ¾ teaspoon dried thyme, ½ teaspoon ground red pepper, ¼ teaspoon each salt and pepper, and ⅛ teaspoon each ground nutmeg and cinnamon. Rub over 2 split, skinned Cornish hens. Bake at 350° for 30 minutes or until juices run clear. Serves 4.

CARIBBEAN SWEET POTATO-AND-BLACK BEAN SALAD

Preparation time: 25 minutes
Cooking time: 6 minutes

1 cup (½-inch) cubed peeled sweet potato
¼ cup banana chutney (such as Busha Browne's Original)
2 tablespoons fresh lime juice
2 teaspoons olive oil
1 teaspoon Dijon mustard
⅛ teaspoon salt
⅛ teaspoon pepper
1 garlic clove, minced
½ cup sliced green onions, divided
1 (15-ounce) can black beans, rinsed and drained
3 cups torn spinach

1. Steam sweet potato, covered, 5 minutes or until tender; cool. Combine chutney and next 6 ingredients in a large bowl; stir well with a whisk. Add sweet potato, ¼ cup onions, and beans; stir well to coat. Place 1 cup spinach on each of 3 plates; top each with ⅔ cup bean mixture. Sprinkle evenly with remaining ¼ cup onions. Yield: 3 servings.

CALORIES 265 (14% from fat); FAT 4.2g (sat 0.6g, mono 2.3g, poly 0.7g); PROTEIN 11.2g; CARB 49.7g; FIBER 8.9g; CHOL 0mg; IRON 5.1mg; SODIUM 489mg; CALC 147mg

And You Don't Even Need a Sauce

Throw-together pastas are quick and creative after-work answers to "What's for dinner?"

Picture this: You rush in your front door after tackling rush-hour traffic. You need dinner on the table in less than an hour. And, it has to be something to satisfy the entire family.

The last-minute solution to such a dilemma is usually a big bowl of pasta with an easy sauce. The fastest of all are throw-together pasta toppings that are amenable to lightning-fast assembly using ingredients almost always on standby in the pantry or refrigerator.

RIGATONI CAPRESE

This dish is based on the classic salad of tomatoes, fresh mozzarella, and basil that hails from the island of Capri—hence the name "Caprese."

- 6 cups hot cooked rigatoni, penne, or ziti (about 12 ounces uncooked pasta)
- 4 cups chopped plum tomato (about 2½ pounds)
- 1½ cups fresh basil leaves, thinly sliced
- 1 cup (4 ounces) diced fresh mozzarella cheese
- 2 tablespoons extra-virgin olive oil
- 1 tablespoon capers
- 1 teaspoon salt
- ½ teaspoon freshly ground pepper
- 1 garlic clove, crushed
- ⅓ cup (1½ ounces) grated fresh Parmesan or Romano cheese

1. Combine first 4 ingredients in a large bowl. Combine oil and next 4 ingredients in a small bowl; stir well with a whisk. Pour over pasta mixture; toss gently. Sprinkle with Parmesan cheese; toss well. Yield: 5 servings (serving size: 2 cups).

CALORIES 390 (29% from fat); FAT 12.5g (sat 5g, mono 5.3g, poly 1.2g); PROTEIN 16g; CARB 54g; FIBER 4.5g; CHOL 25mg; IRON 3mg; SODIUM 553mg; CALC 233mg

PASTA WITH ARUGULA AND SHAVED PARMESAN

(pictured on page 114)

Arugula is a peppery green found next to the fresh herbs in your supermarket. You can substitute spinach, but it won't have the same bite.

- 2¼ cups chopped plum tomato
- ¼ cup chopped pitted kalamata olives
- 1½ tablespoons extra-virgin olive oil
- ½ teaspoon dried crushed red pepper
- ¼ teaspoon salt
- ¼ teaspoon freshly ground pepper
- 2 garlic cloves, minced
- 4 cups hot cooked gemelli or fusilli (about 8 ounces uncooked pasta twists)
- 3 cups torn trimmed arugula
- 2 ounces shaved fresh Parmesan cheese

1. Combine first 7 ingredients in a large bowl. Add pasta and arugula; toss gently. Place 2 cups pasta mixture in each of 4 bowls, and sprinkle with cheese. Yield: 4 servings.

CALORIES 352 (28% from fat); FAT 11.1g (sat 3.3g, mono 5.6g, poly 1.2g); PROTEIN 14.1g; CARB 49.8g; FIBER 3.1g; CHOL 10mg; IRON 3.1mg; SODIUM 469mg; CALC 240mg

PENNE WITH SPINACH, FETA, AND OLIVES

Substitute ziti, rigatoni, or any other medium-sized pasta for the penne. Any kind of olive may be used instead of kalamatas, but the flavor won't be as intense.

- 2 tablespoons extra-virgin olive oil
- 1 tablespoon balsamic vinegar
- 3 garlic cloves, crushed
- 6 cups hot cooked penne (about 12 ounces uncooked tube-shaped pasta)
- 2 cups chopped spinach
- ¼ cup chopped pitted kalamata olives
- 2 tablespoons capers
- ¾ cup (3 ounces) crumbled feta cheese

1. Combine first 3 ingredients in a large bowl. Add pasta and remaining ingredients; toss well. Yield: 4 servings (serving size: 2 cups).

CALORIES 434 (25% from fat); FAT 12.2g (sat 3.7g, mono 3.5g, poly 4.2g); PROTEIN 14.1g; CARB 67g; FIBER 3.5g; CHOL 13mg; IRON 4.5mg; SODIUM 595mg; CALC 124mg

THESE THROW-TOGETHER PASTAS require no separate sauce and will become regular features in your household. But first, you must stock all the right ingredients. Luckily, stocking an Italian pantry is as easy as a little forethought. Almost any supermarket or gourmet-food shop carries everything you will need: anchovy paste, balsamic vinegar, capers, chicken broth, clam juice, olive oil, olives, plum tomatoes, sun-dried tomatoes, and, of course, dried pasta in all its varieties. Throw in just a few ingredients from the fridge—even if it's only a generous handful of chopped parsley or basil leaves. Add flash-boiled shrimp and scallops, and you have a dish dressed well enough for company.

PASTA WITH ASIAGO CHEESE AND SPINACH

(pictured on page 4)

Substitute fusilli, penne, or any other medium-sized pasta for the cavatappi.

- 3 cups boiling water
- 4 ounces sun-dried tomatoes, packed without oil (about 2 cups)
- 2 tablespoons extra-virgin olive oil
- ⅛ teaspoon salt
- ⅛ teaspoon freshly ground pepper
- 2 garlic cloves, crushed
- 6 cups hot cooked cavatappi (about 12 ounces uncooked ridged, spiral pasta)
- 1 (10-ounce) bag fresh spinach, torn
- ¾ cup (3 ounces) grated Asiago cheese
- ½ cup (2 ounces) finely grated fresh Parmesan cheese

1. Combine boiling water and sun-dried tomatoes in a bowl; let stand 30 minutes. Drain and chop.
2. Combine tomatoes and next 4 ingredients in a large bowl. Add pasta and spinach; toss. Sprinkle with cheeses; toss. Yield: 8 servings (serving size: 2 cups).

CALORIES 302 (28% from fat); FAT 9.3g (sat 3.6g, mono 4g, poly 0.9g); PROTEIN 14.4g; CARB 41.8g; FIBER 2.5g; CHOL 16mg; IRON 2.7mg; SODIUM 606mg; CALC 257mg

---

WISE BUYS

These pasta dishes will taste only as good as the ingredients you use—so choose the highest-quality products, including:

- Real Parmesan cheese that comes in a wedge or chunk as opposed to the grated kind that comes in a can;
- Extra-virgin olive oil rather than pure olive oil or vegetable oil;
- Intensely flavored olives such as kalamata or niçoise instead of generic canned black olives;
- Fresh basil and parsley, not dried.

FUSILLI WITH BROCCOLI RABE AND POTATOES

Broccoli rabe resembles broccoli but has bigger leaves, smaller florets, and a peppery bite. You can substitute spinach or broccoli.

- 1 cup low-salt chicken broth
- 1½ tablespoons extra-virgin olive oil
- ½ teaspoon dried crushed red pepper
- ⅛ teaspoon black pepper
- 3 garlic cloves, minced
- 2 cups cubed red potato (about 1 pound)
- 2 pounds broccoli rabe, trimmed
- 4 cups hot cooked fusilli or gemelli (about 8 ounces uncooked short twisted spaghetti)
- ½ cup (2 ounces) grated fresh Parmesan cheese

1. Combine first 5 ingredients in a large bowl.
2. Place potato in a saucepan, and cover with water; bring to a boil. Reduce heat, and simmer 7 minutes or until potato is tender. Drain. Steam broccoli rabe, covered, 5 minutes. Cool. Squeeze out excess water, and coarsely chop. Add potato, broccoli rabe, and pasta to broth mixture in bowl; toss well. Top with cheese. Yield: 4 servings (serving size: 2 cups).

CALORIES 428 (23% from fat); FAT 10.9g (sat 3.8g, mono 5.1g, poly 1.0g); PROTEIN 17.9g; CARB 65.3g; FIBER 4.9g; CHOL 12mg; IRON 4.3mg; SODIUM 316mg; CALC 250mg

---

FARFALLE WITH RED CAESAR DRESSING

- ¼ cup (1 ounce) grated fresh Parmesan cheese
- 2 tablespoons extra-virgin olive oil
- 1½ tablespoons Worcestershire sauce
- 1 tablespoon lemon juice
- 1 tablespoon anchovy paste
- ⅛ teaspoon freshly ground pepper
- 2 garlic cloves, crushed
- 1 (10¾-ounce) can tomato puree
- 6 cups hot cooked farfalle (about 5 cups uncooked bow tie pasta)
- ½ cup chopped fresh parsley

1. Combine first 8 ingredients in a large bowl; stir well with a whisk. Add pasta; toss well. Sprinkle with parsley. Yield: 4 servings (serving size: 1½ cups).

CALORIES 422 (23% from fat); FAT 10.7g (sat 2.4g, mono 5.9g, poly 1.4g); PROTEIN 14.9g; CARB 67.4g; FIBER 5.3g; CHOL 5mg; IRON 4.1mg; SODIUM 994mg; CALC 129mg

---

ZESTY SPAGHETTI WITH SEAFOOD

- 1 cup seeded diced plum tomato (about 4 medium)
- ⅓ cup clam juice
- ¼ cup chopped fresh flat-leaf parsley
- ¼ cup extra-virgin olive oil
- 1 teaspoon grated lemon rind
- 3 tablespoons fresh lemon juice
- 2 teaspoons chopped fresh or ½ teaspoon dried dill
- 2 teaspoons fresh or 1 teaspoon dried thyme
- ½ teaspoon salt
- ½ teaspoon pepper
- 2 quarts water
- ¾ pound medium shrimp, peeled and deveined
- ¾ pound sea scallops, quartered
- 5 cups hot cooked spaghetti or linguine (about 12 ounces uncooked pasta)

1. Combine first 10 ingredients in a large bowl.
2. Bring water to a boil in a large saucepan. Add shrimp and scallops; cook 2 minutes or until done. Drain. Add shrimp, scallops, and pasta to tomato mixture; toss well. Yield: 6 servings (serving size: 1½ cups).

CALORIES 350 (29% from fat); FAT 11.1g (sat 1.5g, mono 6.9g, poly 1.6g); PROTEIN 24.2g; CARB 37.4g; FIBER 2.5g; CHOL 83mg; IRON 3.6mg; SODIUM 384mg; CALC 59mg

LINGUINE WITH GOAT CHEESE AND FENNEL

    1   cup boiling water
    ¼   cup sun-dried tomatoes, packed
        without oil
    ¼   cup chopped fresh flat-leaf
        parsley
    3   tablespoons chopped fresh basil
    2   tablespoons extra-virgin olive
        oil
    1   tablespoon fresh lemon juice
    3   ounces goat cheese, crumbled
    5   cups hot cooked linguine
        (about 10 ounces uncooked
        pasta)
    1   cup thinly sliced fennel bulb
        (about 1 small bulb)

1. Combine boiling water and sun-dried tomatoes in a bowl; let stand 15 minutes. Drain and chop.
2. Combine tomatoes and next 5 ingredients in a large bowl. Add linguine and fennel; toss well. Yield: 4 servings (serving size: 1½ cups).

CALORIES 402 (28% from fat); FAT 12.7g (sat 4.3g, mono 6.1g, poly 1.2g); PROTEIN 13.6g; CARB 58.5g; FIBER 2g; CHOL 19mg; IRON 3.7mg; SODIUM 358mg; CALC 154mg

LIGHTEN UP

A Lesson in Light

A Tennessee professor asks us to reduce the fat and calories in her favorite chicken casserole.

Nashville reader Sue Tully remembers the culinary repertoire she shared with her seven college roommates back in the '70s as less than encyclopedic. "We didn't know much about cooking, but we all knew how to make this one particular chicken casserole. It was cheap, it was simple, and it was delicious," she says. Unfortunately, with its two cans of cream soups and a stick of butter, the roommate recipe now seems

heavier than a Led Zeppelin tape. Giving it our best college try, we trimmed the fat by more than half with just a few simple switches. To update the casserole, we added some cremini mushrooms to replace those little pieces of mushroom in the soup can. Does it pass? Now a college English professor, Tully gives it an A+.

COLLEGE CHICKEN CASSEROLE

Leftover chicken (or a deli-roasted chicken) will work just as well in this recipe, particularly if you're in a hurry. Just increase the canned chicken broth to 2 cups, and skip the first step.
—*Sue Tully, Nashville, Tennessee*

    6   cups water
    ½   cup dry white wine
    1½ teaspoons dried basil
    2   garlic cloves, halved
    1   (10½-ounce) can low-salt chicken
        broth
    6   chicken breast halves (about
        2¼ pounds)
    4   chicken thighs (about 1 pound)
   Cooking spray
    4   cups sliced cremini mushrooms
        (about 8 ounces)
    ¼   cup all-purpose flour
    1   cup 1% low-fat milk
    ½   teaspoon salt
    ¼   teaspoon pepper
    2   cups herb-seasoned stuffing mix
    3   tablespoons light butter, melted

1. Combine first 5 ingredients in a Dutch oven; bring to a boil. Add chicken; cover, reduce heat, and simmer 30 minutes or until tender. Remove chicken with a slotted spoon; bring broth mixture to a boil. Cook until reduced to 4 cups (about 30 minutes). Pour reduced broth mixture into a zip-top plastic bag. Snip off 1 corner of bag; drain 2 cups mixture into a 2-cup glass measure, stopping before fat layer reaches the opening. Reserve remaining mixture for another use. Discard fat.
2. Remove and discard skin and bones from chicken; shred chicken with 2

forks to measure 4½ cups meat. Place in a 13 x 9-inch baking dish coated with cooking spray.
3. Preheat oven to 400°.
4. Place a large skillet coated with cooking spray over medium-high heat. Add mushrooms; sauté 5 minutes. Remove from skillet. Place flour in skillet; gradually add milk, stirring with a whisk until blended. Add 2 cups broth mixture; cook over medium heat 12 minutes or until slightly thick, stirring constantly with a whisk. Stir in mushrooms, salt, and pepper; pour over chicken.
5. Combine stuffing mix and butter; sprinkle over mushroom mixture. Cover and bake at 400° for 20 minutes. Uncover and bake casserole 10 additional minutes or until bubbly. Yield: 6 servings.

CALORIES 425 (30% from fat); FAT 14.3g (sat 5.2g, mono 4.6g, poly 2.7g); PROTEIN 54.2g; CARB 19.2g; FIBER 1.9g; CHOL 158mg; IRON 4mg; SODIUM 572mg; CALC 108mg

BEFORE & AFTER	
SERVING SIZE	
1 serving	
CALORIES	
666	425
FAT	
32.8g	14.3g
PERCENT OF TOTAL CALORIES	
44%	30%
SODIUM	
2,115mg	572mg
HOW WE DID IT	

Rather than using the two kinds of cream soups that were called for in the original recipe, we made a white sauce from scratch by using the broth from the boiled chicken and a small amount of low-fat milk. For the crunchy topping, we used stuffing mix and light butter, but significantly cut the amounts.

The Gathering Place, Part II

Turn your dinner table into a world cruise, and be sure to bring some of your friends along for the trip.

On page 103 you discovered why it's important for us to get back to the idea of gathering with friends and family for dinner and companionship.

Here, the inspiration comes from two favorite tropical delights—St. Thomas in the Caribbean and Kailua-Kona on the "Big Island" of Hawaii. The menus developed from the cuisines of these islands emphasize the naturally abundant produce without sending you in search of hard-to-find ingredients.

The only trick is obtaining the cooperation of your guests because these meals, by design, are too labor-intensive for one person. Everyone must pitch in.

MENU

ROASTED CHICKEN WITH
PINEAPPLE-CURRY SAUCE

WAIMEA FRIED RICE

VEGETABLE STIR-FRY WITH
TROPICAL VINAIGRETTE

LYCHEE SORBET WITH FRUIT
SALSA

ROASTED CHICKEN WITH PINEAPPLE-CURRY SAUCE

⅓ cup diagonally sliced peeled fresh lemon grass
6 garlic cloves, chopped
1 (4-inch) piece peeled fresh ginger, thinly sliced
1 (5-pound) roasting chicken
Cooking spray
1½ cups water
1 teaspoon olive oil
¾ cup diced Vidalia or other sweet onion
1 tablespoon curry powder
1 tablespoon thinly sliced peeled fresh lemon grass or ¾ teaspoon grated lemon rind
1 tablespoon grated peeled fresh ginger
2 garlic cloves, minced
¾ cup low-salt chicken broth
¼ cup thawed pineapple-orange juice concentrate, undiluted
1 (8-ounce) carton plain low-fat yogurt
1 tablespoon fish sauce
¼ teaspoon coconut extract

1. Preheat oven to 350°.
2. Combine first 3 ingredients. Remove and discard giblets and neck from chicken. Rinse chicken with cold water; pat dry. Trim excess fat. Spoon lemon grass mixture into body cavity. Lift wing tips up and over back; tuck under chicken. Place chicken, breast side down, on a rack coated with cooking spray. Pour 1½ cups water into a shallow roasting pan; place rack in pan. Insert meat thermometer into meaty part of thigh, making sure not to touch bone. Bake at 350° for 1 hour and 55 minutes or until thermometer registers 180°. Cover chicken loosely with foil; let stand 10 minutes. Discard skin.
3. Heat oil in a saucepan over medium heat. Add onion and curry; sauté 5 minutes. Stir in thinly sliced lemon grass, grated ginger, and garlic; sauté 3 minutes. Stir in broth and concentrate; bring to a boil. Reduce heat; simmer 3 minutes. Strain mixture through a sieve, reserving sauce. Discard solids.
4. Spoon yogurt onto several layers of heavy-duty paper towels; spread to ½-inch thickness. Cover with additional paper towels; let stand 5 minutes. Scrape into a bowl using a rubber spatula; stir in fish sauce and coconut extract. Gradually add hot pineapple sauce to yogurt mixture, stirring constantly with a whisk. Cover; keep warm.
5. Place a zip-top plastic bag inside a 2-cup glass measure. Pour pan drippings into bag; let stand 10 minutes (fat will rise to top). Seal bag; carefully snip off one bottom corner of bag. Drain pan drippings into yogurt mixture, stopping before fat layer reaches opening; discard fat. Stir well.
6. Serve chicken with pineapple-curry sauce. Yield: 6 servings (serving size: 4 ounces chicken and about ⅓ cup sauce).

CALORIES 229 (32% from fat); FAT 8.2g (sat 2.3g, mono 3.1g, poly 1.6g); PROTEIN 27.9g; CARB 9.8g; FIBER 0.8g; CHOL 79mg; IRON 1.6mg; SODIUM 332mg; CALC 103mg

---

WAIMEA FRIED RICE

4 cups water
1 cup uncooked long-grain brown rice
1 tablespoon dark sesame oil
3 tablespoons thinly sliced lemon grass or 2¼ teaspoons grated lemon rind
3 garlic cloves, minced
1 jalapeño pepper, seeded and finely chopped
½ cup diced celery
⅓ cup diced red bell pepper
4 teaspoons grated peeled fresh ginger
1 cup chopped pineapple
1 tablespoon finely chopped fresh or 1 teaspoon dried mint
1 tablespoon minced fresh cilantro
1 tablespoon fish sauce
1 teaspoon rice vinegar
¼ teaspoon salt

1. Bring water to a boil in a medium saucepan; add rice. Cover, reduce heat, and simmer 25 minutes. Drain and place rice in a shallow dish. Chill 30 minutes.
2. Heat oil in a large nonstick skillet over medium-high heat. Add lemon grass, garlic, and jalapeño; sauté 30 seconds. Add celery, bell pepper, and ginger; sauté 30 seconds. Add rice, and cook until thoroughly heated, stirring occasionally. Stir in pineapple and remaining ingredients. Yield: 6 servings (serving size: ¾ cup).

CALORIES 158 (19% from fat); FAT 3.4g (sat 0.5g, mono 1.3g, poly 1.3g); PROTEIN 3.1g; CARB 29.3g; FIBER 1.9g; CHOL 0mg; IRON 0.8mg; SODIUM 327mg; CALC 18mg

Vegetable Stir-Fry with Tropical Vinaigrette

2 tablespoons rice vinegar
2 tablespoons thawed pineapple-orange juice concentrate, undiluted
2 teaspoons minced shallots
2 teaspoons lemon juice
1 teaspoon cornstarch
1 teaspoon Worcestershire sauce
1 teaspoon honey
2 garlic cloves, minced
1 teaspoon olive oil
Cooking spray
¾ cup chopped green onions
1 cup (¼-inch) diagonally sliced carrot
1 cup julienne-cut yellow bell pepper
1 cup julienne-cut red bell pepper
3 cups small broccoli florets
1 cup fresh bean sprouts

1. Combine first 8 ingredients in a blender; cover and process until smooth. Heat oil in a wok or large nonstick skillet coated with cooking spray over medium-high heat. Add onions, and stir-fry 1 minute. Add carrot and bell peppers; stir-fry 1 minute. Add broccoli; cover and cook 2 minutes. Add vinegar mixture and sprouts; bring to a boil, and cook, uncovered, 30 seconds, stirring constantly. Yield: 6 servings (serving size: about ¾ cup).

CALORIES 56 (18% from fat); FAT 1.1g (sat 0.2g, mono 0.6g, poly 0.3g); PROTEIN 2.7g; CARB 10.8g; FIBER 3g; CHOL 0mg; IRON 1.3mg; SODIUM 31mg; CALC 43mg

Lychee Sorbet with Fruit Salsa

(pictured on page 116)

Lychees (often spelled 'litchis') are small, delicate fruits quite common in Hawaii.

2 cups water
½ cup sugar
1 tablespoon grated peeled fresh ginger
2 (20-ounce) cans whole seedless lychees in heavy syrup, undrained
Fruit Salsa
Fresh mint sprigs (optional)

1. Combine first 3 ingredients in a medium saucepan; bring to a boil. Remove from heat; strain mixture through a double-layer cheesecloth-lined sieve into a bowl. Discard solids.
2. Strain lychees through a colander into a bowl, reserving ½ cup liquid; discard remaining liquid. Combine lychees and ½ cup liquid in a blender; cover and process until smooth. Strain through a double-layer cheesecloth-lined sieve into bowl over ginger mixture. Discard pulp.
3. Pour mixture into the freezer can of an ice-cream freezer; freeze according to manufacturer's instructions. Spoon into a freezer-safe container; cover and freeze 1 hour or until firm. Serve with Fruit Salsa. Garnish, if desired. Yield: 6 servings (serving size: ⅔ cup sorbet and ½ cup salsa).

CALORIES 219 (1% from fat); FAT 0.3g (sat 0g, mono 0.1g, poly 0.1g); PROTEIN 1.5g; CARB 54.2g; FIBER 2.7g; CHOL 0mg; IRON 1.4mg; SODIUM 11mg; CALC 31mg

Fruit Salsa:

1½ cups chopped strawberries
¾ cup finely chopped peeled mango
¾ cup finely chopped pineapple
1 teaspoon minced fresh mint
¼ to ½ teaspoon coarsely ground pepper

1. Combine all ingredients in a small bowl; cover and chill. Yield: 3 cups (serving size: ½ cup).

CALORIES 34 (8% from fat); FAT 0.3g (sat 0g, mono 0.1g, poly 0.1g); PROTEIN 0.4g; CARB 8.6g; FIBER 1.6g; CHOL 0mg; IRON 0.3mg; SODIUM 1mg; CALC 9mg

---

> **MENU**
>
> SPICED SPINACH AND SHRIMP
>
> LAMB SHANKS FRENCHIE
>
> FUNGI FOSTER

Spiced Spinach and Shrimp

(pictured on page 115)

1½ tablespoons chopped peeled fresh lemon grass
1 teaspoon chopped fresh or ¼ teaspoon dried thyme
¼ teaspoon salt
¼ teaspoon pepper
1 garlic clove, minced
1½ teaspoons olive oil, divided
12 medium shrimp, peeled and deveined (about 8 ounces)
4 teaspoons finely chopped seeded serrano chile, divided
⅓ cup finely diced lean Canadian bacon (about 3 ounces)
¼ teaspoon ground nutmeg
1½ cups chopped green onions
12 cups prepackaged fresh spinach (about 8 ounces)
2 teaspoons balsamic vinegar
1 teaspoon cornstarch
1 tablespoon chopped fresh parsley

1. Combine first 5 ingredients. Heat 1 teaspoon oil in a nonstick skillet over medium-high heat. Add 2 teaspoons lemon grass mixture and shrimp; sauté 1 minute. Stir in 1 teaspoon chile, and sauté 30 seconds. Remove from skillet.
2. Add ½ teaspoon oil to a Dutch oven. Add bacon, remaining lemon grass mixture, 2 teaspoons chile, nutmeg, and onions; sauté 1 minute. Stir in spinach; cover and cook 1 minute.
3. Firmly press spinach mixture in a sieve over a bowl; reserve liquid. Combine vinegar and cornstarch. Combine spinach liquid and vinegar mixture in skillet over medium heat; bring to a boil (mixture will be thick). Add shrimp; toss to coat. Remove skillet from heat.
4. Combine parsley and 1 teaspoon chile. Arrange ⅓ cup spinach mixture

on each of 6 plates; top with 2 shrimp. Sprinkle evenly with parsley mixture. Yield: 6 servings.

CALORIES 101 (28% from fat); FAT 3.1g (sat 0.7g, mono 1.4g, poly 0.6g); PROTEIN 12.5g; CARB 7.5g; FIBER 5.2g; CHOL 50mg; IRON 4.4mg; SODIUM 433mg; CALC 149mg

LAMB SHANKS FRENCHIE

3 (1-pound) lamb shanks
½ teaspoon salt, divided
¼ teaspoon black pepper, divided
Cooking spray
1½ cups water, divided
6 small peeled sweet potatoes, each cut lengthwise into 4 wedges
1 teaspoon olive oil
3 cups chopped red bell pepper
2 cups chopped onion
2 teaspoons dried thyme
⅛ teaspoon ground cloves
3 garlic cloves, minced
½ cup tomato paste
2 cups dry red wine
1½ cups (½-inch-thick) sliced celery
½ teaspoon dried crushed red pepper
1 tablespoon water
2 teaspoons cornstarch
8 cups torn kale (about 1 bunch)

1. Preheat oven to 350°.
2. Trim fat from lamb. Sprinkle lamb with ¼ teaspoon salt and ⅛ teaspoon black pepper. Place in a shallow roasting pan coated with cooking spray. Add ½ cup water. Bake at 350° for 1 hour and 15 minutes. Remove from oven; cool. Remove meat from bones, and chop; discard bones, fat, and gristle. Add 1 cup water to pan, scraping pan to loosen browned bits. Place a zip-top plastic bag inside a 2-cup glass measure. Pour drippings into bag; let stand 10 minutes (fat will rise to top). Seal bag; carefully snip off one bottom corner of bag. Drain drippings into a bowl, stopping before fat layer reaches opening; discard fat. Reserve broth.
3. Place potato on a baking sheet coated with cooking spray. Bake at 350° for 45 minutes or until tender.
4. Heat oil in a large nonstick skillet over medium-high heat. Add bell pepper and onion; sauté 1 minute. Stir in thyme, cloves, and garlic; cook 1½ minutes. Add tomato paste; sauté 5 minutes or until paste begins to brown, stirring constantly. Stir in wine, celery, crushed red pepper, ¼ teaspoon salt, and ⅛ teaspoon black pepper. Bring to a boil; cover, reduce heat, and simmer 30 minutes.
5. Combine 1 tablespoon water and cornstarch. Add lamb, reserved broth, and cornstarch mixture to pepper mixture. Bring to a boil; cook 1 minute or until thick, stirring occasionally.
6. Steam kale, covered, for 6 minutes or until tender. Divide kale evenly among 6 plates. Arrange 4 potato wedges on kale; top wedges with 1⅓ cups lamb mixture. Yield: 6 servings.

CALORIES 512 (16% from fat); FAT 9.3g (sat 2.7g, mono 3.5g, poly 1.4g); PROTEIN 42.4g; CARB 67.3g; FIBER 10.3g; CHOL 114mg; IRON 7.8mg; SODIUM 389mg; CALC 236mg

LEMON GRASS

Lemon grass is one of the most important flavorings in Thai cooking and one that has found its way into other cuisines as well. It's a long, thin, light-green stalk, not unlike a green onion. As its name implies, it has a distinct lemon flavor with herbal undertones. To use, discard the tough outer leaves and about 2 to 3 inches of the thick root end. This will leave the tender stalk, which can be sliced or chopped.

FUNGI FOSTER (CORNMEAL PUDDING WITH CARAMEL CRUNCH)

In the Caribbean, fungi refers to a versatile cornmeal mush. We lightened the texture to create something more like a soufflé and crisscrossed the top with strands of caramelized sugar.

1¼ cups 2% reduced-fat milk, divided
¾ cup evaporated skim milk
1 (3-inch) cinnamon stick
6 tablespoons yellow cornmeal
¼ cup egg substitute
2 teaspoons cornstarch
1 tablespoon sugar
¼ cup raisins
1 cup plus 2 tablespoons vanilla low-fat yogurt
½ cup sugar
2 teaspoons hot water
⅛ teaspoon ground cinnamon

1. Combine ¾ cup 2% milk, evaporated milk, and cinnamon stick in a medium-size, heavy saucepan; cook over medium-high heat to 180° or until tiny bubbles form around edge (do not boil). Discard cinnamon stick. Combine ¼ cup 2% milk and cornmeal; add to milk mixture, stirring with a whisk. Cook 5 minutes over medium heat, stirring constantly. Combine ¼ cup 2% milk, egg substitute, cornstarch, and 1 tablespoon sugar in a bowl; gradually add to cornmeal mixture, stirring constantly with a whisk. Add raisins; cook over medium heat until very thick (about 4 minutes), stirring constantly. Remove from heat.
2. Spoon 3 tablespoons yogurt onto each of 6 dessert plates, and top each with ⅓ cup pudding.
3. Place ½ cup sugar in a small, heavy saucepan. Cook over medium-high heat 4 minutes or until sugar dissolves. Cook for an additional 30 seconds or until golden. Gradually stir in water and ground cinnamon. Drizzle about 1 tablespoon caramelized sugar mixture over each serving. Yield: 6 servings.

CALORIES 218 (7% from fat); FAT 1.8g (sat 1g, mono 0.5g, poly 0.1g); PROTEIN 8.1g; CARB 43.5g; FIBER 0.9g; CHOL 7mg; IRON 1mg; SODIUM 107mg; CALC 240mg

The Case for the Egg

For too many years, eggs took a beating. Turns out they're not the nutritional bad guys after all.

Back in the 1970s, as we naively enjoyed our omelets, custards, and quiches, researchers began uncovering troubling links between diet and disease. The deeper they delved, the louder their cries grew about the link between saturated fat and cholesterol and the risk of heart disease. Suddenly, the cholesterol-rich egg was a dietary hoodlum.

Two decades later, however, more and more studies are revealing that for most people, fears about eggs have been exaggerated. Even those who still argue that consumption of eggs needs to be limited agree that saturated fat, not dietary cholesterol, has the major impact on blood-cholesterol levels.

More important, scientists have confirmed in humans what they observed in animal studies decades ago: Response to dietary cholesterol is highly individual. Only about one-third of the population is what's known as responders—people particularly sensitive to high-cholesterol foods.

Many scientists believe how you respond to cholesterol is genetically determined. If a relative died of heart disease and your blood cholesterol is more than 200 mg/dl, for example, a cheese-filled omelet may not be your best daily breakfast choice. Because an easy test for cholesterol sensitivity doesn't exist yet, the American Heart Association (AHA) still urges restraint with eggs and other cholesterol-rich foods. (One egg contains about 215 milligrams of cholesterol, which is two-thirds of the 300-milligram daily limit that the AHA recommends.)

Even so, no one is suggesting that you go eggless, unless you're particularly sensitive to dietary cholesterol. Eggs can be a part of a healthful diet. In fact, AHA guidelines allow up to four eggs a week.

The reasons are simple: At only 70 calories per egg, they're an almost ideal low-fat source of protein. Each egg has about 4.5 grams of fat, of which only one-quarter is saturated—about the same amount as a cup of 1% milk. Eggs also are inexpensive and contain modest amounts of riboflavin, iron, calcium, phosphorus, zinc, and vitamins A, B_6, and B_{12}.

So lighten up and enjoy an occasional soufflé, omelet, or quiche. Most people can savor those foods and still stay within the AHA guidelines, especially if they watch what they pair with their eggs.

FAMILY FRITTATA

(pictured on page 113)

1 teaspoon olive oil
Cooking spray
1 cup finely chopped red onion
1 cup chopped green bell pepper
2 garlic cloves, minced
3 cups thinly sliced yellow Finnish potato or red potato (about 1 pound)
¾ teaspoon salt
¼ teaspoon black pepper
⅛ teaspoon ground red pepper
6 large eggs
2 tablespoons minced fresh parsley
1 tablespoon freeze-dried chives
½ cup finely chopped tomato
Parsley sprigs (optional)

1. Heat oil in a 10-inch cast-iron skillet coated with cooking spray over medium heat. Add onion, bell pepper, and garlic; sauté 5 minutes. Arrange potato over onion mixture; sprinkle with salt, black pepper, and red pepper. Cover, reduce heat to medium-low, and cook 20 minutes or until potato is tender.
2. Preheat broiler. Combine eggs, parsley, and chives in a medium bowl; stir well with a whisk. Pour over vegetables; cook over medium heat 10 minutes or until almost set. Top with tomato; broil 4 minutes or until browned and set. Garnish with parsley sprigs, if desired. Yield: 6 servings.

CALORIES 175 (33% from fat); FAT 6.4g (sat 1.8g, mono 2.6g, poly 0.9g); PROTEIN 8.7g; CARB 21.2g; FIBER 2.4g; CHOL 221mg; IRON 1.6mg; SODIUM 365mg; CALC 42mg

STRATA MILANO WITH GORGONZOLA

This is an easy and elegant make-ahead brunch dish.

2 bacon slices
3¼ cups 1% low-fat milk
1 cup part-skim ricotta cheese
½ cup (2 ounces) Gorgonzola cheese or other blue cheese, crumbled
1 teaspoon salt
½ teaspoon ground red pepper
5 large eggs
1¾ cups diced plum tomato
1 cup finely chopped red onion
1½ teaspoons dried rosemary
1 (16-ounce) loaf sourdough French bread baguette, cut into 1-inch slices and toasted
Cooking spray
2 teaspoons paprika
2 tablespoons (½ ounce) grated fresh Parmesan cheese

1. Cook bacon in a small nonstick skillet over medium-high heat until crisp; crumble and set aside.
2. Combine milk and next 5 ingredients; stir with a whisk until well-blended. Combine bacon, tomato, onion, and rosemary. Arrange half of bread slices in a single layer in a 13 x 9-inch baking dish coated with cooking spray. Spoon half of tomato mixture evenly over bread slices. Pour half of milk mixture over tomato mixture. Repeat procedure with remaining bread, tomato mixture, and milk mixture.

Sprinkle with paprika and cheese. Cover and chill 8 hours or overnight.

3. Preheat oven to 350°.

4. Uncover; bake at 350° for 45 minutes or until set. Yield: 10 servings.

CALORIES 287 (29% from fat); FAT 9.3g (sat 4.4g, mono 3.1g, poly 1.1g); PROTEIN 15.5g; CARB 34g; FIBER 1.9g; CHOL 129mg; IRON 1.9mg; SODIUM 739mg; CALC 252mg

EGGS FLORENTINE

3 (10-ounce) packages frozen chopped spinach, thawed, drained, and squeezed dry
Cooking spray
6 large eggs
3 tablespoons all-purpose flour
¼ teaspoon salt
⅛ teaspoon ground red pepper
2 cups 1% low-fat milk
⅓ cup (1½ ounces) grated fresh Parmesan cheese
¼ teaspoon paprika
6 English muffins, split and toasted
¼ teaspoon coarsely ground black pepper

1. Preheat oven to 350°.

2. Press spinach into bottom of a 13 x 9-inch baking dish coated with cooking spray. Form 6 (3-inch) indentations in spinach using the back of a spoon or bottom of a large custard cup. Break an egg into each indentation.

3. Combine flour, salt, and red pepper in a medium saucepan. Gradually add milk, stirring with a whisk until blended. Place milk mixture over medium heat, and cook until thick (about 8 minutes), stirring constantly. Remove from heat; add cheese, stirring until cheese melts.

4. Pour cheese sauce over eggs and spinach; sprinkle with paprika. Bake at 350° for 25 minutes or until egg yolks are almost set. Cut spinach-egg mixture into 6 portions; serve each portion over 2 English muffin halves, and sprinkle with black pepper. Yield: 6 servings.

CALORIES 363 (25% from fat); FAT 9.9g (sat 3.6g, mono 3g, poly 1.7g); PROTEIN 21.5g; CARB 48.2g; FIBER 4.7g; CHOL 229mg; IRON 5.9mg; SODIUM 756mg; CALC 475mg

SESAME-AND-ROASTED EGGPLANT SOUFFLÉ

Serve this Middle Eastern-inspired soufflé with pita bread and a sliced cucumber salad for a light supper.

Cooking spray
3 cups cubed peeled eggplant (about 12 ounces)
2 teaspoons dark sesame oil
3 garlic cloves
2 tablespoons all-purpose flour
1 cup 1% low-fat milk
2 large eggs, lightly beaten
2 tablespoons chopped fresh or 2 teaspoons dried parsley
1 tablespoon fresh lemon juice
1 tablespoon tahini (sesame-seed paste)
½ teaspoon salt
⅛ teaspoon pepper
4 large egg whites
½ teaspoon cream of tartar
½ teaspoon sesame seeds

1. Preheat oven to 400°.

2. Cut a piece of foil long enough to fit around a 1½-quart soufflé dish, allowing a 1-inch overlap; fold foil lengthwise into thirds. Lightly coat one side of foil and bottom of dish with cooking spray. Wrap foil around outside of dish, coated side against dish, allowing it to extend 4 inches above the rim to form a collar; secure with string or masking tape.

3. Combine eggplant, oil, and garlic in a bowl; toss gently to coat. Place eggplant mixture on a jelly-roll pan coated with cooking spray, spreading evenly. Bake at 400° for 30 minutes.

4. Place flour in a medium saucepan. Gradually add milk, stirring with a whisk until well-blended. Bring to a boil over medium heat; cook 2 minutes or until thick, stirring constantly.

5. Place eggs in a large bowl. Gradually add hot milk mixture to eggs, stirring constantly with a whisk. Combine milk mixture, eggplant mixture, parsley, and next 4 ingredients in a blender or food processor; cover and process until smooth. Return mixture to bowl.

6. Beat egg whites and cream of tartar at high speed of a mixer until stiff peaks form. Gently stir one-fourth of egg white mixture into eggplant mixture. Gently fold in remaining egg white mixture. Pour mixture into prepared soufflé dish, and sprinkle sesame seeds evenly over soufflé. Bake at 400° for 10 minutes. Reduce oven temperature to 375° (do not remove soufflé from oven), and bake for 40 additional minutes or until puffy and golden. Carefully remove foil collar, and serve immediately. Yield: 6 servings.

CALORIES 163 (44% from fat); FAT 8g (sat 1.8g, mono 2.9g, poly 2.3g); PROTEIN 10.6g; CARB 12.7g; FIBER 1.5g; CHOL 113mg; IRON 1.5mg; SODIUM 417mg; CALC 136mg

DAWNING OF A NEW EGG

Scientists and ranchers have been fooling around with the diets of hens to see how diet might affect the nutritional profile of an egg. Although not a whole lot can be done to dramatically lower the cholesterol level of eggs, experts are making other healthful changes.

VITAMIN E: By feeding the hens a vitamin- and mineral-enriched vegetarian diet, a company called Eggland's Best has produced eggs that contain higher levels of the antioxidant vitamin E. If you're willing to pay more for these eggs, this is one way to include more fat-soluble vitamin E in your diet.

OMEGA-3 FATS: The fat profile of the yolk can be altered by adding essential fatty acids (the polyunsaturated "good" fats) to a hen's diet. Eggs are already low in saturated fat. But in some areas of the country, you can now buy EggsPlus from Pilgrim's Pride of Dallas. These are eggs rich in omega-3 fats, the polyunsaturated fats found in fish. (But if you eat fish twice a week, you're probably getting enough of these heart-healthy fats.)

RUSTIC VEGETABLE QUICHE

1 cup all-purpose flour, divided
3½ tablespoons ice water
1 teaspoon sugar
½ teaspoon salt, divided
3 tablespoons vegetable
    shortening
Cooking spray
2 bacon slices
1 cup chopped red potato
½ cup chopped onion
½ cup (2 ounces) shredded reduced-
    fat, reduced-sodium Jarlsberg
    cheese
¼ cup thinly sliced green onions
1½ cups 1% low-fat milk
⅛ teaspoon ground red pepper
3 large eggs
¼ teaspoon paprika

1. Lightly spoon flour into a dry measuring cup; level with a knife. Combine ¼ cup flour and ice water, stirring with a whisk until well-blended. Combine ¾ cup flour, sugar, and ¼ teaspoon salt in a bowl; cut in shortening with a pastry blender or 2 knives until mixture resembles coarse meal. Add ice water mixture; toss with a fork until moist. Gently press mixture into a 4-inch circle on heavy-duty plastic wrap; cover with additional plastic wrap. Roll covered dough into an 11-inch circle; chill 10 minutes.
2. Preheat oven to 400°.
3. Remove top sheet of plastic wrap; fit dough into a 9-inch pie plate coated with cooking spray. Remove remaining sheet of plastic wrap. Fold edges of dough under; flute. Pierce bottom and sides of dough with a fork; bake at 400° for 8 minutes. Cool on a wire rack. Reduce oven temperature to 375°.
4. Cook bacon in a large nonstick skillet over medium heat until crisp. Remove bacon from skillet; crumble. Add potato and onion to bacon drippings in skillet; sauté 10 minutes or until tender. Remove from heat. Arrange potato mixture, bacon, cheese, and green onions in prepared crust. Combine milk, ¼ teaspoon salt, pepper, and eggs; stir well with a whisk. Pour milk mixture into crust; sprinkle with paprika. Bake at 375° for 45 minutes or until a knife inserted 1 inch from center comes out clean; let stand 10 minutes. Yield: 8 servings.

CALORIES 257 (40% from fat); FAT 11.3g (sat 3.6g, mono 4.1g, poly 2g); PROTEIN 12g; CARB 26.6g; FIBER 1.3g; CHOL 119mg; IRON 1.6mg; SODIUM 360mg; CALC 182mg

---

THE PERFECT HARD-BOILED EGG

Here's a no-fail formula for hard-boiled eggs. Place eggs in a saucepan, and cover with cold water. Bring to a boil; turn off heat, cover, and let eggs stand in the hot water for 15 minutes. Rinse with cold water. Gently crack shells, and peel under running water, starting with the large end. Older eggs are better for hard-boiling than the freshest ones.

AVGOLEMONO
(GREEK LEMON SOUP)

Whisked eggs give this famous Greek soup a velvety-smooth texture.

2 cups low-salt chicken broth
1 cup water
3 tablespoons fresh lemon juice
2 large eggs, lightly beaten
1 cup hot cooked long-grain rice
½ teaspoon salt
⅛ teaspoon white pepper
6 lemon slices

1. Heat broth and water in a medium saucepan over medium-high heat. Gradually add hot broth mixture and lemon juice to eggs, stirring constantly with a whisk. Return egg mixture to pan. Cook over medium heat until slightly thick (about 15 minutes), stirring constantly. Remove from heat; stir in rice, salt, and pepper. Ladle soup into 6 bowls; serve with lemon slices. Yield: 6 servings (serving size: ⅔ cup).

CALORIES 74 (27% from fat); FAT 2.2g (sat 0.8g, mono 0.6g, poly 0.2g); PROTEIN 3.8g; CARB 9.6g; FIBER 0.2g; CHOL 72mg; IRON 0.5mg; SODIUM 252mg; CALC 18mg

---

EGG-AND-TUNA SALAD SANDWICHES

4 hard-cooked large eggs, chopped
1 (6-ounce) can chunk light tuna
    in water, drained
2 tablespoons minced red onion
3 tablespoons light mayonnaise
2 tablespoons Dijon mustard
½ teaspoon freshly ground pepper
10 (1-ounce) slices whole-wheat
    bread
5 large red leaf lettuce leaves
5 (¼-inch-thick) slices tomato
1¼ cups alfalfa sprouts

1. Combine first 6 ingredients in a bowl. Spread ½ cup egg mixture over 5 bread slices. Top each with 1 lettuce leaf, 1 tomato slice, ¼ cup alfalfa sprouts, and 1 bread slice. Yield: 5 servings.

CALORIES 294 (30% from fat); FAT 9.8g (sat 2.3g, mono 2.5g, poly 3.4g); PROTEIN 19.5g; CARB 34.8g; FIBER 4.8g; CHOL 184mg; IRON 4mg; SODIUM 697mg; CALC 176mg

---

CURRIED DEVILED EGGS ON WHOLE-WHEAT CRACKERS

6 hard-cooked large eggs
1 tablespoon freeze-dried chives
3 tablespoons fat-free mayonnaise
1½ tablespoons 2% small-curd
    low-fat cottage cheese
2 teaspoons fresh lime juice
1½ teaspoons curry powder
¼ teaspoon ground cumin
⅛ teaspoon ground red pepper
¼ teaspoon paprika
12 reduced-fat whole-wheat
    crackers (such as Keebler
    reduced-fat wheat Toasteds)

1. Peel and slice eggs in half lengthwise. Mash yolks; stir in chives and next 6 ingredients. Spoon about 1 tablespoon yolk mixture into each egg white half. Cover and chill 1 hour. Sprinkle with paprika; serve with crackers. Yield: 12 servings (serving size: 1 filled egg half and 1 cracker).

CALORIES 57 (49% from fat); FAT 3.1g (sat 0.8g, mono 1.1g, poly 0.6g); PROTEIN 3.7g; CARB 3.4g; FIBER 0.3g; CHOL 106mg; IRON 0.4mg; SODIUM 118mg; CALC 16mg

CLASSIC CUSTARD

6 large eggs
½ cup sugar
¼ teaspoon salt
4 cups 1% low-fat milk
1½ teaspoons vanilla extract
½ teaspoon almond extract
Cooking spray

1. Preheat oven to 325°.
2. Combine first 3 ingredients in a large bowl; stir well with a whisk.
3. Cook milk in a large, heavy saucepan over medium-high heat to 180° or until tiny bubbles form around edge (do not boil). Remove milk from heat, and gradually add to egg mixture, stirring constantly with a whisk. Stir in vanilla and almond extracts. Pour mixture into a deep 2-quart soufflé dish coated with cooking spray. Place dish in a 13 x 9-inch baking pan, and add hot water to pan to a depth of 1 inch. Bake at 325° for 50 minutes or until a knife inserted in center of custard comes out almost clean. Remove dish from pan; serve custard warm or chilled. Yield: 7 servings (serving size: ¾ cup).

CALORIES 185 (29% from fat); FAT 6g (sat 2.3g, mono 2.1g, poly 0.7g); PROTEIN 10.1g; CARB 21.6g; FIBER 0g; CHOL 195mg; IRON 0.7mg; SODIUM 210mg; CALC 194mg

For the Love of Chèvre

Tart, creamy, and lower in fat than cream cheese, goat cheese is capturing our fancy.

The American love affair with *chèvre* has been a bit slow in blooming. Today, there are more than 100 goat-cheese producers nationwide, according to the American Dairy Goat Association. And they're all struggling to keep pace with America's increasing taste for goat cheese—consumption has tripled over the last few years.

There's more demand than supply, part of which is simple physics: A goat typically produces less than a gallon of milk a day, compared with about eight from a cow. But it's also because many goat-cheese producers are small farm operations in the French tradition.

Creamy and crumbly, soft goat cheese comes from the farm in cones, discs, or logs—sometimes rolled in herbs. Other styles are similar to cow's-milk cheeses: hard Cheddar, Jack, Parmesan, a ricottalike *fromage blanc,* and a surface-ripened cheese that is comparable to Brie. And while goat cheese is somewhat pricey—ranging from $4 for 3 ounces to $12 for 8 ounces—its flavor allows a little to go a long way.

BLACK BEAN-AND-GOAT CHEESE TORTILLA STACKS

1 teaspoon extra-virgin olive oil
4 garlic cloves, minced
2 (15-ounce) cans black beans, rinsed and drained
¼ cup water
2 tablespoons chopped fresh cilantro
1 tablespoon sun-dried tomato paste
¼ teaspoon salt, divided
¼ teaspoon coarsely ground pepper, divided
1 (14½-ounce) can plum tomatoes, undrained
¼ cup dry red wine
12 (6-inch) corn tortillas
¾ cup (3 ounces) crumbled goat cheese
Fresh Tomato-and-Corn Salsa

1. Heat oil in a large nonstick skillet over medium-high heat. Add garlic and black beans; sauté 2 minutes. Remove from heat; stir in water, cilantro, tomato paste, ⅛ teaspoon salt, and ⅛ teaspoon pepper. Reserve 1 cup bean mixture; set remaining mixture aside.
2. Place tomatoes, wine, ⅛ teaspoon salt, and ⅛ teaspoon pepper in a blender; cover and process until smooth. Reserve 1 cup tomato mixture. Pour remaining mixture into a bowl; set aside.
3. Place reserved 1 cup bean mixture and reserved 1 cup tomato mixture in blender; process until smooth. Set tomato-bean mixture aside.
4. Preheat oven to 350°.
5. Place 2 tortillas, side by side, on a foil-lined baking sheet. Spoon 3 tablespoons tomato-bean mixture over each tortilla; top each with 2 tablespoons remaining bean mixture, 1 tablespoon goat cheese, and 1 tortilla. Repeat procedure 4 times ending with tortillas. Gently press top of each tortilla stack.
6. Bake at 350° for 15 minutes or until thoroughly heated. Cut each stack into 4 wedges. Spoon remaining tomato mixture over wedges, and top with Fresh Tomato-and-Corn Salsa. Yield: 8 servings (serving size: 1 wedge, 2½ tablespoons sauce, and ¼ cup salsa).

CALORIES 253 (19% from fat); FAT 5.4g (sat 2.1g, mono 1.8g, poly 1g); PROTEIN 10.9g; CARB 43.7g; FIBER 6.4g; CHOL 9mg; IRON 3mg; SODIUM 595mg; CALC 178mg

Fresh Tomato-and-Corn Salsa:

½ cup fresh corn kernels (about 1 ear)
1¼ cups chopped tomato
½ cup chopped fresh cilantro
¼ cup chopped red onion
¼ cup chopped green onions
¼ cup fresh lemon juice
1 teaspoon hot pepper sauce
½ teaspoon olive oil
¼ teaspoon salt
¼ teaspoon ground cumin

1. Steam corn, covered, 2 minutes, and cool. Combine corn and remaining ingredients in a large bowl. Yield: 2 cups (serving size: ¼ cup).
Note: The salsa can be made a day in advance. Cover and chill.

CALORIES 24 (23% from fat); FAT 0.6g (sat 0.1g, mono 0.5g, poly 0.2g); PROTEIN 0.8g; CARB 4.8g; FIBER 1g; CHOL 0mg; IRON 0.5mg; SODIUM 86mg; CALC 11mg

Goat cheese's appeal isn't limited to only taste—it has a nutritional basis, too. Soft, fresh *chèvre* (SHEHV-ruh) has 20% fewer calories than cream cheese (76 per ounce compared to 99) and 30% fewer than Cheddar (76 per ounce to 114). Its 6 grams of fat per ounce weighs in well below cream cheese's 10 grams and Cheddar's 9.4.

RIGATONI WITH GOAT CHEESE, SUN-DRIED TOMATOES, AND KALE

½ cup sun-dried tomato sprinkles
2 cups boiling water
½ teaspoon chili oil (or vegetable oil)
¼ cup minced shallots
6 garlic cloves, minced
4 cups coarsely chopped kale
½ teaspoon dried oregano
⅛ teaspoon salt
⅛ teaspoon freshly ground pepper
6 cups cooked rigatoni (about 12 ounces uncooked pasta)
½ cup (2 ounces) crumbled goat cheese

1. Combine tomato sprinkles and boiling water in a bowl; let stand 30 minutes. Drain tomatoes in a sieve over a bowl, reserving ½ cup liquid.
2. Heat oil in a large nonstick skillet over medium-high heat. Add shallots and garlic; sauté 1 minute. Add kale; sauté 3 minutes or until wilted. Add sun-dried tomatoes; sauté 2 minutes. Add reserved ½ cup liquid, oregano, salt, and pepper. Reduce heat; simmer 3 minutes or until kale is tender.
3. Combine pasta, kale mixture, and goat cheese in a large bowl; toss well. Yield: 4 servings (serving size: 1½ cups).
Note: Substitute 1 cup thawed frozen chopped kale for fresh, if desired.

CALORIES 396 (13% from fat); FAT 5.8g (sat 2.7g, mono 1.2g, poly 1.3g); PROTEIN 15.7g; CARB 72.3g; FIBER 4.4g; CHOL 13mg; IRON 4.4mg; SODIUM 484mg; CALC 200mg

SMOKED-SALMON, GOAT-CHEESE, AND FRESH-DILL FRITTATA

You can tell if the frittata is ready by gently shaking the pan (be sure to use a potholder). If the middle wiggles, cook a little longer. If it's fairly firm, the frittata is done.

Cooking spray
2½ cups shredded peeled baking potato or refrigerated shredded hash brown potatoes
¼ teaspoon salt
¼ teaspoon pepper
6 large egg whites
2 large eggs
½ cup (2 ounces) crumbled goat cheese
3 ounces thinly sliced smoked salmon, cut into ¼-inch-wide strips
1 tablespoon chopped fresh dill

1. Preheat oven to 350°.
2. Heat a large nonstick ovenproof skillet coated with cooking spray over medium-high heat. Add potato; sauté 5 minutes or until golden brown. Sprinkle with salt and pepper.
3. Combine egg whites and next 3 ingredients in a medium bowl, and stir well with a whisk. Spread egg mixture evenly over potato in skillet, and cook 2 minutes or until edges are set and bottom is lightly browned. Sprinkle with dill.
4. Bake frittata at 350° for 5 minutes. Broil 3 minutes or until center is set. Carefully loosen frittata with a spatula; gently slide frittata onto a platter. Cut into 4 wedges. Yield: 4 servings.

CALORIES 202 (30% from fat); FAT 6.8g (sat 3.2g, mono 2.1g, poly 0.7g); PROTEIN 16.2g; CARB 18.5g; FIBER 1.6g; CHOL 128mg; IRON 1.5mg; SODIUM 589mg; CALC 100mg

SICILIAN PASTA PIE

2 teaspoons olive oil, divided
Cooking spray
2 cups thinly sliced onion
½ cup (2 x ¼-inch) julienne-cut red bell pepper
4 garlic cloves, minced
2 cups quartered cherry tomato
¼ cup dry red wine
3 tablespoons chopped pitted kalamata olives
2 tablespoons sun-dried tomato sprinkles
¼ teaspoon black pepper
1 (14.5-ounce) can diced tomatoes, undrained
6 cups hot cooked linguine (about 10 ounces uncooked pasta)
½ cup (2 ounces) crumbled goat cheese

1. Heat 1 teaspoon oil in a nonstick ovenproof skillet coated with cooking spray over medium heat. Add onion; sauté 3 minutes. Add bell pepper and garlic; sauté 5 minutes. Add cherry tomato; sauté 2 minutes. Add wine and next 4 ingredients; reduce heat, and simmer 5 minutes. Combine tomato mixture and pasta in a bowl; toss to coat.
2. Preheat oven to 350°.
3. Wipe skillet with paper towels. Coat skillet with cooking spray, and add remaining 1 teaspoon oil. Arrange cheese in skillet, and top with pasta mixture. Cover with foil coated with cooking spray, pressing firmly. Wrap handle of skillet with foil; bake at 350° for 30 minutes. Remove from oven, and let stand for 10 minutes. Invert pie onto a large plate. Cut into 6 wedges. Yield: 6 servings.

CALORIES 270 (17% from fat); FAT 5.2g (sat 1.9g, mono 2g, poly 0.7g); PROTEIN 9.3g; CARB 47.5g; FIBER 4.1g; CHOL 8mg; IRON 2.8mg; SODIUM 271mg; CALC 88mg

ROSEMARY-ROASTED POTATOES WITH GOAT CHEESE

10 cups cubed yellow Finnish potato or baking potato (about 4 pounds)
2 tablespoons chopped fresh or 2 teaspoons dried rosemary
3 tablespoons balsamic vinegar
1 tablespoon olive oil
½ teaspoon salt
¼ teaspoon pepper
6 garlic cloves, chopped
Cooking spray
¾ cup (3 ounces) crumbled goat cheese

1. Preheat oven to 400°.
2. Combine first 7 ingredients in a large zip-top plastic bag, turning well to coat. Arrange potato on a large jelly-roll pan coated with cooking spray. Bake at 400° for 45 minutes or until browned. Place in a large bowl; sprinkle with cheese, tossing well. Yield: 8 servings (serving size: 1 cup).

CALORIES 215 (18% from fat); FAT 4.2g (sat 1.9g, mono 1.7g, poly 0.3g); PROTEIN 5.3g; CARB 40.3g; FIBER 3g; CHOL 9mg; IRON 0.8mg; SODIUM 273mg; CALC 68mg

MEDITERRANEAN GOAT-CHEESE SANDWICHES

You can usually find olive paste in your grocery store's condiment section.

1 (8-ounce) loaf French bread
2 ounces (½ cup) goat cheese
1 tablespoon olive paste (such as Oliva da Sanremo)
1 cup trimmed arugula or fresh spinach
4 (⅛-inch-thick) slices red onion, separated into rings
4 (⅛-inch-thick) slices tomato
6 basil leaves, thinly sliced
½ teaspoon chopped capers
1 teaspoon balsamic vinegar
½ teaspoon olive oil
⅛ teaspoon freshly ground pepper

1. Slice bread in half lengthwise. Spread cheese over cut side of bottom half; spread olive paste evenly over cheese. Arrange arugula and next 4 ingredients on top. Drizzle with vinegar and olive oil. Sprinkle with pepper. Top with top half of loaf. Cut crosswise into 4 pieces. Yield: 4 sandwiches.

CALORIES 225 (21% from fat); FAT 5.2g (sat 2.7g, mono 1.6g, poly 0.8g); PROTEIN 7.8g; CARB 35.3g; FIBER 1.8g; CHOL 15mg; IRON 1.5mg; SODIUM 570mg; CALC 112mg

READER RECIPES

Steaking Their Claims

From meatballs to chili, our readers sent us their favorite beef recipes.

AUNT JENNY'S SLOW-COOKER MEATBALLS

These meatballs are good served over egg noodles.
—Elizabeth Spencer, East Leroy, Michigan

1½ pounds extra-lean ground beef
1 cup dry breadcrumbs
½ cup egg substitute or 4 egg whites
⅓ cup chopped fresh parsley
2 tablespoons minced fresh onion
⅓ cup ketchup
2 tablespoons brown sugar
1 tablespoon lemon juice
1 (16-ounce) can jellied cranberry sauce
1 (12-ounce) bottle chili sauce
Parsley sprigs (optional)

1. Combine first 5 ingredients; shape mixture into 30 (1½-inch) meatballs.
2. Combine ketchup and next 4 ingredients in an electric slow cooker; gently stir in meatballs. Cover with lid; cook on low-heat setting for 8 to 10 hours. Garnish with parsley, if desired. Yield: 10 servings (serving size: 3 meatballs and about 2 tablespoons sauce).

CALORIES 263 (14% from fat); FAT 4.1g (sat 1.4g, mono 1.7g, poly 0.3g); PROTEIN 18.7g; CARB 37.1g; FIBER 0.9g; CHOL 39mg; IRON 2.9mg; SODIUM 721mg; CALC 47mg

MARINATED FLANK STEAK WITH CRANBERRY-RASPBERRY SALSA

My family and friends are convinced that this is one of those gourmet recipes that requires hours of slaving in the kitchen. I just put all the ingredients in a slow cooker and let it cook itself.
—Dana Misner, Woodbury, Minnesota

¼ cup chili sauce
¼ cup lime juice
3 drops hot pepper sauce
1 (1.25-ounce) package low-sodium taco seasoning
2 pounds flank steak
¾ cup (2-inch) sliced green onions
½ cup cilantro sprigs
1 tablespoon chopped seeded jalapeño pepper
1 tablespoon lime juice
1 teaspoon ground cumin
1 (12-ounce) carton cranberry-raspberry crushed fruit (such as Ocean Spray)
16 (8-inch) flour tortillas

1. Combine first 4 ingredients in a small bowl. Trim fat from steak. Place steak in an electric slow cooker; add chili sauce mixture, turning steak to coat. Cover with lid, and cook on high-heat setting for 1 hour. Reduce heat setting to low; cook 9 hours.
2. Combine onions, cilantro, and jalapeño pepper in a food processor, and pulse 5 times or until finely chopped. Add 1 tablespoon lime juice, cumin, and crushed fruit; process until smooth. Spoon salsa mixture into a bowl; cover and chill.
3. Remove steak from slow cooker, discarding cooking liquid. Shred steak. Heat tortillas according to package directions. Spread about 1½ tablespoons salsa over each tortilla. Spoon about ½ cup shredded steak down center of each tortilla; roll up. Yield: 16 servings (serving size: 1 filled tortilla).

CALORIES 278 (24% from fat); FAT 7.4g (sat 2.3g, mono 3g, poly 1.5g); PROTEIN 12.8g; CARB 38.3g; FIBER 2g; CHOL 21mg; IRON 2.7mg; SODIUM 451mg; CALC 70mg

BEEF AND GARLIC

Garlic has a lot of health benefits, so I like to use it as much as I can in cooking. You only need a little bit to add flavor to this Asian-style dish.
—Dragoljub Cenic, New York, New York

1   pound boned sirloin steak, cut into ¼-inch strips
1   garlic clove, minced
Cooking spray
3   cups sliced bok choy
¼   cup thinly sliced green onions
1   cup diced tomato
⅓   cup beef broth
3   tablespoons low-sodium soy sauce
1   tablespoon oyster sauce
⅛   teaspoon pepper

1. Combine beef and garlic in a bowl; chill 10 minutes. Place a large nonstick skillet coated with cooking spray over medium-high heat until hot. Add beef mixture; sauté 5 minutes or until beef is done. Remove beef from pan; keep warm. Combine bok choy and green onions in skillet; sauté 2 minutes. Add beef, tomato, and remaining ingredients; simmer 3 minutes or until slightly thick. Yield: 4 servings (serving size: 1 cup).

CALORIES 189 (0% from fat); FAT 6.2g (sat 2.2g, mono 2.4g, poly 0.4g); PROTEIN 27g; CARB 6g; FIBER 1.3g; CHOL 73mg; IRON 4.2mg; SODIUM 748mg; CALC 74mg

CROCK-POT CHILI

This is my children's favorite meal. What more can I say?
—Patti A. Jensen, Wiltshire, England

1   pound ground round
1   cup chopped onion
½   cup chopped green bell pepper
¼   cup dry red wine or water
1   tablespoon chili powder
1   teaspoon sugar
1   teaspoon ground cumin
¼   teaspoon salt
1   garlic clove, minced
1   (15-ounce) can kidney beans, undrained
1   (14.5-ounce) can Mexican-style stewed tomatoes with jalapeño peppers and spices, undrained
6   tablespoons (1½ ounces) shredded reduced-fat extra-sharp Cheddar cheese

1. Cook ground round in a large non-stick skillet over medium-high heat until brown, stirring to crumble. Add onion and next 7 ingredients; cook 7 minutes or until onion is tender. Place meat mixture in an electric slow cooker, and stir in beans and tomatoes. Cover with lid, and cook on low-heat setting 4 hours. Spoon into bowls; sprinkle with cheese. Yield: 6 servings (serving size: 1¼ cups chili and 1 tablespoon cheese).

Note: The chili can be made on the stovetop if you don't have a slow cooker. After adding the beans and the tomatoes, bring to a boil. Reduce heat; simmer, partially covered, 1½ hours.

CALORIES 243 (21% from fat); FAT 5.6g (sat 2.3g, mono 1.8g, poly 0.5g); PROTEIN 25.5g; CARB 22.9g; FIBER 3.1g; CHOL 49mg; IRON 4.1mg; SODIUM 637mg; CALC 154mg

CHARLIE'S BEEF-AND-ZUCCHINI DISH

My late father-in-law, Charlie, used to make this recipe all the time, and it's one of my husband's favorites.
—Lisa Mahatadse, Moorpark, California

1   pound extra-lean ground beef
Cooking spray
3   cups diced zucchini (about 3 small)
2   garlic cloves, minced
1   teaspoon dried Italian seasoning
2   (8-ounce) cans tomato sauce
1   cup (4 ounces) shredded reduced-fat sharp Cheddar cheese, divided
2½ cups hot cooked rice

1. Cook beef in a large nonstick skillet over medium-high heat until browned; stir to crumble. Drain well.
2. Wipe skillet with a paper towel. Coat with cooking spray; place over medium-high heat. Add zucchini and garlic; sauté 5 minutes. Add beef, seasoning, and tomato sauce; bring to a boil. Reduce heat; simmer 5 minutes. Remove from heat. Add ⅔ cup cheese; stir until cheese melts. Serve over rice. Sprinkle with remaining ⅓ cup cheese. Yield: 5 servings (serving size: 1 cup beef mixture, ½ cup rice, and about 1 tablespoon cheese).

CALORIES 355 (26% from fat); FAT 10.3g (sat 4.6g, mono 3.6g, poly 0.5g); PROTEIN 30.3g; CARB 35.2g; FIBER 2.4g; CHOL 71mg; IRON 4.2mg; SODIUM 759mg; CALC 250mg

JUNE

Celebrate with Cooking Light

Try our field-tested party plan with crowd-pleasing recipes that lend themselves to lots of hands.

It's a dilemma readers tell us about constantly: They want to enjoy their friends more, but they can't seem to find the time. A dinner would be great, but their lives are so rushed that entertaining seems out of the question. Who has the time and energy, not to mention the accouterments?

We've found an answer to the dilemma. The idea is simple: Invite some friends over for an informal dinner, and tell them they're going to help make it. *Cooking Light* provides the recipes and the road map to make everything happen easily and without stress. It's casual and easy, gets everyone involved, inspires conversation, and—best of all—keeps you from having to create a dinner single-handedly.

Start the evening by setting up a restaurant-style station for each recipe, complete with the necessary ingredients, measuring spoons, bowls, and so on. As guests arrive outfit them with a drink, an appetizer, and an apron, then gently guide them into the kitchen. That's all it'll take to get the magic started. What a great new way to socialize!

TEX-MEX BLACK BEAN DIP

Serve with homemade flour tortilla chips (cut flour tortillas into wedges, and toast in the oven at 350° for 8 to 10 minutes or until browned).

- 1 teaspoon vegetable oil
- ½ cup chopped onion
- 2 garlic cloves, minced
- ½ cup diced tomato
- ⅓ cup bottled picante sauce
- ½ teaspoon chili powder
- ½ teaspoon ground cumin
- 1 (15-ounce) can black beans, drained
- ¼ cup (1 ounce) shredded reduced-fat Monterey Jack cheese
- ¼ cup chopped fresh cilantro
- 1 tablespoon fresh lime juice

1. Heat oil in a medium nonstick skillet over medium heat. Add onion and garlic; sauté 4 minutes or until tender. Add tomato and next 4 ingredients; cook 5 minutes or until thick, stirring constantly. Remove from heat; partially mash with a potato masher. Add cheese, cilantro, and lime juice, stirring until cheese melts. Serve warm or at room temperature. Yield: 1⅔ cups (serving size: 2 tablespoons).

CALORIES 42 (21% from fat); FAT 1.0g (sat 0.4g, mono 0.2g, poly 0.2g); PROTEIN 2.6g; CARB 6.2g; FIBER 1.0g; CHOL 2mg; IRON 0.6mg; SODIUM 136mg; CALC 30mg

ROASTED BELL PEPPER-AND-OLIVE PIZZA

Make this appetizer ahead of time, and put it in the oven just before your guests arrive so it can be served hot.

- 2 large red bell peppers
- 2 large yellow bell peppers
- ½ cup sliced green olives
- ¼ cup chopped fresh parsley
- 2 teaspoons drained capers
- 2 teaspoons red wine vinegar
- ¾ teaspoon olive oil
- ⅛ teaspoon black pepper
- 2 (1-pound) Italian cheese-flavored pizza crusts (such as Boboli) or focaccias
- 6 tablespoons (1½ ounces) freshly grated Parmesan cheese

1. Preheat broiler. Cut bell peppers in half lengthwise; discard seeds and membranes. Place bell pepper halves, skin sides up, on a foil-lined baking sheet, and flatten with hand. Broil 15 minutes or until blackened. Place in a zip-top plastic bag, and seal. Let stand 15 minutes. Peel and cut into strips. Combine bell peppers, olives, and next 5 ingredients in a bowl.
2. Preheat oven to 350°.
3. Divide bell pepper mixture evenly among pizza crusts; sprinkle with cheese. Bake at 350° for 7 minutes or until cheese melts. Cut each pizza into 12 wedges. Yield: 12 servings (serving size: 2 wedges).

CALORIES 104 (28% from fat); FAT 3.2g (sat 1.5g, mono 0.8g, poly 0.1g); PROTEIN 4.6g; CARB 15.5g; FIBER 2.1g; CHOL 2mg; IRON 0.9mg; SODIUM 301mg; CALC 62mg

CAVATAPPI WITH SPINACH, GARBANZO BEANS, AND FETA

Have your guests chop the spinach while the pasta cooks; then they can toss all the ingredients together in a big bowl.

    8 cups coarsely chopped
         spinach
    8 cups hot cooked cavatappi
         (about 12 ounces uncooked
         spiral-shaped pasta)
    1 cup (4 ounces) crumbled feta
         cheese
    ¼ cup olive oil
    2 tablespoons fresh lemon
         juice
    ½ teaspoon salt
    ½ teaspoon black pepper
    2 (19-ounce) cans chickpeas
         (garbanzo beans) or other
         white beans, drained
    4 garlic cloves, crushed
Freshly ground pepper
Lemon wedges (optional)

1. Combine first 10 ingredients in a large bowl, tossing well to coat. Garnish with lemon wedges, if desired. Yield: 12 servings (serving size: 1⅓ cups).
Note: You can substitute penne or any other short pasta for the spiral-shaped cavatappi.

CALORIES 288 (27% from fat); FAT 8.6g (sat 2.3g, mono 4.2g, poly 1.3g); PROTEIN 11.2g; CARB 42.2g; FIBER 4.4g; CHOL 9mg; IRON 3.6mg; SODIUM 334mg; CALC 106mg

SHRIMP KEBABS WITH JALAPEÑO-LIME MARINADE

    4 pounds large shrimp, peeled,
         deveined, and butterflied
    1 cup thawed orange juice
         concentrate, undiluted
    2 teaspoons grated lime rind
    ½ cup fresh lime juice
    ½ cup honey
    4 teaspoons ground cumin
    ½ teaspoon salt
    6 garlic cloves, minced
    4 jalapeño peppers, seeded and
         chopped
    4 red bell peppers, cut into 1-inch
         cubes
Lime wedges (optional)
Cooking spray

1. Combine first 9 ingredients in a large zip-top plastic bag; seal and marinate in refrigerator 30 minutes. Remove shrimp from bag, reserving marinade. Thread shrimp, bell pepper cubes, and lime wedges (if desired) onto 12 skewers.
2. Prepare grill or broiler. Place skewers on grill rack or broiler pan coated with cooking spray; cook 4 minutes on each side or until shrimp are done, basting frequently with reserved marinade. Yield: 12 servings (serving size: 1 kebab).
Note: You can substitute 3 pounds of skinned, boned chicken breast or pork tenderloin, cut into 1-inch cubes, for the shrimp, if preferred.

CALORIES 217 (10% from fat); FAT 2.4g (sat 0.4g, mono 0.4g, poly 0.9g); PROTEIN 24.2g; CARB 25.1g; FIBER 0.7g; CHOL 172mg; IRON 3.7mg; SODIUM 269mg; CALC 80mg

GREEN BEANS PROVENÇALE

To chop parsley, put it in a cup and then use kitchen scissors to snip it into pieces.

    2 pounds fresh green beans, cut
         into 1½-inch pieces
   24 small cherry tomatoes, halved
    ½ cup chopped red onion
    ¾ cup chopped fresh parsley
    ¼ cup water
    ¼ cup white wine vinegar
    2 tablespoons grated Parmesan
         cheese
    2 tablespoons olive oil
    ½ teaspoon dried thyme
    ½ teaspoon pepper
    2 garlic cloves, minced

1. Steam beans, covered, 8 minutes or until crisp-tender; drain. Plunge beans into cold water; drain. Combine beans, tomatoes, and onion in a medium bowl.
2. Combine parsley and remaining 7 ingredients; stir until well-blended. Pour over vegetables, tossing gently to coat. Serve at room temperature. Yield: 12 servings (serving size: 1 cup).

CALORIES 56 (43% from fat); FAT 2.6g (sat 0.5g, mono 1.7g, poly 0.3g); PROTEIN 2g; CARB 7.2g; FIBER 2.1g; CHOL 0mg; IRON 1.2mg; SODIUM 25mg; CALC 48mg

MOCHA PUDDING CAKE

Pop this cake in the oven as you enjoy the main course. It should be ready by the time you finish.

    1 cup all-purpose flour
    1 cup sugar, divided
    6 tablespoons unsweetened cocoa,
         divided
  1½ tablespoons instant coffee granules
    2 teaspoons baking powder
    ¼ teaspoon salt
    ½ cup 1% low-fat milk
    3 tablespoons vegetable oil
    1 teaspoon vanilla extract
Cooking spray
    1 cup boiling water
    1 cup plus 2 tablespoons vanilla
         low-fat ice cream

Continued

1. Preheat oven to 350°.
2. Lightly spoon flour into a dry measuring cup; level with a knife. Combine flour, ⅔ cup sugar, ¼ cup cocoa, coffee granules, baking powder, and salt in a bowl. Combine milk, oil, and vanilla in a bowl; add to flour mixture, and stir well. Spoon batter into an 8-inch square baking dish coated with cooking spray.
3. Combine remaining ⅓ cup sugar and 2 tablespoons cocoa. Sprinkle over batter. Pour 1 cup boiling water over batter (do not stir). Bake at 350° for 30 minutes or until cake springs back when touched lightly in center (cake will not test clean when a wooden pick is inserted in center). Serve warm with ice cream. Yield: 9 servings (serving size: 1 [3-inch] square of cake and 2 tablespoons ice cream).
Note: This recipe is easy to double. Spoon it into a 13 x 9-inch baking dish; bake at the same temperature for the same amount of time.

CALORIES 221 (25% from fat); FAT 6.1g (sat 1.7g, mono 1.6g, poly 2.3g); PROTEIN 3.5g; CARB 38.2g; FIBER 0.4g; CHOL 3mg; IRON 1.3mg; SODIUM 154mg; CALC 90mg

LEMON-LIME CREAM TART

This dessert can be made up to three days ahead of time. It was a big hit at all our gatherings.

44 reduced-fat vanilla wafers
3 tablespoons sugar
2 tablespoons stick margarine or butter, softened
1 large egg white
Cooking spray
1 tablespoon grated lemon rind
6 tablespoons fresh lemon juice
2 tablespoons fresh lime juice
3 large eggs, lightly beaten
1 (14-ounce) can low-fat sweetened condensed milk
1 cup frozen reduced-calorie whipped topping, thawed and divided
10 lemon rind strips (optional)
Mint leaves (optional)

1. Preheat oven to 325°.
2. Place wafers in a food processor; process until finely ground. Add sugar, margarine, and egg white; pulse 2 times or just until combined.
3. Press crumb mixture into bottom and up sides of a 9-inch round tart pan coated with cooking spray. Bake at 325° for 15 minutes or until lightly browned. Cool on a wire rack.
4. Combine grated lemon rind, juices, eggs, and milk in a bowl, stirring with a whisk until blended. Pour mixture into prepared crust. Bake at 325° for 30 minutes or until filling is set. Cool completely. Top with whipped topping. Garnish with lemon rind strips and mint, if desired. Yield: 10 servings (serving size: 1 wedge and about 1½ tablespoons whipped topping).

CALORIES 270 (27%% from fat); FAT 8.2g (sat 2.2g, mono 2.4g, poly 1.5g); PROTEIN 6.7g; CARB 43.4g; FIBER 0.6g; CHOL 71mg; IRON 0.2mg; SODIUM 173mg; CALC 15mg

LAST HURRAH

The Meal is the Message

To err is human, so on National Forgiveness Day use our peacemaking po' boy to make amends.

In 19th-century New Orleans, "peacemaker" sandwiches were used to smooth over romantic quarrels. One party gave the other half a French roll slathered in butter and filled with fried oysters. Those were more robust times.

Nonetheless, with National Forgiveness Day, the fourth Sunday in June, rolling around once again, we thought some kind of alimentary amends-making should be available. So we took the peacemaker and turned it into something that really says "let's put this behind us." Actually it's now more like a po' boy, a kind of distant relative of the peacemaker. But the thought behind it is still kind. You'll forgive us for taking healthful liberties.

HAM-AND-OYSTER PO' BOYS

¼ cup all-purpose flour
2 large egg whites, lightly beaten
1 tablespoon water
½ cup dry breadcrumbs
12 shucked oysters, drained
1½ teaspoons vegetable oil
2 cups shredded iceberg lettuce
3 tablespoons low-fat tartar sauce
1 tablespoon fresh lemon juice
6 ounces thinly sliced smoked ham
8 (¼-inch-thick) slices tomato
4 (2½-ounce) hoagie rolls with sesame seeds, split and lightly toasted
4 lemon wedges (optional)

1. Place flour in a shallow dish. Combine egg whites and water in a small bowl. Place breadcrumbs in another shallow dish. Dredge oysters in flour. Dip oysters in egg white mixture, and dredge in breadcrumbs.
2. Heat oil in a large nonstick skillet over medium heat. Add breaded oysters to skillet; sauté 5 minutes on each side or until golden brown. Remove from heat.
3. Combine lettuce, tartar sauce, and lemon juice in a medium bowl. Arrange 1½ ounces ham and 2 tomato slices over bottom half of each roll; top each with 3 oysters, ½ cup lettuce mixture, and top halves of rolls. Garnish with lemon wedges, if desired. Serve immediately. Yield: 4 sandwiches.

CALORIES 416 (20% from fat); FAT 9.2g (sat 2.2g, mono 2.7g, poly 3.3g); PROTEIN 21.8g; CARB 60.7g; FIBER 2.7g; CHOL 51mg; IRON 6.3mg; SODIUM 1,421mg; CALC 111mg

Cinnamon Roles

This world-famous spice is finally making its American breakaway from the confines of toast and sticky buns.

As we continue in our never-ending search for new tastes, cinnamon is finding its way into savory dishes of all kinds. The spice's distinctive notes blend harmoniously with almost every kind of meat and fish, and perk up grains and vegetables in ways that can truly surprise your palate. The transformative genius of cinnamon has fascinated cooks around the world.

Technically, what we Americans buy in the supermarket, whether powdered or in sticks, is not "true" cinnamon *(Cinnamomum zeylanicum)*. It's cassia *(Cinnamomum cassia)*, dubbed "false" cinnamon by the French. The difference between the two is slight, being produced from similar kinds of trees. The flavor of cassia is somewhat stronger and coarser, but you have to pay close attention to notice. In Mexico and France, the milder taste of true cinnamon (called *canela*) is preferred, but the spice siblings have been so mixed and substituted over the last 4,000 years that in the United States, they're considered commercially interchangeable.

PICADILLO

This traditional Latin dish consists of a ground meat-tomato sauce flavored with sweet spices, raisins, olives or capers, and almonds. Serve it with warm flour tortillas.

- 1 teaspoon vegetable oil
- 1½ cups chopped onion
- 1 jalapeño pepper, seeded and finely chopped
- 1 large garlic clove, minced
- 1 pound ground sirloin
- 1½ cups chopped peeled Granny Smith apple (about 1 large)
- ½ cup water
- ¼ cup sliced pimento-stuffed olives
- ¼ cup raisins
- ¾ teaspoon salt
- ¼ teaspoon pepper
- 2 (3-inch) cinnamon sticks
- 1 (14.5-ounce) can diced tomatoes, undrained
- 3 tablespoons slivered almonds, toasted

1. Heat oil in a large Dutch oven over medium-high heat. Add onion; sauté 3 minutes. Add jalapeño pepper and garlic; sauté 1 minute. Add beef, and sauté 3 minutes or until browned, stirring to crumble. Stir in apple and next 7 ingredients; bring to a boil. Reduce heat, and simmer, uncovered, 30 minutes or until sauce is slightly thick. Remove from heat, discard cinnamon sticks, and stir in almonds. Yield: 5 servings (serving size: about 1 cup).

CALORIES 240 (30% from fat); FAT 8.1g (sat 2.2g, mono 3.7g, poly 1.2g); PROTEIN 21.7g; CARB 21.5g; FIBER 4.5g; CHOL 55mg; IRON 3.8mg; SODIUM 580mg; CALC 65mg

CINNAMON-APRICOT GLAZED SALMON

(pictured on page 149)

- 2 tablespoons low-sodium soy sauce
- 1 tablespoon minced peeled fresh ginger
- 2 (3-inch) cinnamon sticks
- 1 (12-ounce) can apricot nectar
- 4 (6-ounce) salmon fillets (about 1 inch thick)

1. Combine first 4 ingredients in a saucepan, and bring to a boil. Reduce heat, and simmer mixture until reduced to ¾ cup (about 30 minutes).

Strain apricot mixture through a sieve over a bowl, and discard solids.

2. Preheat broiler. Place salmon fillets on a broiler pan lined with foil; broil 5 minutes. Brush fish with ¼ cup apricot mixture. Broil 3 minutes or until lightly browned and fish flakes easily when tested with a fork. Serve fish with remaining apricot mixture. Yield: 4 servings (serving size: 5 ounces fish and about 2 tablespoons sauce).

CALORIES 357 (39% from fat); FAT 15.6g (sat 2.7g, mono 7.5g, poly 3.4g); PROTEIN 39g; CARB 12.2g; FIBER 0.5g; CHOL 123mg; IRON 1.1mg; SODIUM 291mg; CALC 16mg

VENETIAN FISH SALAD

- 2 tablespoons all-purpose flour
- 4 (6-ounce) orange roughy or other white fish fillets
- 2 teaspoons olive oil
- 1⅓ cups chopped tomato
- 1½ teaspoons grated orange zest
- ½ cup fresh orange juice
- ⅓ cup coarsely chopped red onion
- 1 teaspoon balsamic vinegar
- ½ teaspoon ground cinnamon
- ½ teaspoon salt
- 4 cups gourmet salad greens
- 1 ounce thinly sliced prosciutto or ham, cut into ½-inch-wide strips

1. Sprinkle flour over fish. Heat oil in a large nonstick skillet over medium heat until hot. Add fish; cook 3 minutes on each side or until fish flakes easily when tested with a fork. Remove fish from skillet, and keep warm.

2. Combine tomato and next 6 ingredients in a bowl. Combine 1 cup tomato mixture and salad greens in a large bowl; toss well.

3. Arrange 1 cup salad greens mixture on each of 4 plates; top each serving with 1 fillet and ¼ cup tomato mixture. Top evenly with prosciutto. Yield: 4 servings.

CALORIES 240 (18% from fat); FAT 4.8g (sat 0.6g, mono 3.1g, poly 0.5g); PROTEIN 35.9g; CARB 12.1g; FIBER 2.2g; CHOL 49mg; IRON 1.8mg; SODIUM 548mg; CALC 35mg

Caramelized Pork over Lettuce

Serve this Vietnamese-inspired dish with rice or Asian noodles (such as udon).

- 2 tablespoons sugar
- 2 tablespoons water
- 2 tablespoons fish sauce
- 1½ teaspoons vegetable oil, divided
  - Cooking spray
- 1½ pounds boned pork loin, cut into 1-inch cubes
- 1 (10½-ounce) can low-salt chicken broth
- ¼ teaspoon black pepper
- 1 (3-inch) cinnamon stick
- 2 cups (2-inch) sliced green onions
- 6 cups shredded romaine lettuce
- ¼ cup rice vinegar
- ¼ cup thinly sliced fresh basil
- ¼ cup minced fresh cilantro

1. Place sugar in a small, heavy saucepan over medium heat; cook 5 minutes or until golden (do not stir). Add water and fish sauce (mixture will splatter); remove from heat.
2. Heat 1 teaspoon oil in a large skillet coated with cooking spray over high heat. Add pork, and cook 4 minutes or until browned on all sides. Remove pork from skillet. Stir broth into skillet, scraping skillet to loosen browned bits. Return pork to skillet; add caramelized sugar mixture, black pepper, and cinnamon stick. Bring to a boil; cover, reduce heat, and simmer 1½ hours or until pork is tender. Remove from skillet, and keep warm.
3. Heat remaining ½ teaspoon oil in skillet; add green onions. Sauté 2 minutes or until lightly browned. Add to pork mixture; keep warm.
4. Combine lettuce and remaining 3 ingredients in a large bowl; toss well. Serve pork mixture over lettuce mixture. Yield: 6 servings (serving size: ½ cup pork and 1 cup lettuce mixture).

CALORIES 234 (39% from fat); FAT 10g (sat 3.3g, mono 4.2g, poly 1.5g); PROTEIN 25.8g; CARB 8.7g; FIBER 2.2g; CHOL 69mg; IRON 2.2mg; SODIUM 618mg; CALC 60mg

Mediterranean Spaghetti

Sweet spices such as cinnamon and nutmeg balance the pungent feta and Parmesan cheeses to give a bold, intriguing flavor to a familiar meat-and-pasta dish.

- ½ pound lean ground beef
- 2 cups chopped onion
- 1½ teaspoons dried oregano
- 2 garlic cloves, minced
- ½ cup dry red wine
- ¼ cup water
- ¾ teaspoon ground cinnamon
- ½ teaspoon salt
- ⅛ teaspoon ground nutmeg
- ⅛ teaspoon pepper
- 1 (14.5-ounce) can stewed tomatoes, undrained
- ¼ cup all-purpose flour
- 2 cups 1% low-fat milk
- ¼ teaspoon ground nutmeg
- 1 cup (4 ounces) crumbled feta cheese
- 2 tablespoons grated Parmesan cheese, divided
- 1 large egg, lightly beaten
- 2 tablespoons dry breadcrumbs, divided
  - Cooking spray
- 4 cups cooked spaghetti (about 8 ounces uncooked pasta)
  - Fresh oregano sprigs (optional)

1. Preheat oven to 375°.
2. Heat a large nonstick skillet over medium-high heat. Add first 4 ingredients, and sauté 5 minutes. Add wine and next 6 ingredients. Bring mixture to a boil; reduce heat, and simmer 10 minutes or until thick.
3. Combine flour, milk, and ¼ teaspoon nutmeg in a medium saucepan; bring to a boil. Reduce heat, and cook 7 minutes or until thick, stirring constantly. Remove milk mixture from heat. Stir in feta cheese, 1 tablespoon Parmesan cheese, and egg.
4. Sprinkle 1 tablespoon breadcrumbs in a 2-quart casserole coated with cooking spray. Place 2 cups spaghetti in casserole; top with 2 cups beef mixture and 1 cup milk mixture. Repeat layers. Combine remaining 1 tablespoon Parmesan cheese and 1 tablespoon breadcrumbs; sprinkle over casserole. Bake at 375° for 30 minutes or until golden brown. Let stand 5 minutes. Garnish with fresh oregano, if desired. Yield: 6 servings (serving size: about 1⅓ cups).

CALORIES 365 (23% from fat); FAT 9.4g (sat 4.8g, mono 2.7g, poly 0.7g); PROTEIN 22.2g; CARB 47.4g; FIBER 3.2g; CHOL 80mg; IRON 3.7mg; SODIUM 709mg; CALC 281mg

Stifado

Stifado (stee-FAH-doh) is a Greek casserole stew containing wine, garlic, and cinnamon.

- 1 teaspoon vegetable oil
- 1½ pounds boned rump roast, cut into 1-inch cubes
- 2 teaspoons dried oregano
- 3 garlic cloves, minced
- ½ cup dry red wine
- ¾ teaspoon ground cinnamon
- 1 tablespoon sugar
- 2 tablespoons red wine vinegar
- ¾ teaspoon salt
- 4 whole cloves
- 1 (14.5-ounce) can no-salt-added stewed tomatoes, undrained
- 1 (14¼-ounce) can fat-free beef broth
- 6 cups (⅓-inch-thick) sliced onion, separated into rings

1. Heat oil in a Dutch oven over medium-high heat. Add half of beef, and cook 5 minutes or until browned, turning occasionally. Remove from pan, and keep warm. Repeat procedure with remaining beef cubes.
2. Return beef cubes to pan. Add oregano and garlic; cook 1 minute. Stir in wine and next 7 ingredients; bring to a boil. Cover, reduce heat, and simmer 1 hour. Add onion, and bring to a boil. Partially cover, reduce heat, and simmer 1 hour or until beef is tender. Discard cloves. Yield: 6 servings (serving size: 1 cup).

CALORIES 245 (21% from fat); FAT 5.6g (sat 1.8g, mono 2.1g, poly 0.7g); PROTEIN 28.3g; CARB 18.5g; FIBER 2.3g; CHOL 65mg; IRON 3.5mg; SODIUM 371mg; CALC 62mg

CHINESE RED-COOKED CHICKEN THIGHS

Red-cooking is a popular Chinese technique of braising meat or poultry in a soy-based mixture containing spices such as cinnamon. The method gives dishes a reddish color and subtle flavor.

¼ cup sherry
3 tablespoons sugar
3 tablespoons low-sodium soy sauce
1 tablespoon water
1 teaspoon fennel seeds, crushed
5 (¼-inch) slices peeled fresh ginger
3 orange rind strips
2 (3-inch) cinnamon sticks
8 chicken thighs (about 2 pounds), skinned
2 ounces uncooked bean threads (cellophane noodles)
1 cup boiling water

1. Combine first 8 ingredients in a Dutch oven; bring to a boil. Reduce heat; simmer, uncovered, 10 minutes. Add chicken; partially cover, and simmer 45 minutes, turning chicken occasionally. Discard cinnamon sticks and orange rind.
2. Combine noodles and boiling water in a bowl; let stand 5 minutes or until soft. Drain. Serve chicken over noodles. Yield: 4 servings (serving size: 2 chicken thighs and 1 cup noodles).

CALORIES 283 (31% from fat); FAT 9.8g (sat 2.6g, mono 3.6g, poly 2.2g); PROTEIN 27.3g; CARB 17.6g; FIBER 0.1g; CHOL 92mg; IRON 1.5mg; SODIUM 386mg; CALC 31mg

ROASTED CHICKEN WITH MEXICAN MOLE SAUCE

1 (10½-ounce) can low-salt chicken broth, divided
2 (6-inch) corn tortillas, torn
2 teaspoons vegetable oil, divided
½ cup chopped onion
½ teaspoon dried oregano
1 large garlic clove, minced
2 tablespoons chili powder
1 tablespoon all-purpose flour
1 (14.5-ounce) can no-salt-added stewed tomatoes, undrained
1 tablespoon unsweetened cocoa
2 tablespoons peanut butter
1 tablespoon cider vinegar
1 teaspoon sugar
1 teaspoon ground cinnamon
½ teaspoon salt
⅛ teaspoon ground cloves
8 skinned chicken quarters (about 3 pounds)
Cooking spray
4 teaspoons sesame seeds, toasted

1. Preheat oven to 350°.
2. Bring 1 cup chicken broth to a boil in a saucepan. Add tortillas; remove from heat.
3. Heat 1 teaspoon oil in a large nonstick skillet over medium-high heat. Add onion, and sauté 3 minutes. Add oregano and garlic; cook 30 seconds. Stir in chili powder and flour; cook 30 seconds. Stir in tortilla mixture; bring to a boil. Remove from heat; cool slightly. Combine tortilla-onion mixture, tomatoes, and next 7 ingredients in a blender or food processor; process until smooth.
4. Heat 1 teaspoon oil in skillet over medium-high heat until hot. Add tomato mixture, and cook 2 minutes (do not stir). Stir in remaining broth; reduce heat, and simmer 5 minutes, stirring frequently.
5. Place chicken quarters, meaty sides up, in a 13 x 9-inch baking dish coated with cooking spray. Pour tomato mixture over chicken. Insert meat thermometer into meaty part of thigh, making sure not to touch bone. Bake at 350° for 40 minutes or until thermometer registers 180°. Sprinkle chicken with sesame seeds. Yield: 8 servings (serving size: 1 chicken quarter and about ⅓ cup sauce).

CALORIES 407 (38% from fat); FAT 17g (sat 4.2g, mono 6.1g, poly 4.5g); PROTEIN 50.7g; CARB 11.6g; FIBER 1.6g; CHOL 146mg; IRON 3.3mg; SODIUM 363mg; CALC 84mg

SPICY SESAME-CRUSTED CHICKEN

In this dish, chicken breast halves are marinated in a sweet-and-savory spice rub and sautéed with a sesame-seed coating, giving them a nutty flavor and crisp crust.

1 tablespoon sugar
1 tablespoon low-sodium soy sauce
1 tablespoon chopped peeled fresh ginger
1 teaspoon ground cinnamon
1 teaspoon pepper
½ teaspoon fennel seeds, crushed
¼ teaspoon salt
1 garlic clove, crushed
4 (4-ounce) skinned, boned chicken breast halves
2 tablespoons all-purpose flour
1 large egg white, lightly beaten
2 tablespoons sesame seeds
2 teaspoons vegetable oil
2 tablespoons water
1 tablespoon fresh lemon juice
1 tablespoon low-sodium soy sauce
Continued

1. Combine first 8 ingredients in a large zip-top plastic bag; add chicken. Seal bag; marinate in refrigerator 8 hours.
2. Remove chicken from bag; dredge in flour. Dip chicken in egg white; sprinkle with sesame seeds. Heat oil in a large nonstick skillet over medium-high heat. Add chicken, and cook 4 minutes on each side or until done.
3. Combine water, juice, and 1 tablespoon soy sauce; drizzle over chicken. Yield: 4 servings (serving size: 1 chicken breast half and 1 tablespoon sauce).

CALORIES 211 (26% from fat); FAT 6g (sat 1.1g, mono 1.9g, poly 2.4g); PROTEIN 28.4g; CARB 9g; FIBER 0.8g; CHOL 66mg; IRON 2.1mg; SODIUM 430mg; CALC 72mg

The Turkey of Summer

Benjamin Franklin wanted it to be the national bird. But the bald eagle won out, and the turkey found itself evolving instead into a national dish—and one served primarily during only a couple of holiday months. Up until about 1980, half of U.S. turkey consumption occurred between October and December.

That trend has changed dramatically, however. The National Turkey Federation reports that last year the summer and spring quarters commanded nearly half (46%) of the turkey market. The traditional high season accounted for 34%.

The reasons are obvious: Americans have cut back on beef but that doesn't mean they want an uninterrupted diet of chicken and fish. Turkey has a robust flavor, so it makes a nice switch, and it's versatile enough to pep up summer meals. And with precut, precooked, economically priced turkey on the market, it's not as if you have to roast a 20-pounder all day long during the heat of summer. As Americans are apparently learning, Ben Franklin was on to a good thing.

APRICOT-NUT TURKEY-SALAD SANDWICHES

1½   cups shredded cooked turkey (about 6 ounces)
¼   cup thinly sliced celery
¼   cup light mayonnaise
2   tablespoons chopped unsalted cashews
2   tablespoons chopped dried apricots
2   tablespoons chopped green onions
2   tablespoons raisins
2   tablespoons plain low-fat yogurt
⅛   teaspoon salt
⅛   teaspoon black pepper
4   leaf lettuce leaves
8   (1-ounce) slices pumpernickel bread

1. Combine first 10 ingredients in a bowl. Place a lettuce leaf on each of 4 bread slices. Spread ½ cup turkey mixture on each of 4 bread slices; top with remaining bread slices. Yield: 4 sandwiches.

CALORIES 286 (23% from fat); FAT 7.2g (sat 1.3g, mono 2.5g, poly 2.3g); PROTEIN 17.6g; CARB 40.2g; FIBER 4.4g; CHOL 35mg; IRON 2.7mg; SODIUM 541mg; CALC 81mg

TURKEY TENDERLOINS WITH PAPAYA SALSA

1¼   cups diced peeled papaya
½   cup diced red onion
½   cup halved cherry tomatoes
2   tablespoons chopped fresh cilantro
1   teaspoon grated lime rind
1½   tablespoons fresh lime juice
1   teaspoon grated peeled fresh ginger
¼   cup raspberry or white wine vinegar
2   tablespoons fresh lime juice
1½   tablespoons Dijon mustard
1   tablespoon chopped fresh or 1 teaspoon dried rosemary
1   tablespoon minced fresh or 1 teaspoon dried thyme
2   teaspoons olive oil
2   (½-pound) turkey tenderloins
Cooking spray

1. Combine first 7 ingredients in a bowl; toss well. Cover and chill.
2. Combine vinegar and next 6 ingredients in a large zip-top plastic bag. Seal bag; marinate in refrigerator 30 minutes. Remove turkey from bag, reserving marinade. Preheat broiler. Place turkey on a broiler pan coated with cooking spray; broil 10 minutes on each side or until turkey is done, basting frequently with marinade. Cut tenderloins into thin slices, and serve with papaya salsa. Yield: 4 servings (serving size: 3 ounces turkey and ½ cup salsa).

CALORIES 200 (26% from fat); FAT 5.8g (sat 1.2g, mono 2.2g, poly 1g); PROTEIN 26.1g; CARB 10.2g; FIBER 1.7g; CHOL 59mg; IRON 2mg; SODIUM 227mg; CALC 47mg

GLAZED TURKEY CUTLETS AND BELL PEPPERS

¼   cup low-salt chicken broth
3   tablespoons balsamic vinegar
2   teaspoons honey
¼   teaspoon salt
¼   teaspoon black pepper
1   pound (¼-inch-thick) turkey breast cutlets
2   teaspoons olive oil
2   garlic cloves, minced
1   red bell pepper, seeded and cut into strips
1   green bell pepper, seeded and cut into strips
4   cups hot cooked rice

1. Combine first 3 ingredients in a bowl.
2. Sprinkle salt and black pepper over both sides of cutlets. Heat oil in a large nonstick skillet over medium-high heat until hot. Add garlic; sauté 30 seconds. Add cutlets; cook 2 minutes on each side or until done. Remove from skillet; keep warm. Reduce heat to medium; add peppers, and sauté 2 minutes. Add broth mixture to skillet; cook 30 seconds, stirring constantly. Spoon sauce and peppers over cutlets. Serve with rice. Yield: 4 servings (serving size: 3 ounces turkey, ⅓ cup bell peppers, and 1 cup rice).

CALORIES 291 (14% from fat); FAT 4.6g (sat 1g, mono 2g, poly 0.8g); PROTEIN 29.5g; CARB 31.2g; FIBER 1.4g; CHOL 68mg; IRON 3mg; SODIUM 227mg; CALC 32mg

SPICY TURKEY FAJITAS

1 cup (1-inch) diagonally sliced
 green onions
2 teaspoons vegetable oil
½ teaspoon garlic powder
½ teaspoon paprika
½ teaspoon ground allspice
¼ teaspoon salt
⅛ teaspoon ground red pepper
1 pound (¼-inch-thick) turkey
 breast cutlets, cut into
 ¼-inch-wide strips
4 (8-inch) flour tortillas
1 teaspoon vegetable oil
2 large ripe plantains (about
 1¼ pounds), peeled and thinly
 sliced
⅛ teaspoon ground red pepper

1. Combine first 8 ingredients in a zip-top plastic bag; seal bag, and shake well to coat. Marinate in refrigerator 20 minutes.
2. Warm tortillas according to package directions.
3. Heat 1 teaspoon oil in a large non-stick skillet over medium-high heat. Add plantains; sauté 5 minutes or until golden. Add ⅛ teaspoon red pepper; stir well. Remove plantains from skillet; keep warm. Add turkey mixture to skillet; sauté 4 minutes or until turkey is done. Divide turkey mixture evenly among tortillas, and roll up. Serve with plantains. Yield: 4 servings (serving size: 1 fajita and ½ cup plantains).

CALORIES 408 (19% from fat); FAT 8.7g (sat 1.7g, mono 2.7g, poly 3.5g); PROTEIN 31.9g; CARB 51.2g; FIBER 2.2g; CHOL 68mg; IRON 3.8mg; SODIUM 448mg; CALC 94mg

TURKEY FRIED RICE

3 tablespoons light brown sugar
1 teaspoon minced peeled fresh
 ginger
¼ teaspoon dried crushed red
 pepper
½ cup rice vinegar
3 tablespoons low-sodium soy sauce
2 tablespoons water
1 tablespoon crunchy peanut
 butter

2 teaspoons vegetable oil
1 pound (¼-inch-thick) turkey
 breast cutlets, cut into thin
 strips
2 garlic cloves, minced
4 cups cooked rice
¼ cup chopped green onions
3 tablespoons chopped unsalted,
 dry-roasted peanuts
Sliced green onions (optional)

1. Combine first 7 ingredients in a bowl; stir with a whisk until blended.
2. Heat oil in a large nonstick skillet over medium-high heat. Add turkey and garlic; stir-fry 3 minutes or until turkey is done. Add rice; stir-fry 2 minutes. Remove from skillet, and keep warm.
3. Add vinegar mixture to skillet; bring to a boil, and cook 3 minutes. Return turkey mixture to skillet; stir-fry 1 minute. Remove from heat; stir in ¼ cup chopped green onions and peanuts. Garnish with sliced green onions, if desired. Yield: 6 servings (serving size: 1 cup).

CALORIES 318 (18% from fat); FAT 6.4g (sat 1.2g, mono 2.4g, poly 2.2g); PROTEIN 23g; CARB 40.1g; FIBER 1.2g; CHOL 46mg; IRON 2.5mg; SODIUM 307mg; CALC 38mg

Strawberry Winners

Fresh strawberries make summer dessert winners.

Strawberries belong to America, where they grow in every state, including Alaska. Most are red, plump, and juicy descendants of an American hybrid perfected in the late 19th century. Strawberries encapsulate the very spirit of our country, achieving greatness without pretense. They inspire a sense of celebration, too, as witnessed by all the strawberry festivals held across the country. Almost all the events crown their own queen, and it's no wonder the berries are linked to beauty: They're sweet to the taste, delicately perfumed, and shaped like hearts.

GLAZED-STRAWBERRY CREAM PIE SQUARES

1⅓ cups graham cracker crumbs
 (about 9 cookie sheets)
3 tablespoons sugar
2 tablespoons stick margarine or
 butter, melted
1 tablespoon vanilla extract
Cooking spray
1½ cups 1% low-fat milk
⅓ cup sugar
5 tablespoons cornstarch, divided
¼ teaspoon salt
1 large egg, lightly beaten
½ cup low-fat sour cream
1 tablespoon stick margarine or
 butter
2 teaspoons vanilla extract,
 divided
2½ cups quartered strawberries
2 tablespoons water
1 tablespoon lemon juice
½ cup sugar
6 cups halved strawberries

1. Preheat oven to 350°.
2. Combine first 4 ingredients in a bowl; toss with a fork until moist. Press into bottom of an 11 x 7-inch baking dish coated with cooking spray. Bake at 350° for 10 minutes; cool on a wire rack.
3. Combine milk and ⅓ cup sugar in a medium, heavy saucepan; cook milk mixture over medium-high heat to 180° or until tiny bubbles form around edge (do not boil). Remove from heat. Combine 3 tablespoons cornstarch, salt, and egg in a bowl; stir with a whisk until smooth. Gradually add hot milk mixture; return milk mixture to pan. Bring to a boil over medium heat; cook 1 minute, stirring constantly. Remove from heat; stir in sour cream, 1 tablespoon margarine, and 1 teaspoon vanilla. Spread over crust; cover with plastic wrap. Chill.
4. Combine quartered strawberries and water in a medium saucepan; bring to a boil, mashing strawberries with a potato masher. Strain mixture through a sieve over a bowl, reserving 1 cup strawberry liquid; discard solids in sieve. Stir lemon juice into strawberry liquid.

Continued

5. Combine ½ cup sugar and remaining 2 tablespoons cornstarch in saucepan; add reserved strawberry liquid, stirring with a whisk. Bring to a boil, and cook 1 minute, stirring constantly. Remove from heat, and stir in remaining 1 teaspoon vanilla. Combine strawberry mixture and strawberry halves in a large bowl, tossing to coat. Spoon over chilled custard mixture. Cover and chill at least 2 hours. Yield: 9 servings.

CALORIES 294 (26% from fat); FAT 8.4g (sat 2.6g, mono 3.1g, poly 2.1g); PROTEIN 4.2g; CARB 50.7g; FIBER 3.7g; CHOL 31mg; IRON 1.3mg; SODIUM 238mg; CALC 94mg

OLD-FASHIONED STRAWBERRY SHORTCAKES

3½ cups halved strawberries, divided
⅓ cup sugar
⅓ cup orange juice
2 teaspoons vanilla extract
1 teaspoon lemon juice
1¼ cups all-purpose flour
3 tablespoons sugar
1 teaspoon baking powder
¼ teaspoon baking soda
⅛ teaspoon salt
3 tablespoons chilled stick margarine or butter, cut into small pieces
½ cup low-fat buttermilk
Cooking spray
6 tablespoons frozen reduced-calorie whipped topping, thawed
Whole strawberries (optional)

1. Combine 1 cup strawberry halves, ⅓ cup sugar, orange juice, vanilla, and lemon juice in a bowl; mash with a potato masher. Stir in remaining 2½ cups strawberry halves. Cover and chill.
2. Preheat oven to 425°.
3. Lightly spoon flour into dry measuring cups; level with a knife. Combine flour and next 4 ingredients in a bowl; cut in margarine with a pastry blender or 2 knives until mixture resembles coarse meal. Add buttermilk, stirring just until moist (dough will be sticky).

4. Turn dough out onto a lightly floured surface; knead lightly 4 times with floured hands. Pat dough into a 6 x 4-inch rectangle. Cut into 6 squares. Place 1 inch apart on a baking sheet coated with cooking spray. Bake at 425° for 12 minutes. Cool on a wire rack.
5. Split shortcakes in half horizontally using a serrated knife; place each bottom half on a dessert plate. Spoon ¼ cup strawberry mixture over each bottom half. Top with shortcake tops; spoon ¼ cup strawberry mixture over each top. Top each serving with 1 tablespoon whipped topping; garnish with whole strawberries, if desired. Yield: 6 servings.

CALORIES 270 (24% from fat); FAT 7.2g (sat 1.9g, mono 2.7g, poly 2.1g); PROTEIN 4.3g; CARB 47.3g; FIBER 3g; CHOL 0mg; IRON 1.7mg; SODIUM 183mg; CALC 93mg

STRAWBERRY-SPICE CAKE WITH CREAM CHEESE FROSTING

1½ cups sugar
¼ cup stick margarine or butter, softened
2 large eggs
1 large egg white
2¼ cups all-purpose flour
¾ teaspoon baking powder
¾ teaspoon baking soda
¾ teaspoon ground cinnamon
½ teaspoon salt
⅛ teaspoon black pepper
⅛ teaspoon ground cloves
¾ cup chopped strawberries
¾ cup low-fat buttermilk
1½ teaspoons vanilla extract
Cooking spray
Cream Cheese Frosting
2 cups sliced strawberries

1. Preheat oven to 350°.
2. Beat sugar and margarine at medium speed of a mixer until well-blended (about 5 minutes). Add eggs and egg white, 1 at a time, beating well after each addition. Lightly spoon flour into dry measuring cups; level with a knife. Combine flour and next 6 ingredients in a bowl. Mash chopped strawberries with a potato masher; combine

mashed strawberries, buttermilk, and vanilla. Add flour mixture to sugar mixture alternately with mashed strawberry mixture, beginning and ending with flour mixture. Pour batter into a 13 x 9-inch baking pan coated with cooking spray. Bake at 350° for 30 minutes or until a wooden pick inserted in center comes out clean. Cool cake in pan on a wire rack.
3. Spread cake with Cream Cheese Frosting; arrange sliced strawberries over top of cake. Store loosely covered in refrigerator. Yield: 16 servings.

CALORIES 292 (14% from fat); FAT 4.5g (sat 1g, mono 1.8g, poly 1.3g); PROTEIN 5.5g; CARB 57.8g; FIBER 1.2g; CHOL 30mg; IRON 1.1mg; SODIUM 275mg; CALC 80mg

Cream Cheese Frosting:

2 teaspoons stick margarine or butter, softened
½ (8-ounce) block fat-free cream cheese, chilled
¼ teaspoon vanilla extract
¼ teaspoon lemon juice
3 cups sifted powdered sugar

1. Combine first 4 ingredients in a large bowl, and beat at high speed of a mixer until fluffy. Add powdered sugar; beat at low speed just until blended (do not overbeat). Yield: 1⅓ cups.

STRAWBERRY WAFFLES WITH BUTTERED STRAWBERRY SAUCE

1 cup all-purpose flour
2 teaspoons sugar
1 teaspoon baking powder
⅛ teaspoon salt
1 cup sliced strawberries
2 tablespoons 1% low-fat milk
1 tablespoon vegetable oil
¼ teaspoon vanilla extract
1 large egg
Cooking spray
Buttered Strawberry Sauce

1. Lightly spoon flour into a dry measuring cup; level with a knife. Combine

flour and next 3 ingredients in a medium bowl; make a well in center of mixture. Place strawberries and next 4 ingredients in a blender; process until smooth. Add strawberry mixture to flour mixture, stirring just until moist.

2. Coat a waffle iron with cooking spray; preheat. Spoon about ¼ cup batter per 4-inch waffle onto hot waffle iron; spread batter to edges. Cook 5 to 6 minutes or until steaming stops; repeat with remaining batter. Serve hot with warm Buttered Strawberry Sauce. Yield: 6 servings (serving size: 1 waffle and ½ cup sauce).

CALORIES 231 (22% from fat); FAT 5.7g (sat 1.1g, mono 1.9g, poly 2.1g); PROTEIN 4g; CARB 41.2g; FIBER 2.8g; CHOL 37mg; IRON 1.7mg; SODIUM 86mg; CALC 72mg

Buttered Strawberry Sauce:

¼ cup sugar
2 teaspoons cornstarch
1 teaspoon lemon juice
1 (11.5-ounce) can strawberry-banana nectar
1 tablespoon stick margarine or butter
½ teaspoon vanilla extract
2½ cups sliced strawberries

1. Combine first 4 ingredients in a medium saucepan. Bring to a boil; cook 1 minute, stirring constantly. Remove from heat; stir in margarine, vanilla, and strawberries. Yield: 3 cups (serving size: ½ cup).

STRAWBERRY-BUTTERMILK ICE CREAM

Strawberry extract enhances the flavor of this recipe, but it can be omitted.

2¼ cups strawberries
½ cup sugar
¼ cup thawed orange juice concentrate, undiluted
2 teaspoons vanilla extract
1 teaspoon strawberry extract (optional)
1 large ripe banana
2 cups low-fat buttermilk

1. Place first 6 ingredients in a food processor; process until smooth. Combine strawberry mixture and buttermilk in freezer can of an ice-cream freezer; freeze according to manufacturer's instructions. Spoon ice cream into a freezer-safe container; cover and freeze 1 hour or until firm. Yield: 11 servings (serving size: ½ cup).

CALORIES 94 (9% from fat); FAT 0.9g (sat 0.5g, mono 0.2g, poly 0.1g); PROTEIN 2.1g; CARB 19.7g; FIBER 1.3g; CHOL 0mg; IRON 0.2mg; SODIUM 24mg; CALC 62mg

READER RECIPES

Tailored Tex-Mex

Our readers share recipes that capture Mexican and Tex-Mex flavors with a few homespun twists.

BLACK BEAN SALAD

—Cathey Brown, Parker, Colorado

1½ tablespoons minced fresh cilantro
1 tablespoon chopped fresh parsley
1 tablespoon fresh lime juice
¼ teaspoon salt
¼ teaspoon black pepper
1 (15-ounce) can black beans, rinsed and drained
½ cup chopped tomato
¼ cup diced peeled avocado
2 tablespoons chopped green onions
1 tablespoon chopped seeded jalapeño pepper
4 cups gourmet salad greens

1. Combine first 5 ingredients in a large bowl; stir well with a whisk. Add beans and next 4 ingredients; toss well. Cover and chill 2 hours. Serve over salad greens. Yield: 4 servings (serving size: ½ cup bean mixture and 1 cup salad greens).

CALORIES 112 (17% from fat); FAT 2.1g (sat 0.4g, mono 1g, poly 0.4g); PROTEIN 6.8g; CARB 18.3g; FIBER 4.2g; CHOL 0mg; IRON 2.3mg; SODIUM 320mg; CALC 46mg

CONFETTI-STUFFED BURRITOS

These burritos have a nontraditional filling, so my husband and I both can enjoy them.
—Jody Williams, St. Joseph, Michigan

2½ cups (½-inch) cubed peeled sweet potato
¾ cup low-salt chicken broth
½ cup coarsely chopped onion
2 garlic cloves, minced
¾ cup fresh corn kernels (about 2 ears)
¾ cup drained canned black beans, partially mashed
½ cup chopped red bell pepper
¼ cup minced fresh cilantro
1½ tablespoons fresh lime juice
¾ cup canned fat-free refried beans
8 (8-inch) flour tortillas
½ cup fat-free sour cream
½ cup bottled salsa
Chopped fresh cilantro (optional)

1. Preheat oven to 350°.
2. Combine sweet potato and broth in a large nonstick skillet. Bring to a simmer over medium-low heat; cover and cook 7 minutes or until tender. Add chopped onion and garlic; cook 2 minutes. Add corn and next 4 ingredients; simmer, uncovered, 6 minutes or until thoroughly heated. Combine sweet potato mixture and refried beans in a medium bowl. Spoon about ½ cup sweet potato mixture down center of each tortilla, and roll up. Place burritos in a 13 x 9-inch baking dish; cover with foil.
3. Bake at 350° for 15 minutes or until thoroughly heated. Serve each burrito with 1 tablespoon sour cream and 1 tablespoon salsa. Sprinkle each burrito with chopped fresh cilantro, if desired. Yield: 8 servings.

CALORIES 251 (14% from fat); FAT 3.8g (sat 0.6g, mono 1.4g, poly 1.5g); PROTEIN 8.1g; CARB 46.4g; FIBER 4.6g; CHOL 0mg; IRON 2.6mg; SODIUM 328mg; CALC 87mg

TURKEY ENCHILADAS

Every year we rent a villa in the mountains above Acapulco. I love the food. At first, I couldn't quite imagine pecans in an enchilada. But trust me, it tastes great.

—Michelle Battin, Washington, Michigan

 2 teaspoons stick margarine or butter
 ¼ cup chopped onion
 3 tablespoons chopped pecans, divided
 1 (8-ounce) block fat-free cream cheese, softened
 1 tablespoon fat-free milk
 ¼ teaspoon salt
 ¼ teaspoon ground cumin
 2 cups chopped cooked turkey breast (about ½ pound)
 ¼ cup chopped fresh cilantro
 6 (8-inch) flour tortillas
 Cooking spray
 1½ cups fat-free milk
 ½ cup fat-free sour cream
 ¼ cup chopped pickled jalapeño peppers
 1 (10¾-ounce) can condensed reduced-fat, reduced-sodium cream of chicken soup, undiluted
 ½ cup (2 ounces) shredded part-skim mozzarella cheese

1. Preheat oven to 350°.
2. Melt margarine in a large nonstick skillet over medium-high heat. Add onion and 2 tablespoons pecans; cook 3 minutes or until onion is tender and pecans are toasted. Remove from heat.
3. Combine cream cheese and next 3 ingredients in a large bowl. Stir in onion mixture, turkey, and cilantro. Spread about ⅓ cup turkey mixture onto each tortilla; roll up, and place, seam sides down, in a 13 x 9-inch baking dish coated with cooking spray.
4. Combine 1½ cups milk, sour cream, jalapeños, and soup in a bowl. Spoon soup mixture over tortillas. Cover with foil; bake at 350° for 35 minutes. Remove foil; sprinkle with mozzarella and remaining 1 tablespoon pecans. Bake an additional 5 minutes

or until cheese melts. Yield: 6 servings (serving size: 1 enchilada).

CALORIES 376 (27% from fat); FAT 11.1g (sat 2.8g, mono 4.4g, poly 2.9g); PROTEIN 27.8g; CARB 38.7g; FIBER 1.9g; CHOL 46mg; IRON 2.4mg; SODIUM 977mg; CALC 320mg

CHEESE-AND-CHICKEN ENCHILADAS

We lightened the original version by using reduced-fat cheese and cream cheese. It's so good you can't even tell the difference.

—Nancy Krogman, Ridgecrest, California

 Cooking spray
 1 cup chopped onion
 1½ cups shredded cooked chicken breast (about ½ pound)
 1 cup (4 ounces) shredded reduced-fat sharp Cheddar cheese, divided
 1 cup bottled picante sauce
 3 ounces ⅓-less-fat cream cheese (Neufchâtel) (about ⅓ cup)
 1 teaspoon ground cumin
 8 (6-inch) flour tortillas
 1½ cups bottled green taco sauce

1. Preheat oven to 350°.
2. Place a large nonstick skillet coated with cooking spray over medium heat until hot. Add onion, and sauté 6 minutes or until tender. Add chicken, ½ cup Cheddar cheese, picante sauce, cream cheese, and cumin. Cook 3 minutes or until cheese melts. Spoon about ⅓ cup chicken mixture down center of each tortilla, and roll up. Place enchiladas in a 13 x 9-inch baking dish; drizzle with taco sauce, and sprinkle with remaining ½ cup Cheddar cheese. Cover and bake at 350° for 15 minutes or until cheese melts. Serve immediately. Yield: 8 servings (serving size: 1 enchilada).

CALORIES 305 (24% from fat); FAT 8.2g (sat 3.7g, mono 2.6g, poly 1.3g); PROTEIN 15.4g; CARB 40.4g; FIBER 1.5g; CHOL 34mg; IRON 2mg; SODIUM 922mg; CALC 194mg

CHICKEN-SPINACH ENCHILADA CASSEROLE

I enjoy cooking healthfully for my husband and my 1-year-old son, Cole.

—Shanna Fuller, Branson, Missouri

 Cooking spray
 1 (8-ounce) package mushrooms, sliced
 4 (4-ounce) skinned, boned chicken breast halves
 1½ cups (6 ounces) shredded reduced-fat sharp Cheddar cheese, divided
 1 cup low-fat sour cream
 ¼ teaspoon salt
 ¼ teaspoon black pepper
 1 (10¾-ounce) can condensed reduced-fat, reduced-sodium cream of mushroom soup, undiluted
 8 (8-inch) flour tortillas
 1 (10-ounce) package frozen chopped spinach, thawed, drained, and squeezed dry

1. Preheat oven to 350°.
2. Place a large nonstick skillet coated with cooking spray over medium-high heat until hot. Add mushrooms; sauté 4 minutes. Remove from skillet. Recoat skillet with cooking spray; place over medium-high heat until hot. Add chicken; cook 4 minutes on each side or until done. Remove chicken from skillet; let cool slightly. Cut chicken into 1-inch cubes. Combine chicken, ¾ cup cheese, sour cream, salt, pepper, and one-half can mushroom soup.
3. Warm tortillas according to package directions. Spoon about ⅓ cup chicken mixture down center of each tortilla; roll up. Place in a 13 x 9-inch baking dish coated with cooking spray; top with remaining soup, spreading evenly. Layer mushrooms and spinach over tortillas; sprinkle with remaining ¾ cup cheese. Bake, covered, at 350° for 30 minutes. Uncover; bake an additional 5 minutes or until thoroughly heated. Yield: 8 servings (serving size: 1 enchilada).

CALORIES 356 (32% from fat); FAT 12.7g (sat 5.6g, mono 3.9g, poly 2.2g); PROTEIN 26.3g; CARB 33.5g; FIBER 3g; CHOL 61mg; IRON 3.1mg; SODIUM 679mg; CALC 336mg

Cinnamon-Apricot Glazed Salmon (page 141)

Farmers' Market Chicken (page 159)

Glazed Plum-Raspberry Kuchen (page 154)

Yellow-Pepper Soup (page 158)

*Green Bean-and-Tomato
Salad with Roasted-Tomato
Dressing (page 159)*

Provençale Pepper-Chicken Salad (page 163)

Minestrone Ragoût over Polenta (page 164)

Grilled Vegetables with Balsamic Vinaigrette (page 156)

Kuchen, Kaffee, und Kultur

These German-style coffeecakes are irresistible on both sides of the Atlantic.

Kaffee und Kuchen is in a sacred ritual that's at the heart of German food, one that cuts across lines of class, age, and occupation.

Translated, it's "coffee and cake," but this is about as accurate as describing "afternoon tea" in England as a cup of leaves steeped in hot water. Kaffee und Kuchen (KOO-khen) is the quintessential *Mittagspause,* the pause in the middle of the day, and from 2 to 4 in the afternoon, it's the primary activity of an amazing number of Germans.

Kuchens are flat cakes, baked on baking sheets and usually cut into 2 x 4-inch rectangles. But other pans and shapes are also used, especially in other countries. The variety is as staggering as it is seasonal: Most kuchens are made with fruit in season—particularly strawberries. In the winter, dried fruits are used, along with such standbys as chocolate, custards, and poppy seeds.

And not all kuchens are sweet. Swabia, the southwestern section of Germany that is home to some of the country's best food, is known for its *Zwiebelkuchen,* or onion cake, a hearty fall specialty that is most frequently served at dinnertime.

Think of kuchen as coffeecake if you want, or think of it as an easily prepared delicacy with an Old World flavor.

PLUM-STREUSEL KUCHEN

Almost every German cook's repertoire contains a plum kuchen. Any type of plum will work in this recipe.

- 1⅔ cups all-purpose flour, divided
- ½ cup sugar
- ½ teaspoon ground cinnamon
- 1 tablespoon vegetable oil
- 2 teaspoons light-colored corn syrup
- ⅓ cup sugar
- 1 teaspoon baking powder
- ¼ teaspoon salt
- ¼ cup chilled stick margarine or butter, cut into small pieces
- ½ cup plain fat-free yogurt
- 2 tablespoons water
- 1½ teaspoons vanilla extract
- ¾ teaspoon grated lemon rind
- 1 large egg, lightly beaten
- Cooking spray
- 2 cups sliced plums (about ¾ pound)

1. Preheat oven to 400°.
2. Lightly spoon flour into dry measuring cups; level with a knife.
3. Place ⅓ cup flour, ½ cup sugar, and cinnamon in a food processor; pulse mixture 2 or 3 times. With processor on, slowly add oil and corn syrup through food chute, processing until mixture resembles coarse meal. Remove streusel mixture from food processor, and set aside.
4. Place remaining 1⅓ cups flour, ⅓ cup sugar, baking powder, and salt in food processor; pulse mixture 2 or 3 times. Add margarine; process until mixture resembles coarse meal. Place margarine mixture in a large bowl.
5. Combine yogurt and next 4 ingredients, stirring with a whisk. Stir yogurt mixture into margarine mixture until blended. Spoon batter into a 9-inch round cake pan coated with cooking spray. Sprinkle half of streusel mixture evenly over batter. Top with plums, arranging in a circular pattern. Sprinkle remaining streusel mixture evenly over plums.
6. Bake at 400° for 45 minutes or until a wooden pick inserted in center comes out clean. Cool on a wire rack. Yield: 9 servings.

CALORIES 258 (27% from fat); FAT 7.7g (sat 1.5g, mono 3.1g, poly 2.5g); PROTEIN 4.2g; CARB 43.6g; FIBER 1.4g; CHOL 25mg; IRON 1.3mg; SODIUM 144mg; CALC 67mg

APPLE-RAISIN STREUSEL KUCHEN

- 5 cups chopped peeled Golden Delicious or Rome apple (about 4 large)
- Cooking spray
- 2 tablespoons granulated sugar, divided
- 1½ cups all-purpose flour
- ⅓ cup granulated sugar
- 1¼ teaspoons baking powder
- ¼ teaspoon baking soda
- ¼ teaspoon salt
- ⅛ teaspoon ground cinnamon
- ⅛ teaspoon ground nutmeg
- ¾ cup low-fat buttermilk
- ¼ cup egg substitute
- 2½ tablespoons vegetable oil
- 1½ teaspoons grated lemon rind
- ½ cup raisins
- ½ cup packed brown sugar
- 3 tablespoons all-purpose flour
- ½ teaspoon ground cinnamon
- ¼ teaspoon ground nutmeg
- 2½ tablespoons chilled stick margarine
- 2 teaspoons light-colored corn syrup

1. Preheat oven to 475°.
2. Arrange apple in a single layer on a jelly-roll pan coated with cooking spray, and sprinkle with 1 tablespoon granulated sugar. Bake at 475° for 8 minutes, stirring well. Sprinkle with 1 tablespoon granulated sugar; bake an additional 7 minutes or until apple is slightly soft. Let cool.
3. Reduce oven temperature to 375°. Lightly spoon 1½ cups flour into dry measuring cups; level with a knife. Combine flour, granulated sugar, and next 5 ingredients. Combine buttermilk and next 3 ingredients, stirring well with a whisk. Add to flour mixture, stirring just

Continued

until moist. Gently fold in apples and raisins. Spoon mixture into a 10-inch springform pan coated with cooking spray; place pan on a baking sheet.

4. Combine brown sugar and next 3 ingredients; cut in margarine and corn syrup with a pastry blender or 2 knives until mixture resembles coarse meal. Sprinkle evenly over batter in pan. Bake at 375° for 50 minutes or until a wooden pick inserted in center comes out clean. Cool on a wire rack. Yield: 10 servings.

CALORIES 280 (23% from fat); FAT 7.1g (sat 1.3g, mono 2.3g, poly 2.7g); PROTEIN 3.8g; CARB 52.3g; FIBER 2.5g; CHOL 0mg; IRON 1.6mg; SODIUM 149mg; CALC 80mg

ALMOND-APRICOT KUCHEN

Chop dried apricots using kitchen shears coated with cooking spray.

    ⅔ cup coarsely chopped dried
        apricots
    ½ cup boiling water
    1 cup low-fat buttermilk
    ¾ cup packed brown sugar
    ⅓ cup egg substitute
    3 tablespoons vegetable oil
    1¼ teaspoons vanilla extract
    ¼ teaspoon almond extract
    2 cups all-purpose flour
    ⅓ cup sliced almonds, ground
    1¼ teaspoons baking powder
    ¾ teaspoon baking soda
    ¼ teaspoon salt
       Cooking spray
    2 tablespoons sliced almonds
    1 tablespoon granulated sugar

1. Combine apricots and boiling water in a bowl; cover and let stand 30 minutes. Drain well.
2. Preheat oven to 375°.
3. Combine rehydrated apricots, buttermilk, and next 5 ingredients. Lightly spoon flour into dry measuring cups; level with a knife. Combine flour and next 4 ingredients in a bowl. Add apricot mixture, stirring just until moist.
4. Pour batter into a 10-inch springform pan coated with cooking spray. Sprinkle with 2 tablespoons sliced

almonds and granulated sugar. Bake at 375° for 30 minutes or until a wooden pick inserted in center comes out clean. Cool on a wire rack. Yield: 12 servings.

CALORIES 220 (25% from fat); FAT 6.2g (sat 1.1g, mono 2.4g, poly 2.2g); PROTEIN 4.7g; CARB 37.3g; FIBER 1.2g; CHOL 0mg; IRON 2mg; SODIUM 160mg; CALC 84mg

PEACH-STREUSEL KUCHEN

To peel the peaches, place them in boiling water for 30 seconds and then plunge them into cold water. The skins should peel off easily.

    1⅓ cups all-purpose flour
    ½ cup granulated sugar
    ¾ teaspoon baking powder
    ½ teaspoon ground ginger
    ¼ teaspoon baking soda
    ¼ teaspoon salt
    ½ cup plain fat-free yogurt
    ¼ cup water
    2 tablespoons vegetable oil
    2 teaspoons vanilla extract
    ¼ teaspoon almond extract
    1 large egg, lightly beaten
       Cooking spray
    ¾ cup all-purpose flour
    ⅔ cup packed brown sugar
    1 teaspoon ground cinnamon
    ¼ teaspoon salt
    ¼ cup chilled stick margarine or
        butter, cut into small pieces
    1 tablespoon light-colored corn
        syrup
    3 cups sliced peeled ripe peaches
        (about 2 pounds)

1. Preheat oven to 375°.
2. Lightly spoon 1⅓ cups flour into dry measuring cups; level with a knife. Combine flour and next 5 ingredients in a bowl. Combine yogurt and next 5 ingredients; add to flour mixture, stirring just until moist. Spoon batter into a 13 x 9-inch baking pan coated with cooking spray, spreading evenly.
3. Lightly spoon ¾ cup flour into a dry measuring cup; level with a knife. Combine flour, brown sugar, cinnamon, and ¼ teaspoon salt; cut in margarine and corn syrup with a pastry

blender or 2 knives until mixture resembles coarse meal. Combine ½ cup streusel mixture and peaches in a bowl; arrange peach mixture evenly over batter. Sprinkle with remaining streusel mixture. Bake at 375° for 50 minutes or until a wooden pick inserted in center comes out clean. Cool on a wire rack. Yield: 12 servings.

CALORIES 250 (24% from fat); FAT 6.8g (sat 1.3g, mono 2.6g, poly 2.5g); PROTEIN 3.7g; CARB 43.9g; FIBER 1.3g; CHOL 19mg; IRON 1.5mg; SODIUM 188mg; CALC 58mg

GLAZED PLUM-RASPBERRY KUCHEN

(pictured on page 150)

Any type of plum will work in this yeast-based kuchen.

    1 package dry yeast
    ¼ cup sugar, divided
    ½ cup warm water (105° to 115°)
    2¾ cups all-purpose flour
    ½ teaspoon salt
    ¼ cup stick margarine or butter,
        melted
    1 large egg, lightly beaten
       Cooking spray
    2 cups sliced plums
    ⅓ cup sugar
    1 cup fresh raspberries
    3 tablespoons seedless raspberry
        jam, melted

1. Dissolve yeast and 1 tablespoon sugar in warm water in a small bowl; let stand 5 minutes. Lightly spoon flour into dry measuring cups; level with a knife. Place flour, 3 tablespoons sugar, and salt in a food processor; pulse 3 times or until blended. With processor on, slowly add yeast mixture, margarine, and egg through food chute; process until dough forms a ball. Process mixture 1 additional minute.
2. Turn dough out onto a lightly floured surface; knead lightly 4 or 5 times. Place dough in a large bowl coated with cooking spray, turning to coat top. Cover and let rise in a warm place (85°), free from drafts, 1 hour or until doubled in bulk.

3. Preheat oven to 425°.
4. Punch dough down. Pat dough into a 12-inch pizza pan coated with cooking spray, and place pan on a large foil-lined baking sheet. Arrange plum slices in concentric circles over dough, gently pressing slices into dough. Sprinkle ⅓ cup sugar over plum slices, and top with raspberries. Bake at 425° for 20 minutes or until puffy and edges are well-browned. Remove from oven, and drizzle with melted jam. Cool on a wire rack. Yield: 12 servings.

CALORIES 220 (20% from fat); FAT 4.8g (sat 0.9g, mono 2g, poly 1.4g); PROTEIN 4.2g; CARB 40.6g; FIBER 2.3g; CHOL 18mg; IRON 1.6mg; SODIUM 150mg; CALC 12mg

DRIED-CHERRY STREUSEL KUCHEN

This lightly spiced coffeecake with a streusel topping may be the most familiar kuchen to Americans.

- ¼ cup all-purpose flour
- ¼ cup packed brown sugar
- ¼ teaspoon ground cinnamon
- 1½ tablespoons chilled stick margarine or butter
- 1⅔ cups all-purpose flour
- ¼ cup granulated sugar
- 3 tablespoons brown sugar
- 1½ teaspoons baking powder
- ½ teaspoon baking soda
- ¼ teaspoon salt
- ⅔ cup low-fat buttermilk
- ⅓ cup egg substitute
- 3 tablespoons vegetable oil
- 1 tablespoon amaretto (almond-flavored liqueur) or water
- 2½ tablespoons vanilla extract
- 1 teaspoon grated lemon rind
- ¼ teaspoon almond extract
- ¾ cup dried tart red cherries
- Cooking spray

1. Preheat oven to 375°.
2. Lightly spoon ¼ cup flour into a dry measuring cup; level with a knife. Combine flour, ¼ cup brown sugar, and cinnamon in a bowl; cut in margarine with a pastry blender or 2 knives until mixture resembles coarse meal. Set streusel mixture aside.
3. Lightly spoon 1⅔ cups flour into dry measuring cups; level with a knife. Combine flour and next 5 ingredients in a large bowl. Combine buttermilk and next 6 ingredients, stirring with a whisk. Add buttermilk mixture to flour mixture, stirring until blended. Gently fold in dried cherries. Spoon batter into a 9-inch round cake pan coated with cooking spray. Sprinkle streusel mixture evenly over top.
4. Bake at 375° for 30 minutes or until a wooden pick inserted in center comes out clean. Cool on a wire rack. Yield: 10 servings.

CALORIES 242 (24% from fat); FAT 6.4g (sat 1.3g, mono 2g, poly 2.6g); PROTEIN 4.2g; CARB 40.1g; FIBER 1.2g; CHOL 0mg; IRON 1.7mg; SODIUM 167mg; CALC 80mg

Summer-Ready Pantry

When fresh summer ingredients and pantry staples come together, good things happen.

Getting a summer pantry in order is like reorganizing a closet. Each year, take stock of the basics on hand, then make a list of what you need to update for the hot months ahead. Try replacing the winter must-haves, such as lasagna noodles and cans of beef broth, with smaller, lighter pastas and vegetable broth. Stock up on orzo, penne, and Arborio rice. Keep pine nuts in the refrigerator to kick-start fresh pestos or to toss into a salad. And always have good quality olive oil and lots of garlic nearby to accent all the fresh summer vegetables.

Once you've got the summer basics stocked, focus on what's fresh and new. The farmers' market is a weekend must, although at this time of year even the grocery bins are bursting with the primary hues and flavors of the season's harvest. Here are a few recipes that make the most of your summer pantry.

MENU SUGGESTION

GRILLED FLANK STEAK WITH HOISIN SAUCE

Sesame-soy glazed noodles*

Steamed snow peas and sliced carrots

*Heat 1 tablespoon dark sesame oil in a large nonstick skillet over medium-high heat. Add 3 cups hot cooked vermicelli, tossing gently. Add ½ cup sliced green onions and 1 teaspoon grated peeled fresh ginger; sauté 3 minutes. Remove from heat, and stir in 2 tablespoons low-sodium soy sauce. Serves 4.

GRILLED FLANK STEAK WITH HOISIN SAUCE

- 1 (1-pound) flank steak
- ½ cup hoisin sauce
- 3 tablespoons fresh orange juice
- 3 tablespoons sherry
- 2 tablespoons grated peeled fresh ginger
- 1 tablespoon Dijon mustard
- 1 tablespoon honey
- 1 tablespoon dark sesame oil
- 1½ teaspoons freshly ground black pepper
- Cooking spray

1. Trim fat from steak. Combine hoisin sauce and next 7 ingredients in a 2-cup glass measure; reserve ¾ cup hoisin mixture. Pour remaining hoisin mixture in a zip-top plastic bag. Add steak to bag; seal. Marinate in refrigerator 4 to 8 hours. Remove steak from bag, discarding marinade.
2. Prepare grill. Place steak on grill rack coated with cooking spray; grill 8 minutes on each side or until desired degree of doneness, basting frequently with reserved hoisin mixture. Let stand 3 minutes. Cut steak diagonally across grain into thin slices. Yield: 4 servings (serving size: 3 ounces).

CALORIES 285 (47% from fat); FAT 14.8g (sat 5.9g, mono 6g, poly 1.1g); PROTEIN 22.5g; CARB 14g; FIBER 0.4g; CHOL 60mg; IRON 2.5mg; SODIUM 443mg; CALC 17mg

Pasta Salad with Cannellini Beans and Tuna

Canned beans and bottled roasted bell peppers team up with asparagus and tomatoes in this main-dish pasta salad.

 3 cups uncooked penne (about 10 ounces tube-shaped pasta)
 1 cup (2-inch) sliced asparagus (about ½ pound)
 2 tablespoons fresh lemon juice
 2 tablespoons olive oil
 1 tablespoon stone-ground mustard
 1 tablespoon minced pitted green olives
 1 tablespoon water
 ½ teaspoon black pepper
 ¼ teaspoon salt
 1 cup chopped tomato
 1 (15-ounce) can cannellini beans or other white beans, rinsed and drained
 1 (7-ounce) bottle roasted red bell peppers, drained and sliced
 1 (6-ounce) can chunk light tuna in water, drained

1. Cook pasta in boiling water 6 minutes. Add asparagus; cook an additional 6 minutes. Drain pasta mixture. Rinse with cold water; drain well.
2. Combine lemon juice and next 6 ingredients. Combine pasta mixture, olive mixture, tomato, and remaining ingredients in a bowl; toss gently. Yield: 6 servings (serving size: 1½ cups).

CALORIES 259 (24% from fat); FAT 7g (sat 1g, mono 3.9g, poly 1.4g); PROTEIN 13.4g; CARB 36.3g; FIBER 3.7g; CHOL 8mg; IRON 2.9mg; SODIUM 393mg; CALC 40mg

Tomatoes Stuffed with Orzo-Feta Salad

The key is to use the best tomatoes you can find.

 2 cups cooked orzo (about 1 cup uncooked rice-shaped pasta)
 1½ cups diced cucumber
 1 cup chopped fresh parsley
 ½ cup (2 ounces) crumbled feta cheese
 ¼ cup diced red onion
 1 tablespoon chopped fresh chives
 1 tablespoon extra-virgin olive oil
 1 tablespoon balsamic vinegar
 1 tablespoon fresh lemon juice
 ¼ teaspoon salt
 ⅛ teaspoon black pepper
 4 large tomatoes

1. Combine first 11 ingredients in a large bowl. Remove cores from tomatoes. Cut each tomato into 8 wedges, cutting to, but not through, the other end. Place 1 tomato on each of 4 plates; top each with 1¼ cups orzo mixture. Yield: 4 servings.

CALORIES 273 (26% from fat); FAT 7.8g (sat 2.8g, mono 3.4g, poly 0.9g); PROTEIN 9.6g; CARB 42.9g; FIBER 4.3g; CHOL 13mg; IRON 3.6mg; SODIUM 331mg; CALC 115mg

Grilled Vegetables with Balsamic Vinaigrette

(pictured on page 152)

 ¼ cup balsamic vinegar
 2 tablespoons honey
 1 tablespoon olive oil
 1 teaspoon coarsely ground black pepper
 ½ teaspoon salt
 4 garlic cloves, minced
 4 plum tomatoes, halved
 2 zucchini, cut lengthwise into ¼-inch slices
 1 (1-pound) eggplant, cut crosswise into 1-inch-thick slices
 1 red bell pepper, cut into 8 wedges
 1 onion, cut into 2-inch-thick wedges
 1 small bunch kale (about 8 ounces)
 Cooking spray

1. Combine first 6 ingredients in a bowl.
2. Combine tomatoes and next 5 ingredients in a bowl. Divide vinegar mixture and vegetable mixture evenly between 2 large zip-top plastic bags. Seal; marinate in refrigerator 1 hour, turning bags occasionally.

3. Remove vegetables from bags, reserving marinade. Prepare grill. Place vegetables on grill rack coated with cooking spray; grill 7 minutes on each side or until onion is tender, basting with reserved marinade. Yield: 8 servings (serving size: 1 cup).

CALORIES 87 (24% from fat); FAT 2.3g (sat 0.3g, mono 1.3g, poly 0.4g); PROTEIN 2.7g; CARB 16.6g; FIBER 2.6g; CHOL 0mg; IRON 1.5mg; SODIUM 168mg; CALC 71mg

Roasted Red Pepper-Lentil Bisque

 3 cups water
 1 cup diced carrot
 ⅔ cup dried lentils
 ½ cup sun-dried tomatoes, packed without oil (about 13)
 1 bay leaf
 1 (14½-ounce) can plum tomatoes, undrained
 4 cups (1-inch) pieces red bell pepper
 1 tablespoon olive oil
 8 garlic cloves, peeled
 1 cup dry red wine
 1 teaspoon ground cumin
 ½ teaspoon salt
 1 tablespoon fresh lemon juice

1. Combine first 5 ingredients in a large saucepan; bring to a boil. Partially cover, reduce heat, and simmer 30 minutes, stirring occasionally. Discard bay leaf. Place mixture in a blender; process until smooth. Add plum tomatoes; process until smooth. Return mixture to pan; cover and set aside.
2. Preheat oven to 400°.
3. While lentil mixture simmers, combine bell pepper, oil, and garlic on a foil-lined jelly-roll pan. Bake at 400° for 30 minutes, stirring after 15 minutes. Place bell pepper mixture, wine, cumin, and salt in blender; process until smooth. Stir into lentil mixture; cook over medium heat 5 minutes or until thoroughly heated. Stir in lemon juice. Yield: 8 servings (serving size: 1 cup).

CALORIES 125 (18% from fat); FAT 2.5g (sat 0.4g, mono 1.4g, poly 0.5g); PROTEIN 6.8g; CARB 21.4g; FIBER 3.9g; CHOL 0mg; IRON 3.1mg; SODIUM 353mg; CALC 46mg

PASTA WITH THREE-HERB PESTO

Any kind of dried pasta will work in this vegetarian main dish.

    3 cups fresh basil leaves
    ½ cup fresh parsley sprigs
    ¼ cup fresh oregano leaves
    2 tablespoons pine nuts, toasted
    1 tablespoon grated fresh
       Parmesan cheese
    ¼ teaspoon salt
    4 garlic cloves
    2 tablespoons olive oil
    8 cups mixed hot cooked pasta
       (such as farfalle, penne, and
       shells)

1. Place first 7 ingredients in a food processor, and process until smooth. With processor on, slowly pour oil through food chute; process until well-blended. Toss with pasta. Yield: 6 servings (serving size: 1⅓ cups).

CALORIES 337 (21% from fat); FAT 8g (sat 1.3g, mono 4.2g, poly 1.7g); PROTEIN 11g; CARB 55.6g; FIBER 3.4g; CHOL 1mg; IRON 3.5mg; SODIUM 123mg; CALC 79mg

SUMMER RISOTTO

    2 (14½-ounce) cans vegetable broth
    1 tablespoon olive oil
    2 teaspoons margarine or butter
    1 cup diced onion
    1 cup (¼-inch) cut green beans
    ½ cup chopped red bell pepper
    ½ cup diced carrot
    1 tablespoon chopped fresh
       flat-leaf parsley
    1 tablespoon chopped fresh basil
    2 garlic cloves, minced
    1 cup uncooked Arborio rice or
       other short-grain rice
    ½ cup dry white wine
    1 tablespoon grated fresh
       Parmesan cheese
    ¼ teaspoon black pepper
Minced fresh flat-leaf parsley
    (optional)

1. Bring broth to a simmer in a saucepan (do not boil). Keep warm over low heat.

2. Heat olive oil and margarine in a large Dutch oven over medium-high heat. Add onion and next 6 ingredients; sauté 6 minutes or until tender. Add rice, and cook 2 minutes, stirring constantly. Stir in wine and 1 cup simmering broth; cook 3 minutes or until the liquid is nearly absorbed, stirring constantly. Add remaining broth, ½ cup at a time, stirring constantly until each portion of broth is absorbed before adding the next (about 25 to 30 minutes total). Stir in Parmesan cheese and black pepper; garnish with minced parsley, if desired. Yield: 4 servings (serving size: about 1 cup).

CALORIES 287 (22% from fat); FAT 7.0g (sat 1.6g, mono 3.6g, poly 1.0g); PROTEIN 5.8g; CARB 50.4g; FIBER 2.8g; CHOL 2mg; IRON 3mg; SODIUM 972mg; CALC 54mg

LIGHTEN UP

Daughter Knows Best

A 15-year-old Florida reader challenges us to trim the fat and calories from her dad's favorite corn bread.

Because 15-year-old Kyleen Rogers of Eustis, Florida, and her 11-year-old sister, Kara, complained once too often about their mother's cooking, Mom issued them a challenge: "If you don't like it, then you cook it." Challenge accepted. At least once a week Kyleen and Kara prepare dinner—lightly. But there's one high-fat family favorite that no one can resist: a recipe for Texas corn bread containing copious amounts of sour cream, Cheddar cheese, oil, and butter. In lightening this recipe, we trimmed 266 calories from each serving, and cut the fat by a Texas-sized three-quarters.

LIGHT TEXAS CORN BREAD

If you don't have self-rising cornmeal mix, stir 2 teaspoons baking powder and ½ teaspoon salt into 1½ cups plain cornmeal.

    1½ cups self-rising yellow cornmeal
       mix
    2 tablespoons sugar
    5 tablespoons light butter, melted
       and divided
    1 cup chopped onion
    1 cup chopped green bell pepper
    1 cup fat-free sour cream
    1 cup no-salt-added cream-style
       corn
    ½ cup (2 ounces) shredded reduced-
       fat extra-sharp Cheddar cheese
    1 large egg, lightly beaten
    2 large egg whites, lightly beaten
Cooking spray

1. Preheat oven to 425°.
2. Combine cornmeal mix and sugar in a large bowl; set aside. Combine 3 tablespoons butter, onion, and next 6 ingredients in a medium bowl; stir well with a whisk. Add to cornmeal mixture, stirring just until moist. Pour batter into a 13 x 9-inch baking pan coated with cooking spray. Bake at 425° for 28 minutes or until a wooden pick inserted in center comes out clean. Brush with remaining 2 tablespoons melted butter. Yield: 12 servings.

CALORIES 141 (29% from fat); FAT 4.6g (sat 2.4g, mono 0.6g, poly 0.4g); PROTEIN 6.1g; CARB 20g; FIBER 0.6g; CHOL 29mg; IRON 1.2mg; SODIUM 283mg; CALC 104mg

BEFORE & AFTER	
SERVING SIZE	
1 piece	
CALORIES	
407	141
FAT	
34g	4.6g
PERCENT OF TOTAL CALORIES	
75%	29%
CHOLESTEROL	
131mg	29mg

Now Appearing in a City Near You

Farmers' markets are proliferating nationwide, giving millions of Americans their own connection to the farm.

The farmers' market is an old idea that has become a modern trend, growing like summer zucchini. According to a U.S. Department of Agriculture survey, the number of farmers' markets swelled nearly 40%, to about 2,400, between 1994 and 1996. Every week, nearly a million people visit farmers' markets.

The personality of each farmers' market is as distinct as the landscape where it evolved. West Coast markets have encouraged organic growers; the Santa Fe market is known for traditional and ethnic foods of the Southwest. Wherever they are, farmers' markets humanize cities with simple, authentic exchanges between the folks who buy and the folks who grow, the cooks and the consumers. In the bargain, they help small local farmers stay in business and preserve lands devoted to agriculture.

Chefs rely on farmers' markets for inspiration, and for seeking out the freshest, most sensually appealing foods to rouse creativity and appetites. But you won't see the pros unless you're an early bird: Chefs shop before dawn and have gone back to their kitchens while the morning is still fresh.

As you walk, you round out your menu. Young cucumbers, unwaxed, and bunches of Christmas-red radishes inspire a sandwich of fresh salad vegetables and shrimp. Summer's abundance of yellow squash and zucchini will simmer with chicken in a light summertime ragoût. Red potatoes and green beans will put a spin on a potato salad seasoned with fresh basil and tomatoes. Yellow bell peppers and Yukon gold potatoes will blend in a golden soup.

YOU BUY, YOU CARRY

When you're shopping at a farmers' market, keep these tips in mind:
• Bring your own bags and some rigid containers for fragile produce like berries.
• Pack things carefully—you don't want your watermelon bearing down on your peaches.
• If you live in a hot climate, you might want to bring an ice chest to keep things cool until you get home.
• Bring lots of small bills and change.
• Don't buy at the first stand—part of the pleasure is the shopping experience, and you don't know where the freshest fruit and the best prices will be found.
• Shop often and get to know the growers, so you'll know who has the freshest stuff.
• Learn to follow your nose. The air-conditioned atmosphere of a supermarket inhibits the scents of produce; in an open-air market, one sniff can tell you how ripe that cantaloupe is.

To find out more about farmers' markets or how to support them in your community, call the American Farmland Trust at 202/659-5170. You can find their Web site at www.farmland.org. You can also contact your local agricultural cooperative extension for information.

MENU

YELLOW-PEPPER SOUP

GREEN BEAN-AND-TOMATO SALAD WITH ROASTED-TOMATO DRESSING

FARMERS' MARKET CHICKEN

VANILLA-POACHED PEACHES

YELLOW-PEPPER SOUP

(pictured on page 151)

2 teaspoons olive oil
⅔ cup chopped onion
⅓ cup diced celery
1¾ cups low-salt chicken broth
1¼ cups water
¾ cup cubed peeled Yukon gold or red potato
¼ teaspoon salt
¼ teaspoon dried thyme
⅛ teaspoon black pepper
2 medium-size yellow bell peppers, seeded, halved, and cut into quarters (about ¾ pound)
Chopped fresh parsley (optional)

1. Heat olive oil in a large saucepan over medium-low heat. Add onion and celery; cook 7 minutes or until onion is soft. Add broth and next 6 ingredients; bring to a boil. Cover, reduce heat, and simmer 40 minutes or until vegetables are tender.
2. Place half of bell pepper mixture in a blender, and process until smooth. Pour pureed bell pepper mixture into a large bowl. Repeat procedure with remaining bell pepper mixture. Spoon soup into bowls; garnish with parsley, if desired. Yield: 4 servings (serving size: 1 cup).

CALORIES 78 (37% from fat); FAT 3.2g (sat 0.7g, mono 1.7g, poly 0.3g); PROTEIN 2.7g; CARB 10.7g; FIBER 1.8g; CHOL 12mg; IRON 1mg; SODIUM 206mg; CALC 24mg

GREEN BEAN-AND-TOMATO SALAD WITH ROASTED-TOMATO DRESSING

(pictured on page 151)

1 large ripe tomato, halved
Cooking spray
1 tablespoon chopped fresh basil
1 tablespoon extra-virgin olive oil
2 teaspoons red wine vinegar
½ teaspoon sugar
½ teaspoon Worcestershire sauce
¼ teaspoon salt
⅛ teaspoon black pepper
2 cups trimmed green or wax beans (about ½ pound)
4 cups torn romaine lettuce
1 cup halved cherry tomatoes
¼ cup sliced red onion, separated into rings

1. Preheat broiler. Place large tomato halves on a broiler pan coated with cooking spray. Broil 10 minutes or until blackened. Cool 10 minutes; peel and core. Combine roasted tomato, basil, and next 6 ingredients in a blender; process until smooth.
2. Steam beans, covered, 7 minutes or until crisp-tender; rinse with cold water, and drain. Place 1 cup lettuce on each of 4 plates. Arrange beans, tomatoes, and onion over lettuce. Spoon 3 tablespoons dressing over each salad. Yield: 4 servings.

CALORIES 83 (43% from fat); FAT 4g (sat 0.5g, mono 2.5g, poly 0.5g); PROTEIN 2.8g; CARB 11g; FIBER 3.5g; CHOL 0mg; IRON 1.6mg; SODIUM 169mg; CALC 49mg

FARMERS' MARKET CHICKEN

(pictured on page 150)

3 tablespoons tomato paste
¼ teaspoon salt
¼ teaspoon black pepper
1 (10½-ounce) can low-salt chicken broth
1 garlic clove, minced
2 tablespoons Italian-seasoned breadcrumbs
4 (4-ounce) skinned, boned chicken breast halves

1 tablespoon olive oil
1 cup diced carrot
1 cup diced red onion
1 cup diced yellow squash
1 cup diced zucchini
2 tablespoons dry vermouth
4 cups hot cooked long-grain rice
2 teaspoons chopped fresh rosemary

1. Combine first 5 ingredients in a medium bowl; stir well with a whisk.
2. Place breadcrumbs in a shallow dish; dredge chicken in breadcrumbs. Heat olive oil in a large nonstick skillet over medium-high heat; add chicken, and sauté 6 minutes on each side. Remove chicken from skillet. Add carrot and next 4 ingredients to skillet; sauté 5 minutes, stirring occasionally. Return chicken to skillet, and add broth mixture. Bring mixture to a boil; cover, reduce heat, and simmer 15 minutes. Serve chicken and vegetable mixture over rice; sprinkle with rosemary. Yield: 4 servings (serving size: 1 chicken breast half, 1 cup rice, and ¾ cup vegetables).

CALORIES 454 (12% from fat); FAT 6g (sat 1.2g, mono 2.9g, poly 0.7g); PROTEIN 33.9g; CARB 64.6g; FIBER 4g; CHOL 67mg; IRON 3.8mg; SODIUM 376mg; CALC 79mg

VANILLA-POACHED PEACHES

You can substitute 1 teaspoon vanilla extract for the vanilla bean; just stir it in after the mixture is reduced.

1 cup water
⅓ cup sugar
1 (3½-inch) piece vanilla bean, split lengthwise
3 large ripe peaches, peeled, pitted, and quartered
2 tablespoons strawberry preserves
4 teaspoons chopped pistachios

1. Combine first 3 ingredients in a medium nonaluminum saucepan; bring to a boil. Reduce heat; add peaches, and simmer 7 minutes or until tender. Remove peaches with a slotted spoon; place in a shallow dish. Bring cooking liquid to a boil; cook until reduced to ½ cup (about 7 minutes). Discard

vanilla bean; pour syrup over peaches. Cool to room temperature.
2. Combine preserves and 4 teaspoons peach syrup; stir with a whisk. Place 3 peach quarters and 1½ tablespoons peach syrup in each of 4 dishes; top each serving with 2 teaspoons strawberry mixture and 1 teaspoon pistachios. Yield: 4 servings.

CALORIES 132 (10% from fat); FAT 1.4g (sat 0.2g, mono 0.9g, poly 2g); PROTEIN 1.1g; CARB 31g; FIBER 1.5g; CHOL 0mg; IRON 0.3mg; SODIUM 4mg; CALC 9mg

---

MENU

COOL-AS-A-CUCUMBER SHRIMP SANDWICH

HERBED POTATO SALAD WITH GREEN BEANS AND TOMATOES

STRAWBERRY-ORANGE MÉLANGE

RASPBERRY LEMONADE

COOL-AS-A-CUCUMBER SHRIMP SANDWICH

⅓ cup minced green onions
¼ cup tub-style light cream cheese, softened
¼ cup light mayonnaise
¼ cup plain low-fat yogurt
1 teaspoon fresh dill
½ teaspoon garlic salt
¼ teaspoon black pepper
6 (1½-ounce) French bread rolls
1½ pounds large shrimp, cooked and peeled
1 cup thinly sliced cucumber
½ cup thinly sliced radishes
6 curly leaf lettuce leaves

1. Combine first 7 ingredients in a bowl. Cut rolls in half horizontally. Spread cream cheese mixture over cut sides of rolls; arrange shrimp on bottom halves of rolls. Arrange cucumber and radishes over shrimp; top with lettuce leaves and roll tops. Yield: 6 servings.

CALORIES 270 (21% from fat); FAT 6.3g (sat 2g, mono 1.4g, poly 2.3g); PROTEIN 23.7g; CARB 27.5g; FIBER 1.2g; CHOL 176mg; IRON 3.9mg; SODIUM 751mg; CALC 98mg

Herbed Potato Salad with Green Beans and Tomatoes

This is a great salad to make ahead—the flavor gets more intense after chilling. Store leftover salad in the refrigerator in an airtight container for up to three days.

2½ pounds small red potatoes, quartered
2 cups (2-inch) cut green beans (about ½ pound)
1 cup chopped fresh basil
½ cup thinly sliced green onions
¼ cup white wine vinegar
1 tablespoon olive oil
2 teaspoons Dijon mustard
½ teaspoon salt
½ teaspoon black pepper
6 garlic cloves, crushed
2 cups diced seeded tomato

1. Place potatoes in a Dutch oven; cover with water. Bring to a boil; cook 10 minutes. Add beans, and cook 6 minutes or until tender. Drain.
2. Combine basil and next 7 ingredients in a large bowl. Add potato mixture; toss well. Add tomato, and toss gently. Cover and chill. Yield: 10 servings (serving size: 1 cup).

CALORIES 118 (13% from fat); FAT 1.7g (sat 0.2g, mono 1g, poly 0.3g); PROTEIN 3.5g; CARB 23.3g; FIBER 3.1g; CHOL 0mg; IRON 2mg; SODIUM 161mg; CALC 39mg

Strawberry-Orange Mélange

A microwave speeds up the preparation of this fresh-fruit sauce.

4 navel oranges (about 2 pounds)
1 tablespoon sugar
1 tablespoon cornstarch
¼ cup fresh orange juice
1 tablespoon fresh lemon juice
2 cups sliced strawberries
½ teaspoon vanilla extract
¼ teaspoon almond extract
2 cups vanilla low-fat ice cream
Mint sprigs (optional)

1. Peel and section oranges over a bowl; squeeze membranes to extract juice. Set sections aside, and reserve ¼ cup juice. Discard membranes. Chop orange sections.
2. Combine sugar and cornstarch in a 1-quart glass measure. Add reserved orange juice, ¼ cup fresh orange juice, and lemon juice, stirring with a whisk until well-blended. Stir in chopped oranges. Microwave mixture at HIGH 2 minutes and 45 seconds or until thick, stirring after 2 minutes. Stir in strawberries and extracts. Serve over ice cream. Garnish with mint, if desired. Yield: 4 servings (serving size: ½ cup fruit and ½ cup ice cream).

CALORIES 176 (15% from fat); FAT 2.9g (sat 1.6g, mono 0.8g, poly 0.3g); PROTEIN 3.7g; CARB 35.7g; FIBER 7.8g; CHOL 0mg; IRON 0.4mg; SODIUM 32mg; CALC 139mg

Raspberry Lemonade

3 cups cold water, divided
1 cup fresh raspberries
1 (6-ounce) can thawed lemonade concentrate, undiluted
Mint sprigs (optional)

1. Combine ¾ cup water and raspberries in a blender; process until smooth. Strain mixture through a sieve into a medium bowl; discard seeds. Combine raspberry liquid, 2¼ cups water, and lemonade concentrate in a pitcher; chill. Garnish with mint, if desired. Yield: 4 servings (serving size: 1 cup).

CALORIES 92 (3% from fat); FAT 0.3g (sat 0g, mono 0g, poly 0.1g); PROTEIN 0.4g; CARB 23.6g; FIBER 2.5g; CHOL 0mg; IRON 0.5mg; SODIUM 2mg; CALC 10mg

Knife Tricks

A chef's knife is one of the most important tools in the kitchen.

For virtually any kind of cutting, the broad, tapered heft of the chef's knife (also known as a French knife) makes it the instrument of choice. The best are high-carbon stainless steel, at least 8 inches but preferably 10 or 12 inches in length. The handle can be made of wood or plastic, but be sure it's well-riveted to clasp the full length of the metal extension from the blade. Also, make sure it feels balanced and right for your hands. You may pay from $80 to $120 for a top brand, but you'll never regret spending extra for quality.

Sautéed Striped Bass with Summer Vegetables

You can substitute any firm, white-fleshed fish fillets for the bass.

4 (6-ounce) striped bass fillets, skinned
½ teaspoon salt, divided
¼ teaspoon black pepper
1 tablespoon olive oil, divided
Cooking spray
1 cup (2 x ¼-inch) julienne-cut yellow squash
1 cup (2 x ¼-inch) julienne-cut zucchini
1 cup (2 x ¼-inch) julienne-cut carrot
1 cup vertically sliced red onion
¾ cup julienne-cut fennel stalks
¼ cup chopped fresh basil
1 tablespoon white wine vinegar
½ teaspoon dried thyme
3 garlic cloves, minced
Fresh basil sprigs (optional)

1. Sprinkle fish evenly with ¼ teaspoon salt and black pepper.
2. Heat 1 teaspoon oil in a large nonstick skillet coated with cooking spray over medium-high heat until hot. Add

fish; cook 3 minutes on each side or until fish flakes easily when tested with a fork. Remove from skillet; keep warm.

3. Combine remaining ¼ teaspoon salt, 2 teaspoons oil, yellow squash, and next 8 ingredients; toss well. Wipe skillet with paper towels; recoat with cooking spray. Add vegetable mixture; sauté 4 minutes or until crisp-tender. Serve fish over vegetables; garnish with basil, if desired. Yield: 4 servings (serving size: 1 fillet and ¾ cup vegetable mixture).

CALORIES 269 (34% from fat); FAT 10.1g (sat 1.8g, mono 5g, poly 2.2g); PROTEIN 34.1g; CARB 9.5g; FIBER 2.3g; CHOL 116mg; IRON 3.8mg; SODIUM 427mg; CALC 190mg

---

MENU SUGGESTION

PAN-SEARED SCALLOPS WITH GINGER-ORANGE SPINACH

*Romaine-bell pepper salad with dates**

Breadsticks

*Combine 4 cups torn romaine lettuce, ½ cup yellow bell pepper strips, and ⅓ cup sliced pitted dates. Add ⅓ cup light Italian dressing; toss well. Sprinkle with 1 tablespoon grated Parmesan cheese. Serves 4.

PAN-SEARED SCALLOPS WITH GINGER-ORANGE SPINACH

- 1 tablespoon julienne-cut peeled fresh ginger
- 1 tablespoon sliced green onions
- 4 garlic cloves, minced
- 20 sea scallops (about 1½ pounds)
- ½ cup vodka
- ¼ cup dry vermouth
- 1 teaspoon stick margarine or butter
- 1 teaspoon grated orange rind
- ⅓ cup fresh orange juice
- 1½ pounds chopped fresh spinach
- ½ teaspoon salt
- ⅛ teaspoon black pepper
- Cooking spray

1. Combine first 3 ingredients in a small bowl.

2. Place scallops in a shallow dish. Add vodka, vermouth, and half of ginger mixture; toss gently. Cover and marinate in refrigerator 30 minutes.

3. Melt margarine in a large skillet over high heat. Add remaining ginger mixture, and sauté 30 seconds. Add orange rind and juice; bring to a boil. Stir in spinach, salt, and pepper; cook 2 minutes or until spinach wilts. Remove from skillet, and keep warm.

4. Remove scallops from marinade, reserving marinade. Place skillet coated with cooking spray over high heat until hot. Add scallops; cook 1½ minutes on each side or until golden brown. Remove from skillet; keep warm. Add reserved marinade to skillet. Bring to a boil; cook until sauce is reduced to ¼ cup (about 5 minutes).

5. Arrange scallops over spinach mixture; drizzle with sauce. Yield: 4 servings (serving size: 5 scallops, ¾ cup spinach mixture, and 1 tablespoon sauce).

CALORIES 233 (13% from fat); FAT 3.3g (sat 0.5g, mono 0.5g, poly 1g); PROTEIN 36.2g; CARB 17.1g; FIBER 10.2g; CHOL 56mg; IRON 7.5mg; SODIUM 799mg; CALC 302mg

---

THREE-PEPPER QUESADILLAS

- 1 cup finely chopped yellow bell pepper
- 1 cup finely chopped red bell pepper
- ½ cup chopped Vidalia or other sweet onion
- 1 tablespoon finely chopped seeded jalapeño pepper
- ½ teaspoon ground cumin
- ½ teaspoon salt
- ¼ teaspoon freshly ground pepper
- Cooking spray
- 8 (6-inch) corn tortillas
- 1 cup (4 ounces) shredded reduced-fat Monterey Jack cheese

1. Combine first 7 ingredients in a bowl.

2. Place a large skillet coated with cooking spray over medium-high heat until hot. Add 1 tortilla; top with ¼ cup bell pepper mixture. Sprinkle with ¼ cup cheese; top with 1 tortilla. Cook 2 minutes on each side or until golden, pressing down with a spatula. Repeat procedure with remaining tortillas, bell pepper mixture, and cheese. Yield: 4 servings (serving size: 1 quesadilla).

CALORIES 225 (29% from fat); FAT 7.2g (sat 3.4g, mono 1.9g, poly 0.9g); PROTEIN 12.2g; CARB 30g; FIBER 4.3g; CHOL 19mg; IRON 2mg; SODIUM 558mg; CALC 327mg

---

LOOK SHARP

Keep your knife sharp—a dull blade can slip and cause more injury than a sharp one. You can sharpen your knives in several ways. We recommend using a **whetstone** or a **sharpening steel**.

To use a whetstone, draw the blade across at a 20-degree angle, alternating sides five or six times. Moisten the stone with water or oil if you wish. Some people prefer using a slotted stand or frame, which holds the whetstone in place. You simply pull the knife blade, held perpendicularly, repeatedly through the slot in the frame until the blade is sharp (or follow the manufacturer's instructions). Electric knife sharpeners have whetstones mounted on two grinding pads; all you have to do is pull the knife through.

A sharpening steel sharpens and realigns the cutting edge of the blade. Frequent use of this tool will maintain a good blade edge for up to two years, at which point you may need to resharpen your knives with a whetstone.

To use a sharpening steel, grip the knife, sharp edge down, in one hand and the steel in the other. Cross them, then place the blade against the steel at a 20-degree angle, and pull it along the entire length of the steel. Repeat several times on both sides of the knife.

Nothing gets a blade duller than poor storage. Always keep your knives in a wooden block or on a strong magnetic wall rack. Never store knives loose in a drawer; banging against other metals is a surefire road to ruin. Also, don't put knives in the dishwasher—the heat affects the blades, and they won't sharpen as well. (The dishwasher is bad for wooden handles, too.)

CHOP CHOP

When you chop with a chef's knife, your objective is to create uniform-size pieces that will cook evenly. Here are the most efficient ways to cut some common foods.

To mince garlic, start by separating the head into individual cloves with your hands. Smash the garlic clove under the blade of the chef's knife by hitting it with the palm of your hand; this breaks open and releases the peel. With your fingers on the knife tip, rock the knife through the garlic until it is minced.

To cut bell peppers into julienne strips, start by cutting the pepper in half vertically and scraping out all the seeds and membranes. Then place pepper halves, skin sides down, on the cutting board.

Cut pepper halves into ¼-inch strips, making sure you keep the blade tip on the cutting board while pushing the blade through the peppers. **To dice the peppers,** simply turn the julienne strips sideways so that they're at a right angle to the blade, and cut into the size specified in the recipe.

To chop zucchini, cut off the blossom end. Then cut the zucchini into ¼-inch lengthwise strips. Cut off the stem end, leaving 3 or 4 (¼-inch) strips. **To dice zucchini,** cut the stack of strips lengthwise down the middle. Turn strips sideways, and cut them into large, medium, or small cubes as desired.

To chop herbs, wash them in cold water, then snip off the stems and pat dry with paper towels. Hold the herbs tightly together on the cutting board with one hand; as you cut, move the fingertips of this hand to the blade. Use your other hand to hold the blade on the cutting board, rocking the knife up and down and scraping the herbs into a pile as you cut.

To chop an onion, slice in half vertically, leaving the root end intact. Place, cut side down, on cutting board. Make several vertical cuts through onion, cutting to but not through root end. Turn onion a quarter, and make even crosswise cuts through it.

To cut corn off the cob, peel and discard silks and shucks. Stand the corn cob on end, and cut the kernels off the cob using a sawing motion.

ZUCCHINI PARMESAN

1 pound zucchini, cut lengthwise
    into ¼-inch-thick slices
6 garlic cloves, peeled
Olive oil-flavored cooking spray
½ cup Italian-seasoned breadcrumbs
¼ cup (1 ounce) grated fresh
    Parmesan cheese
1 cup 2% reduced-fat milk
½ cup fat-free ricotta cheese
½ teaspoon black pepper
¼ teaspoon salt
⅛ teaspoon ground nutmeg
1 large egg, lightly beaten
1 cup chopped cherry tomatoes
¼ cup chopped fresh basil leaves
1½ teaspoons vegetable oil

1. Preheat broiler. Lightly coat zucchini and garlic with cooking spray; place on a baking sheet coated with cooking spray. Broil 5 minutes or until garlic and zucchini are lightly browned. Remove garlic from baking sheet; mince. Set zucchini aside. Combine garlic, breadcrumbs, and Parmesan cheese; set aside. Combine milk and next 5 ingredients in a medium bowl, stirring with a whisk. Combine tomatoes, basil, and oil in a bowl; set aside.
2. Preheat oven to 400°.
3. Spread ½ cup milk mixture in bottom of an 11 x 7-inch baking dish coated with cooking spray. Arrange zucchini slices over milk mixture to cover bottom of dish; top with ⅓ cup breadcrumb mixture and ½ cup milk mixture. Repeat layers, ending with zucchini. Top with tomato mixture, and sprinkle with remaining breadcrumb mixture. Bake at 400° for 45 minutes or until bubbly and brown. Yield: 6 servings.

CALORIES 135 (31% from fat); FAT 4.6g (sat 1.8g, mono 1.8g, poly 0.4g); PROTEIN 9.8g; CARB 15.4g; FIBER 0.9g; CHOL 45mg; IRON 1.1mg; SODIUM 486mg; CALC 176mg

PROVENÇALE PEPPER-CHICKEN SALAD

(pictured on page 151)

Herbes de Provence is an assortment of dried herbs commonly used in the South of France. The blend can usually be found in small clay crocks in the spice section of large supermarkets. A good substitute is ¼ teaspoon each of dried basil, rosemary, and thyme.

4 (4-ounce) skinned, boned
    chicken breast halves
1 teaspoon dried herbes de
    Provence
¼ teaspoon salt
¼ teaspoon black pepper
2 garlic cloves, minced
Olive oil-flavored cooking spray
¾ cup chopped green onions
1 (1 x ¼-inch) julienne-cut green
    bell pepper
1 (1 x ¼-inch) julienne-cut red bell
    pepper
1 (1 x ¼-inch) julienne-cut yellow
    bell pepper
¼ cup sun-dried tomato sprinkles
¼ cup balsamic vinegar
1 tablespoon extra-virgin olive oil
2 garlic cloves, minced
6 cups gourmet salad greens
¼ cup niçoise olives

1. Place each chicken breast half between 2 sheets of heavy-duty plastic wrap. Flatten each to ½-inch thickness, using a meat mallet or rolling pin. Combine herbes de Provence and next 3 ingredients; rub mixture over both sides of chicken.
2. Place a large nonstick skillet coated with cooking spray over medium-high heat until hot. Add chicken; cook 3 minutes on each side or until done. Remove from skillet. Recoat skillet with cooking spray. Add onions and bell peppers; sauté 5 minutes or until tender.
3. Combine tomato sprinkles and next 3 ingredients; stir well with a whisk. Place 1½ cups salad greens on each of 4 plates. Cut each chicken breast half into slices, and place evenly on top of greens; top each with ½ cup bell pepper mixture. Drizzle 2 tablespoons vinegar mixture over each salad; top each with 1 tablespoon olives. Yield: 4 servings.

CALORIES 220 (27% from fat); FAT 6.5g (sat 1.1g, mono 3.6g, poly 1.1g); PROTEIN 29.5g; CARB 11.5g; FIBER 3.2g; CHOL 66mg; IRON 3.3mg; SODIUM 418mg; CALC 81mg

HOLD ON

Grip the handle of your knife in a way that feels comfortable. The traditional manner is to hold the knife by the handle with your thumb and index finger gripping the part nearest the blade and your other fingers curled around the bottom of the handle. Use whatever technique works best for you, but always remember to remain relaxed with the knife—don't strangle it.

It takes two hands to use a good knife properly; one hand guides it, while the other hand holds the food against the cutting board. The guiding hand keeps the knife from slipping and helps control the size of the pieces. Cut with smooth, even strokes. Grip the food with three fingertips and your thumb, and curl your fingertips back for safety. Keep the knife point touching the cutting board, and lift the heel of the knife to move the food along.

Your knuckles are simply a guide for the next cut; always move the knife blade slightly away from your knuckles on the downstroke. After each cut, move your hand back to reposition the food, and repeat.

The motion of the knife should originate from your wrist rather than your elbow. The weight of the knife does most of the work, so it's not necessary to use a lot of downward pressure as you cut.

FRESH CORN-CILANTRO SALAD

- 5 cups fresh corn kernels (about 10 ears)
- 1½ cups finely chopped onion
- 1½ cups chopped red bell pepper
- 1 tablespoon minced peeled fresh ginger
- 4 garlic cloves, minced
  Olive oil-flavored cooking spray
- ⅔ cup chopped fresh cilantro
- ¼ cup red wine vinegar
- 2 tablespoons minced shallots
- 1 tablespoon minced seeded jalapeño pepper
- 4 teaspoons extra-virgin olive oil
- ¼ teaspoon salt
- ⅛ teaspoon black pepper

1. Combine first 5 ingredients. Place a large nonstick skillet coated with cooking spray over medium-high heat until hot. Add corn mixture, and sauté 8 minutes or until corn begins to brown. Remove from heat.
2. Combine cilantro and remaining 6 ingredients in a jar; cover tightly, and shake vigorously. Combine corn mixture and cilantro mixture in a large bowl; cover and chill. Yield: 8 servings (serving size: ¾ cup).

CALORIES 130 (26% from fat); FAT 3.7g (sat 0.5g, mono 2g, poly 0.8g); PROTEIN 4.1g; CARB 24.3g; FIBER 4.4g; CHOL 0mg; IRON 1.3mg; SODIUM 93mg; CALC 21mg

CUTTING BOARD SALSA

A bowl sitting next to your cutting board comes in handy as you finish chopping and dicing the ingredients for this citrusy-hot Mexican-style salsa. It's delicious with tortilla chips or as a topping for Three-Pepper Quesadillas (page 161).

- 2 cups diced tomato
- ½ cup diced peeled jicama
- ½ cup diced onion
- ½ cup diced radishes
- ⅓ cup chopped seeded peeled cucumber
- ¼ cup fresh orange juice
- 2 tablespoons chopped fresh mint
- 2 tablespoons chopped fresh cilantro
- 2 tablespoons fresh lime juice
- 2 teaspoons chopped seeded jalapeño pepper (about 1 small)
- ½ teaspoon salt

1. Combine all ingredients in a large bowl, and toss gently. Cover and chill. Yield: 3½ cups (serving size: ¼ cup).

CALORIES 16 (11% from fat); FAT 0.2g (sat 0g, mono 0g, poly 0.1g); PROTEIN 0.5g; CARB 3.6g; FIBER 0.6g; CHOL 0mg; IRON 0.3mg; SODIUM 103mg; CALC 7mg

INSPIRED VEGETARIAN

Skillet Time

These quick one-pan dinners will help you make the most of your summer weeknights.

How many times have you dragged yourself home after a long day at work, shuffled into your kitchen, and stared blankly at your refrigerator, hoping for dinner to magically materialize?

Here's your solution: a variety of tasty but easy-to-prepare vegetarian skillet suppers.

But don't forget to get set up properly. It's actually quite easy. Obviously, you need a reliable sauté pan. Equally important is stocking a versatile foundation pantry with a variety of beans, pasta, and grains. This will reduce the need to stop at the store, and give you many more options for each meal. But the real secret for these summer dishes lies in the creative selection of fresh vegetables such as zucchini, tomatoes, bell peppers, or eggplant, and one or more fresh herbs to truly kick in that summery taste.

MINESTRONE RAGOÛT OVER POLENTA

(pictured on page 152)

- 2 teaspoons olive oil
- 1 cup diced peeled eggplant
- ½ cup chopped onion
- ½ cup chopped green bell pepper
- ½ cup chopped red bell pepper
- ⅓ cup chopped carrot
- 1 teaspoon dried Italian seasoning
- ¼ teaspoon fennel seeds
- ¼ teaspoon dried crushed red pepper
- 1 garlic clove, minced
- 1 (14½-ounce) can Italian-style stewed tomatoes, undrained and chopped
- 1 cup hot cooked orzo (about ½ cup uncooked rice-shaped pasta)
- 1 cup chopped fresh spinach
- ⅓ cup chopped fresh basil
- ½ teaspoon salt
- 1 (16-ounce) tube polenta, cut into 12 slices
  Cooking spray
  Fresh basil sprigs (optional)

1. Heat oil in a large nonstick skillet over medium-high heat. Add eggplant and next 8 ingredients; sauté 5 minutes. Stir in tomatoes; cook 3 minutes. Stir in orzo, spinach, chopped basil, and salt; cook 1 minute.
2. Preheat broiler. Place polenta on a baking sheet coated with cooking spray; broil 3 minutes on each side. Serve ragoût over polenta; garnish with basil sprigs, if desired. Yield: 4 servings (serving size: 1 cup ragoût and 3 polenta slices).

CALORIES 206 (14% from fat); FAT 3.3g (sat 0.4g, mono 1.7g, poly 0.5g); PROTEIN 7.3g; CARB 46g; FIBER 5.2g; CHOL 0mg; IRON 3.6mg; SODIUM 773mg; CALC 86mg

PASTA SKILLET WITH TOMATOES AND BEANS

2 teaspoons olive oil
2 cups chopped tomato
2 garlic cloves, minced
3 cups hot cooked angel hair pasta (about 6 ounces uncooked)
½ cup chopped fresh basil
½ teaspoon salt
¼ teaspoon black pepper
1 (15½-ounce) can chickpeas (garbanzo beans), drained
½ cup (2 ounces) grated Asiago or Parmesan cheese
2 tablespoons balsamic vinegar
Fresh basil sprigs (optional)

1. Heat oil in a large nonstick skillet over medium-high heat. Add chopped tomato and garlic; sauté 2 minutes. Add pasta and next 4 ingredients; cook 2 minutes. Place mixture in a bowl; stir in cheese and vinegar. Garnish with basil sprigs, if desired. Yield: 4 servings (serving size: 1¼ cups).

CALORIES 376 (21% from fat); FAT 8.9g (sat 3.1g, mono 3.4g, poly 1.6g); PROTEIN 17.5g; CARB 57.8g; FIBER 4.9g; CHOL 15mg; IRON 4.3mg; SODIUM 624mg; CALC 211mg

SMOTHERED SQUASH AND PINTO BEANS

2 teaspoons olive oil
½ cup chopped onion
2 teaspoons minced seeded jalapeño pepper
2 garlic cloves, minced
1 cup (½-inch-thick) sliced yellow squash
1 cup (½-inch-thick) sliced zucchini
½ cup fresh corn kernels
1 (16-ounce) can pinto beans, drained
1 (14.5-ounce) can diced tomatoes, undrained
3 thyme sprigs
½ cup (2 ounces) shredded Monterey Jack cheese
2 cups hot cooked long-grain rice

1. Heat oil in a large skillet over medium-high heat. Add onion, jalapeño pepper, and garlic; sauté 2 minutes. Stir in squash and zucchini; sauté 2 minutes. Add corn and next 3 ingredients; cover, reduce heat, and simmer 10 minutes. Discard thyme; sprinkle with cheese. Serve over rice. Yield: 4 servings (serving size: 1 cup squash mixture and ½ cup rice).

CALORIES 337 (20% from fat); FAT 7.5g (sat 3.2g, mono 3.1g, poly 0.7g); PROTEIN 13.7g; CARB 55.2g; FIBER 5.7g; CHOL 11mg; IRON 3.9mg; SODIUM 432mg; CALC 198mg

TUSCAN SKILLET SUPPER

2 teaspoons olive oil
1 cup chopped zucchini
½ cup sliced onion
½ cup sliced celery
½ cup diced red bell pepper
1 teaspoon dried oregano
2 garlic cloves, minced
1 cup diced tomato
1 (15-ounce) can cannellini beans or other white beans, rinsed and drained
2 rosemary sprigs
1 cup chopped spinach
½ cup (2 ounces) shredded part-skim mozzarella cheese
½ teaspoon salt
⅛ teaspoon black pepper

1. Heat oil in a large nonstick skillet over medium-high heat. Add zucchini and next 5 ingredients; sauté 2 minutes. Stir in tomato, beans, and rosemary; cook 2 minutes. Stir in spinach and remaining 3 ingredients; cook 1 minute or until spinach wilts and cheese begins to melt. Discard rosemary. Yield: 4 servings (serving size: 1¼ cups).

CALORIES 205 (29% from fat); FAT 6.7g (sat 2g, mono 2.8g, poly 1.3g); PROTEIN 11.4g; CARB 27.1g; FIBER 4.8g; CHOL 8mg; IRON 3.4mg; SODIUM 932mg; CALC 170mg

Global Grazing

Sit down for dinner with some friends overseas, and come away with new, healthy ways to eat.

The globalization of the world's cuisines is generally viewed as a negative. But some good news is emerging from this culinary cross-pollination. Instead of simply exporting our burgers and fries, we're importing foods, cooking styles, and mealtime traditions from around the world—many of which tend to be as healthful as they are enjoyable.

From the Japanese, we've discovered soy foods such as tofu, a plant protein that's versatile, flavor-absorbing, and nutritionally dazzling. From the Italians, we've adopted olive oil, which has proven to be the heart-friendliest of the fats. But sampling from the smorgasbord of the world's delights—even if you're selecting the most body-beneficial fare and customs—may not guarantee a healthful diet.

Food anthropologists stress that foreign food traditions are about more than fat grams and vitamin tallies. In many cultures, the normal meal is attended by several generations; our meals often include whoever happens to be in the room at the moment. Our meals lack connections.

The other lesson to be learned from the world's kitchens: the importance of seasonality and variety. Variety is the number-one dietary guideline, and if we targeted that, everything else would follow. We're used to having everything all the time so we take things for granted, and we eat the same stuff over and over. Cultures that don't have that bounty must stick with the season, so over the course of a year, their diets are more varied than ours. That diversity gives you the most nutrients, along with more interesting, satisfying flavors.

MOHAMBRA

This Lebanese spread is typically part of a mezze *platter, along with other spreads and salads. Serve at room temperature with pita wedges.*

2 pounds red bell peppers (about
   4 medium)
Cooking spray
1 cup chopped onion
½ cup chopped walnuts
1 tablespoon ground cumin
⅛ teaspoon ground red pepper
3 garlic cloves, minced
½ teaspoon salt
1 teaspoon honey
9 (6-inch) pitas, each cut into
   8 wedges

1. Preheat broiler. Cut bell peppers in half lengthwise, discarding seeds and membranes. Place pepper halves, skin sides up, on a foil-lined baking sheet; flatten with hand. Broil 3 inches from heat 12 minutes or until blackened. Place peppers in a zip-top plastic bag, and seal. Let stand 15 minutes. Peel peppers. Place bell peppers in a food processor; process until smooth.
2. Place a large nonstick skillet coated with cooking spray over medium-high heat until hot. Add onion and next 4 ingredients; sauté 8 minutes. Stir in bell pepper puree, salt, and honey; cook 5 minutes. Cool. Place onion mixture in food processor, and process until smooth. Serve with pita wedges. Yield: 18 servings (serving size: 2 tablespoons dip and 4 pita wedges).
Note: Store dip in an airtight container in refrigerator for up to 1 week.

CALORIES 98 (27% from fat); FAT 3g (sat 0.4g, mono 0.8g, poly 1.6g); PROTEIN 3.3g; CARB 15.3g; FIBER 1.7g; CHOL 0mg; IRON 2mg; SODIUM 176mg; CALC 26mg

---

VIETNAM. The Vietnamese table features lots of condiments, little dishes, and lettuce leaves—each diner takes a leaf; adds such things as rice noodles, bits of grilled meat or seafood, fresh herbs, and light sauces; rolls it up; and eats it, burrito-style. Flavors are bright, featuring fresh mint, cilantro, chiles, lemon grass, and the essential dipping sauce called *nuoc cham* (fermented-fish sauce with fresh lime juice, vinegar, garlic, chiles, and sugar).

GREECE. The landmark study that first trumpeted the healthfulness of the Mediterranean diet was from the Greek island of Crete. The traditional diet in Crete derived 40% to 50% of its calories from fat—but it was almost entirely from olive oil—and the Cretans had the lowest incidence of heart disease in the Western world. But they also had a very high activity level.

   The Greek diet is based on wheat, with bread as a staple. Meat is typically saved for special occasions. Otherwise, rural Greeks eat fish; lots of fruit, vegetables, and garlic; and some sheep and goat cheeses. They also enjoy red wine. Most of these components have gotten positive reviews in the medical community.

INDIA. India's cuisine varies greatly by region. But grain-based foods are the foundation of all the cuisines, and meat is typically scarce. About 80% of Indians are Hindu and, therefore, are vegetarians, while a significant minority are Muslims, who don't eat pork. But the wealthier, urban Indians are eating more meat and consuming more calories, and, in turn, are getting fatter. The mortality rate due to cardiovascular disease in India is among the highest in the world.

LEBANON/MIDDLE EAST. Middle Easterners share the Mediterranean emphasis on grains and olive oil. Unique, though, is the custom of eating *mezze*—lots of small plates of food. Instead of one big hunk of something, you get a little of this and a little of that, and a lot of tastes and textures.

CHINA. True Chinese cuisine relies on plenty of rice and fiber-rich vegetables, with just enough meat and fat for flavor. The typical Chinese approach to food encourages balance and creativity. The Chinese value texture, and they strive to balance the four primary flavors: sweet, sour, salty, and bitter. That's why they have a lot of smaller dishes in the same meal.

   The Chinese—and the rest of the world, for that matter—can teach us to take joy in our meals.

July · August

California Story

Decades in the making, the Golden State's bold and bountiful cuisine has become one of the world's finest, and changed the way all of us eat—for the better.

For more than 25 years now, California cuisine has been evolving and gaining a reputation. But what exactly is California cuisine? Short answer: an emphasis on fresh, locally grown produce with a decided preference for vegetables, fruits, and grains over meat and fat, and a passion for assimilating multicultural influences. But there's also an expanded definition that's as rich, complex, and evocative as the state itself. Primarily stemming from a Mediterranean sensibility, California cuisine is a healthy obsession with the quality of what you eat on a daily basis. It's planning menus around what looks best that day and season, in the market or the garden.

FLANK-STEAK FAJITAS WITH SPICY GARDEN VEGETABLES

Marinade:

- ⅓ cup minced fresh cilantro
- ⅓ cup fresh lime juice
- ⅓ cup water
- 4 teaspoons dried oregano
- 1 tablespoon ground cumin
- ½ teaspoon salt
- ¼ teaspoon black pepper
- ¼ teaspoon dried crushed red pepper
- 5 garlic cloves, minced

Fajitas:

- 1 cup vertically sliced onion
- 1 (1-pound) flank steak, cut into strips
- Cooking spray
- 1 cup red bell pepper strips
- 1 cup julienne-cut yellow squash
- 1 cup julienne-cut zucchini
- 1 cup fresh corn kernels (about 2 ears)
- 6 (10-inch) fat-free flour tortillas
- 2 cups chopped tomato
- 2 tablespoons low-fat sour cream

1. To prepare marinade, combine first 9 ingredients in a small bowl.
2. To prepare fajitas, combine ⅓ cup marinade, onion, and steak in a large zip-top plastic bag; seal. Set remaining marinade aside. Marinate steak mixture in refrigerator 1 hour, turning occasionally. Remove steak mixture from bag; discard marinade.
3. Place a large nonstick skillet coated with cooking spray over medium-high heat until hot. Add steak mixture, and stir-fry 5 minutes. Place steak mixture in a large bowl, and keep warm.
4. Add bell pepper, squash, zucchini, corn, and remaining marinade to skillet; stir-fry 5 minutes or until vegetables are crisp-tender. Add to steak mixture; toss gently.
5. Warm tortillas according to package directions. Arrange 1 cup steak mixture, ⅓ cup tomato, and 1 teaspoon sour cream down center of each tortilla; roll up. Yield: 6 servings.

CALORIES 345 (27% from fat); FAT 10.3g (sat 4.2g, mono 4g, poly 0.7g); PROTEIN 19.9g; CARB 45.5g; FIBER 4.4g; CHOL 42mg; IRON 5.9mg; SODIUM 685mg; CALC 61mg

CALIFORNIA CRAB POT STICKERS WITH KIWI SAUCE

California has become well-known for its kiwifruit, previously grown primarily in New Zealand. The kiwi is pureed here for an unusual sauce.

Filling:

- 1 pound lump crabmeat, drained and shell pieces removed
- ¼ cup minced green onions
- 1 tablespoon low-sodium soy sauce
- 1 teaspoon grated peeled fresh ginger
- ¼ teaspoon chile puree with garlic sauce
- 2 (10-ounce) packages frozen chopped spinach, thawed, drained, and squeezed dry
- 1 large egg white, lightly beaten
- 1 garlic clove, crushed

Pot stickers:

- 30 won ton wrappers
- 2 tablespoons cornstarch
- ½ cup water
- 1 tablespoon oyster sauce
- ½ teaspoon chile puree with garlic sauce
- ¼ teaspoon grated orange rind
- 2 tablespoons vegetable oil, divided

Kiwi sauce:

- 3 peeled kiwifruit (about ¾ pound)
- ⅓ cup soft tofu, drained
- 2 tablespoons seasoned rice vinegar

1. To prepare filling, combine first 8 ingredients in a large bowl.
2. To prepare pot stickers, working with 1 won ton wrapper at a time (cover remaining wrappers with a damp towel to keep them from drying), spoon about 1 tablespoon crabmeat mixture into center of each wrapper. Moisten edges of dough with water, and bring 2 opposite corners to

center, pinching points to seal. Bring remaining 2 corners to center, pinching points to seal. Pinch 4 edges together to seal. Gently flatten pot sticker using fingertips. Place pot stickers on a large baking sheet sprinkled with cornstarch.

3. Combine ½ cup water, oyster sauce, ½ teaspoon chile puree, and grated orange rind.

4. Heat 1 tablespoon oil in a large nonstick skillet over medium-high heat. Add half of pot stickers; cook 1 minute on each side or until browned. Add half of oyster sauce mixture to skillet; cover and cook 2 minutes. Uncover and cook 1 minute or until liquid evaporates. Remove from skillet. Wipe skillet clean with a paper towel. Repeat procedure with remaining 1 tablespoon oil, pot stickers, and oyster sauce mixture.

5. To prepare kiwi sauce, combine kiwifruit, tofu, and vinegar in a blender; process until smooth. Serve sauce with pot stickers. Yield: 10 appetizer servings (serving size: 3 pot stickers and 2 tablespoons sauce).

CALORIES 183 (22% from fat); FAT 4.4g (sat 0.7g, mono 1.1g, poly 2g); PROTEIN 14.5g; CARB 21.3g; FIBER 2.7g; CHOL 48mg; IRON 2.7mg; SODIUM 425mg; CALC 138mg

GRILLED-SEA BASS TACOS WITH FRESH-PEACH SALSA

Sea bass is abundant in California coastal waters, but any firm white fish such as halibut, grouper, or snapper will work.

Peach salsa:

    3 cups coarsely chopped peeled
         peaches (about 6 small
         peaches)
    1 cup diced red onion
    ¼ cup fresh lemon juice
    3 tablespoons minced fresh
         cilantro
    2 tablespoons minced shallots
    1 teaspoon chopped seeded
         serrano chile
    1 teaspoon honey
    ¼ teaspoon salt

Grilled sea bass:

    1 (1-pound) sea bass fillet
         (about 2 inches thick)
Cooking spray
    ¼ teaspoon salt
    ⅛ teaspoon black pepper

Tacos:

    8 taco shells
    2 cups shredded green cabbage
         or packaged coleslaw mix
    ½ cup minced fresh cilantro

1. To prepare peach salsa, combine first 8 ingredients in a bowl; toss gently.

2. To prepare grilled sea bass, place fish on grill rack coated with cooking spray; grill 6 minutes on each side or until fish flakes easily when tested with a fork. Sprinkle fish with ¼ teaspoon salt and pepper.

3. To prepare tacos, warm taco shells according to package directions. Cut fish into 8 pieces; place 1 piece of fish in each taco shell. Top each taco with ¼ cup peach salsa, ¼ cup shredded cabbage, and 1 tablespoon cilantro. Yield: 4 servings (serving size: 2 tacos).

CALORIES 334 (27% from fat); FAT 10.2g (sat 1.8g, mono 4g, poly 3.4g); PROTEIN 25.2g; CARB 36.6g; FIBER 4.4g; CHOL 78mg; IRON 3.6mg; SODIUM 510mg; CALC 140mg

CURRIED SANTA BARBARA SHRIMP SALAD

(pictured on page 185)

    ½ cup fat-free mayonnaise
    1 tablespoon curry powder
    1 tablespoon fresh lime juice
    1 teaspoon minced peeled fresh
         ginger
    ¾ cup sake (rice wine), divided
    ½ cup golden raisins
    1 pound large shrimp, peeled and
         deveined
    4 cups diced Asian pear or ripe pear
    1½ cups diced peeled mango
    6 tablespoons slivered almonds,
         toasted
    8 cups gourmet salad greens

1. Combine first 4 ingredients in a small bowl. Cover and chill.

2. Combine ½ cup sake and raisins in a glass measure; microwave at HIGH 1 minute or until boiling. Let stand 30 minutes. Drain.

3. Bring remaining ¼ cup sake to a boil in a nonstick skillet; add shrimp. Cover, reduce heat, and cook 2 minutes or until shrimp are done. Remove from heat; drain.

4. Combine mayonnaise mixture, raisins, shrimp, pear, mango, and almonds. Serve over salad greens. Yield: 4 servings (serving size: 2 cups salad greens and 1½ cups shrimp salad).

CALORIES 393 (17% from fat); FAT 7.5g (sat 0.9g, mono 3.6g, poly 1.9g); PROTEIN 22.8g; CARB 64.8g; FIBER 9.7g; CHOL 129mg; IRON 5.1mg; SODIUM 512mg; CALC 155mg

EVER CHANGING, EVER GOOD

California cuisine seems to constantly re-invent itself. Previously obscure ingredients are today commonly found in mainstream supermarkets.

Favorable climate means California cooks get to work with more fresh materials than can be found in any other state. More than 75 major commercial food crops provide more than half the entire country's larder. California is the nation's primary supplier of, among other things, almonds, artichokes, avocados, grapes, kiwifruit, olives, prunes, raisins, and walnuts.

In addition, the state has ample cattle ranches, lamb and poultry producers—and 840 miles of coastline producing Santa Barbara shrimp, lobster, oysters, abalone, and other seafood.

Despite its relatively recent prominence, the roots of California cuisine run deep—all the way back to the Native American tribes who found there an Eden of hunting and gathering.

Asian Primavera with Udon Noodles

4 cups hot water
3 cups dried porcini mushrooms (about 2 ounces)
8 ounces uncooked udon noodles (thick, round fresh Japanese wheat noodles) or spaghetti
2 tablespoons low-sodium soy sauce
½ teaspoon black pepper
1½ tablespoons dark sesame oil
1 cup cubed extra-firm tofu (about 4 ounces)
¼ cup chopped peeled fresh lemon grass
2 tablespoons minced peeled fresh ginger
2 garlic cloves, minced
2 cups (1-inch) julienne-cut zucchini
1 cup sliced button mushrooms
1 cup sliced shiitake mushroom caps
8 cups thinly sliced bok choy leaves
¼ cup minced fresh cilantro

1. Combine hot water and dried mushrooms; let stand 20 minutes. Drain mushrooms through a sieve over a bowl, reserving soaking liquid and mushrooms.
2. Cook noodles in boiling water in a large saucepan 3 minutes, omitting salt and fat; drain. Return noodles to pan. Add reserved soaking liquid, soy sauce, and pepper; bring to a boil, and cook 8 minutes or until liquid is absorbed. Stir in reserved porcini mushrooms.
3. Heat oil in a wok or large nonstick skillet. Add tofu and next 3 ingredients; stir-fry 30 seconds. Add zucchini, button mushrooms, and shiitake mushrooms; stir-fry 2 minutes. Add bok choy; stir-fry 3 minutes or until wilted.
4. Spoon 1½ cups noodle mixture into each of 4 shallow bowls; top each with 1½ cups zucchini mixture. Sprinkle each with 1 tablespoon cilantro. Yield: 4 servings.

CALORIES 383 (19% from fat); FAT 8.1g (sat 1.2g, mono 2.5g, poly 3.5g); PROTEIN 15.2g; CARB 63g; FIBER 5.8g; CHOL 0mg; IRON 6.3mg; SODIUM 347mg; CALC 212mg

California Tabbouleh in an Artichoke Bowl

Two of California's great crops—artichokes and garlic—come together in this fresh vegetarian dish.

4 large artichokes (about 1 pound each)
2 garlic cloves, halved
3 lemon slices
½ cup uncooked bulgur or cracked wheat
1 cup boiling water
2 cups diced tomato
½ cup frozen baby lima beans
½ cup chopped green onions
½ cup chopped fresh flat-leaf parsley
¼ cup chopped fresh mint
¼ cup fresh lemon juice
2 tablespoons sliced ripe olives
1 tablespoon extra-virgin olive oil
½ teaspoon salt
½ teaspoon black pepper
2 garlic cloves, minced

1. Cut off stem from each artichoke; remove bottom leaves, and discard. Trim about ½ inch from top of each artichoke. Place artichokes, stem ends down, in a large Dutch oven filled two-thirds with water. Add garlic halves and lemon slices; bring to a boil. Cover, reduce heat, and simmer 40 minutes or until a leaf near center of each artichoke pulls out easily. Remove artichokes from pan; discard cooking liquid, garlic, and lemon. Remove center leaves and furry thistles with a spoon, and discard. Set artichokes aside.
2. Combine bulgur and boiling water in a medium bowl. Cover and let stand 45 minutes. Drain. Combine bulgur, tomato, and remaining 10 ingredients in a large bowl.
3. Spoon 1 cup tabbouleh into center of each artichoke. Yield: 4 servings.

CALORIES 171 (24% from fat); FAT 4.6g (sat 0.7g, mono 2.9g, poly 0.7g); PROTEIN 6.5g; CARB 30.8g; FIBER 5.5g; CHOL 0mg; IRON 2.8mg; SODIUM 413mg; CALC 73mg

Gazpacho with Avocado and Cumin Chips

1½ cups bottled Bloody Mary mix (such as Major Peters)
1½ cups finely diced tomato
1 cup finely diced yellow bell pepper
¾ cup chopped seeded peeled cucumber
¾ cup finely diced red onion
2 tablespoons fresh lime juice
1 teaspoon red wine vinegar
1 teaspoon Worcestershire sauce
½ teaspoon freshly ground black pepper
2 garlic cloves, crushed
1 (5.5-ounce) can low-sodium vegetable juice
1 (5.5-ounce) can tomato juice
¾ cup diced peeled avocado
¾ cup chopped green onions
Cumin Chips

1. Combine first 12 ingredients in a large nonaluminum bowl. Cover and chill. Serve with avocado, green onions, and Cumin Chips. Yield: 6 servings (serving size: 1 cup soup, 2 tablespoons avocado, 2 tablespoons green onions, and 4 tortilla chips).

CALORIES 129 (27% from fat); FAT 3.8g (sat 0.6g, mono 2g, poly 0.7g); PROTEIN 3g; CARB 22.8g; FIBER 3.4g; CHOL 0mg; IRON 2mg; SODIUM 571mg; CALC 75mg

Cumin Chips:

4 (6-inch) corn tortillas, each cut into 6 wedges
Cooking spray
½ teaspoon ground cumin

1. Preheat oven to 350°.
2. Place tortilla wedges on a large baking sheet. Lightly coat wedges with cooking spray, and sprinkle with cumin. Bake at 350° for 10 minutes or until chips are lightly browned and crisp. Yield: 2 dozen (serving size: 4 chips).

BANANA-DATE CRÈME BRÛLÉE

Southern California dates are grown in Indio, located near Palm Springs.

    1   cup whole pitted dates (about 8
        ounces)
    1   cup evaporated skim milk
    ¾   cup sliced ripe banana
    ½   cup 2% reduced-fat milk
    2   tablespoons sugar
    2   teaspoons vanilla extract
    1   teaspoon ground cinnamon
    ¼   teaspoon salt
    2   large eggs
    2   large egg whites
        Cooking spray
    1   tablespoon sugar

1. Preheat oven to 300°.
2. Combine first 8 ingredients in a blender, and process until smooth (about 2 minutes). Add eggs and egg whites to blender; process just until smooth. Divide mixture evenly among 6 (6-ounce) ramekins or custard cups coated with cooking spray.
3. Place ramekins in a 13 x 9-inch baking pan; add hot water to pan to a depth of 1 inch. Bake at 300° for 55 minutes or until a knife inserted in center comes out clean. Remove ramekins from pan, and sprinkle each with ½ teaspoon sugar.
4. Preheat broiler. Place ramekins on a jelly-roll pan, and broil 3 minutes or until sugar melts. Yield: 6 servings.

CALORIES 226 (10% from fat); FAT 2.6g (sat 0.9g, mono 0.9g, poly 0.3g); PROTEIN 8.1g; CARB 45.1g; FIBER 4g; CHOL 77mg; IRON 1mg; SODIUM 198mg; CALC 176mg

Spanish Made Easy

The exciting international flavors of the Caribbean come from many sources—but none older than Spain.

Island cooking throbs with the flavors of Africa, Europe, and the Americas. But Spain's influence has the longest reach—all the way back to Columbus. Pork, oranges, bananas, plantains, red wine, olive oil, garlic, bell peppers, and almonds all arrived with explorers and conquistadors.

The Caribbean, in turn, had a culinary impact of its own. Columbus took the tomato home, where it distinguished itself by becoming essential to Mediterranean cuisine.

Native foods such as taro root, sweet potato, calabaza squash, and pumpkin are the heart of Caribbean cooking, but the Iberian imports give it soul. The Spanish trinity of sautéed garlic, onion, and bell peppers forms the base for soups, stews, and rice dishes, and garlic-spiked chorizo sausage is so full of pep that a few slices can bring a soup of beans and bananas to life.

SWEET POTATO-PLANTAIN BAKE

    7   cups (½-inch) cubed peeled sweet
        potato (about 2¼ pounds)
    2   cups sliced very ripe plantain
        (about 1 pound)
    ⅓   cup packed brown sugar
    ¼   cup fat-free milk
    ¼   cup low-fat sour cream
    ¼   teaspoon ground allspice
        Cooking spray
    ¼   cup whole pitted dates, chopped
    ¼   cup slivered almonds, toasted

1. Preheat oven to 350°.
2. Place potato in a saucepan, and cover with water; bring to a boil. Reduce heat; simmer 7 minutes. Add plantain; simmer 7 minutes or until very tender. Drain well. Return potato and plantain to pan. Add sugar and next 3 ingredients; beat 2 minutes at high speed of a mixer until smooth. Spoon into a 1½-quart baking dish coated with cooking spray. Sprinkle with dates and almonds. Bake at 350° for 30 minutes or until thoroughly heated. Yield: 8 servings (serving size: ¾ cup).

CALORIES 283 (10% from fat); FAT 3.2g (sat 0.8g, mono 1.3g, poly 0.5g); PROTEIN 3.9g; CARB 63.6g; FIBER 4.7g; CHOL 3mg; IRON 1.4mg; SODIUM 29mg; CALC 63mg

PICADILLO EMPANADITAS

Empanadas are pastry turnovers filled with savory meats and/or vegetables. Our smaller versions, eaten as appetizers, are called empanaditas. Picadillo is a traditional Cuban mixture of ground beef and seasonings.

    ¼   pound ground round
    3   tablespoons finely chopped
        onion
    3   tablespoons finely chopped
        green bell pepper
    1   garlic clove, minced
    3   tablespoons raisins,
        chopped
    2   tablespoons diced pimento
    1   tablespoon capers, chopped
    1   tablespoon tomato paste
    ½   teaspoon bottled habanero sauce
        or other hot sauce
    ⅛   teaspoon salt
    1   (10-ounce) can refrigerated
        pizza crust
        Cooking spray

1. Preheat oven to 425°.
2. Cook beef in a small nonstick skillet over medium-high heat until browned, stirring to crumble. Drain well, and return beef to skillet. Add onion, bell pepper, and garlic; sauté 5 minutes or until tender. Remove from heat; stir in raisins and next 5 ingredients.
3. Divide pizza crust dough into 18 portions; cover dough, and let rest 5 minutes. Shape each portion into a ball, and roll each into a 3-inch circle on a lightly floured surface. Spoon 2 level teaspoons of beef mixture onto half of each dough circle. Moisten edges of dough with water. Fold dough over beef filling, and press edges together to seal.
4. Place empanaditas on a large baking sheet coated with cooking spray. Lightly coat tops of empanaditas with cooking spray. Bake at 425° for 10 minutes or until lightly browned. Yield: 9 appetizer servings (serving size: 2 empanaditas).

CALORIES 114 (14% from fat); FAT 1.8g (sat 0.5g, mono 0.7g, poly 0.4g); PROTEIN 3.9g; CARB 17.8g; FIBER 0.4g; CHOL 8mg; IRON 0.5mg; SODIUM 267mg; CALC 4mg

Sautéed Shrimp with Calabaza and Spicy Ginger Relish

Spicy ginger relish:

⅓ cup finely chopped red bell pepper
2 tablespoons mango nectar
1 tablespoon minced crystallized ginger
1 tablespoon finely chopped green onions
1 teaspoon lemon juice
⅛ teaspoon minced seeded habanero pepper or dried crushed red pepper

Remaining ingredients:

2 teaspoons olive oil, divided
½ cup minced fresh mint
¼ cup minced fresh thyme
1 tablespoon thawed orange juice concentrate
2 teaspoons coriander seeds, crushed
½ teaspoon salt
¼ teaspoon black pepper
6 garlic cloves, minced
1¼ pounds large shrimp, peeled and deveined
1 calabaza or butternut squash (about 1¼ pounds), cut in half
½ cup fat-free, less-sodium chicken broth
2 tablespoons brown sugar
¼ teaspoon salt
⅛ teaspoon ground allspice

1. To prepare spicy ginger relish, combine first 6 ingredients in a small bowl; let stand at room temperature 1 hour.
2. Combine 1 teaspoon oil, mint, and next 6 ingredients in a food processor; process until smooth. Combine mint mixture and shrimp in a large zip-top plastic bag; seal bag. Marinate in refrigerator 40 minutes, turning bag occasionally.
3. Preheat oven to 400°.
4. Place squash, cut sides down, on a baking sheet. Bake at 400° for 40 minutes or until very tender. Peel squash; discard seeds and membrane. Mash pulp. Combine squash, broth, and remaining 3 ingredients in a food processor; process until smooth. Keep warm.
5. Remove shrimp mixture from bag. Heat remaining 1 teaspoon oil in a large nonstick skillet over medium-high heat. Add shrimp mixture; sauté 3 minutes on each side or until done. Serve over squash puree; top with spicy ginger relish. Yield: 4 servings (serving size: 4 ounces shrimp, ½ cup squash puree, and 1 tablespoon relish).

CALORIES 234 (17% from fat); FAT 4.5g (sat 0.8g, mono 2.1g, poly 1g); PROTEIN 23.8g; CARB 25.6g; FIBER 2.3g; CHOL 162mg; IRON 4.5mg; SODIUM 679mg; CALC 143mg

Beef Stew with Cuban Coffee Gravy

1 pound boned rump roast
¼ teaspoon salt
¼ teaspoon coarsely ground black pepper
1½ cups strong brewed coffee
1 cup no-salt-added beef broth
½ cup finely chopped onion
⅓ cup dry red wine
2 garlic cloves, minced
1 cup diced peeled taro root or potato
1 cup sliced mushrooms
¼ cup whole pitted dates, chopped
1 tablespoon capers
2 cups hot cooked long-grain rice
½ cup shredded chayote or yellow squash

1. Trim fat from beef; cut beef into 1-inch cubes. Sprinkle with salt and pepper. Heat a large saucepan over medium-high heat. Add beef, and cook 5 minutes or until browned. Add coffee and next 4 ingredients; bring to a boil. Cover, reduce heat, and simmer 45 minutes.
2. Add taro root and next 3 ingredients to pan; bring to a boil. Cover, reduce heat, and simmer 20 minutes. Serve over rice; top with chayote. Yield: 4 servings (serving size: 1¼ cups stew, ½ cup rice, and 2 tablespoons chayote).

CALORIES 351 (13% from fat); FAT 4.9g (sat 1.7g, mono 1.9g, poly 0.3g); PROTEIN 30.1g; CARB 44.9g; FIBER 3g; CHOL 65mg; IRON 4.5mg; SODIUM 383mg; CALC 35mg

Chorizo-Banana Bean Soup

Sausage and banana may seem like an odd combination, but the spicy chorizo and the sweet flavor of bananas work beautifully together. This soup tastes even better the next day once the flavors have blended.

1 cup dried red beans (about 6 ounces)
1 cup dried black beans (about 6 ounces)
1½ teaspoons olive oil
1⅓ cups diced smoked chorizo sausage (about 4 ounces)
½ cup diced carrot
⅓ cup diced onion
⅓ cup diced green bell pepper
1 teaspoon minced seeded habanero pepper
4 garlic cloves, minced
3⅓ cups water
1 (16-ounce) can fat-free, less-sodium chicken broth
2 bay leaves
¾ cup chopped seeded plum tomato
½ teaspoon salt
¼ teaspoon black pepper
¼ cup mashed ripe banana

1. Sort and wash beans; place beans in a large Dutch oven. Cover with water to 2 inches above beans; bring to a boil, and cook 2 minutes. Remove from heat; cover and let stand 1 hour. Drain; return beans to pan.
2. Heat oil in a large nonstick skillet over medium-low heat. Add sausage and next 5 ingredients; sauté 15 minutes or until vegetables are tender. Add 3⅓ cups water and broth to beans in pan; bring to a boil. Stir in sausage mixture and bay leaves; return to a boil. Cover, reduce heat, and simmer 1½ hours or until beans are tender. Add tomato, salt, and black pepper; simmer 15 minutes. Stir in banana, and remove from heat. Remove bay leaves. Yield: 8 servings (serving size: 1 cup).

CALORIES 223 (24% from fat); FAT 5.9g (sat 1.8g, mono 2.6g, poly 0.8g); PROTEIN 12.4g; CARB 31.6g; FIBER 5.9g; CHOL 11mg; IRON 3mg; SODIUM 399mg; CALC 56mg

Warm Mojo Salsa

Mojo *("mo-yo" in the Caribbean) is a condiment consisting of garlic, oil, and a citrus juice—usually lime.*

- 1 tablespoon vegetable oil
- 1 teaspoon annatto (achiote seed) (optional)
- 4 garlic cloves, minced
- 3 tablespoons fresh orange juice
- 3 tablespoons fresh lime juice
- 2 cups diced seeded plum tomato (about 4 small)
- 1 tablespoon minced fresh basil
- 1 tablespoon minced fresh chives
- ¼ teaspoon salt
- ¼ teaspoon black pepper

1. Combine oil and annatto (if desired) in a saucepan; cook over low heat 5 minutes. Remove from heat; let stand 10 minutes. Strain through a sieve over a bowl; discard seeds. Heat 1½ teaspoons oil mixture in pan; discard remaining oil mixture. Add garlic; sauté 3 minutes. Add orange juice and lime juice; bring to a simmer. Stir in tomato and remaining ingredients; remove from heat. Serve warm over grilled fish or chicken. Yield: 2¼ cups (serving size: 2 tablespoons).

Note: This salsa can be made up to two days ahead of time; cover and chill. Reheat in the microwave or in a saucepan over medium heat. If you do not use the annatto, use only 1½ teaspoons oil.

CALORIES 11 (37% from fat); FAT 0.5g (sat 0.1g, mono 0.1g, poly 0.2g); PROTEIN 0.3g; CARB 1.7g; FIBER 0.3g; CHOL 0mg; IRON 0.1mg; SODIUM 35mg; CALC 3mg

Chocolate-Orange Flan

- ½ cup sugar
- Cooking spray
- 1¼ cups 1% low-fat milk
- 2 tablespoons Dutch process cocoa
- 2 tablespoons dark rum
- 1 teaspoon grated orange rind
- 2 large egg yolks
- 1 large egg white
- 1 (14-ounce) can fat-free sweetened condensed milk

1. Preheat oven to 300°.
2. Place sugar in a medium, heavy skillet over medium heat; cook until sugar dissolves. Continue cooking an additional 1½ minutes or until golden. Immediately pour into a 9-inch quiche dish coated with cooking spray, tipping quickly until caramelized sugar coats bottom of dish.
3. Combine 1% milk and remaining 6 ingredients in a food processor; process until smooth. Pour milk mixture over caramelized syrup in dish. Place dish in a shallow roasting pan, and add hot water to pan to a depth of 1 inch. Bake at 300° for 1 hour or until a knife inserted in center of flan comes out clean. Remove dish from roasting pan, and cool 30 minutes on a wire rack. Cover and chill at least 3 hours. Place a plate upside down on top of dish, and invert flan onto plate. Drizzle any remaining caramelized syrup over flan. Yield: 9 servings (serving size: 1 wedge).

CALORIES 201 (8% from fat); FAT 1.8g (sat 0.7g, mono 0.5g, poly 0.2g); PROTEIN 5.8g; CARB 40.1g; FIBER 0g; CHOL 50mg; IRON 0.4mg; SODIUM 70mg; CALC 160mg

Caribbean Storm

- 2 cups fresh orange juice
- ¾ cup papaya or mango nectar
- ¼ cup white rum
- ¼ cup blue curaçao liqueur
- ⅛ teaspoon freshly grated nutmeg

1. Combine first 3 ingredients in a pitcher; chill. Fill 4 glasses with ice cubes; add ¾ cup orange juice mixture to each glass. Slowly pour 1 tablespoon liqueur down inside of each glass (do not stir before serving). Sprinkle evenly with nutmeg. Yield: 4 servings.

CALORIES 171 (1% from fat); FAT 0.2g (sat 0.1g, mono 0g, poly 0.1g); PROTEIN 0.8g; CARB 21g; FIBER 0.3g; CHOL 0mg; IRON 0.2mg; SODIUM 2mg; CALC 11mg

Latin School

Here's a quick rundown of what you'll need to take your taste buds on a Caribbean tour.

Annatto: Also known as achiote seed; used mainly to add a golden color to dishes such as rice, stews, and sauces. This seed is starting to show up more frequently in the spice section of supermarkets.

Calabaza: Often called Cuban or West Indian pumpkin in produce markets. Round in shape, it can range in color from green to light red-orange. Its flesh is brilliant orange and has a sweet flavor. Butternut squash can be substituted for calabaza.

Chorizo: Spicy, garlic-seasoned, dried pork sausage used more as a flavoring agent than a main ingredient. It can be found prepackaged in the refrigerated meat section. If chorizo is unavailable, you can substitute turkey kielbasa.

Curaçao [KOO-rah-sao]: An orange-flavored, clear or blue-tinted liqueur made from the dried peel of bitter orange. It is produced on its namesake island.

Plantain: A popular cousin of the banana, it's found in the produce section of most supermarkets. When green and hard, plantains are used much like potatoes; when dark and ripe, they turn soft and sweet.

Taro Root: Starchy, potato-like tubers with brown, fibrous skin and grayish-white flesh. It's usually found in the produce section of supermarkets or at Latin-American markets. Any type of potato is a suitable substitute.

Cool Desserts from Hot Cooks

Five celebrated cooks show how to capture the season in desserts you won't believe.

Summer days are when rules relax, when time ticks more slowly, when memories are made. The perfect summer dessert is like a summer day—indulgent and easy.

Think about it: The season for tree-ripened peaches is short. Ice cream melts in a moment on a hot August afternoon. Summer sweets are fleeting pleasures, meant to be eaten fast, before they disappear anyway—which is the way it should be.

Summer desserts should be light. In that spirit, we've collected the favorite low-fat desserts from five leading food experts, cookbook writers, and restaurateurs who know about what's hot, what's cool, and what can amaze with less than two grams of fat.

VIENNESE CARAMEL CUSTARD

(pictured on page 186)

For Nick Malgieri, director of the baking program at Peter Kump's New York Cooking School, a Viennese version of the classic caramel custard is the perfect summer solution.

1¼ cups sugar, divided
½ teaspoon fresh lemon juice
½ teaspoon water
2½ cups fat-free milk
6 large egg whites
2 large eggs
1 tablespoon vanilla extract
Thin lemon slices (optional)

1. Preheat oven to 300°.
2. Combine ½ cup sugar and lemon juice in a small, heavy saucepan over medium-high heat; cook until sugar dissolves. Continue cooking an additional 4 minutes or until golden. Immediately pour into 6 (4-ounce) ramekins, tipping quickly until caramelized sugar coats bottom of cups.
3. Combine ½ cup sugar and ½ teaspoon water in a large, heavy saucepan over medium-high heat; cook until sugar dissolves. Continue cooking about 4 minutes or until golden, and set aside.
4. Heat remaining ¼ cup sugar and milk over medium-high heat in a small, heavy saucepan to 180° or until bubbles form around the edge (do not boil). Gradually add hot milk mixture to sugar mixture in large saucepan, stirring constantly with a whisk. Cook over medium-high heat until sugar melts. Remove from heat.
5. Combine egg whites and eggs in a large bowl, stirring well with a whisk. Gradually add hot milk mixture to eggs, stirring constantly with a whisk. Stir in vanilla extract. Pour into prepared ramekins. Place ramekins in a shallow roasting pan; add hot water to pan to a depth of 1 inch. Bake at 300° for 45 minutes or until a knife inserted in center comes out clean. Remove from pan; cool completely on a wire rack. Cover and chill at least 3 hours.
6. Loosen edges of custards with a knife or rubber spatula. Place a dessert plate, upside down, on top of each ramekin; invert custards onto plates. Drizzle syrup over custards; garnish with lemon slices, if desired. Yield: 6 servings.

CALORIES 245 (7% from fat); FAT 1.9g (sat 0.7g, mono 0.7g, poly 0.3g); PROTEIN 9g; CARB 47.4g; FIBER 0g; CHOL 76mg; IRON 0.3mg; SODIUM 128mg; CALC 137mg

LEMON-GINGER ICE CREAM

Atlanta cooking teacher and cookbook author Shirley Corriher created this brightly flavored lemon-ginger ice cream with a secret ingredient for incredibly creamy texture—fat-free sour cream. The result provides so much of the textural luxury of full-fat premium ice cream you'd swear it was hand-cranked on a back porch at sunset.

¾ cup packed light brown sugar
2 tablespoons light-colored corn syrup
2 tablespoons minced crystallized ginger (optional)
2 teaspoons vanilla extract
1½ teaspoons grated lemon rind
⅛ teaspoon salt
2 (16-ounce) cartons fat-free sour cream
2 (8-ounce) cartons lemon low-fat yogurt
Lemon rind strips (optional)

1. Combine first 8 ingredients in a food processor, and process until smooth, scraping sides of bowl occasionally.
2. Pour mixture into the freezer can of an ice-cream freezer; freeze according to manufacturer's instructions. Spoon ice cream into a freezer-safe container; cover and freeze 1 hour or until firm. Garnish with lemon rind strips, if desired. Yield: 11 servings (serving size: ½ cup).
Note: Crystallized ginger can be found with the spices in the supermarket. If you're not a fan of ginger, omit it. We tested the recipe without the ginger and got a nice lemon taste.

CALORIES 187 (1% from fat); FAT 0.3g (sat 0.2g, mono 0.1g, poly 0g); PROTEIN 7.4g; CARB 36.1g; FIBER 0g; CHOL 0mg; IRON 0.5mg; SODIUM 122mg; CALC 68mg

MANGO-LIME ICE

Rick Bayless, owner of the award-winning Frontera Grill and Topolo-bampo in Chicago, draws on the cuisine of Mexico. This tropical fruit ice gets its tangy flavor from the lime and is perfect after a spicy meal.

    2   cups chopped peeled ripe
          mango (about 1½ pounds)
    1¼ cups sugar
    1   cup water
    ⅓   cup fresh lime juice
    1½ tablespoons grated orange rind

1. Combine ingredients in a food processor; process until smooth. Press mango mixture through a sieve over a bowl, reserving liquid; discard pulp.
2. Pour mango mixture into the freezer can of an ice-cream freezer; freeze according to manufacturer's instructions. Spoon mixture into a freezer-safe container; cover and freeze 1 hour or until firm. Yield: 8 servings (serving size: ½ cup).

CALORIES 151 (1% from fat); FAT 0.1g (sat 0g, mono 0.1g, poly 0g); PROTEIN 0.3g; CARB 39.4g; FIBER 0.6g; CHOL 0mg; IRON 0.1mg; SODIUM 1mg; CALC 7mg

STRAWBERRIES WITH BROWN SUGAR AND BALSAMIC VINEGAR

This easy recipe is one of Nathalie Dupree's favorite "stand-bys."

    2   cups halved small strawberries
    2   tablespoons brown sugar
    1½ teaspoons balsamic vinegar
    ⅛   teaspoon black pepper
    ½   cup lemon low-fat yogurt
    Fresh mint leaves (optional)

1. Combine first 4 ingredients in a bowl; cover and marinate in refrigerator 30 minutes. Spoon ½ cup strawberry mixture into each of 4 bowls; top each with 2 tablespoons yogurt. Garnish with fresh mint leaves, if desired. Yield: 4 servings.

CALORIES 80 (6% from fat); FAT 0.5g (sat 0.1g, mono 0.1g, poly 0.1g); PROTEIN 1.6g; CARB 18.3g; FIBER 2g; CHOL 0mg; IRON 0.4mg; SODIUM 22mg; CALC 52mg

BLACKBERRY SOUP WITH PEACHES AND BERRIES

Pastry chef Lindsey Shere of Chez Panisse in Berkeley, California, created this refreshing, simple soup one summer as the result of an overgrown blackberry patch.

    3½ cups blackberries, divided
    ½   cup water
    6   tablespoons sugar, divided
    1   tablespoon kirsch (cherry brandy)
    2   cups sliced peeled peaches

1. Combine 2½ cups blackberries and ½ cup water in a medium nonaluminum saucepan. Bring to a simmer; cover and cook 15 minutes or until blackberries are very soft. Press blackberry mixture through a sieve over a small bowl, reserving liquid; discard seeds. Combine blackberry liquid, 3 tablespoons sugar, and kirsch; cover and chill at least 2 hours.
2. Combine 3 tablespoons sugar and peaches; toss gently to coat. Spoon ¼ cup blackberry mixture into each of 6 shallow soup bowls. Arrange ⅓ cup peach slices and about 2½ tablespoons blackberries over each serving. Yield: 6 servings.

CALORIES 123 (3% from fat); FAT 0.4g (sat 0g, mono 0.1g, poly 0.2g); PROTEIN 1g; CARB 30.4g; FIBER 7g; CHOL 0mg; IRON 0.5mg; SODIUM 0mg; CALC 30mg

Ahead of the Curve

Vegetarian influences are changing menus in restaurants across America. Try these trendsetters in your own home.

The number of vegetarian offerings in restaurants is soaring. Small ethnic restaurants as well as hip bistros are serving creative vegetarian fare, and in many cases are stressing the use of organically grown produce.

Unlike in the past, many restaurants can accommodate requests for meatless versions of their meat-based dishes. Plus, more high-end restaurants are devoting larger chunks of their menus to vegetarian dishes, sometimes with multiple-course meatless meals.

There's more extensive use of grains and noodles. Quinoa, basmati rice, cracked wheat, and barley are taking the place of plain rice, and noodles of all sizes and shapes are showing up nearly everywhere.

You'll find that many restaurants are reducing their emphasis on poultry and beef. Instead, they're beefing up their vegetable and starch side dishes.

Fusion cooking has found its way onto vegetarian menus in virtually every corner of the country. Afghan, Ethiopian, Vietnamese, Lebanese, Mexican, and other influences are not only healthful, but also generally inexpensive.

LINGUINE WITH ARUGULA AND SUN-DRIED TOMATOES

    2   tablespoons olive oil
    1   cup thinly sliced onion
    3   cups chopped trimmed arugula
    ½   cup canned vegetable broth
    ⅓   cup chopped sun-dried tomatoes,
          packed without oil
    ½   teaspoon ground red pepper
    2   garlic cloves, minced
    4   cups hot cooked linguine
          (about 8 ounces uncooked
          pasta)
    ¼   cup (1 ounce) grated Asiago or
          fresh Parmesan cheese

1. Heat oil in a large nonstick skillet over medium-high heat. Add onion, and sauté 4 minutes or until tender. Add arugula and next 4 ingredients; cook 3 minutes. Add linguine; cook 2 minutes or until thoroughly heated. Sprinkle with cheese; toss well. Yield: 4 servings (serving size: 1¼ cups).

CALORIES 339 (27% from fat); FAT 10.2g (sat 2.3g, mono 5.7g, poly 1.1g); PROTEIN 11.7g; CARB 50.9g; FIBER 2g; CHOL 7mg; IRON 2.3mg; SODIUM 372mg; CALC 148mg

SAMOSA QUESADILLAS

2 teaspoons olive oil
1 cup very thinly sliced cabbage
½ cup chopped onion
½ cup chopped carrot
1 tablespoon curry powder
1 teaspoon minced peeled fresh
   ginger
2 garlic cloves, minced
1 cup mashed cooked peeled
   potato
¼ cup frozen green peas, thawed
1 tablespoon low-sodium soy sauce
8 (6-inch) fat-free flour tortillas
1 cup (4 ounces) shredded
   Muenster cheese

1. Preheat oven to 350°.
2. Heat oil in a large nonstick skillet over medium-high heat. Add cabbage and next 5 ingredients; sauté 3 minutes or until cabbage is crisp-tender. Remove from heat; stir in potato, peas, and soy sauce.
3. Place 4 tortillas on a large baking sheet. Spread about ½ cup potato mixture over each tortilla; top each with ¼ cup cheese and a tortilla. Bake at 350° for 15 minutes or until thoroughly heated. Cut each into 4 wedges. Yield: 4 servings (serving size: 1 quesadilla).

CALORIES 349 (29% from fat); FAT 11.2g (sat 5.8g, mono 4.2g, poly 0.5g); PROTEIN 11.8g; CARB 51.3g; FIBER 4.3g; CHOL 27mg; IRON 3.9mg; SODIUM 831mg; CALC 236mg

SPICY WHITE-BEAN SPREAD

Serve as a dip with raw vegetables or with a crusty baguette.

3 tablespoons fresh lime juice
2 tablespoons extra-virgin olive oil
1 teaspoon ground cumin
2 (16-ounce) cans navy beans,
   drained
2 garlic cloves, chopped
1 jalapeño pepper, seeded and
   chopped
¾ cup minced red bell pepper
¾ cup minced fresh cilantro
¼ cup minced green onions
½ teaspoon salt

1. Place first 6 ingredients in a food processor, and pulse 2 times or until well-blended. Pour bean mixture into a large bowl; stir in bell pepper and remaining ingredients. Yield: 3½ cups (serving size: 1 tablespoon).

CALORIES 19 (24% from fat); FAT 0.5g (sat 0.1g, mono 0.4g, poly 0.1g); PROTEIN 0.8g; CARB 2.8g; FIBER 0.5g; CHOL 0mg; IRON 0.3mg; SODIUM 48mg; CALC 7mg

CHICKPEA-AND-CORN PATTIES

Serve these patties with salsa, either a commercial brand or one from our fresh salsa recipes that start on page 194.

2 teaspoons olive oil, divided
1½ cups fresh corn kernels (about
   3 ears)
1 cup chopped onion
1 teaspoon minced fresh or
   ¼ teaspoon dried thyme
1 (19-ounce) can chickpeas
   (garbanzo beans), rinsed and
   drained
½ cup fresh breadcrumbs
3 tablespoons cornmeal, divided
½ teaspoon salt
¼ teaspoon ground red pepper
Cooking spray

1. Heat 1 teaspoon oil in a large nonstick skillet over medium-high heat. Add corn, onion, and thyme; sauté 2 minutes. Place onion mixture, chickpeas, breadcrumbs, 2 tablespoons cornmeal, salt, and red pepper in a food processor. Pulse 2 times or until combined and chunky. Divide chickpea mixture into 4 equal portions, shaping each into a ½-inch-thick patty; dredge chickpea patties in remaining 1 tablespoon cornmeal.
2. Heat remaining 1 teaspoon oil in a large nonstick skillet coated with cooking spray over medium-high heat. Add patties, and cook 5 minutes. Carefully turn patties; cook 5 minutes or until golden. Yield: 4 servings.

CALORIES 253 (19% from fat); FAT 5.4g (sat 0.7g, mono 2.4g, poly 1.6g); PROTEIN 10.3g; CARB 44.1g; FIBER 5.9g; CHOL 0mg; IRON 3mg; SODIUM 488mg; CALC 54mg

SPICY TOFU AND NOODLES WITH MUSHROOMS

1 cup boiling water
1 (0.5-ounce) package dried wood
   ear or shiitake mushrooms
1 tablespoon vegetable oil
½ cup finely chopped onion
½ cup finely chopped carrot
½ cup thinly sliced green onions
2 teaspoons minced peeled fresh
   ginger
1 teaspoon chile-garlic sauce (such
   as Lee Kum Kee)
2 garlic cloves, minced
1 tablespoon cornstarch
1 tablespoon water
2½ cups cooked rice vermicelli
1 tablespoon low-sodium soy
   sauce
1 tablespoon hoisin sauce
1 teaspoon sugar
2 teaspoons rice vinegar
1 (12.3-ounce) package firm tofu,
   cubed (about 2 cups)
12 Bibb lettuce leaves
½ cup hoisin sauce
¼ cup pine nuts, toasted

1. Combine boiling water and mushrooms in a bowl; cover and let stand 15 minutes. Drain and chop mushrooms.
2. Heat oil in a large skillet over medium-high heat. Add mushrooms, chopped onion and next 5 ingredients; sauté 3 minutes. Combine cornstarch and 1 tablespoon water in a small bowl. Add cornstarch mixture, vermicelli, and next 5 ingredients to skillet; sauté 2 minutes or until sauce is thick. Spoon ⅓ cup tofu mixture onto each lettuce leaf; drizzle 2 teaspoons hoisin sauce over each serving. Sprinkle each serving with 1 teaspoon pine nuts. Yield: 12 servings.

CALORIES 160 (28% from fat); FAT 4.9g (sat 0.7g, mono 1.3g, poly 2.1g); PROTEIN 5.7g; CARB 24.7g; FIBER 1.4g; CHOL 0mg; IRON 3.2mg; SODIUM 290mg; CALC 65mg

STUFFED PORTOBELLO MUSHROOMS

Marinated mushrooms:

½ cup chopped fresh cilantro
¼ cup fresh lime juice
1 tablespoon olive oil
2 teaspoons dried oregano
1 teaspoon black pepper
4 garlic cloves, minced
4 large portobello mushrooms, gills and stems removed

Stuffing:

1 teaspoon olive oil
½ cup diced red bell pepper
½ cup diced yellow bell pepper
½ cup diced onion
4 cups (½-inch) cubed sourdough bread (about 6 [1-ounce] slices)
½ cup (2 ounces) shredded reduced-fat Monterey Jack cheese
¼ cup minced fresh parsley
2 tablespoons water
2 large eggs, lightly beaten
2 tablespoons grated Parmesan cheese

1. To prepare marinated mushrooms, combine first 6 ingredients in a large zip-top plastic bag. Add mushrooms; seal and marinate in refrigerator 15 minutes.
2. Preheat oven to 350°.
3. To prepare stuffing, heat 1 teaspoon oil in a large nonstick skillet over medium-high heat until hot. Add bell peppers and onion; sauté 3 minutes. Combine bell pepper mixture and bread cubes in a large bowl; stir in Jack cheese and next 3 ingredients.
4. Drain mushrooms; discard marinade. Place mushroom caps, stem sides up, on a baking sheet. Spoon 1 cup stuffing into each mushroom cap, and sprinkle each with 1½ teaspoons Parmesan cheese. Bake at 350° for 25 minutes or until stuffing is lightly browned and mushrooms are tender. Yield: 4 servings.

CALORIES 277 (35% from fat); FAT 10.7g (sat 3.8g, mono 4.5g, poly 1.3g); PROTEIN 15.8g; CARB 31.7g; FIBER 3.5g; CHOL 123mg; IRON 4mg; SODIUM 433mg; CALC 250mg

LEBANESE FATOUSH SALAD

1 cup red bell pepper strips
1 cup green bell pepper strips
1 cup thinly sliced peeled cucumber
½ cup thinly sliced onion
2 tablespoons chopped fresh mint
2 tablespoons chopped fresh cilantro
2 tablespoons fresh lemon juice
2 teaspoons extra-virgin olive oil
½ teaspoon salt
¼ teaspoon black pepper
2 tomatoes, cut into ¼-inch-thick wedges (about ½ pound)
1 (6-inch) pita, toasted and torn into bite-size pieces

1. Combine all ingredients in a bowl, and toss gently to coat. Yield: 4 servings (serving size: 1 cup).

CALORIES 97 (29% from fat); FAT 3.1g (sat 0.4g, mono 1.7g, poly 0.4g); PROTEIN 2.2g; CARB 16.2g; FIBER 3.6g; CHOL 0mg; IRON 1.7mg; SODIUM 350mg; CALC 31mg

Portable Power

Snacking and skipping meals are a part of life these days. Vending-machine cuisine doesn't have to be your only option.

We've become such a nation of on-the-go nibblers that one of the major requirements of food in the '90s is that it be portable. With a little planning, you can pull a delicious, healthy snack out of your briefcase that will bridge the space between rush hour and midnight oil.

The major payoff is in your mouth—who can resist the allure of scones, biscotti, muffins? But making your own between-meals snacks also placates your head and body because you're in charge of your own engine.

You shouldn't make a habit of missing regular meals, of course, but let's stay real. And if you want to do that, these snacks are real good.

WHOLE-WHEAT PECAN MUFFINS

1 cup whole-wheat flour
½ cup all-purpose flour
½ cup stone-ground yellow cornmeal
1½ teaspoons baking powder
½ teaspoon baking soda
½ teaspoon salt
1¼ cups low-fat buttermilk
½ cup packed brown sugar
2 tablespoons stick margarine or butter, melted
1 teaspoon almond extract
2 large egg whites
Cooking spray
⅓ cup chopped pecans

1. Preheat oven to 375°.
2. Lightly spoon flours into dry measuring cups; level with a knife. Combine flours and next 4 ingredients in a medium bowl; make a well in center of mixture. Combine buttermilk and next 4 ingredients; stir with a whisk. Add to flour mixture, stirring just until moist.
3. Spoon batter into 12 muffin cups coated with cooking spray; sprinkle with nuts. Bake at 375° for 20 minutes or until muffins spring back when touched lightly in center. Remove from pans immediately. Yield: 1 dozen (serving size: 1 muffin).

CALORIES 161 (28% from fat); FAT 5g (sat 0.6g, mono 2.3g, poly 1.3g); PROTEIN 4.1g; CARB 26.1g; FIBER 2.2g; CHOL 0mg; IRON 1.1mg; SODIUM 200mg; CALC 80mg

SNACKS TO GO

Most of these breads and snack bars will stay moist and fresh-tasting for a couple of days if they are stored properly. Let the muffins, scones, and bars cool completely. Divide into individual portions, and wrap each portion in a piece of heavy-duty plastic wrap. These snacks can be frozen for up to one month. Thaw them at room temperature, or reheat in the microwave for 30 seconds. Store the granola in individual zip-top plastic bags for quick grab-to-go snacks.

CINNAMON-RAISIN OATMEAL BARS

- 3 cups quick-cooking oats
- 1 cup raisins
- ⅔ cup packed brown sugar
- ⅓ cup sliced almonds
- ⅓ cup water
- ¼ cup sesame seeds
- ¼ cup stick margarine or butter, melted
- 2 tablespoons nonfat dry milk
- 1½ teaspoons ground cinnamon
- Cooking spray

1. Preheat oven to 400°.
2. Combine all ingredients except cooking spray in a food processor; process until combined. Press oat mixture into a 13 x 9-inch baking pan coated with cooking spray. Bake at 400° for 20 minutes or until lightly browned. Cool in pan on a wire rack. Yield: 16 bars (serving size: 1 bar).

CALORIES 174 (31% from fat); FAT 6.1g (sat 1g, mono 2.7g, poly 2g); PROTEIN 3.9g; CARB 27.8g; FIBER 2.4g; CHOL 0mg; IRON 1.5mg; SODIUM 44mg; CALC 64mg

CARROT-CAKE BARS

- ⅔ cup packed brown sugar
- 2 tablespoons stick margarine or butter, softened
- ¾ cup low-fat buttermilk
- 1 teaspoon vanilla extract
- 2 large egg whites
- ¾ cup whole-wheat flour
- 1½ cups regular oats
- 2 teaspoons baking powder
- 1 teaspoon ground cinnamon
- ¼ teaspoon baking soda
- ¼ teaspoon salt
- 1 cup shredded carrot
- ½ cup raisins
- Cooking spray

1. Preheat oven to 350°.
2. Beat sugar and margarine at medium speed of a mixer until well-blended (about 5 minutes). Add buttermilk, vanilla, and egg whites; beat well. Lightly spoon flour into a dry measuring cup; level with a knife. Combine flour and next 5 ingredients; gradually add to sugar mixture, beating just until blended. Stir in carrot and raisins.
3. Pour batter into an 11 x 7-inch baking dish coated with cooking spray. Bake at 350° for 33 minutes or until a wooden pick inserted in center comes out almost clean. Cool in pan on a wire rack. Yield: 1 dozen (serving size: 1 bar).

CALORIES 121 (17% from fat); FAT 2.3g (sat 0.5g, mono 0.8g, poly 0.7g); PROTEIN 3.1g; CARB 23.3g; FIBER 2g; CHOL 0mg; IRON 1mg; SODIUM 138mg; CALC 68mg

BANANA-WALNUT SCONES

Try these scones for extra protein, vitamin E, and potassium.

- 3 cups all-purpose flour
- ½ cup packed brown sugar
- 2 teaspoons baking powder
- ½ teaspoon salt
- ¼ teaspoon baking soda
- 3 tablespoons chilled stick margarine or butter
- ¼ cup low-fat buttermilk
- 1 teaspoon vanilla extract
- 2 large egg whites
- 1 cup mashed ripe banana (about 2 medium)
- Cooking spray
- ⅓ cup coarsely chopped walnuts
- 1 tablespoon brown sugar

1. Preheat oven to 400°.
2. Lightly spoon flour into dry measuring cups; level with a knife. Combine flour and next 4 ingredients in a bowl; cut in margarine with a pastry blender or 2 knives until mixture resembles coarse meal.
3. Combine buttermilk, vanilla, and egg whites; stir well with a whisk. Add buttermilk mixture and banana to flour mixture, stirring just until moist (dough will be wet and sticky).
4. Turn dough out onto a lightly floured surface; with floured hands, knead lightly 4 times. Pat dough into a 9-inch circle on a baking sheet coated with cooking spray. Sprinkle walnuts and 1 tablespoon brown sugar over dough, pressing gently into dough. Cut into 12 wedges, cutting into, but not through, dough. Bake at 400° for 20 minutes or until golden. Yield: 1 dozen (serving size: 1 scone).

CALORIES 210 (23% from fat); FAT 5.3g (sat 0.8g, mono 1.7g, poly 2.5g); PROTEIN 5g; CARB 35.8g; FIBER 1.6g; CHOL 0mg; IRON 1.8mg; SODIUM 233mg; CALC 66mg

POWER BISCOTTI

Peanut butter takes the place of margarine or butter, adding flavor as well as protein and B vitamins.

- 2 cups all-purpose flour
- ¾ cup sugar
- ¾ teaspoon baking soda
- ¼ teaspoon salt
- ⅓ cup chunky peanut butter
- 1 teaspoon vanilla extract
- 2 large eggs, lightly beaten
- 2 large egg whites, lightly beaten
- Cooking spray

1. Preheat oven to 325°.
2. Lightly spoon flour into dry measuring cups; level with a knife. Combine flour and next 3 ingredients in a large bowl. Combine peanut butter and next 3 ingredients in a medium bowl, stirring well with a whisk; add to flour mixture, stirring just until blended.
3. Turn dough out onto a lightly floured surface; shape dough into a 10-inch-long roll. Place on a baking sheet coated with cooking spray; flatten to 1-inch thickness. Bake at 325° for 35 minutes. Remove from baking sheet; cool 10 minutes on a wire rack. Reduce oven temperature to 300°.
4. Cut roll diagonally into 18 (½-inch) slices. Place slices, cut sides down, on baking sheet. Bake at 300° for 20 minutes. Turn cookies over; bake an additional 20 minutes (cookies will be slightly soft in center but will harden as they cool). Remove from baking sheet; cool completely on a wire rack. Yield: 1½ dozen (serving size: 1 cookie).

CALORIES 122 (23% from fat); FAT 3.1g (sat 0.7g, mono 1.4g, poly 0.8g); PROTEIN 3.9g; CARB 19.8g; FIBER 0.5g; CHOL 25mg; IRON 0.8mg; SODIUM 121mg; CALC 7mg

CRUNCHY GRANOLA WITH DRIED FRUIT

Coconut, almonds, and sunflower kernels abound in this no-oil recipe. And a ½-cup serving provides about 15% of the U.S. Daily Value for iron.

    1   cup boiling water
    ½   cup sweetened dried cranberries
        (such as Craisins)
    ¼   cup packed brown sugar
    1   (6-ounce) bag dried mixed
        tropical fruit
    3   cups regular oats
    ½   cup sliced almonds
    ½   cup roasted sunflower kernels
    ¼   cup flaked sweetened coconut
    2   tablespoons nonfat dry milk
    1   teaspoon ground cinnamon

1. Preheat oven to 300°.
2. Combine first 4 ingredients in a bowl, and let stand 15 minutes. Combine oats and remaining 5 ingredients; stir into dried-fruit mixture. Spread oat mixture in a jelly-roll pan, and bake at 300° for 1 hour, stirring every 15 minutes. Cool granola to room temperature. Store in an airtight container. Yield: 6 cups (serving size: ½ cup).

CALORIES 224 (28% from fat); FAT 7g (sat 1.4g, mono 2.3g, poly 2.9g); PROTEIN 6.3g; CARB 36.4g; FIBER 3.4g; CHOL 0mg; IRON 2.2mg; SODIUM 19mg; CALC 58mg

SUPER MORNING SHAKE

    2   tablespoons nonfat dry milk
    2   tablespoons honey
    1   (8-ounce) carton vanilla low-fat
        yogurt
    1   (8-ounce) can pineapple chunks
        in juice, undrained
    ½   cup ice cubes

1. Combine first 4 ingredients in a blender, and process until smooth. With blender on, add ice cubes, 1 at a time; process until smooth. Yield: 2 servings (serving size: 1¼ cups).

CALORIES 228 (6% from fat); FAT 1.6g (sat 1g, mono 0.4g, poly 0.1g); PROTEIN 8.9g; CARB 46.5g; FIBER 0.5g; CHOL 7mg; IRON 0.7mg; SODIUM 117mg; CALC 307mg

COOKING CLASS

The Herbs of Summer

Nature's finest seasonings are at their fresh and flavorful peak—and perfect for your table.

Whether you grow them yourself or get them from the grocer, fresh herbs provide the ultimate spark of flavor in any great dish. Plus, they can transform even the ordinary into the memorable.

What's the source of this famous gustatory power? Aromatic oils released when the herbs are cut or cooked. While dried herbs have more concentrated flavors, only with the fresh ones can the real imprint of taste, aroma, and nuance be appreciated.

More so than almost any other ingredient, fresh herbs must be added with great calculation for their delicate potency. In general, cut and cook fresh herbs as late in the process as possible—freshness fades all too quickly.

MENU SUGGESTION

THAI CRAB CAKES WITH CILANTRO-PEANUT SAUCE

Lemon-ginger coleslaw *

*Combine ¼ cup lemon juice, 2 tablespoons sugar, 2 tablespoons cider vinegar, 2 tablespoons water, 2 teaspoons grated fresh ginger, ¼ teaspoon salt, and 1 teaspoon dark sesame oil; toss with 4 cups prepackaged slaw mix and ½ cup chopped green onions. Serves 4.

THAI CRAB CAKES WITH CILANTRO-PEANUT SAUCE

    1¼ cups fresh breadcrumbs
    1   cup fresh bean sprouts, chopped
    ¼   cup finely chopped green onions
    ¼   cup coarsely chopped fresh cilantro
    2   tablespoons fresh lime juice
    ⅛   teaspoon ground red pepper
    1   large egg, lightly beaten
    1   large egg white, lightly beaten
    1   pound lump crabmeat, shell
        pieces removed
    2   teaspoons olive oil, divided
        Cooking spray
        Cilantro-Peanut Sauce

1. Combine first 9 ingredients in a bowl; cover and chill 1 hour. Divide mixture into 8 equal portions, shaping each into a ½-inch-thick patty.

2. Heat 1 teaspoon oil in a large non-stick skillet coated with cooking spray over medium heat until hot. Add 4 patties; cook 3 minutes on each side or until lightly browned. Remove patties from skillet, and keep warm. Wipe skillet clean with paper towels, and recoat with cooking spray. Repeat procedure with remaining 1 teaspoon oil and 4 patties. Serve with Cilantro-Peanut Sauce. Yield: 4 servings (serving size: 2 patties and 3 tablespoons sauce).

CALORIES 315 (30% from fat); FAT 10.5g (sat 1.8g, mono 4.7g, poly 2.6g); PROTEIN 30.6g; CARB 25.4g; FIBER 1.8g; CHOL 169mg; IRON 3.1mg; SODIUM 784mg; CALC 169mg

Cilantro-Peanut Sauce:

    ¼   cup balsamic vinegar
    2½ tablespoons granulated sugar
    2   tablespoons brown sugar
    2   tablespoons low-sodium soy
        sauce
    ½   teaspoon dried crushed red pepper
    ⅛   teaspoon salt
    1   garlic clove, minced
    2   tablespoons creamy peanut butter
    ½   cup chopped fresh cilantro
    2   tablespoons chopped fresh mint

1. Combine first 7 ingredients in a small saucepan, and bring to a boil, stirring frequently. Remove from heat. Add peanut butter, and stir with a whisk until smooth. Cool; stir in cilantro and mint. Yield: ¾ cup.

Caribbean Chicken Shish Kebabs

Caribbean rub:

2 jalapeño peppers, halved and seeded
2 garlic cloves, peeled
¾ cup chopped fresh parsley
¼ cup minced fresh thyme
¼ cup chopped onion
2 tablespoons fresh lime juice
1 teaspoon curry powder
¼ teaspoon salt
⅛ teaspoon black pepper

Shish kebabs:

8 skinned, boned chicken thighs (about 1½ pounds)
1 tablespoon chopped fresh thyme
¼ teaspoon salt
⅛ teaspoon black pepper
2 red bell peppers, quartered
Cooking spray

Remaining ingredients:

1 teaspoon olive oil
1 cup uncooked basmati rice
¾ cup water
1¼ cups fat-free, less-sodium chicken broth
2 tablespoons flaked sweetened coconut, toasted
4 lime wedges

1. To prepare Caribbean rub, drop jalapeño and garlic through food chute with food processor on, and process until minced. Add parsley and next 6 ingredients; process until well-blended, scraping sides of bowl occasionally.
2. To prepare shish kebabs, trim fat from chicken. Sprinkle 1 tablespoon thyme, ¼ teaspoon salt, and ⅛ teaspoon black pepper over chicken; roll up. Thread 4 chicken rolls and 4 bell pepper pieces alternately onto 2 (12-inch) skewers. Brush 2 tablespoons Caribbean rub over kebab. Place kebab in a 13 x 9-inch baking dish. Repeat procedure with remaining chicken rolls, remaining bell peppers, and 2 tablespoons Caribbean rub. Cover and marinate in refrigerator 3 hours.
3. Prepare grill. Place kebabs on grill rack coated with cooking spray; grill 12 minutes on each side or until chicken is done.
4. Heat oil in a saucepan coated with cooking spray over medium-high heat until hot. Add remaining Caribbean rub; sauté 1 minute. Add rice, water, and broth; bring to a boil. Cover; reduce heat. Simmer 15 minutes or until liquid is absorbed. Let stand, covered, 10 minutes. Fluff with a fork.
5. Place 1 cup rice on each of 4 serving plates. Arrange 2 chicken rolls and 2 bell pepper pieces on each serving of rice; sprinkle each with 1½ teaspoons coconut. Serve with lime wedges. Yield: 4 servings.
Note: If using wooden skewers, soak skewers in water 30 minutes before assembling kebabs.

CALORIES 436 (21% from fat); FAT 10.2g (sat 3.2g, mono 3.1g, poly 2g); PROTEIN 38.8g; CARB 45.5g; FIBER 2.6g; CHOL 143mg; IRON 6.1mg; SODIUM 493mg; CALC 70mg

Chicken Quesadillas with Fruit Salsa and Avocado Cream

Cooking spray
1⅓ cups shredded carrot
1 cup thinly sliced green onions
1 cup (4 ounces) shredded Monterey Jack cheese with jalapeño peppers, divided
8 (8-inch) fat-free flour tortillas
2 cups chopped ready-to-eat roasted skinned, boned chicken breasts (such as Tyson; about 2 breasts)
½ cup fresh cilantro
Fruit Salsa
Avocado Cream

1. Place a large nonstick skillet coated with cooking spray over medium-high heat until hot. Add carrot and onions; sauté 5 minutes or until tender. Sprinkle 2 tablespoons cheese over each of 4 tortillas, and top evenly with carrot mixture. Top each tortilla with ½ cup chicken, 2 tablespoons cilantro, 2 tablespoons cheese, and a tortilla.
2. Place skillet coated with cooking spray over medium heat until hot. Add 1 quesadilla, and cook 2 minutes on each side or until quesadilla is browned. Repeat with remaining quesadillas. Cut each quesadilla into 6 wedges. Arrange 4 quesadilla wedges on each of 6 plates. Top each serving with ⅔ cup Fruit Salsa and about 3 tablespoons Avocado Cream. Yield: 6 servings.

CALORIES 408 (28% from fat); FAT 12.5g (sat 4.9g, mono 5.4g, poly 1.2g); PROTEIN 20.6g; CARB 55.8g; FIBER 5.6g; CHOL 38mg; IRON 2.2mg; SODIUM 888mg; CALC 218mg

Fruit Salsa:

2 cups coarsely chopped peeled ripe papaya or mango (about 1 large)
1½ cups coarsely chopped peeled kiwifruit (about 3 kiwifruit)
¾ cup fresh corn kernels (about 1 ear)
½ cup chopped red onion
½ cup minced fresh cilantro
3 tablespoons fresh lime juice
1 tablespoon minced seeded jalapeño pepper
¼ teaspoon salt

1. Combine all ingredients in a small bowl; cover and chill. Yield: 4 cups.

Avocado Cream:

1 peeled medium avocado, pitted and cut into chunks
½ cup fat-free sour cream
2 tablespoons fresh lime juice
2 tablespoons minced fresh cilantro

1. Place first 3 ingredients in a blender; process until smooth. Spoon pureed mixture into a small bowl; stir in cilantro. Cover and chill. Yield: 1⅓ cups.

❶ *The stems on parsley and cilantro are soft and can be used in recipes. Simply place the bunch on a cutting board, and chop with a sharp knife.*

❷ *Thyme and rosemary have woody stems you don't want to use. To remove the leaves in one quick motion, hold the top of each stem with one hand, then strip off the leaves with the fingertips of your other hand.*

❸ *Mint, oregano, tarragon, and sage also have unusable stems, which should be discarded. The leaves of these herbs can be easily pinched off one at a time.*

Handling tip: Herbs with large leaves, such as basil, are often thinly sliced, or chiffonaded. To chiffonade, stack several leaves on a cutting board. Roll up lengthwise, then cut crosswise. ▼

◀ **Fresh-cut, then what?** Shake herbs quickly under cold running water, and dry on paper towels. Large bunches of herbs such as parsley and cilantro can be washed ahead of time, wrapped loosely in a wet paper towel, and stored in a zip-top plastic bag.

Or store a bunch, stems down, in a glass of water with a plastic bag over the leaves in the refrigerator for up to one week, changing the water every other day.

WARM BEEF-AND-POTATO SALAD WITH BÉARNAISE DRESSING

12 **small red potatoes, quartered**
   (about 1¾ pounds)
 4 **shallots, quartered**
 2 **teaspoons olive oil**
Cooking spray
 2 **(4-ounce) beef tenderloin steaks**
   (¾ inch thick)
¼ **cup chopped shallots**
¼ **cup dry white wine**
¼ **cup white wine vinegar**
¼ **cup water**
 3 **tablespoons chopped fresh tarragon**
 2 **tablespoons creamy mustard**
   blend (such as Dijonnaise)
 1 **tablespoon chopped fresh chives**

1. Preheat oven to 375°.
2. Combine potatoes and quartered shallots in a 13 x 9-inch baking dish; drizzle with oil, and toss gently. Bake at 375° for 50 minutes or until tender, stirring occasionally. Cool slightly.
3. Place a large nonstick skillet coated with cooking spray over medium-high heat until hot. Add steaks; cook 3 minutes on each side or until desired degree of doneness. Remove steaks from skillet; keep warm.
4. Add chopped shallots and next 4 ingredients to skillet. Bring to a boil; cook until reduced to ½ cup (about 2 minutes). Strain through a colander into a bowl; discard solids. Add mustard blend to wine mixture; stir well with a whisk.
5. Cut steaks into thin slices. Combine potato mixture, beef, and wine mixture in a large bowl; toss gently to coat. Sprinkle with chives. Serve immediately. Yield: 4 servings (serving size: 1 cup).

CALORIES 280 (25% from fat); FAT 7.9g (sat 2.1g, mono 3.5g, poly 1.2g); PROTEIN 16.5g; CARB 36.1g; FIBER 3.7g; CHOL 35mg; IRON 4.4mg; SODIUM 153mg; CALC 38mg

BASIL Hardy and prolific, basil is a member of the mint family and a perfect choice for a beginner's garden. Varieties range from lemon to opal to cinnamon, but sweet basil is the most common. It tastes like a cross between licorice and cloves when fresh. Basil is commonly used in Mediterranean cooking and is most familiar in Italian pesto, but is also found in the cuisines of Southeast Asia, especially in Thai dishes.

CILANTRO Cilantro, the bright-green leaves and stems of the coriander plant, has a lively, pungent fragrance. This herb is sometimes called Chinese parsley because its use in Asia can be compared to the use of parsley in other parts of the world. It's also widely used in Mexican and Caribbean cooking. Cilantro is susceptible to heat, so add it at the end of the cooking process. It's at its best in cold dishes such as salsas or spring rolls.

MINT This old-fashioned herb is creeping its way into more recipes, although it is by no means as versatile as basil, cilantro, and parsley. Always a winner in mint tea, this herb can add a refreshing lift to salsas, chutneys, and meats. It's commonly found in Middle Eastern lamb dishes, Indian chutneys, and Asian foods.

OREGANO Often associated with Italian cuisine, this herb goes well with tomato-based dishes using basil and capers and is one of the predominant flavors in pizza sauces. Oregano can be used almost anywhere basil is used—in conjunction with it or alone. It's a wonderful addition to marinades and makes a beautiful garnish.

PARSLEY The most popular of the more than 30 varieties of this herb is the curly-leaf variety (often used as a garnish), but flat-leaf or Italian parsley has a stronger flavor and is preferred for cooking. Parsley gives a kick, not to mention color, to almost any dish—especially pastas, pizza, focaccia, soups, and stews.

ROSEMARY The new wave of Mediterranean cuisine makes rosemary the hip herb. A perennial, it can grow to bushlike proportions, especially in the Southwest, where the climate is dry. It's often paired with garlic in marinades and savory dishes such as chicken, lamb, and potatoes, and lends itself surprisingly well to desserts such as ice creams, sorbet, and pudding. Rosemary leaves are quite tough; they can be simmered in soups and sauces, then removed before serving.

SAGE This herb has had a hard time finding a home beyond turkey dressing, but it's still worth a place in your kitchen. A musty mint taste and aroma permeate sage's narrow, oval, gray-green leaves. It goes well with poultry and pork, but also try it in baked goods such as our Fresh-Sage Drop Scones (page 183). Its full flavor develops best when cooked.

TARRAGON A classic component of béarnaise sauce, this refreshing, aniselike herb is also commonly used in French cooking with chicken, fish, and vegetables. Tarragon is often paired with dill and parsley, but it should be combined sparingly with other herbs because its distinctive taste can dominate. It wilts quickly, so use it immediately after picking.

THYME The minty, lightly lemony aroma from this herb's tiny gray-green leaves has given thyme a large role in French, Cajun, and Caribbean cuisines (it's the key ingredient in Caribbean "jerk" seasoning, for example). Add thyme during cooking; its powerful taste develops best at high temperatures.

POTATO-PESTO BAKE

- 1 tablespoon slivered almonds, toasted
- 2 garlic cloves
- 1 cup fresh basil leaves
- 1 cup fresh parsley sprigs
- 2 tablespoons fat-free, less-sodium chicken broth
- 2 tablespoons (½ ounce) finely grated fresh Romano cheese
- 2 tablespoons lemon juice
- 4 teaspoons olive oil, divided
- ½ teaspoon salt
- Cooking spray
- 6 cups (⅛-inch-thick) sliced red potatoes (about 2 pounds), divided
- 2 tablespoons (½ ounce) finely grated fresh Romano cheese, divided
- ½ cup fat-free, less-sodium chicken broth

1. Preheat oven to 425°.
2. Drop almonds and garlic through food chute with food processor on; process until minced. Add basil and parsley; process until finely chopped. Add 2 tablespoons broth, 2 tablespoons cheese, lemon juice, 2 teaspoons oil, and salt; process until smooth.
3. Spread remaining 2 teaspoons oil in an 11 x 7-inch baking dish coated with cooking spray. Arrange 2 cups potatoes in bottom of baking dish; spread 3 tablespoons basil mixture over potatoes, and sprinkle with 2 teaspoons cheese. Repeat procedure with 2 cups potatoes, 3 tablespoons basil mixture, and 2 teaspoons cheese. Top with 2 cups potatoes.
4. Microwave ½ cup broth at HIGH 1½ minutes or until very hot. Pour over potatoes; spread remaining basil mixture over potatoes. Cover with foil; bake at 425° for 45 minutes. Uncover; sprinkle with remaining 2 teaspoons cheese, and bake an additional 15 minutes or until tender. Yield: 6 servings (serving size: ¾ cup).

CALORIES 175 (27% from fat); FAT 5.3g (sat 1.3g, mono 3g, poly 0.5g); PROTEIN 5.8g; CARB 27.4g; FIBER 3.3g; CHOL 5mg; IRON 2.8mg; SODIUM 277mg; CALC 100mg

Tabbouleh with Oranges and Sunflower Seeds

- ¾ cup uncooked bulgur or cracked wheat
- 2 cups boiling water
- 2 navel oranges
- 1 tablespoon sugar
- 1½ tablespoons olive oil
- ¼ teaspoon salt
- ¼ teaspoon black pepper
- 1 cup chopped fresh parsley
- ¾ cup chopped fresh mint
- ¾ cup diced seeded peeled cucumber
- ½ cup coarsely chopped red onion
- 2 navel oranges, each peeled and cut crosswise into 10 (¼-inch-thick) slices
- 2 tablespoons sunflower seeds

1. Combine bulgur and boiling water in a large bowl. Cover and let stand 30 minutes; drain.
2. Peel and section 2 oranges over a bowl; squeeze membranes to extract juice. Set sections aside, and reserve ¼ cup juice. Discard membranes. Combine reserved orange juice, sugar, and next 3 ingredients; stir with a whisk.
3. Add orange sections, parsley, and next 3 ingredients to bulgur mixture; stir well. Add orange juice mixture; toss gently to coat. Cover and chill at least 2 hours.
4. Arrange 4 orange slices on each of 5 serving plates; top with 1 cup tabbouleh. Sprinkle evenly with sunflower seeds. Yield: 5 servings.

CALORIES 204 (28% from fat); FAT 6.3g (sat 0.8g, mono 3.4g, poly 1.7g); PROTEIN 5.3g; CARB 35.2g; FIBER 10g; CHOL 0mg; IRON 1.8mg; SODIUM 131mg; CALC 83mg

Pan-Seared Pork Cutlets with Nectarine Salsa

- 2 teaspoons chili powder
- 1 teaspoon ground coriander
- ½ teaspoon ground cumin
- ½ teaspoon paprika
- ¼ teaspoon salt
- ¼ teaspoon freshly ground black pepper
- 8 (2-ounce) pork loin cutlets
- 1 teaspoon olive oil
- Cooking spray
- ½ cup bottled salsa
- ¼ cup apricot preserves
- 4 cups sliced peeled nectarines
- ¼ cup chopped fresh cilantro
- 2 tablespoons chopped fresh oregano

1. Combine first 6 ingredients; rub mixture over both sides of pork. Heat oil in a large nonstick skillet coated with cooking spray over medium-high heat. Add pork, and sauté 2 minutes on each side or until done. Remove from pan; keep warm.
2. Add salsa and preserves to skillet; bring to a boil. Cook 1 minute. Stir in nectarines, cilantro, and oregano; cook 1 minute or until thoroughly heated. Serve salsa with pork. Yield: 4 servings (serving size: 2 cutlets and 1 cup salsa).

CALORIES 322 (31% from fat); FAT 11g (sat 1.6g, mono 4.1g, poly 1.1g); PROTEIN 25.5g; CARB 32.6g; FIBER 4.7g; CHOL 68mg; IRON 2.7mg; SODIUM 327mg; CALC 60mg

Thai Eggplant Dip

- 1 (1-pound) eggplant
- ⅓ cup golden raisins, chopped
- 2 tablespoons water
- 2 tablespoons chopped fresh basil
- 2 teaspoons fresh lemon juice
- 1 teaspoon olive oil
- ¼ teaspoon black pepper
- ⅛ teaspoon salt
- 1 garlic clove, minced
- 4 (6-inch) pitas
- ½ cup (2 ounces) shredded part-skim mozzarella cheese
- 3 tablespoons grated Parmesan cheese

1. Preheat oven to 425°.
2. Pierce eggplant several times with a fork, and wrap in foil. Place eggplant on a baking sheet, and bake at 425° for 1 hour. Cool slightly. Peel and seed eggplant, and mash with a potato masher.
3. Combine raisins and 2 tablespoons water in a small bowl. Cover with plastic wrap; vent. Microwave at HIGH 30 seconds. Let stand, covered, 10 minutes; drain. Add raisins, basil, and next 5 ingredients to eggplant; stir well.
4. Preheat broiler. Sprinkle pitas with cheeses; broil 2 minutes or until cheese melts. Cut each pita into 6 wedges; serve with dip. Yield: 24 servings (serving size: 1 pita wedge and 1 tablespoon dip).

CALORIES 48 (19% from fat); FAT 1g (sat 0.5g, mono 0.4g, poly 0.1g); PROTEIN 1.7g; CARB 7.7g; FIBER 1.2g; CHOL 2mg; IRON 0.4mg; SODIUM 41mg; CALC 43mg

Fresh-Sage Drop Scones

- 1 cup all-purpose flour
- 1 cup yellow cornmeal
- 2 teaspoons baking powder
- ¼ teaspoon salt
- ¼ teaspoon black pepper
- 1 cup (4 ounces) shredded sharp Cheddar cheese
- ¼ cup minced green onions
- 2 tablespoons chopped fresh sage
- 1½ teaspoons chopped fresh thyme
- 1 cup 1% low-fat milk
- Cooking spray
- 12 fresh sage leaves

1. Preheat oven to 400°.
2. Lightly spoon flour into a dry measuring cup; level with a knife. Combine flour and next 4 ingredients in a large bowl. Stir in cheese and next 3 ingredients. Add milk, stirring just until moist. Drop dough by 2 level tablespoons 2 inches apart onto baking sheets coated with cooking spray. Gently press 1 sage leaf into top of each scone.
3. Bake at 400° for 20 minutes or until golden brown. Serve warm. Yield: 1 dozen (serving size: 1 scone).

CALORIES 129 (26% from fat); FAT 3.7g (sat 2.2g, mono 1g, poly 0.2g); PROTEIN 5.1g; CARB 18.4g; FIBER 1g; CHOL 11mg; IRON 1.2mg; SODIUM 183mg; CALC 143mg

Berried Treasures

Sweet, juicy blueberries are in their prime—and just in time.

Mother Nature knew what she was doing when she arranged for blueberries to peak in August. When summer's most slothful days hit and the weather turns stagnant, these small, plump treasures have the ability to add refreshing sweetness back into your life. Not to mention color.

We don't have that many blue foods, and the deep hues of the berries can stimulate an almost Pavlovian craving, best invoked in foods such as coffeecakes, cobblers, pancakes, and ices. The fresh succulence of the berries pops flavor into your mouth that will make you forget the heat—or at least be glad it arrives with such pleasant distractions.

BLUEBERRY-BEAUJOLAIS ICE

2   cups Beaujolais or other fruity
      red wine
1   cup sugar
2½ cups blueberries

1. Combine wine and sugar in a medium saucepan. Bring to a boil; cook until sugar dissolves, stirring occasionally. Add blueberries; return to a boil. Cook 1 minute. Remove from heat, and cool. Spoon blueberry mixture into a blender; process until smooth. Cover and chill.
2. Pour mixture into the freezer can of an ice-cream freezer; freeze according to manufacturer's instructions. Spoon into a freezer-safe container; cover and freeze at least 1 hour. Yield: 8 servings (serving size: ½ cup).

CALORIES 164 (1% from fat); FAT 0.2g (sat 0g, mono 0g, poly 0.1g); PROTEIN 0.4g; CARB 32.2g; FIBER 2.1g; CHOL 0mg; IRON 0.3mg; SODIUM 8mg; CALC 8mg

PEACH-BLUEBERRY COBBLER

Prepare the biscuit topping while the fruit mixture bakes in the oven.

½   cup sugar
1   tablespoon cornstarch
½   teaspoon grated lemon rind
¼   teaspoon ground cinnamon
3   cups coarsely chopped peeled
      peaches
2   cups blueberries
1   tablespoon lemon juice
½   teaspoon vanilla extract
Cooking spray
1   cup all-purpose flour
3   tablespoons sugar
¾   teaspoon baking powder
⅛   teaspoon baking soda
¼   teaspoon salt
2   tablespoons chilled stick
      margarine or butter, cut into
      small pieces
6   tablespoons low-fat buttermilk
Mint sprigs (optional)

1. Preheat oven to 400°.
2. Combine first 4 ingredients in a large bowl. Add peaches and next 3 ingredients; toss gently. Spoon mixture into an 8-inch square baking dish coated with cooking spray. Bake at 400° for 15 minutes.
3. Lightly spoon flour into a dry measuring cup; level with a knife. Combine flour and next 4 ingredients in a medium bowl; cut in margarine with a pastry blender or 2 knives until mixture resembles coarse meal. Add buttermilk, and stir just until flour mixture is moist.
4. Turn dough out onto a lightly floured surface; knead lightly 3 times. Roll to about ¼-inch thickness; cut into 16 biscuits using a 2-inch biscuit cutter.
5. Remove baking dish from oven; arrange biscuits on top of hot fruit mixture. Bake an additional 20 minutes or until biscuits are golden. Garnish with mint sprigs, if desired. Yield: 8 servings (serving size: ½ cup cobbler and 2 biscuits).

CALORIES 212 (15% from fat); FAT 3.5g (sat 0.6g, mono 1.3g, poly 1.1g); PROTEIN 2.8g; CARB 43.8g; FIBER 3.2g; CHOL 0mg; IRON 1mg; SODIUM 135mg; CALC 50mg

BLUEBERRY PANCAKES

1   cup all-purpose flour
2   tablespoons sugar
1¼   teaspoons baking powder
¼   teaspoon baking soda
¼   teaspoon salt
½   teaspoon grated orange rind
1   cup orange juice
2   tablespoons fat-free milk
2   tablespoons vegetable oil
1   large egg, lightly beaten
1   cup blueberries

1. Lightly spoon flour into a dry measuring cup; level with a knife. Combine flour and next 4 ingredients in a bowl. Combine orange rind and next 4 ingredients in a bowl; add to flour mixture, stirring until smooth.
2. Spoon ¼ cup batter onto a hot nonstick griddle or nonstick skillet; top with a heaping tablespoon blueberries. Turn pancake when top is covered with bubbles and edges look cooked. Repeat procedure with remaining batter and blueberries. Yield: 4 servings (serving size: 2 pancakes).

CALORIES 269 (29% from fat); FAT 8.6g (sat 1.7g, mono 2.6g, poly 3.7g); PROTEIN 5.8g; CARB 43g; FIBER 2.6g; CHOL 56mg; IRON 2mg; SODIUM 249mg; CALC 114mg

---

KEEPING THE BLUES AROUND

Blueberries don't ripen after picking and can deteriorate quickly. Plan to use them within one or two days of purchase. To store for up to two days, arrange unwashed berries in a shallow pan lined with paper towels. Top with more paper towels, cover with plastic wrap, and refrigerate.

Curried Santa Barbara Shrimp Salad (page 169)

Thai Scallops with Asparagus (page 197)

Viennese Caramel Custard (page 174)

Plum Pinwheel Tart (page 191)

Roast Chicken with Plums and Almonds (page 189)

Blueberry Pound Cake (page 197)

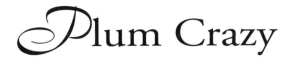

Plum Crazy

No matter which plum you pick, these recipes will guarantee success with this summer-cooking classic.

A bite into a plum is splendorous. The skin is tart and a little rough. Yet the flesh is sweet, soft, juicy. When you cook plums, something magical happens. The sweetness of the flesh, tartness of the skin, and spectrum of colors come together in harmony.

Deciding which plum to buy, however, can be daunting. You never know which of the more than 250 varieties might turn up in the produce section on any given summer day. How can you know which variety to choose? Fact is, all plums taste about the same: sweet flesh inside tart skins. The choices are not so much about flavor as appearance or seasonal availability.

It may seem odd, but most plums wind up as prunes. These "prune plums," also often called blue or European plums, are very small—about twice the size of a grape—and very grainy to the taste. Almost all the ones we eat fresh or cook with, however, are part of a general type known as Japanese plums.

Japanese plums fall into three major categories: red, black, and green. The black Angeleno and Friar and red Santa Rosa are the top sellers. Green-skinned plums were developed primarily for export to Asia where they're popular for pickling, but they've caught on with Americans, too. Each of the three types is suitable for everything from tarts to entrées. And although some plums will change color as they ripen—green to yellow, yellow to red, and so on—the sugar content remains the same once picked.

July is when the largest number of varieties of plums usually matures. Plum breeders are working on creating a whole new family of plum-related fruits. Apriums, pluots, and plumcots—all crosses between plums and apricots—will start vying for your attention at the produce counter soon.

ROAST CHICKEN WITH PLUMS AND ALMONDS

(pictured on page 188)

If you can't find green-skinned plums, substitute a firm plum of any color. Soft plums will give less successful results.

- 1 (4-pound) roasting chicken
- 1 teaspoon grated lemon rind
- ½ teaspoon ground coriander
- ¼ teaspoon black pepper
- Cooking spray
- ½ cup dry sherry
- ½ cup fat-free, less-sodium chicken broth
- ¼ cup fresh lemon juice
- 2 tablespoons honey
- 1 garlic clove, minced
- 9 large shallots, peeled and halved
- 6 firm green-skinned plums, pitted and quartered
- ¼ cup blanched almonds, toasted
- Thyme sprigs (optional)

1. Preheat oven to 350°.
2. Remove and discard giblets and neck from chicken. Rinse chicken under cold water; pat dry. Trim excess fat. Lift wing tips up and over back; tuck under chicken.
3. Sprinkle chicken with lemon rind, coriander, and pepper. Place on a rack coated with cooking spray; place rack in a shallow roasting pan coated with cooking spray. Combine sherry and next 4 ingredients in a bowl; reserve ½ cup sherry mixture for sauce. Insert a meat thermometer into meaty part of thigh, making sure not to touch bone. Bake at 350° for 30 minutes; baste with some of sherry mixture. Bake an additional 45 minutes, basting every 15 minutes. Add shallots to pan; bake an additional 15 minutes, and baste. Add

plums and almonds; bake an additional 15 minutes or until thermometer registers 180° (about 1 hour and 45 minutes total). Place chicken on a platter; place shallots, plums, and almonds around chicken using a slotted spoon. Cover loosely with foil; let stand 10 minutes.
4. Place roasting pan over a stove-top burner. Add reserved ½ cup sherry mixture to pan; bring to a boil over medium heat, scraping pan to loosen browned bits. Reduce heat; simmer 5 minutes. Cool slightly. Place a zip-top plastic bag inside a 2-cup glass measure. Pour drippings into bag; let stand 10 minutes (fat will rise to the top). Seal bag; carefully snip off 1 corner of bag. Drain drippings into a bowl, stopping before the fat layer reaches the opening. Discard fat. Remove foil from chicken; remove and discard skin. Serve sauce with chicken. Garnish with thyme sprigs, if desired. Yield: 6 servings (serving size: 3 ounces chicken, 3 shallot halves, 4 plum quarters, about 3 almonds, and 2 tablespoons sauce).

CALORIES 268 (34% from fat); FAT 10g (sat 2.1g, mono 4.6g, poly 2.2g); PROTEIN 26.7g; CARB 18.7g; FIBER 2.1g; CHOL 76mg; IRON 1.5mg; SODIUM 77mg; CALC 38mg

GETTING PLUM PLUMS

Ripe plums yield slightly to the touch, but don't squeeze. Let the fruit sit in your palm. It should give a little.

If you buy firmer fruit, though, don't put it in the refrigerator or the kitchen window—put it in a paper bag in a dark place for a day or two. The paper bag traps ethylene, the gas that naturally ripens fruit, but the bag also lets the fruit breathe. And if you really want to see a huge difference in ripening, put a fruit that produces lots of natural ethylene, like an apple or a pear, in the bag with the plums. That really speeds up the process.

Although the plums may taste sweeter after a few extra days of ripening off the tree, it's actually a trick on your palate. The sugar level remains the same after picking, but the acidity falls, so it only *seems* sweeter.

SWEET-AND-SOUR RED CABBAGE WITH PLUMS

To complement the reddish purple hue of the cabbage, select a red-skinned plum, such as Santa Rosa, or a deep purple- to black-skinned variety, such as Friar. Serve with ham, pork loin, or roast chicken.

    2 bacon slices
    1 cup chopped onion
    6 cups shredded red cabbage
    2 cups sliced ripe red-skinned
       plums (about 6 medium)
    ½ cup balsamic vinegar
    ½ teaspoon caraway seeds
    3 tablespoons sugar
    ½ teaspoon black pepper

1. Cook bacon in a large nonstick skillet over medium heat until crisp. Remove bacon from skillet; crumble. Add onion to bacon drippings in skillet; sauté 5 minutes. Add cabbage and next 3 ingredients; reduce heat, and cook 20 minutes or until cabbage is tender, stirring occasionally. Add bacon, sugar, and pepper; cook an additional 10 minutes. Yield: 4 servings (serving size: 1 cup).

CALORIES 150 (16% from fat); FAT 2.7g (sat 0.7g, mono 1.2g, poly 0.5g); PROTEIN 3.9g; CARB 31.1g; FIBER 4.8g; CHOL 4mg; IRON 1.1mg; SODIUM 96mg; CALC 69mg

BAKED PLUMS MADEIRA

Marsala, sherry, or port can be substituted for the Madeira.

    6 ripe plums (any variety), pitted
       and quartered
    Cooking spray
    3 tablespoons sugar
    1 tablespoon grated orange rind
    3 tablespoons Madeira wine or
       fresh orange juice
    2 tablespoons fresh orange
       juice
    ¼ teaspoon ground cinnamon
    3 cups vanilla low-fat frozen
       yogurt
    1½ tablespoons pine nuts, toasted

1. Preheat oven to 450°.
2. Place plum quarters in an 11 x 7-inch baking dish coated with cooking spray. Combine sugar and next 4 ingredients. Drizzle orange juice mixture over plums. Bake at 450° for 20 minutes. Serve plums over yogurt; top with pine nuts. Yield: 6 servings (serving size: 4 plum quarters, ½ cup yogurt, and about ½ teaspoon pine nuts).

CALORIES 178 (21% from fat); FAT 4.2g (sat 1.7g, mono 0.9g, poly 1.4g); PROTEIN 4.3g; CARB 33.7g; FIBER 1.5g; CHOL 10mg; IRON 0.5mg; SODIUM 34mg; CALC 103mg

THREE-PLUM UPSIDE-DOWN CAKE

Any ripe plum will work in this recipe. But arranging different-colored plums in the pan creates a stained-glass effect when you turn the cake.

    2 tablespoons stick margarine or
       butter
    1 cup sugar, divided
    3 tablespoons triple sec
       (orange-flavored liqueur) or
       orange juice
    2 ripe red-skinned plums, halved
       and pitted
    2 ripe purple- or black-skinned
       plums, halved and pitted
    2 ripe green-skinned plums,
       halved and pitted
    ¾ cup all-purpose flour
    1 teaspoon baking powder
    ⅛ teaspoon salt
    ½ cup 1% low-fat milk
    1 tablespoon stick margarine or
       butter, melted
    1 teaspoon grated orange
       rind
    1 teaspoon vanilla extract
    2 large egg yolks
    4 large egg whites

1. Preheat oven to 350°.
2. Melt 2 tablespoons margarine in a 9-inch cast-iron or heavy ovenproof skillet over medium heat. Add ½ cup sugar and liqueur; cook until sugar dissolves. Remove from heat. Arrange plum halves, cut sides up, in skillet.

3. Lightly spoon flour into dry measuring cups; level with a knife. Combine flour, baking powder, and salt in a bowl. Add milk and next 4 ingredients; stir with a whisk until smooth.
4. Beat egg whites at high speed of a mixer until foamy. Gradually add remaining ½ cup sugar, 1 tablespoon at a time, beating until stiff peaks form. Gently stir one-fourth of egg white mixture into batter; gently fold in remaining egg white mixture.
5. Pour batter into skillet, and spread evenly over plums. Bake at 350° for 45 minutes or until a wooden pick inserted in center comes out clean. Cool in skillet 5 minutes. Place a plate upside down on top of skillet, and invert cake onto plate. Serve warm or at room temperature. Yield: 8 servings.

CALORIES 253 (22% from fat); FAT 6.2g (sat 1.4g, mono 2.6g, poly 1.6g); PROTEIN 4.5g; CARB 43.1g; FIBER 1.3g; CHOL 55mg; IRON 0.8mg; SODIUM 123mg; CALC 65mg

TRIPLE-PLUM SALSA

Serve this colorful salsa with grilled chicken, fish, or pork.

    ¼ cup finely chopped red onion
    2 tablespoons chopped fresh
       cilantro
    1 tablespoon minced seeded
       jalapeño pepper
    1 teaspoon grated lime rind
    1 tablespoon fresh lime
       juice
    2 teaspoons minced peeled fresh
       ginger
    2 teaspoons vegetable oil
    2 ripe red-skinned plums, pitted
       and diced
    2 ripe green-skinned plums, pitted
       and diced
    2 ripe purple- or black-skinned
       plums, pitted and diced

1. Combine all ingredients in a bowl; toss well. Let stand 30 minutes. Yield: 4 cups (serving size: ¼ cup).

CALORIES 20 (32% from fat); FAT 0.7g (sat 0.1g, mono 0.3g, poly 0.3g); PROTEIN 0.3g; CARB 3.6g; FIBER 0.6g; CHOL 0mg; IRON 0.1mg; SODIUM 0mg; CALC 3mg

PLUM PINWHEEL TART

(pictured on page 187)

If you can't find a red-fleshed plum, Santa Rosa plums can be substituted.

Dough:

- ⅔ cup granulated sugar
- 6 tablespoons stick margarine or butter, softened
- 1 teaspoon vanilla extract
- 2 ounces block-style fat-free cream cheese (about ½ cup)
- 1 large egg
- 2 cups all-purpose flour
- ¼ teaspoon salt

Filling:

- Cooking spray
- 4 cups thinly sliced ripe red-fleshed plums (about 12 medium)
- ¼ cup red currant jelly
- 2 tablespoons water
- 1 large egg, lightly beaten
- 1 teaspoon water
- 2 tablespoons turbinado or granulated sugar

1. To prepare dough, combine first 4 ingredients in a large bowl; beat at medium speed of a mixer 2 minutes or until light and fluffy. Add 1 egg; beat at high speed for 1 minute or until very smooth. Lightly spoon flour into dry measuring cups; level with a knife. Combine flour and salt; add to sugar mixture, beating at low speed just until flour mixture is moist. Gently shape into a ball, and place on a sheet of heavy-duty plastic wrap; cover with an additional sheet of plastic wrap. Freeze 2 hours. Remove dough from freezer; immediately roll dough, still covered, into a 14-inch circle. Remove bottom sheet of plastic wrap. Place dough on a large baking sheet coated with cooking spray; remove top sheet of plastic wrap.
2. Preheat oven to 400°.
3. To prepare filling, arrange plum slices over dough, leaving a 3-inch border. Combine jelly and 2 tablespoons water in a small microwave-safe dish. Microwave at HIGH 30 seconds or until jelly melts; brush plums. Fold 3-inch border of dough over plums, pressing gently to seal (dough will partially cover plums).
4. Combine 1 egg and 1 teaspoon water. Brush dough with egg mixture; sprinkle with turbinado sugar. Bake at 400° for 25 minutes or until lightly browned. Cool on baking sheet 5 minutes. Carefully slide tart onto a platter using a spatula. Yield: 10 servings (serving size: 1 wedge).

CALORIES 293 (26% from fat); FAT 8.6g (sat 1.7g, mono 3.7g, poly 2.5g); PROTEIN 5.3g; CARB 49.6g; FIBER 2.1g; CHOL 45mg; IRON 1.4mg; SODIUM 189mg; CALC 31mg

PLUM ICE CREAM WITH PLUM-COGNAC SAUCE

- 3 cups diced ripe red- or purple-skinned plums (about 6 plums)
- ¾ cup sugar
- 2½ cups 2% reduced-fat milk
- 2 tablespoons cognac or apple juice
- ¼ cup slivered almonds, toasted

1. Combine plums and sugar in a medium saucepan; cook over medium heat 5 minutes or until plums are tender and sugar is dissolved. Place plum mixture in a food processor; process until smooth. Strain plum mixture through a sieve into a bowl to measure 2¼ cups puree, and discard solids. Cover and chill completely.
2. Combine 1½ cups plum puree and milk in the freezer can of an ice-cream freezer; freeze according to manufacturer's instructions. Spoon ice cream into a freezer-safe container; cover and freeze until firm (about 1 hour).
3. Combine remaining ¾ cup plum puree and cognac in a bowl. Spoon over ice cream, and sprinkle with almonds. Yield: 8 servings (serving size: ½ cup ice cream, 1½ tablespoons sauce, and 1½ teaspoons almonds).

CALORIES 172 (18% from fat); FAT 3.4g (sat 1.1g, mono 1.7g, poly 0.5g); PROTEIN 3.6g; CARB 31.3g; FIBER 1.7g; CHOL 6mg; IRON 0.2mg; SODIUM 39mg; CALC 104mg

SO MANY PLUMS, SO LITTLE TIME

Here are a few of the most common plums and their peak seasons. All can be eaten fresh or cooked. In general, late-season plums are sweeter; early-season plums tend to make better jams because of the higher tartness of the skins.

MAY

Black Beaut: black skin, a yellow to reddish flesh
Red Beaut: bright red skin, yellow flesh; small to medium size

JUNE

Blackamber: purplish black skin, yellow flesh; the first large plum of the season
Santa Rosa: red skin, yellow flesh with gold streaks; an old variety

JULY

Elephant Heart: green to brownish purple skin, beet red flesh; a beautiful variety for tarts
Fortune: red skin, yellow flesh; another large-sized plum
Friar: purplish black skin, yellow flesh; very large (8-ounce average); dramatic color
Frontier: purple skin, deep red flesh; one of Elephant Heart's replacements
Mariposa: purple skin, pink to light purple flesh
Simka: red skin, yellow flesh; similar to the Santa Rosa

AUGUST

Casselman: red skin with yellow flesh; another smaller-sized plum
Kelsey: green skin, yellow flesh; green when ripe
Royal Diamond: red skin, yellow flesh; small in the late season

LATE AUGUST TO SEPTEMBER

Angeleno: dark purple skin, amber flesh
Moyer and French Prune: green skin, yellow flesh; very small plums with high sugar content; excellent for baking; dried to make prunes

GINGERY PLUM JAM

Deep purple-skinned Friar plums lend color and rich flavor to this jam. But the red-skinned Santa Rosa makes a nice, if not tart, substitute.

- 4 **pounds ripe purple-skinned plums, pitted and cut into 1-inch pieces (about 24 plums)**
- 1 **cup water**
- 3 **cups sugar**
- 2 **(3-inch) strips julienne-cut lemon rind**
- 1½ **tablespoons minced peeled fresh ginger**
- 3 **tablespoons fresh lemon juice**

1. Combine plums and water in a Dutch oven; bring to a boil. Reduce heat, and simmer, uncovered, 20 minutes or until tender. Stir in sugar and remaining 3 ingredients. Cook over medium heat 40 minutes until thick or a candy thermometer registers 210°. Stir mixture occasionally. (Do not overcook or mixture will scorch.) Cool. Discard lemon rind. Store in an airtight container in the refrigerator up to 2 weeks. Yield: 4 cups (serving size: 1 tablespoon).

CALORIES 51 (4% from fat); FAT 0.2g (sat 0g, mono 0.1g, poly 0g); PROTEIN 0.2g; CARB 12.9g; FIBER 0.6g; CHOL 0mg; IRON 0mg; SODIUM 0mg; CALC 1mg

LAST HURRAH

Sneaky Zucchini

Keep a close eye on the gardeners lurking in your neighborhood, and leave a light on.

The stated purpose of a little-known nocturnal commemoration called "Sneak Some Zucchini Onto Your Neighbor's Porch Night" is to offset the "overzealous planting of zucchini."

Instead of leaving it on porches, you might consider eating it. Here's a completely unsneaky way to get started.

FRECKLED ZUCCHINI WITH LEMON-DILL CREAM

- 6 **tablespoons plain fat-free yogurt**
- 2 **tablespoons low-fat sour cream**
- 1½ **teaspoons chopped fresh dill**
- 1 **teaspoon fresh lemon juice**
- ⅛ **teaspoon salt**
- 1 **teaspoon vegetable oil, divided**
- 4 **medium zucchini, cut lengthwise into ¼-inch-thick slices (about 1½ pounds)**

1. Combine first 5 ingredients in a small bowl.
2. Heat ½ teaspoon oil in a 12-inch cast-iron skillet over high heat. Add half of zucchini slices; cook 2 minutes on each side or until browned. Remove zucchini from skillet; keep warm. Repeat procedure with remaining ½ teaspoon oil and zucchini slices. Serve with yogurt mixture. Yield: 4 servings (serving size: 1 zucchini and 2 tablespoons cream).

CALORIES 51 (41% from fat); FAT 2.3g (sat 0.8g, mono 0.7g, poly 0.6g); PROTEIN 2.9g; CARB 5.8g; FIBER 0.7g; CHOL 3mg; IRON 0.6mg; SODIUM 93mg; CALC 80mg

---

Why This Man is Smiling

Gus Martin's light Cajun and Creole menu is turning heads and tempting customers at New Orleans' Palace Café.

No city in America packs unwanted weight onto a man faster than New Orleans. Just ask Gus Martin. His weight ballooned to 329 pounds after he returned to his hometown in 1982 from a six-year stint in the Army and resumed the cooking career he'd begun as a teenager. By the time his weight peaked three years ago, recalls Martin, he'd developed "an appetite for destruction. I felt really bad. I was on my way to a heart attack."

When Jamie Shannon, executive chef at Commander's Palace, began talking about losing weight, Martin decided to join him. The two men took turns cooking more healthful meals for each other, and Martin resumed exercising seriously. Shannon suggested that Commander's begin offering its customers a separate light menu drawn from the sort of food he and Martin were feeding each other. Martin had already dropped about 50 pounds, and colleagues dubbed the new menu "Gus Light."

Since then, Martin has lost another 50 pounds and moved on from Commander's Palace to become executive chef at Dickie Brennan's Palace Café, adjacent to the French Quarter. But he took his workouts—two hours a day, five days a week—and the idea of an alternative menu with him. The Palace Café Lite Lunch retains the restaurant's Creole and Cajun indulgence without its heavier baggage.

The food reflects Gus' new philosophy. What he wants to do is eat healthfully, continue exercising, and have fun in life. It's all part of eating well.

ROASTED EGGPLANT-AND-RED PEPPER SOUP

2 large red bell peppers
1 (1½-pound) eggplant, cut in half lengthwise
3 cups fat-free, less-sodium chicken broth, divided
1½ cups chopped onion
¼ cup thinly sliced fresh basil
½ teaspoon salt
⅛ teaspoon black pepper
Cilantro sprigs (optional)

1. Preheat broiler. Cut bell peppers in half lengthwise; discard seeds and membranes. Place pepper halves, skin sides up, on a foil-lined baking sheet; flatten with hand. Place eggplant halves, skin sides up, on baking sheet. Broil peppers and eggplant 15 minutes or until blackened. Place peppers in a zip-top plastic bag; seal. Let stand 10 minutes. Peel peppers. Scoop out eggplant pulp. Discard shells.
2. Combine 1 cup broth and onion in a medium saucepan; bring to a boil. Reduce heat; simmer 5 minutes. Add remaining 2 cups broth, bell peppers, and eggplant pulp; simmer 10 minutes. Place bell pepper mixture in a blender; process until smooth. Return pureed mixture to pan. Stir in basil, salt, and black pepper. Garnish with cilantro sprigs, if desired. Yield: 4 servings (serving size: 1¼ cups).

CALORIES 94 (15% from fat); FAT 1.6g (sat 0.7g, mono 0.4g, poly 0.4g); PROTEIN 5g; CARB 17.8g; FIBER 4g; CHOL 4mg; IRON 1.5mg; SODIUM 382mg; CALC 80mg

HICKORY-GRILLED VEGETABLE PLATE

A small amount of hickory chips provides lots of flavor in this recipe.

½ cup hickory wood chips
1 cup balsamic vinegar
4 portobello mushroom caps
2 (8-ounce) yellow squash, halved lengthwise and cut into 2-inch pieces
2 (8-ounce) zucchini, halved lengthwise and cut into 2-inch pieces
1 (1-pound) eggplant, cut crosswise into 8 slices
4 plum tomatoes, halved lengthwise
1 Vidalia or other sweet onion, cut into 4 wedges
1½ tablespoons olive oil
½ teaspoon salt
¼ teaspoon black pepper
Cooking spray
2 cups trimmed arugula (about 4 ounces)
¼ cup chopped fresh basil
¼ cup chopped fresh oregano
¼ cup chopped fresh cilantro
2 tablespoons chopped fresh thyme

1. Soak wood chips in water 30 minutes. Drain well.
2. Bring vinegar to a boil in a small saucepan; cook until reduced to ¼ cup (about 8 minutes).
3. Combine mushrooms and next 5 ingredients in a large bowl. Add oil, salt, and pepper; toss well to coat.
4. Prepare grill. Place wood chips over hot coals. Place mushrooms, squash, zucchini, eggplant, and onion on grill rack coated with cooking spray; grill 5 minutes. Turn vegetables; add tomatoes. Grill 5 minutes or until vegetables are tender.
5. Arrange ½ cup arugula, 3 yellow squash pieces, 3 zucchini pieces, 2 eggplant slices, 2 tomato halves, 1 mushroom cap, and 1 onion wedge on each of 4 plates. Combine basil and remaining 3 ingredients in a small bowl; sprinkle evenly over vegetables. Drizzle 1 tablespoon vinegar over each serving. Yield: 4 servings.

CALORIES 150 (38% from fat); FAT 6.4g (sat 0.9g, mono 3.9g, poly 0.9g); PROTEIN 5.5g; CARB 23g; FIBER 5.7g; CHOL 0mg; IRON 3.3mg; SODIUM 324mg; CALC 139mg

GRILLED PINEAPPLE WITH MANGO COULIS

12 (½-inch-thick) slices fresh pineapple (about 1 pineapple)
Cooking spray
1 cup orange sections (about 1 large orange)
1 cup pink grapefruit sections (about 1 large grapefruit)
Mango Coulis

1. Prepare grill. Place pineapple on grill rack coated with cooking spray, and grill 2½ minutes on each side or until tender.
2. Arrange 3 pineapple slices, ¼ cup orange sections, and ¼ cup grapefruit sections on each of 4 plates. Serve each with ¼ cup Mango Coulis. Yield: 4 servings.

CALORIES 206 (7% from fat); FAT 1.5g (sat 0.1g, mono 0.2g, poly 0.4g); PROTEIN 2g; CARB 51.8g; FIBER 5.8g; CHOL 0mg; IRON 1.1mg; SODIUM 4mg; CALC 50mg

Mango Coulis:

¾ cup cubed peeled ripe mango
½ cup fresh orange juice
1 tablespoon fresh lemon juice
1 tablespoon honey
¼ teaspoon ground allspice
¼ teaspoon ground cinnamon
¼ teaspoon ground nutmeg
¼ teaspoon dried crushed red pepper

1. Combine all ingredients in a blender; process until smooth. Pour through a sieve over a bowl. Reserve liquid; discard solids. Yield: 1 cup (serving size: ¼ cup).

ROASTED-BEET SALAD

8   beets (about 2 pounds)
5   tablespoons rice vinegar, divided
¼   teaspoon salt, divided
¼   teaspoon freshly ground black
    pepper, divided
8   cups gourmet salad greens
    (about 8 ounces)
2   teaspoons olive oil
1   (⅛-inch-thick) slice red onion,
    separated into rings

1. Preheat oven to 375°.
2. Trim off beet stems and roots. Wrap each beet in foil; bake at 375° for 45 minutes or until tender. Cool beets to room temperature; peel and cut into ¼-inch-thick slices. Combine beets, 4 tablespoons vinegar, ⅛ teaspoon salt, and ⅛ teaspoon pepper in a bowl; toss well.
3. Combine remaining 1 tablespoon vinegar, ⅛ teaspoon salt, ⅛ teaspoon pepper, salad greens, and oil in a large bowl; toss well. Place 2 cups salad greens mixture on each of 4 plates; top evenly with beets and onion rings. Yield: 4 servings.

CALORIES 107 (23% from fat); FAT 2.7g (sat 0.5g, mono 1.6g, poly 0.5g); PROTEIN 4.3g; CARB 17.6g; FIBER 3.2g; CHOL 0mg; IRON 2.5mg; SODIUM 276mg; CALC 66mg

TRICOLORED SHRIMP PLATE

2   red bell peppers
2   yellow bell peppers
24   jumbo shrimp, peeled and
      deveined (about 1½ pounds)
1   tablespoon Lemon Grass Oil,
      divided
1   teaspoon dried crushed red pepper
2   garlic cloves, minced
Cooking spray
1½   (10-ounce) bags fresh spinach

1. Preheat broiler. Cut bell peppers in half lengthwise; discard seeds and membranes. Place pepper halves, skin sides up, on a foil-lined baking sheet; flatten with hand. Broil 15 minutes or until blackened. Place in a large zip-top plastic bag; seal. Let stand 15 minutes. Peel and cut into ½-inch strips.
2. Combine shrimp, 2 teaspoons Lemon Grass Oil, crushed red pepper, and garlic in a large zip-top plastic bag; seal and marinate in refrigerator 30 minutes. Heat a large nonstick skillet coated with cooking spray over medium-high heat. Add shrimp mixture, and sauté for 1½ minutes on each side. Remove shrimp from skillet.
3. Heat remaining 1 teaspoon Lemon Grass Oil in skillet; add spinach, and cook 1 minute or until spinach wilts, stirring frequently. Divide spinach evenly among 4 plates; top evenly with roasted peppers and shrimp. Yield: 4 servings.

CALORIES 213 (27% from fat); FAT 6.5g (sat 0.7g, mono 2.7g, poly 0.8g); PROTEIN 29.7g; CARB 10g; FIBER 5.6g; CHOL 194mg; IRON 7mg; SODIUM 277mg; CALC 180mg

Lemon Grass Oil:

1   cup olive oil
½   cup sliced peeled fresh lemon
      grass (about 1 bulb)

1. Combine oil and lemon grass in a saucepan; cook 5 minutes over medium heat. Remove from heat. Store in an airtight container in refrigerator. Yield: 1 cup.

ORANGE SORBET

Gus makes this with the juice of satsumas (mandarin-type oranges that are grown in Louisiana) when they're in season. But it's just as good with juice from navel oranges.

1   cup sugar
1   cup water
2   tablespoons light-colored corn
      syrup
3   cups fresh orange juice

1. Combine first 3 ingredients in a saucepan. Bring to a boil over medium-high heat; cook 45 seconds or until sugar dissolves. Remove from heat; cool completely. Stir in orange juice.
2. Pour mixture into the freezer can of ice-cream freezer, and freeze according to manufacturer's instructions. Spoon into a freezer-safe container; cover and freeze 1 hour or until firm. Yield: 8 servings (serving size: ½ cup).

CALORIES 154 (1% from fat); FAT 0.1g (sat 0g, mono 0.1g, poly 0g); PROTEIN 0.6g; CARB 38.8g; FIBER 0.2g; CHOL 0mg; IRON 0.1mg; SODIUM 7mg; CALC 9mg

Super Salsas

Fresh tomatoes bring out the best in these zesty Mexican-style sauces.

Bumper crops of tomatoes and other vegetables and fruits are filling gardens and grocery aisles this season. And in much of the country, the abundance inspires the best salsas of the year. That's not just good news for chip-and-dip appetizer trays; these flavorful Mexican-derived sauces *(salsa)* can also do a power pep-up on fish, chicken, pork, beef, and even steamed or grilled vegetables. And here's more good news: You can store them in an airtight container in the refrigerator for up to one week.

TOMATO-BASIL SALSA

2   cups chopped seeded peeled
      tomato
¼   cup chopped fresh basil
2   tablespoons chopped red onion
2   tablespoons red wine vinegar
¼   teaspoon salt
⅛   teaspoon black pepper

1. Combine all ingredients in a bowl. Yield: 2 cups (serving size: ¼ cup).

CALORIES 11 (16% from fat); FAT 0.2g (sat 0g, mono 0g, poly 0.1g); PROTEIN 0.5g; CARB 2.5g; FIBER 0.6g; CHOL 0mg; IRON 0.2mg; SODIUM 77mg; CALC 5mg

CORN-AND-JICAMA SALSA

Serve with grilled fish or chicken.

- 2 cups fresh corn kernels (about 4 ears)
- 1 cup finely chopped peeled tomato
- ½ cup finely chopped peeled jicama
- ¼ cup chopped onion
- 1 tablespoon minced fresh cilantro
- ¼ teaspoon salt
- ¼ teaspoon paprika
- ¼ teaspoon black pepper
- 1 (4-ounce) can chopped green chiles, drained

1. Combine all ingredients in a large bowl. Yield: 4 cups (serving size: ¼ cup).

CALORIES 23 (12% from fat); FAT 0.3g (sat 0g, mono 0.1g, poly 0.1g); PROTEIN 0.8g; CARB 5.2g; FIBER 0.9g; CHOL 0mg; IRON 0.2mg; SODIUM 47mg; CALC 3mg

SALSA RANCHERA

Serve with low-fat tortilla chips, grilled meat, or poultry. This is the most traditional salsa, because it goes so well with almost anything.

- 2 cups chopped seeded peeled tomato
- ⅓ cup chopped green onions
- 2 tablespoons minced fresh cilantro
- 2 tablespoons canned chopped green chiles
- 2 tablespoons fresh lime juice
- 1 teaspoon minced seeded jalapeño pepper
- ⅛ teaspoon salt
- ⅛ teaspoon black pepper
- 2 garlic cloves, minced
- Dash of ground cumin

1. Combine all ingredients in a bowl. Yield: 2 cups (serving size: ¼ cup).

CALORIES 14 (13% from fat); FAT 0.2g (sat 0g, mono 0g, poly 0.1g); PROTEIN 0.6g; CARB 3.2g; FIBER 0.8g; CHOL 0mg; IRON 0.4mg; SODIUM 45mg; CALC 9mg

---

KILLER TOMATOES

To get you started on what may become a tradition in your house, here are tips and shortcuts from some old salsa-making hands.

- When you purchase whole tomatoes, remember that one pound of tomatoes yields about two cups, chopped and seeded.

- The easiest way to peel tomatoes is to blanch them in boiling water, then plunge into ice water. This process loosens the skin, allowing you to peel it off in strips with a sharp knife.

- To remove seeds, cut the peeled tomato at both ends and push out the seeds using a spoon.

TROPICAL TOMATO SALSA

Serve with grilled fish or poultry. It also pairs nicely with a seafood fajita or a shrimp or scallop burrito.

- 2 tablespoons lime juice
- ¼ teaspoon salt
- ¼ teaspoon black pepper
- ¼ teaspoon grated peeled fresh ginger
- 1 cup diced peeled mango
- 1 cup chopped tomato
- ¼ cup chopped fresh cilantro
- 2 tablespoons chopped shallots
- 2 teaspoons minced seeded jalapeño pepper

1. Combine first 4 ingredients in a medium bowl. Add mango and remaining ingredients; toss gently. Yield: 2 cups (serving size: ½ cup).

CALORIES 44 (6% from fat); FAT 0.3g (sat 0.1g, mono 0.1g, poly 0.1g); PROTEIN 0.9g; CARB 11.1g; FIBER 1.5g; CHOL 0mg; IRON 0.6mg; SODIUM 154mg; CALC 15mg

---

FAST FOOD

World-Class Skillets

Harried cooks from around the globe rely on the one-pan meal for versatility and speed. Think it could work for you?

Stirred up and ready to go, these handy dishes can fly from stove to plate in 30 minutes or less, with no luggage to check or customs to clear. And there's a final bonus: If you need only one pan to cook, you have only one to clean.

RUSSIAN SKILLET STROGANOFF

Preparation time: 10 minutes
Cooking time: 14 minutes

- 1 (¾-pound) flank steak
- 1 tablespoon cornstarch
- 1 teaspoon olive oil
- 2 cups thinly sliced onion
- 1 (8-ounce) package presliced mushrooms
- ½ cup low-salt beef broth
- ½ teaspoon salt
- ¼ teaspoon black pepper
- ¼ cup fat-free sour cream
- 2 tablespoons finely chopped fresh parsley
- 2 cups hot cooked long-grain rice

1. Trim fat from steak; cut steak diagonally across grain into thin slices. Combine steak and cornstarch in a small bowl; toss well. Heat oil in a large nonstick skillet over medium-high heat. Add steak; sauté 5 minutes. Add onion; sauté 1 minute. Add mushrooms; cover and cook 2 minutes. Add broth, salt, and pepper. Reduce heat; simmer, uncovered, 5 minutes. Remove from heat; stir in sour cream and parsley. Serve with rice. Yield: 4 servings (serving size: 1 cup stroganoff and ½ cup rice).

CALORIES 323 (27% from fat); FAT 9.5g (sat 3.6g, mono 4.1g, poly 0.6g); PROTEIN 21.9g; CARB 35.7g; FIBER 2.4g; CHOL 43mg; IRON 3.6mg; SODIUM 371mg; CALC 32mg

MEDITERRANEAN CHICKPEAS WITH VEGETABLES

Preparation time: 10 minutes
Cooking time: 14 minutes

- 1 tablespoon olive oil
- 1 cup diced onion
- 1 garlic clove, minced
- 2 teaspoons dried basil
- ½ teaspoon sugar
- ½ teaspoon black pepper
- ⅛ teaspoon salt
- 2 bay leaves
- 1 (28-ounce) can diced tomatoes, undrained
- 1 (19-ounce) can chickpeas (garbanzo beans), rinsed and drained
- 2 cups (½-inch) diced zucchini
- 2 cups hot cooked long-grain rice
- ¼ cup (1 ounce) grated fresh Parmesan cheese

1. Heat oil in a large nonstick skillet over medium-high heat until hot. Add onion and garlic; sauté 3 minutes. Add basil and next 5 ingredients. Bring to a boil, and reduce heat to medium. Cook 5 minutes, stirring occasionally. Stir in chickpeas; cook 3 minutes. Add zucchini; cover and cook 3 minutes or until zucchini is tender. Discard bay leaves. Serve with rice; sprinkle with cheese. Yield: 4 servings (serving size: 1½ cups vegetable mixture, ½ cup rice, and 1 tablespoon cheese).

CALORIES 374 (19% from fat); FAT 8g (sat 2g, mono 3.6g, poly 1.6g); PROTEIN 15.2g; CARB 63.2g; FIBER 6.1g; CHOL 5mg; IRON 5.2mg; SODIUM 681mg; CALC 220mg

CHINESE SPICY GINGERED BEEF

Preparation time: 15 minutes
Cooking time: 10 minutes

- 1 (¾-pound) flank steak
- 1 tablespoon cornstarch
- 2 teaspoons olive oil
- 1 tablespoon minced peeled fresh ginger
- 2 garlic cloves, minced
- 1 cup halved baby carrots
- ½ cup fat-free beef broth
- 2 tablespoons low-sodium soy sauce
- 1 tablespoon hoisin sauce
- 1 tablespoon dry white wine
- ½ teaspoon dried crushed red pepper
- 1 (8-ounce) can sliced water chestnuts, drained
- 3 cups sliced bok choy (about 6 ounces)
- 2 cups hot cooked long-grain rice

1. Trim fat from steak; cut steak diagonally across grain into thin slices. Combine steak and cornstarch. Heat oil in a large nonstick skillet over medium-high heat until hot. Add steak mixture; sauté 3 minutes. Stir in ginger and garlic; cook 10 seconds. Stir in carrots and next 6 ingredients; cover and cook 4 minutes. Stir in bok choy; cover and cook 2 minutes. Serve with rice. Yield: 4 servings (serving size: 1 cup beef mixture and ½ cup rice).

CALORIES 361 (26% from fat); FAT 10.6g (sat 3.8g, mono 4.9g, poly 0.6g); PROTEIN 21.3g; CARB 43.4g; FIBER 2.6g; CHOL 43mg; IRON 3.7mg; SODIUM 442mg; CALC 88mg

INDIAN CHICKEN CURRY

Preparation time: 15 minutes
Cooking time: 15 minutes

- 4 cups sliced Swiss chard (about 12 ounces)
- 1 pound skinned, boned chicken breast halves, cut crosswise into thin slices
- 1 tablespoon cornstarch
- 1 tablespoon olive oil
- 1 cup diced onion
- 1⅓ cups fat-free, less-sodium chicken broth
- 1 cup sliced baby carrots
- ½ cup light coconut milk
- 1 tablespoon tomato paste
- 2 teaspoons ground cumin
- 1 teaspoon curry powder
- 1 teaspoon ground cinnamon
- ¼ teaspoon salt
- ¼ to ½ teaspoon ground red pepper
- 2 cups hot cooked long-grain rice
- 3 tablespoons chopped unsalted, dry-roasted peanuts

1. Steam Swiss chard, covered, 2 minutes or until crisp tender. Drain.
2. Combine chicken and cornstarch in a small bowl. Heat oil in a large nonstick skillet over medium-high heat until hot. Add onion; stir-fry 2 minutes. Stir in chicken; cook 4 minutes or until browned. Stir in broth and next 8 ingredients; reduce heat to medium, and cook 5 minutes, stirring occasionally. Add Swiss chard; cook 2 minutes. Serve with rice. Sprinkle with peanuts. Yield: 4 servings (serving size: 1 cup chicken curry and ½ cup rice).

CALORIES 392 (24% from fat); FAT 10.4g (sat 2.9g, mono 4.7g, poly 1.8g); PROTEIN 33.6g; CARB 40.1g; FIBER 4.1g; CHOL 66mg; IRON 4.6mg; SODIUM 576mg; CALC 107mg

THAI SCALLOPS WITH ASPARAGUS

(pictured on page 186)

Preparation time: 10 minutes
Cooking time: 8 minutes

1½ pounds sea scallops
1 tablespoon cornstarch
1½ tablespoons olive oil
1½ teaspoons minced peeled fresh ginger
2 garlic cloves, minced
2 cups (2-inch) sliced asparagus (about ½ pound)
½ cup fat-free, less-sodium chicken broth
1 tablespoon fresh lemon juice
1 tablespoon low-sodium soy sauce
1 teaspoon chile puree with garlic sauce
2 tablespoons chopped fresh basil
½ teaspoon grated lemon rind
2 cups hot cooked long-grain rice
Basil sprigs (optional)

1. Combine scallops and cornstarch. Heat olive oil in a large nonstick skillet over medium-high heat. Add scallops; stir-fry 4 minutes. Remove scallops from skillet. Add ginger and garlic; stir-fry 10 seconds. Stir in asparagus and next 4 ingredients; cook, uncovered, 2 minutes.
2. Return scallops to skillet; cover and cook 1 minute. Remove from heat, and stir in chopped basil and lemon rind. Serve with rice. Garnish with basil sprigs, if desired. Yield: 4 servings (serving size: 1 cup scallop mixture and ½ cup rice).

CALORIES 338 (18% from fat); FAT 6.6g (sat 0.9g, mono 3.8g, poly 0.9g); PROTEIN 32.9g; CARB 35.3g; FIBER 2.1g; CHOL 56mg; IRON 2.1mg; SODIUM 474mg; CALC 72mg

LIGHTEN UP

A New True Blue

A Pennsylvania reader asked us to rescue her favorite blueberry pound cake.

Much as she loves blueberries, Pennsylvania reader Nancy Albed says she seldom uses them to bake the high-fat blueberry pound cake recipe that's been a family favorite for the last nine years. So she pleaded with us to "please, help fix this recipe" in time for summer's new blueberry crop. And one more thing, she added: "I've tried lightening it by using applesauce as a fat replacement, but it didn't turn out as good as the original. Can you do it another way?"

No problem. We replaced the butter with a trio of light products—light butter, light cream cheese, and lemon low-fat yogurt—that enhance the berry flavor rather than overshadow it. Those few changes helped slash the fat by more than half. And the subtle hint of lemon in the yogurt and glaze complements the blueberries.

BLUEBERRY POUND CAKE

(pictured on page 188)

2 cups granulated sugar
½ cup light butter
4 ounces block-style ⅓-less-fat cream cheese (Neufchâtel), softened
3 large eggs
1 large egg white
3 cups all-purpose flour, divided
2 cups fresh or frozen blueberries
1 teaspoon baking powder
½ teaspoon baking soda
½ teaspoon salt
1 (8-ounce) carton lemon low-fat yogurt
2 teaspoons vanilla extract
Cooking spray
½ cup powdered sugar
4 teaspoons lemon juice

1. Preheat oven to 350°.
2. Beat first 3 ingredients at medium speed of a mixer until well-blended (about 5 minutes). Add eggs and egg white, one at a time, beating well after each addition. Lightly spoon flour into dry measuring cups; level with a knife. Combine 2 tablespoons flour and blueberries in a small bowl; toss well. Combine remaining flour, baking powder, baking soda, and salt. Add flour mixture to sugar mixture alternately with yogurt, beginning and ending with flour mixture. Fold in blueberry mixture and vanilla; pour cake batter into a 10-inch tube pan coated with cooking spray. Bake at 350° for 1 hour and 10 minutes or until a wooden pick inserted in center comes out clean.
3. Cool cake in pan 10 minutes; remove from pan. Combine powdered sugar and lemon juice in a small bowl; drizzle over warm cake. Cut with a serrated knife. Yield: 16 servings (serving size: 1 slice).

CALORIES 287 (19% from fat); FAT 6.1g (sat 3.4g, mono 1.8g, poly 0.4g); PROTEIN 5.7g; CARB 53.9g; FIBER 1.5g; CHOL 57mg; IRON 1.3mg; SODIUM 227mg; CALC 50mg

BEFORE & AFTER	
SERVING SIZE	
1 slice	
CALORIES	
315	287
FAT	
13.1g	6.1g
PERCENT OF TOTAL CALORIES	
37%	19%

Separation Anxiety

*Set those little yellow kernels free and watch
them—and your spirits—soar.*

Sure, you can eat corn *on* the cob. But do as we did. Cut some off. And when you look at the corn you've scraped from the cob, see a plate of possibilities. We think you'll find that you'll be glad you did.

DOUBLE CORN-AND-HAM CASSEROLE

You can prepare the corn bread in this recipe up to three days ahead (store whole in an airtight container). Serve the casserole as a main dish with a green salad and sliced fresh tomatoes.

Corn bread:

½ cup all-purpose flour
⅓ cup yellow cornmeal
1 tablespoon sugar
1 teaspoon baking powder
½ teaspoon salt
½ cup 1% low-fat milk
1 tablespoon vegetable oil
1 large egg white, lightly beaten
Cooking spray

Casserole:

6 ears shucked corn
1½ cups fat-free, less-sodium chicken broth
1 cup diced lean ham (about 6 ounces)
½ cup chopped green onions
¼ teaspoon salt
¼ teaspoon black pepper
1 cup (4 ounces) shredded reduced-fat sharp Cheddar cheese
1 large egg, lightly beaten
Fresh chives (optional)

1. Preheat oven to 400°.
2. To prepare corn bread, lightly spoon flour into a dry measuring cup; level with a knife. Combine flour and next 4 ingredients in a medium bowl; make a well in center of mixture. Add milk, oil, and egg white to flour mixture; stir just until moist. Spoon batter into an 8-inch square baking pan coated with cooking spray. Bake at 400° for 18 minutes or until a wooden pick inserted in center comes out clean. Cool completely on a wire rack; crumble into a medium bowl.
3. Reduce oven temperature to 350°.
4. To prepare casserole, cut off tops of corn kernels; scrape corn milk and remaining pulp from cobs using the dull side of a knife blade to yield 3 cups. Combine corn and next 5 ingredients in a large saucepan; bring mixture to a boil. Reduce heat, and simmer 12 minutes. Remove corn mixture from heat, and cool.
5. Combine corn mixture, crumbled corn bread, cheese, and egg in a large bowl. Spoon mixture into a 10-inch deep-dish pie plate or 2-quart casserole coated with cooking spray. Bake at 350° for 50 minutes or until golden brown. Let stand 5 minutes before serving. Garnish with chives, if desired. Yield: 6 servings.

CALORIES 222 (31% from fat); FAT 7.7g (sat 2.8g, mono 2.3g, poly 1.5g); PROTEIN 14.2g; CARB 25.7g; FIBER 2.5g; CHOL 50mg; IRON 1.5mg; SODIUM 679mg; CALC 194mg

FRESH-CORN RISOTTO WITH ROASTED PEPPERS AND SAUSAGE

3 yellow bell peppers
5 cups fat-free, less-sodium chicken broth
1 (12-ounce) package frozen bulk turkey sausage, thawed (such as Louis Rich)
1 teaspoon stick margarine or butter
2 cups fresh corn kernels (about 4 ears)
2 garlic cloves, minced
1¼ cups uncooked Arborio or other short-grain rice
¼ cup (1 ounce) grated fresh Parmesan cheese
2 teaspoons chili powder
¼ teaspoon salt
¼ teaspoon ground cumin
¼ teaspoon black pepper
Minced fresh cilantro (optional)

1. Preheat broiler. Cut bell peppers in half lengthwise, and discard seeds and membranes. Place bell pepper halves, skin sides up, on a foil-lined baking sheet, and flatten peppers with hand. Broil 15 minutes or until peppers are blackened. Place peppers in a zip-top plastic bag, and seal bag. Let stand 15 minutes. Peel peppers, and cut into strips.
2. Bring broth to a simmer in a large saucepan (do not boil). Keep warm over low heat.
3. Cook turkey sausage in a Dutch oven over medium-high heat 8 minutes or until sausage is browned, stirring to crumble. Remove sausage from pan, and set aside. Melt margarine in pan over medium heat. Add corn and garlic; sauté 8 minutes. Add rice, and cook 1 minute, stirring constantly. Stir in ½ cup simmering chicken broth, and cook 1 minute or until liquid is nearly absorbed, stirring constantly. Add remaining chicken broth, ½ cup at a time, stirring mixture constantly, and cook until each portion of broth is absorbed before adding the next (about 20 minutes total). Stir in bell pepper strips, sausage, cheese, and next

4 ingredients. Garnish with cilantro, if desired. Yield: 7 servings (serving size: 1 cup).

CALORIES 308 (28% from fat); FAT 9.5g (sat 3.3g, mono 3.4g, poly 2.2g); PROTEIN 16.5g; CARB 41.1g; FIBER 2.7g; CHOL 45mg; IRON 3.1mg; SODIUM 558mg; CALC 97mg

INDIAN CORN PUDDING WITH BACON AND CHIVES

Cooking spray
2 teaspoons yellow cornmeal
1 cup chopped onion
¼ teaspoon salt
¼ teaspoon garlic powder
¼ teaspoon ground red pepper
¼ teaspoon black pepper
4 ounces Canadian bacon, cut into thin strips
3 cups fresh corn kernels (about 6 ears)
1½ cups whole milk, divided
⅓ cup yellow cornmeal
1 large egg
3 tablespoons chopped fresh chives

1. Preheat oven to 350°.
2. Coat a 1½-quart baking dish with cooking spray, and sprinkle with 2 teaspoons cornmeal.
3. Place a large nonstick skillet coated with cooking spray over medium-high heat until hot. Add onion and next 5 ingredients; sauté 3 minutes or until tender. Stir in corn and 1 cup milk. Reduce heat to low; cover and cook 10 minutes, stirring occasionally. Add ⅓ cup cornmeal, stirring with a whisk. Combine remaining ½ cup milk and egg; stir well with a whisk. Add to cornmeal mixture in skillet; stir well. Stir in chives.
4. Spoon mixture into prepared dish. Bake pudding at 350° for 30 minutes or until lightly browned and set. Let stand 15 minutes. Yield: 8 servings (serving size: ½ cup).

CALORIES 143 (26% from fat); FAT 4.1g (sat 1.6g, mono 1.4g, poly 0.6g); PROTEIN 7.9g; CARB 20.5g; FIBER 2.6g; CHOL 41mg; IRON 0.8mg; SODIUM 313mg; CALC 66mg

PORK SAUTÉ WITH SPICY CORN

Here, the corn kernels infuse the milk, giving it extra body and corn flavor.

3 cups fresh corn kernels (about 6 ears)
¾ cup 2% reduced-fat milk
8 (2-ounce) boned center-cut loin pork chops (¼ inch thick)
¼ teaspoon black pepper
¼ cup all-purpose flour
2 teaspoons vegetable oil, divided
Cooking spray
⅓ cup chopped green onions
1 teaspoon finely chopped unsalted, dry-roasted peanuts
1 tablespoon low-sodium soy sauce
2 teaspoons brown sugar
½ teaspoon dried crushed red pepper

1. Combine corn and milk in a large saucepan. Bring to a boil over medium heat; reduce heat, and simmer 20 minutes, stirring frequently. Strain corn mixture through a sieve over a shallow dish, reserving liquid and solids.
2. Sprinkle pork chops with black pepper. Dip one side of each chop in corn liquid; dredge in flour.
3. Heat 1 teaspoon oil in a large nonstick skillet coated with cooking spray over medium-high heat until hot. Place 4 pork chops, floured sides down, in skillet, and cook 2 minutes. Turn pork chops over, and cook 2 minutes or until done. Repeat procedure with remaining 1 teaspoon oil and remaining pork chops. Set pork chops aside, and keep warm.
4. Add onions to skillet, and sauté 30 seconds over medium-high heat. Add reserved corn solids and peanuts; sauté 4 minutes. Add soy sauce, sugar, and red pepper; sauté 4 minutes or until liquid evaporates. Place 2 pork chops on each of 4 plates; top each serving with ½ cup corn mixture. Yield: 4 servings.

CALORIES 350 (30% from fat); FAT 11.7g (sat 3.5g, mono 4.5g, poly 2.6g); PROTEIN 27.2g; CARB 36.7g; FIBER 5.7g; CHOL 62mg; IRON 2mg; SODIUM 225mg; CALC 86mg

CREAMED SALMON WITH FRESH CORN AND DILL

In this recipe, the milk is infused with onion for extra flavor.

1 (¾-pound) salmon fillet (about 1 inch thick)
¼ teaspoon freshly ground black pepper
Cooking spray
4 ears shucked corn
1 cup whole milk, divided
2 (½-inch-thick) slices onion
4 teaspoons all-purpose flour
½ teaspoon salt
¼ teaspoon white pepper
1 tablespoon chopped fresh or 1 teaspoon dried dill
8 (½-inch-thick) slices French bread, toasted

1. Prepare grill or broiler. Sprinkle both sides of salmon with black pepper. Place salmon on a grill rack or broiler pan coated with cooking spray; cook 5 minutes on each side or until fish flakes easily when tested with a fork. Flake salmon, and set aside.
2. Cut off tops of corn kernels; scrape corn milk and remaining pulp from cobs using the dull side of a knife blade. Set kernels and corn milk aside.
3. Combine ¾ cup milk and onion slices in a large saucepan. Bring milk mixture just to a boil over medium heat; cover, reduce heat, and simmer 5 minutes. Discard onion. Add corn and corn milk to pan; cook 5 minutes, stirring frequently.
4. Combine flour and remaining ¼ cup milk in a small bowl, stirring well with a whisk. Add flour mixture, salt, and white pepper to corn mixture in pan; stir well. Cook 7 minutes or until thick, stirring constantly. Remove from heat, and gently stir in salmon and dill. Serve over toasted bread slices. Yield: 4 servings (serving size: 1 cup creamed salmon and 2 toast slices).

CALORIES 434 (24% from fat); FAT 11.6g (sat 3g, mono 4.9g, poly 2.8g); PROTEIN 28.1g; CARB 55.4g; FIBER 5.1g; CHOL 66mg; IRON 2.4mg; SODIUM 673mg; CALC 109mg

WEST INDIES CORN AND CHICKEN

6 ears shucked corn

Spice mixture:

2 teaspoons dried thyme
2 teaspoons coriander seeds, crushed
1 teaspoon paprika
1 teaspoon black pepper
½ teaspoon salt
½ teaspoon garlic powder
½ teaspoon dried orange peel
½ teaspoon ground cumin

Remaining ingredients:

6 skinned, boned chicken thighs (about 1¼ pounds)
1 bacon slice
1 cup chopped onion
½ cup chopped green bell pepper
½ cup chopped celery
1 tablespoon chopped seeded jalapeño pepper
1 cup water
1¼ cups fat-free, less-sodium chicken broth
1 (15-ounce) can black beans, rinsed and drained
1 cup uncooked converted rice
1 teaspoon sesame seeds

1. Cut off tops of corn kernels; scrape corn milk and remaining pulp from cobs using the dull side of a knife blade.
2. To prepare spice mixture, combine first 8 ingredients; divide spice mixture in half. Coat chicken with half of spice mixture.
3. Cook bacon in a large skillet over medium heat until crisp. Remove bacon from skillet; crumble and set aside. Add chicken to bacon drippings in skillet; cook over high heat 4 minutes on each side or until browned. Remove chicken.
4. Add onion, bell pepper, celery, jalapeño, and remaining spice mixture to skillet; sauté 8 minutes or until lightly browned. Add 1 cup water to skillet; scrape skillet to loosen browned bits. Add corn; cook 5 minutes over medium-high heat, stirring frequently. Add broth, beans, and chicken; bring to a boil. Stir in rice. Sprinkle with bacon and sesame seeds. Cover, reduce heat, and simmer 20 minutes. Remove from heat; let stand 5 minutes. Yield: 6 servings (serving size: 1 chicken thigh and 1½ cups corn mixture).

CALORIES 310 (19% from fat); FAT 6.5g (sat 1.6g, mono 1.9g, poly 1.7g); PROTEIN 27.3g; CARB 38.7g; FIBER 5.6g; CHOL 80mg; IRON 3.9mg; SODIUM 452mg; CALC 67mg

SUMMER-GARDEN TART

2 teaspoons olive oil
1 cup vertically sliced Vidalia or other sweet onion
1 cup sliced yellow squash (about 1 medium)
1 tablespoon chopped fresh or 1 teaspoon dried thyme
¼ teaspoon salt
⅛ teaspoon black pepper
3 garlic cloves, minced
1 cup fresh corn kernels (about 2 ears)
½ cup 1% low-fat milk
1 (11.5-ounce) can refrigerated corn bread twists
Cooking spray
1 tablespoon yellow cornmeal
¼ cup (1 ounce) shredded part-skim mozzarella cheese
¼ cup (1 ounce) grated fresh Parmesan cheese
¼ cup chopped fresh parsley

1. Preheat oven to 400°.
2. Heat oil in a nonstick skillet over medium-high heat. Add onion and next 5 ingredients; sauté 7 minutes or until browned. Combine corn and milk in a saucepan over medium heat; cook 13 minutes.
3. Unroll dough (do not separate into strips). Roll dough into a 12 x 10-inch rectangle on a lightly floured surface. Place dough on a baking sheet coated with cooking spray and sprinkled with cornmeal. Crimp edges of dough with fingers to form a rim. Sprinkle mozzarella cheese over crust; top with corn mixture and vegetables. Sprinkle with Parmesan cheese. Bake at 400° for 15 minutes or until crust is golden. Let stand 10 minutes. Sprinkle with parsley. Yield: 6 servings.

CALORIES 279 (39% from fat); FAT 12g (sat 3.5g, mono 4g, poly 4.2g); PROTEIN 8.8g; CARB 34.6g; FIBER 1.8g; CHOL 6mg; IRON 2.1mg; SODIUM 639mg; CALC 118mg

ROASTED-CORN SALAD

3 cups fresh corn kernels (about 6 ears)
1 tablespoon vegetable oil, divided
Cooking spray
2 tablespoons white balsamic vinegar
1 tablespoon Dijon mustard
¼ teaspoon salt
¼ teaspoon black pepper
1 cup chopped seeded tomato
½ cup chopped red bell pepper
½ cup chopped green onions

1. Preheat oven to 425°.
2. Combine corn and 1 teaspoon oil in a jelly-roll pan coated with cooking spray. Bake at 425° for 20 minutes or until browned, stirring occasionally.
3. Combine remaining 2 teaspoons oil, vinegar, and next 3 ingredients in a medium bowl; add corn mixture, stirring well. Stir in tomato, bell pepper, and onions. Serve warm or at room temperature. Yield: 4 servings (serving size: ¾ cup).

CALORIES 154 (32% from fat); FAT 5.4g (sat 0.9g, mono 1.4g, poly 2.4g); PROTEIN 4.5g; CARB 26.4g; FIBER 4.9g; CHOL 0mg; IRON 1.3mg; SODIUM 282mg; CALC 15mg

TUSCAN BREAD SALAD WITH CORN

Summer vegetables and crisp garlic croutons are tossed together with a sweet corn vinaigrette to create this traditional bread salad. Serve immediately, while the croutons are still crisp.

 1 cup fresh corn kernels (about 2 ears)
 ½ cup water
 2 cups (1-inch) cubed Italian bread
 3 garlic cloves, minced
 2 tablespoons white wine vinegar
 2 tablespoons water
 2 tablespoons mango chutney
 1 tablespoon olive oil
 ¼ teaspoon salt
 ¼ teaspoon coarsely ground black pepper
 1 cup chopped seeded peeled cucumber
 1 cup chopped seeded tomato
 ½ cup chopped green onions
 ½ cup chopped yellow bell pepper

1. Combine corn and ½ cup water in a small saucepan, and bring to a boil. Reduce heat, and simmer 10 minutes or until corn is tender. Drain well.
2. Preheat broiler. Combine bread cubes and garlic in a medium bowl; toss well to coat. Arrange bread cubes on a jelly-roll pan, and broil 5 minutes or until lightly browned, stirring once.
3. Combine vinegar and next 5 ingredients in a large bowl. Add corn, cucumber, and next 3 ingredients. Add bread cubes, and toss gently. Serve immediately. Yield: 6 servings (serving size: ¾ cup).

CALORIES 116 (23% from fat); FAT 2.9g (sat 0.4g, mono 1.8g, poly 0.4g); PROTEIN 3g; CARB 20.8g; FIBER 2.2g; CHOL 0mg; IRON 1.1mg; SODIUM 207mg; CALC 20mg

Take a Hike

Thinking of dining in the great outdoors? These pack-along recipes fit the bill.

CHICKEN-PASTA SALAD

Any kind of short pasta can be substituted for farfalle.
—Julie McCollum, Kansas City, Missouri

 4 cups cooked farfalle (about 8 ounces uncooked bow tie pasta)
 2 cups diced ready-to-eat roasted skinned, boned chicken breasts (about 2 breasts) (such as Tyson)
 ¾ cup sliced carrot
 ¾ cup sliced celery
 ½ cup frozen petite green peas, thawed
 ½ cup diced red bell pepper
 3 tablespoons extra-virgin olive oil
 3 tablespoons fresh lemon juice
 2 tablespoons minced fresh parsley
 1 tablespoon Dijon mustard
 1 teaspoon grated lemon rind
 1 teaspoon dried tarragon
 ¼ teaspoon salt
 ¼ teaspoon black pepper

1. Combine first 6 ingredients in a large bowl. Combine olive oil and remaining 7 ingredients; stir well with a whisk. Drizzle vinaigrette over salad, and toss gently. Cover and chill. Yield: 6 servings (serving size: 1⅓ cups).

CALORIES 270 (28% from fat); FAT 8.5g (sat 1.4g, mono 5.4g, poly 1.1g); PROTEIN 14.6g; CARB 33.5g; FIBER 2.4g; CHOL 23mg; IRON 2.1mg; SODIUM 401mg; CALC 31mg

POTATO-PORTOBELLO SALAD

I'm an allergist with a private practice. But before that, I worked for five years as a professional chef. My wife insists that I try to cook healthful recipes. I like to add portobello mushrooms to recipes because they have a nice earthy taste.

—Joseph D'Amore, M.D., Laurel Hollow, New York

 5 cups (¼-inch-thick) sliced red potato (about 2¼ pounds)
 ½ cup sliced green onions
 ¼ cup chopped fresh parsley
 3 tablespoons lemon juice
 2 tablespoons capers
 2 tablespoons extra-virgin olive oil
 1 tablespoon balsamic vinegar
 ½ teaspoon dried basil
 ½ teaspoon dried oregano
 ½ teaspoon dried tarragon
 ¼ teaspoon black pepper
 8 garlic cloves, minced
 2 portobello mushroom caps, thinly sliced

1. Place potato in a saucepan, and cover with water; bring to a boil. Reduce heat, and simmer 10 minutes or until tender; drain. Cool.
2. Combine green onions and next 10 ingredients in a large bowl. Add potato and mushrooms; toss well. Yield: 8 servings (serving size: 1 cup).

CALORIES 119 (27% from fat); FAT 3.6g (sat 0.5g, mono 2.5g, poly 0.4g); PROTEIN 2.8g; CARB 20g; FIBER 2.1g; CHOL 0mg; IRON 1.3mg; SODIUM 177mg; CALC 24mg

"GRAPE" CHICKEN-SALAD SANDWICHES

When summertime rolls around, my friends always ask me to make my chicken salad. I take it to luncheons or picnics or just serve it at home for lunch. Both my 3-year-old and 5-year-old love it.

—Lee Franze, Duncanville, Texas

 ⅔ cup chopped celery
 ½ cup light mayonnaise
 2 tablespoons lemon juice
 ¼ teaspoon salt
 ⅛ teaspoon onion powder
 ⅛ teaspoon garlic powder
 ⅛ teaspoon dried thyme
 ⅛ teaspoon black pepper
 2½ cups cubed cooked chicken breast (about 1½ pounds)
 1½ cups seedless green grapes, halved
 16 (1-ounce) slices white bread

1. Combine first 8 ingredients in a large bowl; stir in chicken and grapes. Spread ½ cup chicken salad over each of 8 bread slices; top with remaining bread slices. Yield: 8 sandwiches.

CALORIES 364 (24% from fat); FAT 9.8g (sat 2.2g, mono 3.1g, poly 3.6g); PROTEIN 31.4g; CARB 35.7g; FIBER 1.7g; CHOL 79mg; IRON 2.4mg; SODIUM 547mg; CALC 61mg

CHOCOLATE-CHIP BUNDT CAKE

I used to be a nanny, but my passion for cooking compelled me to take on a new career. I'm moving to California to attend a culinary school, and hope to become a pastry chef someday. This is a favorite cake from my childhood days that I decided to lighten.

—Jennifer Sivecz, Telford, Pennsylvania

    Cooking spray
 2 teaspoons all-purpose flour
 1 cup fat-free sour cream
 ¾ cup plus 1 tablespoon warm water
 3 tablespoons vegetable oil
 2 teaspoons instant espresso or 4 teaspoons instant coffee granules
 1 (8-ounce) carton egg substitute
 1 (18.25-ounce) package devil's food cake mix (without pudding in the mix)
 1 (3.9-ounce) package chocolate instant pudding mix
 ½ cup semisweet chocolate chips
 1 tablespoon powdered sugar

1. Preheat oven to 350°.
2. Coat a 12-cup Bundt pan with cooking spray, and dust with flour; set aside.
3. Combine sour cream and next 6 ingredients in a large bowl; beat at medium speed of a mixer 3 minutes. Add chocolate chips, and beat batter 30 seconds.
4. Spoon batter into prepared pan. Bake at 350° for 1 hour or until a wooden pick inserted in center comes out clean. Cool in pan 10 minutes on a wire rack. Invert cake onto wire rack, and cool completely. Sprinkle with powdered sugar. Yield: 16 servings.

CALORIES 230 (30% from fat); FAT 7.6g (sat 2.7g, mono 2.9g, poly 2g); PROTEIN 4.3g; CARB 36.7g; FIBER 0.8g; CHOL 0mg; IRON 1.3mg; SODIUM 397mg; CALC 44mg

September

The Ultimate Quick & Easy Pasta Sauce

It's an open secret among connoisseurs of pasta sauces that canned tomatoes are not only faster, but also better. We'll make you a believer.

If you think canned goods have a bad reputation, think again about canned tomatoes. Diced, whole, or crushed, tomatoes protected by metal containers don't go bad, as will even the best of the vine-ripe varieties. Those little cans of tomato paste impart an intensity and thickness to a recipe that would require hours of cooking at home.

And canned tomatoes, in all their forms, provide a consistency of flavor and texture almost impossible to obtain from their fresh counterparts. Many of the tricks used to keep commercially grown tomatoes from perishing on supermarket shelves, such as ripening them with ethylene gas or in warming rooms, also flatten flavor and aroma.

The bottom line: Fresh is nice, but when it comes to a great pasta sauce, canned is king. Faster, better, stronger, tastier. And once you've found just the right combination of ingredients you can use it again and again. Always quick, always easy, it will become the base for many variations.

Our recipe for Ultimate Quick-and-Easy Pasta Sauce (at right) is followed by five recipes for variations. Each incorporates the basic sauce, with modifications indicated in each of the recipes.

ULTIMATE QUICK-AND-EASY PASTA SAUCE

(pictured on page 221)

This easy-to-make sauce is so tasty and versatile, it's used as the basis of all the sauce recipes that follow. You can substitute crushed or whole tomatoes for the diced. Crushed will give you a smooth, thick sauce; whole adds chunkiness. Serve this sauce with your favorite pasta.

  1 teaspoon olive oil
  1 cup chopped onion
  4 garlic cloves, minced
  ½ cup dry red wine or 2 tablespoons
       balsamic vinegar
  1 tablespoon sugar
  1 tablespoon chopped fresh or
       1 teaspoon dried basil
  2 tablespoons tomato paste
  ½ teaspoon dried Italian seasoning
  ¼ teaspoon black pepper
  2 (14.5-ounce) cans diced
       tomatoes, undrained
  2 tablespoons chopped fresh parsley

1. Heat oil in a saucepan or large skillet over medium-high heat. Add onion and garlic; sauté 5 minutes. Stir in wine and next 6 ingredients; bring to a boil. Reduce heat to medium, and cook, uncovered, about 15 minutes. Stir in parsley. Yield: 3 cups (serving size: 1 cup).

CALORIES 126 (16% from fat); FAT 2.3g (sat 0.4g, mono 1.3g, poly 0.5g); PROTEIN 4.1g; CARB 25.2g; FIBER 3.7g; CHOL 0mg; IRON 2.8mg; SODIUM 461mg; CALC 110mg

SICILIAN-STYLE SAUCE

  1 teaspoon olive oil
  ½ pound ultra-lean ground beef
  1 cup chopped onion
  4 garlic cloves, minced
  ½ cup dry red wine or 2 tablespoons
       balsamic vinegar
  ¼ cup golden raisins
  1 tablespoon sugar
  1 tablespoon chopped fresh or
       1 teaspoon dried basil
  2 tablespoons tomato paste
  ½ teaspoon dried Italian seasoning
  ¼ teaspoon black pepper
  2 (14.5-ounce) cans diced
       tomatoes, undrained
  2 tablespoons chopped fresh parsley
  2 teaspoons coarsely chopped pine
       nuts, toasted

1. Heat oil in a saucepan or skillet over medium-high heat. Add beef, onion, and garlic; sauté 5 minutes. Stir in wine and next 7 ingredients; bring to a boil. Reduce heat to medium; cook, uncovered, about 15 minutes. Stir in parsley and nuts. Yield: 4 cups (serving size: 1 cup).

CALORIES 222 (27% from fat); FAT 6.6g (sat 1.8g, mono 3g, poly 1.1g); PROTEIN 15.8g; CARB 27.8g; FIBER 3.5g; CHOL 35mg; IRON 3.6mg; SODIUM 376mg; CALC 92mg

PUTTANESCA SAUCE

  1 teaspoon olive oil
  1 cup chopped onion
  4 garlic cloves, minced
  ½ cup dry red wine or 2 tablespoons
       balsamic vinegar
  1 tablespoon sugar
  1 tablespoon chopped fresh or
       2 teaspoons dried basil
  2 tablespoons tomato paste
  ½ teaspoon dried Italian seasoning
  ¼ teaspoon black pepper
  2 (14.5-ounce) cans diced
       tomatoes, undrained
  ¼ cup chopped pitted green olives
  2 tablespoons chopped fresh parsley
  1 tablespoon capers
  ½ teaspoon anchovy paste
  ¼ to ½ teaspoon dried crushed red
       pepper

1. Heat oil in a saucepan or large skillet over medium-high heat. Add onion and garlic; sauté 5 minutes. Stir in wine and next 6 ingredients; bring to a boil. Reduce heat to medium, and cook, uncovered, about 15 minutes. Stir in olives and remaining ingredients; cook until thoroughly heated. Yield: 3 cups (serving size: 1 cup).

CALORIES 139 (21% from fat); FAT 3.2g (sat 0.5g, mono 1.8g, poly 0.6g); PROTEIN 4.6g; CARB 26.1g; FIBER 4g; CHOL 0mg; IRON 3.2mg; SODIUM 900mg; CALC 120mg

ARRABBIATA SAUCE

This spicy sauce gets its name from arrabbiare, *which means "to get angry" in Italian.*

1   teaspoon olive oil
1   cup chopped onion
4   garlic cloves, minced
½   cup dry red wine or 2 tablespoons balsamic vinegar
1   tablespoon sugar
1   tablespoon chopped fresh or 1 teaspoon dried basil
1   teaspoon dried crushed red pepper
2   tablespoons tomato paste
1   tablespoon lemon juice
½   teaspoon dried Italian seasoning
¼   teaspoon black pepper
2   (14.5-ounce) cans diced tomatoes, undrained
2   tablespoons chopped fresh parsley

1. Heat oil in a saucepan or large skillet over medium-high heat. Add onion and garlic; sauté 5 minutes. Stir in wine and next 8 ingredients; bring to a boil. Reduce heat to medium, and cook, uncovered, about 15 minutes. Stir in parsley. Yield: 3 cups (serving size: 1 cup).

CALORIES 133 (17% from fat); FAT 2.5g (sat 0.4g, mono 1.3g, poly 0.5g); PROTEIN 4.4g; CARB 26.7g; FIBER 4.2g; CHOL 0mg; IRON 3mg; SODIUM 468mg; CALC 112mg

VODKA SAUCE

This sauce is traditionally served over thick, tubular pasta such as penne or rigatoni. Fat-free half-and-half is a new product that performs like the regular kind.

1   teaspoon olive oil
1   cup chopped onion
½   cup chopped prosciutto or lean ham (about 3 ounces)
4   garlic cloves, minced
½   cup dry red wine or 2 tablespoons balsamic vinegar
⅓   cup vodka
1   tablespoon sugar
2   tablespoons tomato paste
¼   teaspoon black pepper
2   (14.5-ounce) cans diced tomatoes, undrained
½   cup fat-free half-and-half (such as Land O' Lakes)
2   tablespoons chopped fresh parsley

1. Heat oil in a saucepan or large skillet over medium-high heat. Add onion, prosciutto, and garlic; sauté 5 minutes. Stir in wine and next 5 ingredients; bring to a boil. Reduce heat to medium, and cook, uncovered, about 20 minutes. Remove from heat. Stir in half-and-half and parsley. Yield: 5 cups (serving size: 1 cup).

CALORIES 121 (22% from fat); FAT 2.9g (sat 0.7g, mono 1.5g, poly 0.5g); PROTEIN 6.9g; CARB 17.3g; FIBER 2.2g; CHOL 10mg; IRON 1.8mg; SODIUM 556mg; CALC 78mg

SALSA DEL SOL

1   teaspoon olive oil
1   cup chopped onion
4   garlic cloves, minced
1   jalapeño pepper, seeded and minced
½   cup dry red wine or 2 tablespoons balsamic vinegar
1   tablespoon sugar
1   tablespoon chopped fresh or 2 teaspoons dried basil
2   tablespoons tomato paste
½   teaspoon ground cumin
½   teaspoon ground cinnamon
¼   teaspoon black pepper
2   (14.5-ounce) cans diced tomatoes, undrained
¼   cup tequila
2   tablespoons chopped fresh parsley
1   tablespoon minced fresh cilantro

1. Heat oil in a saucepan or large skillet over medium-high heat. Add onion, garlic, and jalapeño; sauté 5 minutes. Stir in wine and next 7 ingredients; bring to a boil. Reduce heat to medium, and cook, uncovered, 10 minutes. Stir in tequila, parsley, and cilantro; cook 5 minutes. Yield: 3 cups (serving size: 1 cup).

CALORIES 127 (17% from fat); FAT 2.4g (sat 0.4g, mono 1.3g, poly 0.5g); PROTEIN 4.2g; CARB 25.2g; FIBER 3.9g; CHOL 0mg; IRON 2.9mg; SODIUM 459mg; CALC 109mg

SHRIMP FRA DIAVOLO WITH FETA

Make sure to prepare the pasta and Arrabbiata Sauce (at left) before you sauté the shrimp for this devilishly spicy dish.

1   teaspoon olive oil
24 medium shrimp, peeled and deveined (about 1 pound)
1   tablespoon lemon juice
4   cups hot cooked linguine (about 8 ounces uncooked pasta)
3   cups Arrabbiata Sauce
¾   cup (3 ounces) crumbled feta cheese

1. Heat olive oil in a large nonstick skillet over medium heat. Add shrimp, and sauté 3 minutes or until done. Drizzle shrimp with lemon juice, and set aside.

2. Place 1 cup linguine on each of 4 plates; top each with ¾ cup Arrabbiata Sauce, 6 shrimp, and 3 tablespoons cheese. Yield: 4 servings.

CALORIES 454 (20% from fat); FAT 9.9g (sat 4g, mono 3.1g, poly 1.5g); PROTEIN 30.3g; CARB 61.7g; FIBER 5.4g; CHOL 148mg; IRON 6.4mg; SODIUM 716mg; CALC 243mg

CHICKEN PARMESAN

(pictured on page 226)

This can be put together in a large shallow dish instead of in gratin dishes.

　4　(4-ounce) skinned, boned
　　　chicken breast halves
　½　cup seasoned breadcrumbs
　¼　cup grated Parmesan cheese
　½　teaspoon dried Italian seasoning
　⅛　teaspoon black pepper
　⅓　cup all-purpose flour
　2　large egg whites, lightly beaten
　2　teaspoons olive oil
　4　cups hot cooked spaghetti
　　　(about 8 ounces uncooked
　　　pasta)
　3　cups Ultimate Quick-and-Easy
　　　Pasta Sauce (page 204)
　1　cup (4 ounces) shredded part-
　　　skim mozzarella cheese
Chopped fresh parsley (optional)

1. Place each chicken breast half between 2 sheets of heavy-duty plastic wrap; flatten to ¼-inch thickness using a meat mallet or rolling pin.
2. Combine breadcrumbs and next 3 ingredients in a shallow dish. Dredge 1 chicken breast half in flour. Dip in egg whites; dredge in breadcrumb mixture. Repeat procedure with remaining chicken, flour, egg whites, and breadcrumb mixture.
3. Heat oil in a large nonstick skillet over medium-high heat. Add chicken, and cook 5 minutes on each side or until done.
4. Place 1 cup spaghetti in each of 4 gratin dishes. Spoon ½ cup Ultimate Quick-and-Easy Pasta Sauce over each serving. Top each with 1 chicken breast half. Spoon ¼ cup sauce over each serving. Sprinkle each serving with ¼ cup mozzarella cheese.
5. Preheat broiler. Place gratin dishes on a baking sheet; broil 3 minutes or until cheese melts. Garnish with chopped parsley, if desired. Yield: 4 servings.

CALORIES 614 (19% from fat); FAT 12.8g (sat 5g, mono 4.8g, poly 1.5g); PROTEIN 49.1g; CARB 74.8g; FIBER 5.4g; CHOL 86mg; IRON 6.1mg; SODIUM 937mg; CALC 375mg

PEPPERED TENDERLOIN WITH POLENTA AND PUTTANESCA SAUCE

(pictured on page 222)

　1¼　cups yellow cornmeal
　¼　teaspoon salt
　4　cups water
　6　(4-ounce) beef tenderloin steaks
　　　(1 inch thick)
　1　garlic clove, halved
　1　teaspoon coarsely ground black
　　　pepper
Cooking spray
　3　cups Puttanesca Sauce (page 204)
Fresh flat-leaf parsley sprigs
　　　(optional)

1. Combine cornmeal and salt in a medium saucepan. Gradually add water, stirring constantly with a whisk. Bring to a boil; reduce heat to medium, and cook 15 minutes, stirring frequently. Remove polenta from heat.
2. Rub steaks with garlic; sprinkle with pepper. Place a large nonstick skillet coated with cooking spray over medium-high heat until hot. Add steaks; cook 3 minutes on each side or until desired degree of doneness. Serve each steak over ⅔ cup polenta; spoon ½ cup Puttanesca Sauce over each steak. Garnish with parsley sprigs, if desired. Yield: 6 servings.

CALORIES 345 (25% from fat); FAT 9.6g (sat 3.3g, mono 3.9g, poly 0.8g); PROTEIN 28.4g; CARB 35.8g; FIBER 3.6g; CHOL 70mg; IRON 6.1mg; SODIUM 610mg; CALC 71mg

How Sweet It Is

Next time you get a desperate dessert craving, relax—there's a terrific way to scratch the itch.

MARY ANN'S ORANGE LOAF CAKE

I've found this cake gets a big welcome at potlucks and family gatherings.
　　　　　—Mary Ann McCann,
　　　　　Rosemount, Minnesota

　1　cup sugar
　⅓　cup reduced-calorie stick
　　　margarine, softened
　½　teaspoon orange flavoring
　3　large egg whites
　1　(8-ounce) carton lemon
　　　low-fat yogurt
　1⅔　cups all-purpose flour
　½　cup oat bran
　1　teaspoon grated orange rind
　½　teaspoon baking soda
　¼　teaspoon salt
Cooking spray

1. Preheat oven to 350°.
2. Beat sugar and margarine at medium speed of a mixer until light and fluffy. Add orange flavoring and egg whites; beat well. Add yogurt; beat well. Lightly spoon flour into dry measuring cups, and level with a knife. Combine flour and next 4 ingredients in a small bowl. Gradually add flour mixture to sugar mixture, stirring just until moist.
3. Coat an 8-inch loaf pan with cooking spray; spoon batter into pan. Bake at 350° for 1 hour and 5 minutes or until a wooden pick inserted in center comes out clean. Cool in pan 10 minutes on a wire rack; remove from pan. Cool completely. Yield: 8 servings (serving size: 1 slice).

CALORIES 297 (18% from fat); FAT 5.8g (sat 1.1g, mono 2g, poly 1.7g); PROTEIN 6g; CARB 56.1g; FIBER 1.4g; CHOL 0mg; IRON 1.5mg; SODIUM 264mg; CALC 45mg

PUMPKIN-STREUSEL CHEESECAKE

(pictured on page 221)

Don't worry if your cheesecake has a few cracks. It's normal with this recipe.
—*Marlene Koch, Columbus, Ohio*

Crust:

¾ cup gingersnap crumbs (about 12 cookies, finely crushed)
1 tablespoon light butter, melted
Cooking spray

Filling:

1 cup 1% low-fat cottage cheese
1 (8-ounce) block fat-free cream cheese
1 (8-ounce) tub light cream cheese
1¼ cups granulated sugar
½ cup low-fat sour cream
2 tablespoons cornstarch
2 teaspoons all-purpose flour
1 teaspoon vanilla extract
¾ teaspoon ground cinnamon
½ teaspoon ground ginger
½ teaspoon ground allspice
1 (15-ounce) can pumpkin
4 large egg whites
2 large eggs

Streusel topping:

½ cup gingersnap crumbs (about 8 cookies, finely crushed)
¼ cup all-purpose flour
2 tablespoons brown sugar
1 tablespoon light butter

1. Preheat oven to 375°.
2. To prepare crust, combine ¾ cup crumbs and 1 tablespoon melted butter; toss with a fork until moist. Press into bottom of a 9-inch springform pan coated with cooking spray. Bake at 375° for 5 minutes; cool on a wire rack. Reduce oven temperature to 325°.
3. To prepare filling, place cottage cheese in a blender or food processor; process until smooth. Combine cottage cheese and cream cheeses in a large bowl; beat at high speed of a mixer until smooth. Add granulated sugar and next 8 ingredients; beat well. Add egg whites and eggs, 1 at a time, beating well after each addition. Pour filling into prepared crust; bake at 325° for 1 hour and 20 minutes.
4. To prepare streusel topping, combine ½ cup crumbs, ¼ cup flour, and brown sugar; cut in 1 tablespoon light butter with a pastry blender or 2 knives until mixture resembles coarse meal. Sprinkle over cheesecake, and bake an additional 10 minutes or until set. Cheesecake is done when the center barely moves when pan is jiggled. Remove cheesecake from oven; run a knife around outside edge. Cool to room temperature. Yield: 12 servings (serving size: 1 slice).

CALORIES 287 (28% from fat); FAT 8.8g (sat 4.3g, mono 3.1g, poly 0.9g); PROTEIN 11.2g; CARB 40.7g; FIBER 1.6g; CHOL 64mg; IRON 1.6mg; SODIUM 361mg; CALC 142mg

MOM'S SPECIAL COMPANY CAKE

When I was growing up, my parents would invite friends over on Saturday nights for an evening of cards. After a couple of hours of playing, they would retire to our large front porch to drink coffee and eat a slice of my mother's wonderful cake.
—*Trudy J. Moore, Little Rock, Arkansas*

Cooking spray
1½ cups plus 2 teaspoons all-purpose flour, divided
1¼ cups sugar
½ cup unsweetened cocoa
1¼ teaspoons baking soda
1 teaspoon salt
1 cup low-fat buttermilk
⅓ cup vegetable oil
⅓ cup Grand Marnier or other orange-flavored liqueur
1 (4-ounce) carton egg substitute or 3 large egg whites
1 cup sugar
¼ cup stick margarine or butter
⅓ cup Grand Marnier or other orange-flavored liqueur
¼ cup water

1. Preheat oven 350°.
2. Coat a 6-cup Bundt pan with cooking spray; dust with 2 teaspoons flour.
3. Lightly spoon 1½ cups flour into dry measuring cups; level with a knife. Combine 1½ cups flour, 1¼ cups sugar, cocoa, and next 6 ingredients in a large bowl; beat at low speed of a mixer until moist. Beat 3 minutes at medium speed. Pour batter into pan.
4. Bake at 350° for 50 minutes or until a wooden pick inserted in center comes out clean. Insert a fork into cake, making several holes. Combine 1 cup sugar and remaining 3 ingredients in a saucepan; boil 1 minute. Pour glaze over cake while still in pan. Cool completely; remove from pan. Yield: 16 servings.

CALORIES 272 (27% from fat); FAT 8.2g (sat 1.8g, mono 2.7g, poly 3.2g); PROTEIN 3.3g; CARB 42.2g; FIBER 0.3g; CHOL 0mg; IRON 1.2mg; SODIUM 298mg; CALC 29mg

FRENCH-BREAD PUDDING

At 83, my dad has had enough bread pudding to become very picky about what he likes. So I was thrilled when he pronounced my recipe—my first attempt at a light bread pudding and one of my first attempts at making bread pudding, period—to be the best he's ever tasted.
—*Amanda Dattilio, Phoenix, Arizona*

1½ cups sugar
1 cup raisins
2 tablespoons vanilla extract
2 teaspoons ground cinnamon
1 (8-ounce) carton egg substitute or 6 large egg whites
6 cups (1½-inch) cubed French bread (about 16 ounces)
4 cups 1% low-fat milk
Cooking spray

1. Preheat oven to 350°.
2. Combine first 5 ingredients in a medium bowl. Combine bread and milk in a large bowl, pressing down with a spatula to soak; let stand 2 minutes. Stir sugar mixture into bread mixture. Spoon bread mixture into a
Continued

13 x 9-inch baking dish coated with cooking spray. Bake at 350° for 40 minutes. Cool on a wire rack 10 minutes. Yield: 12 servings.

CALORIES 279 (5% from fat); FAT 1.7g (sat 0.7g, mono 0.6g, poly 0.3g); PROTEIN 7.2g; CARB 58.1g; FIBER 1.5g; CHOL 4mg; IRON 1.4mg; SODIUM 256mg; CALC 129mg

CHOCOLATE MERINGUE KISSES

Whenever I want something chocolate, I can eat these cookies and indulge without all the fat.

—B. J. Grant, Fort Lauderdale, Florida

- ¼ cup unsweetened cocoa
- 1 ounce unsweetened chocolate, coarsely chopped
- ¼ cup sifted powdered sugar
- 1½ tablespoons cornstarch
- 3 large egg whites
- ½ teaspoon instant coffee granules
- ⅔ cup granulated sugar
- 1 teaspoon vanilla extract

1. Preheat oven to 325°.
2. Cover a baking sheet with parchment or wax paper; secure with masking tape.
3. Combine cocoa and chocolate in a food processor; pulse 4 times or until chocolate is finely chopped. Add powdered sugar and cornstarch; pulse 2 times or until well-blended.
4. Beat egg whites and coffee granules in a medium bowl at high speed of a mixer until foamy. Gradually add granulated sugar, 1 tablespoon at a time, beating mixture until stiff peaks form. Fold in cocoa mixture and vanilla. Spoon egg white mixture into a zip-top plastic bag, and seal. Carefully snip off 1 bottom corner of bag. Pipe egg white mixture into 24 portions onto prepared baking sheet, forming pointed mounds 2 inches wide and 1½ inches high. Bake at 325° for 30 minutes or until dry. Carefully remove meringues from paper. Yield: 2 dozen (serving size: 1 kiss).
Note: Store kisses in an airtight container for up to 2 days.

CALORIES 41 (15% from fat); FAT 0.7g (sat 0.4g, mono 0.2g, poly 0g); PROTEIN 0.8g; CARB 8.1g; FIBER 0g; CHOL 0mg; IRON 0.2mg; SODIUM 7mg; CALC 3mg

ANISE-PECAN BISCOTTI

You can make these cookies ahead, and they stay fresh for up to two weeks if you store them in an airtight container. You can also freeze them for up to one month.

—Diane Baron, Bellevue, Washington

- 1 cup granulated sugar
- ¼ cup stick margarine or butter, softened
- ½ teaspoon anise extract
- 2 large eggs
- 2½ cups all-purpose flour
- 1 teaspoon baking soda
- ½ teaspoon salt
- ¼ cup chopped pecans
- Cooking spray
- 2 tablespoons powdered sugar

1. Preheat oven to 350°.
2. Beat first 4 ingredients at medium speed of a mixer until well-blended. Lightly spoon flour into dry measuring cups, and level with a knife. Combine flour, baking soda, and salt; gradually add to sugar mixture, beating until mixture is well-blended. Stir in chopped pecans.
3. Turn dough out onto a baking sheet coated with cooking spray. Shape dough into a 12-inch-long roll; flatten to a ½-inch thickness. Sift powdered sugar over top of dough.
4. Bake at 350° for 35 minutes. Cool 5 minutes on baking sheet. Cut roll diagonally into 24 (¾-inch) slices. Place slices, cut sides down, on baking sheet. Bake at 350° for 10 minutes (cookies will be slightly soft in center but will harden as they cool). Remove from baking sheet; cool completely on a wire rack. Yield: 2 dozen (serving size: 1 cookie).

CALORIES 114 (26% from fat); FAT 3.3g (sat 0.6g, mono 1.5g, poly 0.9g); PROTEIN 2g; CARB 19.2g; FIBER 0.4g; CHOL 18mg; IRON 0.7mg; SODIUM 129mg; CALC 5mg

LIGHTEN UP

Heavy Homework

A Michigan teacher loved her family's birthday cake but wanted to eat it, too.

Michigan reader Dianne Compo says her family is wild about a gooey, messy, layered concoction of chocolate and coconut that has been the birthday cake of choice for the family. But she stopped making the cake a few years ago because it's so rich.

Admittedly it was a tough assignment. Dianne's recipe packed nearly a pound of coconut, a stick of butter, a 12-ounce bag of chocolate chips, a couple of eggs, and ⅓ cup of oil. One slice of the original cake tipped our scales at nearly 600 calories and more than 28 grams of fat. But with a little tinkering—using less oil and fewer eggs and cutting back on the marshmallows, coconut, and chocolate—we managed to shave off about 19 grams of fat and a hefty 295 calories.

CREAMY COCONUT-TOPPED CHOCOLATE CAKE

(pictured on page 223)

Cake:

- 1¼ cups water
- ¾ cup egg substitute or 4 egg whites
- 2 tablespoons vegetable oil
- 1 (18.25-ounce) package chocolate cake mix (pudding in the mix)
- Cooking spray

Coconut topping:

- ½ cup fat-free milk
- ½ cup granulated sugar
- 9 large marshmallows
- 2 cups flaked sweetened coconut
- ½ teaspoon cornstarch

Frosting:

1½ cups sifted powdered sugar
2 tablespoons unsweetened cocoa
2 tablespoons fat-free milk
2 tablespoons stick margarine or butter
¼ cup semisweet chocolate chips
1 tablespoon light-colored corn syrup

1. Preheat oven to 350°.
2. To prepare cake, combine first 4 ingredients in a large bowl, and beat at low speed of a mixer until moist. Beat at medium speed 2 minutes; pour into a 13 x 9-inch baking pan coated with cooking spray. Bake at 350° for 35 minutes or until a wooden pick inserted in center comes out clean. Cool cake completely in pan on a wire rack.
3. To prepare topping, combine ½ cup milk, granulated sugar, and marshmallows in a medium saucepan; cook over medium heat 5 minutes or until marshmallows are melted. Stir in coconut and cornstarch; bring to a boil. Cook 1 minute, stirring constantly. Spread topping evenly over cake; cool.
4. To prepare frosting, combine powdered sugar and next 3 ingredients in a saucepan; bring to a boil over medium-high heat. Remove from heat; add chocolate chips and corn syrup, stirring until chips melt. Spread frosting gently over topping. Cool until set. Yield: 18 servings.

CALORIES 288 (30% from fat); FAT 9.7g (sat 4.8g, mono 2.3g, poly 2g); PROTEIN 3.2g; CARB 49.2g; FIBER 0.5g; CHOL 0mg; IRON 0.5mg; SODIUM 239mg; CALC 18mg

BEFORE & AFTER	
SERVING SIZE	
1 piece	
CALORIES	
583	288
FAT	
28.6g	9.7g
PERCENT OF TOTAL CALORIES	
44%	30%
CHOLESTEROL	
31mg	0mg

How'd He Do That?

If you're skeptical that great taste can share the culinary stage with low fat, take a cooking class from popular chef Terry Conlan. But keep a sharp eye.

Terry Conlan, executive chef at the Lake Austin Spa Resort in Austin, Texas, has a remarkable ability to extract the fat from rich dishes and hide the loss with a brilliant subterfuge of flavors. He makes sure that what you think you see is never what you get.

By analyzing the role fat plays in a recipe, Conlan can select low-fat or fat-free substitutes that he'd never use on their own but that he sees as essential to a structural redesign. He completes the deception with his signature touch: "layers" of bold, diverting flavors from ingredients of uncompromised integrity.

CAESAR SALAD

(pictured on page 222)

Dressing:

¼ cup grated Parmesan cheese
¼ cup fat-free mayonnaise
¼ cup water
2 tablespoons fresh lemon juice
½ teaspoon anchovy paste
½ teaspoon Worcestershire sauce
¼ teaspoon freshly ground black pepper
⅛ teaspoon dry mustard
2 garlic cloves, minced

Salad:

4 (1-ounce) slices French bread, cut into ¾-inch cubes
8 cups torn romaine lettuce

1. Preheat oven to 300°.
2. To prepare dressing, combine first 9 ingredients; stir well with a whisk.
3. To prepare salad, place bread cubes on a baking sheet; bake at 300° for 15 minutes or until toasted. Combine croutons and lettuce in a bowl. Add dressing; toss to coat. Serve immediately. Yield: 4 servings (serving size: 2 cups).

CALORIES 142 (15% from fat); FAT 2.4g (sat 1.2g, mono 0.7g, poly 0.5g); PROTEIN 6.8g; CARB 22.9g; FIBER 2.6g; CHOL 5mg; IRON 2mg; SODIUM 549mg; CALC 126mg

GRILLED TUNA WITH ROASTED-VEGETABLE SAUCE AND CRISPY RISOTTO CAKES

1 red bell pepper (about ½ pound)
3 plum tomatoes, cut in half lengthwise (about ½ pound)
1 small red onion, cut into ½-inch-thick slices
Cooking spray
1 whole garlic head
2 tablespoons stone-ground mustard
1½ tablespoons red wine vinegar
1 tablespoon minced fresh cilantro
1 tablespoon olive oil
¼ teaspoon black pepper
4 pitted green olives
4 pitted ripe olives
2 garlic cloves, minced
4 (6-ounce) tuna steaks (about ¾ inch thick)
¼ teaspoon dried thyme
¼ teaspoon black pepper
⅛ teaspoon salt
Crispy Risotto Cakes

1. Preheat broiler. Cut bell pepper in half lengthwise; discard seeds and membranes. Place bell pepper halves, skin sides up, on a foil-lined baking sheet, and flatten with hand. Place tomatoes and onion on baking sheet. Lightly coat vegetables with cooking spray. Separate
Continued

garlic head into cloves; place on baking sheet. Broil vegetables 15 minutes or until bell pepper is blackened. Place pepper in a zip-top plastic bag; seal. Let stand 15 minutes. Peel pepper. Separate garlic cloves, and squeeze to extract garlic pulp. Discard skins.

2. Place vegetables, garlic pulp, mustard, and next 7 ingredients in a food processor or blender; process until smooth.

3. Prepare grill. Sprinkle fish with thyme, ¼ teaspoon black pepper, and salt. Place fish on a grill rack coated with cooking spray; grill 4 minutes on each side or until desired degree of doneness. Spoon sauce over fish; serve with Crispy Risotto Cakes. Yield: 4 servings (serving size: 5 ounces tuna, ¼ cup sauce, and 3 risotto cakes).

CALORIES 519 (26% from fat); FAT 14.8g (sat 4g, mono 5.3g, poly 3.4g); PROTEIN 49g; CARB 44.2g; FIBER 2.2g; CHOL 70mg; IRON 4.7mg; SODIUM 806mg; CALC 137mg

Crispy Risotto Cakes:

- 1 cup water
- 1 (16-ounce) can fat-free, less-sodium chicken broth
- 1 teaspoon olive oil
- 2 tablespoons minced fresh onion
- 2 tablespoons finely chopped red bell pepper
- ¾ cup uncooked Arborio or other short-grain rice
- 2 garlic cloves, minced
- ¼ cup (1 ounce) grated fresh Parmesan cheese
- 2 tablespoons minced fresh parsley
- ⅛ teaspoon salt
- Olive oil-flavored cooking spray
- ¼ cup all-purpose flour

1. Bring water and broth to a simmer in a saucepan (do not boil). Keep warm over low heat.

2. Heat oil in a large saucepan until hot. Add onion and bell pepper; cook over medium-high heat 2 minutes or until tender. Add rice, and cook 2 minutes, stirring to coat. Add garlic; cook 30 seconds. Stir in ⅔ cup chicken broth; cook 5 minutes or until liquid is nearly absorbed, stirring constantly. Add remaining broth, ⅔ cup at a time, stirring constantly until each portion of broth is absorbed before adding the next (about 20 minutes total). Remove from heat. Stir in cheese, parsley, and salt.

3. Place risotto on a baking sheet coated with cooking spray, forming a ½-inch-thick layer. Chill until set (about 20 minutes). Cut into 12 circles using a 2-inch biscuit cutter. Dust cakes with flour.

4. Place a large nonstick skillet coated with cooking spray over medium-high heat until hot. Add risotto cakes, and cook 2 minutes on each side or until crispy. Yield: 4 servings (serving size: 3 cakes).

CHICKEN ENCHILADAS WITH SPINACH CREAM SAUCE

Conlan garnishes these enchiladas with a dollop of low-fat sour cream and fresh chives. He serves them with a side of black beans.

- 2 poblano chiles
- Cooking spray
- 1½ cups vertically sliced onion, divided
- 2 cups shredded ready-to-eat roasted skinned, boned chicken breasts (about 2 breasts)
- 6 cups fresh spinach leaves
- ¼ cup chopped green onions
- 1 teaspoon ground cumin
- 2 garlic cloves, minced
- 1½ tablespoons masa harina or all-purpose flour
- 1¼ cups fat-free, less-sodium chicken broth
- ⅓ cup chopped fresh cilantro
- 3 ounces ⅓-less-fat cream cheese (Neufchâtel) (about ⅓ cup)
- ⅛ teaspoon salt
- 4 (8-inch) corn tortillas

1. Preheat broiler. Place chiles on a foil-lined baking sheet, and broil 10 minutes or until blackened, turning occasionally. Place in a zip-top plastic bag; seal. Let stand 15 minutes. Peel chiles; cut in half lengthwise. Discard seeds and membranes; slice into strips to measure ⅔ cup.

2. Place a large skillet coated with cooking spray over medium heat until hot. Add 1 cup sliced onion; cook 10 minutes or until golden brown, stirring frequently. Stir in chicken and ⅓ cup chiles; spoon mixture into a bowl.

3. Steam spinach leaves, covered, 5 minutes or until wilted. Place spinach in a colander, pressing with the back of a spoon until barely moist.

4. Preheat oven to 350°.

5. Wipe skillet with paper towels, and recoat with cooking spray. Place over medium-high heat. Add ½ cup sliced onion and green onions; sauté 3 minutes. Stir in cumin and garlic; sauté 30 seconds. Combine masa harina and broth. Add masa mixture, cilantro, cream cheese, and salt to pan; bring to a boil. Reduce heat, and simmer 5 minutes or until cheese melts, stirring constantly. Place cheese mixture, ⅓ cup chiles, and spinach in a food processor; process until smooth. Strain spinach mixture through a colander into a bowl, and discard solids.

6. Divide chicken mixture evenly among tortillas, and roll up. Pour ½ cup spinach sauce in bottom of an 8-inch square baking dish coated with cooking spray. Arrange filled tortillas on top of spinach sauce. Pour remaining spinach sauce over tortillas. Cover and bake at 350° for 10 minutes or until enchiladas are thoroughly heated. Yield: 4 servings (serving size: 1 enchilada with sauce).

CALORIES 265 (27% from fat); FAT 7.9g (sat 3.8g, mono 2.2g, poly 1g); PROTEIN 22.1g; CARB 30g; FIBER 6.8g; CHOL 51mg; IRON 4.2mg; SODIUM 723mg; CALC 205mg

CHICKEN PUPUSAS

Pupusas are traditional masa-and-potato cakes from El Salvador. Conlan tops his with roasted chicken and a tangy slaw.

Slaw:

- 2½ cups prepackaged coleslaw
- ⅓ cup thinly sliced red onion
- ¼ cup thinly sliced radishes
- ¼ cup minced fresh cilantro
- 1 tablespoon minced seeded serrano chile
- 2 tablespoons white wine vinegar
- 1 tablespoon fresh lime juice
- 2 teaspoons sugar
- ½ teaspoon salt

Masa-potato patties:

- 1 cup masa harina or cornmeal
- ⅔ cup water
- 1 cup mashed cooked peeled baking potato (cooked without salt or fat)
- ¼ cup finely diced tomato
- 1 teaspoon chili powder
- ¼ teaspoon salt
- ¼ cup (1 ounce) shredded reduced-fat sharp Cheddar cheese
- 2 teaspoons olive oil
- Cooking spray
- 2⅔ cups shredded ready-to-eat roasted skinned, boned chicken breasts (about 3 breasts)
- ¼ cup bottled salsa
- ¼ cup fat-free sour cream
- 4 lime wedges

1. To prepare slaw, combine first 5 ingredients in a bowl. Combine vinegar, juice, sugar, and salt in a small bowl. Microwave at HIGH 1 minute or until sugar dissolves. Cool slightly. Pour over slaw mixture; toss well. Cover and chill.
2. To prepare masa-potato patties, combine masa and water in a bowl. Knead lightly 3 or 4 times. Add potato and next 4 ingredients to masa mixture; knead lightly 3 or 4 times.
3. Divide masa mixture into 4 equal portions, shaping each into a ½-inch-thick patty. Heat oil in a large nonstick skillet coated with cooking spray over medium heat. Add patties, and cook 3 minutes on each side or until lightly browned. Serve each patty with ½ cup slaw, ⅔ cup chicken, 1 tablespoon salsa, 1 tablespoon sour cream, and 1 lime wedge. Yield: 4 servings.

CALORIES 330 (17% from fat); FAT 6.3g (sat 1.9g, mono 2.8g, poly 1g); PROTEIN 24.1g; CARB 43.9g; FIBER 4.5g; CHOL 49mg; IRON 2.4mg; SODIUM 929mg; CALC 120mg

POSOLE, SWEET POTATO, AND PINEAPPLE SOUP

If you can't find chayote, substitute 1 cup yellow squash. Conlan likes to garnish this soup with queso ranchero (a soft, low-fat Mexican cheese) and baked tortilla chips.

- 1 whole garlic head
- 6 plum tomatoes, halved
- 1 onion, cut into ½-inch-thick slices
- Olive oil-flavored cooking spray
- 4 cups clam juice
- 2 cups (½-inch) cubed peeled sweet potato
- 1 cup (½-inch) cubed peeled baking potato
- 1 cup cubed chayote (about 1 small)
- 1 cup pineapple juice
- 1 tablespoon sugar
- 1 tablespoon canned adobo sauce or chile paste with garlic
- 2 teaspoons dried oregano
- 2 (16-ounce) cans fat-free, less-sodium chicken broth
- 2 garlic cloves, minced
- 1 tablespoon coconut extract
- 1 pound small shrimp, peeled and deveined
- 1 (15.5-ounce) can golden hominy or whole-kernel corn, rinsed and drained

1. Preheat oven to 400°.
2. Remove white papery skin from garlic head (do not peel or separate the cloves). Wrap in foil. Place garlic head, tomatoes (cut sides down), and onion on a baking sheet coated with cooking spray. Lightly coat tomatoes and onion with cooking spray. Bake at 400° for 30 minutes; cool 10 minutes. Separate garlic cloves; squeeze to extract pulp. Discard skins. Place roasted garlic, tomatoes, and onion in a food processor or blender; process until smooth.
3. Combine pureed mixture, clam juice, and next 10 ingredients in a Dutch oven. Bring to a boil; reduce heat, and simmer 12 minutes or until potatoes are tender. Stir in shrimp and hominy; cook 3 minutes or until shrimp are done. Yield: 8 servings (serving size: 1½ cups).

Note: Try topping this dish with any or all of the following: minced fresh onion, minced fresh cilantro, lime wedges, or diced pineapple.

CALORIES 204 (8% from fat); FAT 1.7g (sat 0.4g, mono 0.2g, poly 0.6g); PROTEIN 14.1g; CARB 34.9g; FIBER 2.8g; CHOL 64mg; IRON 2.2mg; SODIUM 754mg; CALC 82mg

BANANA-MANGO CREAM PIE

Crust:

- 12 pieces plain melba toast
- 1 tablespoon granulated sugar
- 2 tablespoons light butter, melted
- Cooking spray

Filling:

- ½ cup granulated sugar
- ½ cup fat-free sweetened condensed milk
- 2 tablespoons cornstarch
- 1 envelope unflavored gelatin
- 1 (12-ounce) can evaporated skim milk
- ½ cup egg substitute
- 1 large egg yolk
- 2 teaspoons vanilla extract
- 2 cups chopped peeled ripe mango (about 2)
- 1¾ cups sliced banana (about 2)

Topping:

- 1 cup fat-free sour cream
- ½ cup powdered sugar
- 1 teaspoon vanilla extract

Continued

1. Preheat oven to 350°.

2. To prepare crust, place melba toast in a food processor, and process until finely crushed. Combine toast crumbs, 1 tablespoon granulated sugar, and butter in a small bowl; toss with a fork until moist. Press crumb mixture into bottom of a 9-inch springform pan coated with cooking spray. Bake at 350° for 5 minutes; cool crust on a wire rack.

3. To prepare filling, combine ½ cup granulated sugar and next 4 ingredients in a medium-size, heavy saucepan. Cook over medium-low heat 10 minutes or until mixture is thick, stirring constantly with a whisk. Combine egg substitute and yolk. Gradually add hot milk mixture to egg mixture, stirring constantly with a whisk. Return milk mixture to pan, and cook over medium-low heat 5 minutes or until mixture is thick, stirring constantly. Remove from heat; stir in 2 teaspoons vanilla.

4. Arrange mango and banana over prepared crust; spoon filling mixture over fruit. Cover and chill 4 hours or until set.

5. To prepare topping, combine sour cream, powdered sugar, and 1 teaspoon vanilla; stir well with a whisk. Spread over filling. Cover and chill 1 hour. Yield: 12 servings (serving size: 1 wedge).

CALORIES 207 (8% from fat); FAT 1.9g (sat 0.9g, mono 0.5g, poly 0.1g); PROTEIN 7.2g; CARB 40.3g; FIBER 1.1g; CHOL 24mg; IRON 0.5mg; SODIUM 114mg; CALC 125mg

CREAMY LEMON TRIFLE

Sponge cake:

Cooking spray
4 **large egg whites**
¼ **teaspoon salt**
1 **cup powdered sugar, divided**
3 **large eggs**
2 **teaspoons grated lemon rind**
⅔ **cup all-purpose flour**
½ **cup Grand Marnier or other orange-flavored liqueur**

Lemon cream:

¾ **cup granulated sugar, divided**
½ **cup water**
2 **tablespoons cornstarch**
1 **teaspoon grated lemon rind**
⅓ **cup fresh lemon juice**
12 **ounces block-style fat-free cream cheese, softened**
1 **(8-ounce) block ⅓-less-fat cream cheese (Neufchâtel), softened**
¾ **cup low-fat sour cream**
1 **(8-ounce) carton frozen fat-free whipped topping, thawed**
Fresh raspberries (optional)
Fresh mint sprigs (optional)

1. Preheat oven to 375°.

2. Line a 15 x 10-inch jelly-roll pan with parchment paper; coat paper with cooking spray.

3. To prepare sponge cake, beat 4 egg whites at high speed of a mixer until soft peaks form. Gradually add salt and ⅔ cup powdered sugar, 1 tablespoon at a time, beating until stiff peaks form. Combine 3 eggs and 2 teaspoons rind; beat until thick and pale (about 3 minutes). Gently fold egg white mixture into egg mixture. Lightly spoon flour into a dry measuring cup; level with a knife. Fold flour into egg mixture. Spoon batter into prepared pan, spreading evenly. Bake at 375° for 12 minutes or until cake springs back when touched lightly in center. Cool in pan 5 minutes on a wire rack. Loosen from sides of pan; turn out onto wire rack. Carefully peel off parchment paper.

4. Combine liqueur and remaining ⅓ cup powdered sugar in a small bowl. Microwave at HIGH 1 minute; stir until sugar dissolves. Brush mixture over cake; cool.

5. To prepare lemon cream, combine ¼ cup granulated sugar, ½ cup water, and next 3 ingredients in a medium nonaluminum saucepan; bring to a boil. Cook 1 minute, stirring constantly. Pour into a bowl; cool to room temperature. Combine remaining ½ cup granulated sugar and cream cheeses in a large bowl; beat until smooth. Beat in cornstarch mixture and sour cream; fold in whipped topping.

6. Tear cake into large pieces; line bottom of a 3-quart straight-sided glass bowl or trifle bowl with 3 cups cake pieces. Spoon 2 cups lemon cream over cake pieces. Repeat procedure 2 times with remaining cake pieces and lemon cream. Cover and chill 8 hours. Garnish with raspberries and mint sprigs, if desired. Yield: 12 servings (serving size: 1 cup).

CALORIES 294 (23% from fat); FAT 7.6g (sat 4.4g, mono 2.4g, poly 0.4g); PROTEIN 8.4g; CARB 41g; FIBER 0.2g; CHOL 78mg; IRON 0.6mg; SODIUM 288mg; CALC 92mg

INSPIRED VEGETARIAN

World's Best

America's favorite international dishes can be as healthful as they are delicious—with the right touch.

The foods we borrow from other countries—then adapt and ultimately turn into dishes of our own—are what make America's culinary landscape exciting. But we also tend to forget where our favorites came from originally: Spaghetti, kebabs, and egg rolls didn't just sprout up in fast-food stands or at corner cafés.

So what is "American" and what isn't? Who cares? The main thing is that in this country, we have incredible access to the cuisines of the world. Restaurants proliferate with offerings from around the globe—Chinese, Vietnamese, Indian, Italian, Mexican—you name the place, we've got their food.

The problem, however, with many international foods is their fat content. Many countries traditionally cook—or deep-fry—their foods with liberal amounts of fat, tropical oils, and lard.

We've used an enlightened hand, especially in traditional vegetarian favorites such as Lentil Dal, without compromising the taste. Who knows? The time might not be that far off when moo shu is more popular than macaroni.

Hot Provençale Wrap

Roasted vegetables:

2 tablespoons red wine vinegar
2 tablespoons lemon juice
1 tablespoon extra-virgin olive oil
2 teaspoons dried herbes de Provence
1 (½-pound) eggplant, cut diagonally into ¼-inch-thick slices
2 small yellow squash, cut diagonally into ¼-inch-thick slices (about ½ pound)
1 zucchini, cut diagonally into ¼-inch-thick slices (about ½ pound)
1 cup thinly sliced fennel bulb (about 1 bulb)
Cooking spray

Pesto:

½ cup fresh parsley leaves
⅓ cup fresh basil leaves
2 tablespoons (½ ounce) grated fresh Parmesan cheese
1 tablespoon pine nuts
2 tablespoons lemon juice
2 tablespoons tahini (sesame-seed paste)
½ teaspoon salt
¼ teaspoon black pepper
1 (16-ounce) can cannellini beans or other white beans, drained
2 garlic cloves

Wrap:

6 (8-inch) fat-free flour tortillas
6 leaf lettuce leaves
¾ cup sliced bottled roasted red bell peppers
½ cup (2 ounces) shredded provolone cheese

1. To prepare roasted vegetables, combine first 8 ingredients in a large zip-top plastic bag; seal and marinate 20 minutes.
2. Preheat broiler. Remove vegetable mixture from bag; discard marinade. Place vegetable mixture on a jelly-roll pan coated with cooking spray. Broil 12 minutes or until tender, stirring occasionally; set aside.
3. Preheat oven to 350°.
4. To prepare pesto, place parsley and next 9 ingredients in a food processor; process until smooth, scraping sides of processor bowl occasionally.
5. To prepare wrap, warm tortillas according to package directions. Spread ¼ cup pesto over each tortilla. Divide lettuce leaves, roasted vegetables, bell peppers, and cheese evenly among tortillas; roll up. Wrap each tortilla in foil; bake at 350° for 8 minutes or until thoroughly heated. Yield: 6 servings.

CALORIES 325 (28% from fat); FAT 10.1g (sat 2.9g, mono 3.6g, poly 2.6g); PROTEIN 13.1g; CARB 49g; FIBER 5.5g; CHOL 8mg; IRON 5mg; SODIUM 834mg; CALC 260mg

Vegetable Moo Shu

You can substitute flour tortillas for the Quick Chinese Pancakes.

1 (0.5-ounce) package dried wood ear mushrooms
2 cups boiling water
1 teaspoon dark sesame oil
1 teaspoon vegetable oil
3 large eggs, lightly beaten
1 tablespoon minced peeled fresh ginger
2 garlic cloves, minced
4 cups thinly sliced green cabbage
1 cup thinly sliced red bell pepper
1 cup diagonally sliced green onions
3 tablespoons rice vinegar
2 tablespoons dry sherry
2 tablespoons low-sodium soy sauce
2 tablespoons hoisin sauce
Quick Chinese Pancakes

1. Combine mushrooms and boiling water in a bowl; cover and let stand 30 minutes or until soft. Drain; slice mushrooms into thin strips.
2. Heat sesame and vegetable oils in a large nonstick skillet or wok over medium-high heat. Add eggs, and stir-fry 2 minutes. Remove eggs from pan. Add ginger and garlic to pan; stir-fry 1 minute. Add mushrooms, cabbage, and bell pepper; stir-fry 2 minutes. Add onions and next 4 ingredients; stir-fry 1 minute. Stir in eggs. Serve with Quick Chinese Pancakes. Yield: 4 servings (serving size: 1½ cups moo shu and 3 pancakes).

CALORIES 377 (27% from fat); FAT 11.4g (sat 2.8g, mono 4.1g, poly 3g); PROTEIN 16.5g; CARB 51.4g; FIBER 4.4g; CHOL 223mg; IRON 4.1mg; SODIUM 567mg; CALC 209mg

Quick Chinese Pancakes:

1¼ cups all-purpose flour
1½ cups fat-free milk
1 tablespoon stick margarine or butter, melted
1 large egg
1 tablespoon minced fresh chives
¼ teaspoon five-spice powder
Cooking spray

1. Lightly spoon flour into dry measuring cups, and level with a knife. Place flour in a medium bowl. Combine milk, margarine, and egg; add milk mixture to flour, stirring with a whisk until blended. Stir in chives and five-spice powder. Cover and chill 1 hour.
2. Place an 8-inch crêpe pan or nonstick skillet coated with cooking spray over medium-high heat until hot. Remove pan from heat, and pour a scant ¼ cup batter into pan; quickly tilt pan in all directions so batter covers bottom of pan. Cook about 1 minute.
3. Carefully lift edge of pancake with a spatula to test for doneness. Pancake will be ready to turn when it can be shaken loose from pan and the underside is lightly browned. Turn pancake over; cook 30 seconds.
4. Place pancake on a towel, and cool. Repeat procedure until all batter is used. Stack pancakes between single layers of wax paper or paper towels to prevent pancakes from sticking. Yield: 12 pancakes.

THREE-BEAN VEGETABLE MOUSSAKA

1   cup (4 ounces) crumbled feta cheese
1   tablespoon chopped fresh or 1 teaspoon dried oregano
½   teaspoon ground cinnamon
2   (12.3-ounce) packages reduced-fat firm tofu, drained
1   (10-ounce) package frozen chopped spinach, thawed, drained, and squeezed dry
1   (8-ounce) container part-skim ricotta cheese
3   garlic cloves, minced
1   (1¼-pound) eggplant, cut lengthwise into ¼-inch-thick slices
    Cooking spray
1   (25.5-ounce) jar fat-free marinara sauce
1   (16-ounce) can cannellini beans or other white beans, drained
1   (15-ounce) can black beans, drained
1   (16-ounce) can kidney beans, drained
2   cups (8 ounces) shredded part-skim mozzarella cheese

1. Preheat oven to 450°.
2. Combine first 7 ingredients in a bowl; stir until well-blended. Set aside. Arrange eggplant on a baking sheet coated with cooking spray. Bake at 450° for 15 minutes or until lightly browned. Reduce oven temperature to 375°.
3. Spread 1 cup marinara sauce in bottom of a 13 x 9-inch baking dish coated with cooking spray. Arrange 5 eggplant slices over marinara; top with 1⅔ cups spinach mixture and cannellini beans. Repeat layers, alternating remaining beans with each layer. Bake at 375° for 20 minutes. Top with cheese; bake 20 minutes or until cheese is browned. Yield: 8 servings.

CALORIES 390 (28% from fat); FAT 12.1g (sat 6.7g, mono 3g, poly 1.5g); PROTEIN 30.5g; CARB 41g; FIBER 7.3g; CHOL 38mg; IRON 5mg; SODIUM 817mg; CALC 478mg

VIETNAMESE SOFT SPRING ROLLS

1½ ounces uncooked bean threads (cellophane noodles)
2   cups shredded romaine lettuce
1   cup shredded carrot
1   cup fresh bean sprouts
⅓   cup crumbled firm tofu
¼   cup thinly sliced green onions
2   tablespoons thinly sliced fresh mint
2   tablespoons fresh cilantro leaves
2   tablespoons thinly sliced fresh basil
1   tablespoon low-sodium soy sauce
1   teaspoon dark sesame oil
6   (8-inch) round sheets rice paper
    Hoisin Dipping Sauce

1. Combine bean threads and hot water to cover in a bowl; let stand 20 minutes. Drain; cut into 2-inch pieces with scissors.
2. Combine bean threads, lettuce, and next 9 ingredients.
3. Add cold water to a large, shallow dish to a depth of 1 inch. Place 1 rice paper sheet in dish of water. Let stand 2 minutes or until soft. Place rice paper sheet on a flat surface. Spread about ½ cup bean thread mixture in center of wrapper. Fold sides of rice paper sheet over filling, and roll up jelly-roll fashion. Gently press seam to seal; place, seam side down, on a serving platter (cover to keep from drying). Repeat procedure with remaining rice paper and bean thread mixture. Slice each roll in half crosswise. Serve with Hoisin Dipping Sauce. Yield: 6 servings (serving size: 1 spring roll and about 2 tablespoons sauce).

CALORIES 173 (8% from fat); FAT 1.5g (sat 0.2g, mono 0.4g, poly 0.6g); PROTEIN 4g; CARB 36.7g; FIBER 2g; CHOL 0mg; IRON 1.6mg; SODIUM 620mg; CALC 48mg

Hoisin Dipping Sauce:

Chile paste with garlic is a bottled condiment that can be found in the Asian food section of large supermarkets.

½   cup hoisin sauce
¼   cup water
2   tablespoons rice vinegar
1   tablespoon low-sodium soy sauce
2   teaspoons chile paste with garlic

1. Combine all ingredients; cover and chill. Yield: about 1 cup (serving size: about 2 tablespoons).

LENTIL DAL

Dal is a traditional Indian dish made with lentils, tomatoes, onions, and spices.

1   tablespoon olive oil
1   cup chopped onion
1   tablespoon minced peeled fresh ginger
1   teaspoon cumin seeds
1   teaspoon ground turmeric
½   teaspoon dried crushed red pepper
4   garlic cloves, minced
2   cups chopped cauliflower florets
2   cups chopped tomato
2½   cups water
1   cup dried lentils
2   tablespoons fresh lime juice
1   tablespoon minced fresh cilantro
¾   teaspoon salt
6   cups hot cooked basmati or long-grain rice

1. Heat olive oil in a large saucepan over medium-high heat. Add onion and next 5 ingredients; sauté 2 minutes. Add cauliflower and tomato; sauté 1 minute. Stir in water and lentils; bring to a boil. Cover, reduce heat, and simmer 35 minutes or until lentils are tender. Stir in lime juice, cilantro, and salt. Serve with rice. Yield: 6 servings (serving size: 1 cup dal and 1 cup rice).

CALORIES 396 (8% from fat); FAT 3.3g (sat 0.4g, mono 1.8g, poly 0.5g); PROTEIN 15.2g; CARB 77.5g; FIBER 7.4g; CHOL 0mg; IRON 5.7mg; SODIUM 320mg; CALC 67mg

A Chicken in Every Bowl

A few liberties and a one-bowl shortcut put these chicken salads on everyone's timetable.

For a salad, traditional chicken salad definitely tips the fat scales. But we love it, so we took some liberties with the traditional formula and created five main-course chicken salads, all of which have less than 10 grams of fat per serving.

They're a breeze to make because all the ingredients can be tossed together in one bowl. And instead of cooking the chicken, you can take a shortcut by using the latest in poultry convenience—precooked, packaged chicken breasts.

CURRIED CHICKEN SALAD WITH PEAS

Preparation time: 20 minutes

- ⅓ cup plain fat-free yogurt
- 2 tablespoons light mayonnaise
- 1 teaspoon curry powder
- ⅛ teaspoon salt
- Dash of ground red pepper
- 8 ounces ready-to-eat roasted skinned, boned chicken breasts, cubed (such as Tyson)
- 1½ cups diced Red Delicious apple
- 1 cup frozen green peas, thawed
- ½ cup thinly sliced celery
- 2 cups shredded romaine lettuce
- 2 tablespoons coarsely chopped dry-roasted peanuts

1. Combine first 5 ingredients in a large bowl; stir well. Add chicken and next 3 ingredients, tossing to coat. Stir in lettuce; sprinkle with peanuts. Yield: 4 servings (serving size: 1¼ cups).

CALORIES 185 (27% from fat); FAT 5.6g (sat 0.9g, mono 2.0g, poly 2.0g); PROTEIN 17.9g; CARB 15.9g; FIBER 2.4g; CHOL 38mg; IRON 1.7mg; SODIUM 488mg; CALC 70mg

TABBOULEH CHICKEN SALAD

Preparation time: 25 minutes
Cooking time: 20 minutes

- 1½ cups uncooked bulgur or cracked wheat
- 1½ cups boiling water
- 8 ounces ready-to-eat roasted skinned, boned chicken breasts, chopped (such as Tyson)
- 1 cup chopped cucumber
- 1 cup diced plum tomato
- ¾ cup chopped fresh parsley
- ¼ cup minced red onion
- ¼ cup lemon juice
- 3 tablespoons water
- 1 tablespoon extra-virgin olive oil
- ½ teaspoon salt
- ¼ teaspoon black pepper

1. Combine bulgur and boiling water in a large bowl. Cover and let stand 20 minutes or until liquid is absorbed. Add chicken and next 4 ingredients.
2. Combine lemon juice and remaining 4 ingredients; stir with a whisk. Add juice mixture to bulgur mixture; toss gently. Yield: 4 servings (serving size: 1½ cups).

CALORIES 300 (16% from fat); FAT 5.4g (sat 0.9g, mono 3.0g, poly 0.9g); PROTEIN 20.6g; CARB 46.2g; FIBER 11.2g; CHOL 35mg; IRON 2.8mg; SODIUM 603mg; CALC 44mg

SMOKED CHICKEN- AND-POTATO SALAD

Preparation time: 15 minutes
Cooking time: 8 minutes

- 5 medium red potatoes, halved and cut into ¼-inch slices (about 4 cups)
- 3 tablespoons white wine vinegar
- 2 tablespoons water
- 1 tablespoon extra-virgin olive oil
- 2 teaspoons Dijon mustard
- ¼ teaspoon salt
- ¼ teaspoon black pepper
- 8 ounces ready-to-eat smoked chicken breasts, cut into julienne strips
- ⅓ cup thinly sliced green onions

1. Place potatoes in a medium saucepan; cover with water. Bring to a boil. Cook 5 minutes; drain and set aside.
2. Combine vinegar and next 5 ingredients in a large bowl; stir with a whisk. Add potatoes, chicken, and onions; toss to coat. Yield: 4 servings (serving size: 1 cup).

CALORIES 242 (18% from fat); FAT 4.8g (sat 1g, mono 2.5g, poly 0.4g); PROTEIN 17.3g; CARB 32.8g; FIBER 3.6g; CHOL 35mg; IRON 2.6mg; SODIUM 527mg; CALC 31mg

TANGY CHICKEN SALAD

Preparation time: 24 minutes

- ¼ cup white wine vinegar
- 2 tablespoons water
- 1 tablespoon extra-virgin olive oil
- ⅛ teaspoon salt
- ¼ teaspoon cracked black pepper
- 8 cups torn romaine lettuce
- 12 ounces ready-to-eat roasted skinned, boned chicken breasts, shredded (such as Tyson)
- 2 cups diced tomato
- ¼ cup finely chopped smoked ham (about 1½ ounces)
- 1 (8¾-ounce) can no-salt-added whole-kernel corn, drained
- ¼ cup (1 ounce) crumbled blue cheese
- Red onion slices (optional)

1. Combine first 5 ingredients in a small bowl; stir well with a whisk. Arrange lettuce and next 4 ingredients evenly on 4 serving plates. Drizzle each with 2 tablespoons dressing; sprinkle each with 1 tablespoon cheese. Garnish with red onion slices, if desired. Yield: 4 servings.

CALORIES 246 (33% from fat); FAT 9g (sat 2.7g, mono 4.2g, poly 1.0g); PROTEIN 26.4g; CARB 15g; FIBER 3.3g; CHOL 65mg; IRON 2.7mg; SODIUM 769mg; CALC 84mg

ASIAN CHICKEN SALAD WITH NOODLES

Preparation time: 10 minutes
Cooking time: 8 minutes

1 tablespoon sugar
3 tablespoons lime juice
3 tablespoons water
3 tablespoons low-sodium soy sauce
2 tablespoons creamy peanut butter
3 garlic cloves, crushed
3 cups hot cooked linguine (about 6 ounces uncooked pasta)
8 ounces ready-to-eat roasted skinned, boned chicken breasts, shredded (such as Tyson)
1½ cups bean sprouts
⅓ cup sliced green onions

1. Combine first 6 ingredients in a large bowl; stir well with a whisk. Add linguine and remaining ingredients, tossing to coat. Yield: 4 servings (serving size: 1½ cups).

CALORIES 308 (17% from fat); FAT 5.9g (sat 1.1g, mono 2.4g, poly 1.8g); PROTEIN 22.3g; CARB 41.4g; FIBER 2.2g; CHOL 35mg; IRON 2.7mg; SODIUM 629mg; CALC 27mg

Getting Better All the Time

You can, in fact, teach an old picnic new tricks.

Picnics are and always have been all about relaxing: the great outdoors, fine weather, extraordinary food, and good company. For children, picnics are grand repasts prepared by mom and lugged by dad to a spacious clearing, preferably near a lazy river, where someone always has a ball to toss, a kite to fly, or a swimsuit to jump into at a moment's notice.

As young adults, we learn that picnics are not only a way to enjoy family but also to discover new friends—often the courting kind. Relationships have a special way of blossoming when taken beyond the bounds of four walls.

Try looking at picnics from yet a third perspective: as challenges to create food both tasty and totable for yourself and your family. Perhaps your palate now demands a basket filled with something more than chips and sandwiches. While the pasta salad and the cake are ready to eat as soon as you make them, they are so much better after a soak in tasty flavor enhancers. And the dip gets even more zing after a night in the fridge. Add the brownies—which hold their firmness and dark sweetness well into the following afternoon—and you've got a great meal for an enjoyable outing.

PASTA SALAD WITH SHRIMP AND BASIL

Any short, small pasta can be substituted for the seashell pasta in this recipe.

1 pound medium shrimp, cooked and peeled
4 cups cooked medium seashell pasta (about 2 cups uncooked pasta)
2 cups chopped plum tomatoes (about 1 pound)
½ cup chopped green bell pepper
⅓ cup fresh lemon juice
¼ cup chopped shallots
¼ cup chopped fresh or 4 teaspoons dried basil
2 tablespoons extra-virgin olive oil
½ teaspoon salt
½ teaspoon black pepper
1 garlic clove, minced

1. Combine all ingredients in a large bowl. Cover and refrigerate at least 8 hours. Yield: 8 servings (serving size: 1 cup).

CALORIES 197 (21% from fat); FAT 4.5g (sat 0.8g, mono 1.2g, poly 2.1g); PROTEIN 13.2g; CARB 25.7g; FIBER 1.5g; CHOL 83mg; IRON 2.8mg; SODIUM 249mg; CALC 30mg

TABBOULEH SALAD WITH TOMATOES AND FETA

1 cup uncooked bulgur or cracked wheat
2 cups boiling water
½ teaspoon salt
¾ cup (3 ounces) crumbled feta cheese with basil and tomato
⅓ cup dried currants or raisins
¼ cup minced green onions
¼ cup minced fresh mint
1 tablespoon chopped fresh or 1 teaspoon dried basil
1 teaspoon grated lemon rind
12 cherry tomatoes, quartered
2 garlic cloves, minced
¼ cup rice vinegar
2 tablespoons water
2 teaspoons extra-virgin olive oil
½ teaspoon salt
½ teaspoon coarsely ground black pepper

1. Combine first 3 ingredients in a large bowl. Cover and let stand 30 minutes. Add cheese and next 7 ingredients. Combine vinegar and remaining 4 ingredients; stir with a whisk. Pour dressing over salad; toss gently to coat. Cover and refrigerate at least 8 hours. Yield: 10 servings (serving size: ½ cup).

CALORIES 98 (28% from fat); FAT 3.1g (sat 1.4g, mono 1.3g, poly 0.3g); PROTEIN 3.4g; CARB 15.5g; FIBER 2.9g; CHOL 8mg; IRON 0.7mg; SODIUM 336mg; CALC 56mg

CLASSIC POTATO SALAD

1½ pounds baking potatoes, halved
½ cup finely chopped red onion
¼ cup finely chopped celery
¼ cup sweet pickle relish
2 hard-cooked large eggs, coarsely chopped
⅓ cup light mayonnaise
2 tablespoons cider vinegar
1 tablespoon Dijon mustard
¼ teaspoon salt
¼ teaspoon black pepper

1. Cook potatoes in boiling water 25 minutes or until potatoes are tender; drain and cool completely.

2. Cut potatoes into ½-inch cubes. Combine potatoes and next 4 ingredients in a large bowl. Combine mayonnaise and remaining 4 ingredients in a small bowl; stir with a whisk. Pour mayonnaise mixture over potato mixture, tossing gently to coat. Cover and refrigerate at least 8 hours. Yield: 6 servings (serving size: ¾ cup).

CALORIES 208 (25% from fat); FAT 5.7g (sat 1.1g, mono 1.7g, poly 2.2g); PROTEIN 5g; CARB 35.1g; FIBER 2.4g; CHOL 75mg; IRON 1.9mg; SODIUM 387mg; CALC 26mg

SOUTHWESTERN SALSA DIP

¾ cup bottled salsa
½ cup fresh cilantro leaves
2 teaspoons extra-virgin olive oil
¼ teaspoon salt
2 drops hot sauce
1 (15-ounce) can black beans, drained

1. Place all ingredients in a food processor; process until smooth. Cover and refrigerate at least 8 hours. Serve chilled or at room temperature with low-fat tortilla chips. Yield: 1½ cups (serving size: 2 tablespoons).

CALORIES 38 (24% from fat); FAT 1g (sat 0.1g, mono 0.6g, poly 0.2g); PROTEIN 2g; CARB 5.6g; FIBER 1.2g; CHOL 0mg; IRON 0.6mg; SODIUM 144mg; CALC 16mg

MOCHA BROWNIES WITH FRESH RASPBERRIES

1 cup sugar
¼ cup vegetable oil
¼ cup coffee low-fat yogurt
1 teaspoon vanilla extract
3 large egg whites, lightly beaten
½ cup all-purpose flour
⅓ cup Dutch process cocoa
1 teaspoon instant espresso or 2 teaspoons instant coffee granules
¼ teaspoon baking powder
¼ teaspoon salt
Cooking spray
2 cups fresh raspberries

1. Preheat oven to 375°.
2. Combine first 5 ingredients in a large bowl, stirring well with a whisk. Lightly spoon flour into a dry measuring cup; level with a knife. Combine flour and next 4 ingredients in a medium bowl; add flour mixture to sugar mixture, stirring just until moist. Pour mixture into a 9-inch square baking pan coated with cooking spray. Bake at 375° for 25 minutes. Cool in pan on a wire rack. Serve with raspberries. Yield: 16 servings (serving size: 1 brownie and 2 tablespoons raspberries).

CALORIES 116 (30% from fat); FAT 3.9g (sat 0.8g, mono 1g, poly 1.7g); PROTEIN 1.9g; CARB 18.8g; FIBER 1.2g; CHOL 0mg; IRON 0.6mg; SODIUM 50mg; CALC 18mg

PIÑA COLADA CAKE

Baking spray with flour
3 tablespoons canned crushed pineapple in juice, drained
2 tablespoons flaked sweetened coconut
1 (18.25-ounce) package light white cake mix
1 cup bottled piña colada drink mix (such as Holland House)
½ cup white rum, divided
3 tablespoons vegetable oil
3 large egg whites
½ cup water
¼ cup sugar

1. Preheat oven to 350°.
2. Coat a 13 x 9-inch baking pan with baking spray; sprinkle with pineapple and coconut.
3. Combine cake mix, drink mix, ¼ cup rum, oil, and egg whites in a large bowl; beat at low speed of a mixer until blended (about 30 seconds). Beat at medium speed 2 minutes. Pour batter into prepared pan. Bake at 350° for 35 minutes or until a wooden pick inserted in center comes out clean. Remove from oven, and place pan on a wire rack.
4. Combine water and sugar in a small saucepan; bring to a boil. Cook 1 minute, and remove from heat. Stir in ¼ cup rum. Pour glaze over warm cake, and cool completely. Store cake loosely covered, and let stand 24 hours. Yield: 12 servings.

CALORIES 269 (19% from fat); FAT 5.8g (sat 1.9g, mono 1.7g, poly 1.9g); PROTEIN 2.9g; CARB 47.7g; FIBER 0.1g; CHOL 0mg; IRON 0.8mg; SODIUM 316mg; CALC 61mg

MARINATED BERRY FIZZ

3 tablespoons honey
1 teaspoon grated lemon rind
2 tablespoons fresh lemon juice
2 cups fresh blackberries
2 cups fresh raspberries
2 cups fresh blueberries
2 cups sliced peeled peaches
2⅔ cups Asti Cinzano or other sweet sparkling wine
16 amaretti cookies

1. Combine first 3 ingredients in a 2-cup glass measure; microwave at HIGH 1½ minutes or until mixture boils. Cover and chill.
2. Combine blackberries and next 3 ingredients in a large bowl. Add honey mixture, stirring well. Cover and marinate in refrigerator at least 4 hours.
3. Spoon 1 cup fruit mixture into each of 8 bowls; pour ⅓ cup wine over each. Serve each with 2 amaretti cookies. Yield: 8 servings.
Note: Sweetened carbonated fruit-flavored bottled water can be substituted for sweet sparkling wine.

CALORIES 245 (7% from fat); FAT 1.8g (sat 0.3g, mono 0.6g, poly 0.7g); PROTEIN 2g; CARB 37.4g; FIBER 7.2g; CHOL 0mg; IRON 0.7mg; SODIUM 15mg; CALC 30mg

Mass. Appeal

Scenery is only part of the story in this storybook Cape Cod town where Portuguese and New England influences unite to give us some of the best seafood along the Atlantic.

Whaling brought the Portuguese to Provincetown, Massachusetts, in the early 1800s, and generations of American palates have been grateful ever since. The infusion of vibrant Mediterranean ingredients into traditional New England seafood dishes energized the city's cuisine as much as the net-laden fishing boats that leave the docks every morning and come back at sunset laden with the sea's bounty.

But in Provincetown, you won't be eating the catch of the day bloated in batter and fried to a nub. Instead, at restaurants such as Pepe's Wharf (started by the late Nils Berg and Howard Mitcham), The Moors, and the Dancing Lobster, you'll learn what mussels, clams, tuna, and other kinds of seafood can really taste like when enhanced with classic Portuguese ingredients. Garlic, onions, olive oil, tomatoes, and sweet and hot peppers meld with exotic spices like saffron, cilantro, allspice, and cinnamon.

GRILLED SHRIMP WITH PIRI-PIRI SAUCE

Piri-piri is a small, hot pepper. Substitute any small, hot, fresh or dried chile pepper.

Grilled shrimp:

- 3 pounds unpeeled jumbo shrimp
- ¼ cup dry white wine
- 1 tablespoon extra-virgin olive oil
- 6 garlic cloves
- 5 small hot red chile peppers, seeded and thinly sliced

Piri-piri sauce:

- ½ cup white wine vinegar
- ¼ cup extra-virgin olive oil
- ½ teaspoon salt
- 4 small hot red chile peppers, seeded and chopped
- Cooking spray

1. To prepare grilled shrimp, peel shrimp, leaving tails intact. Starting at tail end, butterfly each shrimp, cutting to, but not through, backside of shrimp. Combine shrimp, wine, and next 3 ingredients in a large zip-top plastic bag. Seal and marinate in refrigerator 3 hours, turning bag occasionally.
2. To prepare piri-piri sauce, combine vinegar and next 3 ingredients; stir well with a whisk.
3. Prepare grill. Remove shrimp from bag; reserve marinade. Thread shrimp evenly on 6 (12-inch) skewers. Place skewers on grill rack coated with cooking spray. Grill 7 minutes on each side or until done; turn and baste frequently with reserved marinade.
4. Remove shrimp from skewers; toss with ¼ cup piri-piri sauce. Yield: 6 servings (serving size: 5 ounces shrimp). *Note:* Store remaining piri-piri sauce in an airtight container in refrigerator. Bring to room temperature before using.

CALORIES 205 (30% from fat); FAT 6.9g (sat 1.1g, mono 3.6g, poly 1.3g); PROTEIN 29.2g; CARB 3.3g; FIBER 0.2g; CHOL 215mg; IRON 3.7mg; SODIUM 261mg; CALC 82mg

GRILLED TUNA STEAKS WITH GARLIC AND OREGANO

Serve this simple dish with the Portuguese Cucumber Salad (page 220) or the panzanella salad in the menu box.

- ⅓ cup dry white wine
- 1 tablespoon olive oil
- 2 teaspoons dried oregano
- 1 teaspoon salt
- ½ teaspoon freshly ground black pepper
- 2 garlic cloves, minced
- 6 (6-ounce) tuna steaks (about 1 inch thick)
- Cooking spray

1. Combine first 6 ingredients in a large zip-top plastic bag; add tuna steaks. Seal bag; marinate steaks in refrigerator 30 minutes or up to 2 hours. Remove tuna from bag, reserving marinade.
2. Prepare grill or broiler. Place fish on a grill rack or broiler pan coated with cooking spray, and cook 4 minutes on each side or to desired degree of doneness, basting frequently with reserved marinade. Yield: 6 servings (serving size: 1 tuna steak or 5 ounces fish).

CALORIES 278 (35% from fat); FAT 10.8g (sat 2.5g, mono 4g, poly 3.1g); PROTEIN 39.8g; CARB 0.8g; FIBER 0.1g; CHOL 65mg; IRON 2.1mg; SODIUM 458mg; CALC 12mg

Steamed Mussels with Garlic, Wine, and Cilantro

Serve this dish with a loaf of crusty sourdough bread.

- 4 pounds small mussels, scrubbed and debearded
- 1 tablespoon cornmeal
- 1½ teaspoons olive oil
- 8 garlic cloves, thinly sliced
- 1½ cups water
- ¾ cup dry white wine
- ¼ teaspoon freshly ground black pepper
- ½ cup chopped fresh cilantro

1. Place mussels in a large bowl; cover with cold water. Sprinkle with cornmeal; let stand 30 minutes. Rinse mussels; drain.

2. Heat oil in a large stockpot over medium-high heat. Add garlic; sauté 3 minutes. Add water and wine; bring to a boil. Add mussels; cover and cook over medium-high heat 6 minutes or until shells open, stirring well after 3 minutes. Remove from heat; discard any unopened shells. Sprinkle with pepper and cilantro. Remove mussels with a slotted spoon, and arrange in each of 8 shallow bowls. Yield: 8 appetizer servings (serving size: about 12 mussels).

CALORIES 78 (28% from fat); FAT 2.4g (sat 0.4g, mono 1g, poly 0.5g); PROTEIN 8.6g; CARB 5.1g; FIBER 0.4g; CHOL 19mg; IRON 3.3mg; SODIUM 199mg; CALC 35mg

Howard Mitcham's Portuguese Lobster

Be sure and have crusty bread on hand to soak up the juices.

- 5 quarts water
- 2 tablespoons salt
- 4 (1½-pound) whole Maine lobsters
- 1 teaspoon olive oil
- 3 tablespoons brandy
- 2 cups Howard's Tomato Sauce
- 3 tablespoons chopped fresh parsley

1. Bring 5 quarts water and salt to a boil in an 8-quart stockpot; plunge lobsters headfirst, 1 at a time, into water. Return to a boil; cover, reduce heat, and simmer 10 minutes. Drain well.

2. Remove meat from cooked lobster tails and claws; cut lobster meat into large chunks. Discard shell pieces.

3. Heat oil in a large nonstick skillet over medium-high heat. Add lobster; sauté 2 minutes. Pour brandy into one side of skillet. Ignite brandy with a long match; let flames die down. Add Howard's Tomato Sauce and parsley; cook over low heat 3 minutes or just until thoroughly heated. Yield: 4 servings (serving size: 1 cup).

CALORIES 209 (19% from fat); FAT 4.5g (sat 0.7g, mono 2.8g, poly 0.5g); PROTEIN 31.8g; CARB 8.9g; FIBER 1.5g; CHOL 107mg; IRON 1.7mg; SODIUM 875mg; CALC 126mg

Howard's Tomato Sauce

Used in two of our other recipes—Howard Mitcham's Portuguese Lobster and Pepe's Cataplana—this robust sauce also makes a great substitute for marinara in all your favorite pasta dishes.

- 2 tablespoons olive oil
- 3 cups vertically sliced onion
- 1 cup chopped green bell pepper
- 2 garlic cloves, minced
- 1 cup water
- 1 cup dry red wine
- ½ cup chopped fresh parsley
- 1 tablespoon red wine vinegar
- 1 teaspoon salt
- ½ teaspoon sugar
- ¼ teaspoon cumin seeds, crushed
- ¼ teaspoon dried basil
- ¼ teaspoon dried thyme
- ¼ teaspoon dried crushed red pepper
- ¼ teaspoon freshly ground black pepper
- 1 (28-ounce) can whole tomatoes, undrained and coarsely chopped

1. Heat oil in a large Dutch oven over medium heat. Add onion, bell pepper, and garlic; sauté 7 minutes or until tender. Stir in water and remaining ingredients; bring to a boil. Reduce heat, and simmer, uncovered, until mixture is reduced to about 6 cups (about 1½ hours). Yield: 6 cups (serving size: 1 cup).

CALORIES 103 (44% from fat); FAT 5g (sat 0.7g, mono 3.4g, poly 0.6g); PROTEIN 2.4g; CARB 13.7g; FIBER 2.7g; CHOL 0mg; IRON 1.9mg; SODIUM 615mg; CALC 63mg

Pepe's Cataplana

(pictured on page 225)

In Portugal, cataplana *refers to the hinged pan (resembling a clam shell) used to prepare and serve this dish of clams in a spicy sauce. We've substituted turkey kielbasa or chorizo for the traditional* linguiça *(Portuguese sausage).*

- 6 ounces (¼-inch) diagonally sliced turkey kielbasa or chorizo
- 1 cup diced onion
- 1 cup chopped green bell pepper
- 1 cup chopped red bell pepper
- 3 garlic cloves, minced
- 1½ cups coarsely chopped mushrooms
- 1 cup chopped green onions
- 2 cups water
- 2 cups dry white wine
- 2 cups Howard's Tomato Sauce
- 1 (8-ounce) bottle clam juice
- 3 dozen littleneck clams, scrubbed

1. Heat a large nonstick skillet over medium-high heat. Add sausage; sauté 4 minutes. Reduce heat to medium-low. Add diced onion, chopped peppers, and minced garlic; sauté 5 minutes. Add mushrooms and green onions; sauté 2 minutes.

2. Add water and next 3 ingredients; bring to a boil. Reduce heat, and simmer 25 minutes. Add clams; cover and simmer 5 minutes or until clam shells open. Discard any unopened clam shells. Yield: 6 servings (serving size: about 6 clams and 1⅓ cups sauce).

CALORIES 136 (30% from fat); FAT 4.5g (sat 1.4g, mono 1.2g, poly 0.5g); PROTEIN 9.8g; CARB 15.4g; FIBER 2.9g; CHOL 23mg; IRON 8.9mg; SODIUM 581mg; CALC 78mg

Spicy Fish Stew

This is a good example of the melding of two cultures—cod and potatoes are the New England influences, while the tomato base of the stew and the sherry represent the Portuguese.

1½ tablespoons olive oil
2 cups chopped onion
¾ cup chopped green bell pepper
½ teaspoon dried crushed red pepper
3 garlic cloves, minced
4 cups red potato, halved (about 1¼ pounds)
1½ cups chopped seeded peeled tomato
1½ cups clam juice
1 cup dry white wine
1 tablespoon tomato paste
½ teaspoon salt
¼ teaspoon black pepper
1 bay leaf
1½ pounds cod or other lean white fish fillets, cut into 3 x 1-inch pieces
2 tablespoons dry sherry
2 tablespoons minced fresh parsley

1. Heat oil in a Dutch oven over medium-high heat. Add onion and next 3 ingredients; sauté 5 minutes. Add potato and next 7 ingredients; bring to a boil. Reduce heat; simmer 15 minutes. Stir in cod and sherry; cook an additional 15 minutes or until fish flakes easily when tested with a fork. Stir in parsley. Discard bay leaf. Yield: 7 servings (serving size: 1½ cups).

CALORIES 221 (16% from fat); FAT 4g (sat 0.6g, mono 2.3g, poly 0.6g); PROTEIN 20.5g; CARB 26.4g; FIBER 3.2g; CHOL 42mg; IRON 1.5mg; SODIUM 345mg; CALC 47mg

Portuguese Cucumber Salad

2 cups diced seeded cucumber
½ teaspoon salt
2 red bell peppers
4 plum tomatoes, cut in half lengthwise

2½ tablespoons red wine vinegar
2 tablespoons minced fresh cilantro
1 tablespoon extra-virgin olive oil
¼ teaspoon freshly ground black pepper
2 garlic cloves, minced

1. Combine cucumber and salt in a medium bowl; let stand 30 minutes. Place cucumber on several layers of paper towels to drain.
2. Preheat broiler.
3. Cut bell peppers in half lengthwise; discard seeds and membranes. Place peppers and tomatoes, skin sides up, on a foil-lined baking sheet; flatten peppers with hand. Broil 2 minutes or until blackened. Place in a zip-top plastic bag; seal. Let stand 5 minutes. Peel and dice peppers and tomatoes; place in a large bowl. Stir in cucumber, vinegar, and remaining ingredients. Cover and chill. Yield: 6 cups (serving size: ½ cup).

CALORIES 21 (56% from fat); FAT 1.3g (sat 0.2g, mono 0.9g, poly 0.2g); PROTEIN 0.5g; CARB 2.4g; FIBER 0.7g; CHOL 0mg; IRON 0.4mg; SODIUM 101mg; CALC 6mg

Molho Cru (Portuguese Pickle)

Molho cru (muhl-CREW) is a Portuguese condiment served mainly with fish. This dish gets better with age.

1¼ cups diced onion
¾ cup water
½ cup cider vinegar
¾ teaspoon black pepper
½ teaspoon dried crushed red pepper
¼ teaspoon saffron threads
3 tablespoons minced fresh parsley
1½ tablespoons minced fresh cilantro

1. Combine first 6 ingredients; cover and chill at least 24 hours. Stir in parsley and cilantro just before serving. Yield: 2 cups (serving size: ⅓ cup).

CALORIES 19 (5% from fat); FAT 0.1g (sat 0.0g, mono 0.0g, poly 0.1g); PROTEIN 0.5g; CARB 4.7g; FIBER 0.9g; CHOL 0mg; IRON 0.5mg; SODIUM 4mg; CALC 14mg

Procrastination Pays Off

Didn't plan ahead for supper? Running behind schedule getting a meal on the table? You're in luck—dinner's only a simple stir-fry away.

Easy Asian Beef and Noodles

Even if you're very, very late, you'll have time to make this.

1 (8-ounce) rib-eye steak
1 teaspoon dark sesame oil, divided
1 cup (1-inch) sliced green onions
2 cups prepackaged coleslaw
2 (2.8-ounce) packages beef-flavor ramen noodle soup (such as Campbell's)
1½ cups water
1 tablespoon low-sodium soy sauce

1. Trim fat from steak; cut diagonally across grain into thin slices. Heat ½ teaspoon oil in a large nonstick skillet over medium-high heat. Add steak and onions; stir-fry 1 minute. Remove steak mixture from pan; keep warm. Heat ½ teaspoon oil until hot. Add slaw; stir-fry 30 seconds. Remove slaw from pan; keep warm.
2. Remove noodles from packages; reserve 1 seasoning packet for another use. Add 1½ cups water and remaining seasoning packet to pan; bring to a boil. Break noodles in half; add noodles to water mixture. Cook noodles 2 minutes or until most of liquid is absorbed, stirring frequently. Stir in steak mixture, slaw, and soy sauce; cook until thoroughly heated. Yield: 2 servings (serving size: 2 cups).

CALORIES 489 (23% from fat); FAT 12.5g (sat 3.6g, mono 5g, poly 2.5g); PROTEIN 29g; CARB 68.1g; FIBER 4.9g; CHOL 55mg; IRON 6.3mg; SODIUM 1152mg; CALC 80mg

Ultimate Quick-and-Easy Pasta Sauce, page 204

Pumpkin-Streusel Cheesecake, page 207

Caesar Salad, page 209

Peppered Tenderloin with Polenta and Puttanesca Sauce, page 206

Seasoned Tofu Steaks and Vegetable Stir-Fry with Ginger Sauce, page 238

Creamy Coconut-Topped Chocolate Cake, page 208

Apple-Cider Pie, page 267

Pepe's Cataplana, page 219

Barbecue Roasted Salmon, page 230

Butternut-Rice Pilaf, page 230

Glazed Sesame Pork, page 230

Roasted Corn-and-Garlic Couscous, page 231

Chicken Parmesan, page 206

Spicy Roasted-Red Pepper-and-Bean Dip, page 239

Penne with Tofu-Basil Pesto,
page 239

Lemon-Garlic Chicken Thighs, page 231

Roasted Potatoes and Artichokes with Feta, page 231

𝒟alancing Act

The law of low-fat averages means taste and flavor always tip the scales in your favor.

It's far more important that you average 30% or fewer calories from fat over the course of a day, a week, or even a month than it is to hold the line on every bite that goes in your mouth. Effectively combining higher- and lower-fat foods over time means that many favorites—especially meat, fish, and poultry cuts with more naturally occurring fat—don't have to be banished to nutritional Siberia.

Take salmon—and most of us would love to—but some think they can't because 42% of its calories come from fat. But pair the salmon with a starchy side such as our Butternut-Rice Pilaf (6% of calories from fat), and the meal's *total* calories from fat drop to 26%. Even flank steak, with more than 50% of calories from fat, can make the cut. Just link it with a counterbalancing side such as our Thai Coconut Noodles, with only 12% of calories from fat.

ENTRÉE/SIDE	CALORIES	FAT (G)	% FAT
Peppercorn Flank Steak	227	13.0	52
Thai Coconut Noodles	276	3.6	12
Net Balance	503	16.6	30

PEPPERCORN FLANK STEAK

½ cup dry red wine
2 teaspoons Worcestershire sauce
2 garlic cloves, minced
1 (1-pound) flank steak
2 tablespoons mixed peppercorns, crushed
Cooking spray

1. Combine first 3 ingredients in a large zip-top plastic bag. Trim fat from steak. Score a diamond pattern on both sides of steak. Sprinkle peppercorns over both sides of steak, pressing pepper into steak. Add steak to bag; seal and marinate in refrigerator 1 hour. Remove steak from bag; discard marinade.
2. Prepare grill.
3. Place steak on grill rack coated with cooking spray; grill 4 minutes on each side or until desired degree of doneness. Cut steak diagonally across the grain into thin slices. Yield: 4 servings (serving size: 3 ounces).

CALORIES 227 (52% from fat); FAT 13g (sat 5.5g, mono 5.4g, poly 0.4g); PROTEIN 22g; CARB 2.5g; FIBER 0.3g; CHOL 60mg; IRON 2.9mg; SODIUM 85mg; CALC 21mg

THAI COCONUT NOODLES

Rice sticks can be be found in Asian specialty food markets or in the Asian section of most supermarkets.

2 cups snow peas, trimmed (about 8 ounces)
1 (8-ounce) package rice sticks
1 teaspoon dark sesame oil
½ cup chopped green onions
1½ tablespoons minced peeled fresh ginger
2 garlic cloves, minced
½ cup light coconut milk (such as Hokan)
½ cup water
¼ cup tomato paste
1½ teaspoons curry powder
½ teaspoon salt
Dash of ground red pepper
¼ cup minced fresh cilantro

1. Cook snow peas and rice sticks in boiling water 3 minutes. Drain well.
2. Heat oil in a large nonstick skillet over medium heat. Add onions, ginger, and garlic; sauté 2 minutes. Stir in coconut milk and next 5 ingredients; bring to a boil. Cover, reduce heat, and simmer 5 minutes, stirring frequently. Combine snow peas, rice sticks, and green onion mixture in a large bowl; sprinkle with cilantro. Yield: 4 servings (serving size: 2 cups).

CALORIES 276 (12% from fat); FAT 3.6g (sat 1.7g, mono 0.6g, poly 0.6g); PROTEIN 8.4g; CARB 56g; FIBER 2.9g; CHOL 0mg; IRON 3.2mg; SODIUM 338mg; CALC 96mg

ENTRÉE/SIDE	CALORIES	FAT (G)	% FAT
Double-Cheese Meat Loaf	329	13.9	38
Parsnip Mashed Potatoes	160	0.8	5
Net Balance	489	14.7	27

DOUBLE-CHEESE MEAT LOAF

Cooking spray
1 cup chopped onion
6 tablespoons ketchup, divided
2 tablespoons Dijon mustard, divided
1 cup (4 ounces) shredded part-skim mozzarella cheese
½ cup Italian-seasoned breadcrumbs
¼ cup chopped fresh parsley
2 tablespoons grated Parmesan cheese
1 teaspoon dried oregano
¼ teaspoon black pepper
1 large egg, lightly beaten
½ pound lean ground beef
½ pound lean ground pork
½ pound lean ground veal

1. Preheat oven to 375°.
2. Place a medium nonstick skillet coated with cooking spray over medium-high heat. Add onion; sauté 3 minutes. Combine onion, ¼ cup ketchup, 1 tablespoon mustard, mozzarella, and next 6 ingredients in a large bowl. Crumble ground meats over cheese mixture; stir just until blended.
3. Pack mixture into an 8 x 4-inch loaf pan coated with cooking spray. Combine remaining 2 tablespoons ketchup and 1 tablespoon mustard; spread over top of loaf. Bake at 375° for 1 hour or *Continued*

until meat thermometer registers 160°. Let meat stand in pan 10 minutes. Remove meat loaf from pan; cut into 12 slices. Yield: 6 servings (serving size: 2 slices).

Note: Substitute lean ground beef for the ground veal and pork, if desired.

CALORIES 329 (38% from fat); FAT 13.9g (sat 5.6g, mono 5.3g, poly 1.2g); PROTEIN 33.8g; CARB 15.1g; FIBER 1g; CHOL 133mg; IRON 2.4mg; SODIUM 801mg; CALC 196mg

PARSNIP MASHED POTATOES

5 cups (2-inch) peeled cubed
    baking potato (about 2 pounds)
2 cups (2-inch) peeled cubed parsnip
4 garlic cloves
¾ cup low-fat buttermilk
3 tablespoons minced fresh parsley
2 tablespoons minced fresh chives
¾ teaspoon salt
¼ teaspoon black pepper

1. Combine first 3 ingredients in a large saucepan; add water to cover. Bring to a boil; cook 12 minutes or until vegetables are tender. Drain.
2. Combine potato mixture, buttermilk, and remaining ingredients in a large bowl; beat at medium speed of a mixer until smooth. Yield: 6 servings (serving size: ¾ cup).

CALORIES 160 (5% from fat); FAT 0.8g (sat 0.4g, mono 0.2g, poly 0.1g); PROTEIN 4.6g; CARB 34.9g; FIBER 3.6g; CHOL 0mg; IRON 1.4mg; SODIUM 323mg; CALC 73mg

ENTRÉE/SIDE	CALORIES	FAT (G)	% FAT
Barbecue Roasted Salmon	314	14.7	42
Butternut-Rice Pilaf	253	1.7	6
Net Balance	**567**	**16.4**	**26**

BARBECUE ROASTED SALMON

(pictured on page 225)

¼ cup pineapple juice
2 tablespoons fresh lemon juice
4 (6-ounce) salmon fillets
2 tablespoons brown sugar

4 teaspoons chili powder
2 teaspoons grated lemon
    rind
¾ teaspoon ground cumin
½ teaspoon salt
¼ teaspoon ground cinnamon
Cooking spray
Lemon wedges (optional)

1. Combine first 3 ingredients in a zip-top plastic bag; seal and marinate in refrigerator 1 hour, turning occasionally.
2. Preheat oven to 400°.
3. Remove fish from bag; discard marinade. Combine sugar and next 5 ingredients in a bowl. Rub over fish; place in an 11 x 7-inch baking dish coated with cooking spray.
4. Bake at 400° for 12 minutes or until fish flakes easily when tested with a fork. Serve with lemon wedges, if desired. Yield: 4 servings.

CALORIES 314 (42% from fat); FAT 14.7g (sat 2.5g, mono 6.9g, poly 3.3g); PROTEIN 35.3g; CARB 9g; FIBER 1g; CHOL 111mg; IRON 1.5mg; SODIUM 405mg; CALC 30mg

BUTTERNUT-RICE PILAF

(pictured on page 225)

1 teaspoon olive oil
1 cup chopped onion
3 garlic cloves, minced
3 cups (½-inch) peeled cubed
    butternut or other winter
    squash (about 1 pound)
2 cups water
1 cup uncooked long-grain
    rice
½ cup bottled roasted red bell
    peppers, chopped
1 teaspoon dried rubbed
    sage
1 teaspoon lemon juice
½ teaspoon salt
½ teaspoon ground cumin
¼ teaspoon black pepper

1. Heat olive oil in a large saucepan over medium heat. Add onion and garlic; sauté 3 minutes. Add squash, water, and rice; bring to a boil. Cover, reduce heat, and simmer 20 minutes or until liquid is absorbed. Stir in bell peppers

and remaining ingredients. Yield: 4 servings (serving size: 1¼ cups).

CALORIES 253 (6% from fat); FAT 1.7g (sat 0.3g, mono 1g, poly 0.3g); PROTEIN 5.1g; CARB 55.1g; FIBER 2.7g; CHOL 0mg; IRON 3mg; SODIUM 357mg; CALC 82mg

ENTRÉE/SIDE	CALORIES	FAT (G)	% FAT
Glazed Sesame Pork	275	13.9	45
Roasted Corn-and-Garlic Couscous	193	1.5	7
Net Balance	**468**	**15.4**	**30**

GLAZED SESAME PORK

(pictured on page 226)

½ teaspoon salt, divided
¼ teaspoon black pepper
5 (6-ounce) center-cut pork chops
    (about 1 inch thick)
2 teaspoons dark sesame oil
¾ cup low-salt chicken broth
2 tablespoons sesame seeds, toasted
1 tablespoon brown sugar
2 tablespoons red wine vinegar
1 tablespoon Dijon mustard

1. Sprinkle ¼ teaspoon salt and pepper evenly over both sides of pork. Heat oil in a nonstick skillet over medium-high heat. Add pork, and cook 3 minutes on each side or until browned. Add remaining ¼ teaspoon salt, broth, and remaining ingredients; cover, reduce heat, and simmer 20 minutes. Uncover and simmer an additional 20 minutes or until tender. Serve pork with sauce. Yield: 5 servings (serving size: 1 pork chop and about 2 tablespoons sauce).

CALORIES 275 (45% from fat); FAT 13.9g (sat 4.1g, mono 5.9g, poly 2.6g); PROTEIN 31.8g; CARB 3.3g; FIBER 0.2g; CHOL 88mg; IRON 1.7mg; SODIUM 433mg; CALC 46mg

ROASTED CORN-AND-GARLIC COUSCOUS

(pictured on page 226)

3 garlic cloves, peeled
2 cups fresh corn kernels (about 4 ears)
Cooking spray
½ teaspoon salt, divided
1¼ cups fat-free, less-sodium chicken broth
½ cup water
¼ teaspoon black pepper
1¼ cups uncooked couscous
¼ cup chopped green onions
2 tablespoons diced pimento

1. Preheat oven to 425°.
2. Wrap garlic in foil. Place garlic and corn on a jelly-roll pan coated with cooking spray. Sprinkle ¼ teaspoon salt over corn. Bake at 425° for 15 minutes, stirring every 5 minutes. Unwrap garlic, and mince. Combine garlic, corn, broth, water, remaining ¼ teaspoon salt, and pepper in a medium saucepan. Bring to a boil; gradually stir in couscous. Remove from heat; cover and let stand 5 minutes. Fluff with a fork; stir in onions and pimento. Yield: 5 servings (serving size: about 1 cup).

CALORIES 193 (7% from fat); FAT 1.5g (sat 0.3g, mono 0.2g, poly 0.4g); PROTEIN 7.7g; CARB 40.1g; FIBER 3.5g; CHOL 1mg; IRON 1.3mg; SODIUM 277mg; CALC 13mg

Entrée/Side	Calories	Fat (g)	% Fat
Lemon-Garlic Chicken Thighs	258	11.6	40
Roasted Potatoes and Artichokes with Feta	337	7.1	19
Net Balance	**595**	**18.7**	**28**

LEMON-GARLIC CHICKEN THIGHS

(pictured on page 228)

¼ cup fresh lemon juice
2 tablespoons molasses
2 teaspoons Worcestershire sauce
4 garlic cloves, chopped
8 chicken thighs, skinned (about 2 pounds)
Cooking spray
¼ teaspoon salt
¼ teaspoon black pepper

1. Combine first 4 ingredients; add chicken. Cover and marinate in refrigerator 1 hour, turning occasionally.
2. Preheat oven to 425°.
3. Remove chicken from marinade; reserve marinade. Arrange chicken in a shallow roasting pan coated with cooking spray. Pour reserved marinade over chicken; sprinkle with salt and pepper. Bake at 425° for 20 minutes; baste chicken with marinade. Bake an additional 20 minutes or until chicken is done. Yield: 4 servings (serving size: 2 chicken thighs).

CALORIES 258 (40% from fat); FAT 11.6g (sat 3.3g, mono 4.4g, poly 2.6g); PROTEIN 27.3g; CARB 9.9g; FIBER 0.1g; CHOL 98mg; IRON 1.9mg; SODIUM 268mg; CALC 43mg

ROASTED POTATOES AND ARTICHOKES WITH FETA

(pictured on page 228)

2 pounds small red potatoes, quartered
2 (14-ounce) cans artichoke hearts, drained and cut in half
2 tablespoons chopped fresh or 2 teaspoons dried thyme
1 tablespoon olive oil
½ teaspoon salt
¼ teaspoon black pepper
Cooking spray
½ cup (2 ounces) crumbled feta cheese

1. Preheat oven to 425°.
2. Combine first 6 ingredients in a large bowl, tossing well to coat. Arrange potato mixture in a 13 x 9-inch baking pan coated with cooking spray. Bake at 425° for 40 minutes or until potatoes are tender, stirring occasionally. Combine potato mixture and feta cheese; toss well. Yield: 4 servings (serving size: 2 cups).

CALORIES 337 (19% from fat); FAT 7.1g (sat 2.7g, mono 3.2g, poly 0.6g); PROTEIN 14g; CARB 60.8g; FIBER 4.3g; CHOL 13mg; IRON 5.9mg; SODIUM 656mg; CALC 194mg

The Good Stuff

Pretty to look at and simple to make, homemade vinegars pack more flavor into a bottle than any vinegar you'll find on supermarket shelves.

Where can you find an exotic tropical vinegar bursting with the flavors of mango, papaya, mint, and ginger? Or a spicy Asian concoction that's filled with hints of clove, star anise, peppercorn, lemon, and coriander? At home, of course. That's the only place you can truly shape the kind of richly flavored vinegars that add depth to any dish.

Sound like too much fuss? Not at all. Just get a bottle of vinegar—wine, champagne, or rice are the most suitable kinds—and add cut-up fruit, peppercorns, or fresh herbs. That's it. Tuck the mixture away for a few weeks. Flavors from the herbs or fruits will infuse the vinegar, allowing you to enliven recipes without adding fat.

ORANGE-MINT VINEGAR

Splash some of this vinegar into salsa to give it a bright, tangy flavor. Or pour it over fresh fruit or vanilla ice cream for a sweet-and-sour twist on dessert. If you make a vinaigrette, be sure to use a light-flavored olive or vegetable oil so that this vinegar's delicate fruit flavor won't be overshadowed.

2 oranges, divided
1 cup white wine vinegar
½ cup mint leaves, crushed
5 mint sprigs

1. Carefully remove rind from 1 orange, and using a vegetable peeler, making sure to avoid the white pith just beneath the rind. Squeeze ¼ cup juice from orange into a bowl. Combine orange rind, orange juice, vinegar, and *Continued*

mint leaves in a widemouthed jar; cover and let stand 1 week in a cool, dark place, gently shaking jar occasionally.

2. Strain vinegar mixture through a cheesecloth-lined sieve into a glass measure or medium bowl, and discard solids. Pour into a decorative bottle. Cut 5 strips from rind of 1 orange. Add mint sprigs and 5 orange rind strips to bottle. Seal with a cork or other airtight lid; store in a cool, dark place. Yield: 1 cup.

HOW MANY CALORIES? HOW MUCH FAT?

You'll notice we haven't included any nutritional-analysis figures for these vinegar recipes. That's because they contain zero fat and hardly any calories or nutrients.

MANGO-PAPAYA VINEGAR

Serve over fruit or pasta salad.

1   cup rice vinegar
½   cup mint sprigs, crushed
1   teaspoon minced peeled fresh
    ginger
6   (½-inch-thick) peeled mango
    wedges
6   (½-inch-thick) peeled papaya
    slices
1   tablespoon sugar
4   mint sprigs

1. Combine first 5 ingredients in a widemouthed jar; cover and let stand 2 weeks in a cool, dark place, gently shaking jar occasionally.

2. Strain vinegar mixture through a cheesecloth-lined sieve into a glass measure or medium bowl; discard solids. Combine vinegar mixture and sugar in a small nonaluminum saucepan; cook over low heat 5 minutes or until sugar dissolves. Cool. Pour into a decorative bottle; add mint sprigs. Seal with a cork or other airtight lid; store in a cool, dark place. Yield: 1 cup.

ASIAN FIVE-SPICE VINEGAR

Try this vinegar in Thai and Chinese stir-fries or noodle dishes that call for plain rice vinegar, or as a marinade for cucumbers.

1   cup rice vinegar
1   teaspoon coriander seeds
1   teaspoon whole cloves
1   teaspoon broken star anise
    pieces
1   teaspoon minced peeled fresh
    ginger
1   lemon
1   teaspoon pink peppercorns
5   cilantro sprigs

1. Combine first 5 ingredients in a nonaluminum saucepan; simmer over low heat 10 minutes. Remove from heat, and cool. Pour into a widemouthed jar; cover and let stand 2 weeks in a cool, dark place, gently shaking jar occasionally.

2. Strain vinegar mixture through a cheesecloth-lined sieve into a glass measure or medium bowl; discard solids. Cut 1 strip from rind of lemon; cut into very thin slices to equal 1 teaspoon. Pour vinegar into a decorative bottle; add lemon rind strips, peppercorns, and cilantro. Seal with a cork or other airtight lid; store in a cool, dark place. Yield: 1 cup.

VINEGAR SAFETY

Vinegar can corrode metals because it's acidic by nature (usually 4% to 6%), so you'll need to use glass or non-metal containers and lids. On the upside, a high acid content also makes vinegar an unfriendly environment for bacteria, so you don't need to worry about spoilage.

If you buy an unpasteurized vinegar, however, don't be alarmed if a white film forms on top. It's the harmless "mother" used to ferment vinegar. Just peel it off and discard.

HERBES DE PROVENCE VINEGAR

This vinegar contains many of the same herbs commonly found in herbes de Provence, *the dried herb blend used in southern France. Add a small amount to stews, soups, or vinaigrettes.*

1   cup white wine vinegar
¼   cup basil leaves, crushed
¼   cup thyme leaves, crushed
¼   cup oregano leaves, crushed
¼   cup rosemary leaves/needles,
    crushed
2   teaspoons black peppercorns,
    crushed
¼   teaspoon fennel seeds
2   bay leaves, broken in half
2   basil sprigs
2   thyme sprigs
2   oregano sprigs
2   rosemary sprigs
1   bay leaf

1. Combine first 8 ingredients in a widemouthed jar; cover and let stand 2 weeks in a cool, dark place, gently shaking jar occasionally.

2. Strain vinegar mixture through a cheesecloth-lined sieve into a glass measure or medium bowl; discard solids. Pour into a decorative bottle; add basil sprigs and remaining ingredients. Seal bottle with a cork or other airtight lid; store in a cool, dark place. Yield: 1 cup.

GARLIC VINEGAR

Add this one to soups and stews to round out the flavor, or drizzle it over cooked greens. It also gives a subtle hint of garlic to sweet-and-sour cabbage.

1   cup red wine vinegar
2   tablespoons minced shallots
5   garlic cloves, crushed
4   garlic cloves, peeled

1. Combine first 3 ingredients in a widemouthed jar; cover and let stand 2 weeks in a cool, dark place, gently shaking jar occasionally.

2. Strain vinegar mixture through a cheesecloth-lined sieve into a glass measure or medium bowl; discard shallots and crushed garlic cloves. Pour into a decorative bottle. Thread peeled garlic cloves onto a bamboo skewer; place in bottle. Seal with a cork or other airtight lid; store in a cool, dark place. Yield: 1 cup.

TRIPLE-BERRY VINEGAR

Use this vinegar as a marinade, brush it over fish or chicken before grilling, or add a splash to fruit juice or carbonated water.

¼	cup fresh blueberries
¼	cup fresh raspberries
¼	cup frozen cranberries, thawed
8	sage leaves
1	cup white wine vinegar
3	whole cloves
2	(3-inch) cinnamon sticks
1	tablespoon sugar
8	black peppercorns
5	fresh blueberries
5	fresh raspberries
5	frozen cranberries
4	sage leaves

1. Combine first 4 ingredients in a nonaluminum bowl; crush with a spoon. Place berry mixture, vinegar, cloves, and cinnamon sticks in a wide-mouthed jar; cover and let stand 2 weeks in a cool, dark place, gently shaking jar occasionally.
2. Strain vinegar mixture through a cheesecloth-lined sieve into a glass measure or medium bowl; discard solids. Pour vinegar into a small nonaluminum saucepan, and add sugar. Cook 5 minutes over low heat or until sugar dissolves; cool. Pour into a decorative bottle; add peppercorns and remaining ingredients. Seal with a cork or other airtight lid; store in a cool, dark place. Yield: 1 cup.

MAGIC IN A BOTTLE

❶ *Add bruised herbs, slices of fresh fruit, or other flavoring ingredients to a widemouthed jar containing plain vinegar.*

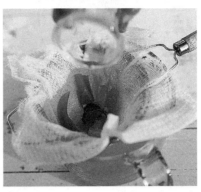

❷ *After one to two weeks—depending on how strong you want the flavor—strain mixture through a cheesecloth-lined sieve into a glass measure or medium bowl.*

❸ *Pour filtered vinegar into a decorative bottle. (You can find bottles such as these at Williams-Sonoma or other kitchenware stores.)*

❹ *Place fresh herbs, garlic, or your preferred ornamental ingredients into decorative bottle. If you've made several types of flavored vinegars, adding fresh samples of some of the ingredients can help in identification. It also gives the vinegars an attractive appearance.*

BRUISING AND MATCHING

Drop a sprig of fresh rosemary or a few leaves of basil into some plain vinegar, and not very much happens. But gently crush the leaves between your fingers, and shazam!—the "bruised" herb begins to release pungent flavors that will seep into the vinegar as it ages. The results are dramatic: Just a little bit goes a long way.

Be sure to match vinegars with the ingredients you add to them. Tart berries or strong-flavored herbs (such as rosemary) can stand up to the boldness of red wine vinegar, while white wine or rice vinegars are best with milder fruits and herbs.

You'll also want to keep the batches small to keep flavors potent. Vinegars made with fruit, for example, stay at their flavor peak for three to six months; vinegars made with herbs do so for about six months. But you can still use these vinegars beyond our recommended time periods—their high acid content keeps them safe indefinitely. They just won't taste as intense.

GARLICKY TOMATO-BASIL VINAIGRETTE

This robust vinaigrette is a perfect light dressing for pasta salads made with fresh vegetables. It's also a tasty marinade for fish, chicken, or beef. Or just toss it, as you would any vinaigrette, with mixed greens.

⅓ cup Garlic Vinegar (page 232)
1½ tablespoons fresh lemon juice
1 tablespoon extra-virgin olive oil
½ teaspoon Dijon mustard
⅛ teaspoon salt
Dash of black pepper
⅓ cup diced seeded plum tomato
2 tablespoons finely chopped fresh basil

1. Combine first 6 ingredients in a medium bowl or jar, and stir well with a whisk. Add tomato and basil; stir well. Cover and chill up to 1 week. Yield: ¾ cup (serving size: 1 tablespoon).

CALORIES 14 (77% from fat); FAT 1.2g (sat 0.2g, mono 0.8g, poly 0.1g); PROTEIN 0.1g; CARB 0.9g; FIBER 0.1g; CHOL 0mg; IRON 0mg; SODIUM 31mg; CALC 2mg

SPICY CITRUS GRILLED SHRIMP

Any of the flavored vinegars can be substituted for the Asian Five-Spice Vinegar.

1½ pounds unpeeled medium shrimp (about 48 shrimp)
2 tablespoons chopped fresh cilantro
3 tablespoons fresh orange juice
½ teaspoon grated lime rind
½ teaspoon grated lemon rind
2 tablespoons fresh lime juice
2 tablespoons fresh lemon juice
2 tablespoons Asian Five-Spice Vinegar (page 232)
1 tablespoon olive oil
¼ teaspoon freshly ground black pepper
Cooking spray

1. Peel shrimp, leaving tails intact.
2. Combine cilantro and next 8 ingredients in a small bowl. Reserve ¼ cup cilantro mixture; set aside. Combine remaining mixture and shrimp in a large zip-top plastic bag; seal and shake to coat. Marinate in refrigerator 1 hour. Thread 6 shrimp onto each of 8 (10-inch) skewers; discard marinade.
3. Prepare grill or broiler. Place kebabs on grill rack or broiler pan coated with cooking spray; cook 3 minutes on each side or until shrimp are done. Remove from grill or broiler; drizzle with reserved ¼ cup cilantro mixture. Yield: 3 servings (serving size: about 16 shrimp).

CALORIES 217 (25% from fat); FAT 6g (sat 0.3g, mono 0.3g, poly 0.6g); PROTEIN 34.7g; CARB 4g; FIBER 0.1g; CHOL 259mg; IRON 4.2mg; SODIUM 254mg; CALC 94mg

CARAMELIZED-ONION FOCACCIA

Adding fruit-flavored vinegar to caramelized onions lends a sweet-tart contrast to simple focaccia.

1½ tablespoons olive oil
7½ cups thinly sliced onion (about 4)
½ cup thinly sliced shallots
3 tablespoons Mango-Papaya Vinegar (page 232)
½ teaspoon dried thyme
¼ teaspoon salt
¼ teaspoon black pepper
1 (14.5-ounce) package focaccia (Italian flatbread)

1. Preheat oven to 400°.
2. Heat olive oil in a large nonstick skillet over medium-low heat. Add onion and shallots; cook 25 minutes or until onion and shallots are golden brown, stirring frequently. Add Mango-Papaya Vinegar and next 3 ingredients; sauté 5 minutes. Arrange caramelized onions over focaccia. Bake at 400° for 8 minutes or until thoroughly heated. Cut focaccia into wedges. Yield: 4 servings.

CALORIES 405 (21% from fat); FAT 9.5g (sat 2.8g, mono 4.7g, poly 1.6g); PROTEIN 13g; CARB 70.6g; FIBER 8.2g; CHOL 0mg; IRON 1mg; SODIUM 676mg; CALC 119mg

---

MENU SUGGESTION

Grilled pork chops with citrus glaze *

White-and-wild rice pilaf

PEACH-PLUM CHUTNEY

*Sprinkle 4 (6-ounce) center-cut loin pork chops with ¼ teaspoon black pepper and ⅛ teaspoon salt. Combine ⅓ cup orange marmalade, 2 tablespoons chopped fresh mint, 2 tablespoons low-sodium soy sauce, and 2 minced garlic cloves. Brush chops with half of marmalade mixture; grill 7 minutes on each side or until done, basting frequently with remaining marmalade mixture. Serves 4.

PEACH-PLUM CHUTNEY

Serve this chutney with grilled chicken or pork chops.

2 tablespoons olive oil
2 cups diced Vidalia or other sweet onion (about 2 small)
1 tablespoon grated orange rind
1 cup fresh orange juice
½ cup Orange-Mint Vinegar (page 231)
6 tablespoons maple syrup
2 tablespoons chopped fresh chives
1½ cups chopped peeled peaches (about 2 large)
1 cup chopped peeled plums (about 2 small)
2 (3-inch) cinnamon sticks

1. Heat oil in a large nonstick skillet over medium heat. Add onion, and sauté 8 minutes. Add orange rind and next 4 ingredients; stir well. Add peaches, plums, and cinnamon sticks; bring to a boil. Reduce heat, and simmer 1 hour or until thick. Discard cinnamon sticks. Cool and store in an airtight container in refrigerator. Yield: 2¼ cups (serving size: ¼ cup).

CALORIES 115 (26% from fat); FAT 3.3g (sat 0.4g, mono 2.3g, poly 0.3g); PROTEIN 1g; CARB 21.7g; FIBER 1.7g; CHOL 0mg; IRON 0.3mg; SODIUM 4mg; CALC 25mg

CAULIFLOWER SALAD WITH ZESTY VINAIGRETTE

3 cups small cauliflower florets
2 cups cooked multicolored rotini (about 4 ounces uncooked corkscrew pasta)
⅓ cup sliced green onions
⅓ cup thinly sliced radishes
¾ cup Garlicky Tomato-Basil Vinaigrette (page 234)
2 tablespoons grated Romano or Parmesan cheese
⅛ teaspoon black pepper

1. Combine first 4 ingredients in a large bowl. Drizzle Garlicky Tomato-Basil Vinaigrette over cauliflower mixture, and toss well. Sprinkle with cheese and pepper; toss. Cover and marinate in refrigerator at least 2 hours. Yield: 5 servings (serving size: 1 cup).

CALORIES 138 (27% from fat); FAT 4.1g (sat 1.1g, mono 2.3g, poly 0.7g); PROTEIN 5.1g; CARB 21.5g; FIBER 2.7g; CHOL 3mg; IRON 1.2mg; SODIUM 130mg; CALC 59mg

TRIPLE-BERRY FRUIT SALAD

1 cup sliced fresh strawberries
½ cup fresh blackberries
½ cup fresh raspberries
2 tablespoons Triple-Berry Vinegar (page 233)
1 tablespoon sugar

1. Combine all ingredients in a small bowl, stirring gently. Cover and chill. Yield: 4 servings (serving size: ½ cup).

CALORIES 45 (6% from fat); FAT 0.3g (sat 0g, mono 0g, poly 0.2g); PROTEIN 0.6g; CARB 10.8g; FIBER 3.6g; CHOL 0mg; IRON 0.4mg; SODIUM 2mg; CALC 15mg

Grace Under Pressure

Can't stand the heat? Get a pressure cooker in your kitchen.

Anyone who's spent too many hours in the kitchen on a hot summer day knows why pressure cookers were invented. Not only do they do their thing in far less time than conventional stovetops, they also don't heat up the place.

Pressure cookers can make the tough tender and, by allowing several items to be cooked together, meld disparate flavors. Especially good for grains, dried beans, and meats, pressure also brings out the best in fare such as risotto, fresh tomatoes, zucchini, and green beans. Fruits find a welcome home in cookers, as do fish such as salmon and tuna.

A second generation of pressure cookers beckons anyone who wants to add an extra measure of speed to meal-making. The old jiggle-top model is still available, but it's been spiffed up and rid of annoying old habits like blowing its top, and your meal, all over the ceiling. Even more advanced are the spring-release-valve models; though more expensive, they are quieter and quicker to decompress. Both are safe, though, and they cook the same inside.

What happens in the pot accounts for the renewed interest. Superheated steam seals in nutrients, requires very little fat, and can put a meal on the table in a half hour.

ORANGE-SCENTED BEET SALAD

6 beets (about 3 pounds)
3 (3-inch) orange rind strips
½ cup fresh orange juice
2 tablespoons cider vinegar
¼ cup sliced green onions
2 tablespoons brown sugar
2 teaspoons grated orange rind
2 teaspoons Dijon mustard
4 cups gourmet salad greens
Orange rind strips (optional)

1. Trim roots and stems from beets; scrub with a brush. Peel beets. Cut beets in half lengthwise; cut into ¼-inch-thick slices. Place beets, 3 orange rind strips, orange juice, and vinegar in a 6-quart pressure cooker. Close lid securely; bring to high pressure over high heat (about 4 minutes). Adjust heat to medium or level needed to maintain high pressure; cook 3 minutes. Remove from heat; place pressure cooker under cold running water. Remove lid.

2. Drain mixture in a colander over a bowl, reserving 1 cup cooking liquid. Discard 3 orange rind strips. Combine 1 cup reserved cooking liquid, beets, onions, and next 3 ingredients in a bowl; toss gently. Place 1 cup greens on each of 4 plates; top with beet mixture. Garnish with additional orange rind strips, if desired. Yield: 4 servings.

CALORIES 142 (4% from fat); FAT 0.6g (sat 0.1g, mono 0.1g, poly 0.2g); PROTEIN 4.9g; CARB 32g; FIBER 3g; CHOL 0mg; IRON 2.7mg; SODIUM 222mg; CALC 70mg

NO PRESSURE ON YOU

Add your ingredients, plus at least a half-cup of whatever liquid the recipe calls for. Lock the lid; bring your cooker to high pressure on the stove. Start the timer, and reduce the heat to the lowest setting required. When the timer goes off, reduce the pressure.

Quick-release action on the spring-valve models lets you do so at the stove; most jiggle tops must be carried to the sink so cool tap water can bring the pressure down. Either method requires only a couple of minutes and stops the cooking process at once. Easiest of all is just letting the cooker sit for about 10 minutes. The pressure will drop while you go about the rest of your meal preparations.

Pressure cookers save you time by cooking foods at above-boiling-point temperatures, usually from 212° to 250°. And the heat stays in the pot, not in your kitchen. Both types of cookers—the traditional jiggle-top from manufacturers such as Presto and the spring-valve from leaders such as Kuhn-Rikon, Magefesa, and Fagor—are safe, but they vary in design, operation, and cost.

JIGGLE-TOP	SPRING-VALVE
Noisy	Little or no hissing
Aluminum	Stainless-steel, triple-ply bottom
Light	Heavy
Must be placed under cold running water for quick release of pressure	Quick pressure-release mechanism can be used on stovetop
About $50 to $70	About $140

CHICKEN-VEGETABLE CHILI

Cooking spray
12 ounces skinned, boned chicken thighs or breast, cut into bite-size pieces
1 cup chopped onion
1 cup chopped red bell pepper
¼ cup chopped seeded jalapeño pepper
¼ cup chopped sun-dried tomatoes, packed without oil
1½ tablespoons chili powder
1 tablespoon ground cumin
2 teaspoons dried oregano
¼ teaspoon ground red pepper
3 garlic cloves, minced
2 cups boiling water
1 cup dried pinto beans (about 6 ounces)
1 cup chopped tomato
1 cup fresh corn kernels (about 2 ears)
½ teaspoon salt

1. Place a 6-quart pressure cooker coated with cooking spray over medium-high heat. Add chicken and onion; sauté 2 minutes. Add bell pepper and next 7 ingredients; sauté 1 minute. Stir in water and beans.
2. Close lid securely; bring to high pressure over high heat (about 4 minutes). Adjust heat to medium-high or level needed to maintain high pressure; cook 25 minutes. Remove from heat; place pressure cooker under cold running water. Remove lid; stir in tomato, corn, and salt. Bring to a boil; cook, uncovered, 5 minutes, stirring frequently. Yield: 6 servings (serving size: 1 cup).

CALORIES 248 (15% from fat); FAT 4g (sat 0.8g, mono 1.1g, poly 1.2g); PROTEIN 20.7g; CARB 35.3g; FIBER 7g; CHOL 47mg; IRON 4.4mg; SODIUM 351mg; CALC 84mg

RISOTTO WITH CORN, ZUCCHINI, AND RED PEPPER

Using a pressure cooker means you don't have to stir this risotto.

1 (16-ounce) can fat-free, less-sodium chicken broth
⅓ cup water
1 tablespoon olive oil
½ cup chopped onion
1 cup uncooked Arborio rice or other short-grain rice
⅛ teaspoon powdered saffron (optional)
1 cup fresh corn kernels (about 2 ears)
1 cup diced zucchini
½ cup finely chopped red bell pepper
⅓ cup (about 1½ ounces) grated fresh Parmesan cheese
¼ teaspoon salt

1. Bring broth and water to a simmer in a medium saucepan; keep warm.
2. Heat oil in a 6-quart pressure cooker over medium heat until hot. Add onion; sauté 2 minutes. Add rice and saffron; sauté 30 seconds. Stir in broth mixture. Close lid securely; bring to high pressure over high heat (about 3 minutes). Adjust heat to medium or level needed to maintain high pressure; cook 3 minutes. Remove from heat; let stand 10 minutes. Place cooker under cold running water. Remove lid; stir in corn, zucchini, and bell pepper. Cook, uncovered, 3 minutes, stirring constantly. Stir in cheese and salt. Yield: 4 servings (serving size: 1¼ cups).

CALORIES 326 (20% from fat); FAT 7.3g (sat 2.6g, mono 3.6g, poly 0.7g); PROTEIN 11.5g; CARB 52.1g; FIBER 2.8g; CHOL 11mg; IRON 2.8mg; SODIUM 560mg; CALC 162mg

THREE-GRAIN SUMMER-VEGETABLE SALAD

Quinoa (KEEN-wah) is not only high in fiber but also higher in protein than any other grain. Millet, usually found in health-food stores, is a tiny, delicate grain that is also rich in protein.

Cooking spray
¼ cup minced fresh onion
1 cup uncooked basmati rice
½ cup uncooked millet
½ cup uncooked quinoa
2 cups water
1 cup apple juice
1 (3-inch) cinnamon stick
1 cup diced peeled Granny Smith apple (about 1 pound)
½ cup raisins
½ cup sliced green onions
½ cup chopped red bell pepper
⅓ cup light mayonnaise
¼ cup minced fresh cilantro
2 tablespoons lemon juice
2 teaspoons curry powder
½ teaspoon salt

1. Place a 6-quart pressure cooker coated with cooking spray over medium-high heat until hot. Add onion, and sauté 1 minute. Add rice,

millet, and quinoa; sauté 30 seconds. Stir in water, apple juice, and cinnamon stick. Close lid securely, and bring to high pressure over medium-high heat (about 4 minutes). Adjust heat to low or level needed to maintain high pressure, and cook 5 minutes. Remove from heat, and place pressure cooker under cold running water. Let stand 7 minutes, and remove lid. Discard cinnamon stick; fluff mixture with a fork. Spoon mixture into a large bowl; cool 5 minutes.

2. Stir in apple and remaining ingredients. Serve salad chilled or at room temperature. Yield: 9 servings (serving size: 1 cup).

CALORIES 212 (15% from fat); FAT 3.6g (sat 0.5g, mono 1g, poly 1.7g); PROTEIN 4.2g; CARB 42.5g; FIBER 2.9g; CHOL 3mg; IRON 3mg; SODIUM 207mg; CALC 30mg

GARLICKY GREEN BEAN-POTATO SALAD

Fresh yellow wax beans can be substituted for the green beans.

1½ pounds yellow Finnish potatoes or red potatoes
¾ cup fat-free, less-sodium chicken broth
2 cups (½-inch) cut green beans (about ½ pound)
10 garlic cloves, peeled
2 tablespoons rice vinegar
2 tablespoons extra-virgin olive oil
2 tablespoons fat-free, less-sodium chicken broth
2 teaspoons Dijon mustard
¼ teaspoon salt
⅛ teaspoon black pepper

1. Cut potatoes into quarters. Cut each piece into ½-inch-thick slices. Pour ¾ cup broth into bottom of a 6-quart pressure cooker; layer potatoes, green beans, and garlic in cooker. Close lid securely; bring to high pressure over high heat (about 9 minutes). Adjust heat to low or level needed to maintain high pressure; cook 3 minutes. Remove from heat; place pressure cooker under cold running water. Remove lid.

2. Drain potato mixture in a colander, reserving garlic cloves; place potato mixture in a large bowl. Combine reserved garlic cloves, vinegar, and remaining 5 ingredients in a blender; process until smooth. Drizzle garlic dressing over potato mixture; toss gently to coat. Yield: 6 servings (serving size: 1 cup).

CALORIES 150 (29% from fat); FAT 4.8g (sat 0.4g, mono 3.3g, poly 0.5g); PROTEIN 3.9g; CARB 23.5g; FIBER 2.9g; CHOL 1mg; IRON 2mg; SODIUM 229mg; CALC 40mg

WHITE BEAN, BASIL, AND TOMATO SOUP

2 cups dried Great Northern beans (about 1 pound)
Cooking spray
1 cup chopped onion
6 garlic cloves, chopped
1 cup diced peeled baking potato
2 teaspoons chopped fresh or ½ teaspoon dried thyme
3 (16-ounce) cans fat-free, less-sodium chicken broth
2 bay leaves
2 cups diced seeded tomato
¼ cup chopped fresh basil
1 tablespoon lemon juice
¾ teaspoon salt
¼ to ½ teaspoon dried crushed red pepper
¼ cup (1 ounce) grated fresh Parmesan cheese

1. Sort and wash beans; set aside. Place a 6-quart pressure cooker coated with cooking spray over medium heat until hot. Add onion; sauté 2 minutes. Add garlic; sauté 1 minute. Add beans, potato, and next 3 ingredients. Close lid securely; bring to high pressure over high heat (about 7 minutes). Adjust heat to medium or level needed to maintain high pressure; cook 35 minutes. Remove from heat; place pressure cooker under cold running water. Remove lid. Discard bay leaves.

2. Partially mash bean mixture. Stir in tomato and next 4 ingredients. Cook, uncovered, over medium heat 5 minutes or until thoroughly heated, stirring frequently. Sprinkle with cheese. Yield: 10 servings (serving size: 1 cup).

CALORIES 183 (7% from fat); FAT 1.4g (sat 0.6g, mono 0.3g, poly 0.3g); PROTEIN 11.8g; CARB 30.5g; FIBER 15.7g; CHOL 4mg; IRON 2.4mg; SODIUM 327mg; CALC 119mg

SPICED SUMMER-FRUIT COMPOTE

Serve warm or cold over frozen vanilla yogurt or angel food cake.

½ cup fresh raspberries
3 peaches, each cut into 8 wedges (about 1 pound)
3 nectarines, each cut into 8 wedges (about ¾ pound)
½ cup mango nectar
2 (3 x 1-inch) orange rind strips
2 (3-inch) cinnamon sticks
¼ cup sugar
2 tablespoons triple sec (orange-flavored liqueur)

1. Combine first 6 ingredients in a 6-quart pressure cooker. Close lid securely, and bring to high pressure over high heat (about 4 minutes). Adjust heat to medium or level needed to maintain high pressure; cook 2 minutes. Remove from heat; place pressure cooker under cold running water. Remove lid; discard orange rind and cinnamon sticks. Stir in sugar and liqueur. Yield: 10 servings (serving size: ½ cup).

CALORIES 74 (4% from fat); FAT 0.3g (sat 0g, mono 0.1g, poly 0.1g); PROTEIN 0.6g; CARB 17.5g; FIBER 1.9g; CHOL 0mg; IRON 0.2mg; SODIUM 0mg; CALC 5mg

Never Too Late for Tofu

Once you let this versatile flavor magnet in the door, you'll have a friend for life.

Tofu comes in a range of textures and flavors: **silken** (excellent for whipping into dips, salad dressings, cheesecakes, and milk shakes); **soft** (also good for mashing and pureeing); and **firm** and **extra-firm** (for crumbling into lasagna, chili, or spaghetti sauce, or for slicing in sautés and stir-fries). And at some supermarkets and Asian food stores, you can even find it smoked, marinated, spiced, fermented, freeze-dried, or deep-fried.

TOFU-AND-VEGETABLE STIR-FRY SALAD

You can substitute an extra-firm reduced-fat tofu for the regular variety.

Vinaigrette:

- ¼ cup seasoned rice vinegar
- 2 tablespoons low-sodium soy sauce
- 1½ teaspoons dark sesame oil
- 1 teaspoon minced peeled fresh ginger
- 2 garlic cloves, minced
- ½ teaspoon sugar
- ⅛ teaspoon dried crushed red pepper

Salad:

- 4 ounces uncooked Chinese-style noodles or angel hair pasta
- 4 cups shredded napa (Chinese) cabbage
- 1½ teaspoons vegetable oil
- 2 cups (2-inch) sliced asparagus (about 1 pound)
- 2 cups red bell pepper strips
- 2 cups diagonally sliced bok choy
- ½ cup chopped green onions
- 1 (12.3-ounce) package extra-firm silken tofu, drained and cut into 2-inch julienne strips

1. To prepare vinaigrette, combine first 7 ingredients in a small bowl.
2. To prepare salad, cook noodles according to package directions; drain and rinse with cold water. Combine 2 tablespoons vinaigrette and noodles; set aside. Combine 2 tablespoons vinaigrette and cabbage; set aside.
3. Heat vegetable oil in a large nonstick skillet over medium-high heat. Add asparagus; stir-fry 5 minutes. Add bell pepper, bok choy, and onions; stir-fry 3 minutes. Add tofu and remaining vinaigrette; remove from heat. Cover and let stand 5 minutes or until tofu is heated.
4. Place 1 cup cabbage mixture on each of 4 plates; top each serving with ½ cup noodle mixture and 1½ cups stir-fry mixture. Yield: 4 servings.

CALORIES 252 (30% from fat); FAT 8.4g (sat 1.4g, mono 2.8g, poly 4.5g); PROTEIN 15g; CARB 31.9g; FIBER 7.1g; CHOL 0mg; IRON 8mg; SODIUM 324mg; CALC 244mg

SEASONED TOFU STEAKS AND VEGETABLE STIR-FRY WITH GINGER SAUCE

(pictured on page 223)

This will wow guests or family on many different levels—it has lots of color, lots of texture, and lots of spice. You might want to double the recipe for the steaks for another meal. Leftover steaks are great stacked on a sandwich with lettuce and a few slices of grilled tomato.

Tofu steaks:

- 1 (12.3-ounce) package reduced-fat firm silken tofu, drained
- ¼ cup all-purpose flour
- 2 tablespoons dry breadcrumbs
- ½ teaspoon dried thyme
- ¼ teaspoon dried dill
- ¼ teaspoon salt
- ¼ teaspoon paprika
- ¼ teaspoon freshly ground black pepper
- 1 large egg, lightly beaten
- 2 teaspoons vegetable oil

Ginger sauce:

- ⅓ cup rice vinegar
- ⅓ cup sugar
- ½ cup water
- 2 tablespoons low-sodium soy sauce
- 1 tablespoon cornstarch
- ¼ cup water
- 1 tablespoon minced peeled fresh ginger

Vegetable stir-fry:

- 1 teaspoon vegetable oil
- 1 cup yellow bell pepper strips
- 1 cup snow peas
- ½ cup chopped plum tomato
- 2 cups cooked angel hair pasta or somen (wheat noodles) (about 4 ounces uncooked pasta)

1. To prepare tofu steaks, cut tofu lengthwise into 4 (½-inch-thick) slices. Place tofu on several layers of heavy-duty paper towels. Cover with additional paper towels; let stand 5 minutes.
2. Combine flour and next 6 ingredients. Dredge each tofu steak in flour mixture. Dip into egg; dredge again in flour mixture. Heat 2 teaspoons oil in a nonstick skillet over medium-high heat. Add tofu steaks; cook 3 minutes on each side. Remove from skillet; cut each steak into 4 wedges. Keep warm.
3. To prepare ginger sauce, combine vinegar and next 3 ingredients in a saucepan; bring to a boil over medium-high heat. Reduce heat, and simmer 3 minutes or until sugar is dissolved. Combine cornstarch and ¼ cup water; stir into sugar mixture. Bring to a boil; cook 1 minute or until thick. Remove from heat; stir in ginger. Keep warm.
4. To prepare stir-fry, heat 1 teaspoon oil in skillet over medium-high heat. Add pepper and peas; stir-fry 2 minutes. Add tomato; stir-fry 1 minute. Serve over pasta; top with ginger sauce and tofu wedges. Yield: 4 servings (serving size: 4 tofu wedges, ½ cup pasta, ½ cup vegetable stir-fry, and ¼ cup ginger sauce).

CALORIES 337 (17% from fat); FAT 6.4g (sat 1.3g, mono 1.8g, poly 2.5g); PROTEIN 15g; CARB 54.3g; FIBER 4.6g; CHOL 55mg; IRON 4.1mg; SODIUM 533mg; CALC 94mg

TOMATO-JALAPEÑO SOUP

*A soft-textured silken tofu is best for
making creamy soups. Because reduced-
fat varieties of tofu are generally firm-
textured, you'll need to use regular tofu
for this recipe. It provides the body and
texture of a cream soup with less than
5 grams of fat.*

- 1 (28-ounce) can plum tomatoes,
  undrained
- 1 (12.3-ounce) package soft silken
  tofu, drained and divided
- 1 teaspoon sugar
- 1 teaspoon olive oil
- ½ cup finely chopped red onion
- 1 garlic clove, minced
- ¼ cup minced fresh or 1 teaspoon
  dried basil
- 1 tablespoon minced seeded
  jalapeño pepper
- 2 teaspoons minced fresh or
  ½ teaspoon dried oregano
- ½ to 1 teaspoon pepper
- ⅛ teaspoon ground cumin
- 1 tablespoon grated fresh
  Parmesan cheese
- 1 tablespoon fresh lemon juice
- ⅛ teaspoon salt

1. Combine plum tomatoes, 1 cup
drained tofu, and sugar in a food
processor; process until smooth. Heat
oil in a large saucepan over medium-
high heat. Add onion and garlic; sauté
4 minutes.

2. Reduce heat to medium, and stir in
tomato mixture, basil, and next 4 ingredients. Cook until thoroughly
heated; cover and keep warm.
3. Combine remaining tofu, Parmesan
cheese, lemon juice, and salt in a
blender; process until smooth.
4. Ladle soup into 4 bowls, and top
with Parmesan cheese mixture. Yield: 4
servings (serving size: 1¼ cups soup
and about 1 tablespoon Parmesan
cheese mixture).

CALORIES 120 (33% from fat); FAT 4.4g (sat 0.9g, mono 1.6g,
poly 1.7g); PROTEIN 8.3g; CARB 14.1g; FIBER 1.9g;
CHOL 1mg; IRON 2.6mg; SODIUM 432mg; CALC 164mg

PENNE WITH TOFU-BASIL PESTO

(pictured on page 228)

*You'll be surprised how tofu picks up
the rich flavors of fresh basil, garlic,
and Parmesan cheese. But what sold
our staff on this dish was the creamy
texture.*

- 1 cup fresh basil leaves
- 1 cup reduced-fat firm silken tofu
  (about 6 ounces)
- ¼ cup (1 ounce) grated fresh
  Parmesan cheese
- 2 tablespoons olive oil
- 2 tablespoons fresh lemon juice
- ½ teaspoon black pepper
- ¼ teaspoon salt
- 1 large garlic clove, minced
- 1 teaspoon olive oil
- 2½ cups sliced cremini mushrooms
- ¼ cup minced shallots
- 4 cups hot cooked penne (about 8
  ounces uncooked tube-shaped
  pasta)

1. Combine first 8 ingredients in a
food processor or blender; process until
smooth. Place pesto in a small nonstick
skillet; cook over low heat until warm.
Remove from heat; keep warm.
2. Heat 1 teaspoon olive oil in a large
nonstick skillet over medium-high
heat. Add mushrooms and shallots;
sauté 4 minutes.

3. Combine penne, pesto, and mushroom mixture in a large bowl; toss.
Yield: 4 servings (serving size: 1¼ cups).

CALORIES 352 (29% from fat); FAT 11.3g (sat 2.5g, mono 6.6g,
poly 1.4g); PROTEIN 14.5g; CARB 48.6g; FIBER 2.1g;
CHOL 5mg; IRON 3.5mg; SODIUM 310mg; CALC 139mg

SPICY ROASTED-RED PEPPER-AND-BEAN DIP

(pictured on page 227)

*Once blended, the tofu in this Tex-
Mex-inspired dip takes on the flavors
of roasted red peppers, jalapeños, lime,
and cumin. Serve with breadsticks,
pita bread, or baked tortilla chips.*

- 1 (7-ounce) bottle roasted red bell
  peppers, drained
- 1 cup reduced-fat firm silken tofu
  (about 6 ounces)
- ⅓ cup fresh parsley leaves
- 2 tablespoons lime juice
- 1 tablespoon extra-virgin olive
  oil
- ½ teaspoon salt
- ½ teaspoon ground cumin
- 2 garlic cloves, crushed
- 1 (16-ounce) can cannellini beans
  or other white beans, rinsed
  and drained
- ½ teaspoon minced seeded
  jalapeño pepper
- Sliced jalapeño pepper (optional)

1. Chop bell peppers to measure ¼
cup; set aside. Place remaining bell
peppers, tofu, and next 7 ingredients in
a food processor; process until smooth.
Spoon mixture into a bowl; stir in reserved ¼ cup bell peppers and minced
jalapeño. Cover and chill. Garnish with
sliced jalapeño, if desired. Yield: 2½
cups (serving size: ¼ cup).

CALORIES 76 (27% from fat); FAT 2.3g (sat 0.3g, mono 1.2g,
poly 0.6g); PROTEIN 4.1g; CARB 10.2g; FIBER 1.2g;
CHOL 0mg; IRON 1.2mg; SODIUM 244mg; CALC 28mg

CREAMY LEMON-LIME TOFU CHEESECAKE

(pictured on page 3)

Find fat-free or low-fat lemon curd on the jelly aisle of the supermarket.

Crust:

1⅓ cups graham cracker crumbs
    (about 8 cookie sheets)
2 tablespoons brown sugar
1 tablespoon reduced-calorie
    stick margarine, melted
Cooking spray

Filling:

1 cup 2% low-fat cottage cheese
⅔ cup tub-style light cream cheese
    (about 5 ounces)
1 (12.3-ounce) package reduced-
    fat firm silken tofu, drained
1 cup granulated sugar
⅓ cup all-purpose flour
½ cup bottled fat-free lemon curd
    (such as Crosse & Blackwell)
2 teaspoons grated lime rind
6 tablespoons fresh lime juice
2 large eggs
1 large egg white

Topping:

1¼ cups low-fat sour cream
½ cup granulated sugar
1 teaspoon grated lemon rind
½ teaspoon vanilla extract
Lemon and lime slices (optional)

1. Preheat oven to 325°.
2. To prepare crust, combine first 3 in-gredients, tossing well with a fork. Sprinkle into bottom of a 9-inch spring-form pan coated with cooking spray.
3. To prepare filling, place cheeses and tofu in a food processor; process until mixture is smooth. Add 1 cup granu-lated sugar, flour, and next 5 ingredients; process until smooth, scraping sides of processor bowl occasionally. Pour into crust. Bake at 325° for 1 hour and 20 minutes or until almost set. Remove from oven.

4. To prepare topping, place sour cream and next 3 ingredients in a small bowl; stir well. Spread over cheesecake, and bake an additional 8 minutes. Turn oven off, and partially open oven door; leave cheesecake in oven 30 min-utes. Remove from oven. Cool 20 minutes on a wire rack; cover and chill 8 hours. Garnish with lemon and lime slices, if desired. Yield: 12 servings.

CALORIES 308 (25% from fat); FAT 8.4g (sat 4.1g, mono 2g, poly 1g); PROTEIN 9.2g; CARB 49.9g; FIBER 0.1g; CHOL 55mg; IRON 1.1mg; SODIUM 282mg; CALC 80mg

TOFU-TAPIOCA PUDDING

3 cups fat-free milk
¾ cup sugar
¼ cup uncooked quick-cooking
    tapioca
¼ teaspoon salt
2 large eggs, lightly beaten
¼ cup fat-free milk
1 cup soft silken tofu, drained
    (about 6 ounces)
1½ teaspoons vanilla extract

1. Combine first 5 ingredients in a saucepan, stirring with a whisk. Let stand 5 minutes. Bring to a boil over medium heat, stirring constantly. Cook 30 seconds, stirring constantly. Pour into a bowl; cool 15 minutes.
2. Combine ¼ cup milk, tofu, and vanilla in a food processor; process 1 minute or until creamy. Fold into tapi-oca mixture. Cover and chill (mixture continues to thicken as it chills). Yield: 8 servings (serving size: ½ cup).

CALORIES 156 (12% from fat); FAT 2g (sat 0.6g, mono 0.7g, poly 0.5g); PROTEIN 6.3g; CARB 28.1g; FIBER 0g; CHOL 57mg; IRON 0.5mg; SODIUM 143mg; CALC 148mg

TOFU-FRUIT SMOOTHIE

½ cup sliced ripe banana
½ cup frozen sweetened sliced
    strawberries, partially thawed
½ cup soft silken tofu, drained
    (about 3 ounces)
½ cup vanilla low-fat yogurt

1. Combine all ingredients in a blender; process until smooth. Serve immediately. Yield: 2 servings (serving size: ¾ cup).

CALORIES 180 (10% from fat); FAT 2g (sat 0.7g, mono 0.5g, poly 0.7g); PROTEIN 6.3g; CARB 36.4g; FIBER 2.1g; CHOL 3mg; IRON 0.9mg; SODIUM 40mg; CALC 147mg

---

THE POWER BEHIND TOFU

The real medicinal hero of tofu is the soybean. But even soybeans have an inner hero called isoflavones. These plant hormones may help battle chronic illness on several fronts. Here's a wrap-up of the benefits.

• **STRONGER BONES:** Preliminary research finds that isoflavones may help protect bone density in post-menopausal women. It's estimated that every gram of soy protein con-tains 1 to 3 milligrams of isoflavones.
• **LOWER CHOLESTEROL LEVELS:** After pooling the results of 38 different stud-ies, a Kentucky researcher concludes that diets rich in soy protein can lower low-density lipoprotein (LDL)—the harmful cholesterol—nearly 13%. In these same studies, soy reduces total cholesterol an average of 9.3%.
• **RELIEF FROM HOT FLASHES:** Scientists in North Carolina find that adding 20 grams of soy protein per day to the diet lessens the severity—but not the number—of hot flashes. Italian researchers, however, find that including soy can cut the number of hot flashes by nearly half.
• **LOWER RISK OF CANCER:** In Asian countries where soy foods are a routine part of the diet, the death rate from breast and prostate cancer is dramatically lower. Isoflavones such as genistein may get the credit. Labora-tory studies find genistein is a potent antioxidant that not only inhibits the growth of cancer cells but also prevents the growth of new blood vessels, which provide the nutrients a cancerous tumor needs to grow.

OCTOBER

Faith in the Future

When Cooking Light *teamed up with an inner-city school to change the eating and fitness habits of its students, what at first seemed like a formidable challenge turned into a remarkable and inspiring success.*

For a week, the magazine's staff and volunteers from around the city allied with Center Street Middle School in Birmingham, Alabama, in a project that unfolded with such dramatic success that it may prove to be a blueprint for healthful retooling of schools across the country. The Center Street Challenge, as we dubbed it, was simply this: To prove that positively intervening to change the eating and fitness habits of schoolchildren was not only possible but doable.

Our basic mission was to create a leaner lunch line that veered away from burgers and fries toward more vegetables, fruits, and lower-fat meats. The project was designed to initiate a shift in eating patterns that would ripple out into the home and the community. Kid by kid, home by home, school by school, lives would get better, stronger, and more enjoyable.

Enchiladas were on the lunch menu on Wednesday. The students examined this new fare, and the magazine and school kitchen staffs watched anxiously from behind the serving line. The initial reaction was tentative as the more cautious eaters poked at the long, sauce-covered cylinders and watched to see if anyone else was going to take a bite. But some already knew about enchiladas and loved them, and others took their cue. Some just took a chance, and before long, even the finicky were cutting up ample bites. And in one remarkable week, over 400 students proved that healthy lives are within everyone's grasp.

CHILI MAC

Although this classic dish had less fat, the kids dug in. "I wish they had this every week," one 13-year-old said. It's also an easy dinner for school nights.

1　pound ground round
½　cup chopped onion
½　cup chopped green bell pepper
3　garlic cloves, minced
2　cups cooked elbow macaroni
　　(about 4 ounces uncooked)
½　cup water
1　tablespoon chili powder
1　teaspoon ground cumin
¼　teaspoon black pepper
1　(14.5-ounce) can whole
　　tomatoes, undrained and
　　chopped
1　(15-ounce) can kidney beans,
　　drained
1　(8¾-ounce) can whole-kernel
　　corn, drained
1　(8-ounce) can tomato sauce
1　(6-ounce) can tomato paste
1　cup (4 ounces) shredded sharp
　　Cheddar cheese

1. Cook first 4 ingredients in a large Dutch oven over medium-high heat until browned, stirring to crumble beef. Drain well; wipe drippings from pan with paper towels. Return beef mixture to pan; stir in macaroni and next 9 ingredients. Bring to a boil; cover, reduce heat, and simmer 20 minutes, stirring occasionally. Spoon onto 8 plates; top with cheese. Yield: 8 servings (serving size: 1 cup beef mixture and 2 tablespoons cheese).

CALORIES 295 (28% from fat); FAT 9.2g (sat 4.4g, mono 3g, poly 0.8g); PROTEIN 22.6g; CARB 32.5g; FIBER 4.2g; CHOL 50mg; IRON 4.3mg; SODIUM 529mg; CALC 151mg

COOKIES FOR THE MULTITUDES

There's nothing like a day in a hot school kitchen to make you appreciate all the hard work that goes on daily in thousands of districts nationwide. The scale of preparation alone can become surreal. These are kitchens where sour cream and yogurt come in 5-pound tubs, bulk cheese in 5- to 10-pound loaves, and Parmesan cheese by the gallon. Each can of beans or tomatoes holds about 7 pounds. Recipes, as you might imagine, acquire a Godzilla-like character that makes dinner preparation for even a large family seem a breeze. Want to make Anzac Biscuits for over 400 kids? Here's what we used:

20　cups all-purpose flour
20　cups oats
20　cups packed brown sugar
10　cups sweetened coconut
3　tablespoons baking soda
3¾　cups water
5　cups stick margarine
2½　cups corn syrup

The larger quantities, of course, have a big effect on preparation. Even using a big Hobart mixer, we had to make the dough in three batches instead of one. And it took three of us to drop the cookies—all 480 of them—onto the baking sheets. To do it, we used one-tablespoon ice-cream scoops, frequently dipped in hot water.

ANZAC BISCUITS

These Australian cookies ("biscuits" down under) were a hit at Center Street.

1　cup all-purpose flour
1　cup regular oats
1　cup packed brown sugar
½　cup shredded sweetened
　　coconut
½　teaspoon baking soda
3　tablespoons water
¼　cup stick margarine or butter,
　　melted

2 tablespoons golden cane syrup (such as Lyle's) or light-colored corn syrup
Cooking spray

1. Preheat oven to 325°.
2. Lightly spoon flour into a dry measuring cup; level with a knife. Combine flour, oats, brown sugar, coconut, and baking soda in a medium bowl. Add water, melted margarine, and syrup; stir well.
3. Drop dough by level tablespoons 2 inches apart onto baking sheets coated with cooking spray. Bake at 325° for 12 minutes or until almost set. Remove from oven; let cookies stand on pans 2 to 3 minutes or until firm. Remove cookies from pans; cool completely on wire racks. Yield: 2 dozen (serving size: 1 cookie).
Note: We found these cookies were much better when made with golden cane syrup. Cane syrup is thicker and sweeter than corn syrup and can be found in supermarkets, in cans, next to the jellies and syrups or in stores specializing in Caribbean and Creole cookery.

CALORIES 98 (27% from fat); FAT 2.9g (sat 1g, mono 0.9g, poly 0.7g); PROTEIN 1.2g; CARB 17.3g; FIBER 0.6g; CHOL 0mg; IRON 0.6mg; SODIUM 59mg; CALC 11mg

SWEET BARBECUE CHICKEN

1 cup packed brown sugar
1 cup bottled barbecue sauce
2 teaspoons dried thyme
1 teaspoon chili powder
1 teaspoon ground red pepper
1 (6-ounce) can apple juice concentrate, thawed and undiluted
12 small chicken leg quarters (about 5¼ pounds), skinned
¾ teaspoon salt
½ teaspoon black pepper
Cooking spray

1. Combine first 6 ingredients in a saucepan. Cook over medium heat 5 minutes or until thoroughly heated, stirring occasionally.
2. Prepare grill or broiler. Sprinkle chicken with salt and pepper. Place on a grill rack or broiler pan coated with cooking spray. Cook 10 minutes on each side. Brush chicken with sauce, and cook an additional 15 minutes or until chicken is done, turning and basting frequently. Yield: 12 servings (serving size: 1 chicken leg quarter).

CALORIES 212 (29% from fat); FAT 6.9g (sat 1.8g, mono 2.4g, poly 1.6g); PROTEIN 18.9g; CARB 17.7g; FIBER 0.3g; CHOL 62mg; IRON 1.7mg; SODIUM 378mg; CALC 30mg

STOVETOP "BAKED BEANS"

1 tablespoon stick margarine or butter
1¼ cups chopped onion
¾ cup chopped green bell pepper
2 garlic cloves, minced
1 cup reduced-calorie ketchup
¼ cup packed brown sugar
¼ cup maple syrup
2 tablespoons Worcestershire sauce
2 teaspoons barbecue smoked seasoning (such as Hickory Liquid Smoke)
2 teaspoons prepared mustard
1 (16-ounce) can red beans, drained
1 (15.8-ounce) can Great Northern beans, drained

1. Melt margarine in a medium saucepan over medium-high heat. Add onion, bell pepper, and garlic; sauté 4 minutes. Stir in ketchup and remaining ingredients; bring to a boil. Reduce heat; simmer 15 minutes, stirring occasionally. Yield: 8 servings (serving size: ½ cup).

CALORIES 179 (10% from fat); FAT 1.9g (sat 0.4g, mono 0.7g, poly 0.7g); PROTEIN 6g; CARB 34.6g; FIBER 3.8g; CHOL 0mg; IRON 2mg; SODIUM 331mg; CALC 53mg

---

WHAT'S FOR LUNCH?

School menus are usually planned many months in advance and rely heavily on district-wide supply considerations, including availability of government commodities such as cheese, beans, etc. We worked with some existing menus, trying to use as many of the regular ingredients and staples as possible, augmented by our own recipes reconfigured for mass servings. When feasible, we did modify some of the regular school items to make them lower in fat: The Spanish rice was prepared with no added fat and with the addition of black beans and garlic powder. Green beans were cooked with no added fat, and corn muffins were served with no butter. The week's menu (recipes with an * are provided):

Monday	Tuesday	Wednesday	Thursday	Friday
• Chili Mac*	• Sweet Barbecue Chicken*	• Turkey Enchiladas*	• Low-fat pizza	• Cheese-Stuffed Potatoes*
• Green beans	• Stovetop "Baked Beans"*	• Spanish rice	• Spinach-Ham Dip* with fresh vegetables	• Garden Salad with Creamy Lemon Dressing*
• Corn muffins	• Coleslaw	• Fresh tomatoes	• Cantaloupe or honeydew wedges	• Rolls
• Apples or grapes	• Rolls	• Frozen-fruit juice bars	• Double-Chocolate Cupcakes*	• Fruit Chunks with Creamy Marshmallow Dip*
• Anzac Biscuits*	• Strawberry Jell-O with bananas	• 2% reduced-fat milk	• 2% reduced-fat milk	• 2% reduced-fat milk
• 2% reduced-fat milk	• 2% reduced-fat milk			

Turkey Enchiladas

Mexican food is always popular, even with teachers, and the turkey was a tasty substitute for chicken.

Cooking spray
¾ cup chopped green bell pepper
½ cup chopped onion
¼ cup all-purpose flour
¾ teaspoon ground coriander
Dash of black pepper
2½ cups chicken broth
1 cup (4 ounces) shredded Cheddar cheese
1 cup fat-free sour cream
3 cups chopped cooked turkey or chicken (about 1½ pounds)
¼ cup bottled salsa
6 (6-inch) flour tortillas

1. Preheat oven to 350°.
2. Place a medium saucepan coated with cooking spray over medium heat until hot; add bell pepper and onion. Sauté 3 minutes or until tender.
3. Lightly spoon flour into a dry measuring cup; level with a knife. Combine flour, coriander, and black pepper in a medium bowl; gradually add broth, stirring with a whisk until well-blended. Add to saucepan; bring to a boil, and cook 3 minutes or until thick, stirring frequently. Remove from heat; stir in cheese and sour cream. Combine 1 cup cheese mixture, turkey, and salsa in a bowl.
4. Spread ½ cup turkey mixture down center of each tortilla; roll up. Place in a 13 x 9-inch baking dish coated with cooking spray. Pour remaining cheese mixture over tortillas. Bake at 350° for 20 minutes or until bubbly. Yield: 6 servings (serving size: 1 enchilada).

CALORIES 448 (28% from fat); FAT 14.1g (sat 6.1g, mono 4.1g, poly 2.7g); PROTEIN 46.7g; CARB 29.5g; FIBER 2g; CHOL 115mg; IRON 4.3mg; SODIUM 738mg; CALC 220mg

Spinach-Ham Dip

To get the students to take the dip, we told them it was "like Ranch dressing." They liked it—even when they discovered the spinach. Serve it warm or cold with raw vegetables and breadsticks.

½ cup fat-free sour cream
1 (8-ounce) block ⅓-less-fat cream cheese (Neufchâtel), softened
1 (8-ounce) carton plain fat-free yogurt
½ teaspoon garlic powder
1¼ cups diced ham (about 6 ounces)
1 (10-ounce) package frozen chopped spinach, thawed, drained, and squeezed dry
1 (2-ounce) jar diced pimento, drained
2 tablespoons grated Parmesan cheese

1. Preheat oven to 375°.
2. Combine first 4 ingredients in a bowl; beat at medium speed of a mixer until smooth. Stir in ham, spinach, and pimento. Spoon mixture into a 1-quart baking dish, and sprinkle with Parmesan cheese. Bake at 375° for 30 minutes or until thoroughly heated. Yield: 3¾ cups (serving size: ¼ cup).

CALORIES 82 (55% from fat); FAT 5g (sat 2.8g, mono 1.6g, poly 0.2g); PROTEIN 5.8g; CARB 3.4g; FIBER 0.6g; CHOL 18mg; IRON 0.6mg; SODIUM 254mg; CALC 72mg

Double-Chocolate Cupcakes

The school kitchen staff was used to making boxed sheet cakes, so these cupcakes were an easy alternative. The students loved them—even low-fat chocolate is still chocolate.

1 (18.25-ounce) package light devil's food cake mix
1 cup water
3 large eggs
Cooking spray
¼ cup semisweet chocolate chips
¼ cup fat-free milk
3 tablespoons unsweetened cocoa
2 cups sifted powdered sugar
2 teaspoons vanilla extract
2 tablespoons powdered sugar

1. Preheat oven to 350°.
2. Combine cake mix, water, and eggs in a bowl; beat at medium speed of a mixer 2 minutes.
3. Divide batter evenly among 24 muffin cups coated with cooking spray. Bake at 350° for 20 minutes or until a wooden pick inserted in center comes out clean. Cool 10 minutes; remove from pans, and cool on a wire rack.
4. Split each cupcake in half horizontally using string or a serrated knife.
5. Combine chocolate chips, milk, and cocoa in the top of a double boiler. Cook over simmering water until chocolate melts, stirring occasionally. Remove from heat; stir in 2 cups powdered sugar and vanilla. Spread 2 teaspoons chocolate mixture over bottom half of each cupcake; top with top halves. Sift 2 tablespoons powdered sugar evenly over tops of cupcakes. Yield: 2 dozen (serving size: 1 cupcake).

CALORIES 155 (17% from fat); FAT 2.9g (sat 1.1g, mono 1g, poly 0.1g); PROTEIN 2.1g; CARB 30.2g; FIBER 0g; CHOL 27mg; IRON 0.3mg; SODIUM 175mg; CALC 8mg

CHEESE-STUFFED POTATOES

This recipe is a good way to keep an inexpensive staple on the lunch menu in a different form. Our message was that potatoes don't have to be French-fried to win over adolescent appetites.

> 6 medium baking potatoes (about 2½ pounds)
> ¾ cup plus 2 tablespoons (3½ ounces) shredded sharp Cheddar cheese
> 1½ cups fat-free sour cream
> ⅓ cup finely chopped green onions
> ¼ teaspoon salt
> Paprika

1. Preheat oven to 400°.
2. Bake potatoes at 400° for 1 hour or until done; cool slightly. Cut each potato open; carefully scoop pulp into a bowl, leaving shells intact. Add cheese and sour cream to pulp, and mash; stir in onions and salt.
3. Increase oven temperature to 450°. Stuff shells with potato mixture, and sprinkle with paprika. Place on a baking sheet; bake at 450° for 15 minutes or until thoroughly heated. Yield: 6 servings.

Microwave Directions: Pierce potatoes with a fork, and arrange in a circle on paper towels in microwave oven. Microwave at HIGH 16 minutes or until done, turning and rearranging potatoes halfway through cooking time. Let stand 5 minutes. Stuff potatoes as directed above, and microwave at HIGH 5 minutes or until thoroughly heated.

CALORIES 314 (16% from fat); FAT 5.7g (sat 3.5g, mono 1.6g, poly 0.2g); PROTEIN 12.4g; CARB 52.3g; FIBER 3.5g; CHOL 17mg; IRON 2.8mg; SODIUM 256mg; CALC 142mg

GARDEN SALAD WITH CREAMY LEMON DRESSING

One of our most pleasant surprises was seeing how much the students enjoyed this salad.

> 7 cups torn romaine lettuce
> ⅔ cup thinly sliced seeded peeled cucumber
> ½ cup thinly sliced carrot
> ⅓ cup sliced green onions
> 6 cherry tomatoes, halved
> ½ cup fat-free sour cream
> 2 tablespoons grated Parmesan cheese
> 1½ tablespoons lemon juice
> 1½ teaspoons water
> 1½ teaspoons vegetable oil
> ¼ teaspoon salt
> ⅛ teaspoon black pepper

1. Combine first 5 ingredients in a large bowl. Combine sour cream and remaining 6 ingredients in a small bowl; stir well with a whisk. Spoon dressing over salad, tossing gently to coat. Yield: 4 servings (serving size: 2 cups).

CALORIES 80 (32% from fat); FAT 2.8g (sat 0.8g, mono 0.8g, poly 1g); PROTEIN 5.3g; CARB 8.7g; FIBER 2.7g; CHOL 2mg; IRON 1.5mg; SODIUM 230mg; CALC 86mg

FRUIT CHUNKS WITH CREAMY MARSHMALLOW DIP

The gooey marshmallow dip made the fresh fruit much more tempting.

> 1 (8-ounce) can unsweetened pineapple chunks
> 2 unpeeled apples, cored and cut into 16 (1-inch) pieces
> 16 tangerine sections (about 2 tangerines)
> 16 seedless green grapes
> 8 fresh strawberries, cut in half lengthwise
> Creamy Marshmallow Dip

1. Drain pineapple chunks in a sieve over a bowl, reserving juice. Set aside 16 pineapple chunks and ¼ cup juice, reserving remaining pineapple and juice for another use. Place ¼ cup pineapple juice in a large bowl, and stir in 16 pineapple chunks, apple pieces, tangerine sections, grapes, and strawberry halves. Chill. Spoon fruit evenly into 8 small bowls; top each with 2 tablespoons Creamy Marshmallow Dip. Yield: 8 servings.

CALORIES 123 (20% from fat); FAT 2.8g (sat 1.6g, mono 0.1g, poly 0.2g); PROTEIN 2.4g; CARB 23.2g; FIBER 2.1g; CHOL 9mg; IRON 0.3mg; SODIUM 90mg; CALC 52mg

Creamy Marshmallow Dip:

> ½ cup tub-style light cream cheese
> ½ cup strawberry low-fat yogurt
> ¼ cup marshmallow creme

1. Combine all ingredients in a medium bowl; beat at low speed of a mixer until well-blended. Cover and chill 2 hours. Yield: 1 cup.

Happy Trails

Move over, gorp. Today there's no limit to how much flavor you can stuff into a backpack.

Trail mix and gorp have given way to portable, power-packed treats such as Banana-Nut Energy Bars, Thai Chicken Roll-Ups, and Sun-Dried Tomato-Parmesan Scones.

A well-prepared snack is a pick-me up in more ways than one. When the meal is aesthetically pleasing, it turns roughing it into something that's not as rough anymore, whether you're backpacking or just out hiking for the day. It enhances the entire experience.

It's also nice to know that traveling first-class doesn't take much extra effort. You can assemble a balanced, backpackable minimeal in the time it takes your hiking socks to finish drying in the dryer.

THAI CHICKEN ROLL-UPS

If you plan on staying outside for longer than two hours, store a blue chill pack along with these roll-ups to keep the filling at a safe temperature.

    2 tablespoons lime juice
    2 tablespoons light mayonnaise
    1 tablespoon reduced-fat peanut
       butter
    ½ teaspoon ground ginger
    ⅛ teaspoon ground red pepper
    1 garlic clove, crushed
    4 (10-inch) flour tortillas
    ½ cup chopped fresh basil
    4 large napa (Chinese) cabbage
       leaves
    6 ounces thinly sliced deli-roasted
       chicken or turkey breast
    1 cup red bell pepper strips

1. Combine first 6 ingredients in a bowl; stir well with a whisk.
2. Spread each tortilla with 1 tablespoon mayonnaise mixture. Top each tortilla with 2 tablespoons chopped basil, 1 cabbage leaf, one-fourth of sliced chicken breast, and ¼ cup bell pepper; roll up. Wrap roll-ups in plastic wrap, and chill thoroughly. Yield: 4 servings.

CALORIES 319 (29% from fat); FAT 10.3g (sat 1.8g, mono 3.9g, poly 4g); PROTEIN 15.9g; CARB 39.8g; FIBER 2.4g; CHOL 2mg; IRON 2.8mg; SODIUM 763mg; CALC 98mg

SUN-DRIED TOMATO-PARMESAN SCONES

    ½ cup boiling water
    2 tablespoons sun-dried tomato
       sprinkles
    2 cups all-purpose flour
    ½ cup grated Parmesan cheese
    2 tablespoons sugar
    1 teaspoon baking powder
    ¾ teaspoon dried oregano
    ½ teaspoon baking soda
    ½ teaspoon salt
    ¾ cup low-fat buttermilk
    2 tablespoons olive oil
    2 large egg whites
Cooking spray

1. Combine boiling water and tomato sprinkles in a bowl; let stand 30 minutes. Drain.
2. Preheat oven to 400°.
3. Lightly spoon flour into dry measuring cups, and level with a knife. Combine flour and next 6 ingredients in a bowl. Combine tomato sprinkles, buttermilk, oil, and egg whites in a bowl. Add tomato mixture to flour mixture, stirring just until moist (dough will be sticky).
4. Turn dough out onto a lightly floured surface; knead lightly 4 times with floured hands. Pat dough into an 8-inch circle on a baking sheet coated with cooking spray. Cut dough into 12 wedges, cutting into, but not through, dough. Bake at 400° for 18 minutes or until golden. Yield: 12 scones.

CALORIES 135 (25% from fat); FAT 3.8g (sat 1.1g, mono 2.1g, poly 0.3g); PROTEIN 4.9g; CARB 20.1g; FIBER 0.6g; CHOL 3mg; IRON 1.1mg; SODIUM 299mg; CALC 94mg

BELL PEPPER-WHITE BEAN SALAD

Give this salad ample time to chill.

    4 cups cooked penne (about 8
       ounces uncooked tube-shaped
       pasta)
    ¾ cup (½-inch) cubed ham (about
       5 ounces)
    ½ cup (2-inch) julienne-cut red bell
       pepper
    ½ cup (2-inch) julienne-cut green
       bell pepper
    ¼ cup (1 ounce) grated Asiago or
       Parmesan cheese
    2 tablespoons diced kalamata
       olives
    2 tablespoons chopped fresh
       parsley
    1 (16-ounce) can cannellini beans
       or other white beans, rinsed
       and drained
    ¼ cup red wine vinegar
    2 tablespoons spicy brown
       mustard
    1 tablespoon olive oil
    ¼ teaspoon freshly ground black
       pepper

1. Combine first 8 ingredients in a large bowl. Combine vinegar and remaining 3 ingredients in a small bowl; stir well with a whisk. Stir into pasta mixture; cover and chill. Yield: 8 servings (serving size: 1 cup).

CALORIES 234 (25% from fat); FAT 6.4g (sat 1.7g, mono 2.3g, poly 1.8g); PROTEIN 11.4g; CARB 32.9g; FIBER 2.3g; CHOL 14mg; IRON 2.6mg; SODIUM 420mg; CALC 71mg

GLACIER PEAKS GRANOLA

This is not only a great snack on the trail, but also a jump-start breakfast when served with milk or yogurt.

    3 cups regular oats
    2 cups sweetened puffed-wheat
       cereal (such as Kellogg's
       Smacks)
    ½ cup wheat bran
    2 tablespoons slivered almonds
    ½ cup applesauce
    ⅓ cup honey
    1 tablespoon vegetable oil
    ½ teaspoon ground cinnamon
    ¼ teaspoon ground ginger
    ½ cup chopped dried apricots
    ½ cup sweetened dried cranberries
       (such as Craisins)

1. Preheat oven to 375°.
2. Combine first 4 ingredients in a large bowl. Combine applesauce and next 4 ingredients in a small saucepan; cook over medium heat 2 minutes or until honey is melted, stirring occasionally. Pour applesauce mixture over oat mixture, stirring to coat. Place mixture in a jelly-roll pan, and bake at 375° for 20 minutes. Gently stir granola, and bake an additional 15 minutes or until dry. Cool; stir in apricots and cranberries. Store in an airtight container. Yield: 7 cups (serving size: ½ cup).

CALORIES 159 (16% from fat); FAT 2.8g (sat 0.4g, mono 0.9g, poly 1g); PROTEIN 3.9g; CARB 32.1g; FIBER 3.5g; CHOL 0mg; IRON 1.8mg; SODIUM 15mg; CALC 20mg

BANANA-NUT ENERGY BARS

½ cup mashed ripe banana
⅓ cup packed brown sugar
¼ cup honey
1 tablespoon vegetable oil
½ teaspoon vanilla extract
1 large egg
½ cup all-purpose flour
1¼ cups multigrain hot cereal (such as Quaker) or quick-cooking oats
¼ cup chopped pecans
½ teaspoon salt
Cooking spray

1. Preheat oven to 350°.
2. Beat first 6 ingredients at medium speed of a mixer until blended. Lightly spoon flour into a dry measuring cup; level with a knife. Gradually add flour, cereal, pecans, and salt to banana mixture; stir until well-blended. Spoon into an 8-inch square baking pan coated with cooking spray. Bake at 350° for 25 minutes. Cool completely on a wire rack. Yield: 12 servings (serving size: 1 bar).

CALORIES 133 (24% from fat); FAT 3.6g (sat 0.5g, mono 1.7g, poly 1.1g); PROTEIN 2.4g; CARB 24.4g; FIBER 1.6g; CHOL 18mg; IRON 0.8mg; SODIUM 106mg; CALC 10mg

Kids Eat the Darndest Things

When your children go trick-or-treating, you know they'll come back loaded with junk food. But there's a seasonably sneaky way to handle those Halloween appetites.

If you want your children to have fun gathering but not gobbling all those Halloween goodies, serve a devilishly delicious dinner *before* the trick-or-treat hour. The menu should include dishes adults enjoy, but that children like, too—so much so that they will waddle out the door so healthfully plumped that they'll have no room for the impending temptations.

MENU

BARBECUE PIZZA BITES

CREAMY BACON DIP

CHICKEN CASSOULET WITH ACORN SQUASH

HALLOWEEN GREEN BEAN SALAD

APPLE 'N SPICE CAKE WITH CARAMEL GLAZE

CANDY APPLE PUNCH

BARBECUE PIZZA BITES

½ pound ground round
½ cup chopped onion
½ cup chopped carrot
⅓ cup barbecue sauce
3 tablespoons brown sugar
¼ teaspoon salt
Dash of black pepper
4 (4-ounce) Italian pizza crusts (such as Boboli)
¼ cup (1 ounce) finely shredded provolone or part-skim mozzarella cheese
2 tablespoons chopped fresh cilantro

1. Preheat oven to 450°.
2. Cook first 3 ingredients in a large nonstick skillet over medium-high heat until browned, stirring to crumble meat. Drain well; return meat mixture to pan. Stir in barbecue sauce and next 3 ingredients; reduce heat, and simmer 5 minutes.
3. Place pizza crusts on a baking sheet. Divide beef mixture evenly among crusts, and sprinkle with cheese. Bake at 450° for 12 minutes or until cheese melts. Sprinkle with cilantro. Cut each pizza into 4 wedges. Yield: 16 servings (serving size: 1 wedge).

CALORIES 78 (25% from fat); FAT 2.2g (sat 0.9g, mono 0.8g, poly 0.3g); PROTEIN 5.2g; CARB 9.2g; FIBER 0.5g; CHOL 10mg; IRON 0.8mg; SODIUM 178mg; CALC 57mg

---

CREAMY BACON DIP

2 (8-ounce) cartons plain fat-free yogurt
6 tablespoons light mayonnaise
¼ cup minced green onions
¼ cup reduced-fat real bacon pieces (such as Hormel)
¼ teaspoon paprika
8 drops hot sauce
2 garlic cloves, crushed
4 ounces low-fat baked tortilla chips (about 24 chips)

1. Spoon yogurt onto several layers of heavy-duty paper towels, spreading to ½-inch thickness. Cover with additional paper towels; let stand 5 minutes. Scrape into a bowl using a rubber spatula. Stir in mayonnaise and next 5 ingredients. Cover and chill. Serve with tortilla chips. Yield: 8 servings (serving size: 3 tablespoons dip and about 3 chips).

CALORIES 132 (30% from fat); FAT 4.4g (sat 0.5g, mono 1.4g, poly 1.5g); PROTEIN 6.5g; CARB 17.5g; FIBER 1.1g; CHOL 10mg; IRON 0.1mg; SODIUM 287mg; CALC 116mg

---

CHICKEN CASSOULET WITH ACORN SQUASH

1 tablespoon stick margarine or butter
2 cups chopped onion, divided
2 garlic cloves, minced
½ cup dry Marsala wine or apple cider
2 tablespoons chopped fresh parsley
¾ teaspoon dried thyme, divided
¾ teaspoon black pepper, divided
½ teaspoon salt, divided
½ teaspoon dried basil
1 (14.5-ounce) can diced tomatoes with basil, garlic, and oregano
2 cups water
2 cups diced peeled acorn squash
1 cup diced carrot
2 (15-ounce) cans Great Northern beans, drained
1 pound skinned, boned chicken breasts
2 bacon slices
½ pound smoked turkey sausage, cut into ¼-inch slices

Continued

1. Melt margarine in a large ovenproof Dutch oven over medium heat. Add 1 cup onion and garlic; sauté 5 minutes. Add Marsala, parsley, ¼ teaspoon thyme, ¼ teaspoon pepper, ¼ teaspoon salt, basil, and tomatoes; bring to a boil. Reduce heat; simmer, covered, 10 minutes. Spoon into a bowl; set aside.

2. Combine remaining ¼ teaspoon salt, 2 cups water, squash, and carrot in Dutch oven; bring to a boil. Reduce heat, and simmer, partially covered, 30 minutes or until vegetables are tender. Partially mash beans with a potato masher; add beans and tomato mixture to pan. Cook over medium-low heat 30 minutes or until thick. Remove from heat.

3. Preheat oven to 325°.

4. Rub chicken with remaining ½ teaspoon thyme and ½ teaspoon pepper; set aside. Cook bacon in a large non-stick skillet over medium-high heat until crisp. Remove bacon from skillet; crumble bacon, and set aside. Add chicken to bacon drippings in skillet; cook 3 minutes on each side or until browned. Remove chicken from skillet; cut into 1-inch pieces. Add 1 cup onion and sausage to skillet; sauté 5 minutes or until lightly browned. Add chicken, crumbled bacon, and sausage mixture to bean mixture in Dutch oven, stirring to combine.

5. Cover and bake at 325° for 1 hour. Uncover and bake an additional 30 minutes. Yield: 8 servings (serving size: 1½ cups).

Note: The squash and bean mixture (steps 1 and 2) can be prepared a day ahead of time; cover and refrigerate.

CALORIES 261 (21% from fat); FAT 6.1g (sat 2.2g, mono 1.9g, poly 1.3g); PROTEIN 25g; CARB 27.8g; FIBER 4.5g; CHOL 50mg; IRON 6mg; SODIUM 817mg; CALC 108mg

HALLOWEEN GREEN BEAN SALAD

Vinaigrette:

- ¼ cup orange juice
- ¼ cup white wine vinegar
- 2 tablespoons water
- 2 teaspoons vegetable oil
- 1 teaspoon prepared horseradish
- 1 teaspoon honey
- 1 teaspoon Dijon mustard
- ¼ teaspoon black pepper

Salad:

- 1½ pounds green beans, trimmed
- 1 cup vertically sliced red onion
- 1 cup peeled orange slices
- 1 cup seedless red grapes, halved

1. To prepare vinaigrette, combine first 8 ingredients in a jar; cover tightly, and shake vigorously. Chill.

2. To prepare salad, steam green beans, covered, 3 minutes or until tender; chill. Combine green beans and next 3 ingredients in a large bowl. Drizzle vinaigrette over salad, tossing gently to coat. Yield: 8 servings (serving size: 1 cup).

CALORIES 68 (19% from fat); FAT 1.4g (sat 0.3g, mono 0.4g, poly 0.6g); PROTEIN 2.1g; CARB 13.6g; FIBER 3.2g; CHOL 0mg; IRON 1mg; SODIUM 26mg; CALC 46mg

APPLE 'N SPICE CAKE WITH CARAMEL GLAZE

- 2 cups all-purpose flour
- 1 teaspoon baking soda
- 1 teaspoon ground cinnamon
- ¼ teaspoon ground nutmeg
- ⅛ teaspoon salt
- ½ cup applesauce
- 1 tablespoon vegetable oil
- 2 teaspoons vanilla extract
- 2 large eggs
- 1 cup sugar
- 1 cup golden raisins
- 1 (20-ounce) can light apple pie filling
- Cooking spray
- ¼ cup fat-free caramel-flavored sundae syrup

1. Preheat oven to 325°.

2. Lightly spoon flour into dry measuring cups; level with a knife. Combine flour and next 4 ingredients in a small bowl; set aside. Combine applesauce, oil, and vanilla in a bowl; set aside. Place eggs in a large bowl, and beat at medium speed of a mixer until foamy. Gradually add sugar, beating well. Add flour mixture and applesauce mixture alternately to egg mixture, beginning and ending with flour mixture; beat well after each addition. Fold in raisins and pie filling.

3. Spoon cake batter into a 10-inch tube pan coated with cooking spray. Bake at 325° for 1 hour and 15 minutes or until a wooden pick inserted in center comes out clean. Cool in pan 10 minutes on a wire rack. Remove from pan; cool completely on a wire rack. Drizzle syrup over top of cooled cake. Yield: 12 servings (serving size: 1 wedge).

CALORIES 266 (8% from fat); FAT 2.4g (sat 0.5g, mono 0.7g, poly 0.8g); PROTEIN 3.7g; CARB 65.5g; FIBER 2.1g; CHOL 36mg; IRON 1.5mg; SODIUM 160mg; CALC 40mg

CANDY APPLE PUNCH

For a toddy version, adults can substitute 1 cup rum for 1 cup water.

- 6 cups cranberry-apple drink
- 3 cups water
- 15 hard cinnamon candies
- 1 (6-ounce) can thawed limeade concentrate, undiluted

1. Combine all ingredients in a large pitcher. Cover and chill 8 hours or until candies are dissolved. Pour mixture into a large Dutch oven, and cook over medium heat until thoroughly heated. Yield: 10 servings (serving size: 1 cup).

CALORIES 166 (0% from fat); FAT 0g; PROTEIN 0.2g; CARB 36.7g; FIBER 0g; CHOL 0mg; IRON 0.2mg; SODIUM 4mg; CALC 12mg

The Squash with the Funny Name

Spaghetti squash is a little of each of its names, and it's as fun to cook as it is delicious to eat.

Is spaghetti squash a pasta? No. It's a squash. Winter variety, gourd family. It gets its name because of one weird quirk: Cut it open and cook it, and the insides separate into long, thin wisps that look amazingly like spaghetti.

The spaghetti squash's slightly sweet, slightly nutty flavor adds wonderful nuances to a range of dishes. Strong flavors and robust salsas complement it perfectly. It's also excellent in frittatas and a surprise ingredient in cakes.

SIMPLE BAKED SPAGHETTI SQUASH

This recipe is the base for all the dishes featured in this story.

1 (3-pound) spaghetti squash

1. Preheat oven to 350°.
2. Cut squash in half lengthwise, and discard seeds. Place squash halves, cut sides down, in a 13 x 9-inch baking dish; add water to dish to a depth of ½ inch. Bake at 350° for 45 minutes or until squash is tender when pierced with a fork.
3. Remove squash from dish, and cool. Scrape inside of squash with a fork to remove spaghetti-like strands. Yield: 5 cups (serving size: 1 cup).

CALORIES 45 (8% from fat); FAT 0.4g (sat 0.1g, mono 0g, poly 0.2g); PROTEIN 1g; CARB 10g; FIBER 2g; CHOL 0mg; IRON 0.5mg; SODIUM 28mg; CALC 33mg

Microwave Squash:

Make sure that your baking dish will fit into the microwave before adding the squash and water.

1 (3-pound) spaghetti squash

1. Cut squash in half lengthwise, and discard seeds. Place squash halves, cut sides down, in a baking dish; add ¼ cup water to dish. Cover with heavy-duty plastic wrap; vent. Microwave at HIGH 15 minutes (or about 5 minutes per pound) or until squash is tender when pierced with a fork.

ORANGE-SPICED SALMON WITH SPAGHETTI SQUASH

Five-spice powder, a piquant mixture of ground spices, can be found in the spice section of large supermarkets or Asian markets.

2 tablespoons dark brown sugar
2 teaspoons grated orange rind
1 teaspoon five-spice powder
¼ teaspoon salt
¼ teaspoon black pepper
3 cups cooked spaghetti squash
Cooking spray
4 (6-ounce) salmon fillets, skinned
4 teaspoons Dijon mustard
Parsley sprigs (optional)

1. Preheat oven to 450°.
2. Combine first 5 ingredients in a bowl. Combine 2 tablespoons sugar mixture and squash; toss gently. Arrange squash in an 11 x 7-inch baking dish coated with cooking spray. Arrange salmon on top of squash; brush with mustard. Sprinkle fish with remaining sugar mixture. Bake at 450° for 15 minutes or until fish flakes easily when tested with a fork. Garnish with parsley sprigs, if desired. Yield: 4 servings (serving size: 1 salmon fillet and ½ cup squash).

CALORIES 336 (40% from fat); FAT 14.8g (sat 2.5g, mono 6.8g, poly 3.2g); PROTEIN 35.7g; CARB 13g; FIBER 1.7g; CHOL 111mg; IRON 1.4mg; SODIUM 402mg; CALC 46mg

SPAGHETTI SQUASH-AND-BLACK BEAN SALSA

Scrape the strands out of the cooked squash and chop them coarsely. Serve with your favorite baked tortilla chips.

3 cups coarsely chopped cooked spaghetti squash
1 cup diced plum tomato
¼ cup thinly sliced green onions
¼ cup fresh lime juice
2 tablespoons minced fresh cilantro
1 teaspoon sugar
⅛ teaspoon salt
1 (15-ounce) can black beans, rinsed and drained
1 jalapeño pepper, seeded and finely chopped

1. Combine all ingredients in a large bowl. Cover and chill. Yield: 5 cups (serving size: ¼ cup).

CALORIES 27 (7% from fat); FAT 0.2g (sat 0g, mono 0g, poly 0.1g); PROTEIN 1.3g; CARB 5.4g; FIBER 1g; CHOL 0mg; IRON 0.4mg; SODIUM 52mg; CALC 11mg

❶ *Cut squash in half with a heavy knife, and scrape out seeds.*

❷ *Place halves in a baking dish, and add water before cooking.*

❸ *Bake until tender when pierced with a fork.*

❹ *Scrape out strands of squash using a fork.*

Also known as "vegetable spaghetti," this squash is available year-round, though peak season is early fall through midwinter. Look for hard, smooth squashes that are pale yellow in color. You can expect to get about 5 cups of spaghetti-like strands from a 3-pound squash.

Store raw, cut spaghetti squash in the refrigerator for up to two days; cover with plastic wrap. Store cooked spaghetti-like strands in an airtight container in the refrigerator for up to two days.

SPAGHETTI SQUASH, LEEK, AND POTATO FRITTATA

⅓ cup 1% low-fat milk
2 tablespoons finely chopped fresh or 2 teaspoons dried basil
¼ teaspoon salt
¼ teaspoon black pepper
5 large egg whites, lightly beaten
2 large eggs, lightly beaten
2 cups cooked spaghetti squash
1 teaspoon stick margarine
Cooking spray
2 cups frozen Southern-style hash brown potatoes, thawed
1 cup thinly sliced leek (about 1 large)
¼ cup (1 ounce) shredded Gruyère or Swiss cheese

1. Combine first 6 ingredients in a large bowl; stir in squash.
2. Melt margarine in a large nonstick skillet coated with cooking spray over medium-high heat. Add hash brown potatoes and leek; sauté 7 minutes or until lightly browned. Add egg mixture to skillet. Cover, reduce heat to low, and cook 10 minutes or until center is almost set. Uncover and sprinkle with cheese.
3. Preheat broiler. Wrap handle of skillet with foil, and broil frittata 5 minutes or until cheese melts. Yield: 4 servings.

CALORIES 202 (29% from fat); FAT 6.5g (sat 2.5g, mono 2.2g, poly 1g); PROTEIN 12.1g; CARB 23.7g; FIBER 1.7g; CHOL 119mg; IRON 1.7mg; SODIUM 315mg; CALC 154mg

SPAGHETTI SQUASH-AND-VEGETABLE GRATIN

1 teaspoon olive oil
3 cups diced zucchini
3 cups sliced mushrooms
¾ cup (3 ounces) shredded part-skim mozzarella cheese, divided
¼ cup chopped fresh parsley
½ teaspoon salt
¼ teaspoon black pepper
2 garlic cloves, minced
1 (14.5-ounce) can no-salt-added stewed tomatoes, undrained and chopped
3 cups cooked spaghetti squash
Cooking spray
½ cup fresh breadcrumbs

1. Preheat oven to 450°.
2. Heat oil in a large nonstick skillet over medium-high heat. Add zucchini and mushrooms; sauté 10 minutes. Remove from heat. Add ¼ cup cheese, parsley, and next 4 ingredients.
3. Combine ¼ cup cheese and squash. Arrange squash mixture in a large gratin dish or shallow 1½-quart baking dish coated with cooking spray. Spoon tomato mixture over squash. Combine remaining ¼ cup cheese and breadcrumbs; sprinkle over tomato mixture. Bake at 450° for 15 minutes or until bubbly. Yield: 6 servings (serving size: about 1 cup).

CALORIES 116 (29% from fat); FAT 3.7g (sat 1.7g, mono 1.3g, poly 0.4g); PROTEIN 6.6g; CARB 15.9g; FIBER 2g; CHOL 8mg; IRON 1.7mg; SODIUM 311mg; CALC 148mg

Spaghetti Squash Slaw with Fresh Herbs

Pair with grilled fish or chicken.

2½ cups cooked spaghetti squash
½ cup finely chopped fresh parsley
¼ cup minced red onion
2 tablespoons finely chopped fresh mint
2 tablespoons finely chopped fresh cilantro
1 tablespoon fresh lime juice
2 teaspoons olive oil
1 teaspoon fresh lemon juice
⅛ teaspoon salt
⅛ teaspoon black pepper

1. Combine all ingredients in a bowl; toss with 2 forks. Cover and chill. Yield: 6 servings (serving size: ½ cup).

CALORIES 38 (40% from fat); FAT 1.7g (sat 0.3g, mono 1.1g, poly 0.2g); PROTEIN 0.7g; CARB 5.5g; FIBER 1.3g; CHOL 0mg; IRON 0.6mg; SODIUM 64mg; CALC 24mg

Greek-Style Salad with Spaghetti Squash

The tangy components of traditional Greek salad—feta cheese, kalamata olives, and oregano—are ideal complements to the subtlety of spaghetti squash. Serve with beef, lamb, or chicken.

3 tablespoons red wine vinegar
2 teaspoons extra-virgin olive oil
1 teaspoon dried oregano
¼ teaspoon salt
¼ teaspoon black pepper
2 garlic cloves, minced
3 cups cooked spaghetti squash
2 cups chopped tomato
1 cup diced cucumber
½ cup (2 ounces) crumbled feta cheese
¼ cup diced green bell pepper
¼ cup diced red onion
2 tablespoons chopped pitted kalamata olives
1 (15.5-ounce) can chickpeas (garbanzo beans), drained

1. Combine first 6 ingredients in a bowl; stir well with a whisk.
2. Combine squash and remaining 7 ingredients in a large bowl. Add vinegar mixture; toss well. Cover and chill. Yield: 8 servings (serving size: 1 cup).

CALORIES 125 (30% from fat); FAT 4.1g (sat 1.4g, mono 1.6g, poly 0.8g); PROTEIN 5.3g; CARB 18.2g; FIBER 3.1g; CHOL 6mg; IRON 1.8mg; SODIUM 261mg; CALC 77mg

Spaghetti Squash Cake with Orange-Cream Cheese Glaze

Have any leftover cooked spaghetti squash? Put it to delicious use in this cake.

Cooking spray
⅓ cup granulated sugar
⅓ cup packed brown sugar
¼ cup stick margarine or butter, softened
¼ teaspoon ground ginger
¼ teaspoon ground cinnamon
2 tablespoons 1% low-fat milk
1 teaspoon vanilla extract
1 large egg
1¼ cups all-purpose flour
1 teaspoon baking powder
⅛ teaspoon salt
1 cup chopped cooked spaghetti squash
Orange-Cream Cheese Glaze
1 tablespoon chopped pecans, toasted

1. Preheat oven to 350°.
2. Coat an 8-inch round cake pan with cooking spray, and line bottom of pan with wax paper. Coat wax paper with cooking spray; set pan aside.
3. Beat granulated sugar and next 4 ingredients at medium speed of a mixer until well-blended. Stir in milk, vanilla, and egg; beat at low speed of mixer until well-blended. Lightly spoon flour into dry measuring cups; level with a knife. Combine flour, baking powder, and salt in a large bowl; stir with a whisk. Stir in sugar mixture and squash. Spoon into prepared cake pan, spreading evenly.

4. Bake at 350° for 35 minutes or until a wooden pick inserted in center comes out clean. Cool in pan 5 minutes. Remove from pan; carefully peel off wax paper. Cool completely on a wire rack. Spoon Orange-Cream Cheese Glaze over top of cake. Sprinkle with pecans. Yield: 8 servings.

CALORIES 283 (26% from fat); FAT 8.2g (sat 2g, mono 3.4g, poly 2.2g); PROTEIN 3.6g; CARB 49.3g; FIBER 0.9g; CHOL 31mg; IRON 1.4mg; SODIUM 184mg; CALC 65mg

Orange-Cream Cheese Glaze:

2 tablespoons ⅓-less-fat cream cheese (Neufchâtel)
½ teaspoon grated orange rind
1 cup sifted powdered sugar
2¼ teaspoons 1% low-fat milk

1. Beat cream cheese and orange rind at medium speed of a mixer until well-blended. Add sugar and milk; beat at low speed until well-blended. Yield: about ½ cup.

INSPIRED VEGETARIAN

New Sauce on the Block

Brown sauces are serious business. When you find a great one, keep it for life.

One of the most critical components of many great dishes is a "mother" sauce—the primary foundation from which hundreds of derivations are born. But in cooking vegetarian dishes, it's a challenge to find a rich, full-flavored vegetarian sauce that could substitute for the meat-based brown sauce. Finally, we have it—a versatile brown sauce that works magic in dozens of dishes.

In this version we've browned mushrooms and other vegetables in a saucepan, then added a few seasonings, wine, and soy sauce for a quick reduction. The soy sauce and mushrooms

Continued

supply the smoky flavor that is normally imparted by the meat.

The ingredients for this sauce are readily available, and they allow you to improvise, not waste. Almost any vegetable trimming can be used, except strongly flavored ones such as broccoli, turnip, or cabbage. (They will take away from the delicate essence of the mushrooms.)

Tomato paste is another simple component almost magically transformed. When browned, the acidity drops, and as the paste caramelizes around the onion, carrot, and celery, it takes on an intense, ruddy color.

GARDEN BROWN SAUCE

- 2 tablespoons olive oil
- 1 cup chopped onion
- 1 cup chopped carrot
- 1 cup chopped celery
- 1 cup sliced mushrooms
- 4 garlic cloves, halved
- ¼ cup tomato paste
- ¼ cup all-purpose flour
- 1 cup dry red wine
- 6 cups water
- 2 tablespoons low-sodium soy sauce
- 2 teaspoons black peppercorns
- 1 teaspoon dried thyme
- ½ teaspoon salt
- 3 bay leaves

1. Heat oil in a saucepan over medium-high heat. Add onion and carrot; sauté 15 minutes or until lightly browned. Add celery, mushrooms, and garlic; cook 10 minutes. Add tomato paste, and sauté 10 minutes or until browned. Add flour, and cook 1 minute. Stir in wine, scraping pan to loosen browned bits. Add water and remaining ingredients. Bring to a boil; reduce heat, and simmer 45 minutes. Strain mixture through a sieve into a bowl, reserving stock. Discard solids. Store in an airtight container for up to 1 week, or freeze for up to 3 months. Yield: 4 cups (serving size: 1 cup).

CALORIES 95 (50% from fat); FAT 5.3g (sat 0.7g, mono 3.8g, poly 0.5g); PROTEIN 1.9g; CARB 10.7g; FIBER 1g; CHOL 0mg; IRON 1.7mg; SODIUM 550mg; CALC 19mg

SPICY WHEAT BERRY ENCHILADAS

You can substitute 3 cups cooked brown rice for the cooked wheat berries.

- 1 cup uncooked wheat berries
- 4 cups water
- 2 teaspoons olive oil
- 2 cups chopped onion
- 1 teaspoon dried oregano
- 1 teaspoon chili powder
- ½ teaspoon ground cumin
- 1 jalapeño pepper, seeded and minced
- 2 cups coarsely chopped spinach
- 2 cups Garden Brown Sauce
- ½ cup chopped fresh cilantro
- 1 tablespoon fresh lime juice
- 8 (8-inch) fat-free flour tortillas
- 2 cups bottled salsa, divided
Cooking spray
- 1 cup (4 ounces) shredded reduced-fat Monterey Jack cheese

1. Place wheat berries in a saucepan, and add 4 cups water; bring to a boil. Reduce heat, and simmer 50 minutes or until tender; drain.
2. Preheat oven to 350°.
3. Heat oil in a large nonstick skillet over medium-high heat. Add onion and next 4 ingredients; sauté 2 minutes. Add spinach and next 3 ingredients. Stir in wheat berries (mixture will be thick).
4. Heat tortillas according to package directions. Spoon about ⅔ cup wheat berry mixture down center of each tortilla; roll up. Spread ½ cup salsa in bottom of a 13 x 9-inch baking dish coated with cooking spray. Place tortillas, seam sides down, in dish. Pour 1½ cups salsa over tortillas; top with cheese. Bake at 350° for 30 minutes. Yield: 8 servings.

CALORIES 298 (18% from fat); FAT 6.1g (sat 2g, mono 2.6g, poly 0.5g); PROTEIN 11.5g; CARB 52.1g; FIBER 6.7g; CHOL 9mg; IRON 3.7mg; SODIUM 754mg; CALC 181mg

EGGPLANT CACCIATORE

- 2 teaspoons olive oil
- 1 cup chopped onion
- 1 cup chopped red bell pepper
- 1 cup chopped green bell pepper
- 2 teaspoons dried Italian seasoning
- ¼ teaspoon dried basil
- 3 garlic cloves, minced
- 3 cups Garden Brown Sauce
- 1 (12-ounce) jar marinara sauce
Cooking spray
- 4 cups (1-inch) cubed peeled eggplant (about 1 pound)
- 4 cups hot cooked linguine (about 8 ounces uncooked pasta)
- ½ cup grated Parmesan cheese

1. Heat oil in a medium saucepan over medium-high heat. Add onion and next 5 ingredients; sauté 3 minutes. Add Garden Brown Sauce and marinara sauce. Reduce heat, and simmer 15 minutes, stirring occasionally.
2. Place a large nonstick skillet coated with cooking spray over medium-high heat. Add eggplant, and sauté 5 minutes or until eggplant is lightly browned. Add onion mixture; reduce heat, and simmer 10 minutes. Serve over linguine; sprinkle with cheese. Yield: 4 servings (serving size: 1 cup pasta, 1½ cups sauce, and 2 tablespoons cheese).

CALORIES 480 (29% from fat); FAT 15.3g (sat 4.7g, mono 6.5g, poly 3.2g); PROTEIN 18.2g; CARB 68.2g; FIBER 9.6g; CHOL 14mg; IRON 6.5mg; SODIUM 961mg; CALC 339mg

TOFU MARSALA

- 2 cups Garden Brown Sauce
- ½ cup sweet Marsala wine, divided
- 2 (12.3-ounce) packages extra-firm tofu, drained
- ¼ cup all-purpose flour
- 2 teaspoons olive oil, divided
- 1 tablespoon fresh lemon juice
- ⅓ cup minced green onions
- 2 tablespoons chopped fresh parsley
- 4 cups hot cooked linguine (about 8 ounces uncooked pasta)
Chopped fresh parsley (optional)

1. Combine Garden Brown Sauce and ¼ cup Marsala in a small saucepan; bring to a boil. Remove from heat, and keep warm.

2. Slice tofu lengthwise into 8 (½-inch-thick) steaks. Dredge in flour. Heat 1 teaspoon oil in a large nonstick skillet over medium-high heat. Add half of tofu; sauté 2 minutes on each side or until browned. Remove from pan, and keep warm. Repeat procedure with 1 teaspoon oil and remaining tofu. Stir in ¼ cup Marsala and lemon juice, scraping pan to loosen brown bits. Stir in brown sauce mixture, onions, and 2 tablespoons parsley. Arrange 1 cup pasta on each of 4 plates; top each with 2 tofu steaks and ½ cup sauce. Garnish with additional parsley, if desired. Yield: 4 servings.

CALORIES 433 (29% from fat); FAT 14.1g (sat 2g, mono 5.5g, poly 5.5g); PROTEIN 22.5g; CARB 56.4g; FIBER 5.3g; CHOL 0mg; IRON 12.6mg; SODIUM 294mg; CALC 210mg

ZESTY BEAN GUMBO

Filé powder (ground sassafras leaves used mainly to flavor and thicken gumbo) can be found in the spice section of your grocery store.

    2 teaspoons olive oil
    1 cup diced onion
    1 cup sliced fresh or frozen okra
    1 cup chopped green bell
         pepper
    ½ cup diced celery
    1 teaspoon filé powder
    ½ teaspoon dried thyme
    ½ teaspoon dried crushed red
         pepper
    2 garlic cloves, minced
 1½ cups Garden Brown Sauce
    1 cup tomato juice
    ½ cup frozen whole-kernel corn,
         thawed
    1 (15-ounce) can no-salt-added
         black beans, drained
    1 (14.5-ounce) can whole
         tomatoes, undrained and
         chopped
    ½ cup chopped green onions
    3 cups hot cooked long-grain rice

1. Heat olive oil in a large saucepan over medium-high heat. Add diced onion and next 7 ingredients; sauté 3 minutes. Stir in Garden Brown Sauce and next 4 ingredients; bring to a boil. Reduce heat, and simmer 20 minutes. Stir in green onions. Serve over rice. Yield: 6 servings (serving size: 1 cup gumbo and ½ cup rice).

CALORIES 266 (13% from fat); FAT 3.7g (sat 0.5g, mono 2.2g, poly 0.6g); PROTEIN 8.8g; CARB 51.6g; FIBER 5.1g; CHOL 0mg; IRON 3.9mg; SODIUM 412mg; CALC 89mg

Crunch Time

If you think your old favorite wheat germ peps you up, you won't believe what it does for chicken, coffeecake, and cookies.

Wheat germ. It's much more than just a breakfast accessory for your morning cereal. With a little imagination, you can turn the nutty flavor and crackling texture of this vitamin-rich "heart" of the wheat berry into an ideal addition to many dishes, either savory or sweet.

Wheat germ is milled out of white flour because it contains small amounts of fat that would limit shelf life, but it's a nutritional bonanza. A quarter-cup carries 130 calories, 12 grams of protein, 4 grams of fiber, and no sodium or cholesterol. It offers about a third of the daily requirement for vitamin E, the wunderkind of antioxidant nutrients. Add to this a little folic acid and a lot of trace minerals—zinc, iron, magnesium, manganese, and chromium—and you've got a powerhouse in each bite. And as for that fat—it's mostly unsaturated and decidedly at the low end of the scale at 4 grams per quarter-cup.

Still, if you're yearning to be trendy, consider wheat germ just for the taste. It provides a subtle new twist to meat loaf and gives a textural boost to coffeecake. Need a quick snack? Try sprinkling a little bit onto a peanut butter sandwich, or stir a couple of spoonfuls into your yogurt. But be sure to save a little for the cereal bowl.

CLASSIC MEAT LOAF

    1 (15-ounce) can chunky garlic-
         and-herb tomato sauce,
         divided (such as Hunt's Ready)
    1 pound ground turkey
    ¼ pound ground round
    ⅔ cup toasted wheat germ
    ½ cup minced fresh onion
    2 tablespoons chopped fresh
         parsley
    1 teaspoon dried oregano
    1 teaspoon dried basil
    ½ teaspoon salt
    1 large egg, lightly beaten
 Cooking spray

1. Preheat oven to 350°.
2. Combine 1 cup tomato sauce, turkey, and next 8 ingredients in a large bowl; stir until well-blended. Place turkey mixture in an 8 x 4-inch loaf pan coated with cooking spray. Brush remaining tomato sauce over top. Bake at 350° for 1 hour and 5 minutes. Let stand 10 minutes. Remove meat loaf from pan. Cut into 12 slices. Yield: 6 servings (serving size: 2 slices).

CALORIES 216 (21% from fat); FAT 5.1g (sat 1.5g, mono 1.3g, poly 1.4g); PROTEIN 25.6g; CARB 15.4g; FIBER 2.9g; CHOL 96mg; IRON 3.4mg; SODIUM 494mg; CALC 79mg

SPICY-MUSTARD CHICKEN BREASTS

    ½ cup plain low-fat yogurt
    2 tablespoons spicy brown
         mustard
    ½ cup toasted wheat germ
    ⅛ teaspoon ground red pepper
    ½ teaspoon salt
    4 (4-ounce) skinned, boned
         chicken breast halves
 Cooking spray

1. Preheat oven to 400°.
2. Combine yogurt and mustard in a shallow dish. Combine wheat germ and pepper in a shallow dish. Sprinkle salt over both sides of chicken. Dip chicken in yogurt mixture; dredge in
Continued

wheat germ mixture. Place chicken on a baking sheet coated with cooking spray. Bake at 400° for 20 minutes or until chicken is done. Yield: 4 servings.

CALORIES 203 (17% from fat); FAT 3.9g (sat 0.9g, mono 1g, poly 1.3g); PROTEIN 31.5g; CARB 9.9g; FIBER 2.3g; CHOL 67mg; IRON 1.9mg; SODIUM 490mg; CALC 80mg

CRANBERRY-STREUSEL-CAKE

Cake:

1½ cups all-purpose flour
¼   cup toasted wheat germ
1½ teaspoons baking powder
½   teaspoon baking soda
1   cup fat-free sour cream
½   cup packed brown sugar
⅓   cup applesauce
¼   cup vegetable oil
1   large egg
¾   cup sweetened dried cranberries (such as Craisins)
Cooking spray

Streusel topping:

¼   cup toasted wheat germ
2   tablespoons all-purpose flour
2   tablespoons brown sugar
½   teaspoon ground cinnamon
1   tablespoon chilled stick margarine or butter

1. Preheat oven to 350°.
2. To prepare cake, lightly spoon 1½ cups flour into dry measuring cups; level with a knife. Combine flour and next 3 ingredients in a large bowl. Combine sour cream and next 4 ingredients in a bowl; stir well with a whisk. Add to flour mixture, stirring just until moist. Fold in dried cranberries. Spoon batter into a 9-inch round cake pan coated with cooking spray.
3. To prepare streusel topping, combine ¼ cup wheat germ and next 3 ingredients in a small bowl; cut in margarine with a pastry blender or 2 knives until mixture resembles coarse meal. Sprinkle streusel topping evenly over batter. Bake at 350° for 50 minutes or until a wooden pick inserted in

center comes out clean. Cool cake on a wire rack. Yield: 9 servings (serving size: 1 wedge).

CALORIES 288 (28% from fat); FAT 8.8g (sat 1.7g, mono 2.7g, poly 3.9g); PROTEIN 6.3g; CARB 45.8g; FIBER 2.2g; CHOL 25mg; IRON 2.2mg; SODIUM 198mg; CALC 74mg

GINGER CRINKLES

You can omit the chopped crystallized ginger and increase the ground ginger to 1½ teaspoons.

⅔   cup packed dark brown sugar
⅓   cup stick margarine or butter, softened
¼   cup molasses
1   large egg white
1   tablespoon chopped crystallized ginger
1⅓ cups all-purpose flour
¾   cup toasted wheat germ
2   teaspoons baking soda
1   teaspoon ground ginger
1   teaspoon ground cinnamon
Cooking spray
2   tablespoons granulated sugar

1. Beat brown sugar and margarine at medium speed of a mixer until light and fluffy. Add molasses and egg white; beat well. Stir in crystallized ginger.
2. Lightly spoon flour into dry measuring cups; level with a knife. Combine flour and next 4 ingredients. Stir into molasses mixture. Cover and freeze 20 minutes.
3. Preheat oven to 350°.
4. Lightly coat hands with cooking spray. Shape dough into 30 balls, about 1 tablespoon each. Roll balls in granulated sugar. Place balls 2 inches apart on baking sheets coated with cooking spray. Bake at 350° for 10 minutes. Cool cookies on pans for 3 minutes. Remove from pans, and cool completely on wire racks. Yield: 2½ dozen (serving size: 1 cookie).

CALORIES 79 (26% from fat); FAT 2.3g (sat 0.5g, mono 0.9g, poly 0.8g); PROTEIN 1.4g; CARB 13.5g; FIBER 0.6g; CHOL 0mg; IRON 0.7mg; SODIUM 113mg; CALC 14mg

KEY LIME SQUARES

Crust:

½   cup all-purpose flour
⅓   cup toasted wheat germ
⅓   cup packed brown sugar
¼   cup stick margarine or butter, softened
Cooking spray

Filling:

1   cup granulated sugar
2   tablespoons all-purpose flour
½   teaspoon baking powder
2   tablespoons tub-style light cream cheese
2   large eggs
1   teaspoon grated Key lime rind or lime rind
¼   cup Key lime juice or lime juice
1   cup frozen reduced-calorie whipped topping, thawed

1. Preheat oven to 350°.
2. To prepare crust, lightly spoon ½ cup flour into a dry measuring cup; level with a knife. Combine flour, wheat germ, and brown sugar in a small bowl; cut in margarine with a pastry blender or 2 knives until well-blended. Press mixture into a 9-inch square baking pan coated with cooking spray. Bake at 350° for 15 minutes. Cool on a wire rack.
3. To prepare filling, combine granulated sugar, 2 tablespoons flour, and baking powder in a medium bowl. Add cream cheese and eggs; beat at high speed of a mixer until well-blended. Stir in rind and juice. Spread filling over crust. Bake at 350° for 25 minutes or until filling is set. Cool on a wire rack. Spread whipped topping evenly over filling. Yield: 9 servings (serving size: 1 square).

CALORIES 251 (30% from fat); FAT 8.3g (sat 2.7g, mono 2.7g, poly 2.1g); PROTEIN 3.9g; CARB 41.8g; FIBER 0.9g; CHOL 51mg; IRON 1.1mg; SODIUM 128mg; CALC 43mg

Sense & Sensibility

Stick with us, and learn the power of moderation when it comes to healthy eating. And try this filet mignon.

At the core of the latest upheaval in the world of food is the relationship between health and flavor, and there's a consumer rebellion that considers fat-free, low-calorie, and low-sodium foods just too puritanical and dull-tasting. Whatever else the information overload on our dining habits has produced, the bottom line has always been that if you don't like it, you won't eat it.

The big problem isn't what we're eating, but how much of it. In 1998, the U.S. Department of Agriculture found that although the percentage of fat in American diets "dramatically lowered" in the last three decades (from 45% in 1965 to 34% in 1995), the intake of fat grams stayed the same or went up. How can this be? You can probably guess. "The total caloric intake was increasing," explains the USDA (United States Department of Agriculture), mostly from extra carbohydrates and, to a lesser extent, from alcohol.

Our recommendation? Stay the moderate course. Sense, sensibility. You don't have to give up anything—least of all the pleasures that come with wonderful food. Balance is not about sacrifice; it is about possibilities. Call us optimists, call us idealists, call us romantics. But always call us for dinner.

LOBSTER-AND-CORN RISOTTO

You can substitute 2 cups cooked shrimp for the lobster.

- 5 cups fat-free, less-sodium chicken broth
- 1 tablespoon olive oil
- ½ cup shallots, minced
- 4 garlic cloves, minced
- 1½ cups uncooked Arborio rice or other short-grain rice
- 2 cups cooked lobster meat, coarsely chopped (about 2 [½-pound] tails)
- 1½ cups fresh corn kernels (about 3 ears)
- ⅓ cup chopped fresh basil
- ¼ cup (1 ounce) grated fresh Parmesan cheese
- 3 tablespoons sherry
- ¼ teaspoon black pepper

1. Bring chicken broth to a simmer in a large saucepan (do not boil). Keep warm over low heat.
2. Heat olive oil in a large saucepan over medium-high heat. Add shallots and garlic; sauté 2 minutes. Add rice; sauté 3 minutes or until translucent, stirring constantly. Stir in ½ cup broth, and cook 3 minutes or until liquid is nearly absorbed, stirring constantly. Add remaining broth, ½ cup at a time, stirring constantly; cook until each portion of broth is absorbed before adding the next (about 30 minutes). Add lobster and remaining ingredients; cook 5 minutes or until thoroughly heated. Yield: 5 servings (serving size: about 1½ cups).

CALORIES 390 (12% from fat); FAT 5.1g (sat 1.4g, mono 2.7g, poly 0.7g); PROTEIN 22.3g; CARB 60.5g; FIBER 2.4g; CHOL 45g; IRON 3.2mg; SODIUM 785mg; CALC 105mg

FILET MIGNON WITH PEPPERCORN MUSTARD SAUCE

(pictured on page 263)

- ¼ teaspoon salt
- ¼ teaspoon coarsely ground or cracked black pepper
- 4 (4-ounce) beef tenderloin steaks (1½ inches thick)
- 1 teaspoon vegetable oil
- ⅓ cup minced shallots
- ½ cup cognac
- ½ cup fat-free beef broth
- ¼ cup green peppercorn mustard or Dijon mustard

1. Sprinkle salt and pepper over steaks. Heat oil in a 9-inch cast-iron skillet over medium-high heat until hot. Add steaks; cook 5 minutes on each side or until desired degree of doneness. Remove steaks from skillet; keep warm. Add shallots to skillet; sauté 30 seconds. Add cognac; cook 10 seconds. Add broth and mustard; stir well. Reduce heat; cook 2 minutes, stirring constantly. Serve steaks with sauce. Yield: 4 servings (serving size: 1 steak and 2 tablespoons sauce).

CALORIES 279 (31% from fat); FAT 9.6g (sat 3.5g, mono 3.7g, poly 1g); PROTEIN 24g; CARB 3.8g; FIBER 0.1g; CHOL 70mg; IRON 3.3mg; SODIUM 656mg; CALC 13mg

THREE-PEPPER BEEF ROAST

- 1 tablespoon cracked black pepper
- 1 teaspoon salt
- 1 teaspoon paprika
- ½ teaspoon white pepper
- ½ teaspoon dried oregano
- ½ teaspoon dried thyme
- ⅛ teaspoon ground red pepper
- 1 (3-pound) boned rib-eye roast
- 2 tablespoons low-sodium soy sauce
Cooking spray

1. Preheat oven to 425°.
2. Combine first 7 ingredients.
3. Trim fat from roast. Brush roast with soy sauce, and rub with pepper mixture. Place roast on a broiler pan
Continued

coated with cooking spray. Insert meat thermometer into thickest portion of roast. Bake at 425° for 10 minutes. Reduce oven temperature to 350° (do not remove roast from oven), and bake an additional hour or until thermometer registers 145° (medium-rare) to 160° (medium).

4. Place roast on a serving platter, and cover with foil. Let stand 10 minutes before slicing. Yield: 10 servings (serving size: 3 ounces).

CALORIES 161 (32% from fat); FAT 5.7g (sat 2.1g, mono 2.5g, poly 0.2g); PROTEIN 24.8g; CARB 0.7g; FIBER 0.2g; CHOL 59mg; IRON 2mg; SODIUM 365mg; CALC 10mg

THAI NOODLES WITH PORK AND SCALLOPS

Black bean sauce can be found in specialty food shops or in the Asian sections of many supermarkets. Brown bean sauce or bean sauce also will work.

Bean sauce:

    3 tablespoons black bean sauce
    3 tablespoons hoisin sauce
    1 tablespoon fish sauce
    2 teaspoons brown sugar

Stir-fry:

  1½ teaspoons vegetable oil
    3 cups thinly sliced onion
  1½ teaspoons sesame oil
    2 teaspoons minced peeled fresh
       ginger
    ¼ teaspoon dried crushed red pepper
    2 garlic cloves, minced
    1 cup chopped green onions
    8 ounces boned pork loin, cut
       into ½-inch pieces
    1 pound bay scallops

Remaining ingredients:

    3 cups hot cooked linguine (about
       6 ounces uncooked pasta)
    ¼ cup chopped fresh cilantro
    2 tablespoons finely chopped
       unsalted, dry-roasted peanuts
    2 tablespoons rice wine vinegar

1. To prepare bean sauce, combine first 4 ingredients; set aside.
2. To prepare stir-fry, heat vegetable oil in a large nonstick skillet over medium-high heat. Add sliced onion, and sauté 6 minutes or until golden brown. Remove onion from skillet; keep warm.
3. Heat sesame oil in skillet over medium-high heat. Add ginger, pepper, and garlic; cook 1 minute. Add green onions; sauté 2 minutes or until onions are soft. Add pork; sauté 5 minutes. Add scallops, and sauté 3 minutes or until scallops are done.
4. Return sliced onion to skillet, and stir in bean sauce. Cook 1 minute or until mixture is thoroughly heated. Place pork mixture in a large bowl. Add pasta, and toss well. Stir in cilantro, peanuts, and vinegar. Yield: 6 servings (serving size: 1 cup).

CALORIES 329 (22% from fat); FAT 7.9g (sat 1.7g, mono 2.9g, poly 2.3g); PROTEIN 27g; CARB 37g; FIBER 3.4g; CHOL 48mg; IRON 2.5mg; SODIUM 554mg; CALC 88mg

FONTINA, CARAMELIZED-ONION, AND PANCETTA PIZZA

(pictured on page 261)

This simple thin-crust pizza recipe was developed by Chicago chef John Hogan.

Pizza Dough
    1 teaspoon olive oil
  1½ ounces pancetta (Italian-style
       bacon) or Canadian bacon,
       chopped
    8 cups sliced onion (about 3 large)
    1 tablespoon chopped fresh thyme
    ½ teaspoon salt
    ½ teaspoon white pepper
    1 tablespoon olive oil, divided
    ¾ cup (3 ounces) shredded fontina
       cheese, divided
Thyme sprigs (optional)
Cracked black pepper (optional)

1. Prepare Pizza Dough according to directions.
2. While dough is rising the second time, heat 1 teaspoon olive oil in a large nonstick skillet over medium-high heat; add pancetta, and sauté 2 minutes. Add onion, thyme, salt, and white pepper; cook 25 minutes or until onion is browned, stirring frequently.
3. Preheat oven to 475°.
4. Brush each prepared pizza crust with 1½ teaspoons oil; top each with half of onion mixture. Sprinkle half of cheese over each pizza. Bake at 475° for 9 minutes or until crusts are crisp. Cut each pizza into 8 wedges. Garnish with thyme sprigs, and sprinkle with black pepper, if desired. Yield: 2 (9-inch) pizzas (serving size: 2 slices).

CALORIES 238 (28% from fat); FAT 7.3g (sat 2.7g, mono 3.4g, poly 0.7g); PROTEIN 8.6g; CARB 34.8g; FIBER 3.1g; CHOL 16mg; IRON 2mg; SODIUM 300mg; CALC 87mg

Pizza Dough:

    1 teaspoon sugar
    1 teaspoon dry yeast (about
       ½ package)
    ¾ cup warm water (105° to 115°)
  2¼ cups all-purpose flour, divided
  1½ teaspoons olive oil
    ½ teaspoon salt
Cooking spray

1. Dissolve sugar and yeast in ¾ cup water in a large bowl; let stand 5 minutes. Lightly spoon flour into dry measuring cups; level with a knife. Stir 2 cups flour, oil, and salt into yeast mixture to form a soft dough. Turn dough out onto a lightly floured surface, and knead until smooth and elastic (about 5 minutes), adding enough of remaining flour, 1 tablespoon at a time, to prevent dough from sticking. Place dough in a large bowl coated with cooking spray, turning dough to coat top. Cover dough, and let rise in a warm place (85°), free from drafts, 40 minutes or until doubled in bulk.
2. Punch dough down. Cover and let rise 40 minutes or until doubled in bulk. Divide dough into 2 equal portions; roll each portion into a 9-inch circle on a lightly floured surface. Place dough circles on a large baking sheet coated with cooking spray. Top and bake according to directions. Yield: 2 (9-inch) pizza crusts.

ZESTY TUNA SANDWICH

¾ cup fat-free mayonnaise
2 garlic cloves, crushed
⅓ cup balsamic vinegar
2 tablespoons olive oil
2 tablespoons molasses
1 teaspoon dried Italian seasoning
¼ teaspoon salt
¼ teaspoon black pepper
⅛ teaspoon ground red pepper
3 yellow bell peppers, each seeded
   and cut into 4 wedges
1 pound tuna steaks
Cooking spray
1 (16-ounce) loaf French bread
4 cups spinach leaves

1. Combine mayonnaise and garlic in
a bowl. Cover and chill.
2. Combine vinegar and next 8 ingredients in a large zip-top plastic bag.
Seal bag, and marinate tuna in refrigerator 30 minutes. Remove bell pepper
and tuna from bag, reserving marinade.
3. Prepare grill or broiler. Place bell
pepper and tuna on a grill rack or
broiler pan coated with cooking spray;
cook 4 minutes on each side or until
bell pepper is tender and tuna is
medium-rare or desired degree of
doneness, basting occasionally with reserved marinade. Cut tuna into 1-inch
chunks.
4. Cut bread loaf in half horizontally,
and spread mayonnaise mixture over
cut sides of bread. Arrange spinach,
bell pepper, and tuna over bottom half
of loaf. Top with remaining half. Cut
loaf into 6 pieces. Yield: 6 servings.

CALORIES 431 (21% from fat); FAT 10.2g (sat 2.1g, mono 5.1g,
poly 2.6g); PROTEIN 26g; CARB 56.5g; FIBER 3.9g;
CHOL 31mg; IRON 4.7mg; SODIUM 979mg; CALC 95mg

SALADE NIÇOISE WITH CHICKEN

1 pound red potatoes, thinly
   sliced (about 3 cups)
¼ cup dry white wine
2 cups (2-inch) cut green beans
   (about ½ pound)
¼ cup minced shallots, divided
2 tablespoons Dijon mustard,
   divided
½ teaspoon dried tarragon
4 (4-ounce) skinned, boned
   chicken breast halves
Cooking spray
3 tablespoons white wine vinegar
2 tablespoons olive oil
1 tablespoon anchovy paste
3 garlic cloves, minced
8 cherry tomatoes, halved
1 tablespoon chopped green
   onions

1. Steam sliced potatoes, covered, 15
minutes or until tender; cool slightly.
Combine potatoes and wine in a bowl;
stir gently to coat. Steam green beans,
covered, 6 minutes or until crisp-tender.
Rinse under cold water; drain.
2. Preheat broiler.
3. Combine 2 tablespoons shallots, 1
tablespoon Dijon mustard, and tarragon in a bowl. Add chicken, tossing
well to coat. Place chicken on a broiler
pan coated with cooking spray, and
broil 6 minutes on each side or until
chicken is done. Cool slightly; slice
into ½-inch strips.
4. Combine 2 tablespoons shallots, 1
tablespoon mustard, vinegar, and next
3 ingredients in large bowl. Add potatoes and green beans; toss gently.
5. Spoon 1¼ cups potato mixture
onto each of 4 plates; top each serving
with one-fourth of chicken strips.
Arrange tomatoes on each salad, and
sprinkle with green onions. Yield: 4
servings.

CALORIES 353 (29% from fat); FAT 11.3g (sat 1.9g, mono 6.3g,
poly 1.4g); PROTEIN 31.8g; CARB 27.8g; FIBER 3.9g;
CHOL 72mg; IRON 3.4mg; SODIUM 820mg; CALC 65mg

ESSENCE OF *COOKING LIGHT*

We've said it for 11 years, and we'll
say it again: *Cooking Light* has always
put flavor first. We want our recipes
to be the best you've ever tasted.
Cooking Light has never been about
puritanical codes, punishing diets, or
denial. Nor have nutritionists, doc-
tors, or other health experts, whose
basic advice has been remarkably
steady: balance, variety, moderation.
These three words are the essence of
Cooking Light.

If sometimes you want Death by
Chocolate or Surf 'n Turf, go for it.
Other times you'll have fresh peaches
or a great pasta. You actually can
have filet mignon and eat it, too—or
Strawberry-Chocolate Meringue
Torte. That's our Big Message.

No single food is verboten or magical; each is part of a continuum. If
the continuum is moderate—a powerful concept which simply means
consciously sifting the alternatives—
then you're going to be healthy and
enjoy life.

PEANUT BRITTLE-APPLE CRISP

(pictured on page 263)

½ cup all-purpose flour
¼ cup granulated sugar
¼ cup packed brown sugar
⅛ teaspoon salt
¼ cup chilled stick margarine or
   butter, cut into small pieces
½ cup coarsely broken peanut brittle
   (about 2 ounces)
7 cups peeled sliced Granny Smith
   apple (about 2 pounds)
3 tablespoons orange marmalade
2 cups low-fat vanilla frozen yogurt

1. Preheat oven to 375°.
2. Lightly spoon flour into a dry measuring cup, and level with a knife.
Combine flour, sugars, and salt in a
bowl; cut in margarine with a pastry
blender or 2 knives until mixture
Continued

resembles coarse meal. Add peanut brittle, stirring to combine.

3. Arrange apple in an 8-inch square baking dish; spoon marmalade over apple. Sprinkle flour mixture over marmalade. Bake at 375° for 40 minutes. Serve warm. Top with yogurt. Yield: 8 servings (serving size: ⅓ cup crisp and ¼ cup yogurt).

CALORIES 281 (25% from fat); FAT 7.8g (sat 2g, mono 2.9g, poly 2.4g); PROTEIN 2.9g; CARB 53g; FIBER 3.2g; CHOL 5mg; IRON 0.8mg; SODIUM 131mg; CALC 69mg

STRAWBERRY-CHOCOLATE MERINGUE TORTE

- 4 large egg whites
- ¼ teaspoon salt
- ¼ teaspoon cream of tartar
- 1 cup sugar
- 2 cups sliced strawberries
- 1 teaspoon sugar
- ¼ cup semisweet chocolate chips, divided
- 2 cups frozen reduced-calorie whipped topping, thawed and divided

1. Preheat oven to 250°.
2. Cover a large baking sheet with parchment paper. Draw 2 (8-inch) circles on paper. Turn paper over, and secure with masking tape.
3. Beat egg whites, salt, and cream of tartar at high speed of a mixer until foamy. Gradually add 1 cup sugar, 1 tablespoon at a time, beating until stiff peaks form.
4. Spread half of mixture into each circle on prepared baking sheet using the back of a spoon. Bake at 250° for 1 hour or until meringues are crisp.
5. Sprinkle strawberries with 1 teaspoon sugar; cover and set aside.
6. Sprinkle each meringue with 1½ tablespoons chocolate chips. Return meringues to oven; turn off heat, and let stand 5 minutes. Spread softened chocolate with a spatula. Cool meringues to room temperature.
7. Place 1 meringue on a serving platter; spread 1 cup whipped topping over top. Arrange half of strawberry mixture

over whipped topping. Top with remaining meringue; spread 1 cup whipped topping over top. Arrange remaining strawberry mixture over whipped topping. Place 1 tablespoon chocolate chips in a small microwave-safe bowl. Microwave at HIGH 1 minute or until chips are soft. Stir chocolate; drizzle over top of torte. Yield: 8 servings (serving size: 1 wedge).

CALORIES 184 (22% from fat); FAT 4.4g (sat 3.3g, mono 0.7g, poly 0.1g); PROTEIN 2.6g; CARB 34.7g; FIBER 1g; CHOL 0mg; IRON 0.3mg; SODIUM 112mg; CALC 19mg

Deli at Your Desk

You say you don't have time for a nourishing breakfast at home anymore? OK, how about at the office?

It's morning—you're going crazy. You've taken your shower, glanced at the newspaper, gotten dressed, fed the dog, made a quick call about an upcoming meeting, and raced to work.

In your office, finally, you catch your breath. Everything got done, somehow, but with one exception: breakfast. But where others would head for the snack machine, you smile and stay put. You reach in your briefcase and pull out the little surprise that will help you survive the usual morning maelstrom. Hello, mouth-watering homemade muffin.

Since 1990, the number of people eating breakfast at work or school has doubled, according to The NPD Group, a research firm that tracks consumer eating habits. So great is the phenomenon it's even picked up its own name: deskfast.

This mini meal gives you a healthful and nutritious catch-up that has the feeling of well-earned indulgence. All it takes is a little planning. The ideal deskfast isn't messy or sticky, doesn't require a fork or knife, and can be whipped up a night or two before. Then it's just pulled from the fridge in the morning.

PROSCIUTTO-AND-PROVOLONE-STUFFED FOCACCIA

Wrap individual slices in aluminum foil, and freeze. Pull one slice out in the morning before going to work, and it should thaw by the time you're ready for a break. Or remove slices from foil and reheat on a paper plate in the microwave at MEDIUM (50% power) about 1 minute.

- 1 package dry yeast (about 2¼ teaspoons)
- 1½ cups warm fat-free milk (105° to 115°)
- 3¼ cups bread flour, divided
- 1 cup semolina or pasta flour
- ¼ cup olive oil
- ½ teaspoon salt
  Cooking spray
- 4 ounces thinly sliced provolone cheese, divided
- 4 ounces thinly sliced prosciutto, divided
- ¼ cup minced fresh chives

1. Dissolve yeast in warm milk in a large bowl; let stand 5 minutes. Lightly spoon flours into dry measuring cups; level with a knife. Stir 3 cups bread flour, semolina, oil, and salt into yeast mixture to form a stiff dough. Turn dough out onto a lightly floured surface. Knead dough until smooth and elastic (about 10 minutes), adding enough of remaining bread flour, one tablespoon at a time, to prevent dough from sticking.
2. Place dough in a large bowl coated with cooking spray, turning to coat top. Cover and let rise in a warm place (85°), free from drafts, 45 minutes or until doubled in bulk. Punch dough down; roll into a 15 x 10-inch rectangle on a lightly floured surface. Place on a large baking sheet coated with cooking spray. Place 2 ounces cheese down the center of the short length of dough; top with 2 ounces prosciutto and 2 tablespoons chives. Fold one short end of dough over filling. Place 2 ounces cheese, 2 ounces prosciutto, and 2 tablespoons chives on top of

fold. Fold remaining short end over filling, pressing firmly to eliminate air pockets; pinch seam and ends to seal. Place on a baking sheet coated with cooking spray. Cover and let rise 45 minutes or until doubled in bulk.

3. Preheat oven to 375°.

4. Uncover dough. Bake at 375° for 20 minutes. Remove from baking sheet; cool on a wire rack. Cut loaf crosswise into 10 slices. Yield: 10 servings.

CALORIES 319 (29% from fat); FAT 10.2g (sat 3.8g, mono 5.2g, poly 1g); PROTEIN 14g; CARB 43.2g; FIBER 1.7g; CHOL 14mg; IRON 2.8mg; SODIUM 370mg; CALC 137mg

CARROT-RAISIN QUICK BREAD

1¾ cups all-purpose flour
1 teaspoon baking soda
¾ teaspoon ground cinnamon
¼ teaspoon baking powder
¼ teaspoon salt
¼ teaspoon ground nutmeg
1 cup coarsely shredded carrot
⅔ cup packed brown sugar
½ cup golden raisins
½ cup fat-free milk
3 tablespoons stick margarine or butter, melted
1 large egg, lightly beaten
Cooking spray

1. Preheat oven to 350°.

2. Lightly spoon flour into dry measuring cups; level with a knife. Combine flour and next 5 ingredients in a large bowl. Combine carrot and next 5 ingredients in a small bowl; add to flour mixture, stirring just until flour mixture is moist.

3. Pour batter into an 8-inch loaf pan coated with cooking spray. Bake at 350° for 1 hour and 5 minutes or until a wooden pick inserted in center comes out clean. Cool bread in pan 10 minutes on a wire rack; remove from pan. Cool on wire rack. Yield: 12 servings (serving size: 1 slice).

CALORIES 174 (19% from fat); FAT 3.6g (sat 0.8g, mono 1.5g, poly 1.1g); PROTEIN 3.1g; CARB 32.9g; FIBER 1.2g; CHOL 19mg; IRON 1.4mg; SODIUM 215mg; CALC 42mg

DOUBLE APPLE-WALNUT SCONES

¼ cup apple juice
½ cup dried currants or raisins
½ cup finely chopped dried apple
1 cup low-fat buttermilk
¼ cup sugar
3 tablespoons stick margarine or butter, melted and cooled
2 cups all-purpose flour
¼ cup coarsely chopped walnuts
1 tablespoon baking powder
1 teaspoon baking soda
¼ teaspoon salt
Cooking spray

1. Preheat oven to 350°.

2. Place ¼ cup apple juice in a small microwave-safe bowl; microwave at HIGH 3 minutes or until juice boils. Remove from microwave. Add currants and dried apple; let stand 15 minutes.

3. Combine apple juice mixture, buttermilk, sugar, and margarine in a large bowl. Lightly spoon flour into dry measuring cups; level with a knife. Combine flour and next 4 ingredients; add to buttermilk mixture, stirring just until moist (dough will be sticky). Drop dough into 12 rounds (about ¼ cup each) onto a baking sheet coated with cooking spray. Bake at 350° for 17 minutes or until golden. Cool on a wire rack. Yield: 1 dozen (serving size: 1 scone).

CALORIES 166 (28% from fat); FAT 5.1g (sat 0.7g, mono 1.6g, poly 2g); PROTEIN 3.6g; CARB 27.4g; FIBER 0.9g; CHOL 0mg; IRON 1.3mg; SODIUM 167mg; CALC 81mg

PEANUT BUTTER-AND-HONEY MUFFINS

1¼ cups all-purpose flour
1 cup whole-wheat flour
1 tablespoon baking powder
¾ teaspoon salt
¼ cup packed brown sugar
⅔ cup honey
½ cup creamy peanut butter
1½ cups fat-free milk
2 large egg whites, lightly beaten
1 large egg, lightly beaten
Cooking spray
1 tablespoon granulated sugar

1. Preheat oven to 400°.

2. Lightly spoon flours into dry measuring cups; level with a knife. Combine flours, baking powder, and salt in a bowl; make a well in center of mixture. Combine brown sugar, honey, and peanut butter; stir well with a whisk. Add milk, egg whites, and egg to honey mixture; stir well. Add honey mixture to flour mixture; stir just until moist. Spoon into 16 muffin cups coated with cooking spray. Sprinkle sugar evenly over tops. Bake at 400° for 18 minutes or until muffins spring back when touched lightly in center. Remove from pans immediately; place on a wire rack. Yield: 16 muffins (serving size: 1 muffin).

CALORIES 180 (24% from fat); FAT 4.7g (sat 0.9g, mono 2.2g, poly 1.4g); PROTEIN 5.9g; CARB 30.6g; FIBER 1.7g; CHOL 14mg; IRON 1.1mg; SODIUM 174mg; CALC 74mg

ORANGE-PECAN MUFFINS

2 cups all-purpose flour
½ cup sugar
2 teaspoons baking powder
¼ teaspoon salt
¼ cup chopped pecans, toasted
1 large egg
2 tablespoons thawed orange juice concentrate
1 teaspoon grated orange rind
¾ cup fat-free milk
3 tablespoons stick margarine or butter, melted
Cooking spray

Continued

1. Preheat oven to 400°.

2. Lightly spoon flour into dry measuring cups; level with a knife. Combine flour and next 3 ingredients in a large bowl. Stir in pecans; make a well in center of mixture. Combine egg and next 4 ingredients; stir well with a whisk. Add to flour mixture, stirring just until moist.

3. Spoon batter into 12 muffin cups coated with cooking spray. Bake at 400° for 22 minutes or until muffins spring back when touched lightly in center. Remove muffins from pans immediately; place on a wire rack. Yield: 1 dozen (serving size: 1 muffin).

CALORIES 167 (28% from fat); FAT 5.2g (sat 0.9g, mono 2.5g, poly 1.5g); PROTEIN 3.5g; CARB 26.9g; FIBER 0.7g; CHOL 19mg; IRON 1.2mg; SODIUM 160mg; CALC 72mg

BLACKBERRY SMOOTHIE

You can use any fresh or frozen berry in this shake. It's easy to take to the office in a small insulated container.

    2 cups fresh or frozen blackberries
    1 cup plain fat-free yogurt
    1 cup apple juice
    ¼ cup honey
    1 large ripe banana

1. Combine all ingredients in a blender; process until smooth. Strain blackberry mixture through a sieve; discard seeds. Yield: 3 servings (serving size: 1½ cups).

CALORIES 265 (3% from fat); FAT 0.8g (sat 0.2g, mono 0.1g, poly 0.2g); PROTEIN 5.7g; CARB 63.2g; FIBER 8.7g; CHOL 2mg; IRON 1.2mg; SODIUM 62mg; CALC 192mg

Taming the Spud

A former Yale medical instructor asked us to tame the ultimate party animal: a decadent twice-baked potato stuffed with spinach and cheese.

When Anne and Andy Lovejoy of Madison, Connecticut, throw their annual open-house party, most of the guests are well-behaved. But each year, one group always goes overboard—the spinach-stuffed potatoes. Although they mean well, with leafy greens promising iron and other nutrients, the excessive spuds just can't help themselves. By the time they hit the buffet table, they're loaded with whole milk and two kinds of cheese. All efforts to reel in the troublesome potatoes, however, have "lacked the flavor of the original version," Anne writes. "Please help!"

Happily, the Lovejoys can rest easy. After a few minor adjustments—a switch to low-fat milk, reduced-fat Cheddar, and light cream cheese—the wayward taters have seen the light.

BEFORE & AFTER	
SERVING SIZE	
1 potato half	
CALORIES	
414	349
FAT	
18.4g	10g
PERCENT OF TOTAL CALORIES	
40%	26%

TWICE-BAKED SPINACH POTATOES

(pictured on page 262)

You can also cook the potatoes in the microwave by piercing them with a fork and arranging them on paper towels. Microwave at HIGH 16 minutes or until done, turning and rearranging potatoes after 8 minutes. Let stand 5 minutes.

    3 large baking potatoes (about
          12 ounces each)
    ½ cup 1% low-fat milk
    ½ cup tub-style light cream cheese
          (about 4 ounces)
  1¾ cups (7 ounces) shredded
          reduced-fat sharp Cheddar
          cheese, divided
    ¼ cup finely chopped onion
    ¼ teaspoon salt
    ¼ teaspoon black pepper
    1 (10-ounce) package frozen
          chopped spinach, thawed,
          drained, and squeezed dry
  Sliced green onions (optional)

1. Preheat oven to 400°.

2. Pierce potatoes with a fork, and bake at 400° for 1 hour and 15 minutes or until tender. Cool. Cut each potato in half lengthwise; scoop out pulp, leaving a ¼-inch-thick shell. Mash pulp with a potato masher.

3. Combine milk and cream cheese in a large bowl; stir with a whisk. Add potato pulp, 1 cup Cheddar cheese, onion, salt, pepper, and spinach; stir well. Spoon potato mixture into shells; sprinkle each half with 2 tablespoons Cheddar cheese. Place stuffed potatoes on a baking sheet; bake at 400° for 15 minutes or until thoroughly heated. Garnish with green onions, if desired. Yield: 6 servings (serving size: 1 potato half).

CALORIES 349 (26% from fat); FAT 10g (sat 5.8g, mono 1.8g, poly 0.4g); PROTEIN 17.5g; CARB 49g; FIBER 4.7g; CHOL 34mg; IRON 3.5mg; SODIUM 501mg; CALC 414mg

Fontina, Caramelized-Onion, and Pancetta Pizza, page 256

Angel Biscuits, page 2??

Twice-Baked Spinach Potatoes, page 260

Filet Mignon with Peppercorn Mustard Sauce, page 255

Peanut Brittle-Apple Crisp, page 257

Mediterranean Chickpea, Tomato, and Pasta Soup, page 271

Rosemary-Herb French Bread, page 269

Autumn Alchemy

Cooking with cider adds a magic to your kitchen that's as old as America and as friendly as a fall afternoon.

What we've always liked about cider is that it gives you the option of drinking an apple if you don't feel like eating one. But what exactly is cider? And is it different from apple juice? Good questions, with lots of different answers. One veteran cider maker and orchard owner told us if the pressed juice is left alone and not filtered, then it's cider. To him, cider means something you can't see through.

A representative for Tree Top Inc., meanwhile, explained that cider is higher in acidity than juice and that different varieties of apples are used for each, depending on the time of year and their availability. Sweet apples such as Red and Golden Delicious normally go into apple juice, whereas tarter varieties like Rome Beauty, Granny Smith, Jonathan, and Winesap are used for making cider.

So they're different. Sort of. Anyone who's ever compared bottles or jugs of nationally marketed brands of apple juice and cider (filtered and pasteurized) knows they look pretty much alike—a clear amber. Similarly, bottled brands of pasteurized but unfiltered juices and ciders are also about the same in appearance: opaque, brownish. Yet some definitely taste different than others—the ciders should be tarter and the juices sweeter—but how they're labeled is up to the manufacturer.

Confused? So is the government, which has set no national standards for distinguishing cider from juice. This accounts for conflicting product names in different parts of the country. Fresh-pressed juice from apples on the West Coast is commonly known as apple juice, whereas on the East Coast, the same thing is called cider, sometimes sweet cider.

No matter the name, you won't confuse cider/juice with "hard cider"—its stronger taste and alcoholic kick are unmistakable. Any cider, by the way, can become hard—fermentation comes naturally if it's not refrigerated.

But cider isn't only a beverage. It can be a real boon to your cooking. Sweet yet acidic, it can be extremely accommodating. As a marinade, for example, cider excels both as a flavoring agent and as a tenderizer, superb for all kinds of meats: beef, pork, poultry, and lamb. It's also good as a sauce base. Consider its function in a dish such as Cider Scalloped Potatoes: The cider complements the sweetness of the potatoes and contributes a welcome tartness. In turn, the cider sauce reacts with the Gouda cheese, which holds the tartness in check while letting the refreshing apple taste come through.

BE SURE IT'S PASTEURIZED

In the old days, all apple cider was unpasteurized: Pick, press, and drink. You can still buy it that way in some areas, or you can make it yourself. But unless you're confident of the cleanliness of the apple source and the water that nourished it, it's much safer to use only pasteurized cider or apple juice. Why? According to Julia Daly, a spokesperson for the U.S. Apple Association, apples are sometimes exposed to strains of the Escherichia coli bacterium. The apple industry is working on a solution to this problem, but in the meantime, just remember to keep your ciders and juices refrigerated.

MENU SUGGESTION

PORK WITH POTATOES, APPLES, AND SOUR CREAM-CIDER SAUCE

Spinach-cauliflower salad*

*Combine 6 cups torn spinach, 1 cup cauliflower florets, and 1 cup sliced mushrooms in a large bowl. Combine 2 tablespoons lemon juice, 1½ teaspoons sugar, 2 teaspoons oil, ½ teaspoon dried thyme, 2 teaspoons water, and ¼ teaspoon cracked black pepper; stir well. Drizzle over salad, tossing to coat. Serves 6.

PORK WITH POTATOES, APPLES, AND SOUR CREAM-CIDER SAUCE

1 (1½-pound) pork tenderloin
1 tablespoon olive oil, divided
1 large onion, cut into 12 wedges
9 small red potatoes, cut in half (about 1¼ pounds)
2 apples, cut into 1-inch cubes (about 1 pound)
1½ cups apple cider
1 cup fat-free, less-sodium chicken broth
½ cup Calvados (apple brandy)
¼ teaspoon salt
⅛ teaspoon black pepper
½ cup low-fat sour cream

1. Preheat oven to 400°.
2. Trim fat from tenderloin. Heat 1 teaspoon oil in a large, ovenproof Dutch oven over medium-high heat. Add pork; cook 8 minutes or until browned, turning occasionally. Remove from pan.
3. Add 2 teaspoons oil to pan. Add onion; sauté 5 minutes. Add pork and potatoes to pan; insert a meat thermometer into thickest portion of pork. Bake, uncovered, at 400° for 15 minutes. Add apples; bake an additional 20 minutes or until potatoes are tender and thermometer registers 160° (slightly pink). Remove pork and potato mixture from pan; keep warm.
4. Add cider and next 4 ingredients to pan, scraping pan to loosen browned

Continued

bits. Bring to a boil over high heat, and cook until reduced to 1 cup (about 8 minutes). Remove from heat. Stir in sour cream, stirring with a whisk until well-blended. Reduce heat; simmer, uncovered, 1 minute. Cut pork into ¼-inch-thick slices. Arrange 3 ounces pork on each of 6 plates; top each serving with 1 cup potato mixture and ¼ cup sour cream sauce. Yield: 6 servings. *Note:* For an alcohol-free version, simply increase the apple cider to 2 cups and omit the Calvados.

CALORIES 366 (20% from fat); FAT 8g (sat 2.9g, mono 3.7g, poly 0.8g); PROTEIN 27.6g; CARB 46.5g; FIBER 4.9g; CHOL 81mg; IRON 3.2mg; SODIUM 252mg; CALC 59mg

CIDER-HOUSE LAMB STEW

3½ pounds boned leg of lamb
 4 cups apple cider, divided
 ½ cup all-purpose flour
 2 tablespoons vegetable oil, divided
Cooking spray
 2 cups chopped onion
 3 garlic cloves, minced
1¼ cups fat-free, less-sodium chicken broth
 ½ cup dry vermouth or white wine
 1 teaspoon salt
 ½ teaspoon black pepper
 4 (3 x 1-inch) lemon rind strips
 3 bay leaves
 1 (3-inch) cinnamon stick
1½ pounds potatoes, cut into 1-inch pieces (about 5 cups)
1¼ cups (1-inch-thick) sliced carrot
1½ cups (1-inch) pieces green bell pepper

1. Trim fat from lamb, and cut lamb into 2-inch cubes. Combine lamb and 3 cups cider in a large zip-top plastic bag; seal and marinate in refrigerator 8 hours or overnight.
2. Drain lamb, discarding marinade. Pat lamb dry with paper towels. Place flour in a large zip-top plastic bag. Place half of lamb in bag; seal bag, shaking to coat. Heat 1 tablespoon oil in a Dutch oven over medium-high heat; add lamb, and cook 5 minutes or until browned. Remove from pan. Add

remaining lamb to bag; seal bag, shaking to coat. Repeat procedure with remaining 1 tablespoon oil and lamb. Remove lamb from pan; set aside.
3. Heat pan coated with cooking spray over medium heat. Add onion and garlic; sauté 6 minutes. Return lamb to pan; add 1 cup cider, broth, and next 6 ingredients. Bring to a boil. Cover, reduce heat, and simmer 1½ hours or until lamb is tender. Add potato and carrot; bring to a boil. Cover, reduce heat, and simmer 15 minutes. Stir in bell pepper; cook 5 minutes or until pepper is crisp-tender. Discard rind strips, bay leaves, and cinnamon stick. Yield: 8 servings (serving size: 1½ cups stew).

CALORIES 416 (23% from fat); FAT 10.5g (sat 3g, mono 3.6g, poly 2.5g); PROTEIN 33.6g; CARB 46.1g; FIBER 4.2g; CHOL 91mg; IRON 5.4mg; SODIUM 476mg; CALC 44mg

HERBED CHICKEN THIGHS WITH CIDER CABBAGE

¾ teaspoon dried oregano
¾ teaspoon ground thyme
½ teaspoon salt
½ teaspoon black pepper
½ teaspoon ground coriander
8 chicken thighs (about 2 pounds), skinned
1 teaspoon olive oil
2 cups apple cider
8 cups sliced red cabbage
1 cup thinly sliced red onion, separated into rings
2 tablespoons red wine vinegar
1 tablespoon sugar

1. Combine first 5 ingredients; rub mixture over chicken. Cover and marinate in refrigerator 30 minutes.
2. Heat oil in a large nonstick skillet over medium-high heat; add chicken, and cook 5 minutes on each side or until browned. Remove chicken from skillet; keep warm. Add cider to skillet, scraping pan to loosen browned bits. Bring to a boil; cook until reduced to 1 cup (about 3 minutes). Remove ½ cup reduced cider from skillet; set aside.
3. Add cabbage and remaining 3 ingredients to skillet; bring to a boil. Cover,

reduce heat to medium, and cook 5 minutes or until cabbage wilts. Return chicken to skillet, nestling chicken into cabbage mixture; add reserved ½ cup reduced cider. Cover and cook over medium-low heat 30 minutes or until chicken is done. Yield: 4 servings (serving size: 2 chicken thighs and 1½ cups cabbage mixture).

CALORIES 296 (22% from fat); FAT 7.1g (sat 1.6g, mono 2.6g, poly 1.7g); PROTEIN 29.2g; CARB 29.6g; FIBER 3.8g; CHOL 113mg; IRON 3.3mg; SODIUM 430mg; CALC 115mg

CIDER SCALLOPED POTATOES

2 tablespoons all-purpose flour
1 cup 1% low-fat milk
1 cup apple cider
½ cup fat-free, less-sodium chicken broth
½ teaspoon salt
¼ teaspoon black pepper
⅛ teaspoon ground nutmeg
½ cup (2 ounces) shredded smoked Gouda cheese
½ cup (2 ounces) shredded reduced-fat Jarlsberg cheese
2 pounds Yukon gold or yellow Finnish potatoes, peeled and thinly sliced

1. Preheat oven to 425°.
2. Place flour in a medium saucepan. Gradually add milk, stirring with a whisk until blended. Stir in cider and next 4 ingredients; bring to a boil over medium heat, stirring constantly. Remove from heat. Combine cheeses in a small bowl. Arrange half of potato slices in a shallow 3-quart casserole, and sprinkle with ½ cup cheese mixture. Arrange remaining potato slices over cheese. Pour cider mixture over potatoes; bake at 425° for 25 minutes. Remove from oven; press potatoes with a spatula. Sprinkle with remaining ½ cup cheese mixture, and bake an additional 20 minutes or until potatoes are tender. Let stand 10 minutes. Yield: 8 servings.

CALORIES 140 (18% from fat); FAT 2.8g (sat 1.7g, mono 0.8g, poly 0.1g); PROTEIN 6.7g; CARB 22.1g; FIBER 1.5g; CHOL 10mg; IRON 0.9mg; SODIUM 274mg; CALC 146mg

APPLE-CIDER PIE

(pictured on page 224)

Crust:

  2 cups all-purpose flour, divided
  ⅓ cup ice water
  ½ teaspoon salt
  ¼ cup chilled stick margarine or
      butter, cut into small pieces
  ¼ cup vegetable shortening

Filling:

  2 cups apple cider
  ⅓ cup sugar
  3 tablespoons cornstarch
  2 tablespoons fresh lemon
      juice
  2 teaspoons vanilla extract
  1¼ teaspoons pumpkin-pie spice
  3 pounds cooking apples (such as
      Braeburn, Rome, or
      McIntosh), peeled and
      quartered
  Cooking spray

Remaining ingredients:

  1 large egg, lightly beaten
  1 tablespoon water
  1 tablespoon sugar

1. To prepare crust, lightly spoon flour into dry measuring cups; level with a knife. Combine ⅓ cup flour and ice water, stirring with a whisk until well-blended. Combine 1⅔ cups flour and salt in a bowl; cut in margarine and shortening with a pastry blender or 2 knives until mixture resembles coarse meal. Add ice water mixture; toss with a fork until moist. Divide dough in half. Gently press each half of mixture into a 4-inch circle on heavy-duty plastic wrap, and cover with additional plastic wrap. Roll one half of dough, still covered, into a 12-inch circle, and chill. Roll other half of dough, still covered, into an 11-inch circle; chill.

2. To prepare filling, bring cider to a boil in a large, heavy saucepan over high heat. Cook until reduced to ½ cup (about 20 minutes). Cool completely.

3. Combine cooled cider, ⅓ cup sugar, and next 4 ingredients in a large bowl. Cut each apple quarter crosswise into ¼-inch-thick slices. Stir apple slices into cider mixture.

4. Preheat oven to 450°.

5. Remove top sheet of plastic wrap from 12-inch circle; invert and fit dough into a 9-inch pie plate coated with cooking spray, allowing dough to extend over edge of plate. Remove top sheet of plastic wrap. Spoon apple mixture into crust, and brush edges of crust lightly with water. Remove top sheet of plastic wrap from 11-inch circle; invert and place on top of apple mixture. Remove top sheet of plastic wrap. Press edges of dough together; fold edges under, and flute.

6. Cut 6 (1-inch) slits into top of pastry using a sharp knife. Combine egg and 1 tablespoon water. Brush top and edges of pie with egg mixture, and sprinkle with 1 tablespoon sugar. Place pie on a baking sheet, and bake at 450° for 15 minutes. Reduce oven temperature to 350° (do not remove pie from oven), and bake an additional 45 minutes or until golden. Cool on a wire rack. Yield: 10 servings.

CALORIES 302 (28% from fat); FAT 9.5g (sat 2.1g, mono 3.5g, poly 2.9g); PROTEIN 2.9g; CARB 52.6g; FIBER 3.9g; CHOL 0mg; IRON 1.5mg; SODIUM 173mg; CALC 16mg

HOT MULLED CRANBERRY-APPLE CIDER

  1 lemon
  1 orange
  3½ cups apple cider
  2½ cups cranberry juice cocktail
  2 (3-inch) cinnamon sticks
  1 teaspoon whole allspice
  6 whole cloves
  1 (¼-inch) piece peeled fresh
      ginger, thinly sliced

1. Carefully remove rind from lemon and orange using a vegetable peeler, making sure to avoid the white pith just beneath the rind. Cut rind into 1 x ¼-inch-thick strips. Combine rind strips, cider, and remaining ingredients in a Dutch oven. Bring mixture to a simmer over medium heat, and cook until reduced to 4 cups (about 30 minutes). Strain mixture through a sieve over a bowl, discarding solids. Yield: 8 servings (serving size: ½ cup).

CALORIES 98 (1% from fat); FAT 0.1g (sat 0g, mono 0g, poly 0.1g); PROTEIN 0.1g; CARB 24.7g; FIBER 0.2g; CHOL 0mg; IRON 0.5mg; SODIUM 6mg; CALC 10mg

NEW AGE WALDORF SALAD

Use a variety of apples for the best flavor in this updated Waldorf salad.

  1 (8-ounce) carton plain low-fat
      yogurt
  2 cups apple cider
  ½ teaspoon celery seeds
  5 cups chopped apple (such as
      Granny Smith, Rome, and/or
      Gala)
  1 cup chopped peeled celeriac
      (celery root)
  ½ cup coarsely chopped pecans,
      toasted
  8 Boston lettuce leaves

1. Spoon yogurt onto several layers of heavy-duty paper towels, and spread to ½-inch thickness. Cover yogurt with additional paper towels, and let stand 5 minutes. Scrape into a bowl using a rubber spatula; cover and chill.

2. Bring cider to a boil in a medium, heavy saucepan over high heat; cook until reduced to ½ cup (about 20 minutes). Cool completely.

3. Combine chilled yogurt, cider, and celery seeds in a large bowl, stirring well with a whisk. Add apple, celeriac, and pecans, tossing gently to coat. Serve salad on lettuce-lined plates. Yield: 8 servings (serving size: ¾ cup).

CALORIES 166 (34% from fat); FAT 6.2g (sat 0.8g, mono 3.3g, poly 1.6g); PROTEIN 4.6g; CARB 26.7g; FIBER 4.1g; CHOL 2mg; IRON 1.2mg; SODIUM 50mg; CALC 74mg

APPLE CIDER-CARAMEL CAKE

Cider "syrup" is folded into this cake for a rich, caramelized flavor.

2¼ cups apple cider, divided
2¼ cups granulated sugar, divided
  1 tablespoon stick margarine or butter
  3 cups sliced peeled cooking apple (such as Braeburn, Rome, or McIntosh)
     Cooking spray
2½ tablespoons dry breadcrumbs
  ½ cup stick margarine or butter, softened
  1 tablespoon grated lemon rind
  1 (8-ounce) block fat-free cream cheese
  3 large eggs
  6 tablespoons fresh lemon juice, divided
  3 cups all-purpose flour
  ½ teaspoon baking soda
  ¼ teaspoon salt
  1 cup low-fat buttermilk
  1 teaspoon vanilla extract
  1 tablespoon powdered sugar

1. Bring 2 cups cider to a boil in a large, heavy saucepan over high heat. Cook until reduced to ½ cup (about 20 minutes). Reduce heat to medium-high; stir in ½ cup granulated sugar. Cook 5 minutes or until sugar dissolves and cider is thick and dark-colored, stirring occasionally. Remove from heat; cool 1 minute. Stir in 1 tablespoon margarine. Stir in apple; cook 15 minutes over medium-high heat or until liquid is absorbed, stirring frequently. Remove from heat; cool. (If apple mixture hardens, place it over low heat until softened).
2. Preheat oven to 325°.
3. Coat a 12-cup Bundt pan with cooking spray; dust with breadcrumbs.
4. Combine 1½ cups granulated sugar, ½ cup margarine, lemon rind, and cream cheese in a large bowl; beat at medium speed of a mixer until well-blended (about 5 minutes). Add eggs, 1 at a time, beating well after each addition. Beat in 2 tablespoons lemon juice. Lightly spoon flour into dry

measuring cups; level with a knife. Combine flour, baking soda, and salt. Add flour mixture to sugar mixture alternately with buttermilk, beginning and ending with flour mixture. Fold in apple mixture. Pour into prepared pan; bake at 325° for 1½ hours or until a wooden pick inserted in center comes out clean. Cool cake in pan 5 minutes; pierce with a wooden skewer in several places.
5. Combine remaining ¼ cup cider, ¼ cup granulated sugar, ¼ cup lemon juice, and vanilla; let stand until sugar dissolves, stirring occasionally. Pour cider mixture over cake in pan, and let stand 10 minutes. Remove from pan, and cool completely on a wire rack. Sift powdered sugar over top of cake. Yield: 18 servings.

CALORIES 286 (22% from fat); FAT 7.1g (sat 1.6g, mono 3g, poly 2g); PROTEIN 5.8g; CARB 50.1g; FIBER 1.2g; CHOL 39mg; IRON 1.3mg; SODIUM 237mg; CALC 68mg

LAST HURRAH

Orderly Disorder

Get Organized Week is a time to get things in order so you'll have time to enjoy your life and make yourself something that tastes great.

MEDITERRANEAN FOCACCIA

This recipe makes 12 (4-inch) focaccias or two (12-inch) focaccias. Kosher salt looks and tastes better, but regular table salt can be used in a pinch.

5¼ cups all-purpose flour, divided
  ½ cup grated Parmesan cheese
  1 teaspoon kosher salt
  1 teaspoon dried rosemary, crushed
  1 package quick-rise yeast
1½ cups very warm water (120° to 130°)

  2 tablespoons olive oil
     Cooking spray
  1 tablespoon cornmeal
  2 teaspoons olive oil
  ½ teaspoon kosher salt
  ¼ teaspoon freshly ground black pepper
  ⅔ cup pimento-stuffed olives, halved
  1 (7-ounce) bottle roasted red bell peppers, cut into ¼-inch strips

1. Lightly spoon flour into dry measuring cups; level with a knife. Combine 5 cups flour, cheese, and next 3 ingredients in a food processor; pulse 2 times or until blended. With processor on, slowly add water and 2 tablespoons oil through food chute; process until dough forms a ball. Turn dough out onto a lightly floured surface. Knead until smooth and elastic (about 5 minutes), adding enough of remaining flour, 1 tablespoon at a time, to prevent dough from sticking.
2. Place dough in a large bowl coated with cooking spray, turning to coat top. Cover and let rise in a warm place (85°), free from drafts, 10 minutes. (Dough will not double in bulk.)
3. Punch dough down; turn out onto a lightly floured surface. Divide dough into 12 equal portions, shaping each portion into a 4-inch circle. Place on 2 large baking sheets coated with cooking spray and dusted with cornmeal. Cover and let rise 40 minutes or until doubled in bulk.
4. Preheat oven to 450°.
5. Uncover dough. Gently brush dough with 2 teaspoons oil. Make indentations in top of dough using the handle of a wooden spoon or your fingertips. Sprinkle with ½ teaspoon salt and black pepper; arrange olives and bell pepper strips as desired on each circle. Bake at 450° for 20 minutes or until golden. Remove from baking sheets; cool on wire racks. Yield: 1 dozen.

CALORIES 261 (19% from fat); FAT 5.6g (sat 1.5g, mono 3.1g, poly 0.6g); PROTEIN 8g; CARB 43.2g; FIBER 1.9g; CHOL 4mg; IRON 3mg; SODIUM 341mg; CALC 82mg

Bread Winners

A pesto-perked loaf, French bread, and the fluffiest of yeast biscuits—our readers share their favorite recipes for leavened bread.

ROSEMARY-HERB FRENCH BREAD

(pictured on page 264)

The machine mixes the dough and allows it to rise. You finish the shaping and baking. Super Bowl Sunday would be just another football party without this bread. When the first loaf comes out of the oven, everyone runs into the kitchen to grab a piece while it's still warm.

—Heather Carter, Fairview, Texas

2¼ cups bread flour
1 package dry yeast (about 2¼ teaspoons)
2 teaspoons sugar
1 teaspoon chopped fresh or dried rosemary
½ teaspoon dried basil
½ teaspoon dried thyme
½ teaspoon dried oregano
½ teaspoon salt
1 cup water
1 teaspoon olive oil
3 tablespoons (¾ ounce) finely shredded fresh Parmesan cheese
1 teaspoon chopped fresh or dried rosemary
¼ teaspoon garlic powder

1. Lightly spoon flour into dry measuring cups; level with a knife. Follow manufacturer's instructions for placing flour and next 8 ingredients into bread pan; select dough cycle, and start bread machine. Remove dough from machine (do not bake).
2. Preheat oven to 350°.
3. Turn dough out onto a lightly floured surface; rub with oil. Shape into a 12-inch long loaf. Place loaf on a baking sheet. Combine cheese, 1 teaspoon rosemary, and garlic powder; sprinkle over top of loaf. Bake at 350° for 45 minutes or until loaf sounds hollow when tapped. Remove from pan; cool on a wire rack. Yield: 1 (1-pound) loaf (serving size: 1 [1-inch] slice).

CALORIES 110 (13% from fat); FAT 1.6g (sat 0.4g, mono 0.6g, poly 0.3g); PROTEIN 3.9g; CARB 19.8g; FIBER 0.2g; CHOL 1mg; IRON 1.4mg; SODIUM 125mg; CALC 26mg

ANADAMA BREAD

My mother's recipe for Anadama Bread was one of the reasons I bought a bread machine. So once I figured out how the machine worked, I adapted her recipe. It still tastes great but contains much less sugar and fat.

—Melodie Esterberg, Rochester, New Hampshire

1½ cups water, divided
⅓ cup yellow cornmeal
1 teaspoon salt
⅓ cup molasses
1½ teaspoons vegetable oil
3 cups all-purpose flour
1 package dry yeast (about 2¼ teaspoons)

1. Combine ½ cup water and cornmeal. Bring 1 cup water and salt to a boil in a small saucepan. Stir in cornmeal mixture, and cook 2 minutes or until thick. Stir in molasses and oil; cool.
2. Lightly spoon flour into dry measuring cups; level with a knife. Follow manufacturer's instructions for placing flour, yeast, and cornmeal mixture into bread pan; select bake cycle. Start bread machine. Yield: 1 (1½-pound) loaf, 12 servings.

CALORIES 158 (6% from fat); FAT 1g (sat 0.2g, mono 0.2g, poly 0.4g); PROTEIN 3.8g; CARB 33.2g; FIBER 1.2g; CHOL 0mg; IRON 2.1mg; SODIUM 199mg; CALC 24mg

WHOLE-WHEAT BREAD

My 9-year-old son is a picky eater. But he always asks for this bread. My daughter loves it, too. Sometimes we go through as many as two loaves a week.

—Jeff Condra, Birmingham, Alabama

2 tablespoons sugar
2 packages dry yeast (about 4½ teaspoons)
2 cups warm water (105° to 115°)
3 cups all-purpose flour
2½ cups whole-wheat flour, divided
3 tablespoons vegetable oil
2 teaspoons salt
Cooking spray
1 tablespoon sunflower seed kernels
1 tablespoon quick-cooking oats
2 tablespoons stick margarine or butter, melted

1. Dissolve sugar and yeast in warm water in a large bowl; let stand 5 minutes.
2. Lightly spoon flours into dry measuring cups; level with a knife. Stir all-purpose flour, 2 cups whole-wheat flour, vegetable oil, and salt into yeast mixture. Turn dough out onto a lightly floured surface. Knead until dough is smooth and elastic (about 8 minutes), adding enough of the remaining whole-wheat flour, 1 tablespoon at a time, to prevent dough from sticking.
3. Place dough in a large bowl coated with cooking spray, turning to coat top. Cover and let rise in a warm place (85°), free from drafts, 45 minutes or until doubled in bulk. Punch dough down; cover dough, and let rest 20 minutes. Divide dough in half. Working with one portion at a time (cover remaining dough to keep from drying), roll each portion into a 6 x 4-inch rectangle on a lightly floured surface. Roll up each rectangle tightly, starting with a long edge, pressing firmly to eliminate air pockets; pinch seams and ends to seal. Place rolls, seam sides down, in 2 (8 x 4-inch) loaf pans coated with cooking spray. Cover and let rise 30 minutes or until doubled in bulk.

Continued

4. Preheat oven to 350°.

5. Uncover dough. Combine sunflower seed kernels, oats, and margarine; brush over loaves. Bake at 350° for 30 minutes or until loaves sound hollow when tapped. Remove from pans; cool on wire racks. Yield: 2 loaves, 12 servings per loaf (serving size: 1 slice).

CALORIES 132 (23% from fat); FAT 3.3g (sat 0.6g, mono 1.0g, poly 1.4g); PROTEIN 3.7g; CARB 22.5g; FIBER 2.2g; CHOL 0mg; IRON 1.3mg; SODIUM 202mg; CALC 8mg

JEFF'S PERFECT PESTO-AND-HERB BREAD

I received a new bread machine as a gift that my fiancé uses to create a most delicious recipe for pesto-and-herb bread. It gets rave reviews from family and friends.

—Elizabeth Murray, Lansing, Michigan

3¼ cups bread flour
3 tablespoons sugar
1 tablespoon dried parsley flakes
1½ teaspoons garlic powder
1½ teaspoons bread machine yeast
1 teaspoon dried oregano
1 teaspoon dried basil
¾ teaspoon salt
1 cup plus 2 tablespoons water
2 tablespoons 1% low-fat milk
2 tablespoons commercial pesto
2 teaspoons olive oil

1. Lightly spoon bread flour into dry measuring cups; level with a knife. Follow manufacturer's instructions for placing flour and remaining ingredients into bread pan. Select European bake cycle, and start bread machine. Yield: 16 servings (serving size: 1 slice).

CALORIES 129 (15% from fat); FAT 2.1g (sat 0.3g, mono 1.1g, poly 0.4g); PROTEIN 3.9g; CARB 23.5g; FIBER 0.2g; CHOL 0mg; IRON 1.7mg; SODIUM 133mg; CALC 25mg

ANGEL BISCUITS

(pictured on page 262)

My husband and I love biscuits but were tired of the canned variety. Then a lady at church gave us this recipe. The dough will keep for several weeks in the refrigerator. It's handy to have on hand for company. Everyone I have shared this recipe with thinks the biscuits are great.

—Linda Turner, Springfield, Missouri

1 package dry yeast (about 2¼ teaspoons)
½ cup warm water (105° to 115°)
5 cups all-purpose flour
¼ cup sugar
1 teaspoon baking powder
1 teaspoon baking soda
1 teaspoon salt
½ cup vegetable shortening
2 cups low-fat buttermilk
Cooking spray
1 tablespoon stick margarine or butter, melted

1. Dissolve yeast in warm water in a small bowl; let stand 5 minutes.
2. Lightly spoon flour into dry measuring cups; level with a knife. Combine flour and next 4 ingredients in a large bowl. Cut in shortening with a pastry blender or 2 knives until mixture resembles coarse meal. Add yeast mixture and buttermilk; stir just until moist. Cover and chill 1 hour.
3. Preheat oven to 450°.
4. Turn dough out onto a heavily floured surface; knead lightly 5 times. Roll dough to ½-inch thickness; cut with a 3-inch biscuit cutter. Place on a baking sheet coated with cooking spray. Brush melted margarine over biscuit tops. Bake at 450° for 13 minutes or until golden. Yield: 2 dozen (serving size: 1 biscuit).

CALORIES 150 (28% from fat); FAT 4.6g (sat 1.2g, mono 1.5g, poly 1.3g); PROTEIN 3.6g; CARB 23.1g; FIBER 0.8g; CHOL 0mg; IRON 1.3mg; SODIUM 183mg; CALC 41mg

FAST FOOD

All You Need Is Soup

Convenience ingredients give these main-dish standouts speedy ease to match their flavors.

The time-honored way to make a base (the soul of any soup) is to simmer stock, but time is the one thing you can't honor when it's 5 p.m. and your family's hungry. So be creative. Combine convenience products such as presliced, frozen, or canned vegetables and canned low-sodium broth or a simple white sauce into a surprisingly quick base. You'll not only expedite dinner, but you'll also banish boredom.

SPICY BLACK BEAN-AND-SAUSAGE SOUP

Preparation time: 10 minutes
Cooking time: 12 minutes

2 (15-ounce) cans black beans, drained and divided
2½ cups water, divided
1 tablespoon olive oil
2 cups diced onion
1 teaspoon chili powder
½ teaspoon ground cumin
¼ to ½ teaspoon hot sauce
¼ teaspoon black pepper
1 garlic clove, minced
6 ounces turkey kielbasa, diced

1. Place 1 cup beans and ½ cup water in a food processor or blender; process until smooth.
2. Heat olive oil in a large Dutch oven over medium-high heat. Add onion, and sauté 4 minutes or until onion is soft. Add bean puree, remaining beans, 2 cups water, chili powder, and next 4 ingredients; bring to a boil. Cover, reduce heat, and simmer 5 minutes, stirring occasionally. Stir in kielbasa, and cook 1 minute or until thoroughly

heated. Yield: 4 servings (serving size: 1½ cups).

CALORIES 291 (26% from fat); FAT 8.3g (sat 2.6g, mono 3.5g, poly 1.5g); PROTEIN 17.8g; CARB 38.9g; FIBER 7g; CHOL 23mg; IRON 7.8mg; SODIUM 789mg; CALC 72mg

CHEESY POTATO FLORENTINE SOUP

Preparation time: 10 minutes
Cooking time: 20 minutes

2 teaspoons stick margarine or butter
2 cups thinly sliced leek (about 2 large)
2 cups frozen Southern-style hash brown potatoes, thawed
1½ cups water
⅛ teaspoon salt
⅛ teaspoon black pepper
1 (16-ounce) can fat-free, less-sodium chicken broth
1 (10-ounce) package frozen chopped spinach, thawed, drained, and squeezed dry
¾ cup (3 ounces) preshredded reduced-fat Mexican blend or Cheddar cheese
¾ cup 1% low-fat milk

1. Melt margarine in a large saucepan over medium-high heat. Add leek, and sauté 4 minutes. Add potatoes and next 5 ingredients. Bring to a boil; reduce heat, and simmer 5 minutes, stirring occasionally.
2. Place half of potato mixture in a food processor or blender; process until smooth. Pour pureed potato mixture into a large bowl. Repeat procedure with remaining potato mixture. Return pureed potato mixture to pan. Stir in cheese and milk; cook 1 minute or until thoroughly heated and cheese melts. Yield: 4 servings (serving size: 1¼ cups).

CALORIES 204 (27% from fat); FAT 6.1g (sat 2.9g, mono 2.2g, poly 1g); PROTEIN 12.8g; CARB 26.9g; FIBER 3.2g; CHOL 9mg; IRON 3mg; SODIUM 514mg; CALC 325mg

CORN-AND-CHICKEN CHOWDER

Preparation time: 5 minutes
Cooking time: 18 minutes

1 tablespoon stick margarine or butter
1 (8-ounce) package presliced mushrooms
¼ cup all-purpose flour
3½ cups 2% reduced-fat milk
1 cup chopped red potato (about 6 ounces)
½ teaspoon dried thyme
½ teaspoon salt
¼ teaspoon black pepper
1 (16-ounce) package frozen whole-kernel corn, thawed
1½ cups shredded ready-to-eat roasted skinned, boned chicken breasts (about 2 breasts)
3 tablespoons chopped green onions, divided

1. Melt margarine in a large Dutch oven over medium-high heat. Add mushrooms; sauté 3 minutes. Stir in flour. Gradually add milk, stirring with a whisk. Add potato and next 4 ingredients; bring to a boil. Stir in chicken and 2 tablespoons green onions; cover, reduce heat, and simmer 15 minutes. Ladle into bowls; sprinkle with green onions. Yield: 4 servings (serving size: 1¾ cups).

CALORIES 376 (23% from fat); FAT 9.4g (sat 3.8g, mono 3.2g, poly 1.9g); PROTEIN 26.4g; CARB 50.7g; FIBER 4.5g; CHOL 52mg; IRON 2.1mg; SODIUM 731mg; CALC 287mg

NEW ENGLAND CLAM CHOWDER

Preparation time: 12 minutes
Cooking time: 20 minutes

2 teaspoons olive oil
1 cup diced onion
½ cup diced celery
2 cups (½-inch) cubed peeled Yukon gold or baking potato (about ¾ pound)
1 cup water
½ teaspoon dried thyme
⅛ teaspoon black pepper
1 (8-ounce) bottle clam juice
1 bay leaf
1 cup 2% reduced-fat milk
1 tablespoon all-purpose flour
1 (6½-ounce) can minced clams, undrained
Chopped fresh parsley (optional)

1. Heat olive oil in a saucepan over medium heat. Add onion and celery; sauté 5 minutes or until onion is soft. Stir in potato and next 5 ingredients. Bring to a boil; cover, reduce heat, and simmer 12 minutes or until potato is tender.
2. Combine milk and flour in a small bowl, stirring with a whisk until smooth. Add flour mixture and clams to saucepan; bring to a simmer. Cook 2 minutes or until mixture begins to thicken, stirring frequently. Discard bay leaf. Ladle soup into bowls; garnish with chopped parsley, if desired. Yield: 4 servings (serving size: 1¼ cups).

CALORIES 184 (19% from fat); FAT 3.9g (sat 1.2g, mono 2.1g, poly 0.4g); PROTEIN 8.4g; CARB 28.5g; FIBER 2.5g; CHOL 20mg; IRON 2.7mg; SODIUM 434mg; CALC 132mg

MEDITERRANEAN CHICKPEA, TOMATO, AND PASTA SOUP

(pictured on page 264)

Preparation time: 10 minutes
Cooking time: 22 minutes

2 teaspoons olive oil
1 cup diced onion
1½ cups water
1 (16-ounce) can fat-free, less-sodium chicken broth
½ teaspoon ground cumin
¼ teaspoon ground cinnamon
¼ teaspoon black pepper
1 (15½-ounce) can chickpeas (garbanzo beans), drained
1 (14.5-ounce) can diced tomatoes, undrained
½ cup uncooked ditalini (very small tube-shaped macaroni)
2 tablespoons chopped fresh parsley

Continued

1. Heat olive oil in a large saucepan over medium-high heat. Add onion, and sauté 3 minutes or until tender. Add water and next 6 ingredients. Bring mixture to a boil; cover, reduce heat, and simmer 5 minutes, stirring occasionally. Add pasta, and cook 9 minutes or until pasta is tender. Stir in parsley. Yield: 4 servings (serving size: 1½ cups).

CALORIES 242 (17% from fat); FAT 4.7g (sat 0.6g, mono 2.2g, poly 1.3g); PROTEIN 11.4g; CARB 39.9g; FIBER 4.6g; CHOL 0mg; IRON 3.6mg; SODIUM 560mg; CALC 79mg

PESTO MINESTRONE WITH TORTELLINI

Preparation time: 10 minutes
Cooking time: 23 minutes

    2 teaspoons olive oil
    1 cup diced onion
  2¼ cups water
    2 cups diced zucchini
    2 cups frozen mixed vegetables
   ¾ teaspoon dried oregano
   ¼ teaspoon black pepper
    2 garlic cloves, minced
    1 (14.5-ounce) can diced
          tomatoes, undrained
    1 (14½-ounce) can vegetable broth
    2 tablespoons commercial pesto
    1 (9-ounce) package fresh three-
          cheese tortellini, uncooked

1. Heat olive oil in a large Dutch oven over medium-high heat. Add onion, and sauté 4 minutes or until tender. Add water and next 7 ingredients; bring to boil. Cover, reduce heat, and simmer 5 minutes or until zucchini is tender.
2. Stir in pesto and tortellini; cover and simmer 6 minutes or until thoroughly heated and pasta is tender. Yield: 6 servings (serving size: 1½ cups).

CALORIES 237 (29% from fat); FAT 7.7g (sat 1.7g, mono 4g, poly 1.4g); PROTEIN 9.3g; CARB 32.7g; FIBER 3.5g; CHOL 20mg; IRON 2mg; SODIUM 682mg; CALC 149mg

Single Times Seven

Because so many of us cook for ourselves, wouldn't it be nice to have a week's worth of great dishes for some solo pampering?

Many single Americans simply opt for meals of convenience: takeout fare, frozen dinners, fast food. But given a suitable recipe, cooking for one can be a richly rewarding experience. Chopping, slicing, and dicing are great ways to relieve stress, and the smell of food cooking in the kitchen is a wonderfully rejuvenating sensation. And what could be better at the end of a long day than to sit down to a wholesome meal?

Maybe we can inspire your culinary creativeness with a full week of meals designed especially for America's millions of singles. All seven suppers are flavorful, low in fat, and economical.

TOMATO, ONION, AND PEPPER STEAK

    4 ounces boned round steak, cut
          into ¼-inch strips
    1 tablespoon low-sodium soy
          sauce
  Cooking spray
    1 cup thinly sliced green bell
          pepper
    1 cup chopped tomato
   ¾ cup sliced onion
   ¼ teaspoon black pepper
   ⅛ teaspoon ground ginger
    2 garlic cloves, minced
   ¾ cup fat-free beef broth
   ¼ cup water
    1 teaspoon cornstarch
   ½ cup hot cooked rice

1. Combine beef and soy sauce in a small bowl; marinate 5 minutes.
2. Heat a large nonstick skillet coated with cooking spray over medium-high heat. Add beef, and sauté 2 minutes. Add bell pepper and next 5 ingredients to skillet. Cover, reduce heat, and simmer 15 minutes.

3. Combine beef broth, water, and cornstarch; stir with a whisk. Add to beef mixture, and simmer, covered, 30 minutes or until beef is tender. Serve over rice. Yield: 1 serving.

CALORIES 420 (14% from fat); FAT 6.6g (sat 1.8g, mono 2.0g, poly 0.8g); PROTEIN 33g; CARB 55.8g; FIBER 6.3g; CHOL 65mg; IRON 6.2mg; SODIUM 572mg; CALC 63mg

STEAK-AND-BEAN BURRITO

  Cooking spray
    2 ounces boned round steak, cut
          into ¼-inch strips
   ⅓ cup chopped onion
    1 garlic clove, minced
   ¾ cup canned black beans, rinsed
          and drained
   ¼ cup fat-free beef broth
   ¼ teaspoon dried crushed red
          pepper
   ⅛ teaspoon ground cumin
    1 (8-inch) flour tortilla
    3 tablespoons fat-free sour cream,
          divided
    2 tablespoons bottled salsa,
          divided
    2 tablespoons finely chopped
          romaine lettuce

1. Heat a nonstick skillet coated with cooking spray over medium-high heat. Add beef, and sauté 2 minutes; remove from pan. Add onion and garlic to pan; sauté 2 minutes. Stir in beans and broth; cook 1 minute. Mash bean mixture with a fork; stir in pepper and cumin.
2. Spread bean mixture over tortilla, and top with 2 tablespoons sour cream, spreading to cover. Place beef strips down center of tortilla; top with 1 tablespoon salsa. Roll up tortilla; place, seam side down, on a microwave-safe plate. Microwave at HIGH 1 minute or until burrito filling is hot. Top with 1 tablespoon sour cream, 1 tablespoon salsa, and lettuce. Yield: 1 serving.

CALORIES 448 (14% from fat); FAT 7.1g (sat 1.7g, mono 2.3g, poly 1.5g); PROTEIN 33.6g; CARB 62.2g; FIBER 8.5g; CHOL 41mg; IRON 5.7mg; SODIUM 1,056mg; CALC 118mg

SPICY PORK-AND-VEGETABLE STIR-FRY

Cooking spray
1 (4-ounce) boned center-cut loin pork chop (about ½ inch thick), cut into 1-inch strips
1 cup small broccoli florets
½ cup thinly sliced red bell pepper
½ cup thinly sliced yellow bell pepper
½ cup vertically sliced onion
1 teaspoon finely grated peeled fresh ginger
1 garlic clove, minced
¼ cup fat-free, less-sodium chicken broth
¼ cup apple juice
2 tablespoons low-sodium soy sauce
1 teaspoon cornstarch
1 teaspoon sugar
¼ teaspoon dried crushed red pepper
½ cup hot cooked rice

1. Heat a large nonstick skillet coated with cooking spray over medium-high heat; add pork, and sauté 2 minutes. Remove pork from skillet. Add broccoli and bell peppers to skillet; stir-fry 2 minutes. Stir in onion, ginger, and garlic; cook 2 minutes.
2. Return pork to pan. Combine chicken broth and next 5 ingredients; stir with a whisk. Add to pork mixture. Reduce heat, and simmer 4 minutes or until sauce thickens. Serve over rice. Yield: 1 serving.

CALORIES 422 (19% from fat); FAT 8.7g (sat 2.6g, mono 3.1g, poly 1.2g); PROTEIN 29.1g; CARB 58g; FIBER 6.3g; CHOL 59mg; IRON 4.7mg; SODIUM 1,189mg; CALC 95mg

SAUTÉED PORK WITH SWEET ONION RELISH AND CORN FRITTERS

1 (4-ounce) boned center-cut loin pork chop (about ¾ inch thick)
¼ teaspoon coarsely ground black pepper
⅛ teaspoon salt
Cooking spray
¼ cup apple juice
1 teaspoon cider vinegar
¼ cup bottled sweet onion relish
Corn Fritters

1. Trim fat from pork; sprinkle pork with pepper and salt. Heat a small skillet coated with cooking spray over medium heat. Add pork; cook 4 minutes on each side or until done. Add juice and vinegar; simmer 3 minutes, turning pork occasionally. Serve warm with relish and Corn Fritters. Yield: 1 serving (serving size: 1 pork chop, ¼ cup relish, and 3 fritters).

CALORIES 430 (25% from fat); FAT 11.9g (sat 3.4g, mono 5.0g, poly 2.4g); PROTEIN 29.4g; CARB 53.6g; FIBER 3.7g; CHOL 59mg; IRON 2.5mg; SODIUM 906mg; CALC 73mg

Corn Fritters:

½ cup frozen whole-kernel corn, thawed
⅓ cup cooked rice
1 tablespoon all-purpose flour
½ teaspoon sugar
¼ teaspoon baking powder
⅛ teaspoon salt
⅛ teaspoon black pepper
1 large egg white
1 teaspoon stick margarine or butter

1. Combine first 7 ingredients in a small bowl. Beat egg white in a medium bowl at high speed of a mixer until stiff peaks form. Fold egg white into corn mixture.
2. Melt margarine in a small nonstick skillet over medium heat. Spoon about ⅓ cup corn mixture per fritter into skillet, shaping each into a ½-inch-thick round patty. Cook 2 minutes on each side or until golden. Serve warm. Yield: 3 fritters.

PARMESAN CHICKEN

1 (6-ounce) skinned chicken breast half
½ teaspoon olive oil
1 tablespoon (¼ ounce) grated fresh Parmesan cheese
⅛ teaspoon dried thyme
⅛ teaspoon dried oregano
⅛ teaspoon salt
Dash of black pepper
Cooking spray
¼ cup fat-free, less-sodium chicken broth

1. Preheat oven to 400°.
2. Brush chicken with olive oil. Combine cheese and next 4 ingredients in a small bowl; sprinkle cheese mixture over both sides of chicken. Place chicken in a shallow dish coated with cooking spray, and pour broth over chicken. Cover and bake at 400° for 40 minutes or until done. Yield: 1 serving.

CALORIES 294 (32% from fat); FAT 10.3g (sat 3.2g, mono 4g, poly 1.3g); PROTEIN 46.1g; CARB 1.5g; FIBER 0.1g; CHOL 122mg; IRON 1.8mg; SODIUM 501mg; CALC 132mg

CHICKEN CAESAR SALAD

3 ounces ready-to-eat roasted skinned, boned chicken breast, chopped (such as Tyson)
2 cups torn romaine lettuce
1 tablespoon (¼ ounce) grated fresh Parmesan cheese
2 tablespoons white wine vinegar
1 tablespoon water
1½ teaspoons olive oil
1 teaspoon fresh lemon juice
⅛ teaspoon black pepper
⅛ teaspoon Dijon mustard
6 fat-free Caesar-flavored croutons

1. Combine first 3 ingredients in a bowl; toss gently. Combine vinegar and next 5 ingredients; stir with a whisk. Add to lettuce mixture; toss well. Top with croutons. Yield: 1 serving.

CALORIES 289 (40% from fat); FAT 12.7g (sat 3.2g, mono 6.8g, poly 1.6g); PROTEIN 31.5g; CARB 8.5g; FIBER 2g; CHOL 77mg; IRON 2.3mg; SODIUM 290mg; CALC 139mg

Herbed Tuna Steak with Black Bean Confetti Relish

Serve the extra relish with baked tortilla chips for a snack.

   1   tablespoon minced shallots
   1   tablespoon lemon juice
   ¼   teaspoon coarsely ground black
        pepper
   ⅛   teaspoon dried tarragon
   ⅛   teaspoon dried oregano
   1   (6-ounce) tuna steak (about
        ¾ inch thick)
Cooking spray
Black Bean Confetti Relish

1. Combine first 6 ingredients in a small dish; cover and marinate in refrigerator 30 minutes.
2. Prepare grill or broiler. Place fish on grill rack or broiler pan coated with cooking spray. Cook 2 minutes on each side or until fish is done. Serve with Black Bean Confetti Relish. Yield: 1 serving (serving size: 1 steak and ½ cup relish).

CALORIES 372 (27% from fat); FAT 11.2g (sat 2.6g, mono 4.5g, poly 2.6g); PROTEIN 45.7g; CARB 21.9g; FIBER 3.4g; CHOL 65mg; IRON 3.9mg; SODIUM 369mg; CALC 33mg

Black Bean Confetti Relish:

   ⅔   cup canned black beans, rinsed
        and drained
   2   tablespoons frozen whole-kernel
        corn
   2   tablespoons diced yellow bell
        pepper
   2   tablespoons diced plum tomato
   1   tablespoon diced red bell pepper
   1   tablespoon minced shallots
   1   tablespoon lemon juice
   1   teaspoon olive oil
   ¼   teaspoon ground cumin
   ¼   teaspoon coarsely ground black
        pepper
   ⅛   teaspoon salt

1. Combine all ingredients in a bowl. Serve relish chilled or at room temperature. Yield: 1 cup (serving size: ½ cup).

CALORIES 116 (23% from fat); FAT 2.9g (sat 0.4g, mono 1.8g, poly 0.5g); PROTEIN 5.8g; CARB 18.5g; FIBER 3.2g; CHOL 0mg; IRON 1.8mg; SODIUM 301mg; CALC 24mg

Good Sports

Inviting your friends over to watch the big game doesn't mean you have to stuff them with chips and beer.

Apparently, there's something in the American spirit that lets us work up appetites while watching others exercise. After all, look at the myriad of gameday fests—World Series parties, Super Bowl soirees, Kentucky Derby galas.

While typical sporting menus are loaded with chips, pretzels, and nuts, here you'll find food far different. But don't worry, it's still stick-to-your-ribs, hearty fare.

GAME-DAY LINEUP

Appetizer
OPPOSING-SIDES
TWO-BEAN DIP

Soups
SPICY GARDEN CHILI *or*
MEXICAN SHRIMP-AND-
CHICKEN SOUP

Sandwiches
SLOW-COOKER
BARBECUE-BEEF
SANDWICHES *or*
THREE-PEPPER FETA
ROLL-UPS

Salad
MIXED GREENS WITH
SUN-DRIED TOMATO
VINAIGRETTE

Dessert
CARAMEL CHEESECAKE

Opposing-Sides Two-Bean Dip

   1   (16-ounce) can Great Northern
        beans, drained
   ½   cup chopped onion, divided
   3   tablespoons grated Parmesan
        cheese
   ½   teaspoon salt, divided
   ½   teaspoon black pepper, divided
   2   small garlic cloves, divided
   1   (15-ounce) can black beans,
        drained
   1   (4.5-ounce) can chopped green
        chiles, drained
   ¼   teaspoon ground cumin

   ½   cup (2 ounces) finely shredded
        reduced-fat sharp Cheddar cheese
   ¼   cup sliced green onion tops
Garlic Pita Chips

1. Combine Great Northern beans, ¼ cup chopped onion, Parmesan cheese, ¼ teaspoon salt, ¼ teaspoon pepper, and 1 garlic clove in a food processor; process until smooth. Spoon white bean mixture into a bowl on one side; set aside.
2. Combine black beans, ¼ cup chopped onion, ¼ teaspoon salt, ¼ teaspoon pepper, 1 garlic clove, chiles, and cumin in a food processor; process until smooth. Spoon black bean mixture into other side of bowl containing white bean mixture.
3. Sprinkle Cheddar cheese and green onions evenly over 2 bean dips. Serve with Garlic Pita Chips. Yield: 12 servings (serving size: about 3 tablespoons dip and 4 chips).

CALORIES 179 (13% from fat); FAT 2.5g (sat 1g, mono 0.3g, poly 0.4g); PROTEIN 7.8g; CARB 29.9g; FIBER 5.4g; CHOL 4mg; IRON 2.2mg; SODIUM 272mg; CALC 111mg

Garlic Pita Chips:

   6   (6-inch) pitas
Butter-flavored cooking spray
   ¼   teaspoon garlic powder

1. Preheat oven to 425°.
2. Coat one side of each pita with cooking spray; sprinkle with garlic powder. Cut each pita into 8 wedges; arrange wedges in a single layer on baking sheets. Bake at 425° for 6 minutes or until golden. Yield: 4 dozen.

SPICY GARDEN CHILI

This chili is best made the day of the party. It thickens over time because the bulgur absorbs some of the liquid. If the chili gets too thick, reheat over medium heat, adding water for desired consistency.

1 tablespoon olive oil
1½ cups chopped onion
1 cup chopped green bell pepper
1 cup chopped mushrooms
3 tablespoons minced seeded jalapeño pepper
2 tablespoons chili powder
2 tablespoons chopped fresh or 2 teaspoons dried oregano
1 teaspoon ground cumin
2 cups water
½ cup uncooked bulgur or cracked wheat
2 (14.5-ounce) cans diced tomatoes, undrained
1 (10¾-ounce) can tomato puree
1 cup frozen whole-kernel corn
1 (16-ounce) can cannellini beans or other white beans, drained
1 (16-ounce) can red beans, drained
9 tablespoons (2¼ ounces) shredded Monterey Jack cheese with jalapeño peppers
9 tablespoons (2¼ ounces) shredded reduced-fat sharp Cheddar cheese
9 tablespoons low-fat sour cream

1. Heat oil in a Dutch oven over medium-high heat. Add onion and next 6 ingredients; sauté 3 minutes. Stir in water and next 3 ingredients; bring to a boil. Reduce heat; simmer 30 minutes or until tender. Stir in corn and beans; cook 5 minutes. Ladle 1 cup chili into each of 9 bowls; top each with 1 tablespoon Monterey Jack, 1 tablespoon Cheddar cheese, and 1 tablespoon sour cream. Yield: 9 servings.

CALORIES 267 (29% from fat); FAT 8.6g (sat 3.7g, mono 3g, poly 1.2g); PROTEIN 13.4g; CARB 38.2g; FIBER 7g; CHOL 16mg; IRON 3.9mg; SODIUM 520mg; CALC 206mg

PREGAME ACTIVITIES

Here's an optional schedule of steps that will simplify game-day preparation.

Up to four days before the game:
1. Make Garlic Pita Chips; store in an airtight container.
2. Complete step 1 of Mexican Shrimp-and-Chicken Soup; freeze broth mixture and chicken separately.

Up to two days ahead:
1. Roast peppers for Three-Pepper Feta Roll-Ups; refrigerate.
2. Make vinaigrette for Mixed Greens with Sun-Dried Tomato Vinaigrette; refrigerate.
3. Shred cheeses for Spicy Garden Chili, and store in zip-top plastic bags; refrigerate.

Day before:
1. Make Opposing-Sides Two-Bean Dip and Caramel Cheesecake; refrigerate both.
2. Remove broth and chicken from freezer; thaw in refrigerator.

Early in the day of the party:
1. Prepare steaks for Slow-Cooker Barbecue-Beef Sandwiches.
2. Make Spicy Garden Chili.
3. Remove Opposing-Sides Two-Bean Dip from refrigerator, and allow to come to room temperature.
4. Finish making Mexican Shrimp-and-Chicken Soup.

MEXICAN SHRIMP-AND-CHICKEN SOUP

½ teaspoon ground cumin
2 cups water
1 teaspoon chili powder
5 teaspoons fresh lemon juice, divided
½ teaspoon salt, divided
½ teaspoon dried oregano
2 (6-ounce) skinned chicken breast halves
2 (16-ounce) cans fat-free, less-sodium chicken broth
2 bay leaves
1 large garlic clove, sliced
1½ pounds red potatoes, peeled and cut into ½-inch cubes
1½ cups (1-inch) cut green beans (about ½ pound)
¾ pound medium shrimp, peeled and deveined
½ cup sliced green onions
2 tablespoons chopped fresh cilantro

1. Place cumin in a Dutch oven; cook over medium heat 30 seconds or until toasted. Add water, chili powder, 3 teaspoons lemon juice, ¼ teaspoon salt, and next 5 ingredients; bring to a boil. Partially cover, reduce heat to medium-low, and simmer 20 minutes or until chicken is done. Remove chicken from pan; place chicken in a bowl, and chill 15 minutes. Strain broth mixture through a sieve into a large bowl; discard solids. Remove chicken from bones; shred meat, and set aside.
2. Return broth mixture to pan. Add potatoes; bring to a boil. Partially cover, reduce heat, and simmer 15 minutes or until tender. Add beans, and simmer 5 minutes. Add chicken and shrimp; simmer 3 minutes or until shrimp are done. Remove from heat; stir in 2 teaspoons lemon juice, ¼ teaspoon salt, onions, and cilantro. Yield: 8 servings (serving size: 1 cup).

CALORIES 162 (11% from fat); FAT 2g (sat 0.5g, mono 0.5g, poly 0.6g); PROTEIN 20.4g; CARB 15g; FIBER 1.9g; CHOL 77mg; IRON 2.3mg; SODIUM 470mg; CALC 47mg

Slow-Cooker Barbecue-Beef Sandwiches

5 tablespoons dark brown sugar, divided
¾ teaspoon black pepper
2 (1-pound) flank steaks
1 cup chopped onion
1 cup tomato paste
3 tablespoons Worcestershire sauce
3 tablespoons molasses
3 tablespoons cider vinegar
1 tablespoon chili powder
1 teaspoon garlic powder
1 teaspoon dry mustard
1 teaspoon ground cumin
½ teaspoon salt
10 (2½-ounce) submarine rolls, split
Red onion slices (optional)
Dill pickle slices (optional)

1. Combine 1 tablespoon brown sugar and pepper; rub over both sides of steaks. Combine ¼ cup brown sugar, onion, and next 9 ingredients in an electric slow cooker. Add steaks; turn to coat. Cover with lid; cook on high-heat setting for 1 hour. Reduce heat setting to low; cook for 7 hours. Remove steaks, reserving sauce in cooker.
2. Shred steaks with 2 forks. Return shredded steak to cooker; stir into sauce. Spoon ½ cup steak mixture onto bottom half of each roll; top with onion and pickles, if desired. Cover with tops of rolls. Yield: 10 servings (serving size: 1 sandwich).

CALORIES 435 (22% from fat); FAT 10.4g (sat 4.2g, mono 4.2g, poly 1.2g); PROTEIN 26g; CARB 57.2g; FIBER 3.1g; CHOL 47mg; IRON 4.9mg; SODIUM 668mg; CALC 77mg

Three-Pepper Feta Roll-Ups

1 cup (4 ounces) crumbled feta cheese
2 tablespoons chopped fresh or 2 teaspoons dried dill
2 tablespoons red wine vinegar
4 red bell peppers, roasted, peeled, and cut into thin strips
2 yellow bell peppers, roasted, peeled, and cut into thin strips
2 orange bell peppers, roasted, peeled, and cut into thin strips
4 garlic cloves, minced
8 (8-inch) flour tortillas
8 curly leaf lettuce leaves

1. Combine first 7 ingredients. Line each tortilla with a lettuce leaf. Spoon ½ cup bell pepper mixture down center of each tortilla; roll up. Yield: 8 servings.

CALORIES 213 (28% from fat); FAT 6.7g (sat 2.7g, mono 2g, poly 1.6g); PROTEIN 7g; CARB 31.5g; FIBER 2.8g; CHOL 13mg; IRON 2.7mg; SODIUM 386mg; CALC 141mg

Mixed Greens with Sun-Dried Tomato Vinaigrette

¼ cup sun-dried tomatoes, packed without oil (about 6)
½ cup boiling water
1 cup chopped seeded peeled tomato
2 tablespoons balsamic vinegar
1 garlic clove, minced
1 tablespoon extra-virgin olive oil
¼ teaspoon salt
¼ teaspoon black pepper
12 cups mixed salad greens
1 cup shredded carrot (about 2)

1. Combine sun-dried tomatoes and boiling water in a bowl; let stand 30 minutes. Drain, reserving water; chop sun-dried tomatoes.
2. Combine sun-dried tomatoes, 1 cup chopped tomato, vinegar, and garlic in a blender; process until smooth. Add reserved tomato liquid, oil, salt, and pepper; process until smooth. Combine greens and carrot in a large bowl; add vinaigrette, tossing well. Yield: 8 servings (serving size: 1½ cups).

CALORIES 44 (41% from fat); FAT 2g (sat 0.3g, mono 1.3g, poly 0.3g); PROTEIN 1.9g; CARB 5.5g; FIBER 2.2g; CHOL 0mg; IRON 1.2mg; SODIUM 118mg; CALC 38mg

Caramel Cheesecake

⅔ cup chocolate graham cracker crumbs (about 5 cookie sheets)
Cooking spray
2 cups fat-free cottage cheese
1 (8-ounce) tub light cream cheese
¾ cup packed brown sugar
½ cup granulated sugar
½ cup fat-free sour cream
¼ cup all-purpose flour
2 teaspoons vanilla extract
2 large eggs
2 large egg whites
¼ cup fat-free caramel sundae syrup, divided
2 (2.07-ounce) chocolate-coated caramel-peanut nougat bars (such as Snickers), chopped and divided

1. Preheat oven to 300°.
2. Sprinkle crumbs into bottom and halfway up sides of a 9-inch springform pan coated with cooking spray.
3. Combine cheeses in a food processor; process 2 minutes or until smooth. Add brown sugar and next 6 ingredients; process just until blended. Pour half of batter into prepared pan. Drizzle with 2 tablespoons syrup; sprinkle with half of chopped candy. Pour remaining batter into pan; drizzle with remaining 2 tablespoons syrup. Bake at 300° for 50 minutes. Sprinkle with remaining chopped candy; bake 10 minutes or until almost set. Turn oven off; let cheesecake stand 1 hour in oven with door closed. Remove cheesecake from oven; cool to room temperature. Cover and chill at least 8 hours. Yield: 12 servings (serving size: 1 wedge).

CALORIES 271 (23% from fat); FAT 6.9g (sat 3.5g, mono 1g, poly 0.5g); PROTEIN 10.9g; CARB 41.8g; FIBER 0.3g; CHOL 49mg; IRON 0.8mg; SODIUM 352mg; CALC 74mg

November

Toward a Tastier Tradition

Americans' changing lifestyles are pushing our traditional Thanksgiving turkey into bold new realms of streamlined looks and full-seasoned flavors.

The question is not whether our traditions should change, but how much fun can we have transforming them. Let's start by dropping some weight—from the turkey. Some may still need the 20-pounder, but most people can cut down to a more manageable 12-pound bird. That's still plenty to feed a dozen of your closest friends and relatives, and maybe leave a little for those leftover raids, but not so much that you'll be dining on turkey for the next month.

Even with a more practical poundage, you still may feel the urge to stuff the bird. The U.S. Department of Agriculture recommends against stuffing before cooking for safety reasons. Consider this advice an opportunity. Instead, just bake our flavorful Sourdough-Sausage Stuffing (page 303) on the side, and season the bird from within by filling the body cavity with spices, herbs, or fruit. Or try seasoning from the outside in: With a smaller bird and a 2-gallon zip-top plastic bag, for instance, marinating becomes an option. Then there's flavoring the turkey by coating it with a pungent spice rub, or even stuffing a mixture of fresh sage, chives, thyme, and parsley under the skin.

Whole turkey breasts, now widely available in supermarkets, are a fantastic alternative for smaller Thanksgiving gatherings. A 5-pound breast will feed up to six people with ample leftovers, and at a cooking time of less than 2 hours, it practically turns roast turkey into fast food. A whole breast costs more per pound than a whole bird, but it's still quite economical.

MENU

FRESH-HERB TURKEY

CRANBERRY-CORN RELISH (PAGE 305)

MAPLE-ORANGE SWEET POTATOES (PAGE 304)

BROCCOLI WITH ALMOND-BREADCRUMB TOPPING (PAGE 305)

SPINACH SALAD WITH BEETS AND ORANGES (PAGE 288)

SOUR CREAM-GREEN ONION FAN TANS (PAGE 282)

BLACK BOTTOM BANANA-CREAM PIE (PAGE 309)

FRESH-HERB TURKEY

1 (12-pound) fresh or frozen whole turkey, thawed
2 tablespoons chopped fresh sage
3 teaspoons chopped fresh chives, divided
2 teaspoons chopped fresh thyme, divided
1 teaspoon chopped fresh parsley
Cooking spray
2¾ cups fat-free, less-sodium chicken broth, divided
⅓ cup dry sherry
2 tablespoons all-purpose flour
2 tablespoons chopped fresh parsley

1. Preheat oven to 350°.
2. Remove giblets and neck from turkey; discard. Rinse turkey thoroughly with cold water; pat dry. Starting at neck cavity, loosen skin from breast and drumsticks by inserting fingers, gently pushing between skin and meat. Combine sage, 2 teaspoons chives, 1 teaspoon thyme, and 1 teaspoon parsley in a small bowl. Rub sage mixture under loosened skin and inside body cavity. Tie ends of legs together with cord. Lift wing tips up and over back; tuck under turkey.
3. Place turkey on a broiler pan coated with cooking spray or on a rack set in a shallow roasting pan. Insert meat thermometer into meaty part of thigh, making sure not to touch bone. Bake at 350° for 3 hours or until thermometer registers 180°. (Cover turkey loosely with foil if it gets too brown.) Remove turkey from oven. Cover loosely with foil; let stand at least 10 minutes before carving.
4. Place a zip-top plastic bag inside a 2-cup glass measure. Pour drippings from pan into bag; let stand 10 minutes (fat will rise to the top). Seal bag; snip off 1 bottom corner of bag. Drain drippings into a medium saucepan, stopping before fat layer reaches opening. Stir in 2½ cups broth and sherry. Bring to a boil; reduce heat, and simmer 10 minutes. Combine ¼ cup broth and flour in a small bowl, stirring well with a whisk. Stir into sherry mixture, and bring to a boil, stirring constantly. Stir in 2 tablespoons parsley, 1 teaspoon chives, and 1 teaspoon thyme. Serve sauce with turkey. Yield: 12 servings (serving size: 6 ounces turkey and ¼ cup sauce).

Note: To substitute a 5-pound turkey breast for a 12-pound turkey, follow the general directions given on page 279. To make sauce, increase total amount of chicken broth to 3 cups and stir 2¾ cups of broth into drippings along with sherry.

CALORIES 264 (14% from fat); FAT 4.1g (sat 1.4g, mono 0.9g, poly 1.2g); PROTEIN 51.4g; CARB 1.7g; FIBER 0.1g; CHOL 142mg; IRON 3.1mg; SODIUM 211mg; CALC 35mg

ORANGE-BOURBON TURKEY

1   (12-pound) fresh or frozen
    whole turkey, thawed
2   cups fresh orange juice (about
    6 oranges)
1   cup water
¾   cup bourbon, divided
⅓   cup molasses
¾   teaspoon salt, divided
4   oranges, peeled
Cooking spray
3   tablespoons all-purpose flour
Orange slices (optional)
Flat-leaf parsley sprigs (optional)

1. Remove giblets and neck from turkey; discard. Rinse turkey thoroughly with cold water; pat dry. Combine orange juice, water, ½ cup bourbon, and molasses in a 2-gallon heavy-duty zip-top plastic bag; add turkey. Seal and marinate in refrigerator 4 to 24 hours, turning bag occasionally. Remove turkey from bag, reserving marinade.
2. Preheat oven to 350°.
3. Tie ends of legs together with cord. Lift wing tips up and over back; tuck under turkey. Sprinkle ½ teaspoon salt into body cavity. Stuff cavity with 4 oranges. Place turkey on a broiler pan coated with cooking spray or on a rack set in a shallow roasting pan. Insert meat thermometer into meaty part of

thigh, making sure not to touch bone. Bake at 350° for 3 hours or until thermometer registers 180°. (Cover turkey loosely with foil if it gets too brown.) Remove turkey from oven. Cover turkey loosely with foil; let stand at least 10 minutes before carving. Discard oranges.
4. Pour reserved marinade into a saucepan; bring to a boil. Skim foam from mixture with a slotted spoon; discard. Reduce heat to medium; cook until reduced to 3½ cups (about 15 minutes). Combine ¼ cup bourbon and flour in a small bowl, stirring well with a whisk. Add to reduced marinade; bring to a boil, and cook 1 minute, stirring constantly. Stir in ¼ teaspoon salt. Serve sauce with turkey. Garnish with orange slices and parsley sprigs, if desired. Yield: 12 servings (serving size: 6 ounces turkey and ¼ cup sauce).
Note: To substitute a 5-pound turkey breast for a 12-pound turkey, omit the 4 peeled oranges used to stuff the whole turkey, then follow the general directions given below.

CALORIES 305 (12% from fat); FAT 4.1g (sat 1.3g, mono 0.9g, poly 1.2g); PROTEIN 51g; CARB 12.8g; FIBER 0.1g; CHOL 142mg; IRON 3.5mg; SODIUM 251mg; CALC 54mg

---

COOKING A WHOLE TURKEY BREAST

For smaller Thanksgiving parties or white-meat-only crowds, a whole turkey breast is a smart alternative to an entire bird. A 5-pound breast can be substituted for the 12-pound bird called for in our recipes with a few minor adjustments.
•Insert a meat thermometer into the meaty part of the turkey breast, making sure it doesn't touch the breastbone.
•Bake the breast at 350° for 1 hour and 45 minutes or until the thermometer registers 170°. Cover the breast loosely with aluminum foil if it gets too brown.
•To carve, slice the breast directly off the bone. Discard skin.
•See specific recipes for any additional changes.

ARIZONA TURKEY WITH CHIPOTLE SAUCE

(pictured on page 2)

If chipotles are unavailable, substitute dried ancho or pasilla chiles.

1   (12-pound) fresh or frozen
      turkey, thawed
1½   teaspoons ground cumin
1   teaspoon chili powder
1   teaspoon dried rubbed sage
¾   teaspoon garlic powder
½   teaspoon ground red pepper
¼   teaspoon ground turmeric
Cooking spray
½   cup boiling water
1   to 2 chipotle chiles
3¾   cups fat-free, less-sodium chicken
      broth, divided
3   tablespoons tomato paste
1   tablespoon Worcestershire sauce
¼   cup all-purpose flour

1. Preheat oven to 350°.
2. Remove giblets and neck from turkey; discard. Rinse turkey thoroughly with cold water; pat dry. Starting at neck cavity, loosen skin from breast and drumsticks by inserting fingers, gently pushing between skin and meat.
3. Combine cumin and next 5 ingredients. Rub mixture under loosened skin and inside body cavity. Tie ends of legs together with cord. Lift wing tips up and over back; tuck under turkey.
4. Place turkey on a broiler pan coated with cooking spray or on a rack set in a shallow roasting pan. Insert meat thermometer into meaty part of thigh, making sure not to touch bone. Bake at 350° for 3 hours or until thermometer registers 180°. (Cover turkey loosely with foil if it gets too brown.)
5. Combine boiling water and chipotle chiles in a small bowl; cover and let stand 30 minutes or until soft. Drain; discard stems, seeds, and membranes. Combine chiles and ½ cup broth in a blender; process until smooth. Set aside.
6. Remove turkey from oven. Cover turkey loosely with foil; let stand at least 10 minutes before carving. Place a
Continued

HOW TO CARVE A TURKEY

❶ *Cut and discard cord used to tie legs. Grab end of one drumstick, and pull it away from bird. To free the leg, follow the contour of bird, cutting underneath the dark thigh meat.*

❷ *Separate drumstick and thigh by severing leg joint. Remove skin. Cut thigh meat off bone. Repeat for drumstick.*

❸ *Remove one side of breast by cutting into center of breast meat and slicing downward along breastbone and rib cage. Remove skin from breast half.*

❹ *Place breast half on cutting surface. Holding it steady with carving fork, slice it against grain.*

zip-top plastic bag inside a 2-cup glass measure. Pour drippings into bag; let stand 10 minutes (fat will rise to the top). Seal bag, and carefully snip off 1 bottom corner of bag. Drain drippings into a medium saucepan, stopping before fat layer reaches opening; discard fat. Add 3 cups broth to drippings. Bring to a boil; cook until reduced to 3 cups (about 6 minutes). Stir in chile mixture, tomato paste, and Worcestershire sauce. Combine remaining ¼ cup broth and flour, stirring with a whisk; add to chile mixture in saucepan. Bring to a boil; reduce heat, and simmer 10 minutes. Strain mixture through a sieve over a bowl; discard solids. Serve sauce with turkey. Yield: 12 servings (serving size: 6 ounces turkey and ¼ cup sauce).

Note: To substitute a 5-pound turkey breast for a 12-pound turkey, follow the general directions given on page 279. To make sauce, increase total amount of chicken broth to 4 cups, and stir 3¾ cups of it into turkey drippings.

CALORIES 277 (14% from fat); FAT 4.3g (sat 1.4g, mono 0.9g, poly 1.2g); PROTEIN 51.7g; CARB 4.2g; FIBER 0.6g; CHOL 142mg; IRON 3.5mg; SODIUM 251mg; CALC 37mg

SPICED TURKEY WITH FRESH-PEAR CHUTNEY

Apple or pineapple juice may be substituted for the pear juice.

    1   (12-pound) fresh or frozen
        whole turkey, thawed
    3   tablespoons pear juice
    2   teaspoons grated peeled fresh
        ginger
    1   teaspoon ground cinnamon
    1   teaspoon ground cloves
    1   teaspoon ground allspice
    2   Granny Smith apples, cored and
        quartered
    1   (2-inch) piece peeled fresh
        ginger, thinly sliced
        Cooking spray
        Fresh-Pear Chutney

1. Remove giblets and neck from turkey; discard. Rinse turkey thoroughly with cold water, and pat dry.

Starting at neck cavity, loosen skin from breast and drumsticks by inserting fingers, gently pushing between skin and meat. Tie ends of legs together with cord. Lift wing tips up and over back; tuck under turkey.

2. Preheat oven to 350°.

3. Combine pear juice and next 4 ingredients. Rub mixture under loosened skin. Stuff cavity with apples and ginger.

4. Place turkey on a broiler pan coated with cooking spray or on a rack set in a shallow roasting pan. Insert meat thermometer into meaty part of thigh, making sure not to touch bone. Bake at 350° for 3 hours or until thermometer registers 180°. (Cover turkey loosely with foil if it gets too brown.) Remove turkey from oven. Cover loosely with foil; let stand 10 minutes before carving. Discard apples and ginger. Serve with Fresh-Pear Chutney. Yield: 12 servings (serving size: 6 ounces turkey and ¼ cup chutney).

Note: To substitute a 5-pound turkey breast for a 12-pound turkey, omit the 2 Granny Smith apples and 2-inch piece of peeled fresh ginger used to stuff the whole turkey, then follow the general directions given on page 279.

CALORIES 310 (12% from fat); FAT 4.3g (sat 1.4g, mono 0.9g, poly 1.2g); PROTEIN 50.9g; CARB 14.7g; FIBER 1.6g; CHOL 142mg; IRON 3.3mg; SODIUM 105mg; CALC 48mg

Fresh-Pear Chutney:

    1   cup chopped red onion
    ⅓   cup packed brown sugar
    ¼   cup currants
    ¼   cup rice vinegar
    ½   teaspoon dried crushed red pepper
    ½   teaspoon minced peeled fresh
          ginger
    ¼   teaspoon ground cinnamon
    ¼   teaspoon ground cloves
    3   cups chopped peeled pear

1. Combine first 8 ingredients in a saucepan; bring to a boil. Cover, reduce heat, and simmer 5 minutes. Remove from heat; cool 10 minutes. Place in a bowl; stir in pear. Yield: 3 cups (serving size: ¼ cup).

CALORIES 55 (3% from fat); FAT 0.2g (sat 0g, mono 0g, poly 0.1g); PROTEIN 0.4g; CARB 13.8g; FIBER 1.5g; CHOL 0mg; IRON 0.3mg; SODIUM 4mg; CALC 14mg

The Yeast Among Us

Aromatic, sensuous, light as cotton candy, and always open to new twists, yeast rolls are the most tempting for guests at those special occasions.

Whatever else is happening around the holiday table, all eyes—and noses, and, ultimately, tongues and tummies—shift attention immediately to the basket of dinner rolls. The classics are fine, but so is the addition of some newer flavor options: buttermilk and oats or sour cream and green onions. And if you're bored with the old Parker House-style, you can twist and twirl the rolls your own way or snip patterns into the tops of them with scissors. Or make cloverleafs, or folds, or just big, luscious loaves. A good roll can have as many variations as you've got appetites.

HERB CLOVERLEAF ROLLS

1 package dry yeast (about 2¼ teaspoons)
2 teaspoons sugar
¼ cup warm water (105° to 115°)
¾ cup 1% low-fat milk
½ cup evaporated skim milk
4 cups bread or all-purpose flour, divided
1½ tablespoons stick margarine or butter, melted
1 teaspoon salt
½ teaspoon dried rosemary
½ teaspoon dried thyme
½ teaspoon dried oregano
¼ teaspoon black pepper
Cooking spray
1 tablespoon water
1 large egg white, lightly beaten

1. Dissolve yeast and sugar in warm water in a large bowl; let stand 5 minutes. Stir in milks. Lightly spoon flour into dry measuring cups; level with a knife. Add 3 cups flour, margarine, and next 5 ingredients to yeast mixture; stir until blended. Turn dough out onto a lightly floured surface. Knead until smooth and elastic (about 10 minutes), adding enough of remaining flour, 1 tablespoon at a time, to prevent dough from sticking to hands.
2. Place dough in a large bowl coated with cooking spray, turning to coat top. Cover and let rise in a warm place (85°), free from drafts, 1 hour or until doubled in bulk. Punch dough down; cover and let rest 10 minutes. Divide into 18 equal portions. Working with 1 portion at a time (cover remaining dough to keep from drying), divide each portion into 3 pieces; shape each piece into a ball. Coat muffin pans with cooking spray; place 3 balls in each muffin cup. Cover; let rise in a warm place, free from drafts, 30 minutes or until doubled in bulk.
3. Preheat oven to 350°.
4. Uncover dough. Combine water and egg white; brush over dough. Bake at 350° for 20 minutes. Serve warm. Yield: 1½ dozen (serving size: 1 roll).

CALORIES 119 (12% from fat); FAT 1.6g (sat 0.3g, mono 0.5g, poly 0.5g); PROTEIN 4.4g; CARB 21.3g; FIBER 0.1g; CHOL 1mg; IRON 1.4mg; SODIUM 158mg; CALC 40mg

BUTTERMILK-OAT ROLLS

(pictured on page 298)

¾ cup regular oats
½ cup boiling water
1 tablespoon sugar
1 package dry yeast (about 2¼ teaspoons)
1½ teaspoons sugar
¼ cup warm water (105° to 115°)
2¼ cups bread or all-purpose flour, divided
¼ cup low-fat buttermilk
1 tablespoon stick margarine melted
¾ teaspoon salt
Cooking spray
1 tablespoon water
1 large egg white, lightly beaten
1 tablespoon regular oats

1. Combine first 3 ingredients; stir until well-blended. Let stand 5 minutes.
2. Dissolve yeast and 1½ teaspoons sugar in warm water; let stand 5 minutes. Lightly spoon flour into dry measuring cups; level with a knife. Add oat mixture, 1¾ cups flour, buttermilk, margarine, and salt to yeast mixture, stirring to form a soft dough. Turn out onto a lightly floured surface. Knead until smooth and elastic (about 8 minutes), adding enough of remaining flour, 1 tablespoon at a time, to prevent dough from sticking to hands. (Dough will be slightly sticky.)
3. Place dough in a large bowl coated with cooking spray, turning to coat top. Cover and let rise in a warm place (85°), free from drafts, 45 minutes or until doubled in bulk. Punch down; cover and let rest 5 minutes. Divide into 12 equal portions. Working with 1 portion at a time (cover remaining dough to keep from drying), shape each into a ball. Place balls in a 9-inch square baking pan coated with cooking spray. Cover; let rise 30 minutes or until doubled in bulk.
4. Preheat oven to 375°. Uncover dough. Combine water and egg white; brush over dough. Sprinkle with oats. Bake at 375° for 25 minutes or until lightly browned. Yield: 1 dozen (serving size: 1 roll).

CALORIES 120 (13% from fat); FAT 1.7g (sat 0.3g, mono 0.6g, poly 0.5g); PROTEIN 3.8g; CARB 22.2g; FIBER 1.3g; CHOL 0mg; IRON 1.4mg; SODIUM 165mg; CALC 13mg

SMOKED-GOUDA ROLLS

1 package dry yeast (about 2¼ teaspoons)
1 tablespoon sugar
¼ cup warm water (105° to 115°)
¾ cup 1% low-fat milk
1 tablespoon stick margarine or butter
1 tablespoon Dijon mustard
3 cups bread or all-purpose flour, divided
½ teaspoon salt
⅛ teaspoon ground red pepper
Cooking spray
¾ cup (3 ounces) shredded smoked Gouda cheese
1 tablespoon water
1 large egg white, lightly beaten
2 teaspoons sesame seeds

1. Dissolve yeast and sugar in warm water in a large bowl; let stand 5 minutes. Combine milk and margarine in a small saucepan over low heat; heat until margarine melts (do not boil). Remove from heat; stir in mustard. Cool milk mixture slightly. Lightly spoon flour into dry measuring cups; level with a knife. Combine yeast mixture, milk mixture, flour, salt, and pepper in a food processor; process 1 minute. Turn dough out onto a lightly floured surface; knead 3 or 4 times.
2. Place dough in a large bowl coated with cooking spray, turning to coat top. Cover and let rise in a warm place (85°), free from drafts, 45 minutes or until doubled in bulk. Punch dough down; cover and let rest 5 minutes. Sprinkle with cheese; knead lightly.
3. Divide dough into 12 equal portions. Working with 1 portion at a time (cover remaining dough to keep from drying), shape each portion into a 10-inch-long rope; tie loosely into a simple knot. Place knots on baking sheets coated with cooking spray. Cover and let rise 30 minutes or until doubled in bulk.
4. Preheat oven to 375°.
5. Uncover dough. Combine 1 tablespoon water and egg white; brush over dough. Sprinkle with sesame seeds. Bake at 375° for 15 minutes or until golden brown. Serve warm. Yield: 1 dozen (serving size: 1 roll).

CALORIES 176 (20% from fat); FAT 4g (sat 1.7g, mono 1.2g, poly 0.7g); PROTEIN 7g; CARB 27.2g; FIBER 0.2g; CHOL 9mg; IRON 1.7mg; SODIUM 217mg; CALC 79mg

ANADAMA ROLLS WITH SAGE

The addition of sage is our new spin, but cornmeal and molasses are characteristic ingredients of this early American yeast bread.

1 package dry yeast (about 2¼ teaspoons)
Dash of sugar
¼ cup warm water (105° to 115°)
¾ cup 1% low-fat milk
¼ cup molasses
3¼ cups bread or all-purpose flour, divided
½ cup yellow cornmeal
2 tablespoons stick margarine or butter, melted
1 teaspoon dried rubbed sage
¾ teaspoon salt
Cooking spray
2 teaspoons water
1 large egg white, lightly beaten

1. Dissolve yeast and sugar in warm water in a large bowl; let stand 5 minutes. Stir in milk and molasses. Lightly spoon flour into dry measuring cups; level with a knife. Add 3 cups flour, cornmeal, and next 3 ingredients to yeast mixture; stir until blended. Turn dough out onto a lightly floured surface. Knead until smooth and elastic (about 10 minutes), adding enough of remaining flour, 1 tablespoon at a time, to prevent dough from sticking to hands.
2. Place dough in a large bowl coated with cooking spray, turning to coat top. Cover and let rise in a warm place (85°), free from drafts, 1 hour or until doubled in bulk. Turn dough out onto a lightly floured surface; punch dough down. Cover and let rest 5 minutes. Divide into 18 equal portions. Working with 1 portion at a time (cover remaining dough to keep from drying), shape each into a ball. Place balls of dough 2 inches apart on baking sheets coated with cooking spray. Cover and let rise 30 minutes or until doubled in bulk.
3. Preheat oven to 350°.
4. Uncover dough. Snip across tops of rolls about ¼-inch deep to make an "X" design, using sharp scissors. Combine 2 teaspoons water and egg white; brush over dough. Bake at 350° for 13 minutes or until golden brown. Serve warm. Yield: 1½ dozen (serving size: 1 roll).

CALORIES 126 (12% from fat); FAT 1.7g (sat 0.4g, mono 0.6g, poly 0.5g); PROTEIN 3.3g; CARB 23.9g; FIBER 0.9g; CHOL 0mg; IRON 1.5mg; SODIUM 123mg; CALC 27mg

SOUR CREAM-GREEN ONION FAN TANS

Three easy steps give these pull-apart rolls their unique shape. They fan out as they bake (hence the name).

1 package dry yeast (about 2¼ teaspoons)
1 teaspoon sugar
¼ cup warm water (105° to 115°)
4¼ cups bread or all-purpose flour, divided
¾ cup 1% low-fat milk
½ cup low-fat sour cream
1 teaspoon salt
¾ teaspoon ground cumin
Cooking spray
3 tablespoons stick margarine or butter, melted and divided
½ cup minced green onions, divided

1. Dissolve yeast and sugar in warm water in a large bowl; let stand 5 minutes. Lightly spoon flour into dry measuring cups; level with knife. Add 4 cups flour, milk, and next 3 ingredients to yeast mixture; stir until blended. Turn dough out onto a lightly floured surface. Knead until smooth and elastic (about 10 minutes), adding enough of remaining flour, 1 tablespoon at a time, to prevent dough from sticking to hands.
2. Place dough in a large bowl coated with cooking spray, turning to coat top. Cover and let rise in a warm place

(85°), free from drafts, 1 hour or until doubled in bulk. Punch dough down; cover and let rest 5 minutes. Divide dough into 3 equal portions. Working with one portion at a time (cover remaining dough to keep from drying), roll each portion into a 12 x 9-inch rectangle on a lightly floured surface. Brush each rectangle with 1½ teaspoons margarine, and sprinkle with about 2½ tablespoons onions. Cut each rectangle lengthwise into 6 (1½-inch) strips. Stack 6 strips, coated sides up, one on top of another. Cut each stack into 8 (1½-inch) sections. Place each stacked section, cut side down, in a muffin cup coated with cooking spray. Brush remaining margarine over dough. Cover and let rise for 30 minutes or until doubled in bulk.

3. Preheat oven to 400°.

4. Bake at 400° for 17 minutes or until golden brown. Serve warm. Yield: 2 dozen (serving size: 1 roll).

CALORIES 113 (21% from fat); FAT 2.6g (sat 0.8g, mono 0.9g, poly 0.7g); PROTEIN 3.5g; CARB 18.7g; FIBER 0.1g; CHOL 2mg; IRON 1.2mg; SODIUM 121mg; CALC 21mg

Food processor variation:

Dissolve yeast and sugar in warm water in a small bowl; let stand 5 minutes. Lightly spoon flour into dry measuring cups; level with a knife. Place 4 cups flour, sour cream, salt, and cumin in a food processor; pulse 2 times or until blended. With processor on, slowly add yeast mixture and milk through food chute; process until dough forms a ball. Process 1 additional minute. Turn dough out onto a lightly floured surface. Knead until smooth and elastic (about 10 minutes); add enough of remaining flour, 1 tablespoon at a time, to prevent dough from sticking to hands. Place dough in a large bowl coated with cooking spray, turning to coat top. Let rise, shape, and bake according to directions above.

INDIVIDUAL BRIOCHE

Traditionally, brioche is served with butter and jam for breakfast, but this classic French bread also makes a rich-tasting dinner roll.

1   package dry yeast (about 2¼ teaspoons)
2   teaspoons sugar
½   cup warm water (105° to 115°)
¼   cup 1% low-fat milk
2   large eggs, lightly beaten
3½ cups bread or all-purpose flour, divided
⅓   cup stick margarine or butter, softened
1   teaspoon salt
Cooking spray
1   tablespoon water
1   large egg white, lightly beaten

1. Dissolve yeast and sugar in warm water in a large bowl; let stand 5 minutes. Stir in milk and 2 eggs. Lightly spoon flour into dry measuring cups; level with a knife. Add 3 cups flour, margarine, and salt to yeast mixture; stir until blended. Turn dough out onto a lightly floured surface. Knead until smooth and elastic (about 10 minutes), adding enough of remaining flour, 1 tablespoon at a time, to prevent dough from sticking to hands.

2. Place dough in a large bowl coated with cooking spray, turning to coat top. Cover dough, and let rise in a warm place (85°), free from drafts, 1 hour or until doubled in bulk. Punch dough down; cover and let rest 5 minutes. Divide dough into 16 equal portions. Working with 1 portion at a time (cover remaining dough to keep from drying), remove 1 rounded teaspoon of dough from each portion, and set aside. Place larger portions of dough in muffin cups coated with cooking spray. Make a deep indentation in the center of each portion using a floured finger. Shape reserved pieces of dough into balls. Press one dough ball into each indentation. Cover and let rise 30 minutes or until doubled in bulk.

3. Preheat oven to 375°.

4. Uncover dough. Combine 1 tablespoon water and egg white; brush over dough. Bake at 375° for 25 minutes or until golden brown. Serve warm. Yield: 16 rolls (serving size: 1 roll).

CALORIES 149 (29% from fat); FAT 4.8g (sat 1g, mono 2g, poly 1.4g); PROTEIN 4.2g; CARB 21.9g; FIBER 0.9g; CHOL 28mg; IRON 1.4mg; SODIUM 205mg; CALC 14mg

Turkey, Pass By

Who says you have to cook the classic on Thanksgiving? This year surprise your guests with an elegant alternative.

What's the solution to making Thanksgiving dinner special? Serve anything *but* the bird. What should you serve? How about a truly rare bird these days—red meat.

A beef tenderloin or rack of lamb makes an impressive centerpiece. Or you might opt for pork. On the other hand, if your heart is set on poultry, you can dazzle your diners with stately stuffed Cornish game hens.

There's an added incentive just for you. Think of the time you'll save in the kitchen by passing on turkey. Most of the above options can be prepared in little more than an hour—about two hours shy of the time it takes to cook a 12-pound bird.

BEEF TENDERLOIN WITH HORSERADISH-AND-ROASTED GARLIC CRUST

Pair this robust dish with a side of creamy mashed potatoes.

1   whole garlic head
Olive oil-flavored cooking spray
⅓   cup prepared horseradish
¼   teaspoon salt
¼   teaspoon dried basil
¼   teaspoon dried thyme
¼   teaspoon black pepper
1   (3-pound) beef tenderloin
Continued

1. Preheat oven to 350°.
2. Remove white papery skin from garlic head (do not peel or separate cloves). Coat with cooking spray; wrap in foil. Bake at 350° for 1 hour; cool 10 minutes. Separate cloves; squeeze to extract garlic pulp. Discard skins. Mash garlic pulp, horseradish, and next 4 ingredients with a fork until blended.
3. Preheat oven to 400°.
4. Trim fat from tenderloin; fold under 3 inches of small end. Rub garlic mixture over roast. Place on a broiler pan coated with cooking spray. Insert a meat thermometer into thickest portion of tenderloin. Bake at 400° for 40 minutes or until thermometer registers 145° (medium-rare) to 160° (medium).
5. Place tenderloin on a platter. Cover and let stand 10 minutes before slicing. Yield: 12 servings (serving size: 3 ounces).

CALORIES 179 (38% from fat); FAT 7.5g (sat 3g, mono 2.8g, poly 0.4g); PROTEIN 24g; CARB 2.5g; FIBER 0.2g; CHOL 70mg; IRON 3.3mg; SODIUM 117mg; CALC 22mg

HERB-ORANGE PORK TENDERLOIN

2 teaspoons ground cumin
1 teaspoon dried thyme
1 teaspoon dried rubbed sage
1 teaspoon ground cinnamon
¼ teaspoon garlic powder
¼ teaspoon salt
2 (1-pound) pork tenderloins
¼ cup orange marmalade
Cooking spray

1. Preheat oven to 425°.
2. Combine first 6 ingredients in a shallow dish. Trim fat from pork. Brush pork with orange marmalade; roll in spice mixture. Place on a broiler pan coated with cooking spray. Insert a meat thermometer into thickest part of pork. Bake at 425° for 25 minutes or until thermometer registers 160° (slightly pink). Cover; let stand 10 minutes before slicing. Yield: 8 servings (serving size: 3 ounces).

CALORIES 155 (17% from fat); FAT 2.9g (sat 1g, mono 1.3g, poly 0.3g); PROTEIN 24g; CARB 7.3g; FIBER 0.2g; CHOL 74mg; IRON 2.2mg; SODIUM 135mg; CALC 25mg

CRANBERRY-CRUSTED RACK OF LAMB WITH ROSEMARY POTATOES

Rack of lamb:

1 (1½-pound) French-cut rack of lamb (about 8 ribs)
2 tablespoons sweetened dried cranberries (such as Craisins)
¾ teaspoon dried rosemary
2 garlic cloves
1 small shallot, peeled and quartered
½ cup seasoned breadcrumbs
¼ teaspoon salt
¼ teaspoon black pepper
2 tablespoons honey mustard
1 teaspoon olive oil

Potatoes:

3 large red potatoes (about 6 ounces each), quartered
2 tablespoons chopped fresh or 2 teaspoons dried parsley flakes
1 teaspoon olive oil
½ teaspoon dried rosemary
⅛ teaspoon salt
⅛ teaspoon black pepper

1. Preheat oven to 425°.
2. To prepare rack of lamb, trim fat from lamb; place lamb, meat side up, on a broiler pan. Insert a meat thermometer into thickest part of lamb, making sure thermometer does not touch bone.
3. Combine cranberries and next 3 ingredients in a food processor; process until cranberries are chopped. Add breadcrumbs, ¼ teaspoon salt, and ¼ teaspoon pepper. Spread mustard over lamb; pat breadcrumb mixture into mustard on lamb. Drizzle with olive oil.
4. To prepare potatoes, combine potatoes and remaining 5 ingredients. Arrange potatoes around lamb. Bake lamb and potatoes at 425° for 40 minutes or until thermometer registers 145° (medium-rare) to 160° (medium). Cover; let stand 10 minutes. Slice lamb into 8 chops. Yield: 4 servings (serving size: 2 lamb chops and 3 potato wedges).

CALORIES 358 (32% from fat); FAT 12.8g (sat 3.8g, mono 5.9g, poly 1.2g); PROTEIN 24.7g; CARB 37.1g; FIBER 2.5g; CHOL 64mg; IRON 4.2mg; SODIUM 752mg; CALC 59mg

GLAZED CORNISH HENS WITH WILD RICE-AND-APRICOT STUFFING

Stuffing:

3 cups fat-free, less-sodium chicken broth
1 cup uncooked wild rice
1 tablespoon stick margarine or butter
1 cup chopped onion
½ cup chopped celery
½ cup chopped fennel bulb
½ cup finely chopped dried apricots
½ teaspoon dried thyme
¼ teaspoon salt
¼ teaspoon paprika
¼ teaspoon black pepper

Glazed hens:

2 (1½-pound) Cornish hens
Cooking spray
¼ cup orange juice
3 tablespoons apricot preserves

Sauce:

¼ cup minced shallots
¾ cup orange juice
½ cup fat-free, less-sodium chicken broth
2 tablespoons lemon juice
½ cup Madeira wine
1 tablespoon cornstarch

Fennel fronds (optional)

1. To prepare stuffing, bring 3 cups broth to a boil in a medium saucepan. Add wild rice; cover, reduce heat, and simmer 50 minutes or until tender. Drain and set aside.
2. Preheat oven to 400°.
3. Melt margarine in a large nonstick skillet over medium heat. Add onion, celery, and chopped fennel; sauté 10 minutes or until tender. Stir in rice, chopped apricots, and next 4 ingredients. Remove from heat.
4. To prepare glazed hens, remove and discard giblets and necks from hens. Rinse hens with cold water, and pat dry. Remove skin, and trim excess fat.

Split hens in half lengthwise. Spoon 4 (1-cup) mounds of wild rice stuffing into a shallow roasting pan coated with cooking spray. Place hen halves, meaty sides up, on top of mounds. Combine ¼ cup orange juice and apricot preserves in a small bowl. Spoon 1½ tablespoons orange juice mixture over each hen half. Bake at 400° for 40 minutes or until juices run clear.

5. To prepare sauce, place a nonstick skillet coated with cooking spray over medium-high heat until hot. Add shallots; sauté 5 minutes or until tender. Add ¾ cup orange juice, ½ cup broth, and lemon juice; bring to a boil over medium-high heat, and cook 5 minutes. Combine Madeira and cornstarch; add to skillet. Bring to a boil; reduce heat, and cook 2 minutes or until thick, stirring constantly. Serve sauce over hens. Garnish with fennel fronds, if desired. Yield: 4 servings (serving size: 1 hen half, 1 cup stuffing, and ¼ cup sauce).

CALORIES 556 (20% from fat); FAT 12.3g (sat 3g, mono 4.4g, poly 3.1g); PROTEIN 43.8g; CARB 68.7g; FIBER 4.2g; CHOL 101mg; IRON 4.2mg; SODIUM 740mg; CALC 81mg

PORK ROAST WITH MARSALA-FRUIT STUFFING

If Marsala wine is not available, use port or sherry instead.

1 (2½-pound) boned pork loin roast

Fruit stuffing:

1 cup sweet Marsala wine
½ cup chopped dried apricots
½ cup chopped pitted prunes
1 tablespoon stick margarine or butter
¼ cup chopped onion
¼ cup chopped celery
2 garlic cloves, chopped
½ cup dry breadcrumbs
¼ teaspoon salt
¼ teaspoon dried marjoram
¼ teaspoon dried thyme
¼ teaspoon dried rubbed sage
¼ teaspoon black pepper

Spice rub:

¼ cup packed brown sugar
2 tablespoons sweet Marsala wine
¼ teaspoon ground allspice

Cooking spray

1. Preheat oven to 400°.
2. Trim fat from roast; set roast aside.
3. To prepare fruit stuffing, combine 1 cup Marsala wine, apricots, and prunes in a saucepan; bring to a boil. Reduce heat to medium; cook 5 minutes. Melt margarine in a nonstick skillet over medium-high heat. Add onion, celery, and garlic; sauté 2 minutes. Remove from heat; stir in apricot mixture, breadcrumbs, and next 5 ingredients. Cut a 1½-inch-wide horizontal slit into the short end of roast; cut through to the other end of roast to form a deep pocket using a long thin knife. Spoon fruit stuffing into pocket; pack, using the handle of a wooden spoon.
4. To prepare spice rub, combine brown sugar, 2 tablespoons Marsala wine, and allspice. Score a diamond pattern on top of roast using a sharp knife; spread spice rub over top. Place roast, rub side up, on a broiler pan coated with cooking spray. Insert a meat thermometer into meaty part of roast. Bake at 400° for 1 hour and 15 minutes or until thermometer registers 160° (slightly pink). Cover and let stand 10 minutes before slicing. Yield: 10 servings (serving size: 3 ounces stuffed pork).

CALORIES 238 (32% from fat); FAT 8.5g (sat 2.7g, mono 3.8g, poly 1.2g); PROTEIN 20.1g; CARB 20.2g; FIBER 1.1g; CHOL 54mg; IRON 1.9mg; SODIUM 190mg; CALC 38mg

Lightning-Fast Lasagnas

The latest wave of no-boil noodles and time-saving standbys has given an old favorite a new lease on speed.

The introduction of no-boil lasagna noodles in the mid-1990s means that today any number of exceptional lasagnas can be put together in a hurry. Beyond those no-boil noodles, the secret to today's speedy lasagnas lies in the use of many other no-fuss ingredients such as preshredded cheeses, frozen chopped spinach, and bottled roasted red peppers. Also, cooking times have been drastically reduced by keeping the number of layers in the lasagna to a minimum and baking the dishes at higher temperatures than customary.

LASAGNA-CHICKEN FLORENTINE

Preparation time: 10 minutes
Cooking time: 35 minutes

1½ tablespoons stick margarine or butter
3 tablespoons all-purpose flour
2 (12-ounce) cans evaporated skim milk
½ teaspoon salt
⅛ teaspoon ground nutmeg
Cooking spray
6 no-boil lasagna noodles
1½ cups shredded cooked chicken breast (about 6 ounces)
1 (10-ounce) package frozen chopped spinach, thawed, drained, and squeezed dry
½ teaspoon freshly ground black pepper, divided
¾ cup (3 ounces) preshredded reduced-fat pizza-blend cheese or Cheddar cheese

Continued

1. Preheat oven to 450°.

2. Melt margarine in a medium saucepan over medium heat. Add flour; cook 30 seconds, stirring constantly. Gradually add milk, stirring with a whisk until blended. Stir in salt and nutmeg; cook until thick, stirring constantly (about 3 minutes).

3. Spread ½ cup sauce in bottom of an 8-inch square baking dish coated with cooking spray. Arrange 2 noodles over sauce; top with half of chicken and half of spinach. Sprinkle with ¼ teaspoon pepper; top with ¾ cup sauce. Repeat layers, ending with noodles. Spread remaining sauce over noodles. Cover and bake at 450° for 25 minutes or until noodles are tender and sauce is bubbly. Uncover and top with cheese; bake an additional 5 minutes. Let stand 5 minutes. Yield: 4 servings.

CALORIES 450 (22% from fat); FAT 11g (sat 4g, mono 4.1g, poly 2.1g); PROTEIN 38.7g; CARB 48.4g; FIBER 3.2g; CHOL 57mg; IRON 3.9mg; SODIUM 782mg; CALC 755mg

Lasagna Primavera

Preparation time: 35 minutes
Cooking time: 35 minutes

- 1½ tablespoons stick margarine or butter
- 1 teaspoon bottled minced garlic
- 2 tablespoons all-purpose flour
- ½ teaspoon salt
- 2 (12-ounce) cans evaporated skim milk
- 2 tablespoons ⅓-less-fat cream cheese (Neufchâtel) (about 1 ounce)
- 1 cup (4 ounces) part-skim ricotta cheese
- 1 cup (4 ounces) preshredded part-skim mozzarella, divided
- ½ teaspoon dried basil
- 1 large egg white
- 2 cups small broccoli florets
- ½ cup prepackaged shredded carrot
- 1 (7-ounce) bottle roasted red bell peppers, drained and chopped
- Cooking spray
- 6 no-boil lasagna noodles
- ½ cup (2 ounces) preshredded fresh Parmesan cheese, divided

1. Preheat oven to 450°.

2. Melt margarine in a medium saucepan over medium heat. Add garlic, and sauté 1 minute. Add flour and salt; cook 30 seconds, stirring with a whisk. Gradually add milk, stirring constantly with a whisk. Bring to a boil; reduce heat, and simmer 3 minutes or until slightly thick, stirring constantly. Remove from heat, and stir in cream cheese until melted. Set aside.

3. Combine ricotta, ¼ cup mozzarella, basil, and egg white in a bowl. Combine broccoli, carrot, and bell peppers. Spread ¼ cup sauce in bottom of an 8-inch square baking dish coated with cooking spray. Arrange 2 noodles over sauce. Spoon half of ricotta mixture over noodle, and top with half of vegetable mixture. Spoon ¾ cup sauce over vegetables; top with ¼ cup Parmesan. Top with 2 noodles, remaining ricotta mixture, remaining vegetable mixture, ¼ cup Parmesan, and 2 noodles, pressing firmly. Spoon remaining sauce over noodles, spreading to cover. Cover and bake at 450° for 25 minutes or until noodles are tender and sauce is bubbly. Uncover and sprinkle with remaining ¾ cup mozzarella; bake an additional 5 minutes. Let stand 5 minutes. Yield: 6 servings.

CALORIES 371 (33% from fat); FAT 13.4g (sat 6.9g, mono 4.2g, poly 1.4g); PROTEIN 26g; CARB 36.2g; FIBER 1.8g; CHOL 38mg; IRON 1.8mg; SODIUM 766mg; CALC 703mg

Antipasto Lasagna

Preparation time: 10 minutes
Cooking time: 35 minutes

- 1 (27.5-ounce) jar fat-free mushroom-and-roasted garlic pasta sauce
- Cooking spray
- 6 no-boil lasagna noodles
- 1 (14-ounce) can artichoke hearts, drained and coarsely chopped
- 1 (7-ounce) bottle roasted red bell peppers, drained and chopped
- ½ cup chopped turkey pepperoni (such as Hormel), divided
- ⅓ cup chopped pitted kalamata olives
- 1 cup (4 ounces) preshredded part-skim mozzarella cheese, divided
- Oregano sprigs (optional)

1. Preheat oven to 450°.

2. Spread ½ cup pasta sauce in bottom of an 8-inch square baking dish coated with cooking spray. Arrange 2 noodles over sauce; top with half of artichokes, half of bell peppers, ¼ cup pepperoni, and half of olives. Sprinkle with ½ cup cheese; top with ¾ cup sauce. Repeat layers, omitting cheese, and ending with noodles. Spread remaining sauce over noodles. Cover and bake at 450° for 30 minutes or until noodles are tender and sauce is bubbly. Uncover and top with remaining ½ cup cheese; bake an additional 5 minutes. Let stand 5 minutes. Garnish with oregano sprigs, if desired. Yield: 4 servings.

CALORIES 375 (20% from fat); FAT 8.4g (sat 3.9g, mono 3.2g, poly 0.8g); PROTEIN 21.7g; CARB 50.7g; FIBER 5.5g; CHOL 37mg; IRON 4.3mg; SODIUM 1,379mg; CALC 285mg

Lasagna Margherite

Preparation time: 15 minutes
Cooking time: 30 minutes

- 1 (26-ounce) jar fat-free tomato-basil pasta sauce
- Cooking spray
- 1 (15-ounce) carton part-skim ricotta cheese
- ⅓ cup chopped fresh basil
- ¼ teaspoon dried crushed red pepper
- ¼ teaspoon salt
- 6 no-boil lasagna noodles
- ½ cup (2 ounces) preshredded fresh Parmesan cheese
- 2 tablespoons chopped fresh basil

1. Preheat oven to 450°.

2. Spread ½ cup pasta sauce in bottom of an 8-inch square baking dish coated with cooking spray. Combine ricotta and next 3 ingredients. Arrange 2 noodles over sauce; top with 1 cup ricotta mixture and ¾ cup sauce. Repeat layers, ending with noodles.

Spread remaining sauce over noodles. Cover and bake at 450° for 25 minutes or until noodles are tender and sauce is bubbly. Uncover and top with Parmesan and 2 tablespoons basil. Bake an additional 5 minutes. Let stand 5 minutes. Yield: 4 servings.

CALORIES 386 (30% from fat); FAT 12.7g (sat 7.6g, mono 3.6g, poly 0.6g); PROTEIN 24g; CARB 42.4g; FIBER 3.7g; CHOL 43mg; IRON 2.8mg; SODIUM 959mg; CALC 620mg

LIGHTEN UP

Taking on Tradition

Our lighter touch helps fulfill a vow to continue a Thanksgiving pumpkin bread tradition.

Every year at Thanksgiving, Hannah Rieland bakes up batches of pumpkin bread for family and friends—a gift they all love. What's even more lovable is the story behind the tradition. "At the ripe old age of 27, I packed my Chevy Vega and headed west to sunny Southern California," says Hannah, now 43. "Being single and new in town, I knew the upcoming Thanksgiving holiday was bound to be a little lonesome. I'll never forget when a coworker at my new job brought in her mother's pumpkin bread. The aroma and taste of the spices in it reminded me of fall back in the Midwest, and I didn't feel so lonely. I knew I had to have that recipe. From that moment on, I vowed to bake pumpkin bread every Thanksgiving for new friends."

She kept her pledge, but these days she's looking for a little help—specifically with the cup of oil and four eggs that go into her recipe. We think we've come up with a pretty good solution, cutting the fat by more than half and knocking off 12% of the calories from fat.

SPICY PUMPKIN BREAD

If you're tempted to fiddle with the spices (maybe substitute pumpkin-pie spice for the allspice, cinnamon, nutmeg, and cloves), think again. We tried it that way in our Test Kitchens, but it wasn't as good. There's just something special about this four-spice combination.

3½ cups all-purpose flour
2 teaspoons baking powder
1 teaspoon ground allspice
1 teaspoon ground cinnamon
1 teaspoon ground nutmeg
¾ teaspoon salt
½ teaspoon baking soda
½ teaspoon ground cloves
1⅓ cups packed brown sugar
¾ cup fat-free milk
⅓ cup vegetable oil
2 teaspoons vanilla extract
2 large eggs
1 (15-ounce) can pumpkin
Cooking spray
⅓ cup chopped walnuts

1. Preheat oven to 350°.
2. Lightly spoon flour into dry measuring cups; level with a knife. Combine flour and next 7 ingredients in a large bowl; make a well in center of mixture. Combine sugar and next 5 ingredients in a bowl; stir well with a whisk until smooth. Add to flour mixture, stirring just until moist.
3. Spoon batter into 2 (8 x 4-inch) loaf pans coated with cooking spray, and sprinkle with walnuts. Bake at 350° for 1 hour or until a wooden pick inserted in center comes out clean. Cool loaves in pans 10 minutes on a wire rack; remove from pans. Cool loaves completely; cut each loaf into 12 slices. Yield: 24 slices (serving size: 1 slice).

CALORIES 161 (26% from fat); FAT 4.7g (sat 0.8g, mono 1.3g, poly 2.3g); PROTEIN 3.1g; CARB 26.9g; FIBER 1.3g; CHOL 18mg; IRON 1.4mg; SODIUM 138mg; CALC 46mg

BEFORE & AFTER	
SERVING SIZE	
1 slice	
CALORIES	
274	161
FAT	
11.7g	4.7g
PERCENT OF TOTAL CALORIES	
38%	26%
CHOLESTEROL	
35mg	18mg
SODIUM	
276mg	138mg

INSPIRED VEGETARIAN

Equal Indulgences

Robust main dishes and creative sides put the garden center stage on a holiday table where everyone can be thankful.

It's always a real challenge to create a vegetarian Thanksgiving menu that tastes as good as what everyone else is having. But it can be done.

Perhaps the most important part of this meal is creating a hearty, vegetable-based entrée. This year, turn to an all-time favorite for the main dish: portobello mushrooms, topped with a sumptuous Harvest-Vegetable Ragoût. But a complete meal means similar attention to the other components, and we've found perfect complements in a nicely spiced Sweet Potato Soup and a palate-freshening Spinach Salad with Beets and Oranges.

We like to end the meal with a classic, and we've borrowed one from France with Pear Clafouti, a traditional and simple Gallic cobbler that says home—and thanks—in all languages. Happy Thanksgiving!

SWEET POTATO SOUP

1 tablespoon vegetable oil
1 cup chopped onion
½ cup chopped celery
2 teaspoons minced peeled fresh
   ginger
¼ teaspoon dried thyme
⅛ teaspoon saffron threads
6 cups chopped peeled sweet
   potato (about 2 pounds)
1 tablespoon grated orange rind
7½ cups vegetable broth
⅛ teaspoon ground red pepper
2 cups chopped spinach

1. Heat oil in a large Dutch oven over
medium-high heat. Add onion and
next 4 ingredients; sauté 5 minutes.
Add sweet potato and orange rind;
sauté 3 minutes. Add broth and red
pepper; bring to a boil. Cover, reduce
heat, and simmer 25 minutes or until
potato is tender. Place half of potato
mixture in a blender or food processor;
process until smooth. Pour pureed
mixture into a bowl. Repeat procedure
with remaining potato mixture. Return
pureed mixture to pan. Stir in spinach,
and cook until thoroughly heated.
Yield: 10 servings (serving size: 1 cup).

CALORIES 119 (18% from fat); FAT 2.4g (sat 0.5g, mono 0.6g,
poly 1.1g); PROTEIN 2.2g; CARB 23.1g; FIBER 3.3g;
CHOL 0mg; IRON 0.9mg; SODIUM 775mg; CALC 36mg

HARVEST-VEGETABLE RAGOÛT

5 teaspoons olive oil, divided
3 cups diced peeled butternut squash
2 cups (½-inch-thick) sliced leek
1½ cups (1-inch-thick) sliced carrot
1½ cups (½-inch-thick) sliced parsnip
1 cup (½-inch-thick) sliced celery
10 garlic cloves, halved
2 bay leaves
2 thyme sprigs
1 tablespoon tomato paste
1 tablespoon all-purpose flour
1 cup dry red wine
½ cup vegetable broth or water
1 (19-ounce) can chickpeas
   (garbanzo beans), drained
¾ teaspoon salt, divided
½ teaspoon black pepper
¼ cup chopped fresh parsley
6 portobello mushrooms
Thyme sprigs (optional)

1. Heat 1 tablespoon oil in a Dutch
oven over medium-high heat. Combine squash and next 5 ingredients;
sauté 8 minutes or until lightly
browned, stirring frequently. Add bay
leaves and 2 thyme sprigs; stir in
tomato paste. Stir in flour and wine;
reduce heat to medium-low, and cook
5 minutes. Stir in broth and chickpeas.
Cover and simmer 20 minutes or until
vegetables are tender. Stir in ½ teaspoon salt, pepper, and parsley. Discard
bay leaves and 2 thyme sprigs.
2. Discard mushroom stems; slice caps.
Heat 2 teaspoons oil in a large nonstick
skillet over medium-high heat. Add
sliced mushrooms, and cook 5 minutes, stirring constantly. Sprinkle with
¼ teaspoon salt. Serve ragoût over
mushrooms. Garnish with additional
thyme sprigs, if desired. Yield: 6 servings (serving size: 1 cup ragoût and ⅔
cup mushrooms).

CALORIES 260 (21% from fat); FAT 6.1g (sat 0.8g, mono 3.2g,
poly 1.3g); PROTEIN 9.9g; CARB 46.2g; FIBER 7.1g;
CHOL 0mg; IRON 5mg; SODIUM 539mg; CALC 124mg

SPINACH SALAD WITH BEETS AND ORANGES

2 navel oranges
6 cups torn spinach
3 cups shredded peeled beets
   (about 1 pound)
1 tablespoon olive oil
2 tablespoons minced shallots
¼ cup raspberry vinegar
¼ teaspoon freshly ground black
   pepper
¼ cup minced fresh chives
¼ cup coarsely chopped walnuts

1. Peel oranges, and cut each crosswise
into 5 slices.
2. Place spinach on a large platter.
Spoon beets onto spinach, and arrange
orange slices on beets. Heat oil in a
nonstick skillet over medium-high
heat. Add shallots, and sauté 1 minute
or until tender. Stir in vinegar and pepper; drizzle over salad. Sprinkle salad
with chives and walnuts. Yield: 6
servings.

CALORIES 122 (41% from fat); FAT 5.6g (sat 0.6g, mono 2.4g,
poly 2.3g); PROTEIN 4.7g; CARB 16.3g; FIBER 5.3g;
CHOL 0mg; IRON 2.4mg; SODIUM 104mg; CALC 93mg

PEAR CLAFOUTI

Cooking spray
1 teaspoon all-purpose flour
2 cups cubed peeled pear
¾ cup all-purpose flour
¼ teaspoon salt
⅛ teaspoon nutmeg
2 cups 1% low-fat milk, divided
½ cup granulated sugar
½ teaspoon vanilla extract
3 large eggs, lightly beaten
2 teaspoons powdered sugar

1. Preheat oven to 375°.
2. Coat a 10-inch deep-dish pie plate
with cooking spray, and dust with 1
teaspoon flour. Arrange pear cubes in
bottom of prepared dish, and set aside.
3. Lightly spoon ¾ cup flour into a
dry measuring cup; level with a knife.
Combine flour, salt, and nutmeg in a
bowl. Gradually add 1 cup milk, stirring with a whisk until well-blended.
Add remaining 1 cup milk, ½ cup
sugar, vanilla, and eggs, stirring until
smooth. Pour batter over pears. Bake at
375° for 35 minutes or until set. Sift
powdered sugar over top. Yield: 6 servings (serving size: 1 wedge).

CALORIES 231 (16% from fat); FAT 4g (sat 1.4g, mono 1.3g,
poly 0.5g); PROTEIN 7.8g; CARB 41.5g; FIBER 1.9g;
CHOL 114mg; IRON 1.3mg; SODIUM 172mg; CALC 122mg

Northern Lights

Slowly but surely, change is coming to this tradition-conscious cradle of French Canadian cuisine.

Cooking lighter is a challenge in northern climates, where high fat intake is part of the culinary and cultural tradition. Yet, recipes are shifting to a somewhat lighter note in Quebec. The changes are not merely inventive, nor are they just waves in the current regional assertiveness against classic French culinary doctrine. They include more fresh ingredients, more seafood, and fewer cream sauces than before. And a few chefs, such as Daniel Vézina, owner of Laurie Raphaël restaurant in Quebec City, have even begun importing some ideas from the United States.

Quebec food writer Rollande Desbois, author of the respected *Cuisine Saveur* cookbook, sees a new lighter style of cooking emerging in the provinces and being emphasized at local restaurants. "Freshness is now the dominant element—valued above all else," she says. "Some chefs have even set aside their freezers. Sauces are much lighter, the consumption of fish is slowly increasing, and sauces made with vegetable juices and purees are becoming more common. Desserts are also lighter, and they are being served in smaller portions."

Some chefs think the shift is being led by a change in consumer tastes. "My clients are eating more greens and more fresh vegetables these days," observes Anne Desjardins, chef and co-owner of L'Eau à la Bouche. "The Quebec Agriculture Department started a campaign 10 years ago to stress locally grown products, and it was a great success. Also, we have new technologies that allow the production of superb greens year-round." One result, Desjardins says, is that her patrons "are starting to appreciate the flavor of the *food* instead of the sauce." It's "not a passing fad," she adds. "These trends are irreversible."

CHICKEN AND BABY CARROTS WITH LEMON AND CHIVES

—Chef Anne Desjardins

½ cup minced fresh chives, divided
4 teaspoons grated lemon rind, divided
6 tablespoons fresh lemon juice, divided
1 tablespoon olive oil, divided
¼ teaspoon salt
¼ teaspoon hot sauce, divided
4 (4-ounce) skinned, boned chicken breast halves
32 baby carrots (about 1 pound)
1 (16-ounce) can fat-free, less-sodium chicken broth
Fresh chives (optional)
Thin lemon slices (optional)

1. Combine ¼ cup minced chives, 2 teaspoons lemon rind, 3 tablespoons lemon juice, 1 teaspoon oil, salt, and ⅛ teaspoon hot sauce in a large zip-top plastic bag; add chicken to bag. Seal and marinate in refrigerator 2 hours. Remove chicken from bag, and pat dry; discard marinade.
2. Heat 2 teaspoons oil in a large skillet over medium heat. Add chicken, and cook 3 minutes on each side. Reduce heat to medium-low. Add remaining 2 teaspoons lemon rind, 3 tablespoons lemon juice, ⅛ teaspoon hot sauce, carrots, and broth; simmer 15 minutes or until carrots are tender. Spoon ⅓ cup sauce onto each of 4 plates; arrange 1 chicken breast half and 8 carrots on top of sauce on each plate. Sprinkle each serving with 1 tablespoon minced chives. Garnish with additional fresh chives and lemon slices, if desired. Yield: 4 servings.

CALORIES 221 (20% from fat); FAT 5g (sat 0.9g, mono 2.9g, poly 0.7g); PROTEIN 29.1g; CARB 14.6g; FIBER 3.8g; CHOL 66mg; IRON 1.5mg; SODIUM 502mg; CALC 53mg

ROASTED HENS WITH RED CABBAGE-APPLE COMPOTE

—Chef Francine Roy

2 (1¼-pound) Cornish hens
¼ teaspoon salt
⅛ teaspoon black pepper
1 tablespoon vegetable oil
1 tablespoon honey
4 fresh rosemary sprigs
2 tablespoons balsamic vinegar
½ cup fat-free, less-sodium chicken broth
¼ cup apple juice
1 tablespoon minced shallots
1 teaspoon stick margarine or butter
¼ teaspoon minced fresh rosemary
Red Cabbage-Apple Compote (page 290)
Crispy Apple Chips (optional) (page 290)

1. Preheat oven to 350°.
2. Remove and discard giblets and necks from hens. Rinse hens with cold water; pat dry. Remove skin; trim excess fat. Split hens in half lengthwise. Sprinkle hens with salt and pepper.
3. Heat oil in a large ovenproof Dutch oven over medium-high heat. Add hens; cook 3 minutes on each side or until browned. Remove from heat. Brush hens with honey. Tuck rosemary sprigs under hen legs. Bake at 350° for 25 minutes or until juices run clear. Remove hens from pan; keep warm.
4. Place pan over high heat. Stir in vinegar, scraping pan to loosen browned bits. Add broth and juice. Bring to a boil; cook until reduced to ½ cup (about 5 minutes). Remove from heat. Stir in shallots, margarine, and minced rosemary. Spoon 2 tablespoons sauce onto each of 4 plates; top each with 1 cup Red Cabbage-Apple Compote and 1 hen half. Garnish with Crispy Apple Chips, if desired. Yield: 4 servings.

CALORIES 459 (25% from fat); FAT 13g (sat 3g, mono 4.2g, poly 4.3g); PROTEIN 29g; CARB 58.1g; FIBER 4.6g; CHOL 82mg; IRON 2.7mg; SODIUM 461mg; CALC 103mg

Continued

Red Cabbage-Apple Compote:

- 1 teaspoon vegetable oil
- 5 cups thinly sliced red cabbage
- 2½ cups diced peeled Granny Smith apple (about ¾ pound)
- 1 cup diced onion
- ¾ cup apple juice
- ½ cup maple syrup
- ¼ cup balsamic vinegar
- ¼ teaspoon salt
- ⅛ teaspoon black pepper

1. Heat oil in a large skillet over medium-high heat. Add cabbage, apple, and onion; sauté 3 minutes. Stir in apple juice and remaining ingredients. Cover, reduce heat to medium, and cook 35 minutes, stirring occasionally. Yield: 4 servings (serving size: 1 cup).

CALORIES 214 (8% from fat); FAT 1.8g (sat 0.3g, mono 0.4g, poly 0.8g); PROTEIN 1.8g; CARB 51.2g; FIBER 4.5g; CHOL 0mg; IRON 1.4mg; SODIUM 163mg; CALC 86mg

Crispy Apple Chips:

- 1 Red Delicious apple, cut into paper-thin slices
- 1 teaspoon sugar

1. Preheat oven to 200°.
2. Cover a baking sheet with parchment paper. Arrange apple slices in a single layer on parchment paper; sprinkle with sugar. Bake at 200° for 1½ hours or until lightly browned. Remove from parchment paper; cool on a wire rack.

SPICED FILLET OF TROUT

—Quebec food writer Rollande Desbois

- 4 (6-ounce) trout fillets
- 1 tablespoon olive oil, divided
- ⅛ teaspoon salt
- ⅛ teaspoon black pepper
- 1 cup fresh breadcrumbs
- 1 teaspoon curry powder
- 1 teaspoon chili powder
- 1 teaspoon pumpkin-pie spice
- ¼ teaspoon dried thyme
- ¼ teaspoon ground red pepper
- ¼ teaspoon ground nutmeg

1. Preheat oven to 450°.
2. Place fillets on a baking sheet. Lightly brush fillets with 1 teaspoon oil; sprinkle with salt and black pepper. Combine breadcrumbs and next 6 ingredients Pat mixture onto fillets; drizzle 2 teaspoons oil evenly over fillets. Bake at 450° for 8 minutes or until fish flakes easily when tested with a fork. Yield: 4 servings.

CALORIES 269 (33% from fat); FAT 10g (sat 1.7g, mono 4.5g, poly 2.5g); PROTEIN 36.1g; CARB 6.9g; FIBER 0.7g; CHOL 97mg; IRON 4mg; SODIUM 183mg; CALC 132mg

SCALLOPS AU VERMOUTH

—Chef James MacGuire

- 1½ cups (3-inch) julienne-cut carrot
- 1½ cups (3-inch) julienne-cut peeled turnips
- 1 cup (3-inch) julienne-cut celery
- 1 cup (3-inch) julienne-cut leek (about 1 large)
- 1 tablespoon olive oil
- ½ cup minced shallots
- 1 pound sea scallops
- ¾ cup dry vermouth
- ¼ teaspoon salt
- ¼ teaspoon hot sauce
- ⅛ teaspoon pepper
- ¼ cup chopped fresh chives
- 1 tablespoon fresh lemon juice

1. Steam first 4 ingredients, covered, 14 minutes or until crisp-tender.
2. Heat oil in a large nonstick skillet over medium-high heat. Add shallots; sauté 2 minutes or until lightly browned. Add scallops; sauté 30 seconds. Add vermouth; cover and cook 3 minutes. Remove scallops from pan with a slotted spoon, reserving vermouth mixture in pan. Divide scallops evenly among 4 plates; top each with ½ cup leek mixture.
3. Add salt, hot sauce, and pepper to vermouth mixture in pan; cook 1 minute. Remove from heat; stir in chives and lemon juice. Spoon 3 tablespoons sauce over each serving. Yield: 4 servings.

CALORIES 206 (20% from fat); FAT 4.5g (sat 0.6g, mono 2.6g, poly 0.7g); PROTEIN 21.2g; CARB 20.3g; FIBER 3.2g; CHOL 37mg; IRON 1.7mg; SODIUM 416mg; CALC 95mg

PANACHE OF SHRIMP AND SNOW PEAS

—Quebec food writer Rollande Desbois

- 2 cups water
- 3 tablespoons minced shallots
- ¼ teaspoon salt
- ¼ teaspoon freshly ground black pepper
- 10 fresh parsley sprigs
- 1 lemon slice
- ½ pound medium shrimp
- ½ pound snow peas (about 2½ cups), trimmed
- 2 tablespoons minced fresh chives
  Tarragon Dressing
- 2 heads Belgian endive, separated into leaves (about ½ pound)

1. Combine first 6 ingredients in a saucepan; bring to a boil. Cook 5 minutes. Add shrimp; cook 3 minutes or until done. Drain liquid; discard liquid and solids. Peel and devein shrimp.
2. Steam snow peas, covered, 3 minutes or until tender. Combine shrimp, snow peas, chives, and Tarragon Dressing in a bowl. Serve on endive-lined plates. Yield: 4 servings (serving size: 1 cup).

CALORIES 145 (38% from fat); FAT 6.1g (sat 0.9g, mono 3.9g, poly 0.8g); PROTEIN 12g; CARB 10.9g; FIBER 2.5g; CHOL 65mg; IRON 3.5mg; SODIUM 365mg; CALC 69mg

Tarragon Dressing:

- 1½ tablespoons extra-virgin olive oil
- 1 tablespoon white wine vinegar
- 1 teaspoon minced fresh or ¼ teaspoon dried tarragon
- ¼ teaspoon salt
- ¼ teaspoon freshly ground black pepper
- 1 garlic clove, crushed

1. Combine all ingredients, stirring with a whisk. Yield: 2 tablespoons.

Melon-and-Maple Soup Perfumed with Ginger

—Chef Anne Desjardins

2 cups cantaloupe balls
¼ cup Muscat or other sweet wine
2½ cups honeydew melon balls
½ cup maple syrup
2 tablespoons fresh lemon juice
1½ teaspoons grated peeled fresh ginger

1. Combine cantaloupe and wine; cover and chill. Combine honeydew and next 3 ingredients in a blender; process until smooth. Pour into a bowl; cover and chill.
2. Pour ⅔ cup honeydew mixture into each of 4 shallow bowls; add ½ cup cantaloupe balls to each. Yield: 4 servings.

CALORIES 193 (2% from fat); FAT 0.4g (sat 0.2g, mono 0g, poly 0g); PROTEIN 1.2g; CARB 45.3g; FIBER 1.9g; CHOL 0mg; IRON 0.8mg; SODIUM 22mg; CALC 43mg

Hot Maple Soufflés

(pictured on page 300)

—Chef Daniel Vézina

1 tablespoon stick margarine or butter, softened
2 tablespoons granulated sugar
3 tablespoons maple syrup
3 tablespoons bourbon
1 cup maple syrup
4 large egg whites
⅛ teaspoon salt
1 teaspoon baking powder
1 tablespoon sifted powdered sugar

1. Preheat oven to 425°.
2. Coat 6 (10-ounce) ramekins with margarine; sprinkle with granulated sugar. Combine 3 tablespoons maple syrup and bourbon in a small microwave-safe bowl; microwave at HIGH 1½ minutes or until mixture boils. Pour about 1 tablespoon bourbon mixture into each prepared ramekin.
3. Cook 1 cup syrup in a medium, heavy saucepan over medium-high heat 8 minutes or until a candy thermometer registers 250°. Beat egg whites and salt at medium speed of a mixer until foamy. Pour hot maple syrup in a thin stream over egg whites, beating at medium speed then at high speed until stiff peaks form. Add baking powder; beat well. Spoon evenly into prepared ramekins; place on a jelly-roll pan. Bake at 425° for 13 minutes or until puffy and set. Sprinkle with powdered sugar. Serve immediately. Yield: 6 servings.

CALORIES 212 (8% from fat); FAT 2g (sat 0.4g, mono 0.8g, poly 0.6g); PROTEIN 2.3g; CARB 47.8g; FIBER 0g; CHOL 0mg; IRON 0.8mg; SODIUM 193mg; CALC 89mg

Baked Apples with Meringue

—Chef James MacGuire

1 tablespoon stick margarine
2 cups chopped McIntosh or other cooking apple (about 2 apples)
1 tablespoon dried currants or raisins
1 tablespoon dark rum
1 teaspoon brown sugar
4 McIntosh or other cooking apples
½ cup maple syrup
½ cup apple cider
2 large egg whites
¼ cup granulated sugar

1. Preheat oven to 350°.
2. Melt margarine in a skillet over medium-high heat. Add chopped apple; sauté 5 minutes. Stir in currants, rum, and brown sugar; cook 1 minute.
3. Core 4 apples, cutting to, but not through, bottoms. Enlarge cavity of each apple by cutting out about 1 inch around inside of core. Peel top half of each apple. Place apples in an 8-inch square baking dish. Spoon ½ cup apple mixture into center of each apple. Pour maple syrup and cider over apples; cover with foil. Bake at 350° for 15 minutes. Remove from oven; uncover dish.
4. Beat egg whites at high speed of a mixer until foamy. Add sugar, 1 tablespoon at a time, beating until stiff peaks form. Spoon into a pastry bag fitted with a star tip; pipe onto tops of apples. Bake at 350° for an additional 20 minutes or until lightly browned. Serve apples with sauce. Yield: 4 servings (serving size: 1 apple and ¼ cup sauce).

CALORIES 302 (11% from fat); FAT 3.6g (sat 0.7g, mono 1.3g, poly 1.1g); PROTEIN 2.1g; CARB 69.2g; FIBER 5g; CHOL 0mg; IRON 1mg; SODIUM 65mg; CALC 44mg

Last Hurrah

Have a Bad Day. Seriously.

"Have a Bad Day Day," which is every November 19, takes off all the pressure, at least one day a year.

Crabby Cajun Dip

2 cups plain low-fat yogurt
2 ounces ⅓-less-fat cream cheese (Neufchâtel) (about ¼ cup)
1 tablespoon Dijon mustard
2 teaspoons anchovy paste
2 teaspoons lemon juice
½ teaspoon dried thyme
½ teaspoon Worcestershire sauce
¼ teaspoon salt
¼ teaspoon black pepper
¼ to ½ teaspoon hot sauce
1 pound lump crabmeat, shell pieces removed
¼ cup minced red bell pepper
¼ cup minced green bell pepper
¼ cup minced green onions

1. Spoon yogurt onto several layers of heavy-duty paper towels; spread to ½-inch thickness. Cover with additional paper towels; let stand 5 minutes. Scrape into a bowl using a rubber spatula; cover and refrigerate.
2. Combine cream cheese and next 8 ingredients, stirring well with a whisk. Stir in yogurt. Stir in crabmeat and remaining ingredients. Yield: 3¾ cups (serving size: ¼ cup).

CALORIES 64 (28% from fat); FAT 2g (sat 0.8g, mono 0.4g, poly 0.4g); PROTEIN 8.4g; CARB 2.8g; FIBER 0g; CHOL 36mg; IRON 0.4mg; SODIUM 284mg; CALC 92mg

Can't Stop Thinking About Tomorrow

Everybody likes turkey for Thanksgiving. Loving it comes the next day.

By the time the candles have been snuffed and the good china put away, what's left of your 20-pounder looks like just one more responsibility. Strip that bird straightaway with a sharp knife, and quickly refrigerate the white and dark meat in separate airtight containers (for up to five days or freeze for up to two months). The challenge is how to serve what you've saved. Look to these recipes for the post-holiday comfort you deserve.

CURRIED TURKEY SOUP

Soup:

- 1 tablespoon stick margarine or butter
- 4 teaspoons curry powder
- 1 teaspoon minced peeled fresh ginger
- 2 garlic cloves, minced
- 4 (16-ounce) cans fat-free, less-sodium chicken broth, divided
- 2 cups chopped onion
- 1 cup chopped leek
- ½ cup diced peeled Golden Delicious apple
- ½ cup diced carrot
- ½ cup diced celery
- 3 cups finely shredded cooked turkey
- 1 tablespoon lemon juice
- ⅛ teaspoon white pepper
- 1 (12-ounce) can evaporated skim milk
- ½ cup all-purpose flour

Remaining ingredients:

- 2¾ cups hot cooked rice
- ¾ cup diced peeled Golden Delicious apple
- ⅓ cup chopped dry-roasted peanuts
- ⅓ cup chopped fresh parsley
- ⅓ cup flaked sweetened coconut, toasted

1. To prepare soup, melt margarine in a large Dutch oven over low heat. Add curry powder, ginger, and garlic; sauté 2 minutes. Add 2 cans broth, onion, and next 4 ingredients; bring to a boil. Reduce heat; simmer 20 minutes or until vegetables are tender.
2. Place half of vegetable mixture in a food processor, and process until smooth. Spoon into a bowl. Repeat procedure with remaining vegetable mixture.
3. Combine vegetable puree, 1 can broth, turkey, and next 3 ingredients in pan; stir well. Combine 1 can broth and flour in a bowl. Stir with a whisk; add to vegetable mixture in pan. Bring to a boil; reduce heat, and simmer 10 minutes or until thick, stirring constantly.
4. Spoon ¼ cup rice into each of 11 bowls; top each with 1 cup soup, about 1 tablespoon diced apple, 1½ teaspoons peanuts, 1½ teaspoons parsley, and 1½ teaspoons coconut. Yield: 11 servings.

CALORIES 267 (25% from fat); FAT 7.5g (sat 2.3g, mono 2.7g, poly 1.8g); PROTEIN 19.3g; CARB 30.1g; FIBER 2.6g; CHOL 36mg; IRON 2mg; SODIUM 555mg; CALC 130mg

THE CLASSIC HOT BROWN

Texas toast is made from extra-thick slices of white bread and is usually sold with other breads.

- 6 (2-ounce) slices Texas toast, lightly toasted
- 12 ounces thinly sliced cooked turkey breast
- 12 (¼-inch-thick) slices tomato (about 2 tomatoes)
- ¼ teaspoon freshly ground black pepper
- Cheddar Cheese Sauce
- 2 bacon slices, cooked and crumbled
- ¼ teaspoon paprika

1. Preheat broiler. Arrange toast in a 13 x 9-inch baking pan or baking dish. Top each toast slice with 2 ounces turkey and 2 tomato slices; sprinkle with pepper. Spoon Cheddar Cheese Sauce evenly over tomatoes; sprinkle with bacon and paprika. Broil until lightly browned. Yield: 6 servings.

CALORIES 331 (18% from fat); FAT 6.8g (sat 2.6g, mono 2.3g, poly 1.2g); PROTEIN 28.3g; CARB 37.3g; FIBER 1.8g; CHOL 60mg; IRON 2.8mg; SODIUM 565mg; CALC 210mg

Cheddar Cheese Sauce:

- 1 teaspoon stick margarine or butter
- 3 tablespoons all-purpose flour
- 1½ cups 1% low-fat milk
- ½ cup (2 ounces) shredded reduced-fat sharp Cheddar cheese
- 1 tablespoon dry sherry
- ¼ teaspoon salt
- ¼ teaspoon ground red pepper
- ⅛ teaspoon onion powder
- 1 (2-ounce) jar diced pimento, drained

1. Melt margarine in a small saucepan over medium heat. Stir in flour; gradually add milk, stirring with a whisk until blended. Cook until thick (about 10 minutes), stirring constantly. Remove from heat; add cheese, stirring until cheese melts. Stir in sherry and remaining ingredients. Yield: 2 cups.

DEVIL IN YOUR POCKET

⅓ cup pineapple preserves
1 tablespoon Dijon mustard
½ teaspoon prepared horseradish
Dash of garlic powder
2 cups chopped cooked turkey
   (about 10 ounces)
½ cup ⅓-less-fat cream cheese,
   (Neufchâtel) (about 2 ounces)
2 (7-inch) pitas, cut in half
24 (¼-inch-thick) slices cucumber
2 cups alfalfa sprouts

1. Combine first 4 ingredients in a bowl. Add turkey; toss gently to coat. Cover; chill 1 hour. Spread 2 tablespoons cream cheese in each pita half; fill each with 6 cucumber slices, ½ cup sprouts, and ½ cup turkey mixture. Serve immediately. Yield: 4 sandwiches.

CALORIES 348 (27% from fat); FAT 10.5g (sat 5.3g, mono 2.8g, poly 1.3g); PROTEIN 26.3g; CARB 35.5g; FIBER 3.9g; CHOL 81mg; IRON 2.8mg; SODIUM 394mg; CALC 78mg

CHUTNEY-TURKEY SALAD ON FOCACCIA

(pictured on page 297)

½ cup finely chopped celery
⅓ cup hot mango chutney
3 tablespoons light mayonnaise
1 teaspoon sesame seeds, toasted
2 cups chopped cooked turkey
   (about 10 ounces)
1 (5.25-ounce) package focaccia
   (Italian flatbread) or 2 (6-inch)
   pitas
Olive oil-flavored cooking spray
1 small zucchini, cut lengthwise
   into 8 (¼-inch) slices
1 (7-ounce) bottle roasted red bell
   peppers, drained and sliced
8 spinach leaves
2 tablespoons reduced-fat Caesar
   dressing
4 teaspoons Dijon mustard

1. Preheat oven to 350°.
2. Combine first 4 ingredients in a medium bowl. Add turkey; toss gently to coat.

3. Cut each bread piece in half horizontally. Coat cut sides of each piece with cooking spray. Place bread slices in a single layer on a jelly-roll pan. Bake at 350° for 12 minutes or until toasted. Spread ½ cup turkey salad over each bottom half. Top with zucchini, peppers, and spinach; drizzle with dressing. Spread mustard over top halves of bread; place on top of sandwiches. Cut each sandwich into 4 wedges. Yield: 4 servings (serving size: 2 wedges).

CALORIES 349 (26% from fat); FAT 10.1g (sat 2.7g, mono 2.6g, poly 3.7g); PROTEIN 26.2g; CARB 38.6g; FIBER 2.8g; CHOL 65mg; IRON 2.5mg; SODIUM 733mg; CALC 65mg

FIERY TURKEY-PÂTÉ CROSTINI

1 tablespoon olive oil
⅔ cup coarsely chopped green
   onions
2 garlic cloves
¼ to ½ teaspoon dried crushed red
   pepper
2 cups chopped cooked turkey
   (about 10 ounces)
½ cup coarsely chopped water
   chestnuts
2 tablespoons light mayonnaise
¾ teaspoon Cajun seasoning
8 (½-inch) pieces crystallized ginger
   or ½ teaspoon ground ginger
2 tablespoons white wine vinegar
1 tablespoon low-sodium soy
   sauce
32 (¼-inch-thick) slices French bread
   baguette (about 1 loaf)

1. Heat oil in a large nonstick skillet over medium-high heat. Add onions, garlic, and pepper; sauté 1 minute. Place onion mixture, turkey, and next 6 ingredients in a food processor; process until well-blended, scraping sides of processor bowl occasionally. Spoon pâté into a bowl; cover and chill at least 8 hours.
2. Spread 1 tablespoon pâté over each bread slice. Yield: 32 crostini.

CALORIES 48 (23% from fat); FAT 1.2g (sat 0.3g, mono 0.5g, poly 0.4g); PROTEIN 3.4g; CARB 5.4g; FIBER 0.3g; CHOL 8mg; IRON 0.5mg; SODIUM 82mg; CALC 8mg

CREAMY TRIPLE-MUSHROOM BISQUE WITH TURKEY

Assorted wild mushrooms can be substituted for either the shiitake or portobello mushrooms.

Cooking spray
1 (3½-ounce) package shiitake
   mushrooms, quartered
1 (6-ounce) package presliced
   portobello mushrooms,
   halved
1 (8-ounce) package button
   mushrooms, quartered
2½ cups chopped cooked dark-meat
   turkey (about 12 ounces)
¼ cup dry red wine
1 teaspoon dried thyme
1 teaspoon balsamic vinegar
½ teaspoon salt
⅛ teaspoon ground red pepper
1 (16-ounce) can fat-free,
   less-sodium chicken broth
½ cup thinly sliced green onions
2 tablespoons chopped fresh
   parsley
3 tablespoons all-purpose flour
2 cups 2% reduced-fat milk
2½ cups cooked long-grain and wild-
   rice blend (such as Uncle Ben's)
½ cup tub-style light cream cheese
Fresh parsley sprigs (optional)

1. Place a large saucepan coated with cooking spray over medium-high heat until hot. Add mushrooms; cover and cook 5 minutes or until mushrooms are tender. Add turkey and next 6 ingredients; bring to a boil. Cover, reduce heat, and simmer 20 minutes. Remove from heat; stir in onions and chopped parsley.
2. Place flour in a small bowl; gradually add milk, stirring constantly with a whisk until well-blended. Add milk mixture to mushroom mixture; bring to a boil. Cook 1 minute or until thick. Reduce heat; add rice and cream cheese, stirring until cheese melts. Garnish with parsley sprigs, if desired. Yield: 8 servings (serving size: 1 cup).

CALORIES 226 (29% from fat); FAT 7.2g (sat 3.2g, mono 1.9g, poly 1.2g); PROTEIN 19.4g; CARB 21.1g; FIBER 1.4g; CHOL 49mg; IRON 2.4mg; SODIUM 415mg; CALC 127mg

White Turkey Chili

1 tablespoon stick margarine or butter
1½ cups chopped onion
½ cup chopped celery
½ cup chopped red bell pepper
1 tablespoon minced seeded jalapeño pepper
1 garlic clove, minced
3 cups chopped cooked turkey (about 15 ounces)
2 (19-ounce) cans cannellini beans or other white beans, drained and divided
2 (16-ounce) cans fat-free, less-sodium chicken broth
1 (4.5-ounce) can chopped green chiles, undrained
1 cup frozen whole-kernel corn
1½ teaspoons ground cumin
1 teaspoon chili powder
½ teaspoon salt
¼ teaspoon black pepper
1 cup 1% low-fat milk
½ cup chopped fresh cilantro

1. Melt margarine in a large Dutch oven over medium-high heat. Add onion and next 4 ingredients; sauté 5 minutes. Add turkey, 1½ cups beans, broth, and next 6 ingredients; bring to a boil. Cover, reduce heat, and simmer 15 minutes.
2. Mash remaining beans. Add mashed beans and milk to turkey mixture. Simmer, uncovered, 20 minutes or until mixture is thick, stirring frequently. Stir in cilantro. Yield: 11 servings (serving size: 1 cup).

CALORIES 217 (19% from fat); FAT 4.6g (sat 1.1g, mono 1.3g, poly 1.6g); PROTEIN 19.6g; CARB 25.1g; FIBER 3.5g; CHOL 33mg; IRON 3.2mg; SODIUM 462mg; CALC 82mg

Slow Cooking for Fast Living

Don't let the slow cooker's name fool you. It can have dinner ready when you get home.

Slow-Roasted Rosemary-and-Garlic Chicken

You'll need at least a 4-quart slow cooker to cook the whole chicken. It also cooks nicely in the larger, oval-shaped cooker.

10 garlic cloves, minced
2 tablespoons chopped fresh rosemary
1 (5- to 6-pound) roasting chicken
5 garlic cloves
4 (3-inch) rosemary sprigs
¼ cup orange juice
1 tablespoon balsamic vinegar

1. Combine minced garlic and chopped rosemary. Remove giblets and neck from chicken; discard. Rinse chicken with cold water; pat dry. Trim excess fat. Starting at neck cavity, loosen skin from breast and drumsticks by inserting fingers, gently pushing between skin and meat. Rub garlic mixture under loosened skin over breast and drumsticks. Place 5 garlic cloves and rosemary sprigs into body cavity. Place chicken, breast side down, in an electric slow cooker. Cover with lid; cook on high heat setting for 1 hour. Reduce heat setting to low; cook 7 hours. Remove chicken from slow cooker, reserving drippings. Discard skin.
2. Place a zip-top plastic bag inside a 2-cup glass measure. Pour drippings into bag; let stand 10 minutes (fat will rise to top). Seal bag; carefully snip off 1 bottom corner of bag. Drain drippings into a small saucepan, stopping before fat layer reaches opening; discard fat.
3. Add orange juice and vinegar to saucepan; bring to a boil. Reduce heat; simmer 10 minutes. Yield: 6 servings (serving size: 3 ounces chicken and ⅓ cup sauce).

CALORIES 175 (33% from fat); FAT 6.4g (sat 1.7g, mono 2.3g, poly 1.5g); PROTEIN 25g; CARB 3g; FIBER 0.2g; CHOL 76mg; IRON 1.3mg; SODIUM 74mg; CALC 27mg

Rioja Chicken

(pictured on page 300)

If you don't want to use the Rioja wine, replace it with another cup of either orange juice or chicken broth. Also, if you're short on time, this chicken dish can be cooked on the high heat setting for 4 hours.

3 tablespoons all-purpose flour
¼ teaspoon salt
¼ teaspoon black pepper
8 chicken thighs (about 3 pounds), skinned
5 garlic cloves, thinly sliced
½ cup pitted prunes (about 3¼ ounces)
¼ cup pimento-stuffed olives
2 tablespoons minced fresh or 2 teaspoons dried thyme
1 tablespoon grated lemon rind
1 bay leaf
1 cup orange juice
1 cup Rioja or other dry red wine
2 tablespoons honey
2 cups hot cooked wild-rice blend or long-grain rice
½ cup chopped fresh parsley

1. Combine first 3 ingredients in a shallow dish. Dredge chicken in flour mixture. Place garlic in bottom of an electric slow cooker. Arrange chicken over garlic; add prunes and next 4 ingredients.
2. Combine orange juice, wine, and honey; pour over chicken. Cover with lid; cook on high heat setting for 1 hour. Reduce heat setting to low; cook 7 hours. Discard bay leaf. Serve over rice. Sprinkle with parsley. Yield: 4 servings (serving size: 2 thighs, 1 cup sauce, ½ cup rice, and 2 tablespoons parsley).

CALORIES 379 (17% from fat); FAT 7.3g (sat 1.7g, mono 2.7g, poly 1.6g); PROTEIN 33g; CARB 46.3g; FIBER 2.7g; CHOL 126mg; IRON 3.8mg; SODIUM 1,009mg; CALC 67mg

PORK ROAST WITH THREE-MUSHROOM RAGOÛT

1 (3½-ounce) package shiitake mushrooms
¼ cup all-purpose flour
1 cup canned crushed tomatoes, divided
2 tablespoons chopped fresh or 2 teaspoons dried thyme
2 (8-ounce) packages button mushrooms, cut in half
1 (8-ounce) package cremini mushrooms, cut in half
1 large onion, cut into 8 wedges
½ ounce sun-dried tomatoes, packed without oil, quartered (about 6)
1¾ pounds boned pork loin roast
½ teaspoon salt
¼ teaspoon black pepper
5 cups hot cooked medium egg noodles (about 4 cups uncooked pasta)

1. Discard shiitake mushroom stems; cut caps into quarters.
2. Lightly spoon flour into a dry measuring cup; level with a knife. Combine flour, ½ cup crushed tomatoes, and thyme in an electric slow cooker; stir well with a whisk. Add mushrooms, onion, and sun-dried tomatoes.
3. Trim fat from pork. Sprinkle pork with salt and pepper; place on top of mushroom mixture. Pour remaining ½ cup crushed tomatoes over pork. Cover with lid; cook on high heat setting 1 hour. Reduce heat setting to low, and cook 7 hours. Remove pork from slow cooker; cut into slices. Serve over noodles. Yield: 5 servings (serving size: 3 ounces pork, 1 cup sauce, and 1 cup noodles).

CALORIES 460 (22% from fat); FAT 11.2g (sat 3.4g, mono 4.4g, poly 1.8g); PROTEIN 34g; CARB 56g; FIBER 6g; CHOL 117mg; IRON 5.6mg; SODIUM 444mg; CALC 62mg

AEGEAN LAMB WITH ORZO

Lamb shoulder is a less expensive cut, but you'll need to trim it well. Expect to trim as much as 1 to 1½ pounds of fat.

4½ pounds lamb shoulder
¼ cup chopped fresh or 4 teaspoons dried oregano
1 tablespoon grated lemon rind
½ teaspoon salt, divided
¼ cup fresh lemon juice
1 (10-ounce) bag fresh spinach, chopped
5 cups hot cooked orzo (about 2½ cups uncooked rice-shaped pasta)
1 cup (4 ounces) crumbled feta cheese
Oregano sprigs (optional)
Lemon slices (optional)

1. Trim fat from lamb. Place lamb in an electric slow cooker; sprinkle with chopped oregano, lemon rind, and ¼ teaspoon salt. Pour in lemon juice; top lamb with spinach. Cover with lid; cook on high heat setting 1 hour. Reduce heat setting to low; cook 7 hours. Remove spinach and lamb from slow cooker, reserving drippings; cool. Remove meat from bones; discard bones, fat, and gristle. Chop meat.
2. Place a zip-top plastic bag inside a 2-cup glass measure. Pour drippings into bag, and let stand 10 minutes (fat will rise to top). Seal bag; carefully snip off 1 bottom corner of bag. Drain drippings into a large bowl, stopping before fat layer reaches opening; discard fat.
3. Add ¼ teaspoon salt, lamb, spinach, orzo, and feta to strained drippings. Garnish with oregano sprigs and lemon slices, if desired. Yield: 8 servings (serving size: 1 cup).

CALORIES 361 (32% from fat); FAT 13g (sat 5.7g, mono 4.4g, poly 1.2g); PROTEIN 29.1g; CARB 30.9g; FIBER 2.4g; CHOL 87mg; IRON 4.6mg; SODIUM 393mg; CALC 141mg

MEXICAN BLACK-BEAN CHILI

You can eliminate the quick-cook method for the black beans if you soak them overnight.

1 pound dried black beans
2 cups chopped onion
1 cup (½-inch) pieces yellow bell pepper
1 cup (½-inch) pieces red bell pepper
1 cup (½-inch) pieces green bell pepper
1 tablespoon chili powder
2 teaspoons cumin seeds
2 teaspoons dried oregano
1 teaspoon salt
½ teaspoon ground cinnamon
1 (15-ounce) can Italian-style tomatoes, undrained and chopped
1½ ounces semisweet chocolate, coarsely chopped
4 garlic cloves, minced
2 jalapeño peppers, seeded and chopped
2 bay leaves
1 cup minced fresh cilantro
1 to 2 teaspoons hot sauce

1. Sort and wash beans; place in a large Dutch oven. Cover with water to 2 inches above beans; bring to a boil, and cook 2 minutes. Remove from heat; cover and let stand 1 hour. Drain beans.
2. Place beans, onion, and next 13 ingredients in an electric slow cooker. Cover with lid, and cook on low heat setting 8 hours. Stir in cilantro and hot sauce. Discard bay leaves. Yield: 6 servings (serving size 1⅓ cups).

CALORIES 362 (11% from fat); FAT 4.4g (sat 1.9g, mono 1.1g, poly 1g); PROTEIN 19.5g; CARB 67g; FIBER 14g; CHOL 0mg; IRON 7.2mg; SODIUM 539mg; CALC 168mg

The Tinkerers' Tales

From soups to meatless chili, our readers find that creative dabbling and using what's at hand are surefire ways to warm up winter meals.

When it comes to following recipes, there are those who go by the book and there are those who tinker. Good thing, too. Here are their results.

CHICKEN-BARLEY SOUP

—*Diane Shingledecker, Lakewood, Colorado*

4½ cups water
1 teaspoon salt
½ teaspoon black pepper
¼ teaspoon poultry seasoning
¼ teaspoon dried oregano
¼ teaspoon dried rosemary
3 pounds chicken pieces, skinned
1 bay leaf
1 cup diced carrot
1 cup diced celery
1 cup diced peeled potato
½ cup diced onion
½ cup diced green bell pepper
½ cup uncooked pearl barley
1 (28-ounce) can diced tomatoes, undrained

1. Combine first 8 ingredients in a 6-quart pressure cooker. Close lid securely, and bring to high pressure over high heat (about 13 minutes). Adjust heat to medium or level needed to maintain high pressure; cook 17 minutes. Remove from heat; let pressure drop. Remove lid. Remove chicken from cooker; cool slightly. Remove chicken from bones, and shred with 2 forks.

2. Return shredded chicken to cooker. Stir in carrot and remaining ingredients. Close lid securely, and bring to high pressure over high heat (about 7 minutes). Adjust heat to medium or level needed to maintain high pressure; cook 3 minutes. Remove from heat; cool under cold water. Remove lid. Discard bay leaf. Yield: 8 servings (serving size: 1½ cups).

CALORIES 249 (24% from fat); FAT 6.5g (sat 1.8g, mono 2.2g, poly 1.6g); PROTEIN 26.6g; CARB 20.8g; FIBER 4g; CHOL 73mg; IRON 2.4mg; SODIUM 546mg; CALC 58mg

SPICY BLACK-AND-RED BEAN SOUP

(pictured on page 299)

To use a slow cooker, combine everything in the pot, and cook on high for the first hour; then turn the temperature down to low, and cook 7 more hours.
—*Marion Ferguson, Birmingham, Alabama*

Cooking spray
1½ cups chopped onion
1¼ cups sliced carrot
2 garlic cloves, minced
3 cups fat-free, less-sodium chicken broth
2 teaspoons sugar
1 (16-ounce) package frozen shoepeg white corn
1 (15-ounce) can red beans or kidney beans, drained
1 (15-ounce) can black beans, drained
1 (14.5-ounce) can Mexican-style stewed tomatoes with jalapeño peppers and spices, undrained
1 (14.5-ounce) can no-salt-added diced tomatoes, undrained
1 (4.5-ounce) can chopped green chiles, undrained

1. Place a large Dutch oven coated with cooking spray over medium-high heat until hot. Add onion, carrot, and garlic; sauté 5 minutes. Stir in broth and remaining ingredients; bring to a boil. Cover, reduce heat, and simmer 2 hours. Yield: 10 servings (serving size: 1 cup).

CALORIES 152 (5% from fat); FAT 0.8g (sat 0.1g, mono 0.1g, poly 0.3g); PROTEIN 7.8g; CARB 30.8g; FIBER 4.2g; CHOL 0mg; IRON 1.9mg; SODIUM 374mg; CALC 52mg

ROASTED-VEGETABLE SOUP

This recipe was inspired by a friend who served me a delicious tomato, potato, and carrot soup one rainy summer day on Martha's Vineyard. I thought the soup might be even better if the vegetables were roasted, and since winter in Buffalo creates the need for a lot of hot soup, I've had plenty of time to perfect the recipe. I like to serve it with a hearty white Tuscan bread and a salad.
—*Anne Graziano, Buffalo, New York*

2½ cups coarsely chopped onion
1 cup chopped carrot
1 tablespoon olive oil
¼ teaspoon salt
¼ teaspoon black pepper
5 plum tomatoes, halved (about 1 pound)
3 garlic cloves, sliced
4 cups vegetable broth (32-ounce carton)
1 cup cubed peeled baking potato
1 teaspoon dried oregano
1 teaspoon dried basil
1 (28-ounce) can whole tomatoes, undrained and chopped

1. Preheat oven to 425°.
2. Combine first 7 ingredients in a jelly-roll pan; toss to coat. Bake at 425° for 30 minutes or until vegetables are tender.
3. Combine broth and remaining 4 ingredients in a large Dutch oven; bring to a boil. Reduce heat; simmer 15 minutes or until potato is tender.
4. Add roasted vegetables to potato mixture. Place half of vegetable mixture in a blender, and process until smooth. Pour pureed mixture into a large bowl; repeat procedure with remaining vegetable mixture. Return to pan; cook 5 minutes or until thoroughly heated. Yield: 10 servings (serving size: 1 cup).

CALORIES 79 (25% from fat); FAT 2.2g (sat 0.3g, mono 1.2g, poly 0.5g); PROTEIN 2.3g; CARB 14.2g; FIBER 2.6g; CHOL 0mg; IRON 1.1mg; SODIUM 598mg; CALC 42mg

(continued on page 301)

Chutney-Turkey Salad on Focaccia
(page 293)

Buttermilk-Oat Rolls (page 281)

Orange-and-Avocado Salsa (page 306)

Spicy Black-and-Red Bean Soup
(page 296)

Maple, Fig, and Marsala Pie (page 309)

Hot Maple Soufflé (page 291)

Rioja Chicken (page 294)

November

TARASCAN SOUP

One of the first meals my wife and I shared before we were married was at this fantastic Mexican restaurant in Santa Barbara, California. We still haven't found a restaurant that comes close to recreating the flavors there, but when we crave great Mexican soup, we do have this recipe.

—*Owen Stayner, Birmingham, Alabama*

 1 tablespoon olive oil
 1 cup chopped onion
 4 large garlic cloves, minced
 1 (28-ounce) can diced tomatoes, undrained
 2 (15-ounce) cans pinto beans, undrained
 2 teaspoons chili powder
 1 teaspoon ground cumin
 ½ teaspoon hot sauce
 ¼ teaspoon salt
 1 (16-ounce) can fat-free, less-sodium chicken broth
 1 cup (4 ounces) shredded reduced-fat Monterey Jack cheese
 16 baked tortilla chips, crushed (about 1 cup)

1. Heat oil in a large Dutch oven over medium-high heat. Add onion and garlic; sauté 3 minutes. Stir in tomatoes; cook 5 minutes. Place beans in a blender or food processor; process until smooth. Add beans, chili powder, and next 4 ingredients to pan; bring to a boil. Reduce heat to medium-low; cook 18 minutes. Serve with cheese and chips. Yield: 8 servings (serving size: 1 cup soup, 2 tablespoons cheese, and about 2 tablespoons chips).

CALORIES 266 (18% from fat); FAT 5.4g (sat 2g, mono 2.3g, poly 0.6g); PROTEIN 15.4g; CARB 40.2g; FIBER 5.9g; CHOL 9mg; IRON 3.7mg; SODIUM 788mg; CALC 212mg

THAI-STYLE PUMPKIN SOUP

If you don't have fresh pumpkin, canned works just as well.

—*Roxanne E. Chan, Albany, California*

 2 (16-ounce) cans fat-free, less-sodium chicken broth
 1 (15-ounce) can pumpkin
 1 (12-ounce) can mango nectar
 ¼ cup reduced-fat chunky peanut butter
 2 tablespoons rice vinegar
 1½ tablespoons minced green onions
 1 teaspoon grated peeled fresh ginger
 ½ teaspoon grated orange rind
 ¼ teaspoon dried crushed red pepper
 1 garlic clove, crushed

1. Combine first 3 ingredients in a large Dutch oven, and bring to a boil. Cover, reduce heat, and simmer 10 minutes. Combine 1 cup pumpkin mixture and peanut butter in a blender or food processor; process until smooth. Add mixture to pan. Stir in vinegar and next 5 ingredients; cook 3 minutes or until thoroughly heated. Ladle into soup bowls. Yield: 6 servings (serving size: 1 cup).

CALORIES 142 (27% from fat); FAT 4.2g (sat 0.9g, mono 1.9g, poly 1.3g); PROTEIN 5.6g; CARB 20.7g; FIBER 4g; CHOL 0mg; IRON 1.4mg; SODIUM 401mg; CALC 29mg

CRAB-AND-CORN CHOWDER

—*Melinda Davis, Oxford, Maryland*

 1 tablespoon olive oil
 ½ cup chopped green onions
 2 cups fresh or frozen corn kernels (about 4 ears)
 2 cups diced red potato
 2 cups fat-free milk
 ¼ teaspoon salt
 ¼ teaspoon Worcestershire sauce
 ⅛ teaspoon black pepper
 1 (16-ounce) can fat-free, less-sodium chicken broth
 1 fresh thyme sprig
 2 tablespoons cornstarch
 1 (5-ounce) can evaporated skim milk
 ½ cup chopped chanterelle or other fresh wild mushrooms (about 2 ounces)
 ½ pound lump crabmeat, shell pieces removed

1. Heat oil in a Dutch oven over medium heat. Add onions; sauté 2 minutes or until tender. Add corn and next 7 ingredients; bring to a boil. Reduce heat; simmer 30 minutes or until potato is tender.
2. Combine cornstarch and evaporated milk in a bowl, stirring with a whisk. Add to soup; simmer 5 minutes or until thick, stirring occasionally. Add mushrooms and crabmeat; remove thyme sprig. Yield: 6 servings (serving size: 1 cup).

CALORIES 220 (16% from fat); FAT 3.8g (sat 0.6g, mono 2g, poly 0.8g); PROTEIN 16.5g; CARB 31.1g; FIBER 2.8g; CHOL 41mg; IRON 1.1mg; SODIUM 452mg; CALC 233mg

VEGETARIAN CHILI

—*Laura Donovan, Horseheads, New York*

 Cooking spray
 2 cups chopped onion
 ¾ cup chopped red bell pepper
 ¾ cup chopped green bell pepper
 1 garlic clove, minced
 1 tablespoon chili powder
 1 teaspoon dried Italian seasoning
 1 (16-ounce) can Great Northern beans, rinsed and drained
 1 (15-ounce) can tomato sauce
 1 (15-ounce) can kidney beans, rinsed and drained
 1 (15-ounce) can black beans, rinsed and drained
 1 (14.5-ounce) can no-salt-added diced tomatoes, undrained
 5 teaspoons grated Parmesan cheese

1. Place a Dutch oven coated with cooking spray over medium-high heat until hot. Add onion and peppers; sauté 10 minutes or until tender. Add garlic; sauté 30 seconds. Add chili powder and next 6 ingredients; bring to a boil. *Continued*

Cover, reduce heat, and simmer 10 minutes or until thoroughly heated. Ladle into soup bowls; sprinkle with cheese. Yield: 5 servings (serving size: 1½ cups chili and 1 teaspoon cheese).

CALORIES 281 (7% from fat); FAT 2.1g (sat 0.6g, mono 0.3g, poly 0.7g); PROTEIN 17g; CARB 53.2g; FIBER 9.5g; CHOL 1mg; IRON 5.8mg; SODIUM 948mg; CALC 155mg

What's in a Name?

Any way it's defined, gingerbread has been pleasing palates throughout the ages.

Today, it seems, just about any recipe that calls for flour, sugar, and ginger is known as gingerbread. Does it matter? Do we appreciate an upside-down, ginger-spiked cake topped with pears any less because of muddled etymology? Take a bite, and get back to us.

QUICK-AND-EASY GINGERBREAD

½   cup granulated sugar
¼   cup butter or stick margarine, softened
½   cup orange juice
⅓   cup molasses
¼   cup egg substitute or 1 egg white
1½ cups all-purpose flour
2   teaspoons ground ginger
½   teaspoon baking powder
½   teaspoon baking soda
½   teaspoon ground cinnamon
¼   teaspoon salt
¼   teaspoon ground nutmeg
Cooking spray
1   teaspoon powdered sugar

1. Preheat oven to 350°.
2. Beat granulated sugar and butter at medium speed of a mixer until well-blended. Add orange juice, molasses, and egg substitute; beat well.
3. Lightly spoon flour into dry measuring cups; level with a knife. Combine flour and next 6 ingredients in a small bowl; gradually add flour mixture to molasses mixture, stirring until well-blended. Pour batter into an 8-inch square baking pan coated with cooking spray. Bake at 350° for 25 minutes or until a wooden pick inserted in center comes out clean. Cool gingerbread in pan on a wire rack. Sprinkle with powdered sugar. Yield: 9 servings (serving size: 1 square).

CALORIES 209 (23% from fat); FAT 5.4g (sat 1.1g, mono 2.3g, poly 1.7g); PROTEIN 3g; CARB 37.6g; FIBER 0.6g; CHOL 0mg; IRON 1.8mg; SODIUM 237mg; CALC 50mg

OLD-FASHIONED CIDER-GINGERBREAD BUNDT CAKE

2½ cups all-purpose flour
1   tablespoon ground ginger
2   teaspoons baking soda
1   teaspoon ground cinnamon
1   teaspoon ground cloves
¼   teaspoon salt
1   cup granulated sugar
¾   cup blackstrap molasses
¾   cup apple cider
½   cup apple butter
¼   cup vegetable oil
¼   cup egg substitute or 1 egg white
1⅓ cups shredded peeled Granny Smith apple (about 1 apple)
Cooking spray
1   tablespoon powdered sugar

1. Preheat oven to 350°.
2. Lightly spoon flour into dry measuring cups; level with a knife. Combine flour and next 5 ingredients in a bowl. Combine granulated sugar and next 5 ingredients in a large bowl; beat at medium speed of a mixer 2 minutes. Add flour mixture; beat until well-blended. Add apple; beat well. Pour batter into a 12-cup Bundt pan coated with cooking spray. Bake cake at 350° for 55 minutes or until a wooden pick inserted in center comes out clean. Cool in pan 10 minutes; invert cake onto a wire rack, and cool completely. Sift powdered sugar over cake. Yield: 16 servings (serving size: 1 slice).

CALORIES 219 (16% from fat); FAT 3.8g (sat 0.7g, mono 1g, poly 1.7g); PROTEIN 2.5g; CARB 44.6g; FIBER 0.9g; CHOL 0mg; IRON 3.8mg; SODIUM 210mg; CALC 141mg

PEAR UPSIDE-DOWN GINGERBREAD CAKE

3   peeled small pears, cored and cut lengthwise into ¼-inch-thick slices (about 1 pound)
2   tablespoons grated peeled fresh ginger, divided
1   tablespoon lemon juice
Cooking spray
2   tablespoons granulated sugar
½   cup packed dark brown sugar
¼   cup butter or stick margarine, softened
1   large egg
½   cup low-fat buttermilk
¼   cup molasses
1   cup all-purpose flour
1   teaspoon baking soda
½   teaspoon ground cinnamon
¼   teaspoon salt
¼   teaspoon dry mustard
¼   teaspoon ground cloves
¼   teaspoon ground nutmeg
1   teaspoon powdered sugar

1. Preheat oven to 350°.
2. Combine pears, 1 tablespoon ginger, and lemon juice. Coat a 9 x 2-inch round cake pan with cooking spray; sprinkle with granulated sugar. Arrange pears in bottom of pan in a circular pattern.
3. Combine brown sugar and butter in a large bowl; beat at medium speed of a mixer until well-blended. Beat in egg. Add buttermilk, molasses, and remaining 1 tablespoon ginger; beat until well-blended. Lightly spoon flour into a dry measuring cup; level with a knife. Combine flour and next 6 ingredients. Add flour mixture to batter; stir until well-blended. Pour over pears. Bake at 350° for 40 minutes or until cake springs back when touched lightly in center. Cool in pan 20 minutes on a wire rack.

Place a plate sprinkled with powdered sugar upside down on top of cake pan; invert cake onto plate. Yield: 8 servings.

CALORIES 244 (26% from fat); FAT 7.1g (sat 1.5g, mono 2.9g, poly 2g); PROTEIN 3.3g; CARB 43.3g; FIBER 1.2g; CHOL 28mg; IRON 1.7mg; SODIUM 323mg; CALC 66mg

GINGER-CHOCOLATE CHIP BISCOTTI

1 teaspoon vanilla extract
2 large eggs
1 large egg white
2 cups all-purpose flour
1 cup sugar
1 teaspoon ground cinnamon
½ teaspoon baking powder
½ teaspoon baking soda
½ teaspoon salt
¼ teaspoon ground cloves
½ cup semisweet chocolate minichips
2 tablespoons chopped crystallized ginger
Cooking spray

1. Preheat oven to 350°.
2. Combine first 3 ingredients in a large bowl; stir with a whisk. Lightly spoon flour into dry measuring cups; level with a knife. Combine flour and next 6 ingredients in a medium bowl. Add flour mixture, minichips, and ginger to egg mixture; stir until well-blended. Divide dough in half, and turn out onto a baking sheet coated with cooking spray. Shape each portion of dough into a 12-inch-long roll; flatten to ½-inch thickness. Bake at 350° for 25 minutes. Remove rolls from baking sheet; cool rolls 10 minutes on a wire rack.
3. Cut each roll diagonally into 18 (½-inch) slices. Place slices, cut sides down, on baking sheet. Bake at 350° for 10 minutes. Turn cookies over; bake an additional 10 minutes (cookies will be slightly soft in center but will harden as they cool). Remove from baking sheet; cool completely on wire racks. Yield: 3 dozen (serving size: 1 cookie).

CALORIES 65 (17% from fat); FAT 1.2g (sat 0.6g, mono 0.4g, poly 0.1g); PROTEIN 1.3g; CARB 12.6g; FIBER 0.2g; CHOL 12mg; IRON 0.5mg; SODIUM 62mg; CALC 9mg

GINGERBREAD PEOPLE COOKIES

2¼ cups all-purpose flour
1½ teaspoons ground ginger
1 teaspoon ground cinnamon
½ teaspoon baking powder
¼ teaspoon baking soda
¼ teaspoon salt
¼ teaspoon ground nutmeg
¼ teaspoon ground cloves
6 tablespoons granulated sugar
¼ cup butter or stick margarine, softened
½ cup molasses
1 large egg white
Cooking spray
2 tablespoons dried currants
1¼ cups powdered sugar
2 tablespoons lemon juice
¼ teaspoon vanilla extract

1. Lightly spoon flour into dry measuring cups; level with a knife. Combine flour and next 7 ingredients in a bowl. Combine granulated sugar and butter in a large bowl; beat at medium speed of a mixer 5 minutes. Add molasses and egg white; beat well. Add flour mixture to sugar mixture; beat at low speed until well-blended. Divide dough in half. Shape each half into a ball; wrap in plastic wrap. Chill 1 hour.
2. Preheat oven to 350°.
3. Working with 1 portion of dough at a time (keep remaining half chilled until ready to use), roll dough to ⅛-inch thickness on a heavily floured surface; cut with a 2½-inch boy or girl cookie cutter. Place gingerbread cookies 1 inch apart on baking sheets coated with cooking spray. Arrange currants on cookies as buttons. Bake at 350° for 8 minutes. Remove from pans; cool on wire racks.
4. Combine powdered sugar, lemon juice, and vanilla in a bowl. Spoon into a decorating bag or a heavy-duty zip-top plastic bag with a tiny hole snipped in 1 corner of bag, and decorate as desired. Yield: 4 dozen (serving size: 1 cookie).

CALORIES 59 (15% from fat); FAT 1g (sat 0.2g, mono 0.4g, poly 0.3g); PROTEIN 0.7g; CARB 11.9g; FIBER 0.2g; CHOL 0mg; IRON 0.5mg; SODIUM 38mg; CALC 13mg

Scene Stealers

Keep your eyes on the supporting cast, not the big star, for the most memorable flavors on the Thanksgiving table.

There's an old show-biz saying: There are no small parts, only small actors. Same with food. The traditional tastes of potato, stuffing, and cranberry are fine, but you can also add new scenes, energizing vegetables and casseroles with unexpected spices or toppings—sesame seed, almond, Parmesan.

SOURDOUGH-SAUSAGE STUFFING

3 turkey Italian sausage links (about 11 ounces)
1 teaspoon olive oil
2 cups chopped onion
2 cups chopped celery
2 tablespoons chopped fresh parsley
2 teaspoons dried rubbed sage
1 teaspoon dried thyme
½ teaspoon salt
½ teaspoon dried marjoram
½ teaspoon black pepper
12 cups (½-inch) cubed sourdough bread (about 1 pound)
1 (16-ounce) can fat-free, less-sodium chicken broth
Cooking spray

1. Preheat oven to 350°.
2. Remove casings from sausage. Heat oil in a large nonstick skillet over medium-high heat; add sausage, and sauté 5 minutes or until browned, stirring to crumble. Add onion and celery; sauté 3 minutes. Stir in parsley and next 5 ingredients. Place sausage mixture in a large bowl; stir in bread and broth. Spoon stuffing into an 11 x 7-inch baking dish coated with cooking spray. Cover and bake at 350° for 15 minutes. Uncover; bake an additional 20 minutes or until golden brown. Yield: 9 servings (serving size: 1 cup).

CALORIES 208 (21% from fat); FAT 5g (sat 1.7g, mono 1.9g, poly 2.4g); PROTEIN 11.9g; CARB 28.9g; FIBER 2.1g; CHOL 30mg; IRON 2.3mg; SODIUM 699mg; CALC 76mg

TWO-CHEESE SCALLOPED POTATOES

1½ cups fat-free milk
1½ cups (6 ounces) shredded reduced-fat extra-sharp Cheddar cheese, divided
1 cup (4 ounces) shredded reduced-fat Monterey Jack cheese, divided
¼ cup ketchup
2 teaspoons Worcestershire sauce
¼ teaspoon black pepper
2½ pounds peeled baking potatoes, cut into ¼-inch-thick slices
2 cups vertically sliced onion
Cooking spray
2 tablespoons chopped fresh parsley

1. Preheat oven to 350°.
2. Combine milk, ¾ cup Cheddar, ½ cup Monterey Jack, and next 3 ingredients. Set aside.
3. Arrange half of potatoes and half of onion in bottom of a 13 x 9-inch baking dish coated with cooking spray. Top with half of milk mixture. Repeat layers; top with remaining ¾ cup Cheddar, ½ cup Monterey Jack, and parsley. Cover and bake at 350° for 1 hour and 15 minutes. Uncover; bake an additional 20 minutes or until potatoes are tender and cheese is browned. Yield: 8 servings (serving size: ¾ cup).

CALORIES 233 (27% from fat); FAT 7.1g (sat 4g, mono 1.9g, poly 0.3g); PROTEIN 14.8g; CARB 28.5g; FIBER 2.5g; CHOL 25mg; IRON 1.2mg; SODIUM 377mg; CALC 377mg

TWICE-BAKED SWEET POTATOES WITH SESAME CRUST

8 small sweet potatoes (about 3 pounds)
¼ cup thawed apple juice concentrate
2 tablespoons fresh lemon juice
1 tablespoon low-sodium soy sauce
1 tablespoon molasses
2 teaspoons grated peeled fresh ginger
¼ cup sesame seeds, toasted
¼ teaspoon ground red pepper
Cooking spray

1. Preheat oven to 375°.
2. Wrap potatoes in foil; bake at 375° for 1 hour or until tender. Cool. Peel and cut each potato into 6 wedges.
3. Combine juice concentrate and next 4 ingredients in a microwave-safe bowl; set aside. Combine sesame seeds and pepper.
4. Place potato wedges on a jelly-roll pan coated with cooking spray. Brush wedges with apple juice mixture; sprinkle with sesame seed mixture. Bake at 375° for 15 minutes or until golden brown. Microwave remaining apple juice mixture at HIGH 30 seconds or until hot; drizzle over potato. Yield: 8 servings (serving size: 6 wedges).

CALORIES 221 (12% from fat); FAT 2.9g (sat 0.4g, mono 0.9g, poly 1.2g); PROTEIN 3.5g; CARB 46.4g; FIBER 5.1g; CHOL 0mg; IRON 1.8mg; SODIUM 74mg; CALC 87mg

MAPLE-ORANGE SWEET POTATOES

2½ pounds peeled sweet potatoes, cut into ¼-inch-thick slices
⅓ cup fresh orange juice
¼ cup maple syrup
2 tablespoons brown sugar
1 tablespoon stick margarine or butter, melted
½ teaspoon salt
⅛ teaspoon ground cloves
¼ cup chopped pecans, toasted

1. Place potato slices in a 2-quart casserole. Combine juice and next 5 ingredients; pour mixture over potatoes. Cover loosely with plastic wrap; microwave at HIGH 10 minutes. Stir after 5 minutes. Uncover and microwave at HIGH 5 minutes or until potato is tender. Sprinkle with pecans. Yield: 10 servings (serving size: ½ cup).

CALORIES 173 (18% from fat); FAT 3.5g (sat 0.5g, mono 1.8g, poly 1g); PROTEIN 2g; CARB 34.4g; FIBER 3.4g; CHOL 0mg; IRON 0.8mg; SODIUM 146mg; CALC 33mg

CARAMELIZED PEARL ONIONS

1 tablespoon stick margarine or butter
1 tablespoon sugar
1 (16-ounce) package frozen pearl onions, thawed
1⅔ cups coarsely chopped red bell pepper
1 teaspoon chopped fresh or ¼ teaspoon dried rosemary
½ teaspoon salt
¼ teaspoon black pepper

1. Melt margarine in a nonstick skillet over medium-high heat. Add sugar and onions; sauté 8 minutes or until golden brown. Stir in bell pepper and remaining ingredients; sauté 2 minutes. Yield: 6 servings (serving size: ½ cup).

CALORIES 62 (30% from fat); FAT 2.1g (sat 0.4g, mono 0.9g, poly 0.7g); PROTEIN 1g; CARB 11g; FIBER 1.2g; CHOL 0mg; IRON 0.8mg; SODIUM 225mg; CALC 31mg

LEMON-DILL CARROTS

1 teaspoon olive oil
3 cups diagonally sliced carrot
¼ cup fat-free, less-sodium chicken broth
1 teaspoon grated lemon rind
1 tablespoon fresh lemon juice
½ teaspoon celery salt
¼ teaspoon black pepper
1 tablespoon minced fresh or 1 teaspoon dried dill

1. Heat oil in a large nonstick skillet over medium-high heat. Add carrot; sauté 2 minutes. Stir in broth and next 4 ingredients. Cover; reduce heat to medium-low, and cook 10 minutes or until carrots are tender, stirring occasionally. Remove from heat; stir in dill. Yield: 6 servings (serving size: ½ cup).

CALORIES 33 (25% from fat); FAT 0.9g (sat 0.1g, mono 0.6g, poly 0.1g); PROTEIN 0.7g; CARB 6.1g; FIBER 1.8g; CHOL 0mg; IRON 0.4mg; SODIUM 214mg; CALC 20mg

Broccoli with Almond-Breadcrumb Topping

6 cups chopped broccoli
⅓ cup dry breadcrumbs
2 tablespoons grated Parmesan cheese
2 tablespoons finely chopped almonds
1 teaspoon dried basil
1 teaspoon dried oregano
¼ teaspoon salt
¼ teaspoon black pepper

1. Preheat oven to 450°.
2. Cook broccoli in boiling water 2 minutes, and drain. Rinse with cold water; drain well. Place broccoli in an 11 x 7-inch baking dish. Combine breadcrumbs and remaining 6 ingredients; sprinkle breadcrumb mixture over broccoli. Bake at 450° for 15 minutes or until breadcrumbs are golden brown. Yield: 8 servings (serving size: ¾ cup).

CALORIES 52 (29% from fat); FAT 1.7g (sat 0.4g, mono 0.7g, poly 0.4g); PROTEIN 3.4g; CARB 7.3g; FIBER 2.5g; CHOL 1mg; IRON 1.1mg; SODIUM 153mg; CALC 69mg

Cranberry-Corn Relish

¼ cup diced red onion
2 tablespoons minced fresh cilantro
1 (16-ounce) can whole-berry cranberry sauce
1 (15.25-ounce) can whole-kernel corn, drained
1 (4.5-ounce) can chopped green chiles, undrained

1. Combine all ingredients in a bowl. Cover and chill at least 30 minutes. Yield: 3½ cups (serving size: ¼ cup).

CALORIES 75 (2% from fat); FAT 0.2g (sat 0g, mono 0.1g, poly 0.1g); PROTEIN 0.9g; CARB 19g; FIBER 0.5g; CHOL 0mg; IRON 0.3mg; SODIUM 87mg; CALC 5mg

Seduced by Citrus

With citrus dishes so delicious, you'll never just peel an orange again to get your holiday vitamin C.

Have you given any thought to how you're going to stay healthy during the holiday frenzy? Probably not. After all, you take your vitamins, and there will be no shortage of things to eat. With all the activity, you could get into a bigger problem than you realize and wind up in a nutritional downswing.

Rather than just peel an orange, why not put the full range of citrus to use in recipes that will make your buffet something to remember? Citrus adds freshness to salads, salsas, desserts—even entrées. And our simple citrus tips on page 340 will make it even easier to add this nutritional ally to your holiday dishes.

Mediterranean Orange Roughy

2 teaspoons olive oil
1⅔ cups vertically sliced onion
1 cup chopped orange sections (about 3 oranges)
1½ teaspoons chopped fresh or ½ teaspoon dried oregano
¼ teaspoon salt
¼ teaspoon black pepper
8 pitted ripe olives, halved
1 garlic clove, minced
4 (6-ounce) orange roughy or other white fish fillets
⅓ cup fat-free, less-sodium chicken broth
1 teaspoon grated orange rind

1. Preheat oven to 450°.
2. Heat oil in a large nonstick skillet over medium-high heat. Add onion, and cook 7 minutes or until lightly browned, stirring occasionally. Remove from heat. Stir in orange sections and next 5 ingredients.
3. Arrange fillets in a single layer in a 13 x 9-inch baking dish. Combine broth and rind; pour over fish. Spoon onion mixture over fish. Bake at 450° for 15 minutes or until fish flakes easily when tested with a fork. Yield: 4 servings (serving size: 5 ounces fish and ⅓ cup onion topping).

CALORIES 190 (21% from fat); FAT 4.5g (sat 0.5g, mono 3.1g, poly 0.4g); PROTEIN 26.4g; CARB 10.6g; FIBER 3.2g; CHOL 34mg; IRON 0.9mg; SODIUM 365mg; CALC 40mg

Mexican Black Bean-and-Citrus Salad

Tangelos, a cross between grapefruit and tangerines, add a rich, tart flavor to this bean salad. If you can't find this citrus hybrid, substitute oranges or tangerines. Serve this salad with chicken, fish, or pork.

1 tablespoon olive oil
1 cup diced onion
1 cup diced red bell pepper
2 teaspoons grated tangelo rind
¼ cup fresh tangelo juice
3 tablespoons fresh lime juice
1 teaspoon sugar
½ teaspoon salt
½ teaspoon ground cumin
¼ teaspoon hot sauce
1½ cups tangelo sections (about 8 tangelos)
¼ cup finely chopped fresh cilantro
2 (15-ounce) cans black beans, rinsed and drained

1. Heat oil in a nonstick skillet over medium-high heat. Add onion and bell pepper; sauté 5 minutes or until tender.
2. Combine rind and next 6 ingredients in a bowl. Combine onion mixture, tangelo, cilantro, and beans in a bowl. Add juice mixture; toss. Yield: 6 servings (serving size: about ¾ cup).

CALORIES 174 (16% from fat); FAT 3.1g (sat 0.5g, mono 1.7g, poly 0.5g); PROTEIN 8.3g; CARB 30.9g; FIBER 6.5g; CHOL 0mg; IRON 2.4mg; SODIUM 418mg; CALC 56mg

ORANGE-AND-AVOCADO SALSA

(pictured on page 298)

Serve this salsa with grilled chicken, pork, or tortilla chips.

    1   cup chopped orange sections
          (about 3 oranges)
    ½   cup diced peeled avocado
    ¼   cup thinly sliced spinach
    3   tablespoons chopped red onion
    2   tablespoons chopped fresh
          cilantro
    2   tablespoons fresh lime juice
    1   tablespoon minced seeded
          jalapeño pepper
    ¼   teaspoon salt

1. Combine all ingredients in a bowl; toss well. Yield: 2 cups (serving size: ½ cup).

CALORIES 59 (46% from fat); FAT 3g (sat 0.5g, mono 1.8g, poly 0.4g); PROTEIN 1.1g; CARB 8.5g; FIBER 2.8g; CHOL 0mg; IRON 0.5mg; SODIUM 153mg; CALC 29mg

FIELD SALAD WITH TANGERINES, ROASTED BEETS, AND FETA

    2   beets (about ½ pound)
    ½   teaspoon grated tangerine rind
    6   cups gourmet salad greens
    1   cup tangerine sections (about
          3 tangerines)
    ¼   cup (1 ounce) crumbled feta or
          blue cheese
    ¼   cup fresh tangerine juice
    ¼   teaspoon black pepper
    1   tablespoon fresh lemon juice
    2   teaspoons extra-virgin olive oil
    ⅛   teaspoon salt
    ⅛   teaspoon Dijon mustard

1. Preheat oven to 425°.
2. Leave root and 1 inch of stem on beets; scrub with a brush. Place beets on a baking sheet lined with foil; bake at 425° for 45 minutes or until tender. Cool slightly. Peel beets; cut each into 8 wedges.
3. Combine rind and next 3 ingredients in a large bowl. Combine tangerine juice and next 5 ingredients; stir

well with a whisk. Pour over salad mixture, and toss to combine. Place salad mixture evenly on 4 plates; top with beets. Yield: 4 servings (serving size: 1½ cups salad and 4 beet wedges).

CALORIES 120 (32% from fat); FAT 4.2g (sat 1.4g, mono 2.1g, poly 0.4g); PROTEIN 4.1g; CARB 18.6g; FIBER 3.3g; CHOL 6mg; IRON 1.7mg; SODIUM 220mg; CALC 89mg

SPICED CITRUS COMPOTE

    1   cup water
    ⅓   cup sugar
    ¼   cup grapefruit rind strips
    ¼   cup orange rind strips
    2   tablespoons dried sweet cherries
    ¼   teaspoon whole cloves
    ¼   teaspoon whole allspice
    1   (3-inch) cinnamon stick
    2   cups pink grapefruit sections
          (about 2 large grapefruit)
    1½ cups orange sections (about
          4 oranges)
    ¾   cup tangerine sections (about 2
          tangerines)

1. Combine first 8 ingredients in a small saucepan. Bring to a boil; cover, reduce heat, and simmer 10 minutes. Strain mixture through a sieve into a bowl; discard solids.
2. Combine sugar mixture and citrus sections in a large bowl. Cover and chill at least 3 hours. Yield: 6 servings (serving size: ⅔ cup).

CALORIES 98 (2% from fat); FAT 0.2g (sat 0g, mono 0.1g, poly 0.1g) PROTEIN 1g; CARB 25g; FIBER 2.9g; CHOL 0mg; IRON 0.1mg; SODIUM 0mg; CALC 30mg

CITRUS MEDLEY WITH POUND CAKE TRIANGLES

Tangerines can be substituted for the tangelos. Red navel or any other type of orange can be substituted for the blood orange.

    ⅓   cup fresh tangelo juice
    ¼   cup fresh blood orange juice
    2   tablespoons golden raisins
    2   tablespoons sugar
    2   teaspoons finely chopped fresh
          mint
    1½ cups tangelo sections (about 8
          tangelos)
    1½ cups blood orange sections (about
          8 blood oranges)
    6   (1-ounce) slices fat-free pound
          cake
    2   tablespoons stick margarine or
          butter, melted

1. Combine first 5 ingredients in a small saucepan. Bring to a boil; cook 1 minute. Remove from heat. Gently stir in tangelo and orange sections. Cool completely.
2. Brush both sides of cake slices with margarine. Place a large nonstick skillet over medium-high heat until hot. Add cake slices; cook 2 minutes on each side or until lightly browned. Cut each cake slice in half diagonally. Serve cake with fruit mixture. Yield: 6 servings (serving size: 2 cake triangles and ½ cup fruit).

CALORIES 195 (18% from fat); FAT 3.9g (sat 0.8g, mono 1.7g, poly 1.2g); PROTEIN 2.2g; CARB 38.4g; FIBER 4.5g; CHOL 0mg; IRON 0.9mg; SODIUM 187mg; CALC 54mg

---

VITAMIN C

Vitamin C, our staunch ally, helps keep the immune system humming. But that's only the beginning of this key vitamin's role. It also helps combat free radicals, those renegade metabolic waste products and environmental agents that contribute to aging and disease. And C is instrumental in collagen formation, which maintains healthy skin, bones, and muscle.

You'll find that vitamin C is abundant—and not just in tablets or canned juices. Winter is a booming citrus season. Grocery-store fruit bins are brimming with the fresh stuff: oranges, tangerines, grapefruits—all terrific sources of vitamin C. Just one medium orange (75 milligrams) or grapefruit (78 milligrams) more than meets the vitamin's Recommended Daily Allowance of 60 milligrams.

$\mathscr{A}$ Crust You Can Trust

Everybody wishes for an easy, homemade crust that puts pies back on the holiday table—without all the fat. Wish granted.

Unfortunately, whether they're frozen or homemade, most piecrusts do have something in common: They're incredibly high in fat and calories. Typically, the crust is responsible for more fat and calories than the filling. Far more. In an average apple pie, for example, the crust contributes 70% of the fat and more than half the calories of each slice.

Do we have to live with this? Can nothing be done? Here's a crust that's a snap to make and adaptable enough for all our best fillings. It stands up to a side-by-side blind taste test against the full-fat version, and it's so easy that even an inexperienced baker can pull it off with panache.

At long last, a crust we can trust.

PASTRY CRUST

A slurry is a mixture of flour and liquid (water and vinegar in this recipe). It's the key to this tender low-fat crust. Pie weights can be ordered by mail or found in gourmet kitchen shops. You can also use uncooked dried beans, but save them to reuse as weights. They'll be too hard for cooking.

1   cup all-purpose flour, divided
3   to 4 tablespoons ice water
½   teaspoon cider vinegar
1   tablespoon powdered sugar
¼   teaspoon salt
¼   cup vegetable shortening

1. Preheat oven to 400°.
2. Lightly spoon flour into a dry measuring cup, and level with a knife. Combine ¼ cup flour, ice water, and vinegar, stirring with a whisk until slurry is well-blended.
3. Combine ¾ cup flour, sugar, and salt in a bowl; cut in shortening with a pastry blender or 2 knives until mixture resembles coarse meal. Add slurry; toss with a fork until flour mixture is moist. Gently press mixture into a 4-inch circle on heavy-duty plastic wrap; cover with additional plastic wrap. Roll dough, still covered, into a 12-inch circle; freeze 10 minutes.
4. Remove 1 sheet of plastic wrap; let stand 1 minute or until pliable. Fit dough, plastic-wrap side up, into a 9-inch pie plate or a 9-inch round removable-bottom tart pan. Remove plastic wrap. Press dough against bottom and sides of pan. Fold edges under or flute decoratively. Line bottom of dough with a piece of foil; arrange pie weights on foil. Bake at 400° for 20 minutes or until edge is lightly browned. Remove pie weights and foil; cool on a wire rack. Yield: 1 (9-inch) crust.

Food processor variation:

1. Preheat oven to 400°. Lightly spoon 1 cup flour into a dry measuring cup; level with a knife. Place flour, sugar, and salt in a food processor; pulse 2 times or until combined. Add shortening; pulse 10 times or until mixture is combined. Add ice water and vinegar through food chute, pulsing just until combined (mixture won't form a ball). Gently press mixture into a 4-inch circle on heavy-duty plastic wrap; cover with additional plastic wrap. Roll dough, still covered, into a 12-inch circle; freeze 10 minutes.
2. Remove 1 sheet of plastic wrap; let stand 1 minute or until pliable. Fit dough into a 9-inch pie plate or 9-inch round removable-bottom tart pan. Remove top sheet of plastic wrap. Press dough against bottom and sides of pan. Fold edges under or flute decoratively. Arrange pie weights on a piece of foil in bottom of dough; bake at 400° for 20 minutes or until edge is lightly browned. Remove pie weights and foil; cool on a wire rack. Yield: 1 (9-inch) crust.

PEAR-AND-ALMOND CUSTARD PIE

1   (9-inch) **Pastry Crust**
5   firm, ripe Anjou pears (about 2 pounds), peeled and cored
½   cup packed brown sugar
⅛   teaspoon salt
2   large eggs, lightly beaten
⅔   cup 2% reduced-fat milk
½   teaspoon almond extract
½   teaspoon vanilla extract
2   tablespoons brown sugar
2   tablespoons sliced almonds

1. Prepare and bake Pastry Crust in a 9-inch pie plate. Cool crust completely on a wire rack.
2. Preheat oven to 400°.
3. Cut pears in half lengthwise; cut each half into ⅛-inch-thick slices, keeping slices in order as they are cut. Arrange pear slices in prepared crust in 2 layers. Combine ½ cup brown sugar, salt, and eggs in a bowl; stir well with a whisk. Add milk and extracts; stir well. Pour milk mixture over pears; sprinkle with 2 tablespoons brown sugar and almonds. Place pie plate on a baking sheet. Bake at 400° for 15 minutes. Reduce oven temperature to 350° (do not remove pie from oven); bake an additional 1 hour and 5 minutes or until a knife inserted in center comes out clean. Cool on a wire rack. Yield: 8 servings (serving size: 1 wedge).

CALORIES 268 (28% from fat); FAT 8.3g (sat 2.1g, mono 3g, poly 2.1g); PROTEIN 4.6g; CARB 45.5g; FIBER 3.3g; CHOL 57mg; IRON 1.5mg; SODIUM 143mg; CALC 63mg

The pastry dough can be rolled out and frozen in between sheets of plastic wrap for up to one week. It can also be made ahead, rolled out, placed in a pie plate, and covered tightly and refrigerated for one day.

❶ Stir together ¼ cup flour, ice water, and vinegar to make a slurry.

❷ Combine remaining flour, sugar, and salt in a bowl. Then cut in shortening until the mixture looks like coarse meal.

❸ Add slurry, and toss with a fork until flour mixture is moist.

❹ Gently press dough into a circle on heavy-duty plastic wrap.

❺ Place additional plastic wrap over the dough, and roll into a 12-inch circle. Freeze for 10 minutes.

❻ Remove top sheet of plastic wrap, and let the dough rest for about 1 minute or until it is easy to work with.

❼ Fit dough, plastic-wrap side up, into a 9-inch pie plate or a 9-inch round removable-bottom tart pan. Remove plastic wrap. Fold the edges of the dough under, and flute.

❽ Line the dough with aluminum foil, and fill with pie weights. Bake.

❾ Remove pie weights and foil. Allow the piecrust to cool on a wire rack.

BLACK BOTTOM BANANA-CREAM PIE

(pictured on front cover)

Although slightly unconventional for Thanksgiving, this pie is a refreshing follow-up to the big meal as well as a tempting armchair treat for later that night.

 1 (9-inch) Pastry Crust (page 307)
 3 tablespoons cornstarch, divided
 2 tablespoons sugar
 2 tablespoons unsweetened cocoa
 Dash of salt
 1⅓ cups 1% low-fat milk, divided
 1 ounce semisweet chocolate, chopped
 ½ cup sugar
 ¼ teaspoon salt
 2 large eggs
 1 tablespoon stick margarine or butter
 2 teaspoons vanilla extract
 2 ounces block-style fat-free cream cheese, softened
 2 cups sliced ripe banana (about 2 large bananas)
 1½ cups frozen fat-free whipped topping, thawed
 Chocolate curls (optional)

1. Prepare and bake Pastry Crust in a 9-inch pie plate. Cool completely on a wire rack.
2. Combine 1 tablespoon cornstarch, 2 tablespoons sugar, cocoa, and dash of salt in a small, heavy saucepan; gradually add ⅓ cup milk, stirring with a whisk. Cook 2 minutes over medium-low heat. Stir in chopped chocolate; bring to a boil over medium heat. Reduce heat to low; cook 1 minute, stirring constantly. Spread chocolate mixture into bottom of prepared crust.
3. Combine remaining 2 tablespoons cornstarch, ½ cup sugar, ¼ teaspoon salt, eggs, margarine, and remaining 1 cup milk in a heavy saucepan over medium heat, stirring constantly with a whisk. Bring to a boil. Reduce heat to low, and cook 30 seconds or until thick. Remove from heat. Add vanilla. Beat cream cheese at medium speed of

a mixer until light (about 30 seconds). Add ¼ cup hot custard to cream cheese, and beat just until blended. Stir in remaining custard.
4. Arrange banana slices on top of chocolate layer in crust; spoon custard over bananas. Press plastic wrap onto surface of custard; chill 4 hours. Remove plastic wrap. Spread whipped topping evenly over custard. Garnish with chocolate curls, if desired. Chill until ready to serve. Yield: 8 servings (serving size: 1 wedge).

CALORIES 315 (29% from fat); FAT 10.1g (sat 4.8g, mono 3.4g, poly 2.4g); PROTEIN 6.9g; CARB 49.6g; FIBER 1.6g; CHOL 58mg; IRON 1.4mg; SODIUM 253mg; CALC 94mg

MAPLE, FIG, AND MARSALA PIE

(pictured on page 299)

 1 (9-inch) Pastry Crust (page 307)
 1⅓ cups coarsely chopped dried figs (about 8 ounces)
 ⅓ cup sweet Marsala wine or sweet sherry
 2 tablespoons stick margarine or butter
 ½ cup packed dark brown sugar
 ¼ teaspoon salt
 ½ cup maple syrup
 1 tablespoon cider vinegar
 2 teaspoons vanilla extract
 3 large eggs, lightly beaten

1. Prepare and bake Pastry Crust in a 9-inch pie plate. Cool crust completely on a wire rack.
2. Combine figs and Marsala wine in a medium saucepan; bring to a simmer over medium heat. Cover, reduce heat, and simmer 10 minutes or until liquid is absorbed. Remove from heat; place in a medium bowl. Cool completely.
3. Preheat oven to 350°.
4. Melt margarine in a small, heavy saucepan over low heat. Remove from heat; add brown sugar and salt, stirring until combined. Add maple syrup, vinegar, vanilla, and eggs; stir well. Add to fig mixture; stir well. Spoon fig mixture into prepared crust. Bake at 350°

for 35 minutes or until filling is set. Cool on a wire rack. Yield: 10 servings (serving size: 1 wedge).

CALORIES 273 (28% from fat); FAT 8.5g (sat 2.1g, mono 3.1g, poly 2.4g); PROTEIN 3.9g; CARB 46.8g; FIBER 4.2g; CHOL 66mg; IRON 1.7mg; SODIUM 172mg; CALC 63mg

FRUIT-AND-BERRY STREUSEL PIE

Let the fruit mixture cool before pouring it into the baked crust. The streusel will stay on top instead of sinking into the filling.

 1 (9-inch) Pastry Crust (page 307)
 ¼ cup all-purpose flour
 ¼ cup packed brown sugar
 ½ teaspoon ground cinnamon
 ¼ teaspoon salt, divided
 2 tablespoons chilled stick margarine or butter, cut into small pieces
 1¼ cups water
 ½ cup sugar
 2 tablespoons cornstarch
 2½ cups fresh or frozen cranberries
 ½ cup dried blueberries or dried cherries
 ⅓ cup golden raisins
 1 teaspoon grated lemon rind
 1 tablespoon fresh lemon juice
 1 (16-ounce) can apricot halves in light syrup, drained and sliced into quarters

1. Prepare and bake Pastry Crust in a 9-inch pie plate. Cool completely on a wire rack.
2. Lightly spoon flour into a dry measuring cup; level with a knife. Combine flour, brown sugar, cinnamon, and ⅛ teaspoon salt in a bowl; cut in margarine with a pastry blender or 2 knives until mixture resembles coarse meal. Set aside.
3. Combine remaining ⅛ teaspoon salt, water, sugar, and cornstarch in a saucepan. Bring to a boil, and cook 1 minute, stirring constantly. Add cranberries, and cook over medium heat 10 minutes or until cranberries pop.
Continued

Remove from heat. Stir in blueberries, raisins, rind, and juice. Fold apricots into cranberry mixture. Cool to room temperature.

4. Preheat oven to 400°.

5. Pour fruit mixture into prepared crust. Sprinkle streusel mixture evenly over fruit mixture. Place pie on a baking sheet in lower third of oven. Bake at 400° for 30 minutes. Cool completely on a wire rack. Yield: 10 servings (serving size: 1 wedge).

CALORIES 257 (24% from fat); FAT 6.8g (sat 1.5g, mono 2.4g, poly 2.1g); PROTEIN 2.1g; CARB 47.9g; FIBER 2.2g; CHOL 0mg; IRON 1.2mg; SODIUM 147mg; CALC 16mg

BRANDIED SWEET POTATO TART

- 1 (9-inch) Pastry Crust (page 307)
- 2 cups mashed cooked sweet potato (about 1½ pounds)
- ⅓ cup packed dark brown sugar
- ½ teaspoon pumpkin-pie spice
- ¼ teaspoon salt
- 2 ounces block-style ⅓-less-fat cream cheese (Neufchâtel), softened
- 2 large eggs
- 3 tablespoons brandy
- 1 large egg white
- 3 tablespoons dark brown sugar
- 3 tablespoons light-colored corn syrup
- 1 teaspoon vanilla extract
- Dash of salt
- ¼ cup chopped pecans

1. Prepare and bake Pastry Crust in a 9-inch round removable-bottom tart pan. Cool crust completely on a wire rack.

2. Preheat oven to 325°.

3. Beat sweet potato and next 4 ingredients at medium speed of a mixer until well-blended. Add 2 eggs and brandy; beat until well-blended. Spoon filling into prepared crust.

4. Beat egg white and next 4 ingredients at medium speed of a mixer 2 minutes or until light brown. Pour corn syrup mixture over sweet potato mixture; sprinkle with pecans. Place tart on a baking sheet. Bake at 325° for

1½ hours or until a knife inserted in center comes out clean. Cool completely on a wire rack. Yield: 8 servings (serving size: 1 wedge).

CALORIES 318 (32% from fat); FAT 11.2g (sat 3.1g, mono 4.3g, poly 2.6g); PROTEIN 6.0g; CARB 48.8g; FIBER 3.1g; CHOL 61mg; IRON 1.7mg; SODIUM 221mg; CALC 42mg

PUMPKIN-SWIRL CHEESECAKE TART

- 1 (9-inch) Pastry Crust (page 307)
- ¾ cup fat-free sweetened condensed milk, divided
- 1 (8-ounce) block fat-free cream cheese softened
- 4 ounces block-style ⅓-less-fat cream cheese (Neufchâtel), softened
- 1 tablespoon vanilla extract
- ¼ teaspoon salt
- 2 large eggs, divided
- 1 large egg white
- ⅔ cup canned unsweetened pumpkin
- ½ teaspoon ground cinnamon
- ¼ teaspoon ground ginger
- ¼ teaspoon ground allspice

1. Prepare and bake Pastry Crust in a 9-inch round removable-bottom tart pan. Cool completely on a wire rack.

2. Preheat oven to 300°.

3. Combine ½ cup condensed milk and cream cheeses in a medium bowl; beat at medium speed of a mixer until smooth. Add vanilla, salt, 1 egg, and egg white; beat until combined. Spoon ½ cup cream cheese mixture into a small bowl; add remaining ¼ cup condensed milk, 1 egg, pumpkin, and next 3 ingredients, stirring well with a whisk.

4. Pour remaining cream cheese mixture into prepared crust. Pour pumpkin mixture over cream cheese mixture; swirl together using a knife. Bake at 300° for 50 minutes. Turn oven off; cool tart in closed oven 45 minutes. Remove from oven; cool completely on a wire rack. Cover; chill. Yield: 8 servings (serving size: 1 wedge).

CALORIES 280 (32% from fat); FAT 10.1g (sat 3.9g, mono 3.2g, poly 1.9g); PROTEIN 11.4g; CARB 33.5g; FIBER 1.3g; CHOL 72mg; IRON 1.2mg; SODIUM 427mg; CALC 182mg

FRESH-ORANGE TART

- 1 (9-inch) Pastry Crust (page 307)
- 6 large navel oranges
- ¼ cup sugar
- 1½ tablespoons cornstarch
- ⅛ teaspoon salt
- ½ teaspoon vanilla extract
- 3 tablespoons orange marmalade

1. Prepare and bake Pastry Crust in a 9-inch round removable-bottom tart pan. Cool completely on a wire rack.

2. Peel and section oranges over a bowl, and squeeze orange membranes to extract juice. Set 2 cups sections and ½ cup juice aside; reserve remaining sections and juice for another use. Discard membranes.

3. Combine sugar, cornstarch, and salt in a small saucepan; gradually add reserved ½ cup juice, stirring with a whisk until blended. Bring to a boil over medium heat, stirring constantly. Reduce heat to low; cook 1 minute. Remove from heat; stir in vanilla. Cool, stirring occasionally.

4. Place marmalade in a microwave-safe bowl, and microwave at HIGH 30 seconds or until marmalade melts. Spread marmalade in bottom of prepared crust. Arrange 1 cup orange sections on top of marmalade; spoon ⅓ cup orange filling over sections. Top with remaining orange sections and remaining orange filling. Cover and chill at least 4 hours. Yield: 8 servings (serving size: 1 wedge).

CALORIES 184 (27% from fat); FAT 5.5g (sat 1.4g, mono 1.8g, poly 1.7g); PROTEIN 2.2g; CARB 32.5g; FIBER 2.5g; CHOL 0mg; IRON 0.8mg; SODIUM 115mg; CALC 25mg

December

Another Kind of Warmth

The classic New England farmhouse is the busy hub for holidays filled with the laughter of children, aromas from the kitchen, and the lure of dinner.

A rustic old farmhouse can feel a little forlorn, especially at Christmas, without a lot of people. So when you cook, you do it for a crowd—your own and the one you've invited over. It makes for busy days, but that's the point. With sunup, the chopping and mixing begin in the kitchen, flooding your home with food you can't wait to eat.

With the preliminary chores out of the way and breakfast behind you, it's time to get down to the serious work. Dinner is hours away, and even the best old home can become confining—especially to children. Which is reason to look forward to the snow.

Sure, a new base and fresh powder are good news in New England—all that white stuff means a healthy economy. But snow also keeps people busy. Someone has to go out and shovel the drive, the walk, and the steps. It's a great job for children, and a good way to get them outside and into the day. Even the smaller ones can get bundled up and play.

When you come inside a couple of hours later, the house feels as warm as the bed you left that morning. And the aromas of the cooking set off all the alarms of your appetite. Now the house is full of people, a fire is blazing, the lights on the Christmas tree are twinkling, and the cooking is done. You gather around a sturdy table fairly groaning with the weight of good things to eat. Outside, evening settles in. The world is cold, turning dark: the familiar face of winter. Inside is the place to be.

MENU

PORK AND ROASTED WINTER
VEGETABLES
or
CIDER-BRAISED TURKEY
WITH APPLES

CURRIED BUTTERNUT
SQUASH SOUP

HONEY-CORNMEAL ROUNDS

SAVOY CABBAGE SALAD

PEAR, WALNUT, AND MAPLE
SYRUP PIE

PORK AND ROASTED WINTER VEGETABLES

(pictured on page 320)

Roasted vegetables:

- 6 cups diced peeled beets (about 1 pound)
- 4½ cups (2½-inch) cubed peeled butternut squash (about 1½ pounds)
- 3 cups (1½-inch) cubed turnips (about 1 pound)
- 2 cups chopped onion
- 2 cups (1-inch-thick) sliced carrot
- 1 cup (1½-inch) cubed peeled red potato (about 8 ounces)
- 8 garlic cloves
- Cooking spray
- 1 tablespoon olive oil
- ½ teaspoon salt
- ¼ teaspoon black pepper

Braised pork:

- 2 pounds boned Boston butt pork roast
- 2 teaspoons olive oil, divided
- 1 cup dry white wine
- 1 teaspoon chopped fresh or ¼ teaspoon dried thyme
- ¼ teaspoon salt
- 10 peppercorns
- 2 bay leaves

1. Preheat oven to 450°.
2. To prepare roasted vegetables, place first 7 ingredients in a 13 x 9-inch baking dish coated with cooking spray. Drizzle with 1 tablespoon oil; sprinkle with ½ teaspoon salt and pepper. Bake at 450° for 1½ hours, stirring occasionally.
3. To prepare braised pork, trim fat from pork; cut pork into 2-inch cubes. Heat 1 teaspoon oil in a Dutch oven over medium-high heat. Add half of pork; sauté 5 minutes or until browned on all sides. Remove from pan. Repeat procedure with 1 teaspoon oil and remaining pork. Return pork to pan; add wine and next 4 ingredients. Bring to a boil. Cover, reduce heat, and simmer 1 hour. Uncover; bring to a boil, and simmer 5 minutes. Remove bay leaves. Serve pork with roasted vegetables. Yield: 8 servings (serving size: 1 cup vegetables and about ½ cup pork).

CALORIES 319 (29% from fat); FAT 10.3g (sat 3.1g, mono 5.5g, poly 1.3g); PROTEIN 23.5g; CARB 35g; FIBER 4.9g; CHOL 55mg; IRON 2.9mg; SODIUM 409mg; CALC 102mg

---

CIDER-BRAISED TURKEY WITH APPLES

- 2 (1¼-pound) skinned, boned turkey breast halves
- 1 tablespoon chopped fresh or 1 teaspoon dried thyme
- ½ teaspoon salt, divided
- ¼ teaspoon black pepper
- 1 tablespoon olive oil
- ⅔ cup diced shallots
- 3 Fuji or gala apples (about 1¼ pounds), each cut into 8 wedges
- 1 cup apple cider

1 tablespoon chopped fresh or
  1 teaspoon dried rosemary
3 (10-ounce) bags fresh spinach
2 teaspoons stick margarine
⅛ teaspoon black pepper
¼ cup minced fresh parsley

1. Preheat oven to 400°.
2. Secure turkey halves together at 1-inch intervals with heavy string. Rub surface of turkey with thyme, ¼ teaspoon salt, and ¼ teaspoon pepper. Heat oil in a large ovenproof Dutch oven; add turkey, browning on all sides. Remove from pan. Add shallots; sauté 3 minutes. Add apples; sauté 3 minutes. Return turkey to pan. Stir in cider and rosemary; bring to a boil. Cover and bake at 400° for 30 minutes. Uncover; turn turkey over, and bake an additional 30 minutes or until turkey is done and apples are tender. Remove from oven; let stand 10 minutes.
3. Heat a large nonstick skillet over medium-high heat. Add 4 cups spinach; sauté until spinach wilts. Place in a bowl. Repeat procedure with remaining spinach. Add ¼ teaspoon salt, ⅛ teaspoon pepper, and margarine to spinach; toss.
4. Cut turkey into ¼-inch-thick slices; serve with apple mixture and spinach. Sprinkle with parsley. Yield: 8 servings (serving size: 3 ounces turkey, about ⅓ cup spinach, and ¼ cup apple mixture).

CALORIES 292 (18% from fat); FAT 5.9g (sat 1.3g, mono 2.1g, poly 1.5g); PROTEIN 41.1g; CARB 21.3g; FIBER 11.7g; CHOL 85mg; IRON 9.1mg; SODIUM 450mg; CALC 283mg

CURRIED BUTTERNUT SQUASH SOUP

2 tablespoons olive oil
2 cups chopped onion
2 tablespoons chopped seeded jalapeño pepper
1 teaspoon curry powder
6 cups cubed peeled acorn or butternut squash (about 3 pounds)
4 cups water
1 teaspoon salt
1 cup 2% reduced-fat milk
2 tablespoons dry sherry

1. Heat oil in a Dutch oven over medium heat. Add onion; cover and cook 5 minutes. Stir in jalapeño and curry; cook 2 minutes. Stir in squash, water, and salt; bring to a boil over medium-high heat. Cover, reduce heat, and simmer 30 minutes or until squash is tender.
2. Place half of squash mixture in a blender; process until smooth. Pour pureed squash mixture into a bowl. Repeat procedure with remaining squash mixture. Return pureed squash mixture to pan; stir in milk and sherry. Cook 5 minutes or until thoroughly heated. Yield: 8 servings (serving size: 1 cup).

CALORIES 91 (24% from fat); FAT 2.4g (sat 0.5g, mono 1.3g, poly 0.2g); PROTEIN 2.4g; CARB 16.6g; FIBER 2.2g; CHOL 2mg; IRON 0.9mg; SODIUM 313mg; CALC 83mg

HONEY-CORNMEAL ROUNDS

(pictured on page 319)

We loved the round shape of this bread, but for a standard loaf, you can use 9-inch loaf pans.

3 cups 2% reduced-fat milk
½ cup honey
¼ cup stick margarine or butter
2 cups yellow cornmeal
2 packages dry yeast (about 4½ teaspoons)
7 cups all-purpose flour
2 teaspoons salt
Cooking spray
1 tablespoon yellow cornmeal

1. Combine first 3 ingredients in a medium saucepan; place over medium heat until margarine melts. Cool slightly (to 120° to 130°). Combine 2 cups cornmeal and yeast in a large bowl; add milk mixture, stirring well with a whisk. Lightly spoon flour into dry measuring cups; level with a knife. Add flour and salt to cornmeal mixture; stir until a soft dough forms. Turn dough out onto a lightly floured surface; knead 3 or 4 times. Cover and let rest 15 minutes. Knead until smooth and elastic (about 8 minutes).

2. Place dough in a large bowl coated with cooking spray, turning to coat top. Cover and let rise in a warm place (85°), free from drafts, 50 minutes or until doubled in bulk. Punch dough down; divide dough in half. Coat 2 (9-inch) pie plates or cake pans with cooking spray; dust each with 1½ teaspoons cornmeal. Working with 1 portion at a time (cover remaining half to keep from drying), shape dough into a 7-inch round. Place round, seam side down, in prepared pie plate. Repeat procedure with remaining half of dough. Cover and let rise 20 minutes or until doubled in bulk.
3. Preheat oven to 350°.
4. Lightly score rounds in a spoke pattern using a sharp knife. Bake at 350° for 45 minutes or until rounds sound hollow when tapped. Remove from plates; cool on wire racks. Yield: 2 rounds, 16 wedges per round (serving size: 1 wedge).

CALORIES 173 (12% from fat); FAT 2.3g (sat 0.6g, mono 0.8g, poly 1g); PROTEIN 4.4g; CARB 33g; FIBER 1.3g; CHOL 1.8mg; IRON 1.7mg; SODIUM 175mg; CALC 34mg

SAVOY CABBAGE SALAD

Savoy and napa cabbage each have a more delicate taste and texture than green cabbage, and they offer a refreshing change of pace.

8 cups thinly sliced Savoy or napa (Chinese) cabbage
⅓ cup sliced pitted kalamata olives
1 garlic clove, minced
1 tablespoon extra-virgin olive oil
1 tablespoon fresh lemon juice
⅛ teaspoon salt
⅛ teaspoon black pepper

1. Combine first 3 ingredients in a bowl. Drizzle with oil and juice; toss. Sprinkle with salt and pepper; toss well. Yield: 8 servings (serving size: 1 cup).

CALORIES 41 (53% from fat); FAT 2.4g (sat 0.3g, mono 1.7g, poly 0.3g); PROTEIN 1.5g; CARB 4.9g; FIBER 0.7g; CHOL 0mg; IRON 0.5mg; SODIUM 103mg; CALC 30mg

PEAR, WALNUT, AND MAPLE SYRUP PIE

Comice pears work best, but almost any variety of pear can be used. Toasting the walnuts imparts a deep nutty flavor that contrasts with the maple syrup.

Pastry:

- 2 cups all-purpose flour, divided
- ⅓ cup ice water
- ½ teaspoon salt
- 3 tablespoons chilled stick margarine or butter
- 3 tablespoons vegetable shortening

Filling:

- ⅓ cup packed brown sugar
- ⅓ cup chopped walnuts, toasted
- 3 tablespoons cornstarch
- 1 tablespoon lemon juice
- 4 large Comice pears (about 3 pounds), peeled, cored and cut lengthwise into ½-inch-thick slices
- ¼ cup maple syrup
- 1 teaspoon vanilla extract
- Cooking spray
- 2 teaspoons water
- 1 large egg

1. Preheat oven to 450°.
2. To prepare pastry, lightly spoon flour into dry measuring cups; level with a knife. Combine ⅓ cup flour and ice water, stirring with a whisk until well-blended. Combine 1⅔ cups flour and salt in a bowl; cut in margarine and shortening with a pastry blender or 2 knives until mixture resembles coarse meal. Add ice water mixture; toss with a fork until moist. Divide dough in half. Gently press each half of mixture into a 4-inch circle on heavy-duty plastic wrap; cover with additional plastic wrap. Roll one half of dough, still covered, into a 12-inch circle; freeze 10 minutes. Roll other half of dough, still covered, into an 11-inch circle; freeze 10 minutes.
3. To prepare filling, combine brown sugar, walnuts, and cornstarch in a large bowl. Combine lemon juice and pears in a medium bowl; stir in syrup and vanilla. Stir pear mixture into sugar mixture. Remove 1 sheet of plastic wrap from 12-inch circle; invert and fit dough into a 9-inch pie plate coated with cooking spray, allowing dough to extend over edge of plate. Remove top sheet of plastic wrap. Combine 2 teaspoons water and egg in a small bowl; stir well with a whisk. Spoon pear mixture into prepared crust; brush edges of piecrust lightly with egg mixture. Remove 1 sheet of plastic wrap from 11-inch circle; invert and place on top of pear mixture. Remove top sheet of plastic wrap. Press edges of dough together; fold edges under, and flute.
4. Brush top and edges of pie with egg mixture. Place pie on a baking sheet; cut 5 (1-inch) slits into top of pastry using a sharp knife. Bake at 450° for 15 minutes. Reduce oven temperature to 350° (do not remove pie from oven); bake an additional 45 minutes or until browned. Cool on a wire rack 30 minutes. Serve warm or at room temperature. Yield: 10 servings.

CALORIES 290 (31% from fat); FAT 10g (sat 1g, mono 2.3g, poly 2.8g); PROTEIN 4.6g; CARB 46.9g; FIBER 3.1g; CHOL 22mg; IRON 1.8mg; SODIUM 168mg; CALC 30mg

Every Bog Has Its Day

Who would think the sweet-tart flavor of cranberries starts in a place called a bog? Not that you care when you're slicing the cheesecake.

"Many people think cranberries grow underwater, but it's not true," Dot Angley insists. She should know. Along with the 500 or so other growers from Massachusetts' renowned cranberry farms, she's part of a $1 billion state industry that produced nearly 2.1 million barrels (about 40% of the world's supply) of the tart, bright red berry in 1997.

Cranberries grow in bogs. And bogs—beds of peat, sand, and clay—are dry most of the time. The berries we find in the produce aisle at the grocery store are usually harvested dry, too.

But at certain times of the year, farmers flood their bogs to protect the berries, whose vines are surprisingly delicate. At other times, immersion is used for wet-harvesting. "Once the plants are flooded," Angley explains, "we use machines called water reels to gently knock the berries off the vines. The berries float to the surface, and they're corralled and sent immediately to the processing plant." Wet-harvested berries are only used for juices and jellies.

Cranberries—one of just three commercial fruits native to North America (along with blueberries and Concord grapes)—are flooded for protection against the cold. By filling the bogs in winter, farmers provide a blanket of thick ice that naturally insulates the vines from lethal changes in temperature and also prevents them from dehydrating.

CRANBERRY-GLAZED PORK

- 1 cup fresh cranberries
- 1 cup coarsely chopped peeled cooking apple
- ⅔ cup packed dark brown sugar
- ½ cup water
- ¼ cup finely chopped onion
- 1 tablespoon minced peeled fresh ginger
- 1 teaspoon curry powder
- ⅛ teaspoon ground red pepper
- 2 (¾-pound) pork tenderloins
- ¼ teaspoon salt
- ¼ teaspoon black pepper
- Cooking spray

1. Preheat oven to 350°.
2. Combine first 8 ingredients in a small saucepan; bring to a boil. Cover, reduce heat, and simmer 20 minutes. Uncover and simmer 2 minutes or until thick. Cool 10 minutes. Place in

a blender or food processor; process until smooth. Divide cranberry sauce in half.

3. Trim fat from pork; sprinkle pork with salt and black pepper. Brush with half of cranberry sauce. Place pork on rack of a broiler pan coated with cooking spray; bake at 350° for 30 minutes or until a meat thermometer registers 160° (slightly pink). Serve pork with remaining cranberry sauce. Yield: 6 servings (serving size: 3 ounces pork and 2 tablespoons sauce).

CALORIES 243 (11% from fat); FAT 3.1g (sat 1g, mono 1.3g, poly 0.3g); PROTEIN 24g; CARB 29.5g; FIBER 1g; CHOL 74mg; IRON 2.1mg; SODIUM 164mg; CALC 34mg

SPICY CHICKEN QUESADILLAS WITH CRANBERRY-MANGO SALSA

2   teaspoons olive oil
2   cups sliced mushrooms
1   cup chopped green bell pepper
½   cup chopped red onion
2   cups chopped ready-to-eat roasted skinned, boned chicken breasts (about 3 breasts) or cooked turkey breast
½   teaspoon chili powder
¼   teaspoon ground cumin
8   (8-inch) flour tortillas
½   cup (2 ounces) shredded reduced-fat sharp Cheddar cheese
Cooking spray
Cranberry-Mango Salsa

1. Heat oil in a large nonstick skillet over medium-high heat until hot. Add mushrooms, bell pepper, and onion; sauté 4 minutes or until mushrooms are tender. Add chicken, chili powder, and cumin; sauté 2 minutes or until thoroughly heated.

2. Spread about ½ cup chicken mixture over each of 4 tortillas; top each with 2 tablespoons Cheddar cheese and a tortilla.

3. Coat skillet with cooking spray; place over medium heat until hot. Add 1 quesadilla, and cook 3 minutes on each side or until lightly browned.

Remove from skillet, and keep warm. Repeat procedure with remaining quesadillas. Cut each quesadilla into 3 wedges. Serve with Cranberry-Mango Salsa. Yield: 6 servings (serving size: 2 wedges and ¼ cup salsa).

CALORIES 342 (24% from fat); FAT 9.1g (sat 2.3g, mono 3.8g, poly 2.3g); PROTEIN 18.1g; CARB 47.9g; FIBER 3.8g; CHOL 30mg; IRON 3mg; SODIUM 663mg; CALC 183mg

Cranberry-Mango Salsa:

1   cup finely chopped cranberries
1   cup chopped peeled mango or papaya
¼   cup minced red onion
2   tablespoons minced fresh cilantro
1½   teaspoons honey
1   teaspoon minced seeded jalapeño pepper
¼   teaspoon salt

1. Combine all ingredients in a small bowl; toss well. Yield: 1½ cups (serving size: ¼ cup).

CALORIES 36 (3% from fat); FAT 0.1g (sat 0g, mono 0.1g, poly 0.1g); PROTEIN 0.4g; CARB 9.2g; FIBER 0.8g; CHOL 0mg; IRON 0.2mg; SODIUM 99mg; CALC 8mg

CHEESECAKE WITH CRANBERRY GLAZE

The cheesecake needs to chill eight hours, so plan on making this a day ahead. The Cranberry Glaze can also be made ahead and chilled.

Cooking spray
⅓   cup gingersnap crumbs (about 6 cookies, finely crushed)
1   (16-ounce) carton fat-free cottage cheese
1   (8-ounce) block ⅓-less-fat cream cheese (Neufchâtel), softened
⅔   cup sugar
¼   cup all-purpose flour
1½   teaspoons vanilla extract
½   teaspoon almond extract
2   large eggs
2   large egg whites
1   (8-ounce) carton low-fat sour cream
Cranberry Glaze

1. Preheat oven to 300°.

2. Coat bottom of a 9-inch springform pan with cooking spray; sprinkle with cookie crumbs.

3. Place cheeses in a food processor; process 2 minutes or until smooth, scraping sides of bowl once. Add sugar and next 6 ingredients; pulse just until smooth.

4. Pour cheese mixture into prepared pan; bake at 300° for 1 hour and 10 minutes or until almost set. Turn oven off, and let cheesecake stand in closed oven for 1 hour. Remove cheesecake from oven; cover and chill at least 8 hours. Serve with Cranberry Glaze. Yield: 12 servings (serving size: 1 wedge and 2 tablespoons glaze).

CALORIES 226 (29% from fat); FAT 7.4g (sat 4.1g, mono 2.3g, poly 0.5g); PROTEIN 9.8g; CARB 29.6g; FIBER 0.3g; CHOL 61mg; IRON 0.5mg; SODIUM 254mg; CALC 74mg

Cranberry Glaze:

½   cup sugar
2   teaspoons cornstarch
2   cups fresh cranberries
⅔   cup water

1. Combine sugar and cornstarch in a medium saucepan; stir in cranberries and water. Bring to a boil over medium-high heat; cook 5 minutes or until cranberries pop. Cool. Yield: 1½ cups (serving size: 2 tablespoons).

FRESH TASTE, YEAR-ROUND

While cranberries are in season, it's a good idea to buy extra bags for later use. Simply place them in the freezer and then take them out to prepare fresh cranberry recipes year-round.

STEAMED CRANBERRY PUDDING WITH ORANGE MARMALADE SAUCE

Steamed pudding is a traditional holiday treat, but you have to use a pudding steamer. To order a steamer, call Sweet Celebrations Inc. at 800/328-6722.

1½ cups all-purpose flour
1½ teaspoons baking powder
¾ teaspoon ground cinnamon
¼ teaspoon salt
¼ teaspoon ground ginger
⅛ teaspoon ground nutmeg
⅛ teaspoon ground cloves
⅓ cup granulated sugar
⅓ cup packed dark brown sugar
2 tablespoons stick margarine or butter, melted
1 teaspoon vanilla extract
1 large egg
½ cup 1% low-fat milk
1½ cups coarsely chopped fresh cranberries
½ cup golden raisins
3 tablespoons chopped pecans
Cooking spray
Orange Marmalade Sauce

1. Lightly spoon flour into dry measuring cups; level with a knife. Combine flour and next 6 ingredients in a small bowl.
2. Beat sugars, margarine, vanilla, and egg in a large bowl at medium speed of a mixer until well-blended (about 2 minutes). Add flour mixture to sugar mixture alternately with milk, beginning and ending with flour mixture. Stir in cranberries, raisins, and pecans.
3. Spoon batter into a 6-cup steamed-pudding mold coated with cooking spray. Cover tightly with lid or foil coated with cooking spray; secure foil with a rubber band. Place mold on a shallow rack in a stockpot; add enough hot water to come halfway up sides of mold. Cover and steam over medium-low heat 2½ hours or until a wooden pick inserted in center comes out almost clean, adding additional water as needed. Cool on a wire rack 10 minutes. Invert mold onto a platter; slice pudding. Serve warm with Orange Marmalade Sauce. Yield: 10 servings (serving size: 1 slice pudding and 3 tablespoons sauce).

CALORIES 262 (21% from fat); FAT 6.1g (sat 1.4g, mono 2.7g, poly 1.5g); PROTEIN 5.6g; CARB 47.4g; FIBER 1.3g; CHOL 46mg; IRON 1.6mg; SODIUM 210mg; CALC 134mg

Orange Marmalade Sauce:

1¾ cups 1% low-fat milk
3 tablespoons sugar
1 tablespoon cornstarch
1 large egg
2 tablespoons orange marmalade
1 teaspoon stick margarine or butter, softened
½ teaspoon grated orange rind
½ teaspoon vanilla extract

1. Combine first 4 ingredients in the top of a double boiler; stir well with a whisk. Cook over simmering water until thick (about 6 minutes), stirring constantly. Remove from heat; stir in marmalade and remaining ingredients. Serve warm. Yield: 2 cups (serving size: 3 tablespoons).

SPICED CRANBERRY SAUCE

1 (12-ounce) bag fresh cranberries
1 cup sugar
1 cup water
¼ teaspoon ground cinnamon
⅛ teaspoon ground ginger
Dash of ground nutmeg

1. Combine all ingredients in a medium saucepan, and bring to a boil over medium-high heat. Reduce heat; simmer 10 minutes or until cranberries pop, stirring occasionally. Spoon into a bowl; cover and chill. Yield: 2½ cups (serving size: ¼ cup).

CALORIES 94 (1% from fat); FAT 0.1g (sat 0g, mono 0.1g, poly 0g); PROTEIN 0.1g; CARB 24.4g; FIBER 0.4g; CHOL 0mg; IRON 0.1mg; SODIUM 1mg; CALC 3mg

CRANBERRY-ORANGE RELISH

This lively relish adds zing to roast turkey or a ham sandwich.

1½ cups fresh cranberries
1 small thin-skinned Valencia orange, quartered and seeded
½ cup sugar
3 tablespoons chopped walnuts
1 tablespoon Grand Marnier or other orange-flavored liqueur (optional)

1. Combine cranberries and orange in a food processor; pulse 5 times or until chopped. Combine cranberry mixture, sugar, walnuts, and, if desired, liqueur in a bowl; let stand at least 30 minutes before serving. Cover and store in refrigerator for up to 2 weeks. Yield: 2 cups (serving size: 1 tablespoon).

CALORIES 23 (16% from fat); FAT 0.4g (sat 0g, mono 0.1g, poly 0.3g); PROTEIN 0.3g; CARB 4.7g; FIBER 0.4g; CHOL 0mg; IRON 0mg; SODIUM 0mg; CALC 4mg

Southwestern Salad with Ginger-Sesame Vinaigrette (page 321)

Chicken Enchilada Bake with Mushroom Sauce (page 321)

Sourdough-Pumpkin Strata (page 321)

Classic Beef Tenderloin (page 334)

Barley-Mushroom Pilaf (page 334)

Honey-Cornmeal Round (page 313)

Citrus Granita (page 340)

Lemon-Poached Oranges (page 340)

Cinnamon Sugar Crisps (page 340)

Pork and Roasted Winter Vegetables (page 312)

*Monte Cristo Sandwich
with Sweet Mustard Sauce (page 337)*

December

Something Beautiful, Simple, Communal

In Santa Fe, the sweet aroma of piñon and the flickering light from candles urge people into the crisp desert air for holiday strolls and into the welcoming homes of friends.

Just as in other parts of the country, those who live in Santa Fe hope for a white Christmas. But snow weather is cold weather, especially when night falls. It's a good time to be indoors—and for most that means being home. Wide-planked rustic tables of old polished wood make a fine setting for a holiday feast like the one we offer here.

MENU

SOUTHWESTERN SALAD WITH
GINGER-SESAME VINAIGRETTE

SOURDOUGH-PUMPKIN
STRATA *or*
CHICKEN ENCHILADA BAKE
WITH MUSHROOM SAUCE

PEAR-CORNMEAL CRUNCH
CAKE

RUM-SPIKED WINTER
COMPOTE

SOUTHWESTERN SALAD WITH GINGER-SESAME VINAIGRETTE

(pictured on page 317)

- 10 cups gourmet salad greens
- 1 cup sliced peeled papaya
- ½ cup sliced seeded peeled cucumber
- ½ cup red bell pepper strips
- ½ cup cilantro leaves
- ¼ cup seasoned rice vinegar
- ½ teaspoon grated peeled fresh ginger
- 2 teaspoons dark sesame oil

1. Combine first 5 ingredients in a large bowl. Combine vinegar, ginger, and oil; stir well with a whisk. Pour dressing over salad; toss gently to coat. Yield: 8 servings (serving size: 1 cup).

CALORIES 33 (38% from fat); FAT 1.4g (sat 0.2g, mono 0.5g, poly 0.6g); PROTEIN 1.5g; CARB 4.2g; FIBER 1.8g; CHOL 0mg; IRON 1.1mg; SODIUM 10mg; CALC 36mg

SOURDOUGH-PUMPKIN STRATA

(pictured on page 318)

Assemble this strata the night before and keep it in the refrigerator until ready to bake.

- 6 (1¼-inch) slices sourdough French bread (about 7½ ounces)
- Cooking spray
- 1½ cups (6 ounces) shredded reduced-fat sharp Cheddar cheese, divided
- ½ cup chopped onion, divided
- 1 (4.5-ounce) can chopped green chiles, drained and divided
- 1⅔ cups fat-free milk
- ½ teaspoon dried thyme
- ½ teaspoon dried rubbed sage
- ¼ teaspoon salt
- ¼ teaspoon coarsely ground black pepper
- 1 (15-ounce) can pumpkin
- 2 large eggs
- 2 tablespoons shelled pumpkin seeds (optional)

1. Arrange 2 bread slices in a single layer in a 2-quart soufflé dish coated with cooking spray. Sprinkle with ½ cup cheese, one-third of onion, and one-third of chiles. Repeat layers twice.
2. Combine milk and next 6 ingredients in a blender; process until smooth. Pour over bread layers. Cover with plastic wrap; refrigerate 8 hours.
3. Preheat oven to 350°.

4. Uncover; sprinkle strata with pumpkin seeds, if desired. Bake at 350° for 1 hour and 5 minutes or until a knife inserted in center comes out clean. Let strata stand 10 minutes before serving. Yield: 6 servings (serving size: about 1 cup).

CALORIES 255 (29% from fat); FAT 8.3g (sat 3.9g, mono 2.2g, poly 0.5g); PROTEIN 17g; CARB 28.9g; FIBER 4g; CHOL 94mg; IRON 2.5mg; SODIUM 552mg; CALC 403mg

CHICKEN ENCHILADA BAKE WITH MUSHROOM SAUCE

(pictured on page 317)

- 2 poblano chiles (about 6 ounces)
- 2 Anaheim chiles (about 4½ ounces)
- 1 red bell pepper
- 1 tablespoon olive oil
- 3 cups sliced cremini mushrooms (about 8 ounces)
- 1½ cups sliced shiitake mushrooms (about 1 [3½-ounce] package)
- ½ cup sliced green onions
- 2 garlic cloves, minced
- 2 tablespoons all-purpose flour
- ½ teaspoon dried rubbed sage
- ¼ teaspoon ground cumin
- ¼ teaspoon black pepper
- 1¼ cups fat-free, less-sodium chicken broth
- ½ cup water
- 4 ounces block-style fat-free cream cheese, softened (about ½ cup)
- ½ cup (2 ounces) shredded Monterey Jack cheese
- ¼ cup chopped fresh cilantro
- Cooking spray
- 9 (6-inch) corn tortillas, cut in half
- 2¼ cups chopped skinned roasted chicken breast (about ¾ pound)
- ¼ cup (1 ounce) grated fresh Romano cheese

1. Preheat broiler.
2. Cut chiles and bell pepper in half lengthwise; discard seeds and membranes. Place chile and bell pepper halves, skin sides up, on a foil-lined

Continued

baking sheet; flatten with hand. Broil 5 minutes or until blackened, turning occasionally. Place in a zip-top plastic bag; seal. Let stand 15 minutes; peel and chop chiles and bell pepper.

3. Preheat oven to 350°.

4. Heat oil in a large nonstick skillet over medium heat. Add cremini mushrooms and next 3 ingredients; sauté 5 minutes. Stir in flour and next 3 ingredients; cook 2 minutes. Stir in chopped chiles and bell pepper, broth, and water; simmer 5 minutes or until mixture is thick, stirring constantly. Stir in cream cheese. Remove from heat; stir in Monterey Jack cheese and cilantro.

5. Spoon 1 cup mushroom sauce into an 11 x 7-inch baking dish coated with cooking spray; top with 6 tortilla halves, ¾ cup chicken, and 1 cup mushroom sauce. Repeat layers twice, ending with sauce. Sprinkle with Romano cheese. Cover and bake at 350° for 35 minutes or until mixture is bubbly. Let stand 10 minutes. Yield: 8 servings.

CALORIES 239 (29% from fat); FAT 7.8g (sat 2.9g, mono 3.0g, poly 1.1g); PROTEIN 21.4g; CARB 21.2g; FIBER 3g; CHOL 48mg; IRON 2.2mg; SODIUM 250mg; CALC 204mg

PEAR-CORNMEAL CRUNCH CAKE

1½ cups all-purpose flour
 1 cup packed brown sugar
 ½ cup yellow cornmeal
 ½ cup granulated sugar
 1 tablespoon ground cinnamon
 ¾ teaspoon ground ginger
 ¼ cup stick margarine or butter
 ¼ cup chopped pecans
 1 teaspoon baking powder
 ½ teaspoon baking soda
 ½ teaspoon salt
 1 cup chopped pear
 1 cup fat-free sour cream
 2 teaspoons vanilla extract
 1 teaspoon grated lemon rind
 1 large egg
 1 large egg white
Cooking spray

1. Preheat oven to 350°.

2. Lightly spoon flour into dry measuring cups; level with a knife. Combine flour and next 5 ingredients in a large bowl; cut in margarine with a pastry blender or 2 knives until mixture resembles coarse meal. Remove ¾ cup flour mixture; place in a small bowl. Stir in pecans; set pecan mixture aside.

3. Add baking powder, baking soda, and salt to remaining flour mixture; stir in pear. Combine sour cream and next 4 ingredients; stir well with a whisk. Add to flour mixture, stirring just until moist.

4. Pour batter into a 13 x 9-inch baking pan coated with cooking spray; top with pecan mixture. Bake at 350° for 50 minutes or until a wooden pick inserted in center comes out clean. Cool cake in pan on a wire rack. Yield: 16 servings.

CALORIES 198 (21% from fat); FAT 4.7g (sat 2g, mono 1.8g, poly 0.6g); PROTEIN 3.4g; CARB 35.4g; FIBER 1g; CHOL 22mg; IRON 1.3mg; SODIUM 196mg; CALC 41mg

RUM-SPIKED WINTER COMPOTE

 2 cups fresh cranberries
 1 cup water
 ½ cup white rum
 ½ cup packed brown sugar
 2 (3-inch) cinnamon sticks
2½ cups tangerine or orange sections (about 7 tangerines)
2½ cups grapefruit sections (about 3 grapefruit)

1. Combine first 5 ingredients in a medium saucepan; bring mixture to a boil. Reduce heat, and simmer, uncovered, 5 minutes or until cranberries pop. Add fruit sections, stirring gently. Cover and simmer 4 minutes or until thoroughly heated. Discard cinnamon sticks. Serve warm or at room temperature. Yield: 8 servings (serving size: ¾ cup).

CALORIES 117 (2% from fat); FAT 0.2g (sat 0g, mono 0g, poly 0.1g); PROTEIN 1g; CARB 29.8g; FIBER 2.1g; CHOL 0mg; IRON 0.4mg; SODIUM 6mg; CALC 31mg

Destress Your Holidays

Turn holiday survival into holiday fun with a little help from our TV special.

Through a partnership with Home & Garden Television, we developed an hour-long special, *Cooking Light for the Holidays*. Here's a sampling of the show's featured recipes.

BROWN GRAVY

 ¼ cup all-purpose flour
1½ cups degreased turkey drippings or fat-free, less-sodium chicken broth
 ½ cup water
 ½ cup dry red wine
 ¼ teaspoon ground red pepper
 ¼ teaspoon black pepper

1. Place flour in a small bowl. Gradually add turkey drippings and water, stirring with a whisk until blended. Bring wine to a boil in a medium saucepan over medium-high heat; cook 2 minutes. Add flour mixture; cook 2 minutes or until slightly thick, stirring constantly with a whisk. Remove from heat; stir in peppers. Yield: 8 servings (serving size: ¼ cup).

CALORIES 42 (28% from fat); FAT 1.3g (sat 0.3g, mono 0.3g, poly 0.4g); PROTEIN 3.9g; CARB 3.6g; FIBER 0.1g; CHOL 8mg; IRON 0.6mg; SODIUM 20mg; CALC 5mg

GREEN BEANS AMANDINE

 ¼ cup fat-free margarine
 3 pounds green beans, trimmed
 3 cups fat-free, less-sodium chicken broth
 ¾ teaspoon freshly ground black pepper
 ½ teaspoon salt
 2 tablespoons cornstarch
 ¼ cup water
 2 tablespoons lemon juice
 ¼ cup sliced almonds, toasted

1. Melt margarine in a large skillet over medium-high heat. Add beans; sauté 5 minutes. Add broth, pepper, and salt; bring to a boil. Cover, reduce heat, and simmer 15 minutes. Combine cornstarch and water; add to skillet. Bring to a boil; cook 1 minute, stirring constantly. Stir in juice. Sprinkle with almonds just before serving. Yield: 8 servings (serving size: 1 cup).

CALORIES 89 (17% from fat); FAT 1.7g (sat 0.2g, mono 1g, poly 0.4g); PROTEIN 4.9g; CARB 15.9g; FIBER 4g; CHOL 0mg; IRON 1.9mg; SODIUM 402mg; CALC 72mg

CRANBERRY CHUTNEY

- 1 cup chopped Granny Smith apple
- 1 cup raisins
- 1 cup chopped onion
- 1 cup sugar
- 1 cup white vinegar
- ¾ cup chopped celery
- ¾ cup water
- 2 teaspoons ground cinnamon
- 1½ teaspoons ground ginger
- ¼ teaspoon ground cloves
- 1 (12-ounce) bag fresh or frozen cranberries

1. Combine all ingredients in a large saucepan; bring to a boil. Reduce heat, and simmer, uncovered, 30 minutes or until slightly thick, stirring occasionally. Yield: 4 cups (serving size: ¼ cup).
Note: Store chutney in an airtight container in the refrigerator up to 1 month.

CALORIES 98 (2% from fat); FAT 0.2g (sat 0g, mono 0g, poly 0.1g); PROTEIN 0.6g; CARB 25.6g; FIBER 1.3g; CHOL 0mg; IRON 0.4mg; SODIUM 7mg; CALC 15mg

SOUTHERN CORN BREAD DRESSING

Speckled Corn Bread
- 1 (12-ounce) can refrigerated buttermilk biscuits
- 2 tablespoons dried rubbed sage
- 1 teaspoon poultry seasoning
- ¼ to ½ teaspoon black pepper
- 1 teaspoon stick margarine or butter

Cooking spray
- 1 cup chopped celery
- 1 cup chopped onion
- 4⅔ cups fat-free, less-sodium chicken broth
- 2 large egg whites, lightly beaten

1. Crumble Speckled Corn Bread; set aside. Bake biscuits according to package directions; cool. Tear 8 biscuits into small pieces, reserving remaining 2 for another use. Combine corn bread, torn biscuits, sage, poultry seasoning, and pepper.
2. Preheat oven to 350°.
3. Melt margarine over medium-high heat in a medium nonstick skillet coated with cooking spray. Sauté celery and onion 8 minutes or until tender. Cool slightly. Add vegetable mixture to dressing mixture; gently stir in broth and egg whites. Spoon mixture into a 13 x 9-inch baking dish coated with cooking spray. Bake at 350° for 55 minutes. Yield: 10 servings.

CALORIES 262 (25% from fat); FAT 7.2g (sat 1.6g, mono 3.2g, poly 1.3g); PROTEIN 8.8g; CARB 9.3g; FIBER 1.3g; CHOL 1mg; IRON 3.2mg; SODIUM 782mg; CALC 150mg

Speckled Corn Bread:

- 1 teaspoon stick margarine
Cooking spray
- 1 cup frozen whole-kernel corn, thawed
- 1 cup chopped red bell pepper
- 1⅓ cups self-rising yellow cornmeal mix
- ⅔ cup self-rising flour
- 1 teaspoon sugar
- ⅛ teaspoon ground red pepper
- 1¼ cups fat-free milk
- 2 large egg whites, lightly beaten

1. Preheat oven to 400°.
2. Melt margarine over medium-high heat in a nonstick skillet coated with cooking spray. Sauté corn and bell pepper 8 minutes or until corn is lightly browned and bell pepper is tender; cool.
3. Combine vegetable mixture, cornmeal mix, and next 3 ingredients; add milk and egg whites, stirring until moist. Pour batter into a 9-inch round cake pan coated with cooking spray. Bake at 400° for 30 minutes or until a

wooden pick inserted in center comes out clean. Remove from pan; cool completely on a wire rack. Yield: 12 servings (serving size: 1 wedge).
Note: Substitute 1⅓ cups plain yellow cornmeal, 2 teaspoons baking powder, and ½ teaspoon salt for 1⅓ cups self-rising yellow cornmeal mix, if desired.

CALORIES 100 (9% from fat); FAT 1g (sat 0.2g, mono 0.3g, poly 0.4g); PROTEIN 3.8g; CARB 19.8g; FIBER 0.5g; CHOL 1mg; IRON 1.3mg; SODIUM 381mg; CALC 105mg

MINT-CHOCOLATE TRUFFLES

- ⅓ cup semisweet mint-chocolate chips
- 4 ounces ⅓-less-fat cream cheese (Neufchâtel), softened (about ½ cup)
- 1 (16-ounce) package powdered sugar, sifted
- ¼ cup unsweetened cocoa
- ¼ cup sifted powdered sugar
- 2 tablespoons semisweet mint-chocolate chips

1. Place ⅓ cup chips in a glass bowl; microwave at HIGH 1 minute or until almost melted, stirring until smooth. Cool.
2. Add cheese to melted chips; beat at medium speed of a mixer until smooth. Add 1 (16-ounce) package powdered sugar; beat until well-blended. Press mixture into a 6-inch square on plastic wrap; cover with additional plastic wrap. Chill at least 1 hour.
3. Remove top sheet of plastic wrap; cut mixture into 48 squares. Roll each square into a ball; place on wax paper. Roll half of balls in cocoa; roll remaining balls in ¼ cup powdered sugar.
4. Place 2 tablespoons chips in a heavy-duty zip-top plastic bag; microwave at HIGH 1 minute or until soft. Knead bag until smooth. Snip a tiny hole in corner of bag; drizzle chocolate over balls rolled in cocoa. Serve at room temperature. Yield: 4 dozen (serving size: 1 piece).
Note: Freeze truffles in a single layer in an airtight container for up to 1 month. Thaw at room temperature 1 hour.

CALORIES 58 (22% from fat); FAT 1.4g (sat 0.8g, mono 0.4g, poly 0g); PROTEIN 0.5g; CARB 11.5g; FIBER 0g; CHOL 2mg; IRON 0.1mg; SODIUM 10mg; CALC 3mg

A Pretty Fair Trade

Winter in Key West is like summer in most of the country, and the holidays are celebrated in a way that suits the climate and characters.

Because winter in Key West could pass for summer in many parts of the country, Key West cooks plan their menus accordingly. *Mojos* (Cuban lime sauces) and vinaigrettes are better suited than the heavier sauces and gravies of the Northeast. Tropical fruits loom large in the local cooking, if for no other reason than that most natives grow these delicious fruits on trees in their own backyards.

The proximity to Cuba may be the most profound influence of all. The local enthusiasm for the robust flavors of cumin, garlic, and lime juice stems from Cuba; so does the popularity of black beans and pineapple. Rum figures prominently in Key West cooking and drinking—a reminder of the days when Key Westers smuggled Cuban rum from Havana to the Florida Keys.

MENU

This buffet menu serves about 16 people. The portions are small so that guests can sample everything.

SMOKED-TROUT SPREAD

CHILI-SPICED SMOKED
TURKEY BREAST

ROASTED WHOLE SNAPPER

SWEET POTATO-GRANNY
SMITH APPLE SALAD

CALYPSO RICE AND BEANS

ROLLED GREENS

SEAFOOD SALAD

RUM-ALLSPICE POUND CAKE
WITH AMBROSIA

PASSIONATE WHITE SANGRÍA

LIME SUNSET

SMOKED-TROUT SPREAD

This rich spread is best on plain crackers such as unsalted saltines or Carr's Table Water Crackers.

1	pound smoked trout fillets, skinned
½	cup sliced celery
⅓	cup sliced green onions
⅓	cup part-skim ricotta cheese
¼	cup (2 ounces) tub-style light cream cheese
1	tablespoon stick margarine or butter
1	tablespoon fresh lemon juice
1	teaspoon Worcestershire sauce
½	teaspoon hot sauce
88	water crackers

1. Break trout fillets into large pieces. Place trout and next 8 ingredients in a food processor; process until smooth, scraping sides of processor bowl occasionally. Serve with water crackers. Yield: 2¾ cups (serving size: 2 tablespoons spread and 4 crackers).

CALORIES 95 (25% from fat); FAT 2.6g (sat 0.9g, mono 1.1g, poly 0.2g); PROTEIN 7.2g; CARB 11.1g; FIBER 0.5g; CHOL 9mg; IRON 0.2mg; SODIUM 321mg; CALC 20mg

CHILI-SPICED SMOKED TURKEY BREAST

You don't need a smoker; any covered grill will give the same effect. Simply place the turkey breast on the cool side of the grill and use soaked wood chips.

¼	cup fresh lime juice (about 2 limes)
2	tablespoons olive oil
2	teaspoons unsweetened cocoa
2	teaspoons paprika
2	teaspoons brown sugar
1	teaspoon salt
1	teaspoon dried oregano
1	teaspoon chili powder
1	teaspoon dried thyme
2	garlic cloves, minced
1	(6-pound) whole turkey breast
2	cups mesquite chips
	Cooking spray

1. Combine first 10 ingredients in a small saucepan; bring to a boil. Remove from heat; cool. Combine lime juice mixture and turkey in a large zip-top plastic bag. Seal and marinate in refrigerator 2 hours. Soak wood chips in water at least 30 minutes. Drain well.

2. Preheat gas grill to medium-hot (350° to 400°) using both burners. Turn left burner off. Place wood chips in a disposable foil pan or a foil packet pierced with holes on grill over right burner. Remove turkey from marinade; discard marinade. Place turkey, skin side up, on grill rack coated with cooking spray over left burner. Cover and cook 1½ hours. Turn turkey over; cook 15 minutes or until meat thermometer registers 170°. Remove turkey from grill. Cover loosely with foil; let stand at least 10 minutes before carving. Discard skin. Yield: 16 servings (serving size: 3 ounces).

CALORIES 126 (11% from fat); FAT 1.6g (sat 0.3g, mono 0.7g, poly 0.3g); PROTEIN 25.6g; CARB 0.6g; FIBER 0.1g; CHOL 71mg; IRON 1.4mg; SODIUM 119mg; CALC 13mg

ROASTED WHOLE SNAPPER

We found that an unscented kitchen-size plastic garbage bag was the best container to marinate a fish this large.

1	(8-pound) cleaned whole red snapper (head and tail left intact)

Snapper marinade:

1	cup fresh lime juice (about 8 limes)
1	cup water
½	cup fresh orange juice (about 2 oranges)
1	tablespoon salt

Spice rub:

½	cup (1-inch) sliced green onions
2	tablespoons chopped fresh parsley
1	tablespoon chopped fresh or 1 teaspoon dried thyme

2 tablespoons fresh lime juice
  (about 1 lime)
1 tablespoon olive oil
½ teaspoon salt
½ teaspoon ground allspice
¼ teaspoon black pepper
¼ teaspoon ground red pepper
6 garlic cloves, peeled

Remaining ingredients:

Cooking spray
2 large ripe tomatoes, each cut
  into 8 wedges
2 large onions, each cut into
  8 wedges
1 cup dry white wine

1. Score skin of fish in a diamond pattern. To prepare snapper marinade, combine 1 cup lime juice and next 3 ingredients in an extra-large plastic bag. Add fish; seal and marinate in refrigerator 20 minutes, turning bag once. Remove snapper from bag; discard marinade.
2. Preheat oven to 425°.
3. To prepare spice rub, combine green onions and next 9 ingredients in a food processor or blender; process until smooth. Spread spice rub evenly over both sides of fish. Place fish on a rack coated with cooking spray.
4. Place tomato wedges, onion wedges, and wine in a shallow roasting pan; place rack with fish over vegetables in pan. Cover with foil; bake at 425° for 30 minutes. Uncover and bake an additional 45 minutes or until fish flakes easily when tested with a fork. Remove skin from top side of fish; discard skin. Remove tomato mixture from pan; serve with fish. Yield: 16 servings (serving size: 4 ounces fish and ¼ cup tomato mixture).

CALORIES 173 (16% from fat); FAT 3g (sat 0.6g, mono 1g, poly 0.8g); PROTEIN 30.5g; CARB 4.9g; FIBER 0.8g; CHOL 53mg; IRON 0.6mg; SODIUM 142mg; CALC 58mg

SWEET POTATO–GRANNY SMITH APPLE SALAD

Serve warm or at room temperature.

5 cups (½-inch) cubed peeled sweet
  potato (about 1½ pounds)
1 cup coarsely chopped onion
¼ cup packed brown sugar
¼ cup fresh orange juice
2 tablespoons vegetable oil
1 tablespoon fresh lemon juice
½ teaspoon salt
½ teaspoon black pepper
3 cups (1-inch) cubed Granny
  Smith apple (about 1¼ pounds)

1. Preheat oven to 350°.
2. Combine sweet potato and onion in a 13 x 9-inch baking dish. Combine sugar and next 5 ingredients in a small bowl. Pour over potato mixture; toss well. Cover; bake at 350° for 30 minutes, stirring occasionally. Stir in apple; cover and bake 15 minutes or until apple is tender. Uncover; bake an additional 5 minutes. Yield: 14 servings (serving size: ½ cup).

CALORIES 103 (19% from fat); FAT 2.2g (sat 0.4g, mono 0.6g, poly 1g); PROTEIN 1g; CARB 20.6g; FIBER 2.4g; CHOL 0mg; IRON 0.4mg; SODIUM 92mg; CALC 19mg

CALYPSO RICE AND BEANS

You can substitute a 15-ounce can of black beans for the dried. If you do, omit soaking and cooking procedures in step 1.

1 cup dried black beans

Rice:

1 tablespoon olive oil
1¼ cups chopped onion
1 cup chopped celery
1½ tablespoons minced seeded
   jalapeño pepper
¾ teaspoon salt
4 garlic cloves, chopped
2 bay leaves
1½ cups uncooked basmati rice
3½ cups water

Remaining ingredients:

½ cup chopped red bell pepper
½ cup chopped yellow bell pepper
¾ teaspoon black pepper
½ teaspoon ground cumin
½ teaspoon ground coriander
2 cups diced pineapple
¼ cup minced fresh cilantro

1. Sort and wash beans; place in a medium saucepan. Cover with water to 2 inches above beans; bring to a boil, and cook 2 minutes. Remove from heat; cover and let stand 1 hour. Drain beans; return to pan. Cover beans with 2 inches of water. Bring to a boil over medium-high heat. Reduce heat; simmer 1½ hours or until tender. Drain beans; set aside.
2. To prepare rice, heat oil in a large nonstick skillet over medium-high heat until hot. Add onion and next 5 ingredients; sauté 4 minutes. Add rice; cook 1 minute. Add 3½ cups water; bring to a boil. Cover, reduce heat, and simmer 20 minutes. Add beans; cover and simmer 12 minutes, stirring occasionally. Discard bay leaves.
3. Stir in red bell pepper and next 4 ingredients; cook 6 minutes. Stir in pineapple and cilantro; cook 2 minutes. Yield: 16 servings (serving size: about ⅔ cup).

CALORIES 133 (9% from fat); FAT 1.3g (sat 0.2g, mono 0.7g, poly 0.3g); PROTEIN 4.3g; CARB 26.4g; FIBER 2.7g; CHOL 0mg; IRON 1.8mg; SODIUM 120mg; CALC 31mg

ROLLED GREENS

The name of this South American dish comes from the technique of rolling the collard leaves tightly together to make slicing easier.

3 pounds collards or kale
2 teaspoons olive oil
2 bacon slices, finely diced
8 cups chopped onion
½ teaspoon salt
½ teaspoon black pepper
½ to 1 teaspoon hot pepper sauce

Continued

1. Remove stems from collards. Wash and pat dry. Stack 4 or 5 collard leaves together; roll up, holding tightly, and slice thinly. Repeat procedure with remaining leaves to equal 32 cups.
2. Heat oil in a large Dutch oven until hot. Add bacon; sauté 2 minutes or until lightly browned. Add onion; sauté 2 minutes. Add collards in 4 batches; cook 1 minute after each addition, stirring frequently. Cook an additional 25 minutes or until tender, stirring frequently. Add salt, pepper, and sauce; cook 2 minutes. Yield: 16 servings (serving size: ½ cup).

CALORIES 73 (18% from fat); FAT 1.5g (sat 0.3g, mono 0.7g, poly 0.3g); PROTEIN 2.9g; CARB 13.7g; FIBER 4.2g; CHOL 1mg; IRON 1.4mg; SODIUM 137mg; CALC 226mg

SEAFOOD SALAD

1 pound medium shrimp, peeled
½ pound sea scallops
1 (6-ounce) mahimahi or other firm white fish fillet (about ½ inch thick)
¾ cup diced seeded tomato
¼ cup minced fresh cilantro
3 tablespoons minced shallots
2 tablespoons fresh lime juice
1 tablespoon minced seeded jalapeño pepper
1 teaspoon salt
16 Bibb lettuce leaves

1. Steam shrimp and scallops, covered, 6 minutes or until done. Cool and cut shrimp and scallops into quarters. Steam fish, covered, 8 minutes or until fish flakes easily with a fork. Cool and cut into 1-inch pieces.
2. Combine shrimp, scallops, fish, tomato, and next 5 ingredients in a bowl. Spoon ¼ cup seafood mixture into center of each lettuce leaf; roll up. Yield: 8 servings (serving size: 2 wraps).

CALORIES 102 (11% from fat); FAT 1.3g (sat 0.2g, mono 0.2g, poly 0.5g); PROTEIN 18.1g; CARB 3.9g; FIBER 0.7g; CHOL 90mg; IRON 1.8mg; SODIUM 427mg; CALC 42mg

RUM-ALLSPICE POUND CAKE WITH AMBROSIA

2 cups sugar
⅔ cup stick margarine or butter, softened
2 large eggs
1 large egg white
3 cups all-purpose flour
2 teaspoons baking powder
1 teaspoon baking soda
½ teaspoon ground ginger
½ teaspoon ground allspice
½ teaspoon ground nutmeg
¼ teaspoon salt
1¼ cups low-fat buttermilk
¼ cup dark rum
1 tablespoon grated orange rind
1 teaspoon vanilla extract
Cooking spray
Ambrosia

1. Preheat oven to 375°.
2. Beat sugar and margarine at medium speed of a mixer until well-blended (about 5 minutes). Add eggs and egg white, 1 at a time, beating well after each addition. Lightly spoon flour into dry measuring cups, and level with a knife. Combine flour and next 6 ingredients. Combine buttermilk, rum, orange rind, and vanilla. Add flour mixture to sugar mixture alternately with buttermilk mixture, beginning and ending with flour mixture. Pour batter into a 10-inch tube pan coated with cooking spray.
3. Bake at 375° for 50 minutes or until a wooden pick inserted in center comes out clean. Cool in pan 10 minutes; remove from pan. Cool completely on a wire rack. Serve with Ambrosia. Yield: 18 servings (serving size: 1 slice cake and ¼ cup Ambrosia).

CALORIES 292 (26% from fat); FAT 8.5g (sat 2.2g, mono 3.4g, poly 2.3g); PROTEIN 4.4g; CARB 48.4g; FIBER 2.5g; CHOL 25mg; IRON 1.3mg; SODIUM 259mg; CALC 79mg

Ambrosia:

3 oranges
2 ruby red or pink grapefruit
2 cups strawberry halves
2 kiwifruit, peeled and cut into wedges
¼ cup flaked sweetened coconut

¼ cup dark rum
3 tablespoons brown sugar

1. Peel and section oranges and grapefruit over a bowl; squeeze membranes to extract juice. Add sections to bowl; discard membranes. Stir in strawberries and remaining ingredients. Cover and chill. Yield: 18 servings (serving size: ¼ cup).

CALORIES 50 (11% from fat); FAT 0.6g (sat 0.4g, mono 0.1g, poly 0.1g); PROTEIN 0.6g; CARB 8.9g; FIBER 1.9g; CHOL 0mg; IRON 0.2mg; SODIUM 4mg; CALC 18mg

PASSIONATE WHITE SANGRÍA

Make the sangría ahead of time, and add the ginger ale just before serving.

3 cups pineapple juice
1 cup white grape juice
1 cup passion fruit juice
¼ cup fresh lime juice (about 2 limes)
1 (750-milliliter) bottle Riesling or other slightly sweet white wine
1 (12-ounce) can ginger ale

1. Combine first 5 ingredients in a large pitcher; chill. Add ginger ale, stirring gently. Yield: 10 servings (serving size: 1 cup).

CALORIES 135 (1% from fat); FAT 0.1g (sat 0g, mono 0.1g, poly 0g); PROTEIN 0.5g; CARB 22.7g; FIBER 0.1g; CHOL 0mg; IRON 0.6mg; SODIUM 11mg; CALC 23mg

LIME SUNSET

2 cups pineapple juice
2 cups cranberry juice cocktail
½ cup fresh lime juice
1 (11.5-ounce) can apricot nectar
9 lime slices
2 (12-ounce) cans ginger ale

1. Combine first 5 ingredients in a large pitcher; cover and chill. To serve, add ginger ale; stir gently. Pour over ice. Yield: 9 servings (serving size: 1 cup).

CALORIES 114 (1% from fat); FAT 0.1g (sat 0g, mono 0.1g, poly 0g); PROTEIN 0.4g; CARB 29.7g; FIBER 0.3g; CHOL 0mg; IRON 0.4mg; SODIUM 9mg; CALC 15mg

One Cool Custard

Here's our foolproof guide to crème caramel, a classic dessert no dinner table should be without.

Ever felt a silky smooth, sweet spoonful of crème caramel glide along your tongue and melt inside your mouth? It's almost impossible to suppress the "*mmmm,*" the overwhelming human response. The evidence is split, though, on whether the best thing to do next is consume the rest of the crème caramel in a mad rush of pleasure or toy with it, catlike, nibble by nibble. Or do both. But never neither.

CLASSIC CRÈME CARAMEL

    ⅓ cup sugar
    3 tablespoons water
 Cooking spray
    3 large eggs
    1 large egg white
    2 cups 2% reduced-fat milk
    1 tablespoon vanilla extract
    ⅔ cup sugar
    ⅛ teaspoon salt
 Fresh raspberries (optional)

1. Preheat oven to 325°.
2. Combine ⅓ cup sugar and 3 tablespoons water in a small, heavy saucepan over medium-high heat; cook until sugar dissolves, stirring frequently. Continue cooking until golden (about 4 minutes). Immediately pour into 6 (6-ounce) ramekins or custard cups coated with cooking spray, tilting each cup quickly until caramelized sugar coats bottom of cup. Set aside.
3. Beat eggs and egg white in a medium bowl with a whisk. Stir in milk, vanilla, ⅔ cup sugar, and salt. Divide mixture evenly among prepared custard cups. Place cups in a 13 x 9-inch baking pan; add hot water to pan to a depth of 1 inch. Bake at 325° for 50 minutes or until a knife inserted in center comes out clean. Remove cups from pan. Cover and chill at least 4 hours.
4. Loosen edges of custards with a knife or rubber spatula. Place a dessert plate, upside down, on top of each cup; invert onto plates. Drizzle any remaining caramelized syrup over custards. Garnish with raspberries, if desired. Yield: 6 servings.

CALORIES 212 (18% from fat); FAT 4.3g (sat 1.8g, mono 1.5g, poly 0.4g); PROTEIN 6.5g; CARB 37.6g; FIBER 0g; CHOL 117mg; IRON 0.4mg; SODIUM 131mg; CALC 113mg

PUMPKIN-MAPLE CRÈME CARAMEL

Freshly grated nutmeg gives this dessert its distinctive spiciness. Regular ground nutmeg can be substituted, but the flavor won't be as intense.

    ½ cup granulated sugar
    ¼ cup water
 Cooking spray
    ⅓ cup packed dark brown sugar
    2 tablespoons maple syrup
    3 large eggs
    ½ cup canned pumpkin
    ½ cup 2% reduced-fat milk
    ¼ teaspoon ground nutmeg
    ½ teaspoon vanilla extract
    ⅛ teaspoon salt
    1 (12-ounce) can evaporated skim milk
 Freshly grated nutmeg (optional)

1. Preheat oven to 325°.
2. Combine ½ cup granulated sugar and ¼ cup water in a small, heavy saucepan over medium-high heat; cook until sugar dissolves, stirring frequently. Continue cooking until golden (about 4 minutes). Immediately pour into 6 (6-ounce) ramekins or custard cups coated with cooking spray, tilting each cup quickly until caramelized sugar coats bottom of cup. Set aside.
3. Beat brown sugar, syrup, and eggs in a medium bowl with a whisk. Add pumpkin and next 5 ingredients; stir until well-blended. Divide mixture evenly among prepared custard cups. Place cups in a 13 x 9-inch baking pan; add hot water to pan to a depth of 1 inch. Bake at 325° for 1 hour and 10 minutes or until a knife inserted in center comes out clean. Remove cups from pan. Cover and chill at least 4 hours.
4. Loosen edges of custards with a knife or rubber spatula. Place a dessert plate, upside down, on top of each cup; invert onto plates. Drizzle any remaining caramelized syrup over custards. Garnish with freshly grated nutmeg, if desired. Yield: 6 servings.

CALORIES 230 (13% from fat); FAT 3.3g (sat 1.2g, mono 1.2g, poly 0.4g); PROTEIN 8.4g; CARB 42.2g; FIBER 0.8g; CHOL 114mg; IRON 1.1mg; SODIUM 164mg; CALC 222mg

ALMOND CRÈME CARAMEL

The texture of this crème caramel may remind you of a delicate cheesecake.

    ½ cup sugar
    ¼ cup water
 Cooking spray
    2 tablespoons chopped almonds, toasted
    ⅓ cup sugar
    1 tablespoon all-purpose flour
    4 ounces ⅓-less-fat cream cheese (Neufchâtel), softened (about ½ cup)
    2 large egg whites
    1 large egg
 1½ cups 2% reduced-fat milk
    ¼ teaspoon almond extract

1. Preheat oven to 325°.
2. Combine ½ cup sugar and ¼ cup water in a small, heavy saucepan over medium-high heat; cook until sugar dissolves, stirring frequently. Continue cooking until golden (about 4 minutes). Immediately pour into 6 (6-ounce) ramekins or custard cups coated with cooking spray, tilting each cup quickly until caramelized sugar coats bottom of cup. Sprinkle almonds evenly over caramelized sugar; set aside.
3. Combine ⅓ cup sugar and flour. *Continued on page 329*

Continued on page 329

A crème caramel involves two crucial steps: making the caramel syrup and baking the custard atop the syrup. The custard in a crème caramel can be flavored many ways, but how to make the dessert doesn't change. For exact ingredients, quantities, and cooking times, see the individual recipes.

❶ *Combine sugar and water in a heavy saucepan over medium-high heat, stirring until sugar dissolves.*

❷ *Continue to cook without stirring; after about 2 minutes mixture will start to caramelize and turn light brown. After an additional 1 to 2 minutes the mixture will be a deep golden brown.*

❸ *Immediately pour enough caramel into a ramekin or custard cup to cover the bottom of the cup.*

❹ *Tilt the cup so that its bottom is completely covered with caramel. Repeat for remaining cups.*

❺ *Divide custard mixture (eggs, milk, and flavorings) evenly among prepared cups.*

❻ *Place cups in a 13 x 9-inch baking pan. Carefully add hot tap water to the pan to a depth of 1 inch. Bake at 325° for recommended cooking time.*

❼ *After custards have cooled and chilled, run a thin knife around the edge of each to loosen it from its cup.*

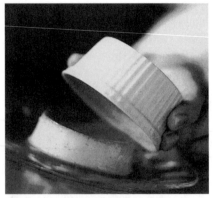

❽ *Place a dessert plate, upside down, on top of each cup. Invert the cup and plate. Lift the cup; the custard should slip out easily with the caramel syrup on top.*

Beat cream cheese at medium speed of a mixer until smooth. Add flour mixture, beating until well-blended. Add egg whites and egg; beat well. Gradually add milk and almond extract, beating well. Divide evenly among prepared custard cups. Place cups in a 13 x 9-inch baking pan; add hot water to pan to a depth of 1 inch. Bake at 325° for 50 minutes or until a knife inserted in center comes out clean. Remove from pan. Cover and chill at least 4 hours.

4. Loosen edges of custards with a knife or rubber spatula. Place a dessert plate, upside down, on top of each cup; invert onto plates. Drizzle any remaining caramelized syrup over custards. Yield: 6 servings.

CALORIES 223 (31% from fat); FAT 7.6g (sat 3.9g, mono 2.6g, poly 0.5g); PROTEIN 6.6g; CARB 32.8g; FIBER 0.3g; CHOL 56mg; IRON 0.4mg; SODIUM 135mg; CALC 99mg

BANANA-NUT CRÈME CARAMEL

⅓ cup granulated sugar
3 tablespoons water
Cooking spray
½ cup mashed ripe banana (about 1 banana)
⅓ cup packed dark brown sugar
2 tablespoons dark rum
¼ teaspoon vanilla extract
⅛ teaspoon salt
1 (12-ounce) can evaporated skim milk
2 large eggs, lightly beaten
4 pecan halves, toasted (optional)

1. Preheat oven to 325°.
2. Combine granulated sugar and 3 tablespoons water in a small, heavy saucepan over medium-high heat; cook until sugar dissolves, stirring frequently. Continue cooking until golden (about 4 minutes). Immediately pour into 4 (6-ounce) ramekins or custard cups coated with cooking spray, tilting each cup quickly until caramelized sugar coats bottom of cup. Set aside.
3. Combine banana and next 6 ingredients, stirring well with a whisk.

Divide mixture evenly among prepared custard cups. Place cups in a 9-inch square baking pan; add hot water to pan to a depth of 1 inch. Bake at 325° for 45 minutes or until a knife inserted in center comes out clean. Remove cups from pan. Cover and chill at least 4 hours.
4. Loosen edges of custards with a knife or rubber spatula. Place a dessert plate, upside down, on top of each cup; invert onto plates. Drizzle any remaining caramelized syrup over custards. Top with toasted pecan halves, if desired. Yield: 4 servings.

CALORIES 274 (13% from fat); FAT 3.9g (sat 1g, mono 1.6g, poly 0.6g); PROTEIN 10g; CARB 51.2g; FIBER 0.9g; CHOL 114mg; IRON 1.1mg; SODIUM 209mg; CALC 277mg

IRISH CREAM-ESPRESSO CRÈME CARAMEL

⅓ cup sugar
3 tablespoons water
Cooking spray
2 large eggs
1 large egg white
½ cup sugar
3 tablespoons Irish cream liqueur (such as Bailey's)
1 tablespoon instant espresso or 2 tablespoons instant coffee granules
⅛ teaspoon salt
1 (12-ounce) can evaporated skim milk
Chopped chocolate-covered coffee beans (optional)

1. Preheat oven to 325°.
2. Combine ⅓ cup sugar and 3 tablespoons water in a small, heavy saucepan over medium-high heat; cook until sugar dissolves, stirring frequently. Continue cooking until golden (about 4 minutes). Immediately pour into 4 (6-ounce) ramekins or custard cups coated with cooking spray, tilting each cup quickly until caramelized sugar coats bottom of cup. Set aside.
3. Beat eggs and egg white in a medium bowl with a whisk. Stir in ½

cup sugar, liqueur, espresso, salt, and milk. Divide mixture evenly among prepared custard cups. Place cups in a 9-inch square baking pan; add hot water to pan to a depth of 1 inch. Bake at 325° for 55 minutes or until a knife inserted in center comes out clean. Remove cups from pan. Cover and chill at least 4 hours.
4. Loosen edges of custards with a knife or rubber spatula. Place a dessert plate, upside down, on top of each cup; invert onto plates. Drizzle any remaining caramelized syrup over custards. Garnish with chopped coffee beans, if desired. Yield: 4 servings.

CALORIES 305 (15% from fat); FAT 5g (sat 2g, mono 1.6g, poly 0.4g); PROTEIN 11g; CARB 54.7g; FIBER 0g; CHOL 114mg; IRON 0.7mg; SODIUM 229mg; CALC 264mg

TROUBLESHOOTING

Here's how to avoid the most common problems when making crème caramel—plus a few other helpful tips.
To keep the sugar from crystallizing, stir as little as possible after it has melted. If some caramel crystallizes on the side of the pan, wash the crystals down with a wet pastry brush. Never touch or taste hot caramel.

Even after the caramel is removed from the heat, it can burn quickly. If it has a blackish-brown color, it's probably burned and it's best to start over.

Pouring the custard mixture into the custard cups can be messy. To make pouring easier, mix the ingredients in a bowl with a spout, or mix them in a regular bowl and transfer it to a 4-cup glass measuring cup.

Oven temperatures vary, so check the custards for doneness 5 minutes before the end of the recommended cooking time. And remember, custard continues to cook as it cools.

If the crème caramel has not been thoroughly chilled (we recommend at least 4 hours), some of the caramel may stick to the bottom of the cup. If so, just scrape out the remaining syrup with a rubber spatula.

What, Us Worry?

For National Stress-Free Family Holidays Month, all you really gotta do is grab a nibble and chill.

No one is arguing that National Stress-Free Family Holidays Month at this time of year doesn't encompass an oxymoron of the highest magnitude. But just because something is impossible doesn't mean it can't be done. All you have to do is come home for the holidays, grab an endlessly comforting ooey-gooey treat, put your feet up, and chill.

MAKE-AHEAD OOEY-GOOEY STICKY BUNS

(pictured on page 1)

Don't let the name stress you. All you have to do is mix up the dough, shape the rolls, then let them rise in the refrigerator overnight. Too demanding a schedule? You can make them impromptu the same day by letting the dough rise in a warm place for about an hour.

    1   package dry yeast (about 2¼
          teaspoons)
    1   teaspoon granulated sugar
    ¼   cup warm water (105° to 115°)
    4   cups all-purpose flour, divided
    ¼   cup granulated sugar
    1   teaspoon ground nutmeg
    ¾   teaspoon salt
    1   cup evaporated skim milk,
          divided
    ¼   cup water
    1   large egg, lightly beaten
        Cooking spray
    1¼ cups packed dark brown sugar,
          divided
    ⅓   cup dark corn syrup
    2   tablespoons stick margarine or
          butter
    ¾   cup chopped pecans
    1   tablespoon ground cinnamon

1. Dissolve yeast and 1 teaspoon granulated sugar in ¼ cup warm water in a small bowl; let stand 5 minutes. Lightly spoon flour into dry measuring cups; level with a knife. Place 3¾ cups flour, ¼ cup granulated sugar, nutmeg, and salt in a food processor; pulse 2 times or until blended. Combine ⅔ cup milk, ¼ cup water, and egg. With processor on, slowly add milk mixture and yeast mixture through food chute; process until dough forms a ball. Process an additional minute. Turn dough out onto a lightly floured surface; knead until smooth and elastic (about 8 minutes); add enough of remaining flour, 1 tablespoon at a time, to prevent dough from sticking to hands.
2. Place dough in a large bowl coated with cooking spray, turning to coat top. Cover and let rise in a warm place (85°), free from drafts, 45 minutes or until doubled in bulk. Combine remaining ⅓ cup milk, 1 cup brown sugar, corn syrup, and margarine in a small saucepan; bring to a boil, stirring constantly. Remove from heat. Divide pecans evenly between 2 (9-inch) round cake pans coated with cooking spray. Top each with half of brown sugar mixture.
3. Punch dough down; let rest 5 minutes. Roll into a 24 x 10-inch rectangle on a lightly floured surface; coat entire surface of dough with cooking spray. Combine remaining ¼ cup brown sugar and cinnamon in a small bowl; sprinkle evenly over dough. Beginning with a long side, roll up jelly-roll fashion; pinch seam to seal (do not seal ends of roll). Cut roll into 24 (1-inch) slices, using string or dental floss. Arrange 12 slices, cut sides up, in each pan. Cover with plastic wrap coated with cooking spray, and let rise in refrigerator 8 to 24 hours or until doubled in bulk.
4. Preheat oven to 375°.
5. Bake rolls at 375° for 23 minutes. Run a knife around outside edges of pans. Place a plate upside down on top of each pan; invert onto plate. Yield: 2 dozen (serving size: 1 bun).

CALORIES 188 (19% from fat); FAT 4g (sat 0.5g, mono 2.1g, poly 1g); PROTEIN 3.7g; CARB 35.1g; FIBER 1g; CHOL 10mg; IRON 1.5mg; SODIUM 110mg; CALC 51mg

Mixer Variation:

Combine yeast mixture, 3 cups flour, granulated sugar, nutmeg, and salt in a large bowl. Add ⅔ cup milk, ¼ cup water, and egg. Beat at medium speed of a mixer until blended. Turn dough out onto a lightly floured surface; knead until smooth and elastic (about 8 minutes); add enough of remaining flour, 1 tablespoon at a time, to prevent dough from sticking to hands. Proceed to step 2.

LIGHTEN UP

Hasta la Vista, Fat

We've helped Becky Bramlage say good riddance to unwanted fat and calories in a cherished Mexican Chicken Casserole.

We began by substituting all-white breast meat for the light and dark chicken used in the original recipe. Then, to retain the cheesiness of the casserole's filling, we replaced the half-and-half with a combination of evaporated skim milk and light cream cheese. Finally, we topped everything off with reduced-fat Cheddar and crumbled tortilla chips. The result? It's great!

MEXICAN CHICKEN CASSEROLE

    1   cup fat-free, less-sodium chicken
          broth
    2   (4.5-ounce) cans chopped green
          chiles, divided
    1¾ pounds skinned, boned chicken
          breasts
    2   teaspoons olive oil
    1   cup chopped onion
    1   cup evaporated skim milk
    1   cup (4 ounces) shredded
          Monterey Jack cheese
    ¼   cup (2 ounces) tub-style light
          cream cheese
    1   (10-ounce) can enchilada sauce

12 (6-inch) corn tortillas
Cooking spray
½ cup (2 ounces) shredded reduced-
  fat extra-sharp Cheddar cheese
1 ounce tortilla chips, crushed
  (about 6 chips)

1. Combine broth and 1 can of chiles in a large skillet; bring to a boil. Add chicken; reduce heat, and simmer 15 minutes or until chicken is done, turning once. Remove chicken from cooking liquid, reserving cooking liquid; cool chicken. Shred meat with two forks; set aside.
2. Preheat oven to 350°.
3. Heat oil in a large nonstick skillet over medium-high heat. Add 1 can of chiles and onion; sauté 3 minutes or until soft. Add reserved cooking liquid, milk, and next 3 ingredients; stir well. Stir in shredded chicken; cook 2 minutes. Remove from heat.
4. Place 4 tortillas in bottom of a 2-quart casserole coated with cooking spray. Spoon 2 cups chicken mixture over tortillas. Repeat layers twice, ending with chicken mixture. Sprinkle with Cheddar cheese and chips. Bake at 350° for 30 minutes or until thoroughly heated. Let stand 10 minutes before serving. Yield: 8 servings (serving size: 1 cup).

CALORIES 369 (28% from fat); FAT 11.4g (sat 5g, mono 3.8g, poly 1.4g); PROTEIN 35.6g; CARB 31.3g; FIBER 3g; CHOL 79mg; IRON 2.4mg; SODIUM 479mg; CALC 360mg

BEFORE & AFTER	
SERVING SIZE	
1 cup	
CALORIES	
519	369
FAT	
27.2g	11.4g
PERCENT OF TOTAL CALORIES	
47%	28%
CHOLESTEROL	
99mg	79mg
SODIUM	
502mg	479mg

First Class for Santa

Saint Nick needs love this time of year just like the rest of us. What he doesn't need is extra baggage.

Although Santa needs his share of fun fuel for all those takeoffs and landings, rest assured he's not looking for any unnecessary weight on the rooftop. But that doesn't mean he wants a saltine cracker and a grape. Santa goes first class—would you want it any other way? So leave him something a little sweet, a lot special, and loaded with love. He can carry that around the world.

LEMON-FROSTED SUGAR COOKIES

You may want to start this recipe early in the day because the dough requires about 4 hours to chill.

Cookies:

1 cup granulated sugar
½ cup stick margarine or butter, softened
1 large egg
1 large egg white
1 tablespoon fat-free milk
1 teaspoon grated lemon rind
1 teaspoon vanilla extract
2 cups all-purpose flour
¼ cup toasted wheat germ
1 teaspoon baking powder
½ teaspoon baking soda
⅛ teaspoon salt

Frosting:

2 cups powdered sugar
1 tablespoon fat-free milk
1 tablespoon fresh lemon juice
¼ teaspoon vanilla extract
Food coloring (optional)
Assorted sugar sprinkles (optional)

1. To prepare cookies, beat granulated sugar and margarine in a large bowl at medium speed of a mixer until well-blended (about 4 minutes). Add egg and next 4 ingredients, beating well. Lightly spoon flour into dry measuring cups; level with a knife. Combine flour and next 4 ingredients in a bowl. Add flour mixture to sugar mixture, stirring well. Spoon dough onto plastic wrap; flatten to a 1½-inch thickness. Cover tightly with plastic wrap; chill 4 hours or overnight.
2. Preheat oven to 400°.
3. Roll dough to a 15 x 12-inch rectangle on a heavily floured surface. Cut dough into 20 (3-inch) squares using a sharp knife. Place cookies 2 inches apart on ungreased baking sheets. Bake at 400° for 8 minutes or until golden. Immediately remove cookies from sheets using a wide spatula; cool on wire racks.
4. To prepare frosting, combine powdered sugar and next 3 ingredients. Stir in food coloring, if desired. Spread about 2 teaspoons frosting over each cookie or place frosting in a small zip-top plastic bag. Snip a tiny hole in one corner, and drizzle over cookies. Sprinkle with assorted sugar sprinkles, if desired. Yield: 20 cookies (serving size: 1 cookie).

CALORIES 188 (24% from fat); FAT 5.1g (sat 1g, mono 2.1g, poly 1.6g); PROTEIN 2.2g; CARB 33.8g; FIBER 0.6g; CHOL 11mg; IRON 0.8mg; SODIUM 131mg; CALC 21mg

Giant Oatmeal-Raisin Cookies

1 cup sugar
¼ cup stick margarine or butter, softened
2 large eggs
¾ cup applesauce
1 teaspoon vanilla extract
2 cups all-purpose flour
½ teaspoon baking soda
½ teaspoon pumpkin-pie spice
¼ teaspoon salt
1 cup regular oats
1 cup golden raisins
½ cup chopped pecans
Cooking spray

1. Preheat oven to 375°.
2. Beat sugar and margarine in a large bowl at medium speed of a mixer until well-blended (about 4 minutes). Add eggs, 1 at a time, beating well after each addition. Add applesauce and vanilla; beat well.
3. Lightly spoon flour into dry measuring cups; level with a knife. Combine flour and next 3 ingredients in a bowl. Add to sugar mixture; beat well. Stir in oats, raisins, and pecans.
4. Drop dough into 24 mounds 2 inches apart onto baking sheets coated with cooking spray. Bake at 375° for 14 minutes or until golden brown. Remove cookies from sheets; cool on wire racks. Yield: 2 dozen (serving size: 1 cookie).

CALORIES 148 (27% from fat); FAT 4.4g (sat 0.7g, mono 2.1g, poly 1.2g); PROTEIN 2.6g; CARB 25.4g; FIBER 1.3g; CHOL 18mg; IRON 0.9mg; SODIUM 80mg; CALC 11mg

Orange Fig Bars

Dough:

6 tablespoons stick margarine or butter, softened
¼ cup sugar
¼ cup honey
1 teaspoon vanilla extract
1 large egg
1¾ cups all-purpose flour
1 teaspoon baking powder
¼ teaspoon salt

Filling:

2 cups dried figs (about 12 ounces)
1 tablespoon grated orange rind
¼ cup boiling water
2 tablespoons sugar
2 tablespoons honey
2 tablespoons fresh orange juice

Remaining ingredients:

Cooking spray
1 teaspoon fat-free milk
1 large egg yolk, lightly beaten

1. To prepare dough, beat margarine at medium speed of a mixer until smooth. Add ¼ cup sugar; beat 2 minutes. Add ¼ cup honey, vanilla, and egg; beat until well-blended. Lightly spoon flour into dry measuring cups; level with a knife. Combine flour, baking powder, and salt in medium bowl. Add flour mixture to egg mixture, stirring just until moist. Divide dough in half; gently press each half of dough into a square on plastic wrap. Cover with additional plastic wrap; chill 8 hours.
2. Preheat oven to 375°.
3. To prepare filling, place figs and orange rind in a food processor; process until minced. Combine boiling water, 2 tablespoons sugar, and 2 tablespoons honey, stirring until sugar dissolves. Stir in orange juice. With processor on, slowly add orange juice mixture to fig mixture through food chute. Process until well-blended, scraping sides of bowl occasionally; set aside.
4. Working with one portion of dough at a time (cover remaining dough to keep from drying), roll each portion to a 9-inch square on a heavily floured surface. Fit one portion of dough into a 9-inch square baking pan coated with cooking spray. Spread fig mixture evenly over dough in pan. Place remaining square of dough on top of filling. Combine milk and egg yolk in a small bowl, stirring with a whisk; brush over top of dough.
5. Bake at 375° for 30 minutes or until top is golden. Cool 30 minutes on a wire rack. Remove from pan; cool completely. Transfer to a flat surface or cutting board, and cut into bars using a sharp, heavy knife. Yield: 20 servings (serving size: 1 bar).

CALORIES 156 (25% from fat); FAT 4.3g (sat 0.9g, mono 1.8g, poly 1.3g); PROTEIN 2.2g; CARB 28.9g; FIBER 3.2g; CHOL 22mg; IRON 1mg; SODIUM 100mg; CALC 45mg

Gingersnaps

2½ cups all-purpose flour, divided
1 tablespoon ground ginger
2 teaspoons baking soda
1 teaspoon ground cinnamon
¼ teaspoon black pepper
⅛ teaspoon salt
½ cup stick margarine or butter, softened
¾ cup granulated sugar, divided
½ cup packed dark brown sugar
¼ cup molasses
1 large egg
1 large egg white
Cooking spray

1. Lightly spoon flour into dry measuring cups; level with a knife. Combine 2 cups flour, ginger, baking soda, cinnamon, pepper, and salt. Beat margarine, ½ cup granulated sugar, and brown sugar at medium speed of a mixer until light and fluffy. Add molasses; beat 2 minutes. Add egg and egg white; beat until fluffy. Stir in flour mixture until well-blended. Shape dough into a ball with floured hands; add enough of remaining flour, 1 tablespoon at a time, to prevent dough from sticking. Wrap in plastic wrap; chill 1 hour.
2. Preheat oven to 375°.
3. Shape dough into 30 balls with floured hands. Roll balls in ¼ cup granulated sugar; place 2 inches apart on baking sheets coated with cooking spray. Bake at 375° for 12 minutes. Immediately remove cookies from sheets to a wire rack; cool completely. Yield: 2½ dozen (serving size: 1 cookie).

CALORIES 109 (27% from fat); FAT 3.3g (sat 0.7g, mono 1.4g, poly 1g); PROTEIN 1.5g; CARB 18.6g; FIBER 0.3g; CHOL 7mg; IRON 0.8mg; SODIUM 136mg; CALC 13mg

TOFFEE CANDY APPLES

You'll need a candy thermometer and wooden sticks to make these treats. Also, be sure to use a heavy saucepan.

8   Granny Smith apples
1½ cups packed dark brown sugar
⅓   cup water
⅓   cup dark corn syrup or molasses
2   tablespoons stick margarine or butter
1   tablespoon white vinegar

1. Wash and dry apples; remove stems. Insert a wooden stick into stem end of each apple; set aside.
2. Line a baking sheet with foil.
3. Combine sugar and remaining 4 ingredients in a medium saucepan. Bring to a boil over medium heat; cover and cook 3 minutes. Uncover and continue cooking, without stirring, until mixture reaches 280° (about 8 minutes).
4. Remove from heat. Quickly dip apples in sugar mixture; allow excess to drip off. Place apples, stick sides up, on prepared pan; cool completely. Yield: 8 servings.

CALORIES 301 (10% from fat); FAT 3.3g (sat 0.6g, mono 1.3g, poly 1g); PROTEIN 0.3g; CARB 71.8g; FIBER 4.3g; CHOL 0mg; IRON 1mg; SODIUM 66mg; CALC 46mg

HOT SPICED FRUIT PUNCH

Leave Santa a note to reheat this aromatic punch in the microwave.

4   cups cranberry-raspberry drink
2   cups orange-strawberry-banana juice
1   teaspoon whole allspice
2   orange-and-spice tea bags
5   (3 x ¾-inch) lemon rind strips
1   (3-inch) cinnamon stick
¼   cup sweetened dried cranberries (such as Craisins)
¼   cup diced dried apricots
2   tablespoons sugar
Cinnamon sticks (optional)

1. Combine first 6 ingredients in a large saucepan, and cook 30 minutes over medium-low heat. Remove from heat; let stand 30 minutes. Strain mixture; discard solids. Return juice mixture to pan; stir in cranberries, apricots, and sugar. Cook over medium-low heat 30 minutes, stirring occasionally. Pour into mugs; serve with a cinnamon stick, if desired. Yield: 8 servings (serving size: ¾ cup).

CALORIES 151 (1% from fat); FAT 0.1g (sat 0g, mono 0g, poly 0.1g); PROTEIN 0.5g; CARB 38.6g; FIBER 0.6g; CHOL 0mg; IRON 0.6mg; SODIUM 10mg; CALC 16mg

Stranded Where We Wanted to Be

The snow started falling on the morning of the 23rd, the day family and friends were scheduled to arrive for our annual Christmas at the cabin. Although only a light snow at first, the front was shaping up to be a massive one, and naturally had caught everyone, especially the weather service, by surprise.

Somehow, miraculously, everyone arrived by nightfall. And in our joyous reunion, the giddiness of relief only intensified our usual holiday cheer. The snow that fell upon us seemed like celebratory confetti in a ticker-tape parade.

We had long ago learned the wisdom of laying in vast quantities of foodstuffs for the holidays as the nearest decent grocery store was an hour's drive over the pass. In late afternoon the snow stopped abruptly, the skies cleared, the drifts glittered in the evening light as if studded with flakes of mica. We decorated the tree and prepped Christmas Eve dinner, everyone contributing food, dishes, and general kitchen mayhem. Never had we been more grateful for our bounty, never had cooking been more festive. We sat down to an extraordinary feast, and our first toast was to holiday travelers: May they all make it safely home for Christmas.

CREAMY TURNIP SOUP

2   teaspoons stick margarine or butter
3½ cups chopped leek
¾   cup chopped shallots (about 5 ounces)
4   cups diced peeled turnips (about 1½ pounds)
2   cups water
3   (16-ounce) cans fat-free, less-sodium chicken broth
¾   cup whole milk
¼   teaspoon black pepper

1. Melt margarine in a large Dutch oven over medium-high heat. Add leek and shallots; sauté 4 minutes. Add turnips; sauté 2 minutes. Stir in water and broth; bring to a boil. Reduce heat; simmer 30 minutes or until turnips are tender.
2. Place one-third of turnip mixture in a blender; process until smooth. Pour pureed mixture into a large bowl; repeat procedure with remaining turnip mixture. Return puree to pan; stir in milk and pepper. Cook until thoroughly heated. Ladle into soup bowls. Yield: 8 servings (serving size: 1¼ cups).

CALORIES 95 (18% from fat); FAT 1.9g (sat 1.1g, mono 0.6g, poly 0.2g); PROTEIN 4.6g; CARB 14.9g; FIBER 1.8g; CHOL 6mg; IRON 1.3mg; SODIUM 435mg; CALC 80mg

CLASSIC BEEF TENDERLOIN

(pictured on page 318)

- 1 (3½-pound) trimmed beef tenderloin
- 1½ cups dry vermouth, divided
- ¼ cup extra-virgin olive oil
- ½ cup minced shallots
- 3 tablespoons minced fresh or 1 tablespoon dried tarragon
- 1 tablespoon minced fresh or 1 teaspoon dried thyme
- 1½ teaspoons salt
- ½ teaspoon black pepper
- 3 garlic cloves, minced
- Cooking spray
- 1¼ cups fat-free, less-sodium chicken broth
- 2 tablespoons tomato paste
- 1 teaspoon prepared horseradish

1. Fold under 3 inches of small end of tenderloin; tie tenderloin with string at 2-inch intervals. Combine ½ cup vermouth, oil, and next 6 ingredients in a large zip-top plastic bag. Add tenderloin to bag; seal. Marinate in refrigerator at least 8 hours, turning bag occasionally.
2. Preheat oven to 450°.
3. Remove tenderloin from bag; discard marinade. Place tenderloin on a broiler pan coated with cooking spray. Insert a meat thermometer into thickest portion of tenderloin. Bake at 450° for 35 minutes or until thermometer registers 145° (medium-rare) to 160° (medium). Place tenderloin on a platter, reserving drippings. Cover tenderloin with foil; let stand 10 minutes. Remove string before slicing.
4. Place 1 cup vermouth in a saucepan; bring to a boil, and simmer until reduced to ½ cup (about 9 minutes). Stir in broth; bring to a boil, and simmer 10 minutes. Stir in reserved drippings, tomato paste, and horseradish. Serve sauce with tenderloin. Yield: 8 servings (serving size: 3 ounces meat and about ¼ cup sauce).

CALORIES 209 (42% from fat); FAT 9.7g (sat 3.3g, mono 4.4g, poly 0.5g); PROTEIN 24.8g; CARB 2.9g; FIBER 0.2g; CHOL 71mg; IRON 3.3mg; SODIUM 244mg; CALC 12mg

HONEY-APPLE TURKEY WITH GRAVY

- 1 (12-pound) fresh or frozen turkey, thawed
- ½ cup packed brown sugar
- ½ cup water
- 4 cups apple juice
- ¼ cup cider vinegar
- ½ teaspoon salt
- ¼ teaspoon black pepper
- Cooking spray
- ½ cup fat-free, less-sodium chicken broth
- ¼ cup Calvados (apple brandy)
- 3 tablespoons honey
- ¼ cup all-purpose flour

1. Remove and discard giblets and neck from turkey. Rinse turkey with cold water; pat dry. Trim excess fat. Lift wing tips up and over back; tuck under turkey.
2. Combine sugar and water in a medium saucepan; cook 5 minutes over medium heat or until sugar dissolves. Remove from heat; stir in apple juice and next 3 ingredients. Combine turkey and juice mixture in a large oven cooking bag; seal and marinate in refrigerator 24 hours. Remove turkey from bag, reserving 2¾ cups marinade; discard remaining marinade.
3. Preheat oven to 325°.
4. Place turkey on a broiler pan coated with cooking spray or on a rack set in a shallow roasting pan. Insert a meat thermometer into meaty part of thigh, making sure not to touch bone. Bake at 325° for 3 hours and 10 minutes or until thermometer registers 180°, basting occasionally with 2 cups marinade. (Cover turkey loosely with foil if it gets too brown.)
5. Remove turkey from oven. Cover turkey loosely with foil; let stand at least 10 minutes before carving. Discard skin.
6. Place a zip-top plastic bag inside a 2-cup glass measure. Pour drippings into bag; let stand 10 minutes (fat will rise to the top). Seal bag; carefully snip off 1 bottom corner of bag. Drain drippings into a medium saucepan, stopping before fat layer reaches opening; discard fat. Add ½ reserved cup marinade, broth, brandy, and honey to pan. Combine remaining ¼ cup marinade and flour in a small bowl, stirring with a whisk; add to gravy mixture in saucepan. Bring to a boil; reduce heat, and simmer 15 minutes, stirring frequently. Serve gravy with turkey. Yield: 12 servings (serving size: 6 ounces turkey and 2 tablespoons gravy).

CALORIES 328 (11% from fat); FAT 4.1g (sat 1.4g, mono 0.9g, poly 1.2g); PROTEIN 50.9g; CARB 19g; FIBER 0.2g; CHOL 142mg; IRON 3.4mg; SODIUM 175mg; CALC 39mg

BARLEY-MUSHROOM PILAF

(pictured on page 318)

Barley and shiitake mushrooms add a nutty flavor to this high-fiber take on rice pilaf.

- 4 cups water
- 1 cup uncooked pearl barley
- 3 (3½-ounce) packages fresh shiitake mushrooms
- Cooking spray
- 1 tablespoon olive oil
- 2 cups chopped onion
- 1½ cups chopped red bell pepper
- ¾ cup chopped yellow bell pepper
- ½ cup fat-free, less-sodium chicken broth
- ¼ cup chopped fresh flat-leaf parsley
- 1 tablespoon chopped fresh or 1 teaspoon dried thyme
- 1 teaspoon salt
- ¼ teaspoon freshly ground black pepper
- ¾ cup (3 ounces) grated Monterey Jack or fresh Parmesan cheese, divided

1. Bring 4 cups water to a boil in a large saucepan. Add barley; cover, reduce heat, and simmer 45 minutes. Remove from heat; let stand, covered, 5 minutes.
2. Preheat oven to 350°.
3. Remove and discard stems from mushrooms; slice mushroom caps. Heat a large nonstick skillet coated

with cooking spray over medium-high heat until hot. Add mushrooms; sauté 3 minutes. Remove from skillet. Heat oil in skillet over medium heat. Stir in onion; cover and cook 6 minutes. Add bell peppers; cover and cook 2 minutes. Stir in cooked barley, mushrooms, broth, and next 4 ingredients.

4. Spoon half of barley mixture into an 11 x 7-inch baking dish coated with cooking spray; sprinkle with half of cheese. Repeat layers. Cover and bake at 350° for 45 minutes. Yield: 8 servings (serving size: ¾ cup).

CALORIES 182 (26% from fat); FAT 5.2g (sat 2.1g, mono 2.4g, poly 0.5g); PROTEIN 8.1g; CARB 27.5g; FIBER 5.9g; CHOL 7mg; IRON 1.9mg; SODIUM 353mg; CALC 150mg

ROASTED WINTER VEGETABLES

3 cups (1-inch) cubed peeled rutabaga (about 1½ pounds)
2 cups (1-inch) cubed peeled turnips (about 1 pound)
2 cups (1-inch) pieces fennel bulb (about 1 large)
2 cups (1-inch-thick) sliced parsnip (about ½ pound)
3 garlic cloves, halved
1½ tablespoons extra-virgin olive oil
¾ teaspoon salt
⅛ teaspoon ground nutmeg
⅛ teaspoon freshly ground black pepper
¼ cup chopped fresh flat-leaf parsley
2 teaspoons chopped fresh or ½ teaspoon dried thyme

1. Preheat oven to 400°.
2. Combine first 5 ingredients in a large bowl. Add oil, salt, nutmeg, and pepper; toss well. Arrange vegetables in a single layer on a jelly-roll pan. Bake at 400° for 45 minutes or until tender and lightly browned, stirring occasionally. Remove from oven; add parsley and thyme, tossing well. Yield: 8 servings (serving size: ¾ cup).

CALORIES 80 (33% from fat); FAT 2.9g (sat 0.4g, mono 1.9g, poly 0.3g); PROTEIN 2g; CARB 13.1g; FIBER 2g; CHOL 0mg; IRON 1.3mg; SODIUM 258mg; CALC 73mg

SQUASH-SWISS CHARD GRATIN

Swiss chard is a member of the beet family and is grown for its dark green leaves and reddish, celery-like stalks. Oyster mushrooms add a peppery flavor to this robust winter squash casserole.

1½ pounds Swiss chard
¼ cup water
2 cups chopped oyster mushrooms (about 8 ounces)
1 cup fat-free, less-sodium chicken broth
1 teaspoon salt, divided
¼ teaspoon freshly ground black pepper, divided
5 cups cubed peeled butternut squash (about 1½ pounds)
1 tablespoon finely chopped fresh or 1 teaspoon dried rubbed sage
1 tablespoon olive oil
½ teaspoon paprika
4 garlic cloves, chopped
Olive oil-flavored cooking spray
¼ cup warm 2% reduced-fat milk
½ cup dry breadcrumbs
1 tablespoon reduced-calorie margarine, melted

1. Preheat oven to 450°.
2. Remove stems and center ribs from Swiss chard. Bring ¼ cup water to a boil in a large Dutch oven. Add Swiss chard; cover, reduce heat to medium, and cook 5 minutes or until tender. Drain. Plunge Swiss chard into ice water; drain. Squeeze until barely moist; pat dry, and coarsely chop to measure 2 cups.
3. Combine mushrooms and broth in a large skillet over medium-high heat. Bring to a boil; cover, reduce heat, and cook 3 minutes or until mushrooms are tender. Add Swiss chard; cook 8 minutes or until liquid is absorbed, stirring constantly. Stir in ½ teaspoon salt and ⅛ teaspoon pepper; remove from heat.
4. Combine ½ teaspoon salt, ⅛ teaspoon pepper, squash, and next 4 ingredients in a large bowl. Spread squash mixture evenly on a jelly-roll pan coated with cooking spray. Bake at

450° for 20 minutes or until squash is tender. Remove from oven.
5. Reduce oven temperature to 375°.
6. Combine squash mixture and milk in a large bowl. Mash squash mixture with a potato masher; fold in Swiss chard mixture. Spoon mixture into an 11 x 7-inch baking dish coated with cooking spray. Combine breadcrumbs and margarine; sprinkle over casserole. Cover and bake at 375° for 15 minutes. Yield: 8 servings (serving size: ¾ cup).

CALORIES 66 (29% from fat); FAT 2.1g (sat 0.4g, mono 1.3g, poly 0.2g); PROTEIN 2g; CARB 11.4g; FIBER 1.4g; CHOL 1mg; IRON 1mg; SODIUM 380mg; CALC 48mg

PUMPKIN YEAST ROLLS

1 cup canned pumpkin
2 teaspoons vanilla extract
1 package dry yeast (about 2¼ teaspoons)
2 tablespoons brown sugar
¾ cup warm fat-free milk (105° to 115°)
5 cups bread flour, divided
¼ cup stick margarine or butter, softened
1 teaspoon salt
1 teaspoon cider vinegar
¼ teaspoon ground nutmeg
1 large egg
Cooking spray

1. Combine pumpkin and vanilla; set aside.
2. Dissolve yeast and sugar in milk in a large bowl; let stand 5 minutes. Lightly spoon flour into dry measuring cups; level with a knife. Add 2 cups flour, pumpkin mixture, margarine, and next 4 ingredients to yeast mixture; beat at medium speed of a mixer until smooth. Stir in 2 cups flour to form a sticky dough. Turn dough out onto a lightly floured surface. Knead dough until smooth and elastic (about 10 minutes); add enough of remaining flour, 1 tablespoon at a time, to prevent dough from sticking to hands.
3. Place dough in a large bowl coated with cooking spray, turning to coat
Continued

top. Cover dough, and let rise in a warm place (85°), free from drafts, 1 hour or until doubled in bulk.

4. Coat 24 muffin cups with cooking spray. Punch dough down, and divide in half. Working with 1 portion at a time (cover remaining dough to keep from drying), divide each portion into 12 equal pieces; shape each piece into a ball. Place 1 ball in each muffin cup. Cover and let rise 30 minutes or until doubled in bulk.

5. Preheat oven to 350°.

6. Uncover dough; bake at 350° for 20 minutes or until lightly browned. Remove from pans; cool on wire racks. Yield: 2 dozen (serving size: 1 roll).

CALORIES 134 (18% from fat); FAT 2.7g (sat 0.5g, mono 1g, poly 0.9g); PROTEIN 4.2g; CARB 22.8g; FIBER 0.5g; CHOL 9mg; IRON 1.5mg; SODIUM 128mg; CALC 19mg.

APPLE-CRANBERRY COBBLER

Fruit mixture:

½ cup sugar
¾ cup fresh orange juice (about 3 oranges)
¼ cup water
¾ teaspoon pumpkin-pie spice
1 (12-ounce) bag fresh or frozen cranberries
6 cups cubed peeled Rome apple (about 2½ pounds)
¼ cup dark rum
Cooking spray

Topping:

1 cup all-purpose flour
¼ cup sugar
1 teaspoon baking powder
¼ teaspoon baking soda
¼ teaspoon salt
¼ cup chilled stick margarine or butter, cut into small pieces
⅔ cup low-fat buttermilk
1 teaspoon grated orange rind
2 teaspoons sugar

1. Preheat oven to 400°.

2. To prepare fruit mixture, combine first 5 ingredients in a large saucepan.

Bring to a boil over medium-high heat, stirring occasionally. Reduce heat; simmer 10 minutes or until cranberries pop and mixture is slightly thick. Cool slightly; stir in apple and rum. Spoon fruit mixture into a 3-quart casserole coated with cooking spray.

3. To prepare topping, lightly spoon flour into a dry measuring cup; level with a knife. Combine flour and next 4 ingredients in a bowl. Cut in margarine with a pastry blender or 2 knives until mixture resembles coarse meal. Combine buttermilk and orange rind in a bowl; add to flour mixture. Stir just until moist.

4. Spoon topping in 8 equal portions over fruit mixture; sprinkle evenly with 2 teaspoons sugar. Bake at 400° for 35 minutes or until filling is bubbly and topping is golden brown. Yield: 8 servings.

CALORIES 274 (22% from fat); FAT 6.6g (sat 1.4g, mono 2.7g, poly 2g); PROTEIN 2.9g; CARB 53.2g; FIBER 3.2g; CHOL 0mg; IRON 1mg; SODIUM 239mg; CALC 74mg

SPARKLING CITRUS CIDER

2½ cups fresh orange juice (about 8 oranges)
1½ cups fresh tangerine juice (about 6 tangerines)
1 (25.4-ounce) bottle sparkling apple cider, chilled
¼ cup grenadine

1. Strain orange and tangerine juices through a cheesecloth-lined colander into a large bowl; discard pulp. Combine juices and cider in a large pitcher. Pour ¾ cup into each of 8 glasses. Slowly pour 1½ teaspoons grenadine down inside of each glass (do not stir before serving). Yield: 8 servings.

CALORIES 102 (2% from fat); FAT 0.2g (sat 0g, mono 0g, poly 1g); PROTEIN 0.8g; CARB 25g; FIBER 0.4g; CHOL 0mg; IRON 0.5mg; SODIUM 5mg; CALC 22mg

FAST FOOD

Feed the Hustle

When the going gets tough, the tough may go shopping, but the wise carve out a half-hour for a decent meal.

SHRIMP AND ARTICHOKES OVER PARMESAN GRITS

Preparation time: 30 minutes
Cooking time: 18 minutes

2 teaspoons olive oil
½ cup chopped onion
1 (9-ounce) package frozen artichoke hearts, thawed
3½ cups fat-free, less-sodium chicken broth, divided
1½ pounds large shrimp, peeled and deveined
2 garlic cloves, minced
1 teaspoon dried oregano
1 teaspoon grated lemon rind
1 teaspoon fresh lemon juice
¼ teaspoon salt
¼ teaspoon black pepper
¾ cup uncooked quick-cooking grits
⅓ cup grated Parmesan cheese

1. Heat oil in a large nonstick skillet over medium-high heat. Add onion and artichokes; sauté 5 minutes. Add 1 cup broth, shrimp, and garlic; sauté 6 minutes. Add oregano and next 4 ingredients. Remove from heat; cover and keep warm.

2. Bring remaining 2½ cups broth to a boil in a medium saucepan. Slowly stir in grits; reduce heat to low. Cook 7 minutes or until thick and creamy, stirring occasionally. Stir in cheese. Spoon ½ cup grits into each of 4 bowls; top with 1 cup shrimp mixture. Yield 4 servings.

CALORIES 341 (18% from fat); FAT 7g (sat 2.1g, mono 2.6g, poly 1.2g); PROTEIN 35.9g; CARB 32.5g; FIBER 2.4g; CHOL 199mg; IRON 4.8mg; SODIUM 912mg; CALC 185mg

Japanese Beef and Noodles Big Bowl

Preparation time: 20 minutes
Cooking time: 15 minutes

2 large egg whites
1 large egg
8 cups fat-free beef broth
¼ cup low-sodium soy sauce
2 tablespoons sugar
1 tablespoon grated peeled fresh ginger
8 ounces beef tenderloin, cut into 2 x ¼-inch slices
1½ cups (1-inch) sliced green onions
4 cups hot cooked soba (buckwheat noodles) or angel hair pasta (about 8 ounces uncooked)
2 cups fresh bean sprouts

1. Beat egg whites and egg at medium speed of a mixer 1 minute; set aside.
2. Combine broth and next 3 ingredients in a large saucepan; bring to a boil. Reduce heat; add beef and onions. Simmer 1 minute. Add egg mixture without stirring; cook 1 minute. Remove from heat; gently stir. Place 1 cup of noodles in each of 4 large soup bowls; add 2 cups of beef mixture and ½ cup sprouts. Yield: 4 servings.

CALORIES 389 (12% from fat); FAT 5.4g (sat 1.9g, mono 1.9g, poly 0.4g); PROTEIN 28g; CARB 55.4g; FIBER 1.5g; CHOL 90mg; IRON 4mg; SODIUM 742mg; CALC 54mg

Farfalle with Wild-Mushroom Sauce

Preparation time: 25 minutes
Cooking time: 15 minutes

1 tablespoon olive oil
1 cup diced onion
6 cups sliced cremini mushrooms (about 1 pound)
4 cups thinly sliced shiitake mushroom caps (about ½ pound)
1 cup sliced oyster mushroom caps (about 3½ ounces)
½ teaspoon dried thyme
¼ teaspoon salt
⅛ teaspoon black pepper
¾ cup fat-free, less-sodium chicken broth
¼ cup dry vermouth or white wine
2½ teaspoons bottled minced garlic
4 cups hot cooked farfalle (about 8 ounces uncooked bow tie pasta)
½ cup (2 ounces) finely shredded fresh Parmesan cheese
4 teaspoons chopped fresh chives

1. Heat oil in a large nonstick skillet over medium heat. Add onion; sauté 5 minutes. Add cremini mushrooms and next 5 ingredients; sauté 5 minutes. Stir in broth, vermouth, and garlic; reduce heat to medium-low, and cook 5 minutes.
2. Combine mushroom mixture and pasta in a large bowl; toss well. Sprinkle each serving with cheese and chives. Yield: 4 servings (serving size: 2 cups pasta, 2 tablespoons cheese, and 1 teaspoon chives.)

CALORIES 425 (19% from fat); FAT 9g (sat 3.1g, mono 3.7g, poly 1.2g); PROTEIN 19.4g; CARB 68g; FIBER 5.1g; CHOL 10mg; IRON 5.6mg; SODIUM 479mg; CALC 211mg

Gnocchi with Canadian Bacon-Tomato Sauce

Preparation time: 8 minutes
Cooking time: 19 minutes

2 teaspoons olive oil
1 cup chopped onion
¾ cup diced lean Canadian bacon (about 4 ounces)
1 teaspoon dried rubbed sage
1 teaspoon bottled minced roasted garlic
½ teaspoon dried oregano
1 teaspoon sugar
¼ teaspoon black pepper
2 (14.5-ounce) cans no-salt-added diced tomatoes
1 (16-ounce) box vacuum-packed gnocchi with potato (such as Bellino)
4 teaspoons grated Parmesan cheese

1. Heat oil in a large nonstick skillet over medium-high heat. Add onion and next 4 ingredients; sauté 4 minutes. Add sugar, pepper, and tomatoes; reduce heat to medium, and cook 10 minutes, stirring occasionally.
2. Cook gnocchi according to package directions, omitting salt. Divide gnocchi evenly among 4 shallow bowls; top each with ¾ cup sauce and 1 teaspoon cheese. Yield: 4 servings.

CALORIES 319 (15% from fat); FAT 5.4g (sat 1.4g, mono 2.8g, poly 0.4g); PROTEIN 12.6g; CARB 55.6g; FIBER 3.9g; CHOL 17mg; IRON 1.9mg; SODIUM 898mg; CALC 78mg

Monte Cristo Sandwich with Sweet Mustard Sauce

(pictured on page 320)

Preparation time: 10 minutes
Cooking time: 12 minutes

¼ cup red currant jelly
2 tablespoons Dijon mustard
1 tablespoon orange juice
1 tablespoon water
⅔ cup egg substitute
½ cup fat-free milk
¼ teaspoon salt
¼ teaspoon black pepper
4 (1-ounce) slices cooked turkey breast
4 (1-ounce) slices cooked ham
4 (1-ounce) slices 50%-less-fat Jarlsberg or Swiss cheese
8 (1-ounce) slices white bread
Cooking spray
1½ teaspoons powdered sugar

1. Combine first 4 ingredients in a saucepan over low heat, stirring well with a whisk. Cook until jelly melts.
2. Combine egg substitute and next 3 ingredients in a shallow dish.
3. Place one slice each of turkey, ham, and cheese on each of 4 bread slices. Top with remaining bread slices. Dip both sides of each sandwich into egg substitute mixture. Place in a large nonstick skillet coated with cooking spray over medium-high heat. Reduce
Continued

heat to medium; cook 3 minutes on each side or until golden. Sprinkle with powdered sugar. Serve sandwiches with sauce. Yield: 4 servings (serving size: 1 sandwich and 2 tablespoons sauce).

CALORIES 394 (18% from fat); FAT 7.7g (sat 2.5g, mono 2g, poly 0.9g); PROTEIN 33g; CARB 46.3g; FIBER 1.2g; CHOL 54mg; IRON 2.8mg; SODIUM 1,282mg; CALC 348mg

New Year's Eve 1-2-3

Everybody needs to be somewhere when the year comes to an end. Why not at home, among friends, with a buffet dinner that's incredibly easy to make?

CALIFORNIA CHICKEN SANDWICH

Preparation time: 30 minutes
Cooking time: 15 minutes

- ⅓ cup fat-free mayonnaise
- 2 tablespoons thawed orange juice concentrate
- 1 teaspoon lime juice
- ½ teaspoon ground cumin
- ⅛ teaspoon hot sauce
- 4 (4-ounce) skinned, boned chicken breast halves
- ¼ teaspoon salt
- ⅛ teaspoon black pepper
- Cooking spray
- 8 (1½-ounce) slices diagonally cut sourdough bread, toasted
- 4 small romaine lettuce leaves
- 2 plum tomatoes, each cut lengthwise into 4 slices
- 1 peeled avocado, cut into 8 wedges

1. Combine first 5 ingredients in a small bowl.
2. Sprinkle chicken with salt and pepper. Place a large nonstick skillet coated with cooking spray over medium-high heat; add chicken. Cook 5 minutes on each side. Reduce heat to low; cover and cook 5 minutes or until done. Remove from heat. Cut chicken diagonally across grain into thin slices.
3. Spread 1 tablespoon mayonnaise mixture on each of 4 bread slices. Top with 1 lettuce leaf, 1 sliced chicken breast half, 2 tomato slices, 2 avocado wedges, and remaining bread slices. Yield: 4 servings.

CALORIES 432 (19% from fat); FAT 8.9g (sat 1.8g, mono 4.4g, poly 1.5g); PROTEIN 35.2g; CARB 52.8g; FIBER 2.8g; CHOL 66mg; IRON 3.7mg; SODIUM 951mg; CALC 112mg

Bid adieu to the old year. Perhaps the idea of spending the eve in a tux or gown at a four-star restaurant doesn't ring your chimes.

Your choice: a New Year's Eve celebration at home with people you actually care about kissing when the clock turns midnight. Not only a sane option, but also utterly doable.

Try this three-course, make-ahead buffet supper for eight. That's four hors d'oeuvres, three main dishes, and four desserts—all created from recipes using no more than three ingredients each (not including salt, pepper, and water).

Easy to prepare before guests arrive, these dishes free up your time for more important activities, such as popping champagne corks and waving "so long" to the year. Also, your guests will feel freer—to mingle and serve themselves at their own pace throughout the evening. Make sure to stack up lots of little plates, though. Frequent return trips to the buffet table are as certain as the passing of each hour.

It's safe to assume that because New Year's Eve falls on the heels of all the traditional holiday feasts, everyone is already pumpkined-, hammed-, and turkeyed-out. So even without announcing that your dinner is actually low in fat and calories, an evening of sampling and nibbling won't cause any next-day resolutions to lower the numbers on the scale. In fact, the only numbers to keep in mind are 1-2-3. Until the Times Square ball begins to fall. Then make it 3-2-1.

SHISH KEBABS WITH ONIONS AND POMEGRANATE MOLASSES

Pomegranate molasses is a thick syrup made from reduced pomegranate juice, sugar, and lemon. You can find it in your supermarket in the international food section or at a Middle Eastern food market. It's also excellent brushed on roasted chicken and pork.

- 2 pounds boned leg of lamb
- 6 tablespoons pomegranate molasses or hoisin sauce, divided
- ½ cup grated fresh onion
- ½ teaspoon salt
- ¼ teaspoon black pepper
- 1 onion, quartered and separated into pieces

1. Trim fat from lamb. Cut lamb into 60 (¾-inch) pieces. Combine lamb, 3 tablespoons molasses, grated onion, salt, and pepper in a large zip-top plastic bag, and seal. Marinate in refrigerator 8 hours, turning bag occasionally. Remove lamb from bag, and discard marinade.
2. Thread 4 lamb cubes and 4 onion pieces alternately onto each of 15 (6-inch) skewers.
3. Preheat broiler. Place kebabs on a broiler pan; broil 3 minutes on each side or until desired degree of doneness. Pour 3 tablespoons molasses evenly over kebabs. Yield: 15 servings (serving size: 1 kebab).

CALORIES 81 (23% from fat); FAT 2.1g (sat 0.7g, mono 0.8g, poly 0.2g); PROTEIN 9.8g; CARB 5.3g; FIBER 0.4g; CHOL 29mg; IRON 0.9mg; SODIUM 194mg; CALC 9mg

RADISH WREATH WITH WHIPPED CUMIN GOAT CHEESE

24 radishes with leaves (about 2 large bunches)
¼ cup (2 ounces) goat cheese
1 teaspoon water
¼ teaspoon salt
¼ teaspoon ground cumin

1. Remove leaves from radishes, leaving 1 inch of stem; scrub with a brush. Wash and drain leaves; arrange leaves in a circle on a platter. Cut radishes in half lengthwise. Combine cheese and remaining 3 ingredients in a small bowl; stir with a rubber spatula until smooth. Spread cheese mixture evenly over cut sides of radishes. Arrange radishes on leaves. Yield: 24 servings (serving size: 2 radish halves).

CALORIES 7 (64% from fat); FAT 0.5g (sat 0.4g, mono 0.1g, poly 0g); PROTEIN 0.4g; CARB 0.3g; FIBER 0g; CHOL 2mg; IRON 0mg; SODIUM 52mg; CALC 13mg

SCALLOPS IN SHIITAKES

The scallops can either be cut in half horizontally or crosswise to fit into the mushroom caps.

24 medium shiitake mushroom caps (about 1½-inch diameter)
¼ teaspoon freshly ground black pepper
12 medium sea scallops, cut in half (about 1 pound)
2 tablespoons commercial pesto

1. Preheat oven to 450°.
2. Arrange mushroom caps in a shallow baking dish. Sprinkle pepper into mushroom caps. Place 1 scallop half into each mushroom cap. Spoon ¼ teaspoon pesto onto each scallop half. Bake at 450° for 10 minutes or until scallops are done. Yield: 8 servings (serving size: 3 stuffed mushrooms).

CALORIES 99 (27% from fat); FAT 3g (sat 0.6g, mono 1.2g, poly 0.6g); PROTEIN 12.3g; CARB 7.5g; FIBER 1.8g; CHOL 18mg; IRON 2.1mg; SODIUM 138mg; CALC 48mg

SMOKED-SALMON QUESADILLAS

¾ cup tub-style light cream cheese with chives and onions (about 6 ounces)
8 (8-inch) fat-free flour tortillas
8 ounces smoked salmon, coarsely chopped
¼ teaspoon freshly ground black pepper

1. Spread cream cheese evenly over 4 tortillas. Divide salmon among tortillas, and sprinkle with pepper. Top each with remaining tortillas, pressing gently. Heat a nonstick skillet over medium-high heat. Cook each quesadilla 2 minutes on each side. Cut each quesadilla into 6 wedges. Yield: 8 servings (serving size: 3 wedges).

CALORIES 182 (21% from fat); FAT 4.2g (sat 2.5g, mono 1.3g, poly 0.3g); PROTEIN 9.4g; CARB 25.8g; FIBER 1.8g; CHOL 22mg; IRON 0.3mg; SODIUM 660mg; CALC 33mg

ROQUEFORT MOUSSE AND CRUDITÉS

While perfect with celery, this dip is marvelous with any crudité.

8 celery stalks with leaves
1 (16-ounce) carton fat-free cottage cheese
¾ cup (3 ounces) crumbled Roquefort or other blue cheese
⅛ teaspoon freshly ground black pepper

1. Finely chop 2 tablespoons celery leaves; reserve stalks.
2. Place leaves, cottage cheese, blue cheese, and pepper in a blender or food processor; process 1½ minutes or until smooth. Spoon into a bowl; cover and chill 1 hour. Cut celery stalks into sticks or as desired. Serve with mousse. Yield: 8 servings (serving size: ¼ cup mousse and 1 celery stalk).

CALORIES 79 (35% from fat); FAT 3.1g (sat 2g, mono 0.8g, poly 0.1g); PROTEIN 10.1g; CARB 3.2g; FIBER 0.6g; CHOL 10mg; IRON 0.2mg; SODIUM 393mg; CALC 102mg

PROSCIUTTO, MANGO, AND PARMESAN SALAD

4 cups coarsely chopped peeled mango (about 4 mangoes)
4 ounces thinly sliced prosciutto, coarsely chopped
3 ounces shaved Parmigiano-Reggiano cheese
¼ to ½ teaspoon freshly ground black pepper

1. Combine all ingredients in a bowl; toss gently. Yield: 15 servings (serving size: ⅓ cup).

CALORIES 64 (32% from fat); FAT 2.3g (sat 1.2g, mono 0.8g, poly 0.2g); PROTEIN 4g; CARB 7.7g; FIBER 0.7g; CHOL 8mg; IRON 0.2mg; SODIUM 205mg; CALC 72mg

CRISP FENNEL-ORANGE SALAD

To save time on party day, make this salad the day before you plan to serve it.

6 large navel oranges
2 tablespoons extra-virgin olive oil
¼ teaspoon salt
¼ teaspoon black pepper
2 (1-pound) fennel bulbs with stalks

1. Grate 1½ tablespoons rind; set aside. Peel and section oranges over a bowl to measure 3 cups; squeeze membranes to extract juice. Set sections aside, reserving ½ cup juice. Discard membranes. Combine grated rind, reserved juice, oil, salt, and pepper in a blender; process until smooth.
2. Trim tough outer leaves from fennel; mince feathery fronds to measure ¼ cup. Remove and discard stalks. Cut fennel bulb in half lengthwise; discard core. Cut halves crosswise into thin slices to measure 3 cups. Combine sliced fennel, orange sections, and juice mixture; toss gently. Sprinkle with fronds. Yield: 12 servings (serving size: ½ cup).

CALORIES 53 (41% from fat); FAT 2.4g (sat 0.3g, mono 1.7g, poly 0.2g); PROTEIN 1.2g; CARB 7.8g; FIBER 2.1g; CHOL 0mg; IRON 0.7mg; SODIUM 51mg; CALC 45mg

LEMON-POACHED ORANGES

(pictured on page 319)

    4 cups water
    1 cup sugar
    ¼ cup grated lemon rind (about
         4 large lemons)
    ⅔ cup fresh lemon juice (about
         4 lemons)
    7 navel oranges (about 4 pounds),
         each peeled and cut crosswise
         into 4 slices

1. Combine first 4 ingredients in a
Dutch oven. Add orange slices; bring to
a boil. Reduce heat to medium-low;
cook 5 minutes. Remove slices with a
slotted spoon; place in a bowl. Cook
juice mixture over medium-high heat
15 minutes (until slightly syrupy); pour
over oranges. Cover; chill at least 4
hours. Yield: 14 servings (serving size: 2
orange slices and about ¼ cup syrup).

CALORIES 89 (1% from fat); FAT 0.1g (sat 0g, mono 0g,
poly 0.1g); PROTEIN 0.7g; CARB 23.2g; FIBER 2.9g;
CHOL 0mg; IRON 0.1mg; SODIUM 0mg; CALC 29mg

CITRUS GRANITA

(pictured on page 319)

    ⅔ cup fresh lemon juice (about
         4 lemons)
    3 cups water
    1 cup sugar
    1 cup fresh orange juice (about
         4 oranges)

1. Combine all ingredients in a saucepan.
Bring to a boil over medium-high heat;
cook 1 minute or until sugar dissolves,
stirring constantly. Remove from heat;
cool. Pour into a 13 x 9-inch baking dish;
cover and freeze at least 8 hours or until
firm. Remove from freezer; scrape mixture with a fork until fluffy. Store remaining granita in an airtight container; cover
and freeze up to 1 month. Yield: 7 cups
(serving size: ½ cup).

CALORIES 66 (0% from fat); FAT 0g; PROTEIN 0.2g;
CARB 17.2g; FIBER 0g; CHOL 0mg; IRON 0mg;
SODIUM 0mg; CALC 3mg

FOUR SIMPLE CITRUS TIPS

**Making citrus rind strips with a
channel knife or vegetable peeler—**
*Remove the strips before sectioning or
juicing. Peel gently, being careful not
to include the bitter white pith layer
attached to the underside of the rind.*

Creating grated citrus rind—*Always
grate rind before sectioning or juicing. Hold the fruit firmly. Push
down on a handheld grater, but not
too hard. Just take off the color, not
the white pith.*

Sectioning fresh citrus—*Peel fruit,
then cut between white membranes to
expose flesh. Hold fruit over a bowl
to catch the juices that drip down.*

Extracting more juice—*Take the leftover membranes after sectioning and
squeeze.*

RUM-MARINATED DRIED
FRUIT

    3 (8-ounce) packages dried mixed
         fruit, coarsely chopped
    ¾ cup sugar
    3 cups water
    1 cup dark rum

1. Combine all ingredients in a 2-
quart jar with a lid. Cover tightly;
shake vigorously. Store in a cool, dark
place for at least 3 days. Yield: 14 servings (serving size: ½ cup).

CALORIES 220 (0% from fat); FAT 0g; PROTEIN 0.8g;
CARB 44.8g; FIBER 0g; CHOL 0mg; IRON 1.6mg;
SODIUM 10mg; CALC 18mg

CINNAMON SUGAR CRISPS

(pictured on page 319)

    32 won ton wrappers
    1½ tablespoons stick margarine or
          butter, melted
    8 teaspoons cinnamon sugar

1. Preheat oven to 400°.
2. Arrange wrappers on baking sheets;
brush evenly with margarine. Sprinkle
each wrapper with ¼ teaspoon cinnamon sugar. Bake at 400° for 5 minutes
or until crisp. Cool on wire racks.
Yield: 8 servings (serving size: 4 crisps).

CALORIES 123 (19% from fat); FAT 2.6g (sat 0.5g, mono 1g,
poly 0.9g); PROTEIN 3.2g; CARB 21.5g; FIBER 0.3g;
CHOL 3mg; IRON 1.5mg; SODIUM 208mg; CALC 30mg

Month-by-Month Index

A month-by-month listing of every food story with recipe titles that appeared in the magazine in 1998. See page 348 for the General Recipe Index.

General Recipe Index

A listing by major ingredient, food category, and/or regular column for every recipe that appeared in the magazine in 1998.

Menu Index

Each menu includes recipes from the magazine and appropriate generic items to round out the meal.
Refer to the page number with each menu to locate the recipe.

Acknowledgments and Credits

CONTRIBUTING RECIPE
DEVELOPERS:

Nancy Baggett
Pat Baird
Colleen Dunn Bates
Bev Bennett
Pasquale Bruno
Holly Berkowitz Clegg
Ying Chang Compestine
Terry Conlan
Leslie DeDominic
Dave DiResta
Linda West Eckhardt
Janet Fletcher
Jim Fobel
Joanne Foran
Rozanne Gold
Kathy Gunst
Jeanne Jones
Barbara Kafka
Jeanne Kelley
Jean Kressy
Karen A. Levin
Susan Herrmann Loomis
Marianne Marinelli
Gus Martin
Janet Mendel
Paulette Mitchell

Jill Nussinow
Greg Patent
Bettina Perez
Elizabeth Perez
Marge Perry
Steven Petusevsky
Victoria Abbott Riccardi
Elizabeth Riely
Sandra Rudloff
Donna Shields
Martha Rose Shulman
Nina Simonds
Kathleen Desmond Stang
Sandy Szwarc
Elizabeth J. Taliaferro
Jennifer Viegas
Robin Vitetta-Miller
Robb Walsh
Kenneth Wapner
Connie Welch

CONTRIBUTING PHOTO STYLISTS:

Amy Nathan: pages 93, 94, 96

Mary Jane Sawyer: page 58

CONTRIBUTING PHOTOGRAPHERS:

Jim Bathie: pages 262, 299

Hornick/Rivlin: page 58

Deborah Jones: pages 93, 94, 96

Randy Mayor: pages 221, 223, 298

Howard L. Puckett: pages 38, 40, 59, 60, 93,
95, 96, 113, 115, 149, 151, 185, 222, 300,
317, 318

METRIC EQUIVALENTS

The recipes that appear in this cookbook use the standard United States method
for measuring liquid and dry or solid ingredients (teaspoons, tablespoons, and cups).
The information in the following charts is provided to help cooks outside the U.S.
successfully use these recipes. All equivalents are approximate.

EQUIVALENTS FOR DIFFERENT TYPES OF INGREDIENTS

A standard cup measure of a dry or solid ingredient will
vary in weight depending on the type of ingredient.
A standard cup of liquid is the same volume for any type of
liquid. Use the following chart when converting standard
cup measures to grams (weight) or milliliters (volume).

Standard Cup	Fine Powder (ex. flour)	Grain (ex. rice)	Granular (ex. sugar)	Liquid Solids (ex. butter)	Liquid (ex. milk)
1	140 g	150 g	190 g	200 g	240 ml
¾	105 g	113 g	143 g	150 g	180 ml
⅔	93 g	100 g	125 g	133 g	160 ml
½	70 g	75 g	95 g	100 g	120 ml
⅓	47 g	50 g	63 g	67 g	80 ml
¼	35 g	38 g	48 g	50 g	60 ml
⅛	18 g	19 g	24 g	25 g	30 ml

LIQUID INGREDIENTS BY VOLUME

¼ tsp						=	1 ml	
½ tsp						=	2 ml	
1 tsp						=	5 ml	
3 tsp	=	1 tbls			=	½ fl oz	=	15 ml
		2 tbls	=	⅛ cup	=	1 fl oz	=	30 ml
		4 tbls	=	¼ cup	=	2 fl oz	=	60 ml
		5⅓ tbls	=	⅓ cup	=	3 fl oz	=	80 ml
		8 tbls	=	½ cup	=	4 fl oz	=	120 ml
		10⅔ tbls	=	⅔ cup	=	5 fl oz	=	160 ml
		12 tbls	=	¾ cup	=	6 fl oz	=	180 ml
		16 tbls	=	1 cup	=	8 fl oz	=	240 ml
		1 pt	=	2 cups	=	16 fl oz	=	480 ml
		1 qt	=	4 cups	=	32 fl oz	=	960 ml
						33 fl oz	=	1000 ml = 1 l

DRY INGREDIENTS BY WEIGHT
(To convert ounces to grams, multiply the number of ounces by 30.)

1 oz	=	¹⁄₁₆ lb	=	30 g
4 oz	=	¼ lb	=	120 g
8 oz	=	½ lb	=	240 g
12 oz	=	¾ lb	=	360 g
16 oz	=	1 lb	=	480 g

LENGTH
(To convert inches to centimeters, multiply the number of inches by 2.5.)

1 in			=	2.5 cm			
6 in	=	½ ft	=	15 cm			
12 in	=	1 ft	=	30 cm			
36 in	=	3 ft	=	1 yd	=	90 cm	
40 in			=	100 cm	=	1 m	

COOKING/OVEN TEMPERATURES

	Fahrenheit	Celsius	Gas Mark
Freeze Water	32° F	0° C	
Room Temperature	68° F	20° C	
Boil Water	212° F	100° C	
Bake	325° F	160° C	3
	350° F	180° C	4
	375° F	190° C	5
	400° F	200° C	6
	425° F	220° C	7
	450° F	230° C	8
Broil			Grill